Lost in the Shadow of the Word

Lost in the Shadow of the Word

Space, Time, and Freedom in Interwar Eastern Europe

✦

Benjamin Paloff

NORTHWESTERN UNIVERSITY PRESS
EVANSTON, ILLINOIS

the modern language initiative

THIS BOOK IS MADE POSSIBLE BY A COLLABORATIVE GRANT
FROM THE ANDREW W. MELLON FOUNDATION.

Northwestern University Press
www.nupress.northwestern.edu

Printed in the United States of America

10 9 8 7 6 5 4 3 2 1

Library of Congress Cataloging-in-Publication Data

Names: Paloff, Benjamin, author.
Title: Lost in the shadow of the word : space, time, and freedom in interwar Eastern Europe / Benjamin Paloff.
Description: Evanston, Illinois : Northwestern University Press, 2016. | Includes bibliographical references and index.
Identifiers: LCCN 2016007597 | ISBN 9780810134133 (pbk. : alk. paper) | ISBN 9780810134140 (cloth : alk. paper) | ISBN 9780810134157 (e-book)
Subjects: LCSH: Slavic literature—20th century—History and criticism. | Space and time in literature. | Modernism (Literature)
Classification: LCC PG509.S65 P35 2016 | DDC 891.8—dc23
LC record available at https://lccn.loc.gov/2016007597

For Anna Barańczak
and for Stanisław Barańczak, in memoriam

Who includes diversity and is Nature,
Who is the amplitude of the earth and the coarseness and sexuality of the earth,
and the great charity of the earth, and the equilibrium also,
Who has not look'd forth from the windows the eyes for nothing, or whose brain
held audience with messengers for nothing,
Who contains believers and disbelievers, who is the most majestic lover,
Who holds duly his or her triune proportion of realism, spiritualism, and of the
æsthetic or intellectual,
Who having consider'd the body finds all its organs and parts good,
Who, out of the theory of the earth and of his or her body understands by subtle
analogies all other theories,
The theory of a city, a poem, and of the large politics of these States;
Who believes not only in our globe with its sun and moon, but in other globes with
their suns and moons,
Who, constructing the house of himself or herself, not for a day but for all time,
sees races, eras, dates, generations,
The past, the future, dwelling there, like space, inseparable together.

—Walt Whitman, "Kosmos"

CONTENTS

ACKNOWLEDGMENTS

I have accumulated so many debts of gratitude in the making of this book that any attempt to repay them here seems a fool's errand. I will give it a shot nonetheless.

In its earliest development, this text was a doctoral dissertation. My advisors in that endeavor—Stephanie Sandler, William Mills Todd III, and Jonathan Bolton—provided exceptional guidance and support then and have continued to do so in the years since. Michał Paweł Markowski, my dear friend and teacher, was an informal addition to my committee, and he has been an inspirational partner in addressing the intersections of philosophy and literature. The project benefitted at its formative stages from conversations that had definite beginnings but no end: Alexander Spector, Rebecca Reich, Emily van Buskirk, Jacob Edmond, Janusz Margański, and Peter Zusi—thank you for your unwavering generosity. The late Svetlana Boym deserves special mention for her inspiring turns of mind and excellent cheer. Konstantin Azadovskii, Jerzy Jarzębski, the late Elena Shvarts, and Ol'ga Sedakova helped shape my thinking over the course of several visits to St. Petersburg, Moscow, and Kraków. I am grateful to Nikita Zabolotskii for all his insights into his father's work, as well as for the lunch over which they were conveyed.

Of course, no project of this kind gets very far without the often anonymous labors of library and archival specialists. It is a pleasure to acknowledge the assistance of Jagiellonian University's Polish Institute, Kraków; the Polish Academy of Sciences and the Adam Mickiewicz Museum of Literature, Warsaw; the Museum of Czech Literature and the Institute for Czech Literature, Prague; the Harvard College Library; Yale University's Beineke Library; Princeton's Firestone Library; and especially the Institute for Russian Literature (Pushkinskii Dom) of the Russian Academy of Sciences.

Lost in the Shadow of the Word started taking its current shape during a three-year Junior Fellowship with the Michigan Society of Fellows, and it owes a great deal to the joyful, insistently interdisciplinary discussions among the historians, cosmologists, ecologists, poets, anthropologists, and philosophers who passed through the society during my time there. I would especially like to thank Donald Lopez and Hussein Fancy.

Ultimately, one is always writing for his or her readers, and mine have been particularly attentive, supportive, and demanding. Mikhail Krutikov read and commented on every page of my later drafts. Anton Shammas offered sage advice on the text's main arguments. Caryl Emerson, Bożena Shallcross, and Thomas Seifrid carefully picked over the entire book and helped me see what was missing, misplaced, or misconceived at precisely the points where I needed fresh eyes. My two extraordinary research assistants, Jenny Zhang and Jamie Parsons, on many occasions liberated me from the dark enclosure of my own prose.

Portions of chapter 5 have appeared in early versions: "Denatured Spirits: Shame and Doubling in Witold Gombrowicz and Richard Weiner," in *New Perspectives on Polish Culture: Personal Encounters, Public Affairs,* edited by Tamara Trojanowska et al. (New York: PIASA Books, 2011); and "Zaraźliwy śmiech: Tożsamość i infekcja w *Bakakaju*" (Contagious Laughter: Identity and Infection in Gombrowicz's *Bakakaj*), in *Witold Gombrowicz, Nasz współczesny,* edited by Jerzy Jarzębski (Krakow: Universitas, 2010). It is a pleasure to acknowledge the editors' kindness and support.

In 2015, the American Comparative Literature Association awarded *Lost in the Shadow of the Word* its Helen Tartar First Book Subvention Prize. I am tremendously grateful to ACLA and the awards committee for honoring this book, and for doing so in memory of one of the outstanding editors in the field.

There are so many more of you to thank, and we are only at the beginning.

A NOTE ON TRANSLATIONS, TRANSLITERATIONS, AND OTHER TRACES

The following study draws on primary sources originally written in Czech, Polish, and Russian. Unless otherwise noted, all translations are my own. I have generally followed the Library of Congress standard for transliteration of Cyrillic into Roman script, though names that appear commonly in English (e.g., Dostoevsky, Tolstoy, Shklovsky) appear in their more familiar form. For readers keen to consider quoted material in the original, this is provided, untransliterated, in the notes.

In chapters 3 and 4, in-text citations from lyric poems appear in a literal English translation. Since these literal glosses cannot convey the formal virtues of the poems or the wealth of information that the form suggests, especially for the reader who does not have facility with the Cyrillic alphabet, I have supplied an appendix with lyric translations and annotations for three of the poems: Osip Mandel'shtam's "I returned to my city . . ." and "No, never was I anyone's contemporary . . ." and Nikolai Zabolotskii's "Red Bavaria."

Lost in the Shadow of the Word

Introduction

> A man who wants the truth becomes a scholar; a man who wants to give free play to his subjectivity may become a writer; but what should a man do who wants something in between?
>
> —Robert Musil

This book is about in-betweenness. Not in the sense that might apply generally to literary studies, where we often find ourselves hunting down conceptual antinomies and paradoxes within the text—though many of the fictional heroes, lyric subjects, and authors discussed here may indeed strike us as existing between social, political, sexual, or even biological categories.[1] My interest here will be much narrower. Specifically, this book is about being suspended in the kind of in-betweenness that is engendered by indeterminacy in space and time. More specifically still, it argues that the new understanding of space and time that emerged at the turn of the last century fundamentally changed the representation of individual subjectivity in Eastern European literature.

Another, more ambitious way of describing this book's central aim is that it provides a comprehensive diagnosis of what we mean when we characterize Eastern European Modernism as uncanny, strange, or simply "Kafkaesque." In the Western imaginary, Central and Eastern Europe have long been nests not only of darkness and foreboding, of vampires and filicidal tsars named "Terrible," but of inscrutability itself. The enduring repeatability of Winston Churchill's formulation about Russia being "a riddle wrapped inside a mystery inside an enigma" echoes the critical tendency to present diverse writers and artists, including those who observe a rigorous consistency of purpose and method, in terms of their "absurdism."[2] But this puzzlement on the part of readers, which is then ascribed retroactively to the theme of puzzlement on the part of writers, is the peculiar province of a strain of Eastern European Modernism that has been generalized, in reductive terms like "Kafkaesque," to apply to the whole. I intend to ground the "Kafkaesque" in the specificity of its cultural moment by examining its origins in a spatial-temporal predicament—the predicament of in-betweenness.

By treating late Modernism in terms of space and time, I am therefore setting aside the popular use of the word "Kafkaesque" to describe a logical paradox or an interminable bureaucratic nightmare.[3] Or, more accurately, the term's conventional application to epistemological, spiritual, or legal dilemmas is already inscribed within Kafka's universe, where the boundlessness of the narrative construct means that there is *no outside to escape to*. Tzvetan Todorov calls this "a *generalized fantastic,*" a story world that no longer recognizes its most uncanny elements as unusual at all and thus "swallows up the entire world of the book and the reader along with it."[4] In Todorov's reading, Kafka builds a home within the uncanny—a *Heim* within the *Unheimliche,* as it were. Where Todorov errs is in his assertion that Kafka's "oneiric logic [. . .] no longer has anything to do with the real."[5] For Kafka provides every indication that he is not merely inventing a story world. The textual construct models a reality that the author believes to be our own, though veiled behind its own representation, a reality that Bruno Schulz defines as "the shadow of the word" and Kafka as "only a bad mood of God, a bad day of his." When Max Brod suggested that there may yet be hope in other worlds, Kafka is said to have replied with sly sincerity, "Oh, plenty of hope, an infinite amount of hope—but not for us."[6]

Why space and time? In the first place, the rethinking of space and time in the early decades of the twentieth century so pervaded popular print, the visual arts, and the public imagination that what we have come to know as literary Modernism would be inconceivable without it. Physicists, mathematicians, and philosophers working on space and time, and including Albert Einstein, Henri Poincaré, Edmund Husserl, and Henri Bergson, among many others, enjoyed international celebrity in their day. "No other single event [. . .] has had a greater impact on both popular and scholarly attitudes toward the production of knowledge," Hans Gumbrecht has remarked, "than Einstein's publication of his theory of relativity."[7]

This impact, however, could also be profoundly traumatic. Suddenly confronted with Cubism and special relativity, not to mention stirrings of a revolutionary End of History, the first decades of the new century thrust Europe into a general bewilderment, a sense that the world had become incomprehensible. Or as Michael Beddow puts it apropos his reading of Thomas Mann, "Scientific knowledge, identified in the nineteenth century as the domain of 'hard' facts and plain, no-nonsense certainties, had in the space of a few years become a region in which the gulf between fundamental reality and common-sense notions of what is real and true had grown almost unbridgeably wide."[8] Thomas Vargish and Delo E. Mook offer the delightful term "epistemic trauma" for this "peculiar strangeness or alienation from common sense" that relativity theory thrust upon us by challenging not who we are but *how* we are.[9] A central claim of my own study is that writers in Central and Eastern Europe approached this "epistemic trauma" in ways peculiar to their geopolitical and cultural circumstance, representing the inescapability of the very same aspects of space and time in which major Western authors recognized a potential for freedom.

This key difference is initially elided by the similarities in how Modernists treat space and time across the European continent. Texts that arose directly from this cultural moment are notable for having reawakened a largely dormant approach to literary representation, one in which the linear development and strictly delineated story worlds that had become standard over the preceding century surrendered ground to the epic wandering and episodic adventure more familiar from earlier literary artifacts, especially *Don Quixote* and Sentimentalist fiction. In what Milan Kundera has called "the depreciated legacy of Cervantes," space and time are not merely stable platforms for our external, ostensibly objective observation of events, as they are in scientific positivism and its literary correlate, the Realist novel. Rather, the unified space-time of these texts bends around its hero. The world he inhabits reflects his own movement through it; it mirrors, in effect, his own troubled interiority. This is what Kundera means when he writes that Kafka's accomplishment was "that seamless fusion of dream and reality," "that supremely lucid gaze set on the modern world, along with the most unfettered imagination."[10] We need only recall the hero of *The Trial* (1915) stumbling numbly through a mysterious and opaque criminal process, though we might just as easily point to the revelation of Robert Walser's *Jakob von Gunten* (1909), whose eponymous hero suddenly announces to himself, "I am living in a fairy tale and am no longer a cultured being in an age of culture."[11]

Kundera offers what has since become a familiar pantheon of European Modernists who revive Cervantes's legacy, making the hero's subjective adventure through space and time the centerpiece of novelistic discourse once again: Mann, James Joyce, Marcel Proust, and Robert Musil, as well as Hermann Broch and Witold Gombrowicz.[12] In Kundera's view, these authors successfully subverted the Realist imperative to provide social, physical, or even psychological verisimilitude. Instead, we encounter the author's willful manipulation of the text's spatial-temporal construct and a sense that the world of the text arises from the hero's participation in it. I will sometimes refer to this spatial-temporal construct, both in the sense of how we represent it to ourselves (experience, in whatever form) and how we represent it to each other (text, in whatever form), as "milieu," following Michel Foucault's stripped-down definition as "[t]he space in which a series of uncertain elements unfold," though Foucault generously notes that he is borrowing his concept from Isaac Newton and Jean-Baptiste Lamarck.[13] (Newton will resurface in chapter 2, Lamarck in chapter 3.)

Changes in the milieu of everyday experience naturally lead to changes in the milieu of representation. Hugh Kenner explains why in his treatment of

Ulysses, noting that when a major reconceptualization allows for new possibilities in science and philosophy, as occurred with the emergence of non-Euclidean geometry, "the queer things mathematicians do with this freedom have a way of turning back toward the familiar world, and describing it from a new angle."[14] This "new angle" continues to draw the attention of scholars of Proust, Mann, and Joyce.[15] As it was emerging in literature, reimagining how space and time behave in the text, the "new angle" was already being theorized, first by György Lukács (1885–1971), a Jewish-Hungarian philosopher writing in German, and subsequently by Mikhail Bakhtin (1895–1975), a Russian philosopher whose extensive readings in German had led him, at a crucial moment in his intellectual development, to Lukács. Taken together, their investigations into literature's spatial-temporal framework constitute a forceful assault on the strictures of Realist representation, albeit one that Lukács would subsequently repudiate. Just as significantly, their work effectively presents an aesthetics of freedom within an inherently unfree signifying system—the literary text.

I provide a detailed discussion of how Lukács and Bakhtin construct this freedom in chapter 1. And if it had meant the same thing for writers in Central and Eastern Europe as it did for Proust, Joyce, and Mann, portraying a world of epic adventure within the overdevelopment and hyperdefinition of modern European society, this freedom might well have been my book's focus. Several recent studies of Western European literature, in fact, suggest not only that textual space and time have lately been awarded a great deal of scholarly space and time but that this attention is inextricably bound to the notion of freedom. In *Time, Space, and Motion in the Age of Shakespeare,* for example, Angus Fletcher has demonstrated how deeply Western literature associates the breakdown of spatial-temporal boundaries with individual freedom, both physical and metaphysical, an association that persists in our reading of Modernism in Western Europe.[16] The very fact that time passes, and that in the process it carries away the force of an initial impression or experience, is itself subverted in Michael Clune's treatment of Proust, Vladimir Nabokov, and others.[17] Likewise, for Martin Hägglund the desire to suspend time's passing is predicated on an acceptance that it passes in the first place, so that the heroes of Proust, Nabokov, and Virginia Woolf enjoy access to the past while remaining rooted in an experiential present.[18] If we read Modernism's encounter with the Einsteinian revolution solely on the basis of Western European manipulations of space-time in the literary text, we might easily agree with Stephen Kern's assertion that "modernists' subversions always implied a positive reworking, and thus their resistance to chronology was complemented by an affirmation of techniques for ordering experience based on the workings of consciousness."[19] The potential for a simple gesture, such as dipping a madeleine into a cup of tea, to fuse the adult consciousness to childhood memory (*Swann's Way,* 1913); or for a single day's journey through Dublin to dilate into an echo of an ancient hero quest (*Ulysses,* 1922); or for a visit to an alpine sanatorium to become a lasting reprieve from modern time (*The Magic Mountain,* 1924)—all of these instances suggest an excitement about the reevaluation of spatial-temporal strictures, Modernism's "imperative to make the phenomenal world new," as Sara Danius describes it.[20]

Despite the enduring interest of writers like Proust and Joyce, of course, European Modernism, in the East as well as in the West, is hardly wanting for specimens of strict definition, spatial-temporal and otherwise. Programmatic definition is the central task, after all, of the aesthetic manifesto, the mission statement of literary luminaries and like-minded colleagues that, in its proliferation from the fin de siècle through the interwar period, we may regard as the Modernist text par excellence. Thus the literature of spatial-temporal destabilization emerges as a particular strain of Modernist literature, and it is because the freedom explored in this literature looks radically different when we move further east that we can say unequivocally that in-betweenness is not merely another way of describing Modernism writ large. The difference is partially attributable to what Kundera calls the intrusion of History:

> The time was past when man had only the monster of his own soul to grapple with, the peaceful time of Joyce and Proust. In the novels of Kafka, Hašek, Musil, Broch, the monster comes from outside and is called History; it no longer has anything to do with the train the adventurers used to ride; it is impersonal, uncontrollable, incalculable, incomprehensible—and it is inescapable. This was the moment (just after the First World War) when the pleiad of great Central European novelists saw, felt, grasped the *terminal paradoxes* of the Modern Era.[21]

The Soviet Union, Poland, and Czechoslovakia, whose literatures provide the primary texts for this study, were all new geopolitical inventions following World War I, and writers in interwar Central and Eastern Europe were acutely aware of the special challenges they faced in creating a new literature that would both reflect and advance these new realia in the very moment of their becoming. The same challenges, Galin Tihanov has argued, made Eastern and Central Europe the primary incubator for modern literary theory, including the work of Lukács and Bakhtin.[22] In-betweenness is the dark by-product of this creative energy. In probing the potential that Proust, Mann, and Joyce discover in dissolving spatial-temporal boundaries, certain writers in Eastern Europe gradually came to the frightful realization that a system without constraint, any milieu without a boundary, allows no possibility for escape. We become prisoners of our own freedom.

An illustration is in order. Let's imagine that you are living in Moscow in the early 1920s, a time and place where we see an especially marked contrast between, on the one hand, the rhetoric extolling the freedoms of the "new life," and on the other, extreme physical deprivation. You occupy a cramped, dilapidated apartment, and you're lucky to have that. There's been a bloody civil war and a famine that has left millions dead, yet that doesn't keep you from dreaming of just a little more space, a bit more freedom to move around. Of course, there's no chance of your obtaining a bigger apartment in the foreseeable future, yet this is an old-life problem for which the new life provides solutions. A strange peddler shows up and gives you—for free, no less, as a sample!—a liquid formula that instantly makes the apartment bigger. A drop here, a drop there, and your living space expands. At first you are afraid you'll be caught by the housing inspector, but there is nothing to worry about: your apartment no longer conforms to the old rules of space and time. Each expansion of the apartment has no appreciable effect on the building around it. From the street or corridor, no one would have any idea what you've been up to. But then you get carried away, you accidentally drop the liquid, and the apartment expands infinitely, haphazardly, in all directions. Now you're trapped. No matter how far you walk in your own apartment, you will never be able to find the wall, let alone the door.

The word that leaps to mind when we envision such a scenario is "Kafkaesque," though its author, Sigizmund Krzhizhanovskii ("Quadraturin," 1926), would not encounter Kafka's work until 1939. What Krzhizhanovskii, a Russian-Polish theater critic, did have at his disposal was a strong interest in Einsteinian notions of space and time, which his imagination carries to a logical, albeit horrifying, conclusion.[23] Still, Kafka is an effective touchstone for this kind of story, in which the strictures of modern life compel the hero to seek freedom, and that freedom becomes its own prison. If a writer like Proust is relieved when he "finds that above the world of necessity there is the world of freedom," as young Marcel notes, then Kafka discovers that the "world of necessity" might have been preferable to freedom.[24] At least necessity implies enough definition for the hero to be able to locate himself.

The term I sometimes use for this condition is "intermediacy." Even as shorthand for spatial-temporal in-betweenness, and especially for readers who share my skepticism of critical coinages, my use of the term demands some preliminary justification. Evoking the sense of being suspended in-between (while shedding some of that phrase's unwieldiness), intermediacy partakes of both the immediacy of direct intuition and the mediation, or mediacy, of experience and language. The distinction, with echoes in ancient philosophy and its first modern articulation in G. W. F. Hegel, is resisted by the authors treated in this study, who are drawn simultaneously to self-obliteration in the Absolute and radical self-assertion in the experiential world.[25] Whether the hero of narrative fiction or the speaker of the lyric poem, the intermediate subject finds himself caught between the security of definition and the freedom of formlessness, between the power of his own autonomy and the unburdening that comes with his absorption into the Absolute. In the relativistic space-time of this representational construct, the hero can never know precisely where (or when) he is. He is condemned to wander eternally through an environment that is itself transformed by his movements through it.

What I am proposing with my recourse to this term is not an alternative to the well-established critical designations that have been applied to some of these authors to denote their artistic methods (including Expressionism, "noetic" fiction, or lyric avant-garde) or their philosophical investments (Existentialism, Structuralism). Rather, I look to narrow our focus to a rich thematic thread that remains veiled behind these more capacious designations. The inspiration for such a move has been the authors themselves, with their insistent depictions of spatial-temporal in-betweenness, their explicit reflections on being in-between, and their engagement with kindred philosophical discourses, and it is the conceptual structure of in-betweenness in this literature, rather than the shorthand "intermediacy" itself, that I wish to emphasize as the book's central investment.

Nor do I wish the reader to come away from this study with the false impression that its author sees spatial-temporal in-betweenness as the exclusive province of Eastern European literature, or indeed that Eastern Europe can be essentialized at all as a geopolitical entity standing apart from the West.[26] That the kinds of in-betweenness explored in the following pages found such fertile ground in interwar Eastern Europe might even be regarded as a historical accident, the filtering of a pan-European zeitgeist through the specific sociopolitical circumstances of the interbelline East. What interests me here is the precise quality and structure of the uncomfortable sense of entrapment perceived in this literature both in its own time and place and by generations of readers since. Or, to put it in terms more biological than literary, the genes of spatial-temporal destabilization express themselves differently depending on specific environmental conditions.

The term "intermediacy," therefore, can be considered a placeholder, one that holds open a conceptual space and describes its resident ontological condition, thereby unveiling the commonality of a path tread by several writers and given various names in their work, as well as in the philosophical and critical tradition. When Bruno Schulz writes of "cosmic homelessness" in the "half-real regions" of existence, he is describing a condition analogous to what György Lukács calls "transcendental homelessness," "as though every living thing were found somewhere in the middle of time and its movement" (Andrei Platonov), "that intermediate, transitory phase of development" (Witold Gombrowicz) where "everything runs together [and] you don't know where the borders are" (Vítězslav Nezval). Czesław Miłosz refers to "our bifurcation into here and there, into inside and outside, or, if you prefer, into a body imprisoned within its passing and a mind soaring above it," a vision of reality that he at one point pictures as a "spinning mirror." For Osip Mandel'shtam, it's a spread-out fan, an image that resurfaces in Nikolai Zabolotskii. For Richard Weiner, it's "a spiral."

The theme of intermediacy has in fact already been noted, under various guises, by many readers of this literature, who describe how these authors represent "metaphysical superfluity" (Mikhail Epstein), "the intermediate area between perception and symbol" (Natalia Poltavtseva), "the in-between of trace and destination" (Alain Badiou), and the effort "to reconcile subjectivity and objectivity, relativism and absolutism, pluralism and monism" (William Harkins).[27] As Eryk Pieszak writes of Gombrowicz, here the only "real person is someone who is 'suspended in-between.'" What has typically been elided is not the recognition of in-betweenness as a theme in each author, but the ways in which a sustained cross-cultural comparison illuminates the substructure of this theme for all of them.

For these authors, intermediacy is not merely a critical designation but an ontological fact, one that acknowledges both the necessity and the futility of what Erich Fromm termed an "escape from freedom."[28] While the writers I treat in this book were certainly inspired by scientific discovery and influenced by sociopolitical discourse, they are primarily concerned with their metaphysical implications for the individual thinking subject, and this is where I focus my attention. Time and again, these authors bounce between definite form and transformation, a self-contained identity and interpenetration, center and periphery. Unable to achieve an ideal of pure Being, they also find themselves unable to escape from Being. Yet it is their awareness of and occasional revelry in being in-between—between East and West, between the imperialist past and the birth of the new man—that makes these writers and their heroes alluringly strange. For this literature of metaphysical experiment, "between" is truly the "meta" in metaphysics. Existentialist literature need not concern itself with the theme of intermediacy, but intermediacy's implications are inherently existential.

Intermediacy also implies a Faustian bargain, in two distinct senses. It is a constant trade-off, a deal with the devil. And it is intimately bound with the steady march from the old world into the modern. In *Theory of the Novel* (1915, published 1920), Lukács nominates Dante's *Commedia* as the pivot point between the "organic" world represented in Greek epic, a world that fully absorbs the figures represented in it, and the world of the novel, dominated by the individual's struggles against the definitions that modernity has imposed on him. In fact, according to Lukács, the novel arises as a genre precisely in order to represent that struggle, whereas in Dante we see that the world through which the hero passes is his own soul. By destabilizing the spatial-temporal strictures of the literary models and narrative norms they inherited, certain writers of the interwar period likewise found the freedom to present their own subjectivity as both the hero and the setting of their texts. They also discovered, however, that there is no way out. If the Faustian bargain of modern man arises, as Marshall Berman puts it, because he, "as the bearer of a dynamic culture within a stagnant society [. . . ,] is torn between inner and outer life," then what distinguishes the authors of intermediacy from their predecessors and contemporaries is that they are concerned more with the irresolvability of their in-betweenness than with the more convenient exit points provided by Enlightenment rationalism and Romantic spiritualism.[29]

It is in this respect that intermediacy splinters off from so much of Modernist literature, which typically depicts the world now coming into being as the realization of all hopes and dreams or, alternatively, as what Berman calls the "tragedy of development."[30] Like the Modernism to which it belongs, intermediacy still displays the tendency toward tragic self-obliteration inherited from earlier aesthetic and philosophical trends.[31] For, as Berman demonstrates, it is the nature of the developer to destroy himself in the process of creating a new reality: "Ironically, once this developer has destroyed the pre-modern world, he has destroyed his whole reason for being in the world."[32] Romantic and post-Romantic literatures offer many examples, from Goethe's Faust and Dr. Frankenstein's triumph over death—whose product literally rampages through the remnants of the old order and guarantees the demiurge's destruction as a consequence of his act of creation—to the death of the thinking subject in the sublime. The young Lukács explains: "Everything the Romantics wanted to conquer sufficed for no more than a beautiful death. Their life-philosophy was one of death; their art of living, an art of dying."[33]

Yet for writers stuck in between, the new world now coming to life is also dragging them away from a beloved past, even as the persistence of the past makes the new world a grotesque transformation of the old. The spatial dimension of this transformation is treated in chapter 2, which examines intermediacy in the story worlds of Bruno Schulz (1892–1942) and Andrei Platonov (1899–1951), two writers whose entrapment between past and future worlds plays out in an indeterminate journey between a well-defined starting point and an increasingly inchoate periphery. The hero wanders through an expansive landscape, encounters fascinating but fleeting companions and foes, but gets nowhere. His movements through space constitute a flight back and forth between security and freedom, between formal definition and disintegration. Accordingly, the most prominent consequence of spatial intermediacy in this literature is metamorphosis, the destabilization of spatial form.

Every movement in the literature of intermediacy encounters its countermovement; this is how intermediacy preserves itself, through the hero's continuous vacillation between extremes—a dialectic, to be sure, yet an anti-Hegelian one, insofar as it is necessarily devoid of sublimation or progress. What appears as transformation in space meets its countermovement in time, as repetition. These symptoms of intermediacy cannot be divorced from one another. To do so would neutralize intermediacy as such, which arises precisely from the hero's failure to step decisively into home or adventure, past or future, form or formlessness. Just as he serves as an archetype for indeterminate wanderings through narrative space, Don Quixote is emblematic of repetition in narrative time as well; we may even describe Cervantes's novel, following Foucault, as "the first modern work of literature, because in it we see the cruel reason of identities and differences make endless sport of signs and similitudes."[34] Not only is the knight errant a slave to repetition, but his repetitions are themselves recursive: each is a quest for repetition in similitude.

The temporal aspect of intermediacy is the focus of chapter 3, where I discuss the mechanisms by which clear distinctions between past, present, and future break down in the literary artwork. As much as my approach to this problem grows out of my reading of time in Bakhtin, I am "unwriting" Bakhtin in at least one important respect, namely, by restricting my treatment of temporal intermediacy initially to the work of two lyric poets, Osip Mandel'shtam (1891–1938) and Czesław Miłosz (1911–2004). Bakhtin states unequivocally that the time construct of epic literature could be revived in the novel, but not in lyric poetry, which he treats exclusively as the poet's monologic and thoroughly self-contained declaration to his audience.[35] In their removal of temporal constraint, particularly through the adoption of a childlike, naive attitude toward the distinctions that separate one time from another, Mandel'shtam and Miłosz demonstrate both the function of Bakhtinian discourse in the lyric poem and the tragic consequences that this discourse has for the poem's lyric subject.

We might call the stretching and eventual neutralization of time as a delimiting factor in a literary text "time dilation," an important implication of Einsteinian relativity. The time of a moving frame of reference, Einstein theorized, slows down when observed from another frame of reference.[36] In the literature of intermediacy, time often becomes so diffuse as to disappear altogether. As a result, events become maximally "eventful," in Bakhtin's idiosyncratic use of the word: "eventness"—*sobytiinost'*—is the potential for an event to blossom into any number of often unforeseen potential consequences. This is one of the core concepts by which Bakhtin separates the free adventures of Don Quixote from the bulk of European literature that would follow, with its linear, authorially predetermined sequences of causes and effects. Eventness means that anything might happen, and what does happen has little consequence anyway, since it is not being orchestrated by the author.

Gary Saul Morson helps clarify this potential in its practical application with the useful term "sideshadowing." If foreshadowing transmits to the reader the ultimate predestination of the narrative universe, for which the author is both God-the-Creator and God-the-Destroyer, then sideshadowing neutralizes narrative teleology by suggesting alternative outcomes. It produces what Morson calls, in a kindred formulation of intermediacy, the "middle realm" between potential and realized events: "Some nonactual events enjoy their own kind of reality: the temporal world consists not just of actualities and impossibilities but also of real though unactualized possibilities."[37] In the literature of intermediacy, we see these possibilities layered one atop the other, such that the hero or lyric voice inevitably becomes confused as to which reality he occupies. He is condemned to indeterminate, quixotic wanderings through repetitive narrative and poetic cycles. He cannot stop moving, and the more he moves, the more he is faced with his freedom in space and time as an inescapable abyss.[38]

Kafka comes to mind once again, having first drawn a reality of unbounded space and inconsequential time in the last extant chapter of his first, unfinished (and therefore open-ended) novel, *The Man Who Disappeared* (Der Verschollene, 1912; often translated into English as *Amerika*). The title alone is an apt figure for eternal, indeterminate wandering. Forced from his parents' home after impregnating the chamber maid—already fascinated with unfair punishment, Kafka makes a point of telling us that it was *she* who sexually assaulted *him*—Karl Rossman, the novel's protagonist, is sent to the United States. Kafka's America is a space of endless, fanciful adventure, one that features an absurd (if enviably convenient) bridge connecting Boston to New York City.[39] The farther Rossman wanders, the more his actions seem to lose their meaning. No matter what he does, he will be expelled from one living arrangement into another, more expansive one, until he at last finds himself in "the Nature Theater of Oklahoma," an ahistorical, timeless, open space, a stage environment where the theater becomes as large as the world. Action and performance blend together. As in Lukács's reading of Dante or Jorge Luis Borges's "Map of the Empire whose size was that of the Empire," reality and representation merge.[40] Walter Benjamin characterizes the Nature Theater of Oklahoma as a zone in which events lose their power to signify and instead melt into pure gestures, which then seek out meaning, here and throughout Kafka's work, "in ever-changing contexts and experimental groupings."[41] In such a space, Rossman experiences what Bakhtin later calls, in his expanded 1963 reworking of his Dostoevsky study, "the carnival square," where "[a]ll *distance* between people is cancelled, and a distinct carnival category comes to the fore—*free familiar contact between people*."[42] In the Theater of Oklahoma, Kafka's protagonist becomes an eternal wanderer, a performer in an infinite space where there is no difference between performer and audience. Shame, delight, and ideas are shared equally among everyone, and Rossman seems almost to dissolve into the crowd. It is difficult to imagine that the novel could ever have been completed, since there is no clear exit point for the narrative. Rossman's time, whatever that may mean, will never come.

In *The Man Who Disappeared,* Kafka executes an assault on temporality that resonates powerfully with Lukács's observation about the novel, written at approximately the same time, as the medium in which "meaning is separated from life, and hence the essential from the temporal; we might almost say that the entire inner action of the novel is nothing but a struggle against the power of time."[43] Yet this model of absolute freedom in unbounded performance can just as easily become an absolute prison, and Kafka shows us this as well. Time may become so dilated that experience and memory become coexistential, effectively joining interiority and exteriority, which hardly allows for a transcendence of the Self. Quite the contrary: the outer world becomes an immediate reflection of one's own subjectivity, which means the hero is trapped in the world that he himself is.

This is what we find in *The Castle* (Das Schloss, 1922), Kafka's last, also unfinished novel. The space-time construct of *The Castle* is precisely what we have already encountered at the end of *The Man Who Disappeared,* only now the hero dissolves tragically in his own adventure. His name, truncated to Josef K. in *The Trial* (Der Prozess, 1915), is now the utterly anonymous "K." Constantly moving toward the eponymous Castle without ever getting any closer to it, K. spends his time performing meaningless tasks, playing whatever role is demanded by the unseen authorities deep inside the Castle, but none of these roles accords with his own sense of self. K. can neither enter nor exit this milieu.[44] Unbounded narrative space-time becomes, as C. S. Lewis memorably describes his bewitched land of Narnia, a place where "it is always winter [. . .] and never Christmas."[45]

Over the arc of Kafka's career, it is our orientation toward the spatial-temporal construct, and not the construct itself, that changes from delight to despair. At the end of his monumental three-volume study *Indeterminate Thought* (La Pensée indéterminée, 1985–90), Georges Poulet hints at a similar transition from Proust to Kafka, noting that both writers dramatize their "lack of knowledge"—*manque de savoir*—about the reality around them, but whereas Proust fills this lack with his own memory and imagination, Kafka dwells within the lack itself, as an irremediable negativity that is "ultimately the sole means of escaping the rigidly determined nature of the real."[46] Where I would challenge Poulet's description of this shift is in his implication that Kafka presents, or even hopes for, any escape at all. The technologies of the modern era, with their emphasis on ever-increasing velocity and connectivity, only exacerbate the confusion between Self and Other, inside and outside, past and future. In chapter 4, then, we will look at two more poets, Nikolai Zabolotskii (1903–1958) in Soviet Leningrad and

Vítězslav Nezval (1900–1958) in Prague, who experience urban modernity as a space of metamorphosis between times. Through their vision of the city in a state of constant, indeterminate transformation, a reflection of the lyric speaker's own movement through space, we come to recognize how inextricable the spatial and the temporal are from one another.

Blurring the conceptual boundary between the individual and his surroundings naturally leads us to reevaluate the relationship between artist and artwork. After all, if the voices we hear in these texts are always in flux between an absolute individuality and total dissolution in the Absolute, doesn't the gulf between the real author and his imagined construct—that is, between the living, breathing artist and his creation—present an ultimate boundary, one that no metaphysical speculation can ever cross?

Bakhtin's treatment of Dostoevsky suggests otherwise, depicting an author powerless to define his characters, who then behave according to their own volition. The author in Bakhtin's model merely observes his heroes' actions, which take on the hue of fully valid, ethically consequential acts, as if they had occurred in the real world: "For [Dostoevsky], coming to an understanding of the world meant conceiving all its contents as simultaneous *and guessing at their interrelationships in the cross-section of a single moment.*"[47] The freedom that results from this process cannot be absolute; even in Bakhtin's reading of Dostoevsky, the hero's freedom is purchased at the expense of the author, who is reduced to playing the role of a scribe recording his characters' activities.

As difficult as it may be to find a convincing example of the author's expulsion from the literary process in Dostoevsky, whose works are so meticulously plotted and characters so frequently drawn to type, we have a ready-made example in one of Kafka's briefest stories, "The Truth about Sancho Panza" (Die Wahrheit über Sancho Pansa, 1917), which is short enough to quote here in its entirety:

> Without making any boast of it Sancho Panza succeeded in the course of years, by feeding him a great number of romances of chivalry and adventure in the evening and night hours, in so diverting from himself his demon, whom he later called Don Quixote, that his demon thereupon set out, uninhibited, on the maddest exploits, which, however, for the lack of a preordained object, which should have been Sancho Panza himself, harmed nobody. A free man, Sancho Panza philosophically followed Don Quixote on his crusades, perhaps out of a sense of responsibility, and had of them a great and edifying entertainment to the end of his days.[48]

In Kafka's retelling of *Don Quixote,* one of the foundational works to which Bakhtin returns time and again throughout his career, Sancho Panza begins as a reader, whiling away his evenings with chivalric romances, just as Cervantes tells us Don Quixote had done before going mad. Kafka then transforms Sancho into a kind of author: it is Sancho who fills Don Quixote's head with the ideas that spur him to misadventure. In this version, however, Don Quixote is not Sancho's master, but a "demon"—and not anyone's demon, but specifically Sancho's, the demon attached to him personally—*sein Teufel*. Thus it becomes difficult to say whether Sancho's evening reading is for his own benefit or for that of his demon, who in any case should remain attached to the person he torments and have full access to his thoughts and feelings. The demon pays for his knowledge by being unable to act on his own. Later, under the name of Don Quixote, he alters this circumstance by detaching himself from Sancho and embarking on a life of adventure. And yet Sancho recognizes that the demon remains by necessity a part of him. Now that he has exposed the world to this danger, the squire must expiate his *Verantwortlichkeitsgefühl*—his "sense of being responsible"—by following and recording the demon's exploits. In the end, the demon becomes the author of his own adventures. And Sancho, as the demon's reader, is transformed into yet another author, whose reports regarding the activities of Don Quixote we will be privileged, presumably, to read.

Kafka's model is hermeneutical candy. The reader (Sancho) becomes the author, who again becomes a reader, who in turn resumes his authorial activities. In the course of this elliptical movement, the real author (Cervantes) is excluded, but the world itself is not, for Sancho clings to his guilt. Toward whom? According to Bakhtin's notion that "in order to live, one must be unfinalized, open for oneself," responsibility is foremost an openness to the world *for the sake of oneself.*[49] In this enlightened self-interest, the individual realizes his own freedom by not being sealed within himself. In "The Truth about Sancho Panza," it is the fact that Sancho has opened himself to the world, by the very act of loosing his demon upon it, that makes him "a free man." This does not mean, however, that Sancho is wholly detached from his more intrepid subconscious, since he cannot help but compulsively follow his demon's adventures. It is only by observing these adventures that Sancho can satisfy his sense of ethical obligation.

Sancho, in this way, provides us an illustration of Bakhtin's author-as-observer. He cannot control his demon, any more than the ego can master the id, yet the hero, in all his independent action, remains a part of the author. Don Quixote's playing field, meanwhile, is unbounded by time and space. His adventures will almost certainly go on forever. This is a rosy ideal of narrative, but it must break down the moment the hero becomes unsatisfied with his boundless universe and attempts to move beyond it. The realization that this kind of transgression or migration beyond the limits of Being is impossible is not unique to the literature of intermediacy in Central and Eastern Europe, but it is in this body of work that the preoccupation with entrapment in Being becomes its own, self-sustaining concern. Literature thus emerges as both a means of engaging the world and a trace of that very same engagement, the residue of what Maurice Blanchot would later describe, with frequent reference to Kafka, as the "essential solitude" of writing, the "surrender to the interminable" in the textual construct, through which "the writer, drawn out of himself by literature in search of its essence, tries to salvage his relations with the world and himself."[50]

The Polish novelist Witold Gombrowicz (1904–1969) was thinking in a similar vein in 1957 when he reflected that "[t]he story of my becoming is the history of my constant adaptation to my literary works."[51] Reading Gombrowicz alongside two Czech contemporaries, the world-famous Karel Čapek (1890–1938) and his utterly obscure colleague Richard Weiner (1884–1937), chapter 5 examines intermediacy as a "tragedy of development" for the individual hero, author, and reader alike, one in which freedom constantly threatens the identity of anyone who dares pursue it, while identity imposes strictures that compel us to seek out freedom. In these authors, all of the thematic symptoms of spatial-temporal intermediacy, from homelessness and repetition to transformation and doubling, appear in exquisite and unsettling relief.

One can easily imagine other applications of intermediacy as an interpretive paradigm, just as one could test it against other authors or texts than those who appear in the following pages. I suggest some of these other directions in the conclusion. But even a cursory reading of this study will reveal the striking absence of primary texts by women, which warrants comment here, however brief and inadequate my explanation will be for so peculiar a lacuna.

Many women do, in fact, appear on the margins of the story I am about to tell. They include major Modernist writers, such as the Russian poet Anna Akhmatova (1889–1966), and lesser-known figures like Debora Vogel (1902–1942), the Jewish avant-gardist whose correspondence with Bruno Schulz helped effect the latter's turn from graphic art to literature. Neither could be properly characterized as an author for whom in-betweenness occupies a prominent thematic or conceptual position. Akhmatova's lyrics are grounded in relatable social and historical experience, with little or no spatial-temporal destabilization, whereas the spatial-temporal construct of Vogel's lyrical prose is dismantled so thoroughly that her narratives often have no discernible time, place, or character. Writers rooted in the Symbolist movement, such as the Russian poet Zinaida Gippius (1869–1945), are similarly disqualified by their neo-Romantic privileging of the spiritual over the material, while poets like Marina Tsvetaeva (1892–1941), whose oddities might otherwise suggest various forms of in-betweenness, appears to reject spatial-temporal definition altogether.[52] From the opposite direction, many important female writers of the period, including the influential Polish novelist Zofia Nałkowska (1884–1954), hewed more closely to accessible themes and methods, thereby avoiding the obscurity that enshrouded most of my authors in their own lifetimes.

I can speculate, if tentatively, that female writers of the interwar period, a small minority still struggling to define themselves in literatures traditionally dominated by male voices, saw little need to court the anonymity that an exploration of personal and artistic in-betweenness would all but guarantee.[53] But marked as their absence from this international coterie appears to us today—it was utterly unremarkable at (or for) the time—it belies the vital role women would play in advancing the theme of intermediacy in postwar literature, when the troubling and phantasmagoric spatial-temporal construct that engenders intermediacy would have a new, radically different life.

For the Modernist author in the West, writing may allow a path toward escape from the definite present by granting access to other times, and literature serves an unmistakably Aristotelian function by allowing us to experience tragic feelings without having to live through tragic circumstances. This is what Proust means when he extols the power of the author:

> Through him, we become the true Proteus who puts on all forms of life in succession. Exchanging them thus, one for another, we feel that to our being, grown so agile and so strong, these forms of life are only a game, a mask that grieves or grins, but which is never quite real. Our good or bad fortune momentarily looses its tyrannical hold on us, we play with it and with that of others. This is why we feel such happiness when we reach the end of some beautiful novel with a tragic theme.[54]

But what would happen were our escape route—the "end" that brings "happiness"—cut off? What would happen if the tragic dream didn't end, or if the mask, a favored metaphor for several of the authors discussed in this book, could not be removed? What would become of us if we were to discover that there is no way out of these stories, no escape from these masks, except into other masks?

Then we would find ourselves inescapably in between.

Chapter 1

✦

The Metaphysics of Reading In Between

> A remarkable phenomenon: the more our immediacy absorbs us, the more we feel the need to offset it, so that we live, in one and the same moment, within the world and outside it. Hence, when we confront the sideshow of empires, all that remains for us to do is seek a middle term between the skull's grin and serenity.
>
> —E. M. Cioran

Though intermediacy as a theme of interwar Eastern European literature was energized by dramatic shifts in the modern conception of space and time, it is ultimately rooted in a problem fundamental to the philosophy of representation, namely: How can I represent the unity of Being—what Bruno Schulz will call the "extreme monism of substance"—if my knowledge of reality is always divided between inner and outer experience, between the subjective and the objective, and ultimately between the episodic nature of memory and the indifferent continuity of the exterior world? In short, how can I represent this totality when representation itself, whether in literature, the plastic arts, or thought, peels off from and betrays that unity?[1]

While this epistemological dichotomy is ages old, we may just as well ask what it is about European discourses in the early twentieth century that makes them especially fertile ground for representing in-betweenness. The answer lies in changes within the European milieu, in the evolving understanding of how individuals exist in space-time. This was a period when technological, scientific, and philosophical advances were closing in on the monism-dualism divide, albeit from different directions. At the turn of the century, and for the first time in human history, people living in distant villages could imagine that they shared the same time—their respective town clocks were now synchronized—and space, since it was now possible to travel efficiently from one place to another with advance knowledge of when one would depart and when one would arrive.[2] With the advent of the cinematograph, artists, scientists, and the urban public could finally visualize simultaneous action in multiple locations.[3] A world that for centuries had been defined by differences of culture, language, religion, and class was giving way to the highly integrated, multicultural, and urban existence more familiar to us today.

Of course, this modernization was not yet an accomplished fact, and in the interwar period there remained enough tension between a subjective approach to experience, rooted in intuition, and its objective counterpart, based in disinterested observation, for the public disagreements of philosophical partisans to make the international news.[4] In his last major work, Edmund Husserl identified this tension as a "crisis" of knowledge, noting that "the difficulty which has plagued psychology, not just in our time but for centuries—its own peculiar 'crisis'—has a central significance both for the appearance of puzzling, insoluble obscurities in modern, even mathematical sciences and, in connection with that, for the emergence of a set of world-enigmas which were unknown to earlier times."[5] For Husserl, the disciplinary shift of the sciences toward concrete data and mathematical demonstration—he calls this "physicalistic rationalism"—does not relieve humanity of the burden of unraveling "the enigma of subjectivity."[6] On the contrary, the rapid accumulation of knowledge about the world—which Husserl, a mathematician by training, otherwise lauds—makes it all the more urgent for us to understand how we, as individuals, fit into a universe so indifferent to our individuality.

Accordingly, we are not dealing merely with a crisis of knowledge in a scientific sense but with a crisis in the very constitution of subjectivity, what the influential Russian Symbolist poet Aleksandr Blok calls, in a famous 1919 declaration, the "crisis of humanism." Just as Husserl identifies positivist claims toward objectivity as a way of sidelining the subject, Blok sees the crisis, rooted in the Reformation and invigorated by eighteenth-century revolutions, consisting in the individual's being absorbed by the masses.[7] But it is another, later Eastern European thinker, the Romanian philosopher Emil Cioran, who provides some of the most elegant explications of this tension between individuation and universality:

> If I oppose the sole truth of Unity by a necessarily deceptive Multiplicity—if, in other words, I identify the *other* with a phantom—my rebellion is meaningless, since to exist it must start from the irreducibility of individuals, from their condition as monads, circumscribed essences. Every act institutes and rehabilitates plurality, and, conferring reality and autonomy upon *the person,* implicitly recognizes the degradation, the parceling-out of *the absolute*. [. . .] We measure an individual's value by the sum of his disagreements with things, by his incapacity to be indifferent, by his refusal as a subject to tend toward the object.[8]

In a rapidly industrializing society, this "refusal as a subject to tend toward the object"—the rejection of conformity, membership, and even of sympathy with the Other—constitutes a rebellion against the collective. Thus the individual might affirm his own freedom and autonomy. In rebelling, however, the individual must also run up against "the sole truth of Unity," the material fact of our arising from and disintegrating into the same substance, as well as the social interpenetration that is increasingly evident in technological advances and philosophical explanations.

The literature of in-betweenness, then, is a product of this tension between the expansive inner life and the failure of the outer world to reflect it. In his earliest efforts to theorize this problem in literature, Lukács described it as the painful incommensurability of soul and form.[9] The achievement of European Romanticism, Lukács argues, is that it underscored the struggle of essence to make itself fully manifest in a world that was not its equal. Accordingly, in his critical reading of Søren Kierkegaard's engagement to Regine Olsen, Lukács suggests that the Danish philosopher *had to separate* himself from the woman whom he passionately loved, if only to realize his Romantic ideal of separation from his lover and, by so doing, to bring his outer reality into closer alignment with his inner self-concept.[10]

There is a clear line of development from this principle to Lukács's more mature discussion in *The Theory of the Novel*, where he suggests that "[t]he abandonment of the world by God manifests itself in the incommensurability of soul and work, of interiority and adventure—in the absence of a transcendental 'place' allotted to human endeavor."[11] The "world" in question is that which arises in the soul of the character, the inner world that must strive against the efforts of one's milieu to delimit it. "[E]ither the world is narrower," Lukács continues, "or it is broader than the outside world assigned to it as the arena and substratum of its actions."[12]

In Romantic and post-Romantic literature, the "abandonment of the world by God" fuels the Faustian dilemma of modern man, who must become a demiurge in order to reshape the external world in the image of his own interiority. The potential prize is free will as such, the perfect equivalence of inner conception and outer manifestation. If we take this notion to its logical extreme, the boundary between inside and outside, between soul and form, dissolves. Ultimately, the inner world of the subject not only becomes "broader than the outside world assigned to it as the arena and substratum of its actions" but absorbs the outside world entirely.

One cannot expect literary models to achieve such extremes without a wholesale rejection of the representative norms built into the Western tradition. Indeed, many of the Surrealist and Futurist artistic programs of the early twentieth century predicate their claims to total creative freedom on their revolt against a traditional tendency to mold literary space against some semblance of lived praxis. This is the case, for example, with Velimir Khlebnikov's "trans-sense language" (*zaumnyi iazyk*, or simply *zaum*) or Vladimir Mayakovsky's declaration that "the past is cramped," and that we must therefore "toss Pushkin, Dostoevsky, Tolstoy and the rest from the steamship of Modernity."[13] The soul, in a sense, becomes form.[14]

Lukács, however, does not apply his spatial comparison of inner and outer worlds to the avant-garde. Rather, he is interested in developing a method of conceptualizing the spatial-temporal milieu of the literary text as we see it in *Don Quixote*—that is, in the infancy of the European novel. This construct has been, in Kundera's formulation, "depreciated" by the rationalistic privileging of verisimilitude.[15] The figure of Don Quixote offers us an enduring example of the hero or thinking subject as metaphysically in between: he is both a mentally unstable old man and a gallant knight-errant, both a reader infected by the chivalrous tales he has read and the author—by virtue of his wayward performance—of a tale of his own. Through his associative delusions, windmills are transformed into giants, and a ruined beggar becomes his Dulcinea. Except in moments when the contrast between fantasy and reality offers some comic payoff, Cervantes's method carefully prevents the reader from peeking behind the curtain of his artifice, allowing us instead to put real stock in Don Quixote's unreal world, which most often appears to us as he, the hero, would have it. In this sense, Sancho Panza is Don Quixote's first "reader." As we have already seen in Kafka's "The Truth about Sancho Panza," the squire serves first to express our initial doubts, and then to acquiesce to his master's vision in our stead.

What Lukács describes in *The Theory of the Novel* is the failure of Western literature to assimilate this sense of intermediacy. When we do see shades of it again, according to Lukács, it is already the second half of the nineteenth century, and it is not in the West, but in Russia. Thus one of the most provocative assertions in Lukács's book comes in its closing passage: "[The world of the renewed epic] is the sphere of pure soul-reality in which man exists as man, neither as a social being nor as an isolated, unique, pure and therefore abstract interiority [. . .]. It is in the words of Dostoevsky that this new world, remote from any struggle against what actually exists, is drawn for the first time simply as a seen reality."[16] Without offering details as to how Dostoevsky achieves this renewed epic, Lukács leaves the challenge to his readers. He would not perform the necessary analysis himself; in a gesture befitting the Underground Man, he took a sharply Marxist turn, disavowed *The Theory of the Novel,* and produced his masterwork, *History and Class Consciousness,* in 1923. It fell to a young Russian philosopher, Mikhail Bakhtin, to demonstrate how Dostoevsky's narrative universe constitutes a "pure soul-reality," a milieu of maximal freedom.

On its face, Dostoevsky's work seems an unlikely candidate for such potential. His novels are meticulously plotted demonstrations not only of how freedom allows choice but of how our choices lead to inevitable spiritual and social consequences. The interpretations offered by Dostoevsky's best critics of the nineteenth century and early twentieth underscore those consequences and reify the monologic philosophical and ideological positions that Bakhtin would reject. Bakhtin had started a translation of *The Theory of the Novel* in 1921 and abandoned it, having learned that Lukács now rejected the work.[17] The text that Bakhtin subsequently produced, *Problems of Dostoevsky's Creative Work* (Problemy tvorchestva Dostoevskogo, 1929), is an extravagant attempt to out-Lukács Lukács. By taking the Hungarian critic's bait and choosing Dostoevsky for his primary texts, Bakhtin essentially constructs an elaborate escape act within an otherwise self-enclosed and inescapable narrative system.

With Bakhtin's help, the hero will escape from the author, but this escape proves consequential for the reader's milieu as well. The hero's escape from the author also allows the critic to escape an unacceptably hermetic critical tradition; as Mikhail Gasparov puts it, "Bakhtin is the mutiny of the self-asserting reader against the pieties imposed on him."[18] In a sense, Bakhtin provides a mirror for the pointlessly rebellious predilections of Dostoevsky's protagonists, for whom transgression—*prestuplenie,* the word more commonly translated as "crime" in the Russian title of *Crime and Punishment*—is a necessary probing of freedom's limits. Bakhtin transforms Dostoevsky into a box from which he, the reader, then escapes, and in the pure exercise of escaping Dostoevsky Bakhtin turns him into a Modernist aesthetic object, much the same way that Houdini's lockbox, that definitively Modernist amusement, becomes an art object or, at the least, a set piece: a safe from which a man can release himself while blindfolded and chained upside-down is both more and less than a safe.[19]

Bakhtin's reading of Dostoevsky liberates the novelist, meanwhile, from didactic purpose or practical social or ethical critique. Like Kafka's Nature Theater of Oklahoma, the literary text becomes a platform for pure performance, where Dostoevsky's characters and their ideas seem to exist in a free space, independent of the finalizing will of their author.[20] Thus Bakhtin tests the potential of twentieth-century metaphysics to introduce freedom into the locked-down world of the literary text.[21] His now-canonical interpretation represents a sequence of hermeneutic escape acts, each tied to a particular critical or philosophical impasse. Along the way, Bakhtin transforms Dostoevsky the author into Dostoevsky the hero.

Dostoevsky and the Future of Reading

Before Bakhtin, the main currents of Dostoevsky criticism had described a writer who used fiction to animate and illustrate lucid philosophical and social critiques. Numerous early studies paint Dostoevsky as an author who burdens young men with troublesome ideas and invites the reader to witness how those ideas come into moral conflict in—well, if not the *real* world, then the *Realist* world, delineated by rigid temporal constraints and accurately mappable spaces. Witness, for example, the spiritual struggles played out in *Crime and Punishment* (Prestuplenie i nakazanie, 1866), *Demons* (Besy, 1872), and *The Brothers Karamazov* (Brat'ia Karamazovy, 1880), as well as the corresponding readings of their heroes as encapsulations of monologically definable ideas about responsibility and redemption.[22]

So monologic was the tendency in reading Dostoevsky, in fact, that his work had given rise to a critical paradigm that I sometimes call the school of "Dostoevsky *as* ____": the critic will complete the analogy with whatever role best reflects his own interest. This habit of reading Dostoevsky as a reflection of the reader himself was inaugurated by A. F. Koni's canonical essays on Dostoevsky from 1881, composed shortly before the novelist's death. Koni, a celebrated jurist, presented Dostoevsky as a criminologist working in fiction.[23] Four years later, Vladimir Chizh, a psychiatrist, suggested the possibility of reading Dostoevsky as a psychopathologist.[24] Antonii Khrapovitskii and Vladimir Soloviev, a Russian Orthodox bishop and theologian, respectively, advanced the popular notion that Dostoevsky was a kind of religious prophet.[25] It is a tradition that continues into the twenty-first century with philosopher James Scanlan's *Dostoevsky the Thinker*.[26]

Much as he rebels against this critical tradition, Bakhtin nevertheless takes up one of its central tasks, namely, to address the nexus between the metaphysical and the ethical, a problem we see clearly in the oft-repeated précis of Ivan's attitude in *The Brothers Karamazov,* that if there is no God, all is permitted. Given the spiritual struggle in that novel between the brothers Ivan and Alyosha, this formulation has inevitably been interpreted from a Christian theological perspective, but for Bakhtin—as later for the French Existentialists—the premise is metaphysical rather than essentially religious: if God, who instantiates time, is removed, then so too is time. Outside time, individuals enjoy absolute freedom as individuals—"their freedom and self-sufficiency in the very structure of the novel in relation to the author," Bakhtin says of Dostoevsky's characters—but they must also face the ethical meaning, rather than the temporal consequences, of their free choices.[27]

In order to redraw Dostoevsky as Cervantes, Bakhtin had to invent a hermeneutic system that, on the one hand, would free the novelist from the grasp of a critical tradition that had already defined him as a programmatic, even didactic author. On the other hand, Bakhtin would also need to free the fictional hero from Dostoevsky. Such a solution would have to integrate formal and metaphysical elements into a single interpretive process. By freeing the hero from the author, Bakhtin devised a commentary not only on literary process but also on Being as such. In other words, Bakhtin sought an aesthetic argument about literature to support fundamentally metaphysical assertions about Being.

This "ethical-religious" problem in Dostoevsky, as Bakhtin called it, had been ill served by the critical tradition, which tended to reduce the spiritual struggles of Dostoevsky's heroes to a set of social, religious, and psychological critiques mirroring the novelist's expository prose and notebooks. In order for Dostoevsky's work to be truly "ethical," it had to be more than just a narrative illustration of moral precepts.[28] Ethics, for Bakhtin, presupposes a milieu in which individuals can make free choices whose outcomes are not determined in advance, choices fostered by a dialogue among equals, without an authority (or author) standing above them. This is not the sort of thing one typically encounters in carefully plotted Realist fiction by a single author.

Yet the possibility of reading such dialogue in Dostoevsky's novels had already been suggested well before Bakhtin's contribution. In his 1901 lecture "Ivan Karamazov as a Philosophical Type"—not quite the "Dostoevsky *as* ____" critical paradigm, but close—and more notably in his 1914 essay "Russian Tragedy," the religious philosopher Sergei Bulgakov reads Dostoevsky's fiction as a philosophical drama staged for the reader.[29] Then, in his essay "Dostoevsky and the Novel-Tragedy," Viacheslav Ivanov takes Bulgakov's notion of theatricality a step further, cultivating an ethical dimension that emphasizes the intersubjectivity of Dostoevsky's characters: "It is not cognition that is the basis of the Realism supported by Dostoevsky, but 'penetration' [. . .]. Penetration is a certain *transcensus* of the subject [. . .] by which it becomes possible to apprehend the alien 'I' not as an object, but as another subject. This is not a peripheral expansion of the borders of individual consciousness, but a certain movement in the very determining centers of its usual coordination."[30] This is the first time in Russian criticism that Dostoevsky's characters appear as thinking subjects, not merely as puppets manipulated by the author, and Bakhtin recognized the achievement.[31] For Ivanov, the ethical turn in Dostoevsky involves a *transcendence* of self, a recognition that the Other is also an "I," and thus necessarily that the Other has something to say of equal value to the thoughts and ideas of anyone else. For this reason, Ivanov rejects "cognition" (*poznanie*), the absorption of external information by a single consciousness who then forms his own judgments—the very foundation of literary Realism—as the basis of Dostoevsky's Realism. Like Lukács, making the same observation at precisely the same time, Ivanov proposes that Dostoevsky's characters appear fully possessed of their own subjectivity.

Instead of cognition, which simply registers the reality handed to it, Ivanov suggests that Dostoevsky's characters demonstrate "penetration" (*proniknovenie*, which could also be translated as "interpenetration"). The interpenetration of the Self and its Other means that the "I" cannot exist without a "you," and the ideal of a self-contained individuality is thereby revealed as illusion. Instead of *Cogito ergo sum*, Ivanov gives us *Es ergo sum: you* are, therefore *I* am.[32] Ivanov expurgates thought from the Cartesian dictum and declares the existence of one subject dependent on the equally valid existence of another, an ontological interdependence elegantly described by Jean-Luc Nancy as "being singular-plural." As Nancy tells us, "if Being is being-with, then it is, in its being-with, the 'with' that constitutes Being; the with is not simply an addition."[33]

Ivanov offers a productive distinction between cognition, or the individual's absorbing the data of the world into himself, without any threat to his individuality, and penetration, that is, the intersubjectivity of the subject, or the notion that the individual depends on the Other in order to be an individual at all. It is a distinction that will arise time and again throughout our tour of intermediacy. Yet it struck Bakhtin as incomplete, since Ivanov presents it simply as a device used by Dostoevsky to make his otherwise monologic broadcasts more persuasive. Accordingly, Bakhtin's admiration for penetration as an immediate and intuitive process is tempered by his dissatisfaction with Ivanov's failure to explain how it is possible to enact it in a literary text, especially in a body of work so frequently read as a monologic religious or psychosociological critique. For Ivanov, the "testament" (*zavet*) to which Bulgakov refers—an unambiguously religious word—still exists in Dostoevsky, which means essentially that Ivanov's notion of penetration is limited to the author's deep sympathy for his heroes, a spiritual, Christian "act of love."[34] The "dialectic" that Ivanov notes in Dostoevsky's texts is "merely post factum," since the testament remains essential, the dialogue merely illustrative.[35]

Bakhtin found Ivanov's analysis promising but believed it had stopped short. After all, Bakhtin asks, what is the point of recognizing the subjectivity of the Other if the dialogue between subjects will be tyrannized by a supreme authorial design? Bakhtin agrees with Ivanov's approach insofar as both maintain that ethics must begin in freedom. Bakhtin goes further, however, in his conviction that this freedom must be more than an authorial illusion, and that it therefore requires a level of formal innovation much greater than Ivanov's hybrid of novel and tragic drama. The protagonists must be liberated from the author himself, so that "Dostoevsky's protagonists, in the artist's creative design, *are not only objects of the authorial word, but also subjects of their own, immediately significant word*."[36] A new, more radical solution is necessary. Again, we return to the question of becoming—of transformation—as Bakhtin insists that Dostoevsky's ethical-religious worldview is meaningless unless he is able to enact it in a new literary form.[37]

Bakhtin's Dostoevsky: A Prototype for Writing (and Reading) In Between

How, then, is Dostoevsky's ethical-religious worldview made manifest in the world? And is there a productive difference here between the world of lived praxis and the world of the literary text?

Bakhtin seems to have started developing his approach to Dostoevsky in earnest in 1922, a critical moment in his personal biography.[38] After a few years of study in Petrograd and a brief teaching appointment in the small town of Nevel', about five hundred kilometers to the south, he was now recently married and teaching in a secondary school in nearby Vitebsk. The following year, he would be diagnosed with a chronic bone infection in one leg that severely hampered his mobility and, in 1938, required the leg's amputation.

Considering how to manifest the ethical-religious urgency of freedom in Dostoevsky, both for himself as a reader and for a new Soviet society, Bakhtin first drew on Lukács's treatment of Dante in *The Theory of the Novel,* the book whose translation into Russian Bakhtin had just abandoned. Lukács's version of Dante helped Bakhtin understand the difference between real polyphony, a dialogue of multiple voices, each of which represents a subjective and ethically responsible position, and heteroglossia—a purely formal polyphony, the staging of dialogue that is in fact merely the author speaking through various characters. Thus it is through Dante that, in the first chapter of *Problems of Dostoevsky's Creative Work,* Bakhtin understands how the heroes' worlds in Dostoevsky "rest side-by-side on an even plane of coexistence (as do the worlds of Dante) and mutual action (which is absent from Dante's formal polyphony), and not one behind the other as levels of arrangement."[39] That is, Bakhtin adopts Lukács's view that the narrative world of Dante's journey is contained within the soul of the hero himself. This is still not enough for Bakhtin; he notes that the encounter with many characters and their voices in Dante is a purely "formal polyphony," since every not-Dante in the *Commedia,* including Virgil, is subordinate to him, not "side-by-side on an even plane of coexistence." Truly, it is difficult to imagine Francesca di Rimini or any other of the poor souls from the *Inferno* embarking on a spiritual journey comparable to Dante's own.

Bakhtin, like Lukács, was born into a world where the dominant model of reading was through the sequence of plot, which determines the consequence of action. This was the model that Lukács presents as having deflected us from the indeterminate wanderings of Don Quixote. In order to restore us to Cervantes's path—to enact what Albert Camus, whom Bakhtin would later name as an inheritor of Dostoevsky's polyphonic novel, called "the rectification of the actual world"—Bakhtin focused his attention on the literary representation of temporality.[40] If the philosopher could neutralize temporal distinction, he would be able to demonstrate how the novel's characters all share "an even plane of coexistence" rather than "one [plane] behind the other."

Bakhtin drew significant inspiration here from Tadeusz Zieliński, a Polish classical philologist who had instructed him at St. Petersburg University during World War I. Zieliński's work on Greek literature and religion, most notably *The Treatment of Simultaneous Events in the Greek Epic* [Die Behandlung von gleichzeitiger Ereignisse im antiken Epos, 1901], proposes that we read time in ancient texts as reflecting a different experience of time for the texts' authors.[41] For Bakhtin, the notion that literary texts from different epochs could encode an experience of temporality particular to the time and place of their composition proved instrumental. Yet in light of the reading model that Bakhtin was now developing, his former teacher's approach was lacking insofar as it was couched in the terminology of fin-de-siècle psychologism: Zieliński addresses our *impressions* of time, not how time as such is constituted in the real world. Accordingly, Zieliński's model could not show how simultaneity of lived experience could be rendered as true simultaneity in the literary text.

The idea of performance, appropriately, provides Bakhtin's escape route. As Gary Saul Morson and Caryl Emerson have pointed out, Bakhtin's earliest writings do not offer the notion of "unfinalizability," the open-endedness and indeterminacy that keep our choices from being mere playacting.[42] This "unfinalizability," however, would become an essential feature of Bakhtin's transformation of Dostoevsky. By the time he wrote the first version of his Dostoevsky book, Bakhtin had already fashioned himself into a linguistic philosopher of simultaneities, not of beginnings and endings, with a notion of freedom that arises from acts of performance, events rife with "eventness." Acts become meaningful and responsible only when they are not predetermined, when they imply real ethical choice—when, as Morson says, they "are performed in a world in which there are multiple possibilities, in which some things that could happen do not."[43]

While freedom consists in the openness of these performances, it is hardly typical of Dostoevsky's own characters, who often prefer external definition, an identity imposed from outside. Dostoevsky illustrates this most colorfully in *Demons,* when Pyotr Verkhovenskii quotes a silly old man as having rejected talk of atheism by asking, "If there is no God, then what kind of captain am I?"[44] Bakhtin's reading, however, largely dissolves these external definitions by dismissing Dostoevsky's use of plot as an instrument of social and moral consequence.

The conceptual seeds of this solution emerge in two texts from Bakhtin's time in Vitebsk, "Toward a Philosophy of the Act" (K filosofii postupka) and "Author and Hero in Aesthetic Activity" (Avtor i geroi v esteticheskoi deiatel'nosti). In "Toward a Philosophy of the Act," which presents a largely

Formalist critique of Husserlian phenomenology, Bakhtin formulates an understanding of the event as inextricable from the people and things that surround the thinking subject:

> The event may be clear and distinct to the participant in every moment of his action. Does that mean that he understands it logically? Does it mean that the only thing he has a clear view of is general moments and relations transcribed into concepts? No. He clearly sees the unique individuals he loves, as well as the sky, the earth, and the trees, [. . .] and also time, through which he is granted value, the value of these people and these objects, concretely and genuinely affirmed. He also intuits their internal lives and desires; he recognizes the genuine and proper meaning of the interrelations between himself and these people and objects.[45]

The tension conveyed by this passage must remain unresolved: the individual's relation to the event is simultaneously active and passive, both rational and intuitive. His perception of the event covers the full range from the passively visual ("he has a clear view," which in Bakhtin's Russian is a grammatically passive construction) through the actively visual ("he clearly sees") to the even more active penetration of outward appearance and the immediate, intuitive apperception of "internal lives and desires." The value of this internal content, which might otherwise belong solely to the outside observer or Other, arises concurrently with the individual's growing awareness of simultaneity. In Bakhtin's insistence on the interconnectedness of the subject and his surroundings, there is a powerful echo *avant la lettre* of Nancy's notion of "being-with," since the phenomenological understanding of Being toward which Bakhtin gravitates binds existence to events and, more to the point, to eventness. For the individual subject, the vast, open potential of this eventness would in turn remain unknowable if not for "the interrelations between himself and these people and objects."

From the very beginning, then, Bakhtin regards the literary text as a world construct or platform, a milieu at least potentially equal to the one we all contend with every moment of our waking lives. Characters, when fully realized, are fully valid actors within their textual universe; they, like us, exist through their social interactions, a notion that demonstrates Bakhtin's strong interest in phenomenological approaches to sociology, most notably those of Max Scheler.[46] Scheler's writings had a profound influence on the young Bakhtin, whose notebooks for *Problems of Dostoevsky's Creative Work* contain extensive quotations from Scheler's *The Nature of Sympathy* (Wesen und Formen der Sympathie, 1923).[47] According to Scheler, "emotional infection" and "fellow feeling," whose symptoms include contagious laughter or a shared sense of the tragic, are evidence that an individual's thoughts, ideas, and emotions are always bound intuitively to those of others. The notion that ideas move fluidly among thinking subjects constitutes a central thesis of Bakhtin's reading of Dostoevsky, namely, that Dostoevsky's heroes are not in possession of their own ideas. Instead, those ideas bounce among the characters through variegated, "polyphonic" speech—that is, speech that reflects the individual subjectivity of the characters themselves, rather than the finalizing voice of the author.

Whereas Bakhtin saw this mutual infection as a guarantor of the hero's ethical freedom within the text, the literature that actively explores it typically treats it as a source of horror. In the immersion of one subject in another, both lose their distinctiveness and individuality. The hero can move asymptotically toward an ideal of freedom in infection—of a liberation of the Self in the abstract being of the Other—but then he must flee in the opposite direction, toward the equally unattainable ideal of secure enclosure within his individual identity. Bakhtin, like his contemporaries, cannot hope to resolve the incommensurability of soul and form, nor can he turn away from it. In the continuation of the same passage from "Toward a Philosophy of the Act," Bakhtin steps back from a wholehearted endorsement of intuition and infection in favor of a sharper critique of Husserl, whose concepts, however logically derived, remain too flimsy and abstract to convey the meaning of the concrete event, or of Being itself:

> And this event cannot be transcribed in theoretical terms without losing the very meaning of its eventness, the very thing that the act knows responsibly and by which it is oriented. It would be incorrect to assert that this concrete truth of the event, which the agent sees and hears and lives through and understands in the single performance of the responsible act—that this truth is unsaid, that one can only live through it in the moment of the action without being able to express it distinctly and clearly. I assert that language, and not the abstract logical moment in its purity, is far more capable of expressing precisely this truth.[48]

Bakhtin's "eventness" is still underdeveloped here, since the multiplicity of potential outcomes that will later become its hallmark remains absent. Instead, we have the opposite, the concreteness and detail of the act as a singular, lived-through, experienced, and rationally processed event. This singularity is further reified by language, which takes the "truth" of the event and wraps it in a comprehensible, communicable package.

Connecting this passage to the one I quoted earlier, we see how language emerges as the tool by which the individual makes meaning of the events that constitute his Being, which would otherwise get lost in Husserl's "abstract logical moment." This solution is suggested in a note to the section of "Author and Hero in Aesthetic Activity" that attempts to define "The Spatial Form of the Hero." The note reads simply: "Absence of gnoseological reflex and pure idealism (Husserl). Zieliński."[49] If I am interpreting this note correctly, Bakhtin reaches for the classical philologist's textually grounded understanding of time as an antidote to Husserl's "pure idealism." The language of the novel for Bakhtin, as Thomas Seifrid puts it, "provides both the site and the record of humanity's most significant engagement with the world."[50]

This nevertheless presents a serious paradox. On the one hand, Bakhtin objects to the "purity" of experiential reality as it is abstracted by Husserlian phenomenology. He instead posits an infectious model of experience, one in which, for an event to have meaning, the individual or hero must "intuit" the relationships between himself and all those elements (people, things) within his purview. But then these multiple, simultaneous processes—the subject's movement among other subjects, his apperception of everything that, like him, is moving and changing in space and time—have to be "transcribed" into language, and not into abstract logic. How can language bear the weight of Being, when abstract logic cannot? Why must the event be so inclusive, even gluttonous in its consumption of all things and their interrelationships, only to be locked down in what Nietzsche had already bemoaned as "the constraint of language," beyond which thought is impossible?[51]

The answer is that Bakhtin's understanding of language is already moving swiftly toward a concept of unfinalizability; his "language," his word, is in the process of opening. Although Bakhtin has not yet described unfinalizability, it is already intimated in how the hero intuits the inner life of Others, a subject penetrating the subjectivity of other subjects—the very same "penetration" that Bakhtin will later approve in Ivanov's essay on Dostoevsky. This sense is conveyed most powerfully by the repeated characterization of the act as "responsible" (*otvetsvennyi*, which also makes it "crucial"). To what or whom is the act responsible? To the actor, to the people and things around him, as well as to its own "eventness," "the very thing that the act knows responsibly and by which it is oriented." The act, like Being, is ultimately responsible to the world "assigned to it as the arena and substratum of its actions," to the milieu in which it is undertaken.

At least several years before the completion of *Problems of Dostoevsky's Creative Work,* then, Bakhtin was already striving toward a notion of language that is vitally connected to both metaphysics and ethics, Being and responsibility. He was committed to discovering a model of reading in which soul and form coexist, each in its own fullness; in which rational definition and identity do not cancel intuition and interrelation; in which the hero's actions affirm both his metaphysical and his ethical status. This model of authorial discourse exists in and through language, but in the truly polyphonic literary text language remains so open as to assume the same ethical urgency as lived praxis.

Although Bakhtin did not articulate this ideal until the first iteration of his Dostoevsky book, he recognized the impediments that lay before him several years earlier, another strong indication that he was already moving toward a notion of unfinalizability in the earliest period of his professional activity. In "Author and Hero in Aesthetic Activity," Bakhtin states unequivocally that the finality of the authorial word closes the world of the hero, who becomes little more than a prop in the author's narrative game, and that this enclosure all but eliminates any ethical import that the hero's actions might have in a less definition-bound milieu:

> The author not only sees and knows everything that all the heroes, separately and collectively, see and know, but much *more* than they do, in that he knows things to which they theoretically have no access. In the author's always fixed and steady *excess* of vision and knowledge vis-à-vis each of his heroes we find all the moments of the finalization of the whole [. . .]. With finalization, and with the finalization of the event, one cannot live, one cannot act; in order to live, one must be unfinalized, open for oneself—in any case, in all the essential moments of life, one must still hold to value, and not amount merely to one's own availability.[52]

Once again, we return to Lukács's ratio between the world contained within the soul of the hero and the world beyond him. Bakhtin notes that what encloses and "finalizes" the hero is the "excess" of the author's knowledge about him. This excess of knowledge constitutes the hero's outer world and, according to the logic of Lukács's analysis, places strict limits on his ability to act freely, and therefore responsibly. If the event is finalized, then no real act is possible. This is perhaps the earliest suggestion of Bakhtin's central notion of eventness. Unless there is the possibility of multiple outcomes—unless one can choose one act over another, judging the possible outcomes in a world of free ethical choices and their meanings—one cannot truly exist, except perhaps as an illustrative prop in another (the author's) consciousness. By refusing to "merely amount to one's own availability," the hero can potentially seize the excess knowledge of the author. His knowledge of the world now internalized within himself, the world in which the hero acts will be the world that he himself is.

Here is the central critical and metaphysical project of *Problems of Dostoevsky's Creative Work*. Picking up Lukács's suggestion that Dostoevsky is the first modern novelist to reconstitute the kind of freedom for the hero that we see in ancient literature and picaresque novels, Bakhtin constructs a reading that locates such freedom in Dostoevsky and, therefore, seems to write the historical Dostoevsky out of the process of his own authorship.

My treatment of this project as an aesthetics of freedom is amplified once again by biographical data. In 1928, shortly after completing the book, Bakhtin was arrested and charged with counterrevolutionary activity. The sentence of five years' hard labor at Solovki, which almost certainly would have been fatal, was commuted to internal exile on account of his poor health. When the book was published in Leningrad in June 1929—an unusual event, given its author's political disfavor—Bakhtin was already on his way to Kazakhstan.

Intermediacy as Chronotope

That Dostoevsky is a master of plotting simultaneous action in his novels is beyond question. One need look only to the convenient absence of the porter at his station both when Raskolnikov comes to the pawnbroker's house and as he leaves (*Crime and Punishment*), or to Alyosha's sudden realization in *The Brothers Karamazov* that, listening to Ivan's allegory of "The Grand Inquisitor," he has not been keeping an eye on Dmitri. But these instances, like most narrative content in Dostoevsky's fiction, are driven by plot demands, and the very consequentiality of each moment seems to reject what Bakhtin imagines as the author guessing at connections between simultaneous actions.

In 1971, Zbigniew Podgórzec, a Polish journalist and translator of Dostoevsky, asked Bakhtin which twentieth-century authors best echo this vision of the novel. Bakhtin's answers were telling: Camus, Sartre, Kafka, Andrei Belyi.[53] To varying degrees, these writers offer much greater resonance with the critical categories Bakhtin applies to Dostoevsky—among them, polyphony, unfinalizability, and ethical responsibility in a world where the spatial-temporal boundaries that normally produce consequence are disrupted—than they do with Dostoevsky's style or rhetorical methods. But this apparent incompatability between the novelist's devotion to narrative consequence and the philosopher's aesthetics of freedom appears a necessary symptom of what Galin Tihanov persuasively calls Bakhtin's "emancipatory discourses," in which Dostoevsky provides the very construct from which emancipation would be achieved.[54] Bakhtin's strategy for reading Dostoevsky liberates his characters from the ideas that drive them. For Bakhtin, freedom from the possession of ideas—possessing ideas, being possessed by them—means that Dostoevsky's heroes are free within the novels. It also means that Dostoevsky himself, as the hero of Bakhtin's metaphysical adventure, is free within the open, constantly reworked space of Bakhtin's study.Thus we might easily imagine Dostoevsky and Bakhtin conversing together in what the latter called "great time," *bol'shoe vremia*. "Great time" is Bakthin's underinvestigated detemporalization of the canon, a dialogic space wherein the giants of literary production remain in eternal dialogue with one another.[55] It is in "great time" that we might picture Dostoevsky writing a book that unravels Bakhtin and, in the process, re-creates Dostoevsky.

Pending the materialization of such a miracle, we may turn to what Bakhtin calls "chronotope." The chronotope is a formal typology of spatial-temporal norms across the history of Western narrative. The space-time construct of the *Illiad* is particular to the epic, that of *Anna Karenina* is particular to the novel, and so on. Bakhtin coined the term in 1938 simply as a calque of "timespace"—the international form "space-time" had not yet been adopted in Russian—in direct, if ambiguously defensive, reference to Einstein: "This term is used in mathematical science and was introduced by and cultivated by the theory of relativity (Einstein). The special sense that it has in the theory of relativity does not concern us; we will bring it in here—into literary studies—almost as a metaphor (almost, but not entirely)."[56] We may be tempted initially to assume that what the space-time of lived experience is to us, chronotope is to the world of the given narrative genre, but it would be more accurate to say, following Morson and Emerson, that "time and space vary in *qualities*; different social activities and representations of those activities presume different kinds of time and space."[57] That is, having adopted the neo-Kantian perspective that our experience of the world consists in our reading of perceptions, Bakhtin takes a radically non-Kantian turn by assuming a functional equivalence between what perception separates, that is, between material reality and its representation. As Bernhard F. Scholz has suggested, Bakhtin "did not distinguish clearly enough between space and time as forms of immediate reality and as forms of *represented* immediate reality."[58] When Bakhtin writes that the relation between the spatial-temporal construct of lived experience and its equivalent in literature is "almost, but not entirely" metaphorical, he is leaving it to the reader to determine degree.

In my description of intermediacy in interwar Modernism, the chronotopes that interest me belong first to Dante and Cervantes. Bakhtin tells us that the chronotope of the *Commedia* is "vertical": each episode happens, as it were, at the same time, since the poet's inward journey is beyond time. (Bakhtin asserts that, after Dante, the master of this verticality in European literature is Dostoevsky, who uses it to stage simultaneous action.) The chronotope that belongs to *Don Quixote* is a little different, itself a hybrid of the chronotope of the chivalric romance, which occurs in an "alien, miraculous world"—that is, a world where space and time are chronically indefinite, and anything can happen—and the chronotope of the picaresque, the novel of episodic wandering. Between the world wars, the literature of in-betweenness combines these chronotopes into a dynamic whole. The world through which intermediate heroes and lyric voices wander is both "alien" and "miraculous" and, at the same time, recognizable as a historical reality. Episodic repetition, meanwhile, gradually collapses horizontal movement into vertical stasis. The chronotope of intermediacy is one in which we see constant movement and zero progress.

By replacing Dostoevsky's typically cramped and restrictive spaces with performative spaces, and by eliminating Dostoevsky's plots in favor of open-ended atemporality, Bakhtin effectively delineates what was going on in some of the most challenging literature of his own time. The figure that is left in Dostoevsky's place is no longer the familiar author of carefully defined characters, places, and actions, but rather an observer of consubstantiality in an ill-defined milieu. "The fundamental category of Dostoevsky's artistic vision," Bakhtin claims, "was not the moment of coming into being, but *being-with and interaction*. He saw and thought his world chiefly in space, and not in time."[59] While such a reading appears to warp Dostoevsky's fiction, to create freedom in an otherwise deterministic narrative system, Bakhtin's emphasis on consubstantiality and unfinalizability fits the intermediate literature of his own time extremely well.

Still, we must wonder whether the system of freedom Bakhtin describes—a system that is unbounded in space and time, in which one is never entirely independent from, or absorbed entirely into, the collective—can ever foster the freedom he ascribes to it. After all, without boundaries and definitions there is no possibility of escape.

Chapter 2

✦

In Medias Res: On Spatial Intermediacy (Bruno Schulz, Andrei Platonov)

> Space, like time, gives birth to forgetfulness, but does so by removing an individual from all relationships and placing him in a free and pristine state—indeed, in but a moment it can turn a pedant and philistine into something like a vagabond.
>
> —Thomas Mann

Standing before the mint-green façade of the municipal theater in Drohobycz, the boom-and-bust oil town where Bruno Schulz was born, spent most of his life, and died, we have two potential routes by which to return to the main square, where Schulz's father maintained a successful haberdashery before his senility brought both business and family to ruin.[1] Turning north and walking just a few paces up Theater Street, then making a sharp left onto Mazepa—the kind of narrow commercial lane that is typical of these once-prosperous Galician settlements, with their faded stucco, store windows, and narrow balconies occasionally supported by otherworldly atlantids and caryatids—we reach the market square. Continuing around to the square's northwest corner, skirting the stately Town Hall, we arrive at what at the turn of the last century had been the shop of Jakub Schulz, though it would be his wife Henrietta's name displayed on the sign outside, quietly suggesting the dowry that put them in business. The entire journey is no more than 350 meters, a five-minute walk at the leisurely, distracted pace of a young boy.

But if we were to choose another route, crossing the street in front of the theater, we would find ourselves on Podwale. Taking an archaic name for "foundations" or the foot of city walls, Podwale is just a back alley behind the same buildings that beckon along Mazepa, "the reverse side," Schulz tells us, "sort of the inner lining of the four lines of the market square."[2] In the title story of *Cinnamon Shops,* Schulz's narrator—sometimes called Józef, Jacob's prodigal son in the Old Testament, and unmistakably a stand-in for Schulz's boyhood self—takes the latter route when his mother sends him home from the theater to fetch his father's wallet. Any curious child might have done the same. He immediately becomes lost in the lush courtyards and small, back-alley shops—"I call them 'cinnamon shops' for the color of that dark paneling they're adorned with"—though he is just a stone's throw from home.[3]

The narrative architectonics of most of Schulz's stories works from the center out.[4] From the starting point of the given tale we move out toward the periphery, our narrative progress measured against the destabilization of the space that the narrative represents. Jerzy Jarzębski has recently suggested that the center of Schulz's city is the "seat of values" for his conceptual universe, which helps account for the fact that "[t]he road from center to periphery is at the same time the process of unbridling form," as Schulz shows us repeatedly.[5] But the word "periphery" demands a caveat. "Noncenter" would be more accurate, since "periphery" implies a spatial or conceptual border, a discernible boundary that defines the space's limits, and thus also its "center." In the literature of intermediacy, the center of narrative space is always the position of the hero or speaker relative to his moment in narrative time. There is no definite border.

Typically, even the end of the text is inconclusive and elliptical. Like Don Quixote, the hero first abandons security to seek adventure, but the farther he ventures out the more he finds himself along streets that "multiply, intertwine, and replace one another": "Duplicate streets, so to speak, open in the depths of the city—street-doubles, streets that lie and deceive. A bewitched and misguided imagination generates phantom city maps that one would have said he'd long since known quite well, and on which these streets have their places and names, while the night, in its unexhausted fecundity, has nothing better to do than keep providing new, fabricated configurations."[6] Schulz's depiction of the cityscape is typical of his noncenter spaces, which can appear anywhere, even "in the depths of the city," so long as we encounter them at some remove from the speaker's initial position within the narrative. This has the effect of rendering the narrator's journey indeterminate, since the further he goes, the less likely he is to find his way, and the more likely he will get lost in what Schulz subsequently calls, in a chance echo of Bakhtin, "this manifold architectonic polyphony"—that is, narrative dimensions layered one atop another, such that the hero never knows precisely where he is.[7]

Just as space decays in relation to the hero's movements, so too does time. Day or night, the later it gets—and the further we move into the narrative—the more certain the hero is to lose track of time, or else to perceive that time has lost its meaning. With the breakdown of spatial-temporal definition, matter similarly abandons the stability of form, leading to weather so unruly that the city becomes unnavigable. "We became increasingly convinced," Schulz remarks in "The Gale" (Wichura), "that this entire storm was merely the night's Don-Quixotism imitating, in the narrow space of the [stage's] wings, the gale's tragic expanses, its cosmic homelessness, its orphanhood."[8] The link between Don Quixote and "cosmic homelessness" could not have been articulated better by Lukács or Bakhtin, though it is highly unlikely that Schulz was aware of either. Like the adventures of Cervantes's archetypal knight-errant, Schulz's stories are inherently episodic, allowing his hero to retreat to a point of stability and definition, if momentarily, rather than succumb completely to these "tragic expanses" and the disintegration, both physical and metaphysical, they occasion. This also means, however, that the trauma that Schulz consistently associates with wandering out from the stability of the center, especially the trauma of his father's descent into senility and ruin, will be repeated compulsively every few pages, from one story to the next.

This chapter treats spatial intermediacy and its most striking symptom, the material transformation of people and things—that is, changes in how things occupy space. My treatment focuses on Schulz and on the early Soviet author Andrei Platonov, coevals who had no opportunity for mutual acquaintance but who nevertheless address intermediacy as both cosmic inevitability and existential menace. The primary texts for this discussion are Platonov's major novels, *Chevengur* (1926–29) and *The Foundation Pit* (Kotlovan, 1929–30), and Schulz's stories, collected as *Cinnamon Shops* (Sklepy cynamonowe, 1933) and *Sanatorium under the Sign of the Hourglass* (Sanatorium pod klepsydrą, 1937), though I also have recourse to both authors' journalism and theoretical prose.[9] Before we delve into their literary works, however, we must first consider what each author believed his representations to *represent* in the first place.

Bruno Schulz's Spaces: The Reality of Representation

Schulz's spatial descriptions in "Cinnamon Shops" vividly portray a peculiar paradox, namely, that while we can easily identify the ostensible object of Schulz's ekphrasis—he often provides us with the names of streets and landmarks—we would be hard-pressed to map that space as Schulz describes it. This is because the space's geometry is nonlinear; we can conceive of it only by superimposing extra dimensions, which allow streets and buildings to shift position without disturbing the more familiar, and therefore more stable, spaces adjacent to them.[10] Such an approach to the construction of urban space, interior or exterior, is unremarkable in the visual art of the period.[11] For literature, however, it marks a departure from the aesthetics of the Western European precursors of intermediacy, particularly Mann and Proust, even as it borrows liberally from their attitudes toward space and time. In one of his last letters (dated November 6, 1941), Schulz explains to Anna Płockier, a painter then living in nearby Borysław, that Mann and Dostoevsky—for the latter, Schulz points specifically to *The Double* and *The Brothers Karamazov*—"prove how little depends on crossing or maintaining the line of realism, that it is simply a matter of gesture, pose, style. If by realism we mean to understand a certain mundaneness, the ordinariness of the reality described, then these authors are a striking rejection of that definition." [12] Michał Paweł Markowski calls Schulz's approach simply "antirealism," which, rather than communicate the surfaces of things and events to appeal to the reader's physical senses, uses a highly evocative language to express their essence. Not so much a representation of reality in language—and not at all a denial of it—antirealism becomes the proper instantiation of reality *through* language.[13]

The new tendency literalizes what the Realist is more likely to suspend in metaphor and allegory. Krzhizhanovskii's "Quadraturin" might be regarded as emblematic of how this plays out spatially: the story's hero wants a larger apartment, and his apartment literally expands infinitely in all directions without upsetting the surrounding building. But an even more pressing point of reference for the behavior of space in Schulz is Franz Kafka and the endlessly twisting path in *The Castle*. Architectonically, the Castle represents a point of asymptotic approach. K. can close the distance, but the distance is never closed.

The question of what Schulz owes to Kafka has been a topic of debate since the 1930s, when the Polish reviewers of Schulz's second collection of stories, *Sanitorium under the Sign of the Hourglass,* first noted similarities between the two authors.[14] Indeed, reading these authors side by side one cannot help but notice that both bodies of work feature the transformation of a man into an insect—*The Metamorphosis* appeared in 1915, Schulz's "Cockroaches" eighteen years later—or that both regard the figure of the Father as a source of tremendous anxiety, though in Kafka this anxiety stems from the overwhelming surfeit of the Father's authority, whereas in Schulz it is the absence of the Father's authority that torments the narrator.[15]

To the Marxist critics of the immediate postwar period, Schulz's spatial construct could only seem, in the words of the poet Mieczysław Jastrun, a "flight from historical responsibility, from the horror of a historical reality that was soon to destroy our country and burn up centuries of our culture [. . .], an escape [. . .] into the alchemy of words, or else into 'sanatoria under the sign of the hourglass.'"[16] This reaction prompted Artur Sandauer, a vocal opponent of the Socialist Realism that was quickly becoming dogma in Polish literature, to redirect our attention to the *kind* of reality that Schulz portrays precisely and consistently. Schulz's frequent references to "marginal" or "false" time, according to Sandauer, "[. . .] suggest something of an alternative kind of time that enables not only the succession, but also the alternation of events, where one can advance in a couple of directions: not only forward, but into depth. This vision, distinctly post-Einsteinian, determines the specificity and power of such images [. . .] where temporal processes are sort of projected onto the spatial grid."[17] Sandauer does not defend Schulz as a fantasist. Instead, he emphasizes that Schulz has adapted his compositional strategies to a new way of construing reality as such. Sandauer proposes a systemic overlay of space and time inspired by Einstein's (or, more accurately, Hermann Minkowski's) unification of space and time. The movement through one is also the movement through the other, certainly. Yet Sandauer suggests an additional component to Schulz's narrative construct, one that allows us, through an imaginative exercise, to envision additional spatial-temporal dimensions, potentially infinite in number, intricately and inextricably intertwined with those of daily experience. Schulz calls these complementary dimensions by many names, but he does not regard them as pure fantasy or imaginative play. In the post-Einsteinian world-concept to which Schulz refers, reality necessarily includes those spaces and temporalities that we do not experience fully in everyday life, but that nevertheless remain essential components of our reality.

The technology that Schulz nominates as allowing us to unmask the interdimensional quality of space-time is the lyrical word. Not coincidentally, this is also Schulz's reading of the "ingenious artistic act" of Kafka, who, as Schulz explains in his afterword to the Polish translation of *The Trial,* "discovered for these questions, elusive and inexpressible in human language, an as-if adequate corporeality, a sort of substitute material in which he builds and construes the question's structure to its finest details."[18] It would be all too easy to misconstrue what Schulz calls "substitute material" and, subsequently in the same text, "a parallel, double, substitute reality" as being somehow akin to the ur-reality of Platonic metaphysics or, closer to Schulz's own cultural moment, of Symbolist aesthetics. But we have encountered this description before: the same word that Schulz applies to Kafka's narrative construct, *sobowtórny* ("double"), appears in his description of the *ulice sobowtóry* ("street-doubles") in the story "Cinnamon Shops." By Schulz's time, this word was already synonymous in Polish with the phantasmagoria of Dostoevsky's *The Double* (Dvoinik, 1846) and the German Romantic image of the doppelganger. Inscribed within that tradition, this double cannot be taken for a world behind the world. Instead, it refers to real potentials that extend from—and are in fact indispensable components of—the reality we experience every day. The double, whether of a person (Dostoevsky's miserable Goliadkin) or a place (Schulz's streets), draws its signifying power from the fact that it envisions an alternative course for a reality that exists even in its absence. The double is a psycholinguistic construct, analogous to Jacques Lacan's Other, particularly in light of his admonition that *Il n'y a pas d'Autre de l'Autre*—"There is no Other of the Other."[19]

In this regard, where we can make a strong distinction between the narrative constructs of Schulz and Kafka is in the extent to which each author explicitly bridges the gap between the experiential and the potential or mythic. In Schulz's reading of Kafka, the latter's narrative universe is wholly divorced from the biographical reality of its author; it is "a self-contained poetic reality, round, closed on all sides, grounded in itself and staying put."[20] Read in the context of his entire body of work, Schulz's treatment of Kafka suggests a methodological reversal of his own approach to lyrical narrative. Whereas Schulz uses lyrical language to emphasize the nonpresent, unrealized aspects of experience, a process that he terms "the mythicization of reality," Kafka, Schulz tells us, "has an unusually sharp vision of the realistic surface of reality, [. . .] but to him this is a loose, unrooted outer skin that he removes like a delicate covering and places on his own transcendent world, transplants onto his own reality."[21] Despite the idiosyncrasies of Schulz's reading—today we have little trouble appreciating both the biographical foundations and the allegorical pitch of Kafka's writing, especially in light of his *Diary,* letters, and minor works, to which Schulz never had access—this view of Kafka underscores an essential feature of Schulz's art, namely, the double emphasis on the experiential present and those alternative paths of reality that the intellect can access only through imagination, intuition, and memory.

Schulz's approach to art therefore falls in line with the Formalist notion of alienation, estrangement, or *ostranenie,* at least insofar as the poetic word serves to restore our dulled perception of experiential reality.[22] Yet Schulz's notion takes us deeper. If, according to the Formalist model, the experience of art awakens us to a reality we have stopped seeing, for Schulz there is no stepping back from the imagined space, nor indeed any point in doing so, since the spaces we intuit are just as integral to reality as those we experience. Where Formalist defamiliarization alienates us from ourselves in order to allow us to return to ourselves, Schulz allows us no such return.

This alienation from oneself appears in its most reduced version in one of Schulz's earliest extant compositions. "Solitude" (Samotność) offers a map of the thematic substructure of spatial intermediacy by portraying two spaces—one an imagined room, the other a mirror image of the same room—and thus also the simplest form of doubling we know from everyday experience: the confrontation with our own mirror image.

Losing Yourself: Bruno Schulz and the Space of "Solitude"

"Solitude" bookends Schulz's literary career. Probably written in the late 1920s, making it one of his earliest works of fiction, it appears as the penultimate story in his second and final collection, *Sanatorium under the Sign of the Hourglass.*[23] The story begins by imagining briefly what it would be like to be a vermin, in this case a mouse, perhaps a calculated echo of Kafka's Gregor Samsa. Schulz's narrator then asks us whether we, his readers, would like to know *jak wyglądam,* or "how I look": "Sometimes I see myself in the mirror. What a strange, amusing and painful thing! A shame to admit it. I never see myself *en face,* face to face. But a little deeper, I stand there a little further in the depth of the mirror, sort of to the side, sort of in profile, I stand there lost in thought and look to the side. I stand there motionless, looking to the side, sort of behind myself. Our gazes have stopped meeting."[24] This description does little to answer the question "How do I look?" *(Jak wyglądam?).* Rather, it speaks to the issue of "how I *am looking*" *(Jak oglądam?)*—how this speaker, try as he might, is incapable of looking at himself.[25] This inability to meet his own gaze is directly correlated to the spatial construct established in the text. The hero's self-alienation is a psychic extension of his physical isolation from the world, as we see clearly when he goes on to ask: "Must I reveal that my room is walled in? How can that be? Walled in? How would I be able to get out?"[26]

Beyond its construction of an impossible space that allows neither entrance nor egress, "Solitude" raises the question of what happens when someone locked in with himself, his room having no doors, becomes detached from himself, since his displaced image in the mirror will not meet his gaze.[27] In Schulz, the protagonist typically attempts to escape this double isolation—his physical entrapment compounded by his psychic self-alienation—by deconstructing the boundaries that precipitate it. This is precisely what happens in "Solitude." The narrative concludes: "I merely have to imagine a door, a good old door, as in the kitchen of my childhood, with an iron handle and a bolt. There is no room so walled in as not to open to so trusted a door, if only one has strength enough to insinuate it therein."[28] Ending on an uncharacteristic note of optimism, Schulz suggests that the way out of one's isolation is by reestablishing access to remembered spaces, in this case the kitchen recollected from childhood. And the only way this can be achieved is through a practical indifference to what distinguishes one time or space from another.

The point of "Solitude" is to animate the basic tension between identity, on the one hand, and interconnection, on the other, only then to diffuse this tension through a willful failure to differentiate the experiential present from childhood fantasy and memory. By establishing a provisional connection with the past, which Schulz consistently treats as the time of his father's slow demise, he can escape from his isolation in the present. But he also risks losing track of the features that distinguish the present from the past, or the Self from the Other. Here we see the double bind of intermediacy: the escape route always becomes its own trap. In Schulz's distortions of narrative space-time, the narrator creates an escape hatch from his isolation, but his method of escape endangers his very subjectivity, as well as the individuality of those people and things he begins to associate with each other as he grows indifferent to their distinctive features.

A double movement, out from the Self and back to the Self, results in the repetition and circularity we witness throughout Schulz's stories, not only as the narrator moves back and forth between self-singularity in the present and a redoubled integration with lost people and objects but even more obviously in the cyclical nature of the stories themselves. Most of Schulz's narratives are set just after the turn of the twentieth century, when the ten-year-old Schulz witnessed the collapse of his father's mental and physical health, and with it his family's financial security and community standing. In one tale after another, the character of the Father, Jakub, deteriorates both physically and ontologically. He disappears by the end of each text, only to be reconstituted at the beginning of the next.[29] Schulz continuously relives the trauma of losing his father, whose name was, in fact, Jakub. In this way, Schulz's stories play out a Freudian repetition compulsion without any hope of ever "working through" it. The author's search for lost time, as it were, allows him fleeting access to the Father, but it also reifies the Father's absence and unrecoverability.

The overlay of spaces is thus concomitantly an overlay of times, the space of the present infected with a projection of the space of the past. It is also, as we will see more vividly in the examples to come, an overlay of subject and object, a fact that should not be surprising when we consider that our very identity, our self-equivalence, is predicated on the uniqueness of our spatial-temporal coordinates, a uniqueness that intermediacy in space and time corrupts.

At the same time, this reading of Schulz leaves open the question of whether an orientation toward the future would corrupt temporal definitions as effectively as Schulz's orientation toward the past. When it comes to their capacity for destabilizing the present, the Soviet author Andrei Platonov demonstrates that the past and future are functionally equivalent. Comparing the spatial-temporal construct of these two authors, we see that intermediacy in space is the same whether it is the past or the future that invades the present. Spatial intermediacy simply means present space overlaid with nonpresent space. Just as space blurs when we move from the center to the noncenter, time becomes indistinct as we move from the present toward the nonpresent. The "nonpresent" reveals itself in both the literal, conventional sense of "not-now" and in the hyperliteral sense, as "not-here."

What appears as spatial distortion is merely the concurrence of the "here" and the "not-here" in space-time.

The Aporia of the Imagined Future: Andrei Platonov's *The Foundation Pit*

Platonov was, like Schulz, the child of a provincial town far removed from the center of cultural life. Situated some five hundred kilometers south of Moscow, in the heart of the resource-rich Black Earth Region, Voronezh was several times larger than Schulz's Drohobycz, yet hardly less isolated.[30] The ratio between this modest point of origin and the seemingly endless landscape surrounding it is at the very core of both Platonov's worldview and his narrative universe. "His autonomy is the autonomy of an idiosyncratic metaphysician," Joseph Brodsky writes of Platonov, "a materialist, essentially, who tries to comprehend the universe independently, from his vantage—or disadvantage—point of a small muddy provincial town lost like a comma in the infinite book of a vast, sprawling continent."[31]

Neither of them full-time authors, Schulz and Platonov made their livings in large part by reshaping the spaces of the world they had inherited. As a graphic artist, Schulz paid particular attention to representing the world of the past, which continued to exert a psychic pressure on the visual and verbal texts he created in the present. Platonov, meanwhile, worked as a land engineer, specializing in melioration and wilderness conversion. In his youth, he intended quite literally to help shape the world of the future through the grandiose public works projects that transformed the Russian landscape in the early decades of Soviet Communism and that culminated in 1948 in the state plan poetically dubbed "The Great Stalin Program for the Transformation of Nature."[32] By 1926, just as Platonov was beginning work on his sprawling novel *Chevengur*, Viktor Shklovsky had already noted that "these rivers we studied in our geography book—the Voronezh, Bityug, Khoper, Tikhaya Sosna—do not exist" because of the land reclamation projects executed by the likes of "Comrade Platonov."[33]

Platonov's early journalistic writings suggest that, like any true believer in the Soviet experiment, he unified his land work conceptually with ideological ambitions for the Communist world to come, the world that he was then dedicated to building.[34] This optimism, as Stephen Kotkin describes in reference to the First Five-Year Plan, grew out of the conviction that the human domination of nature was as much a scientific inevitability as Communism was a historical one, given "the reliability of scientific planning and the seemingly limitless possibilities afforded by modern technology, when combined with the ultimate science of society, Marxism."[35] By the time the First Five-Year Plan came into effect in 1928, Platonov had already witnessed the disastrous effects of Soviet land reforms, the agricultural underproduction of the New Economic Policy (1921–28), and the increasingly violent clashes between the authorities and the wealthier private farmers, or *kulaks*—a violence vividly portrayed in the climactic passages of *The Foundation Pit,* arguably his masterpiece. All of Platonov's fiction from the late 1920s and 30s reflects these deep anxieties about whether the future he had been promised could ever be fully achieved. *Chevengur* and *The Foundation Pit,* both suppressed until decades after the author's death, offer particularly vibrant instances of a temporal construct oriented toward the imagined future, but with a spatial overlay that is no less tragic than what we find in Schulz's orientation toward the past. In other words, Schulz's intermediacy describes the tragedy of clawing after a past that is continuously receding, since time's inexorable march into the future drags us along with it. Platonov, on the other hand, presents the failure of achieving the future, since the past refuses to let us go completely.

This is especially clear in the underlying spatial conceit of *The Foundation Pit,* the simpler and more elegant of the two novels, though its author left it in a less finished state than its larger, publication-ready cousin.[36] The foundation pit is being excavated in the middle of an anonymous Soviet town, the first phase of construction for a "common house" (*obshchii dom*) "where the whole local class of the proletariat will be settled."[37] The adjective *obshchii* enjoys a privileged position in Platonov's lexicon: he will repeat it and its derived forms throughout the text as a verbal foil to all things individual or particular. But the "common house" is never constructed. In order to accommodate the expanding ranks of the proletariat, the idealized building grows ever larger, requiring a deeper and deeper foundation. Thus Platonov's extended allegory of early Soviet Communism ends, quite literally, with his protagonists being swallowed up in the future's infinitely expanding space.

The novel's characters represent social types whose lives will be impacted by the project. These include Voshchev, the itinerant worker cast out of his small factory, we are told in the novel's opening paragraph, for "his pensiveness amidst the common pace of labor"; Safronov, a doctrinaire laborer; Prushevskii, the terminally depressed foreman; and Nastia, an orphan girl from a bourgeois family who represents the ostensible first wave of the Revolution's beneficiaries. Her speech a grotesque scramble of Leninist and Stalinist clichés—though a little girl, she twice instructs her comrades to "liquidate" and "kill the kulaks as a class"—Nastia is a prime example of how Platonov attaches specific language to certain characters in lieu of exposition. When it comes to describing his characters' physical attributes, Platonov is so sparing that, as Eric Naiman and Eliot Borenstein have noted, they seem to lack a corporeal presence even within the conceptual framework of the narrative.[38] Brodsky goes so far as to suggest that Platonov's characters are trapped within language, that "Platonov speaks of a nation which in a sense has become the victim of its own language; or, to put it more accurately, he tells a story about this very language, which turns out to be capable of generating a fictitious world, and then falls into grammatical dependence on it."[39]

Consistent with Brodsky's sense of entrapment within the creative potential of language, Platonov often burdens his characters with dense spatial-temporal metaphors reflective of the central spatial-temporal metaphor of the foundation pit itself. In a typically lyrical passage, for example, he conveys Voshchev's emotional state as a temporal figure: "In the evenings Voshchev lay back with open eyes and pined about the future [*toskoval o budushchem*], when everything would become universally known [*obshcheizvestnym*] and embedded in a meager feeling of happiness."[40] Most striking among this sentence's remarkable lexical features is how Platonov attaches the "future" *(budushchee)* to the notion of pining, expressed by the verb *toskovat'*, which in its more conventional usage would connote a backward-looking glance, a powerful longing for past experience or a lost object or, at the very least, a counterfactual reality that has not come to pass.[41] The author links verb and object with the equally unconventional preposition *o*, an effective emphasis of the phrase's exceptional design: in neutral speech, the verb should be followed by the preposition *po*, "after" or "along." That is, we pine "after" the object of our nostalgia, since we ourselves come after that object and, like passengers on a train who have missed their stop, can no longer arrive at our intended destination. Platonov's use of the verb shifts its connotative weight from a fantasy of the experiential past (nostalgia) to a certainty about the as-yet-unexperienced future.[42] Voshchev's nostalgia reverses nostalgia's spatial paradigm: here we have arrived on time, but the object for which we would have been nostalgic has failed to meet us.[43]

Spiritual states thus appear in the novel as internal echoes of external space, as Mikhail Epstein indicates in reference to the persistent longing felt by Platonov's characters:

> The emaciated (*toshchie*) long (*toskuiut*) more strongly; "vainness" (*tshcheta*), too, is formed from the same old Slavic root meaning "emptiness." The more emaciated the people, and the more deserted the nation around them, the longer the longing—that feeling of vainness and abandonment with which they encompass nonbeing—that stretches between them. More deeply than in the traditional, noble, "superfluous" men, features of a kind of metaphysical superfluity are glimpsed in Platonov's "emaciated" characters.[44]

Platonov achieves this correspondence between inner and outer experience textually through rhetorical figures of repetition, especially *paregmenon*, or the reiteration of the same word root in multiple forms and inflections. Each new deployment of a given word root becomes a verbal instantiation of the dynamic interconnections and transformations in which Platonov's characters are already embroiled from the outset. Voshchev does not care for universal knowledge for himself, but for everything to be *obshcheizvestnyi*, "universally known," by everyone who will live in the *obshchii dom*, "common house." What he truly calls for here is self-obliteration, the sublimation of his individual consciousness in the collective.

Instead of wishing that the idealized past still awaited him in a future just around the corner, Voshchev conceptualizes the future in past terms, and it is not difficult to understand why. By the time Platonov penned *The Foundation Pit*, the "end of history" heralded by the October Revolution was already a distant memory, but the bountiful Communist future that had been promised was increasingly in doubt. This relationship to past and future evokes two different nostalgic paradigms, which Svetlana Boym distinguishes as "restorative nostalgia," the fantasy of the collective oriented toward the future, and "reflective nostalgia," the fantasy of the individual oriented toward his or her past. As Boym explains, "If restorative nostalgia ends up reconstructing emblems and rituals of home and homeland in an attempt to conquer and spatialize time, reflective nostalgia cherishes shattered fragments of memory and temporalizes space."[45] In other words, what Boym calls "restorative nostalgia" reconstitutes the past as a place to which we can return, if only we can find the way, whereas "reflective nostalgia" refigures those spaces we can readily access as containers for past time. Voshchev fuses these reflective and restorative species of nostalgia together; he spatializes time and temporalizes space, and this is arguably his primary function within the narrative. Temporally, what might otherwise have been a longing for the individual's past is redirected toward a collective future, where "everything would be universally known." Spatially, the future Voshchev imagines must be constructed, as it were, from the ground up, a place where individual history has dissolved into universal consciousness.

The Foundation Pit's strange publication history leaves some doubt as to whether any edition would have conformed fully to its author's vision. It first appeared in 1969, nearly two decades after its author's death, and then only in English translation; it would have to wait almost two more decades before its first publication in its country of origin. Subsequent Russian-language redactions have reflected the strong scholarly biases of their editors. As it is, the novel ends abruptly with the death of Nastia, the orphan girl who is a favorite among those laboring in the foundation pit. Whether we are to take Nastia's death as a suggestion of the fragility of the Soviet future or, what is more, a wholesale condemnation of Stalinism remains uncertain, as it has been throughout the novel. Yet there is considerably less ambiguity in a handwritten valediction that Platonov appended to the first typescript of the original and at some point likely considered the end of the novel:

> Will the Soviet Republic [*esesersha*] perish, like Nastia, or will she grow into a whole person, into a new, historic society? This is the unsettled feeling that constituted the theme of this work while its author was writing it. The author may have been mistaken in portraying the ruin of the socialist generation as a girl's death, but this error arose merely from excessive worry over something precious, the loss of which is tantamount to the destruction not only of all that is past, but of the future as well.[46]

This passage effectively delineates the novel's foundational aporia. Platonov conceives of the Soviet experiment as something started but never finished, and he gives it a feminine ending, so that instead of the conventional *eseser* for "Soviet Union," we have *esesersha,* simultaneously the mother-and-motherland—*rodina-mat'*—and a little girl like Nastia, blending childlike innocence, childish ignorance, and an adult's commitment to ideology and historical vision. In fact, the only time Platonov uses this term in the final text is when it comes out of the mouth of a muzhik—"Hey you, Esesersha is our mother!"—who, when asked whether the Soviet Union is a virgin or a widow, derisively calls out that she is a virgin who needs to be taught a lesson.[47] No longer the Russia of the past nor as yet the Soviet state of the future, Platonov's *esesersha* is caught in between, seemingly incapable of moving backward or forward.[48]

Likewise, Platonov's Soviet Man is a definitively aporetic creation, condemned to indeterminate wandering by his inability to pass into the future. In his major study of Platonov's expansive novel *Chevengur,* Evgenii Iablokov characterizes this indeterminacy as *obratimost',* "reversibility," the quality by which individuals strive toward one goal before reversing course and striving toward its opposite.[49] Such reversal is represented most vibrantly in the Russian tradition by Dostoevsky, where it is typically symptomatic of emotional ambivalence or spite and might best be described by Freud's term "undoing," or the performance of a counteract that might magically "undo" the undesired effect of a preceding act.[50] But unlike what we find in Dostoevsky, Platonov's reversibility is not a symptom of emotional ambivalence or spite. It indicates an aporia, the failure to pass from one place to another, tantamount here to the failure to pass from one time (the present) to another (the future) because of our insurmountable attachment to a third (the past). Nowhere is this more evident than in *The Foundation Pit*'s eponymous metaphor, an excavation that can never be completed, since the building that would fill it can never be large enough to house the masses who would live there. Chiklin, who finds Nastia and takes her in when her mother dies, imagines that "future man will find himself a chamber in that solid house, so as to look out from the high windows on the expansive world awaiting him."[51] Platonov insists that this potential is always just out of reach.

In this literature, space is a non-delimited zone of endless potential and epic adventure, a chronotope comparable to that of *Don Quixote.* It is a manageable milieu, perhaps, if only one can locate its center, construct a zone of concrete definition therein, and from that vantage point survey the possibilities of an "expansive world." It turns out, however, that space cannot be conquered in this way—one is reminded that "the centre cannot hold," Yeats's declaration of Modernist angst—because time has also failed to find its limit.[52] The Einsteinian revolution has already established that time and space are coexistential; you cannot remove the limit on one without doing the same to the other. In *The Foundation Pit,* the proletarian house exists only for "future man," who can never arrive, since time offers no concrete threshold to cross. This unfinalizability means that the leap into the future that is so essential to the Leninist philosophy of history is fundamentally impossible.[53]

On this basis we can begin to question whether the standard classification of Platonov's novel as utopian (or dystopian) is itself critically productive. In my reading, none of Platonov's major works constructs the milieu of classical utopia, the kind most familiar to us, first, from Thomas More's *Utopia* (1516), and in its Modernist reincarnation through Evgenii Zamiatin's *We* (My, 1921), Aldous Huxley's *Brave New World* (1931), and George Orwell's *Nineteen Eighty-Four* (1948). In each of these texts the utopian-dystopian space has a specific, stable border. More's Utopia is an island; Zamiatin's city is bordered by a "green wall"; Huxley's "World State" is dotted with "reservations" and hideaways; and Orwell's hero finds pleasure and solace in proletarian quarters largely outside the authoritarian government's interest. These boundaries are indispensable to the plots of utopian fiction, particularly in the twentieth century, since it is only by crossing the border that the novels' protagonists can effect the escape that they, unique among their fellows, desperately desire.

By contrast, the spatialization of time and temporalization of space in Platonov render both unbounded, foreclosing any possibility of encroachment into another time or space, or even of observing another's actions without becoming entangled in them. This boundlessness is consistent with the worldwide proletarian revolution envisioned by Marx, an inevitability given the fact that historical process for Marx is ultimately global.[54] By the time Platonov was writing *The Foundation Pit,* however, the world proletarian revolution had clearly failed to materialize, giving rise to the novel's fanciful conceit: a physical space, the foundation pit itself, that must expand infinitely from its center. It is a space of constantly shrinking density. Instead of the proletarian house constructed for "future man," Platonov's characters see only *pustota*, "emptiness"; *pustyr'*, "wasteland"; and *pustosh'*, "uncultivated ground." Platonov's space provides his characters with none of the definition they seek, since the space itself has no practical limits.

In fact, Platonov's political ideology is inextricable from his spatial imagination, insofar as he clearly saw new models of space-time as part of a global revolution, a new science for a new society, at the same time as he watched that revolution fail to achieve its aims. Accordingly, just as we can look to Platonov's early journalistic writings for important clues as to his ideological and critical development, the same sources can help us understand how a modern concept of space-time fits into the author's larger worldview.

The World Half Made

Platonov had a general interest in new theories about space-time, and one can reasonably suppose that Einstein's critique of Euclidean space—that Euclidean geometry cannot describe the universe, for if the universe is mapped against infinite Euclidean planes the average density of matter must approach zero—had special resonance for an author and engineer fascinated by spaces.[55] In 1921, Platonov went so far as to explain the significance of Minkowski space-time to the proletarian readers of *Voronezhskaia kommuna,* a regional newspaper to which he contributed regularly. In a brief article entitled "Audible Steps: The Revolution and Mathematics" (Slyshnye shagi: Revoliutsiia i matematika), Platonov declares that "social revolution is the gate to the kingdom of consciousness," and that future sciences "will not be today's science, which rots in universities, laboratories, and libraries. It will be the tempestuous flame of cognition that has gripped every city, every street, every being on our planet."[56]

As he often did in his short articles, the young Platonov, then at work on the poetry collection *Blue Abyss* (Golubaia glubina, 1922), joins the stirring language of early Soviet propaganda to that of speculative philosophy. But much as he does in his fictional prose, Platonov uses this vocabulary in idiosyncratic ways. This is particularly significant with regard to Platonov's use of the word *poznanie*, "cognition," which differs from Viacheslav Ivanov's deployment of the same word vis-à-vis Realist literature. Platonov seems to have in mind the universal "cognition" (*poznanie*) of a collective "consciousness" (*soznanie*). Whereas the "penetration" (*proniknovenie*) that Ivanov highlights as a signature feature of Dostoevsky's art is a sharing of consciousness between individual characters, Platonov's "kingdom of consciousness" is the antiworld of the kingdom of the past, which the Bolshevik revolution has ostensibly swept aside. When Ivanov calls his penetration "a certain *transcensus* of the subject," he anticipates Platonov's notion of universal cognition, though Platonov takes it a step further. If "penetration" describes the process by which the individual transcends himself, thereby recognizing the subjectivity of the Other, then what Platonov projects is an "interpenetration": Ivanov's *transcensus* occurs simultaneously for every subject, subsuming all subjects into a collective consciousness. This is the same kind of consciousness that Voshchev longs for when he imagines all knowledge becoming "universally known" (*obshcheizvestnyi*) in the "common house" (*obshchii dom*) that is to fill the empty space of the foundation pit.

The socialist revolution occasions for Platonov a recognition of vast, universal interconnections, which is precisely why he presents Minkowski space-time as a harbinger of the future science. He explains that space and time are now "identical, they are one," and that "the imperfection of our consciousness lies in the fact that I, for example, was unable to understand this formula right away, at first I sensed it."[57] For Platonov, the collective consciousness ("*our* consciousness") and immediate, universal cognition—in which the bright future of Soviet Communism also consists—will reflect the dissolution of space and time into a single, self-identical Absolute.

Platonov's heroes are, like Schulz's, demiurges, reshaping the story world around them as reflections of themselves, situated, as Natalia Poltavtseva has put it, "in the intermediate area between perception and symbol," where "'real' events and man's 'phantasms' are linked, where imagination and association play an important role, the area in which the 'external' and the 'internal' meet, the signified and the signifier, the sorting of objects into 'real' and 'nonexistent.'"[58] But they do not have the power to finish the world, which they leave half made, a pale reflection of their ideal superimposed on a reality that resists correction. Caught between the "real" and the "nonexistent," between events and "phantasms," these heroes are *demi*-demiurges, trapped in the world they shape and inextricably bound to it, since it shapes them as well. Absent a truly collective consciousness and immediate intuition, Platonov's unified spatial-temporal framework is unbearable. The only way his characters can move through time is by passing constantly through unbounded space, entangled with their surroundings and each other without ever being fully collective or completely individual.

Platonov's heroes, continually searching for a stable center that turns out to be absent or illusory, are condemned to homelessness. Their wandering is a symptom of their intermediacy, the sense that they are stretched between individuality and universality, which the more sensitive among them feel viscerally within themselves, as Voshchev does, in an early passage that is also the novel's only other use of *obshcheizvestnyi*, "universally known" or "known to all":

> Till evening, Voshchev walked silently around the city, as if in anticipation of the moment when the world would become universally

> known. But, as before, the light of the world remained unclear to him, and in the darkness of his body he sensed a quiet place where there was nothing, but where nothing prevented anything from beginning. As though living in absentia, Voshchev did his walking among the people, feeling the increasing strength of his grieving mind and secluding himself all the more in the tightness of his sorrow.[59]

Again, the belated future promises a collective consciousness that stands in stark contrast to Voshchev's feeling of isolation. His anticipation suggests a tenuous connection to that future, one that affords knowledge of what it contains while also forestalling direct access to it. The partialness of this contact with the nonpresent calls for special attention in Platonov, who manifests it with regard to both the future and the past. The past plagues Platonov's heroes, not only through memory but in the physical presence of remnants and ruins of the pre-Revolutionary world that must be cleared away before the future can fully arrive.

In this sense, Platonov's aporia is remarkably, if paradoxically, close to Heidegger's early notion of the transcendent subject, who "surpasses" the people and things around him without ever escaping his own subjectivity. This establishes the failure of passage—into the future, into other subjects—at the center of both *The Foundation Pit* and *Chevengur*. In these novels, Platonov refers frequently to the impossibility of these forms of passage, as well as to how this impossibility (or impassability) is an integral feature of his characters' subjectivity. We see this most clearly in Voshchev's reflections, which, projected through the narrator's thoroughly omniscient telling, give voice to a persistent sense of in-betweenness: "his endurance went on in the world, as though every living thing were found somewhere in the middle of time and its movement: its beginning had been forgotten by everyone, and its end was unknown; only its course remained in all directions."[60] Of the several possible translations of *terpenie*, I have chosen "endurance," though the Russian can also connote suffering on a biblical scale. In fact, Platonov's signature warping of literary language frequently echoes liturgical phrasing for the reader, as Maria Dmitrovskaia has shown, especially when he is referring to time.[61]

Platonov draws out Voshchev's experience in the world (characteristically, a patient acceptance of suffering) beyond the present, and he makes Voshchev aware of that attenuation, the intermediacy of being "in the middle of time and its movement." Voshchev experiences this lack as internal emptiness, the literal nonpresent, a space within the enclosure of his own body, "where nothing prevented anything from beginning." Despite the author's emphasis on potential—a potential embodied in the foundation pit, which by novel's end becomes a mass grave—Voshchev is in constant danger of disappearing altogether; he is already described as nonpresent, "as though living in absentia." If this description is taken literally, Platonov is suggesting through Voshchev that the world of the idealized future will itself constitute "common knowledge" (*obshcheizvestnost'*), since it is the unfathomable nature of the world, the opacity of existence, that makes life tragic.

Among others, however, Voshchev "seclud[es] himself all the more in the tightness of his sorrow." Typical of the principal characters in *The Foundation Pit* and *Chevengur,* he is stuck between the anxiety of his self-singularity—the *-edin-,* "one," in the word *uedinit'sia,* "to seclude oneself"—and his desire to be dissolved in universal awareness.[62] That this problem was felt as personally for Platonov as it clearly was for Schulz is suggested by the cryptoautobiographical threads that the Russian author stitched into his fiction. As several commentators have noted, the novel's very first sentence tells us that Voshchev is the same age as Platonov was at the time he wrote *The Foundation Pit.* Chiklin, whose role as Nastia's rescuer places him at the center of the novel's loose plot, is called "Klimentov" throughout the first manuscript and subsequent typescripts, and Voshchev was also initially called "Klimentov."[63] This suggests that Platonov regarded both characters as potential or partial proxies for the author, whose birth name was Andrei Klimentov. Platonov had assumed his pen name from his father's given name, Platon.

Like Józef, Schulz's own stand-in, Voshchev desperately wishes for a cosmic authority to offer him definition and order, to save him from his intermediacy in space and time. Gazing at the Milky Way, he calls in vain for this authority to interrupt time itself, "to issue a resolution about discontinuing the eternity of time, about the expiation of life's anguish."[64] Thomas Seifrid reads this passage as an indication that "for Platonov time is synonymous with entropy and reveals itself in disintegration rather than progress," which is no doubt true, but only if we conceive of time as endless, as irremediably open-ended.[65] Platonov, however, was of two minds with regard to the nature of time. His heroes are stretched to the breaking point by their own indeterminacy within time, though early essayistic works like "Audible Steps" show that he at least held out some hope for the possibility that time could be mastered, delimited, or "interrupted," restoring the Soviet Man to the modern progress narrative. Voshchev fantasizes not about stopping time altogether, but about neutralizing its "eternity," canceling its unfinalizability, and thereby creating a limit that would make life easier to bear.

One more example will help illustrate the torment of spatial-temporal intermediacy and lead to a more detailed discussion of one of its most consistent thematic symptoms, namely, the hero's sense of orphanhood and homelessness, of being unanchored within his story world. In the following passage, which was ultimately cut from Platonov's handwritten manuscript of *The Foundation Pit,* Voshchev and Chiklin, the two stand-ins for Andrei Klimentov/Platonov, are standing next to the pit when Voshchev hears a song that sweeps him back into his childhood:

> He heard this song in his childhood, the soldiers sang it in the Russo-Japanese War. And now it is being sung again,—and just as in that distant time, the sky was covered in a hazy heat, but the sun shone bleakly over all the deserted decay [var.: over the entire orphanhood] of the earth. That is, Voshchev lives his life in vain—it doesn't change, it's like an arrested childhood, and there is no truth in it in the end. [. . .] The sorrow of the universal condition was starting to torment Voshchev, he felt all exterior life as his own interiority, and he cleared his throat, having opened his mouth for communication.
>
> —Chiklin, so where is Marxism? All around are weak places [var.: people] and a single, empty, eternal time, my health will waste away again . . .
>
> —That's just it!—Chiklin said.—A house is needed here, but there's just an empty space, and you're in need despite yourself. But we'll manage, we'll fill all that emptiness in.[66]

Platonov describes Voshchev as being quite literally stuck in the past, in the "distant time" of his own "arrested childhood." Voshchev is, in a metaphysical sense, immature, a hybrid of an unfinished child consciousness and a more defined, rational adult mind. For this reason, he feels as though he has not actually "lived" his life, though the Russian verb that Platonov uses, *prozhivat'*, is more expressive than our English one because it also carries the semantic weight of "survival" and "living through." Voshchev cannot "live his life through" because that life has no limits to be crossed, no "through" to be measured. The world that has been promised him, which falls under the general heading of "Marxism," has likewise failed to arrive, also because "a single, empty, eternal time" leaves us no threshold to be crossed. Voshchev cannot step out of the past; Marxism cannot step out of the future.

On the same page of the novel's handwritten manuscript, the narrator tells us that the workmen at the foundation pit live mostly in their dreams, where "they saw a world that had already been fully completed."[67] Here is an interesting inversion of representational norms: the dream world is finalized, but the experiential world is not. In Platonov, this unfinalized world reflects the heroes' own immaturity or incompleteness. Like Platonov, the author who tells us in "Audible Steps" that he had felt the unity of space and time before he actually understood it, Voshchev senses an equivalence between exteriority and interiority—"he felt all exterior life as his own interiority"—without knowing what such a connection could mean. Underscoring the spatial model of human subjectivity, in this instance Platonov has rendered "places" in the unrevised text and "people" in the variant text interchangeable in their "weakness."

Because being open to the world means feeling its suffering as one's own, Voshchev experiences the potential of emptiness as torment. He wonders aloud when Marxism will come, presumably to put an end to "empty, eternal time," which is slowly dissolving him. Chiklin, in turn, promises that they will be able to make content where there is none, to replace the emptiness with a house—that is, a construction with definite boundaries to give their lives shape, a home to end their endless wandering. "Emptiness," then, is also the potential for multiple, as-yet-undefined outcomes, that quality of freedom that Bakhtin calls "eventness." Or, to be more precise, "eventness" is the potential that stands before this "nothing," the possibility that anything could happen. This reveals another, deeper dimension of Platonov's spatial overlay, which produces not only the superimposition of one historical or mnemonic time frame over another but also a space of contact between Self and Other, mind and world, where anything can happen. In this regard, Seifrid has noted that both Bakhtin and Platonov attempt to occupy a middle ground between conceptual oppositions, such that "the self/other (or mind/world) dichotomy is overcome in the self's 'dialogic' *exchange* with all that is Other (other selves and the world beyond subjectivity)."[68] Yet the same intermediate space that represents pure potential in Bakhtin comes to mean disintegration and despair for Platonov. His emptiness needs to be filled somehow, even as the space of the foundation pit allegorizes how the emptiness is ever more expansive.

The only way to fill this emptiness is to work against the self-isolation of individual experience, to establish essential contact with others, a principle that Platonov captures beautifully in one of the novel's more mysterious reflections: "The snowy wind died down; the unclear moon appeared in the distant sky, drained of whirlwinds and clouds, in a sky that was so desolate that it admitted an eternal freedom, and so terrible that for freedom one had to have friendship."[69] For Platonov, unabashedly fond of pathetic fallacy, the sky typically represents unbounded freedom, visible but painfully unattainable, just as the bright future of the universal collective is visible but unattainable. Here, emptiness, being "drained" of content, brands the sky as having admitted an eternal freedom. As Miroslav Drozda points out, however, the openness of the sky only underscores the emptiness of space and, with it, the hero's homelessness, since the "vast, boundless exteriors" of Platonov's work allow the hero "no intimate substitute for home," leaving him "exposed to nature as though to a material infinitude, to the universe."[70] Platonov describes the sky as "terrible" or "uncanny" (*zhutko*) *because* it will not afford freedom without "friendship" (i.e., "free and familiar contact" with the Other), which is too slow in coming, and which also represents a threat to individual agency. For Voshchev, the activity of constructing the foundation pit for the world of the future becomes a distraction from this paradox, a means of channeling his otherwise indeterminate energies, but the emptiness that threatens us with orphanhood and homelessness still remains. Unable to achieve either complete separation from the Other or absolute unity with oneself, he is condemned to what Lukács aptly describes as "transcendental homelessness."[71]

Orphanhood, Homelessness, and the Crisis of Fellow Feeling

The transcendental homelessness that Lukács identifies in German Romantic literature receives a surprising remedy in *History and Class Consciousness,* where Lukács confronts the give-and-take of individual freedom, the "specious freedom" that the individual asserts over and against the equally valid interests of others.[72] For Lukács, having abandoned for a time his reflections on freedom in literary representation, the bourgeois conception of individual agency leads inevitably to the enslavement of others. The only path to what Marx called "the realm of freedom" is through an emergent proletarian class consciousness, a sense of our thick interconnection with each other, "conscious action directed towards the comprehended totality of society."[73] Lukács, like Marx, now understands freedom spatially, as a zone of "free and familiar contact," wherein the material inequities and social hierarchies that delimit our freedom are swept aside along with their attendant antinomies, "between subject and object, freedom and necessity, individual and society, form and content, etc."[74] In Russian political philosophy, this reading finds its analogue in Lenin's interpretation of Marx's "future Communism," in which the dictatorship of the proletariat becomes obsolete, since the state itself "withers away" with class consciousness. That is, once the absolute collective is achieved in the social order, the mechanisms of collectivization become unnecessary. Once the absolute collective is achieved in the ontological order, the transformations that result from these deep associations become unnecessary as well.[75]

So conceived, class consciousness would replace restrictive and ultimately false dichotomies with an all-empowering unity. No longer would we suffer from transcendental homelessness, for home would be everywhere. For Schulz and Platonov, as in the literature of intermediacy in general, the spatial aspect of transcendental homelessness is thematized as wandering or rootlessness in space, while its psychosocial aspect appears as orphanhood. Their protagonists seek to remedy this unrootedness by immersing themselves in collectives of various stripes. Inevitably, they find that this sublimation of the Self is just as painful as their isolation had been.

Many of Platonov's major characters, including Nastia in *The Foundation Pit* and Sasha Dvanov in *Chevengur,* are orphans whose desire to build a Communist future is motivated by a need to recover or reconstitute a family lost to them in the past. They are stretched between the here and now, in which they themselves exist, and an atemporal plane when the lost kinsman both *was* and *will be* alive. Accordingly, Platonov's characters seek transformation deliberately in order to draw the dead back into the sphere of the living, thereby neutralizing their sense of homelessness. This is literally the case for the second major character in *Chevengur,* Kopenkin, Platonov's seriocomic take on Don Quixote. Kopenkin is motivated to achieve Communism in Chevengur because he believes that doing so will bring about the resurrection of his deceased beloved, Rosa Luxemburg, the Marxist revolutionary murdered in Berlin in 1919. Yet Kopenkin seeks not only the resurrection of Rosa Luxemburg but also of his own mother, who in his mind already shares the same essence: "Kopenkin loved his mother and Rosa equally, because his mother and Rosa were for him one and the same primal creature, just as the past and future live in his one life."[76] The author has cleverly avoided the use of a plural verb for Luxemburg and his mother: he attaches the singular neuter form *bylo* to them both, calling them *pervoe sushchestvo,* which we can understand as both "primal creature" and "first essence." He reserves the plural for the past and future, which, in an echo of Bergsonian *durée*, "live in his one life."

For Platonov, death can be surmounted by integrating the subject into a universal, monistic essence, a notion rooted firmly in Russian revisions of Western, primarily German philosophy. In *Chevengur,* for instance, we can readily discern the empiriomonism of Aleksandr Bogdanov (1873–1928), who sought to revise dialectical materialism by unifying the spirit level with the material world, thereby achieving an ideal of cognition that "overcomes the dualism" of physical and psychic experience.[77] This was not a fanciful undertaking; Bogdanov was investigating the possibility of reinvigorating the human mind and spirit through science in 1928 when he died performing a blood-transfusion experiment on himself. Concerning the subversion of mortality, Platonov was equally drawn to Nikolai Fedorov (1829–1903), whose articles, collected posthumously as *Philosophy of the Common Task* (Filosofiia obshchego dela, 1906), suggest the possibility of resurrecting the dead through a scientific collectivization of matter. It was through this quasi-monistic lens that Platonov took a particular interest in the widely discussed developments in the theoretical physics of his day, particularly the ideas about the unity of space and time put forward by Minkowski and Einstein.

Yet Platonov's ideas are not, as they may appear from a cursory glance, actually monistic in the world they project. Rather, his major prose expresses the repeated failure of the universe to attain the monistic ideal of his vision of Communism and, in so doing, to redeem the detachment his orphan characters feel vis-à-vis their past losses and future gains. In another sentence cut from the manuscript of *Chevengur,* we once again see Sasha Dvanov choose Communism as the solution to the deaths of his loved ones: "Dvanov thought that he must go to his mother, as well as to his dead brother, not by the direct path of devotion and eternal memories, but by a detour—through Communism and the triumph over nature: then there would be the very best of meetings."[78] Similarly, Kopenkin looks to Communism to restore his beloved Rosa Luxemburg, whom he has never met in life, but whom he conflates with his own mother. For Kopenkin and Dvanov alike, Communism represents the end of days and the arrival of the Kingdom of God on earth—there are multiple references to the Second Coming of Christ, when the dead will rise from the grave, in the finished text—as Platonov states bluntly in the novel's manuscript: "[Kopenkin] completely attached himself to Dvanov's conviction and decided to await the excavation of graves."[79] This expectation imparts a certain urgency to the characters' project of establishing Communism in the town of Chevengur: when it comes to resurrecting the dead, there is literally no time to lose. Of course, they are also tilting at windmills. The grand Communist future in which the dead would be restored to the living is always out of reach. The monistic ideal is just that—an ideal—and we watch it disintegrate time and again into a deflated duality. Such failure to reach the Absolute is all the more frustrating because the ideal can be seen, however dimly, on the other side of the flawed reality that Platonov's characters must endure.

Structurally, the gap between the ideal and lived praxis imbues the text of *Chevengur* with an underlying circularity that, in its structural repetitions and thematic emphasis on return, shows an even stronger, quixotic kinship between Platonov and Schulz. The difficulty of return forms the basic plot point of several of Platonov's shorter masterworks, notably "Fro" (1936), "The Potudan River" (Reka Potudan', 1936), and "The Return" (Vozvrashchenie, 1946). In *Chevengur,* the author emphasizes repetition verbally, as in his abundant use of words bearing the prefix *ezhe-* (*ezheminutno*, "every minute"; *ezhenedel'no,* "every week")—words he evidently didn't think the novel had enough of, because in revising the manuscript he systematically inserted many more of them into the text. Platonov's verbal repetitions also resonate with the macrostructure of the novel, itself composed of largely repetitive episodes in which Dvanov and Kopenkin depart from Chevengur and return, only to depart again. Both protagonists in fact feel spatially oppressed in the town of Chevengur, with its houses crammed together so tightly that there are barely streets, but they have determined that the Communism that is to materialize there is their best hope for the return of the dead.

Conceptually, the Communism that Platonov imagines for Chevengur erases the boundary between life and death, as well as between people, animals, and things. From the very beginning of the novel, death is treated as a continued existence in another space. Sasha Dvanov is an orphan because of his father's fascination with that other world, prompting him to drown himself in the novel's opening passages: "[H]e saw death as another province that spread out under the sky, as if at the bottom of the cool water, and it drew him in."[80] And later, near the book's end, Platonov draws a direct link between this "other province," Sasha Dvanov's need for the Other to compensate for his orphanhood, and the sense that Communism is an eternal existence in another world, as another character, Chepurnyi, believes:

> Alexander Dvanov did not love himself so deeply as to strive after Communism for his own personal life, but he went forward with everyone because everyone was going, and it was frightening to remain alone. He wanted to be with the people, because he had no father or kin of his own. Chepurnyi, on the contrary, was vexed by Communism, the way Dvanov's father had been vexed by the mystery of life after death, and Chepurnyi could not endure the mystery of time and cut the length of history short with the urgent organization of Communism in Chevengur,—just as the fisherman Dvanov could not endure his own life. He had transformed it into death in order to experience in advance the beauty of that world.[81]

Platonov describes Dvanov's need to share in the existence of others, to indulge a Bakhtinian "free and familiar contact," as a response to the death of his father. Along similar lines, Eliot Borenstein suggests that in certain instances Platonov uses the verb *umeret'*, "to die," as a verb of motion. In one of the most peculiar instances of Platonov warping a prepositional phrase, toward the beginning of *Chevengur* Sasha Dvanov, recently orphaned, sits by his father's grave and says, "Not long from now I will die *toward* you."[82] In Borenstein's reading, the use of *umeret'* as a verb of motion "becomes the shortcut to the characters' final destination," which is death, and therefore a reintegration of the family that has been splintered by death.[83]

At the same time, Platonov ties the death of Dvanov's father to Chepurnyi's vision of Communism as a world where one continues to live after one has died. There is a strong sense that although characters die in Platonov—and most of them do—the death of the body does not furnish an escape from Being. The dead not only live on in memory but are reabsorbed into a cosmic cycle from which they could be recalled, whole, if only a universal collective consciousness could be achieved. The failure to achieve this universal collective at one point motivates Chepurnyi, standing over the body of a boy who has just died, to exclaim in frustration, "he is still completely alive inside, it's only on the outside that he has died," and by the end of the novel Platonov's characters, having failed to bring the dead back to join them, must go join the dead.[84] Sasha Dvanov drowns himself in the same lake where his father had drowned himself years before, though this in itself does not bring the narrative to a final conclusion: Prokofii, Sasha's adoptive brother, sets out in search of him, presumably to spin off a new iteration of the same adventures we have already seen, and to leave open the possibility of recalling the dead from their other world.

Platonov often represents this transcendental homelessness through spatial allegories of isolation and self-splitting. In *The Foundation Pit*, for example, Prushevskii, the foreman, experiences his own consciousness as a cramped, walled-in space, and he lives in the hope that someone will eventually succeed in penetrating it:

> Since the age of twenty-five the engineer Prushevskii had felt the constraint of his consciousness and the limit of his further understanding of life, as though a dark wall had appeared in the buffer before his feeling mind. And since then he had suffered, moving along his wall, and was consoled that, in essence, the very central, genuine organization of the matter from which the world and people are derived had been grasped by him,—all of vital science had been laid out right up to the wall of his consciousness, and beyond the wall there was only a tedious place where one couldn't even go. But all the same, it was interesting: might not someone else crawl out beyond the wall?[85]

Prushevskii feels a desperate need to connect with others in order to mitigate his own detachment. This detachment, however, cannot be remedied, since it is from himself that he feels detached. The Freudian disconnect between Prushevskii's consciousness and his unconscious mind—his "feeling mind" (*oshchushchaiushchii um*), which he knows must exist, but which contains psychic material to which he has no access—pains him. His sole consolation is the interconnectedness of all matter, since people and things are made from the same substance, just as Schulz will later characterize his fiction as reflecting "a certain extreme monism of substance, for which particular objects are merely masks."[86] Thus, much as Schulz does in "Solitude," Platonov proposes self-alienation as a potential consolation for one's orphanhood and homelessness, since in the faint presence of "someone else" (*kto-nibud'*), another Prushevskii within his unconscious mind, Platonov holds out the possibility that the Self split between the subject and his double can soothe *his own* loneliness. Like the promise of collective existence colorfully figured by the foundation pit, however, this possibility can never be realized. It remains in the text as pure potential, Prushevskii's hope that this as-yet-unknown self might someday reveal himself to his consciousness.

By the time he wrote *The Foundation Pit,* Platonov had already elaborated his notion of the split self in *Chevengur,* where "a small onlooker" (*malen'kii zritel'*) or "watchman" (*storozh*) appears as a recurring, nonverbal character within the very subjectivity of the novel's heroes: "But in man there also exists a small onlooker—he does not take part in acts, nor in agonies—he is always solitary and maintains his sangfroid. His charge is to see and serve as witness, but he has no right to speak in the person's life, and it is simply unknown why he exists. This corner of a person's consciousness is lit night and day, like the doorman's room in a large house."[87] If the observer cannot take active part in the events described in the novel, why point out his existence at all? For the very reason that the hero who, like Prushevskii, suffers partial detachment from the world also experiences partial detachment from himself, which only spurs him toward communion with the collective or the Absolute. This notion is, like Lukács's transcendental homelessness, rooted in the German Romantic tradition. Thus it seems especially fitting to turn to a German Romantic philosopher, in this case Schelling, for an explanation of why the subject splits himself in the manner we see in Schulz and Platonov:

> Every entity, everything that is, wants to be in itself and out of itself at the same time. It wants to be in itself inasmuch as it posits or collects itself together as what-is, as a subject; to this extent it opposes development and expansion. It wants to be out of itself inasmuch as it desires to be what it is in itself once more, and hence externally. In the first case it is something withdrawn by itself, which sets itself in opposition to what is outside of it; but it sets itself in opposition only in order to reveal and declare itself against this outside as what it is in itself. It cannot, therefore, remain in this withdrawn condition.[88]

Schelling's formulation anticipates the paradox of subjectivity in early Heidegger, for whom the subject's overlap with other subjects is an inherent feature of his subjectivity. In Schulz and Platonov, the hero strives toward self-singularity, "to be in itself," but in doing so he must also turn outward to witness himself from outside, "to be out of itself." One way to perform this operation is through Ivanov's notion of "penetration" vis-à-vis Dostoevsky, which allows the subject to see himself in the reflection of other people and things, but which also presents the risk of being infected with their otherness, that is, of abandoning one's self-singularity. Another, more solipsistic method is self-splitting: by externalizing himself, expropriating himself into a double or observer, the hero becomes his own witness from outside.[89]

Bakhtin idealized this otherwise hellish condition in his reading of Dostoevsky, where "free and familiar contact" does not necessarily obliterate the individual subject. Rather, it reinforces the hero's intersubjectivity (in which subjectivity consists, according to Heidegger) to such an extent that nothing—no idea or feeling—can be ascribed to the individual alone. Indeed, the *individual* subject becomes a contradiction in terms: there must be an appreciable measure of "fellow feeling"—to borrow Max Scheler's term, and a core concept in the genealogy of Bakhtin's reading of Dostoevsky—if subjectivity is to manifest itself at all.[90] Bakhtin is guardedly optimistic that "free and familiar contact" can be achieved, and that the individual will therefore enjoy the "absolute freedom" envisioned by Schelling, if only through unrestricted contact and the fellow feeling that unrestricted contact brings.

The authors of intermediacy make only abortive gestures toward this universality. For both Platonov and Schulz, freedom and the Absolute—and perhaps more accurately freedom *in the* Absolute—are *fata morgana.* The workers in *The Foundation Pit* can dig forever; they know that they want a universal collective, but that does not mean that they will have one.

Similarly, Schulz, whose dying house was located on Drohobycz's market square, can watch as the differences that allow us to distinguish one thing from another, or one façade from the next, melt away, but the collectivization of matter only makes it that much more difficult to reach the singularity of one's home. Miłosz Bukwalt has therefore argued that Drohobycz, as the setting for the author's memory of his father, renders the physical urban space inextricable from the lost time of the Father: "But Schulz's penetration of prehistory is identical with his artistic return to the 'age of genius' of a childhood spent in the mythic space of his native city, his house, and the store and its goods. The urban complex, the domicile, and the emporium of household goods are, for this writer, places sanctified by the traces of his Jewish father's presence."[91] Schulz's Drohobycz is not just a *where;* it is also a *when.*

For Platonov and Schulz, orphanhood and homelessness are fundamental conditions of Being, not contingent states of being. Orphanhood encompasses a detachment that must be redeemed through a connection with others. In this way, one does not feel "like an orphan" among other people, but rather senses the transcendental condition of orphanhood when confronted by them. Platonov thus describes Prushevskii's orphanhood as a feeling felt *toward* other people: "Prushevskii walked to the foundation pit before unknown people. He'd sent a letter to his sister and now wanted to be hard at work, to worry about current matters and to construct some building for someone else's use, if only not to disturb his consciousness, in which he had established a particularly tender indifference, coordinated with death and with a feeling of orphanhood toward the people who remained."[92] In interwar Russia, with so many children left parentless by war, famine, and disease, it is unremarkable that writers would take an interest in orphans, and Platonov is no exception. Nor was Platonov alone in adopting orphanhood as a metaphorical figure; for example, in *The Naked Year* [Golyi god], his 1921 novel of the Russian Civil War, Boris Pil'niak, Platonov's friend and sometime artistic collaborator, offhandedly characterizes the wind as "lone" or "orphan-like"—*sirotlivyi,* from *sirota,* "orphan."[93] What tags Prushevskii's experience of orphanhood as symptomatic of intermediacy is his desire for indifference, that is, for the same kind of emptiness that promises pure potential in Voshchev, for it is only through this indifference in himself that Prushevskii can remain open to the possibility of connection without ceding any of his individual agency. This is why he must bury himself, so to speak, in the organization of space "for someone else's use," one of many instances in which Platonov warps and repurposes Soviet language. At the First Congress of Agricultural Communes in 1919, Lenin had defined Communism as labor performed "conscious of the necessity of working for general use"—that is, "for the common good."[94] Prushevskii knows that he will not see this happen, but he hopes that the future building will redeem the empty space of the foundation pit and connect him, if only by proxy, to future man.

This, we already know, will not happen. The foundation pit will only grow deeper and wider. For Platonov, there will be no great leap into the future, nor an absorption into an immediate, collective consciousness, for the only way his characters can move through time is by moving through space, continuously searching for a stable, illusory center. In the absence of such stability, either in absolute universality or absolute self-singularity, we see an uncomfortable blending of the subject and the world around him. Indifference offers us a way out of the either-or proposition that Lukács defines for the hero when he asserts that the world within the hero's soul "is narrower or it is broader than the outside world assigned to it as the arena and substratum of its actions." In their manipulation of narrative space, Platonov and Schulz do not "assign" a world to their characters at all. Instead, the distinction between their heroes' interiority and the "outside world" dissolves into indifference. Streets and stairwells change course according to the wanderer's predilections and distractions. Spaces and things overlap as the hero willingly fails to distinguish between them. This is why transformation reveals itself as one of the most consistent motifs of this literature of in-betweenness.

By way of arriving at a more robust appreciation of how indifference leads to transformation, consider what is undoubtedly the twentieth century's most notorious instantiation of literary transformation, Kafka's opening sentence in "The Metamorphosis" (Die Verwandlung, 1912): "As Gregor Samsa awoke one morning from uneasy dreams he found himself transformed in his bed into a gigantic insect."[95] While our attention is drawn inexorably to the man-sized insect awaiting us at the end of the sentence, we should try to rest with Mr. Samsa in the middle of the utterance, in that moment when "he found himself," *fand er sich*, if only to ask, "*Who* found *what*?" Is Kafka's hero an insect or a man? The simple answer is that he is both at the same time, a monster, a human consciousness with the hard exoskeleton of a cockroach. Discussions of Samsa's condition frequently note that his name contains the Czech root *sám*, "alone," but it is neither his personal alienation nor his insectile appearance that makes him a monster.[96] What keeps "The Metamorphosis" from being an anecdote about household pests is the fact that Gregor Samsa is both a human being and an insect *at the same time*. Samsa is monstrous because he is a hybrid, a man-insect who recognizes himself as both at once, a feature captured perfectly by Kafka's qualification of the "insect" as *ungeheuer*, which as an adjective means "enormous" or "immense" but as a noun means "monster."[97]

This monstrosity stems from indifference, a term I use in both its psychological and ontological senses. Psychologically, indifference is among the most familiar of the lacks we might sense emotionally, in this case a lack of preference that in its purest form represents a failure a priori to distinguish the merits of one object over another. Ontologically, indifference forms the basis of the identity or self-equivalence of the Absolute, especially in German Idealism.[98] We see the connection between these two senses most vividly in language when we declare that "it's all the same to me," an expression that enjoys near-perfect analogues in Russian (*mne vse ravno*), Polish (*wszystko mi jedno*), Czech (*je mi to jedno*), and, finally, German (*es ist mir gleich*). Each of these common phrases expresses the singularity or, at the very least, the equality of unlike things. As a failure to recognize difference, indifference reveals the power of connecting or associating discrete objects, and it is for this reason that indifference, instead of offering a passive, disinterested psychological response, appears as an active, deliberate exercise among the heroes of intermediate literature. The hero sees unlike people or things and, by refusing to differentiate among them, merges them together. Schulz frequently uses the word *obojętność* in his texts to signify both psychological and ontological indifference. For Platonov, the key word is *ravnodushie,* which litters *The Foundation Pit* and especially *Chevengur.*

Indifference, Transformation, Death: Platonov's *Chevengur*

In *Chevengur*, Platonov portrays an attempt to transform the town of Chevengur into the realization of the Soviet future deep in the Russian steppe, which the author treats as a potentially unbounded space of epic adventure. And rightly so: the boundlessness of space and time, we find, is an essential feature of Platonov's Soviet ideal, since it is only through the erasure of boundaries that man and material can be collectivized into a single consciousness, a monistic whole that will have no end. As Gopner, a minor character, puts it, "the new world will be constructed from eternal material, which will never reach a disposable condition."[99]

The challenge for this project, however, is twofold. First, boundlessness is difficult to achieve, and Platonov's work is as much about the failure to attain the Absolute as it is about the efforts to do so. Second, where some provisional boundlessness becomes evident in his fiction, it necessarily destabilizes the spatial-temporal framework of the world and dislocates the individual hero, stretching him precariously between the collective ideal and his own individuality. Early in his detailed commentary to *Chevengur,* Evgenii Iablokov remarks that the subject of Platonov's novel is precisely the individual's doomed struggle to recover a lost connection to Being: "Platonov wrote his novel about the eternal quest in which we find humanity, 'detached' [*raz"edinennoe*] from Being and plucked out from nature, like a child from its mother; about how [humanity] strives to overcome the terror of orphanhood."[100] Platonov's characters in fact shuttle between ideals of unification—*ob"edinenie*—and complete dispersal or detachment—*raz"edinenie*—because the hero can never fully surrender his individuality.

It is this intermediacy, the construction of Platonov's narratives between the old world of discrete entities and the new world of collective consciousness, that gives rise to the first suggestion of metamorphosis early in *Chevengur*. Here, we repeatedly find Zakhar Pavlovich, an itinerant railroad worker, looking wistfully at machines. Our narrator tells us that Zakhar Pavlovich "truly loved and felt only a finished ware,—that into which man has been transformed by means of labor, and which continues to live an independent life."[101] In Platonov's novel, this notion that labor has turned man into a machine is far more than an old man's capricious fantasy and also more than a materialist ideal of productivity in the young socialist state, but it is also less than a complete and irrevocable transformation. Man is mechanized, but metal is also humanized. For Zakhar Pavlovich machines—particularly trains—are as human as humans are themselves the mechanical instruments of labor. Transformation results from association, indifference to the distinction between unlike entities. To put us out of doubt as to how literally we are to take this blurring of the boundary between man and machine, Platonov goes so far as to have Zakhar Pavlovich engage in a complete, two-way conversation with a locomotive, which serves to illustrate the old man's "fellow feeling" or "sympathy for the locomotive."[102]

For Zakhar Pavlovich, humans are transformed into machines and the train into a human. Zakhar Pavlovich associates himself with mechanical objects so powerfully that he universalizes this association. In the original manuscript of the novel, Platonov initially delineated this transformation explicitly as a means of transcending the mortality—the ultimate boundary—of things: "Zakhar Pavlovich rushed to the workday, so that he might transform as many dead natural things into goods as possible and, through them, make bits of matter with living bodies—similar to a person, and even better than one."[103] Here, as in the text's final redaction, we see that for Zakhar Pavlovich it is the mechanism, the machine, or the instrument that lives and ultimately redeems the mortality of the human body. Thus it is in the creation of useful things that mortality itself is subverted.

But Zakhar Pavlovich's optimism runs aground at the thought that he cannot be certain that the potential of the new world is, in fact, limitless. Like Voshchev in *The Foundation Pit*, Zakhar Pavlovich looks skyward for assurances that never come: "He wanted the world to be truly infinite, so that wheels would always be indispensable and would continuously ready themselves for the common joy, but he was by no means capable of feeling infinitude."[104] This manner of suggesting and then eroding an ideal, of positing the limitlessness of the world and then emphasizing how the ideal has not yet been achieved, is typical of the "reversibility" or "undoing" of Platonov's longer narratives. And there is no doubt about what is ultimately at stake in Platonov's effort to establish an unbounded world: not individual happiness, but the "common joy"—*obshchaia radost'*—of the collective.

The limitlessness of the sky, visible but unreachable, represents the ideal disintegration of boundaries in *Chevengur.* Later in the text, Sasha Dvanov gazes at the sky and senses the mounting isolation of humanity: "Dvanov lay in the grass of Chevengur, and wherever his life would lead, its ends should be among courtyards and people, because there is nothing else besides the grass, which was wilting in the unpopulated space, and sky, which signifies with its indifference the isolated orphanhood of people on earth."[105] Hardly a cheerful ideal, it is an ideal nonetheless. The sky does not differentiate among people and, we sense, scarcely recognizes them at all. For Dvanov, this "indifference" is the means by which the observer recognizes a more fundamental condition, namely, the people's existential homelessness, their "orphanhood," as well as their isolation within that homelessness. It is the same solitude that Voshchev wishes for himself in *The Foundation Pit.*

For some of Platonov's characters, the isolated, undifferentiated mass of humanity on earth represents an ultimate good, as it does for Chepurnyi, who believes that the future has already been attained in Chevengur in spite of the dire living conditions of the orphans who have been brought into the town to realize Communism. This is, of course, absurd, so that elsewhere in the novel Chepurnyi ecstatically explains to Sasha Dvanov how there is no need to establish a post office, since the inhabitants of Chevengur already live as one: "The people live in a heap and see each other in person—tell me, please, what do they need a post office for! Brother, here the proletarians are already closely united!"[106]

Platonov elaborates on this universalism in an overwrought passage later cut from the manuscript of *Chevengur,* which in offering Sasha Dvanov's thoughts in the first person indicates a stronger link between author and hero than we might otherwise see in the later text:

> Then I felt our disastrous time and inevitable death vividly and sorrowfully. I felt sorry for the floundering, unsheltered people, joined together and abandoned [. . .]; in my youth I dreamt about a different, peaceful destiny—about a deep, human consciousness that saw events in the world before they happened,—about the wealth of the universe, which satisfies all thirst for life, and the kind of absolute, loving sense of faith in man's meaning that belongs to the conqueror and savior of tempestuous nature, which destroys its very self.
>
> I thought all this over many times—now I was interested in the transformation of ideas into event.[107]

Platonov explicitly posits the dream of a "deep, human consciousness that saw events in the world before they happened" as an antidote to "our disastrous time and inevitable death." In *Chevengur,* he directs the "wealth of the universe" against the deprivation of "the floundering, unsheltered people, joined together and abandoned." This is at least nominally what transformation is supposed to do for the individuals in the novel. We are not dealing merely with the "transformation of ideas into event," as suggested here, but the creation of a world in which all transformations are unnecessary, since matter and consciousness—"class consciousness," in Lukács's interpretation—emerge from and reconnect us to the same "wealth of the universe." Once matter and consciousness are again subsumed into this "extreme monism of substance"—to borrow Schulz's phrase once more—death itself loses its meaning.

The transformations we see in *Chevengur* are thus largely abortive, and with good reason. Metamorphosis represents the middle term between worlds, between life and death, between self-singularity and absorption into the collective. In *Chevengur,* Platonov constantly suggests the possibility of transformation, but only to emphasize how it is never completed, just as the town of Chevengur is *not* transformed into a Communist Eden. This is because for Platonov transformation depends not only on the associative acts of those who observe from outside but on the associations drawn from within the objects of transformation. In other words, it is not enough for me, the hero of the narrative of in-betweenness, to see strong similarities between a man and a bird; this will not suffice to transform the man into a bird. The man must see himself as a bird as well, so that the observing subject and the observed object are in agreement—so that they, in this essential sense, overlap.

A vivid illustration of this principle comes toward the end of *The Foundation Pit,* set during the violent "dekulakization" of the late 1920s and anticipating the forced land collectivization of the following decade. The animals on the kolkhoz start to behave like good Socialists, organizing their lives around the needs of the collective.[108] In the novel's most remarkable phantasmagoric turn, a bear, Misha, transforms into a blacksmith and becomes Nastia's faithful companion. Platonov treats these instances as natural, even to be expected: "The bear stopped hammering and, having gone off, drank half a bucket of water from thirst. Then, having dried his weary-proletarian face, the bear spat in his paw and again set about the striker's task."[109] Just as the peasants have been collectivized—the kolkhoz speaks as a single voice in the text and thinks as a collective consciousness—so too have the animals.

Misha's transformation into a real worker with a worker's "weary-proletarian face" is never explicitly discussed in the text, nor do the other protagonists react to his human personality with bewilderment or surprise. On the contrary, Platonov subsequently points out how his transformation comes as much from within as from without, since it is rooted in Misha's own association of the animal and the human and his indifference toward what distinguishes one from the other. As he walks with Nastia, the two share a peculiar moment of mutual appreciation: "The girl kept following the bear; she was pleased that an animal is also the working class, and the hammerer looked at her as on a forgotten sister, with whom he had fattened himself at his mother's belly in the summertime forest of his childhood."[110] Which of these images is more unsettling: the bear as representative of an animal working class or Nastia as the sister bear nursing at the belly of the mother bear in the forest? These transformations blur the boundary that would otherwise allow us to distinguish one from the other, bear from girl. In this sense, everyone here is a monster.

In fact, Platonov treats these transformations so naturally that he uses a word directly denoting transformation only once in the novel, as Chiklin is looking upon the corpse of Nastia's mother: "[Her] naked legs were covered in a thick down, almost fur, that had grown from illness and shelterlessness, some kind of ancient, reanimated power had transformed the dead woman, even while she was still alive, into an animal with an overgrown hide."[111] In living like an animal, in her homelessness and "shelterlessness," Nastia's mother has turned into a beast. Again, it is a transformation brought about from within as much as from without, by a touch of the absolute interconnection that for Platonov pervades all things as an "ancient, reanimated power."

Indifference, Transformation, Death: The Schulz Household

Like Platonov, Schulz constructs a story world where spatial and temporal distinctions no longer define us, and he does so as a means of mitigating his protagonist's persistent feeling of homelessness, unrootedness, and orphanhood. In the title story of *Sanitorium under the Sign of the Hourglass,* for example, Schulz's narrator goes to visit his late father at a facility where Jakub remains alive, since "[m]y father's time and my own no longer fit together."[112] But Schulz does not have to wander far from his house to get lost in a tangle of conflated spaces. Remember that the center-out architectonics of Schulz's fiction means that otherwise discrete spaces become confused as we move from the narrative's point of origin, frustrating the hero's effort to return home from his wanderings. Schulz describes this dynamic at the beginning of "Visitation" (Nawiedzenie):

> We lived on the square, in one of those dark houses with blank and blind façades, which are so difficult to distinguish each from the other.
>
> This causes constant errors. Because, having first stepped into the wrong foyer or onto the wrong stairs, one usually got into a veritable labyrinth of alien apartments, passages, of unexpected ex-

> its onto alien courtyards, and one forgot about the initial purpose of the expedition, so that after many days, returning from strange byways and tangled adventures, at some gray dawn, with pricks of conscience one would recall the family home. [113]

Schulz's home is a labyrinth of unbridled fecundity and decay, but as a spatial center it is also more stable than the town periphery, a center-out design according to which, as Jarzębski puts it, "the heart of the city beats here in the very center, where it is associated with wealth, exacting workmanship, the peculiar tangibility of architectural detail, whereas peripheries denote the gradual blurring of form, the erasure of precision in performance, and a rather peculiar abnegation."[114] In "Visitation," Schulz specifies that the difficulty of finding the way home stems not only from the inconstancy of space-time but also from a failure to differentiate one space from another. He emphasizes that the spaces that do not belong to his home are "alien" (*obce*) and "wrong" (*niewłaściwe,* "wrong, inappropriate"; literally, "not one's own"), and yet these spaces are also indistinguishable from the home itself. The fun of "tangled adventures" is mitigated by the "pricks of conscience" that tell the narrator to go back where he belongs.

For Schulz, as for Platonov, "emptiness" (*pustka*), "homelessness" (*bezdomność*), and "orphanhood" (*sieroctwo*) suggest a potential akin to freedom, but it is a melancholic freedom, since it implies the lack of a mythic object—of the lost Father, the lost home—that can never be recovered. Like the equivalent lexical elements in Platonov (*pustota, bezdomnost', sirotstvo*), these words are patterned throughout Schulz's oeuvre. They appear most colorfully in "Nimrod" (Nemrod), a short narrative about Schulz's spiritually significant dog. As a child Schulz did in fact have a small dog by that inauspicious name: "The dominant of his disposition was a kind of vague and fundamental sorrow, orphanhood and helplessness—an inability somehow to fill the emptiness between the sensations of mealtime. [. . .] Even in the depths of sleep, in which he had to satisfy the need to lean and cuddle, using his own person for this purpose, rolled up into a trembling ball—he was kept company by his loneliness and homelessness."[115] Schulz shows himself to be no less committed to pathetic fallacy than Platonov, reading in his dog a metaphysical condition that he might as easily identify in himself. But we must also consider that Schulz assigns comparable spiritual gravity to almost every person or thing that catches his attention, and in this regard "Nimrod" represents a milder version of the self-splitting we have already seen in "Solitude": the dog, with no one to cuddle in his sleep, must cuddle with himself, literally "using his own person for this purpose." Nimrod keeps company with his own *lack* of company, his "loneliness" and "homelessness," which appear as permanent character traits.[116] Of course, Nimrod is not homeless, nor is he presented to us as an orphan. Rather, homelessness and orphanhood are innate and immutable qualities of spirit, and they are tied directly to the "emptiness" that plagues the dog when he is not enjoying the sensual satisfaction of mealtime.

Schelling tells us that transformation is more apparent than essential, occurring only on the surface of things, since everything already shares the same basic essence, Platonov's "ancient, reanimated power." Every being "contains within its concept the possibility of infinitely many things that lie outside of its individual state."[117] Schulz agrees, elaborating on this principle in his oft-cited open letter to Stanisław Ignacy Witkiewicz, in which he defines his "extreme monism of substance":

> *Cinnamon Shops* provides a certain recipe for reality, establishes a certain special kind of substance. The substance of that reality is in a state of constant fermentation, germination, of latent life. There are no objects that are dead, hard, delimited. Everything disperses beyond its borders, lasts only for a moment in a given form, only to abandon it at the first opportunity. Someone may be a person, someone else a cockroach, but that form does not reach down to the essence; it's a role adopted for the moment, only an outer skin that will be tossed off a moment later. What is established here is a certain extreme monism of substance, for which particular objects are merely masks.[118]

Schulz's "recipe for reality," too, occupies an intermediate zone between monistic unity and a dualism where the masks assumed by that reality lead us astray even as we try to navigate it. Outward form appears here as emerging from what Schelling calls "absolute infinity," that is, the "sacred abyss from which everything springs forth and to which everything returns," and where differentiated forms would seem to reflect only fleeting facets of the Absolute.[119] What this means in Schulz's artistic practice is that, as in Platonov, metamorphosis demonstrates the impossibility of an escape from Being, even in death. All of reality is consubstantial, rendering all metamorphosis, as it were, pro forma.

Perhaps Schulz's most stunning instantiation of this principle, and certainly the one that has most consistently drawn comparison with Kafka's poor Gregor Samsa, occurs in "Cockroaches" (Karakony), from *Cinnamon Shops*, in which indifference and association appear explicitly as the vehicles of Jakub's metamorphosis. Or, rather, *metamorphoses*: underscoring the vast potential of form, Schulz executes a double transformation, with Jakub changing simultaneously into a cockroach and a stuffed condor, both of which remind the narrator of his father in appearance and spiritual sensibility. "We should note," Schulz emphasizes at the end of "Mannequins" (Manekiny), "that when they came into contact with this unusual man all things withdrew, as it were, to the root of their being, deconstructed their effect down to their metaphysical core, returned, as it were, to their elemental concept, so then to betray it and tilt into those doubtful, risky, and ambiguous regions that we will here call the regions of the great heresy."[120]

As with Kafka and Platonov, the first question we might ask with regard to Schulz's transformations is *in whom* to locate the indifference that serves as their basis. For Schulz, both psychological and ontological indifference are all-pervasive. That is, indifference, as a failure to recognize salient differences between one thing and another, is evidenced both in the witnesses to transformation and in the transformed subject himself. In the opening paragraph of "Cockroaches," Schulz attempts to move beyond the Father—"At that time my father was already gone"—and leaps immediately into a description of the stuffed condor, which Jakub will ultimately become: "In the cool semidarkness of the drawn curtains, it stood there as in life, on one leg, in the pose of a Buddhist sage, and its bitter face, the withered face of an ascetic, had petrified into an expression of ultimate indifference and abnegation."[121] Schulz's narrator associates this face with his father's and, following deeply ingrained stereotypes of Jewish physiognomy, with old Jewish men in general. We see this association earlier in Schulz, in such stories as "Birds" (Ptaki, his first published prose), as well as in his graphic art. At least as early as 1930, Schulz saw a metaphoric link between condors and the Jewish men of his father's generation, as we see in his drawing "Old Men and a Condor" (Starcy i kondor, circa 1930; figure 2.1).[122]

Schulz is quick to point out that Jakub is similarly indifferent to his corporeal integrity or spiritual sovereignty, stating outright that, with the edges of his world having long since blurred, the Father "could not take root in reality and hovered eternally on the periphery of life, in half-real regions, on the edges of actuality."[123] Schulz's descriptions of physical and metaphorical spaces alike make Jakub's intermediacy unmistakable while also matching it to that of the stuffed bird, the "half-real regions" of Jakub's existence echoing the description of the condor standing a moment earlier "[i]n the cool semidarkness of the drawn curtains." His intermediate status, half in one world while half in another and characterized in terms half-spatial, half-spiritual, eases his association with whatever he comes into contact with, most urgently with the cockroaches, whose movements he seems to imitate, and with the stuffed condor, to which he bears a visual resemblance. This association does not belong to the narrator alone, but is shared by Jakub, who surrounds himself with birds in other stories (to which Schulz alludes at the beginning of "Cockroaches"), and who studies with equal deliberation the dance of those nasty insects: "My father moved with the complicated, multilimbed movement of that strange ritual, in which I recognized with horror an imitation of a cockroachy ceremony. [. . .] His similarity to a cockroach appeared more distinct with every day—my father was changing into a cockroach."[124]

Figure 2.1. Bruno Schulz, "Old Men and a Condor" (Starcy i kondor; c. 1930, pencil on paper). Wojciech Chmurzyński, *Bruno Schulz 1892–1942: Rysunki i archiwalia ze zbiorów Muzeum Literatury im. Adama Mickiewicza w Warszawie* (Warsaw: Muzeum Literatury im. Adama Mickiewicza, 1992). Original in the collection of Muzeum Literatury im. Adama Mickiewicza, Warsaw.

Schulz's use of an imperfective verb—*zamieniał się*, "was changing"—warrants special attention. Krzysztof Stala has pointed out that Schulz very rarely uses perfective verbs, preferring imperfectives to convey the disintegration of time as a continuous process.[125] In like fashion, the use of the imperfective verb, analogous to the progressive aspect in English, initially reveals Jakub's "imitation of a cockroachy ceremony" as a transformation still in progress. It is only after the members of Jakub's household have ratified their own indifference to his transformation that it takes on its most tragic hue, as Schulz's narrator tells us in no uncertain terms in the story's penultimate paragraph: "[W]e stopped distinguishing him; he had merged completely with that dark, uncanny tribe."[126] Thus we can say that Jakub's transformation into a cockroach is a collaborative process. Ontological indifference, as I have said, belongs equally to all things. It is more active than passive, a recognition of our own intractable consubstantiality. The psychological indifference to that which would otherwise distinguish Jakub from cockroaches belongs to both him and his family. The association of his being with "that dark, uncanny tribe" is felt equally by him and by those around him.

We may recall the similar role played by Gregor Samsa's family in "The Metamorphosis": they serve not only as witnesses to Gregor's transformation but to register a reaction, which is more grief, disgust, and resignation than actual surprise. That is, the Samsa family is saddened by what has befallen them, yet it seems to make some sense in their universe. The chief clerk, on the other hand, is quite shocked by the creature he finds in Gregor's room, a fair indication that he does not know Gregor well enough to see the cruel logic of his change.

The transformations we witness in the literature of intermediacy therefore differ substantially from those imposed from without by the gods. They are neither gift nor punishment, nor are they ever any more arbitrary than the shades of similitude from which they arise. Nor, for that matter, are they necessarily permanent, though the unfortunate Mr. Samsa's transformation turns out to be. Instead, the transformed subject is a Nietzschean "cross between plant and ghost," a bodily form infused with a spirit too weak to shore up his selfhood against the world around him.[127]

Caroline Walker Bynum offers a productive distinction between metamorphosis and hybridity, suggesting that the former is a process, whereas the latter is a mixed state: "Metamorphosis breaks down categories by breaching them; hybrid forces contradictory or incompatible categories to coexist and serve as commentary each on the other."[128] In Schulz and Platonov, as well as in other authors who emphasize the in-betweenness of the thinking subject, this metamorphic process results in a hybrid of essence and the many forms by which that essence manifests itself in the world. Hybridity is nothing more than the face of metamorphosis, the essence and its mask, always already on the path to adopting a new mask.[129] It reveals a heretofore hidden interconnection among unlike things.

Schulz first explored this idea in graphic works executed using the painstaking method of *cliché verre,* an etching on transparent material that produces a negative image that can be used to make a positive photographic reproduction. In a manner thematically resonant with Schulz's subsequent writings, *cliché verre* typically discards the original etching; our only access to the image is through its reproductions. Schulz's early cycle of *cliché verre* graphics, *The Book of Idolatry* (Księga Bałwochwalcza, 1920–22), includes two images of the individual caught in midtransformation. *Mademoiselle Circe and Her Troupe* (figure 2.2) and *The Enchanted City II* (figure 2.3) both feature the same figure of a half man, half tiger cowering at the feet of beautiful, imposing women. This man-tiger appears in at least two other works, always in the same position, where being treated like a beast has

Figure 2.2. Bruno Schulz, "Mademoiselle Circe and Her Troupe: Circus" (Mademoiselle Circe i jej trupa: Cyrk, c. 1922; cliché verre). Bruno Schulz, *Księga obrazów,* ed. Jerzy Ficowski (Gdańsk: Słowo/obraz terytoria, 2012).

turned him into a beast.[130] The men in these images seem indifferent to how they are treated; they display the "expression of ultimate indifference and abnegation" that appears on the condor's face in "Cockroaches." And the women they worship are undoubtedly indifferent to them, though a woman's indifference to the men at her feet, a frequent theme in Schulz's graphic art, is once again an *active* indifference reflected in an upturned nose and haughty airs. One can also argue, as Małgorzata Kitowska-Łysiak does, that these images of women, who appear in *The Book of Idolatry* as the sadistic deities of masochistic men, are themselves hybrids of real and mythic figures, evoking the often androgynous representations of gods in the print culture of fin-de-siècle Europe.[131] But here, too, it is reality that undergoes a transformation into myth, since Schulz regularly places real and recognizable faces in his imaginary scenes. (The artist's own face is visible on the man crouching in the lower right center of *The Enchanted City II.*) Such gestures toward the real world do not diminish the fantastic quality of the images but augment it, hinting at the hybridity of an elusive essence and an external form imposed on it, as if arbitrarily. I say "as if" because there is

Figure 2.3. Bruno Schulz, "The Enchanted City II: Revolution in Town" (Zaczarowane miasto II: Rewolucja w mieście, c. 1922; cliché verre). Bruno Schulz, *Księga obrazów,* ed. Jerzy Ficowski (Gdańsk: Słowo/obraz terytoria, 2012).

no obvious associative link between Jakub and cockroaches, and yet both Jakub and his family come to draw the same association. As Schulz himself would elucidate in his open letter to Witkiewicz, we get a powerful sense that everything in Schulz's world shares the same essence, but it is only when all parties are equally indifferent that Jakub's transformations take place.

Jakub is aware of this as well, as he elaborates in "A Treatise on Mannequins: Conclusion" (Traktat o manekinach: Dokończenie):

> Here before our very eyes my father started to construct a picture of his dreamed-of "generatio aequivoca," a kind of generation of creatures only half organic, of a kind of pseudovegetation and pseudofauna, the product of a fantastic fermentation of matter.
>
> These creations were by appearances similar to living creatures, to vertebrates, crustaceans, cephalopods, yet these appearances were deceiving. These were essentially amorphous creatures without an internal structure, the fruits of the imitative tendency of matter,

> which, endowed with memory, habitually repeats its once-adopted forms. Matter is subject to a generally limited morphological range, and a certain store of forms repeats itself constantly in various orders of being.[132]

Schulz's point of reference is Arthur Schopenhauer, who, near the end of book 2 of *The World as Will and Representation* (1818, 1844), describes the spontaneous generation that sees one form arising from, yet still containing, those forms that precede it: "There arise originally through *generatio aequivoca,* subsequently through assimilation to the existing germ, organic humour, plant, animal, man."[133] The creatures that occupy Jakub's world are the same creatures he will also become. Form is simply a temporary outer shell for matter, and since all matter is consubstantial and can adopt any number of outward appearances, these appearances are of necessity deceptive. They provide a false sense of stability in a world of matter always in flux; they cannot adequately reflect the totality of Being. Essence comes to signify both the ever-changing and ungraspable, on the one hand, and on the other hand its precipitate, the temporarily singular creature or being. Schulz has the most fun with this concept when he writes the phrase *w istocie istoty amorfne*, "essentially amorphous creatures." We can render the repetition of *istota* literally as "essences in essence amorphous." Schulz's *antanaclasis*, the transformative repetition of the same word in different meanings, demonstrates verbally how essence, lacking a definitive form, must constantly change forms.

Accordingly, in the passage from "Visitation" quoted earlier, we see that space is subject to the same transformative factors as are objects and people. When we can no longer distinguish one space from another, we ourselves may be lost in indifference, which is why Schulz uses the same verb—*odróżnić*—to convey both the failure to tell one façade from another and, later, his family's indifference toward Jakub. In "Visitation," we already see the ominous presence of cockroaches: "Great cockroaches sat motionless in the corners, their shadows making them enormous."[134] More menacing here, however, is the threat signaled by unstable spaces, where Jakub "felt, without looking, that space was growing over him with the pulsing tangle of wallpaper, full of whispers, hissings, and lisps."[135] The space is described through analogy to *inarticulate* speech, utterances that sound like words but are not. It is in this environment that Jakub's individuality begins to disintegrate. Not surprisingly, toward the end of "Visitation" we find him imitating a stuffed "vulture"—not yet a "condor," but at least in the same family.

In "Cockroaches," the groundwork for Jakub's transformation into the condor and into cockroaches is the same. The idea here is that being or becoming one thing does not preclude Jakub from being or becoming another. Jakub appreciates this fact, and he takes great pleasure in observing it in others. Still early in the story, the narrator addresses the problem to his overburdened mother: "I have wanted to ask you for a long time: is it true that this is he?—And though I did not indicate the condor even with a glance—my mother guessed at once, became quite flustered, and lowered her eyes."[136] Schulz's narrator and his mother have entered the realm of taboo. Jakub has long since associated himself with the stuffed condor, an association his son and wife share but cannot acknowledge openly. The narrator is very clear on this point, stating outright that he has been harboring his suspicion "for a long time." If mother and son are ashamed, it is only because they know that through their indifference—both neglect in a conventional sense, and failure to differentiate in an ontological one—they have contributed to Jakub's defacement.

Once again, temptation by and retreat from this danger help us account for the repetitive structure of Schulz's stories, which frequently begin as attempts to reclaim a connection to Jakub, the Father, and end in a reenactment of the Father disintegrating or fading away, only to be reconstituted and lost again in the next story. Schulz's attempts to neutralize orphanhood backfire, since we cannot control the associative movements that allow us access to the past in the first place. This failure to differentiate allows the past to infect Schulz's narrator, and it also allows people, places, and things to interpenetrate one another in his stories.

For both Schulz and Platonov, transformation promises, but then does not deliver, the possibility of a world in which the dead are recovered and returned to the living. Nor does death constitute an escape from Being. The dead can never be released, nor can they be returned, and the false promises held out by transformation, coupled with the circularity of each repetitive narration, mean that the trauma of that loss is relived with each iteration and only partially mitigated by the hope of another meeting at the beginning of the next cycle. This is why narratives of intermediacy may strike us as unfinished, since in-betweenness, indeterminacy, and unfinalizability are the ultimate objects of these representations. Try as we might to imagine Schulz or Platonov laying their characters to rest, we know that Jakub will be reconstituted in the next story, or that Platonov will resurrect Nastia in a question appended to the manuscript of *The Foundation Pit,* just as Proust crossed out the last sentence of his monumental novel, rewrote the sentence, crossed it out again, and on and on, never able to define the edge of the world he had created.

In Platonov and Schulz, time's unfinalizability is another aspect of this spatial multidimensionality. Hence the monstrosity we see in the literature of intermediacy can also be described temporally, insofar as characters subject to unbounded, open-ended narrative constructs play out what Julia Kristeva has called "a singularly Proustian theme, that of Time placed within men who are transformed later into monstrous beings."[137] The open-endedness of Proust's narrative is monstrous, according to Kristeva, "because it is prolonged past measure in Time. Monster = space-time = characters."[138] The author's own failure to delimit the project of writing in space and time is the final symptom of the text's intermediacy.

Up to this point I have treated the spatial dimension of intermediacy more or less in isolation from its temporal dimension, and I have done so in order to lay bare the thematic substructure by which spatial intermediacy leads to orphanhood and homelessness, then to indifference, association, and ultimately transformation. With the notion of unfinalizability, however, it no longer makes sense to sequester temporality from the discussion, since in spatial overlap we are dealing just as much with intermediacy in time. Schulz, who establishes the intermediate space of "Cockroaches" in reference to "half-real regions" and the "semidarkness" of the room, loses his father in the end to temporal intermediacy as the narrator's mother explains that Jakub has become an endless wanderer in a strange hour that is neither night nor day: "Do not torment me, dear. You know very well that your father travels around the country on business, you know very well that he sometimes arrives home at night only to venture on before dawn."[139]

From Indifference in Space to Naivety in Time

The protagonists of the literature of in-betweenness keep one foot in the familiar world of lived praxis, so they cannot surrender to this open-endedness entirely. Yet they can exploit it, exploding the present by opening it to past and future. In the process, they blur the boundaries that define the individual as such. In a 1936 letter to Andrzej Pleśniewicz, a prominent literary critic, Schulz describes his effort to foster unfinalizability by revolting against time:

> What you write about our artificially protracted childhood—about immaturity—disorients me a little. For it seems to me that the species of art that lies in my heart is actually a regression: it is a return to childhood. If it were possible to reverse course, to reach one's childhood again by some detour, again to have its plenitude and boundlessness—this would be the fulfillment of "the age of genius," of the "messianic times" that have been promised and sworn to us by all mythologies. My ideal is to "mature" into childhood. Now *that* would be a real maturity.[140]

"If it were possible to reverse course," to achieve the "plenitude and boundlessness" of mythology: this is Schulz's authorial project, and it is shared by several of his contemporaries. Naivety regarding the passage of time—a naivety delicately constructed and explicitly stated—does for moments in time what indifference does for distinctions in space. Michał Okłot is quick to point out that this is not "a glorification of the naive creative spontaneity of a child," and I, too, must emphasize that what I call "naivety" is an active effort to unknow definitions, as Okłot explains: "Only through regression towards the mythical origin, the state of 'abundance and limitlessness,' accessed by the peculiarly attuned perception suitable for grasping it, can one redeem the 'degenerated reality' in the time that is yet to come, the messianic time."[141] Schulz's artistic activity thus constitutes a metaphysical project, the goal of which is to transform experiential reality into myth. And because it is an *authorial* project, one that he approached with professional deliberateness, Schulz pursues it even in his literary criticism from the 1930s. In what remains the only monograph devoted to Schulz's considerable output as a reviewer, Marta Bartosik demonstrates that Schulz's ideal of reading was to arrive at a text the way a child might, experiencing "the ambiguity and instability of meanings, their inexhaustibility over a single contact with the text."[142] Along these lines, even Schulz's book reviews typically begin in medias res, quickly relaying the reader's most powerful memories of the experience of reading.[143]

This is a significant point, since it shows how an activity as far removed from childhood memory and the writing of fiction as arts journalism is equally subsumed into Schulz's mythmaking project. Or else, if we are to move toward the extreme that Schulz articulates in his programmatic 1936 essay "The Mythicization of Reality" (Mityzacja rzeczywistości), we are not dealing with mythmaking so much as with a recognition that myth is itself all consuming and inescapable, that "science is nothing more than the construction of a myth about the world, since myth is already built into the very elements, and there is generally no way out beyond myth."[144]

Despite the autobiographical elements of Schulz's fiction, then, we are not to read his work as childhood reminiscence, but as an attempt to recover a child's sense of space and time, as Jan Błoński puts it, "a return to the moment when, in the stream of impressions and emotions, the child senses a higher order and direction (i.e., one that is independent of immediate needs)."[145] Like everything else in Schulz's universe, memory is absorbed into a universal process; the only distinctive feature of childhood experience in Schulz is that the child does not bat an eye at the confusion and interconnectivity he sees everywhere around him. We can even take Błoński's formulation a step further: in the perception of "a higher order and direction," the fictional hero turns his back on the "immediate needs" of experiential reality, trying to leap from the particularity of his existence into the totality of myth. The "immaturity" to which Schulz refers in his letter is Bakhtinian unfinalizability, a systematic and cultivated frustration of temporal definition, a practiced naivety in regard to how time defines us. The protagonist may achieve this naivety by jumping backward or forward in time, effectively short-circuiting past, present, and future. Or he may preserve the unfinalized core of his Being, refusing to mature into cultural, social, or ontological definition. Both directions produce the same result: time no longer serves as a meaningful boundary.

Such naivety is a calculated gesture to counter the possibility that ontological knowledge, in its positive articulation, becomes its own veil. "Essential reality reveals itself only to our naivety," Karl Jaspers tells us, and this is precisely why Schulz and Platonov are preoccupied with the "immature" or "naive" child mind.[146] Indeed, the protagonist of nearly all of Schulz's stories is a hybrid of a mature consciousness and a recollected child self. Within this hybrid, the adult ego provides mature reflections on childhood data, but that data has already been mythologized by the child mind, leaving most suggestions of adult skepticism behind.

The recovery of what Schulz calls "the age of genius" is likewise central to the plot of *Chevengur,* in which Kopenkin approaches his quest for the resurrection of Rosa Luxemburg with a childlike naivety.[147] The naive, childlike adult is a stock figure in Platonov's fiction; we see him or her in Nikita, the protagonist of "The River Potudan," and in the eponymous heroes of both "Fro" and the unfinished novel *Happy Moscow* (Shchastlivaia Moskva, 1933–36). But the most important naive hybrid of the adult and the child in Platonov remains Nastia, the very embodiment of the Soviet future in *The Foundation Pit.* Nastia is a peculiar blend of childlike simplicity and adult pragmatism, at once the fairy-tale sister of the bear-worker Misha and a merciless proponent of Stalinist collectivization, declaring to Chiklin, "Liquidate the kulaks as a class. Long live Lenin, Kozlov and Safronov! Uncle Chiklin, Stalin is only one drop worse than Lenin, and Budennyi two. Greetings to the poor kolkhoz, but not to the kulaks."[148] There is a conspicuous continuity between Nastia's brutally uncompromising ideology and that of the party "activist" who oversees the liquidation of the kulaks. Like Nastia, the activist dehumanizes private landowners, eventually graphing their liquidation against icons for the remaining proletariat: "Instead of people the activist made marks for [their] existence: a bast shoe from the last century, a tin ring from a shepherd's ear, a sack-cloth trouser leg, and other trappings of the laboring but indigent body."[149] For the activist, even the task of charting a state-sanctioned action (the liquidation of the kulaks) requires reference to those features of the past that have persisted into the present.

What I am calling "naivety" should not be confused with simple ignorance. It is rather a stylistic effect with metaphysical and psychological consequences. It is therefore akin to the device that Ol'ga Meerson has identified as *neostranenie* ("non-defamiliarization") in Platonov—that is, the amplification of the uncanny through the author's refusal to acknowledge that anything is out of the ordinary.[150] In its most powerful instantiations, however, even this refusal appears to overstate the author's position vis-à-vis what he describes: so thorough is the hero's immersion in his world that he does not seem to perceive the extraordinary enough to refuse it in the first place. In drawing on his childhood to compose fantastic stories, Schulz was certainly aware that the adult writer was fictionalizing experiences remembered from childhood, just as Proust had done. But in *Remembrance of Things Past* the reader observes Marcel grow up to become the author, whose mature reflections are evident at every turn. Not so in Schulz or Platonov. While all three writers invite us to explain the persistence of the past through Bergsonian durée, what appears in Proust as the pleasure of memory becomes in Schulz and Platonov the painful inescapability of childhood.

In the literature of intermediacy, the endurance of the child mind is manifest as the assignation of magical qualities to everyday things or the failure to distinguish between separate times, places, and objects. But this affectation of naivety is more a device than a condition. Affecting naivety, the hero takes advantage of what Jean Piaget terms "participation," or the child's confusion of his own inner world with the world around him, which "results from a lack of differentiation between the consciousness of the action of the self on the self and the consciousness of the action of the self on things."[151] What is for Piaget a clinical observation in child psychology can also be read as the natural consequence of the literary construct described by Lukács as the hero having a soul "broader than the outside world assigned to it as the arena and substratum of its actions." This blending is symptomatic of Schulz's "age of genius," a deliberate effort on these authors' part to evade or negate the kinds of discrimination that maturity demands.

The Short Circuit of Time and Timelessness

Naivety regarding the passage of time constitutes an active effort to transform experiential reality into myth. In the prose of Bruno Schulz and Andrei Platonov, the child consciousness appears as a nexus between time and timelessness—that is, between the temporal definition that we experience in our everyday lives and the eternity we may hope is just on the other side of history. Difficult as it may be to discuss this neutralization of time without indulging our own nostalgia for childhood experience—and not for any particular experience, but for the *way a child experiences*—both Schulz and Platonov represent this temporal collapse in its tragic aspect, since the abolition of spatial-temporal definitions also cancels the possibility of escape. We cannot hope to eject ourselves from a system that has no boundaries.

This does not mean, however, that Schulz and Platonov do not also convey their fascination, or even delight, at the imaginative play such freedom promises. Platonov's early poems, for example, look exuberantly at the notion that the child contains the future, well before the same notion would necessitate the death of the orphan girl Nastia in *The Foundation*

Pit. In his 1920 poem "Children" (Deti)—an admittedly unimpressive lyric, whose marching trochees and hard rhymes may remind us of a school cheer—the Bolshevik promise of the end of history has already been accomplished, so that man becomes an eternal child living "forever" in timelessness:

> Наши дети не родились,
> Не родятся никогда—
> Через вечность мы пробились,
> Будем биться, жить всегда.
>
> Дети—сладкое бессилие,
> Сказка радостная смерти.
> Мы ж невянущие лилии,
> Мы смеющиеся дети.
>
> [Our children were not born, / Will never be born—/ We've broken through to eternity, /We'll keep breaking, we'll live forever. // Children are a sweet powerlessness, / A joyful fairytale of death. / We are unfading lilies, / We are laughing children.][152]

These quatrains must strike us as profoundly naive in historical context, as Platonov would undoubtedly agree just a few years later. Even as he was writing *Blue Depth,* in fact, Platonov was aware of his own wishful thinking, declaring in the subsequent poem, "The dream of a child is the song of a prophet."[153] This is the sense of the title under which he gathered the stories he was writing simultaneously with these poems, *Notes of Progeny* (Zapiski potomka). Surprisingly nuanced given their propagandist design—they were published with the express intention of disabusing the peasantry of traditional beliefs—the stories' reference to the *potomok,* a term that could just as easily be translated as "offspring" or "child," emphasizes the individual's physical embodiment of a time quite unlike our own. Even in these satirical texts, there is a potential for a darker reading, one that emphasizes imperfective action or progress deferred.[154] More than simply populating the world of the future, the "child" or "progeny" Platonov posits is a new vision of the human as such, a creature in whom temporal divisions collapse on themselves.

Naivety—what I might define as "sweet childish ignorance," but for the fact that so many of us never experience it that way—is a favored instrument in producing this collapse. Here it may be helpful to emphasize the distinction between what I am calling "naivety" and the more general interest in the child mind that we find in the primitivism or "naivism" that roughly coincides with intermediacy in Eastern European literature.[155] While many artists and writers took a formal interest in how children combine words or images, intermediacy uses naivety as a device to collapse time, to deprive time of its power to define the individual subject, and in this way to unveil an ontological condition that is otherwise hidden from view. A simple imitation of childish language or vision would be inadequate to this task, since the invention of a narrative or lyric voice poised between childhood and maturity requires a refined verbal sophistication, one that projects naivety and uses it to cut through temporal boundaries. The naivety of intermediacy, then, is not an affectation of childishness, but a particular way of using language to undermine the temporal distinctions that language itself encodes.

Theodore Adorno's term for this effect is "epic naivety." Epic naivety reflects epic discourse's peculiar ability to fuse myth and narrative, which for Adorno implies a collision of time with timelessness. "The amorphous flood of myth is the eternally invariant," he tells us, "but the *telos* of narrative is the differentiated, and the unrelentingly strict identity in which the epic subject matter is held serves to achieve its non-identity with what is simply identical, with unarticulated sameness: serves to create its differentness."[156] Myth is constant and immutable, always already identical to itself. Narrative, on the other hand, is particular, at least insofar as it attempts to communicate events that are interesting precisely because they represent a sequence of differences. One may "narrate" a myth, but in Adorno's estimation this verbal act does not change the immutability and noncontingency of myth itself. This is because myth occurs beyond time, outside history. The author of an epic narrative uses myth to universalize particular experience, while at the same time he particularizes the otherwise timeless qualities of the myths he employs. Epic naivety, then, allows the storyteller to ignore the paradox of his own enterprise. The speaker of the epic text does not recognize the inherent self-contradiction of particular events narrated in mythic terms. The result, Adorno adds, is a certain "anachronistic element" to epic discourse, which he defines as that "in which what is solid and unequivocal comes together with what is ambiguous and flowing, only to immediately part from it again."[157]

By formulating the difference between epic and narrative in temporal terms, with the universality and timelessness of the epic milieu running counter to the particularity and contingency of modern narrative, Adorno helps us avoid a potential misreading of Schulz, Platonov, and other writers whose textual worlds are similarly poised between historical experience and the eternal. For it would be all too easy to dismiss Schulz's preoccupation with the past as "passéism" (Filippo Tommaso Marinetti's term), just as it would be foolish to describe Platonov's orientation toward the future as "Futurist." Intermediate temporality is neither of these things. Instead of focusing readers' attention on the past or the future, intermediacy requires a delicate fusion of the experiential present, which is our only point of contact with time, with timelessness. Whether that timelessness is located in a mythic past or in an equally mythic future may inflect our reading of the text, but it does not change the underlying construct or our impression of intermediacy as *a detemporalization* of historical contingency.

Bakhtin reaches a similar conclusion in his essay "Epic and Novel" (Epos i roman, 1941). A distinctive feature of the novel as a genre, he explains, is its "zone of maximal contact with the present (with the contemporary) in all its incompleteness," whereas in epic literature "the epic world is divided from the contemporary—that is, from the time of the singer (the author and his audience)—by an absolute epic distance."[158] Although Bakhtin does not share Adorno's distinction between the universal and the particular within epic itself, both thinkers struggle with the idea of an amorphous, universal timelessness (the epic past for Bakhtin, myth for Adorno) in conflict with a specific, differentiated telling of the world (the novelistic word for Bakhtin, narrative per se for Adorno). Recall that Bakhtin's early critique of Husserl in "Toward a Philosophy of the Act" was grounded in precisely this conflict: a universal ideal, Bakhtin argued, cannot adequately capture the particularity of lived experience, but language comes much closer to doing so. By the time he wrote "Epic and Novel," however, Bakhtin had reconfigured his thinking about the novel to emphasize its openness, both in the generic sense of novelistic prose being open to infection by other textual sources and in the temporal sense of its being connected to a present whose outcome is always undetermined. "The epic world," on the other hand, "is thoroughly and completely closed, not only as a real event in the distant past, but also in its own meaning and value: one cannot change it, nor rethink it, nor reevaluate it."[159] As is often the case with Bakthin's most provocative ideas, we find a degree of conceptual slippage: the epic attains an identity—a perfectly closed self-equivalence—that is simultaneously universal and particular. Bakhtin remarks that the whole of the epic past is too massive to tell, but that this "is no disaster, for the structure of the whole is repeated in every part, and every part is complete and circular, like the whole."[160] That is, the epic world is characterized by fractal recursion, with each of its repetitive, self-similar parts serving as a potential seed for an epic text. The episodic narrative repetition in Schulz and Platonov comes immediately to mind.

Between Adorno's concept of epic naivety and Bakhtin's generic division between the epic and the novel, we witness a phase shift in the framing of the basic ontological conflict of identity (the universal or monistic ideal) and difference (the particular manifestation). Adorno sees this conflict operating necessarily within epic discourse itself, and this allows him to treat epic quite broadly, with examples that include modern novels and Greek epics, as well as lyric poems. Bakhtin, meanwhile, sees the conflict occurring *between* genres, separating the national epic from the modern novel. But what if the tension between the universal and the particular occurs not within a given discourse, nor between different kinds of discourse, but between discourse and the reality it tends to represent?

In *The Literary Work of Art* (Das literarische Kunstwerk, 1931), Roman Ingarden, Husserl's most important Polish disciple, argues that the salient difference between real and represented objects is that "every real object is *unequivocally, universally* (i.e., in *every* respect) *determined*."[161] Represented objects always preserve "spots of indeterminacy." No matter how detailed the representation, a literary text will always leave certain features of the object to the imagination, whereas real objects are complete and self-identical. Oddly, this brings us back to Bakhtin's early critique of Husserl, though Ingarden is understandably more sympathetic to Husserl's "abstract logical moment" than Bakhtin had been. Whereas Bakhtin asserts that language captures lived praxis by defining it in the word, Ingarden believes that lived praxis is always already defined, and that language, in its failure to determine every feature of the reality it seeks to represent, is in fact closer to an abstract ideal.

Intermediacy, not surprisingly, arises at the crossroads between these positions. It uses language's capacity for aural and etymological associations to departicularize the particular at the same time as it articulates mythic associations as experiential, narrative fact. This is why the story worlds of Platonov and Schulz seem to hybridize child and adult consciousnesses, blurring the boundary between identity and association and extending the resulting crisis from the domain of the individual to the textual world in which he is represented. Intermediacy shows us the real world, the experience of contingency in time, through the mist of an epic naivety that erases its boundaries. "The mythicization of reality" is Schulz's name for this process.[162]

Schulz tells us that poetry—by which he means lyrical language in general, including that of his own prose—reconnects the reader to the timelessness of myth, from which the word derives its own meaning: "Poetry recovers these lost meanings, restores their place to words, links them according to ancient significations."[163] The word that Schulz uses for the "recovery" of lost signification is rooted in "cognition," *poznanie*: poetry "recovers"—*odpoznaje*—lost meanings by "recognizing" a deep interconnection that is always already contained in everyday reality, yet is veiled by conventional language. As a practical description of literary language's function and purpose, I have already suggested, Schulz shares Shklovsky's notion that art "defamiliarizes" us from reality in order to renew our perception of reality. Meanwhile, the temporal operation that Schulz describes moves well beyond aesthetic experience and situates him at the intersection of Adorno, Bakhtin, and Ingarden.[164] For Schulz, the purpose of the poetic word is, in effect, to reestablish lost connections between mythic timelessness—represented in Schulz by his own memories of childhood and of provincial life in the twilight of the Austro-Hungarian Empire—and the lived experience of the adult who speaks in his stories.

Schulz insisted that the bridge between the individually subjective and the universally objective lay in what he terms, in his open letter to Witkiewicz, "spiritual autobiography or genealogy," or else "private mythology."[165] He recognized it elsewhere among his older contemporaries, in the works of Rainer Maria Rilke—his favorite poet—and in Mann, Proust, and Kafka.[166] As a counterweight to the fragmentary nature of experience, however, Schulz found this "private mythology" incomplete and unreliable, since the writer could discover an originary unity of the Self—an erasure of distinctions between inside and outside, childhood memory and adult consciousness—only at the moment of writing. The task of writing is always the same: to reconstitute, through a systematic inventory of the Self, a unity of subjective and objective experience, which nevertheless evaporates at the moment that writing comes to an end. This again recalls Blanchot's description of writing as an activity or dialogic space, rather than as the text that remains merely as the faint trace of that activity. Thus writing comes to be regarded as the sole means of escaping oneself and, at the same time, as a reification of the need to escape in the first place. Escape becomes its own spectacle, the literary counterpart to the escape artistry that had been a European sensation in the early years of the last century.

Schulz's admiration for Rilke is noteworthy in this connection because, among European writers at the dawn of the twentieth century, we now recognize Rilke among the most impassioned advocates for the notion that the unity of inner and outer experience is the very telos of poetic utterance. Rilke attributed the epistemological split between subjective experience and the outside world to consciousness itself, which screens us off from a spontaneous and transcendental knowledge of the world as animals know it, what Rilke terms, in the eighth of his *Duino Elegies,* "the Open." Heidegger cautions us not to mistake "the Open" for "the unconcealedness of beings that lets beings as such be present," since experiencing the world as an animal does, without a contemplative consciousness, would mean to perceive only its surfaces and, therefore, only its concealedness.[167] Yet Giorgio Agamben's more recent critique of Heidegger demonstrates that the Belgian phenomenologist oscillated between privileging human consciousness and the idealized nonconsciousness of the animal, an oscillation that perfectly captures the intermediacy of the poetic utterance in Schulz.[168] The poetic word connects the writer (and, through the text, the reader) with the Open, thereby offering a glimpse of the world as unmediated by consciousness, yet this "glimpse" is never present to the reader except through the author's conscious (and therefore mediated) representation. No wonder that what Schulz enjoys most consistently in Rilke is the precision with which he seems to crystallize abstract experience.[169]

In his description of "the mythicization of reality," Schulz calls these instances of man-made *poiesis,* of sparks of meaning that arise spontaneously in human language, "short circuits": "The process of making meaning is closely connected with the word. Speech is the metaphysical organ of man. Over the course of time, however, the word stiffens, becomes fixed, stops being a conductor for new meanings. The poet restores conduction through new short circuits, which arise out of accumulation."[170] Schulz asserts that the word is fluid at the moment of its utterance, but that it becomes "fixed" with age. The task of the poet is to restore "conductivity" to words, to reconnect lived praxis to mythic timelessness through "short circuits." At first glance, the notion that consciousness screens us off from an immediate experience of the world may strike us as counterintuitive, since we are accustomed to thinking that consciousness is the very site where our contemplation of the world occurs. A quick reevaluation of this notion, however, reveals its inherent self-contradiction. Contemplation is *not* experience; it occurs after the fact, in discrete episodes of thought that are themselves hybrids of recalled sensations and willful intelligence. Accordingly, contemplation has little in common with the continuous present as it actually happens. This continuity is the engine driving what Schulz describes as the "constant fermentation, germination, of latent life," which one can access only through language.

But not just any language. Language as a direct representation of experience, however illusory later studies of literary Realism have demonstrated that representation to be, for Schulz reproduces the false divisions and definitions—the discontinuities of conscious contemplation, Cioran's "parceling-out of the absolute"—that he sought so intently to erase. Only poetic or lyrical language can reconnect us to the continuum of Being, the deep interconnectedness of space, time, and matter, this "extreme monism of substance." The "mythicization of reality" is therefore also the realization of myth. For Schulz as well as Platonov, poetic language hybridizes myth and narrative (à la Adorno). The world it projects is a hybrid of the epic past and individual experience.[171] Time and again the speaker short-circuits his adult consciousness to his childhood memories, an operation made possible by the narrator's epic naivety with regard to the incommensurability of the two.

Chapter 3

In the Meantime: On Temporal Intermediacy (Osip Mandel'shtam, Czesław Miłosz)

> In point of fact, life shows us remnants of the old surviving in the new at every step, both in nature and in society.
>
> —V. I. Lenin

Bakhtin maintained that, because of its "particular relationship with extraliterary genres," the novel can have a broad "zone of contact" with multiple temporal frames.[1] Lyric poetry, on the other hand, is a closed genre, no longer evolving and incapable of accommodating multiple voices without petrifying them into a single voice. In "Discourse in the Novel," Bakhtin further notes that, although it may draw on heteroglossic source material, poetry "operates in its own language as if it were the one and only language, as if there were no heteroglossia outside it."[2] These and similar pronouncements from Bakhtin as to what makes the novel distinctive as a mode of discourse would seem to negate the possibility of formal intermediacy in the lyric poem—"formal" in the sense of intermediacy consisting in the very language through which it is conveyed.[3] The lyric poem can certainly *allude* to multiple times and places, and there is nothing to prevent it from addressing in-betweenness as a principle of metaphysics. But in these instances the poet refers us out of the text, whose language is otherwise singular and self-contained, as if issuing from the body of the poet alone. Indeed, the Russian word for an extratextual allusion, *ssylka,* also means "exile." Is the only way to connect disparate times and spaces in the lyric poem to leave the poem altogether?

In this chapter, I focus on the temporal side of intermediacy by a decidedly non-Bakhtinian course—that is, through the lyric poem. Several poets working in the interwar period explore intermediacy exclusively as a poetic theme. More importantly, they instantiate intermediacy and its thematic substructure—including homelessness, spatial-temporal displacement, and transformation—formally, through a systematic manipulation of lyrical devices. By mixing registers and voices *naively,* indifferent to the differences between them, the interwar poems of Osip Mandel'shtam (1891–1938) and Czesław Miłosz (1911–2004) offer especially salient examples of intermediacy as both thematic concern and formal construct. In reading a selection of their poems against their philosophical reflections on reality and its representation, we recognize how lyrical language can effect naivety in order to create short circuits across time.

Where Past and Future Meet: Mandel'shtam's Word

Like Bruno Schulz, Mandel'shtam was born into a Jewish mercantile family in Poland in the last decade of the nineteenth century, Mandel'shtam in January 1891, Schulz in July 1892. The poet's father, Emil, who dealt in leather, was considerably more prosperous than Schulz's. When Osip was still a small child, his father's standing in trade allowed him to move the family from Warsaw, the poet's birthplace, first to Pavlovsk, then to Petersburg, which were otherwise barred to Jewish settlement until the eve of the October Revolution. In 1900 the young Mandel'shtam entered the stately new building of the exclusive Tenishevskii School on Mokhovaia Street, in the heart of Petersburg.

Tenishevskii offered a modern Russian education with a curriculum that, while broad, focused on science and commercial skills, though there was also plenty to occupy students interested in humanistic pursuits. Among Mandel'shtam's instructors was Vladimir Gippius, a minor poet to whom Mandel'shtam devotes the closing passages of *The Noise of Time* (Shum vremeni, 1925), the lyrical autobiography whose composition marks the beginning of a five-year hiatus from writing poems. He describes Gippius's principal teaching as "literary spite"—*literaturnaia zlost'*—that is, writing as the ultimate vehicle for dissatisfaction, rejection, and *ressentiment,* as it had been for Dostoevsky's graphomaniac narrator in *Notes from Underground*, who introduces himself fittingly as "a spiteful man."[4] From Tenishevskii Mandel'shtam went on to study in Paris in 1908, where he attended Bergson's lectures at the Sorbonne before returning to Petersburg, a copy of the French philosopher's *Creative Evolution* in hand.[5] Making another trip to Western Europe the following year, he enrolled for a semester at Heidelberg University before financial constraints forced his return to Russia, where he studied at St. Petersburg University and joined Viacheslav Ivanov's circle of young poets and intellectuals.[6] He never completed a degree.

From 1911, Mandel'shtam counted himself among the poets calling themselves "Acmeists," and whose coterie included Anna Akhmatova, his close friend and later a guardian of his artistic legacy, and her husband, the poet Nikolai Gumilev (1886–1921).[7] Formally, the Acmeists had little in common. What they shared, according to an oft-cited, offhand remark from the 1930s, long after their loose association had all but dissolved, was a "nostalgia" or "longing"—*toska*—"for world culture."[8]

In Mandel'shtam's work, this "longing" or "nostalgia" is most evident in the poet's frequent recourse to the themes and images of Hellenic antiquity and medieval Europe. Yet to read Mandel'shtam's lyric approach as strictly backward looking would be to miss the point entirely. As Mikhail Gasparov has demonstrated, Mandel'shtam "asserted that the current reader of poetry is"—much like the note-taking "progeny" of Platonov's early cycle of stories—"a newcomer, since he does not know what the [poet's] contemporaries know, and because of this the poetry of the past is, for him, new and unexpected."[9] The "newcomer"—the same *potomok,* "progeny," "descendent," "child," or "offspring," with a distinct emphasis on *potom,* "later," "afterward"—is, once again, the vessel through which all time flows. The encounter between the reader and the poetic word subverts temporality by importing the past (the text) into the present (the reading) and by orienting itself forever toward the future act of reading. Thus poetry restores, as Schulz puts it, "conductivity to the word."

Throughout his interwar prose, Mandel'shtam insists that the past and future are bound together in the present and that repeated attempts to split them off from one another are both self-deceptive and counterproductive. The seeds of this approach are already evident before the Revolution, however, in the poet's Acmeist manifesto "The Morning of Acmeism" (Utro akmeizma, c.1912), where he castigates Futurists for privileging the materiality of the poetic word at the expense of its "conscious sense," while also taking Symbolists to task for appearing to turn their backs on the materiality of world and word alike.[10] He intensifies his critique in later writings, suggesting in "On the Nature of the Word" (O prirode slova, 1920–22) that critical camps focused on rejection, whether of tradition or of future developments, also seem to reject the complementarity of systems in mathematics: "Much like we have two geometries—one from Euclid, the other from Lobachevskii—there are two potential histories of literature written in two keys: one that speaks only of acquisitions, the other only of losses, and they will both be speaking about the very same thing."[11] Mandel'shtam compares the "two potential histories of literature" to the classical geometry of Euclid and the hyperbolic geometry advanced in the nineteenth century by Nikolai Lobachevskii, which allows for the intersection of parallel lines in curved space. Einstein had used Lobachevskii's geometry to great effect in his special theory of relativity, all the while insisting that it cannot abolish Euclid any more than Einstein himself would abolish Newton.

Mandel'shtam develops his critique further in his essay "*Sturm und Drang*" (Buria i natisk), started in 1922 and published the following year under the generic title "On Contemporary Russian Poetry" (O sovremennoi russkoi poezii). Here he frames the Futurists' rejection of the past—best remembered in Mayakovsky's declaration that "the past is cramped" and that we must therefore "toss Pushkin, Dostoevsky, Tolstoy and the rest from the steamship of Modernity"—as vestiges of Romantic nationalism run amok. At the same time, Mandel'shtam sees the Russian Symbolists, whom he acknowledges as progenitors of the Acmeists, as "pseudo-Symbolists," belated and programmatically old-fashioned relative to their earlier brethren in France and Germany.[12] Both camps strike Mandel'shtam as willfully blind to half of what is going on around them, both in art and in the wider world:

> It is most unfortunate that memory and deed have parted ways so quickly, rather than walking hand-in-hand. The Tomorrow-ists and Passéists have very quickly found themselves in two opposed camps. The Tomorrow-ists have summarily disavowed the past—though this disavowal is nothing more than a matter of diet. On hygienic grounds, they have forbidden themselves to read old poets, or they have read them under the blanket, not admitting it publicly. It is precisely this diet that the Passéists have prescribed themselves as well. I am resolved to affirm that up to the current moment many venerable men of letters have, when pressed, not read their own contemporaries.[13]

Instead of referring conventionally to Futurists and Symbolists, in this passage the poet calls them derisively *budushchniki,* "Tomorrow-ists," and *passeisty,* "Passéists," which is what Marinetti had called the enemies of Futurism. Mandel'shtam ridicules the oppositional politics of these aesthetic camps, much of which he dismisses as public posturing. More than the theatricality of their polemics, however, the poet cannot comprehend how it is that intelligent writers can deliberately ignore literary artifacts and, more importantly still, the aspects of our shared reality that they represent. Both Tomorrow-ism and Passéism are, for Mandel'shtam, fictions that blind us to the fundamental interconnection of past and future.[14]

The exceptions to Mandel'shtam's sometimes biting critique of his predecessors are the Futurist poet Velimir Khlebnikov (1885–1922) and the Symbolist poet Aleksandr Blok (1880–1921). Khlebnikov's philological fascination with neologisms undoubtedly resonated with Mandel'shtam's evolving concept of the poetic word as an instrument that restores unity to temporal disjuncture. And Blok's fondness for mixing linguistic registers drawn from the entire tradition of Slavic verse appealed to Mandel'shtam's sense of the past surviving in the present. The eclecticism of these approaches—Mandel'shtam approves Blok as "the most complex instance of literary eclecticism"—gives Mandel'shtam a point of access to both poets, stripping away the programmatic baggage of their respective aesthetic camps. Mandel'shtam understands this access specifically in spatial-temporal terms:

> Khlebnikov is Futurism's answer to Blok. What do they have to say to one another? Their battle continues even in our day, when neither of them is among the living. Like Blok, Khlebnikov conceived of language as a state, though hardly one in space or geography, but in time. Blok is a contemporary right down to the bone: his time collapses and gets lost, yet nevertheless he remains in the generational consciousness for the contemporaries of his own time. Khlebnikov does not know what a contemporary is. He is a citizen of all history, of the entire system of language and poetry. A kind of idiotic Einstein who does not know how to distinguish which is nearer, a railroad bridge or *The Lay of Igor's Campaign*. Khlebnikov's poetry is idiotic—in the genuine, Greek, inoffensive sense of the word.[15]

Mandel'shtam's reading of these two poets is extremely instructive. Blok invents exquisite confusions by jumping quickly from one image to the next, frustrating our efforts to root the poem in a specific circumstance. By stepping out of time, Mandel'shtam seems to say, Blok always strikes us as our contemporary. Khlebnikov, on the other hand, belongs to all times at once. In calling this poetry "idiotic," Mandel'shtam has in mind the Greek *idiotes,* a "commoner" or "nonprofessional," someone unencumbered by the prejudices of politics or convention. In Mandel'shtam's assessment, Khlebnikov is to time as Blok (or, for that matter, Diogenes of Sinope) is to space: unaffiliated, a cosmopolitan or "citizen of the world."

Other scholars have noted the time construct of Mandel'shtam's poems as having emerged from a syncretic blending of the antithetical notions of historical progress—which regards time as a sequence of discrete moments—and the eternal and undifferentiated Absolute. Thus Nikita Struve describes Mandel'shtam's early and intense desire to feel grounded in history as having conditioned a kind of return to the Symbolist liquidation of time, if by the alternate route of medieval culture, such that "Mandel'shtam completely accepts reality in its absolute Being."[16] In a more recent study, Stuart Goldberg traces the decisive moment in the development of Mandel'shtam's time construct to roughly the same period—the eve of the First World War—but rather than focus on the poet's interest in medieval culture, Goldberg sees Mandel'shtam as having internalized Blok, his "boldness and especially his consummate skill in generating convincing poetic embodiments of the 'inseparability and unfusedness' [Blok's language] of disparate time frames, both mythical and historical."[17] Both his engagement with medieval culture and his reading of Blok clearly had a decisive influence on Mandel'shtam's treatment of temporality and atemporality, of history and eternity. Yet we must also remain vigilant *not* to privilege one over the other. As Mandel'shtam underscores in "*Sturm und Drang*," one side of these oppositions only has meaning in the context of the other.

This is how Mandel'shtam understands his artistic pedigree, but it is not merely a way for the poet to situate himself within the aesthetic debates of his time. The same oppositional model resurfaces when he reflects on his own upbringing. Bookending his remarks on language in *The Noise of Time,* Mandel'shtam draws a decisive contrast between the passionate declamations of his Russian teacher and the language of his home, whether the artificially "literary, Great Russian speech" of his mother, his grandfather's words "composed of unfamiliar noises," or his father's hybrid of the two, neither here nor there, "neither German nor Russian," as if "[his] father had no language, only tongue-tied-ness and languagelessness."[18] This description, a diagnosis of the "Judaic chaos" that suffuses his childhood home, is perhaps the memoir's most frequently quoted, vividly illustrating as it does the child's desire—or the adult's projection of desire onto his child self—for a firmer rooting in his actual space and time. Instead, Mandel'shtam writes that his father "transported me into a completely different age and distant setting," a time and place without clear definition, where Spinoza, Rousseau, and Schiller are in conversation with each other.[19] In Mandel'shtam's revisionist family history, Emil is an anachronistic child of the Western European Enlightenment, a self-fashioned foil to the poet's more Russian-seeming mother. The counterpoints these figures represent in the poet's imagination reflect deeper antinomies—West versus East, rationalism versus spiritualism, the future versus the past—and they set the stage for his writing in the 1920s, which struggles to reconcile binary oppositions, especially that of past and future.

The lyric act in Mandel'shtam does not arrest time. Nor does it privilege the past over the future, or vice versa. Rather, it renders visible the continuity of time's architecture; it provides access to an internal consistency that is otherwise masked by everyday experience. From one day to the next, the mature, sober consciousness is all too ready to acknowledge the Heraclitean truth that "everything flows," and that return is therefore impossible, since "man can never step into the same river twice." But the mature sobriety of this regard is antithetical to the literature of intermediacy in general, and to Mandel'shtam's poems specifically, in which "epic naivety" and "the mythicization of reality" insistently subvert such clean definition in space and time. In their short circuits between present experience and a timelessness projected into the past or future, Mandel'shtam forges a hybrid of experiential reality and the nonpresent that effectively reshapes the experiential world around memory, both cultural and personal. This proves just as tragic for Mandel'shtam as it does for Schulz and Platonov. Once again, the destabilization of spatial-temporal boundaries, initially conceived as facilitating the individual's exercise of will, forecloses any possibility of escape.

This inescapability is already implicated in Mandel'shtam's postulate, stated in "The Morning of Acmeism," that "[e]xistence is the artist's greatest ambition," and that the artist "wants no other paradise than Being."[20] As Emmanuel Levinas would argue in 1935, "Existence is an absolute that is asserted without reference to anything else. It is identity."[21] In other words, there is *no way out* of existence, for there is no *out* that is not already implicated within existence itself. Mandel'shtam would most likely agree, though in the manner of Bakhtin and Lukács he turns his attention most insistently in the 1920s to the world construct within the poem, where reality is constituted by "the word as such."[22]

"The word as such" provides the key to understanding the connection between aesthetics and metaphysics in Mandel'shtam's work from the interwar period. While Gasparov defines the third and final phase of Mandel'shtam's career as beginning in 1924, with the composition of his poem "January 1, 1924" (1 ianvaria 1924) and his subsequent five-year hiatus from writing poems, a major shift in the poet's thinking is already discernible in his aesthetic reflections from the very beginning of the decade. This shift entails a reevaluation of the Acmeist hierarchy of values, which, in High Modernist fashion, privileges the artifacts of high culture, especially those that have survived from antiquity. Mandel'shtam does not toss this hierarchy aside wholesale, but he does reframe his relationship to culture as one of temporal proximity and distance. As in space, our view of events, ideas, or images across time becomes less distinct the further we are removed from them; we can remember the recent past or anticipate the near future with much greater clarity than we can those things that are more distant from us. This, of course, does not mean that events or ideas from the distant past do not continue to affect us. On the contrary, the effort to lay bare the hidden connections between the present and nonpresent becomes that much more urgent and difficult as those connections recede. This is Mandel'shtam's version of the center-out architectonics of narrative space in Schulz and Platonov. In his later lyrics, time past and future are now *moving* targets, their specific significance contingent on the relative position of the speaker in the present.

If we revisit "The Morning of Acmeism," it becomes clear how the project of reintegrating the non-present into the present grows out of Mandel'shtam's early reflections on the lyric word. In contradistinction to the Futurists, whom Mandel'shtam accuses of positioning the word horizontally, "on all fours"—that is, in its own, strictly delimited present, which is also that of the poet—"in Acmeism [the word] for the first time assumes a more worthy vertical position and enters into the Stone Age of its existence."[23] On first reading, we may take this to mean that the Futurists have subjugated the word to their own games, whereas the Acmeists seek to allow the word to speak for itself, to stand on its own. But Mandel'shtam's metaphor is richer. The verticality of the word, the "Stone Age of its existence," demands a much broader understanding of lyric function than anything anticipated by either Futurism's linguistic playfulness or Symbolism's associative unconscious. For Mandel'shtam, the poetic word encompasses the whole history of its denotative and connotative development and deployment, as well as its etymologies and aural echoes. Each word is, in essence, an embodiment of what T. S. Eliot called, in his contemporaneous treatment, "tradition": the ever-evolving totality of lyrical language.[24]

The "word as such"—the word fully possessed of its lyrical potential—gives the poet access to both history and mythology. Thus we find in many of Mandel'shtam's poems not only neoclassical references to myths and legends from the Mediterranean tradition, which do not in themselves distinguish Acmeism from Symbolism, but a richly layered cross-pollination of words based on aural repetitions and etymological puns.[25] In this way, the frequent appearance of paregmenon in Mandel'shtam's poems, his tendency to repeat and transform words and their roots, reflects his "sense of reality"—the artist's *mirooshchushchenie,* as he calls it in "The Morning of Acmeism"—as much as it suggests a simple delight in wordplay. The poetic word is a column erected diachronically across time, bombarding us with the sum of a word's past and future usage and associations, which the younger Mandel'shtam understands spatially as well as temporally: "One can only build in the name of 'three dimensions,' as these are the conditions of any builder. [. . .] To build means to fight emptiness, to hypnotize space."[26] The poet's challenge, then, is not to navigate the dualistic boundary between the real and the ideal, as it had been for the Symbolists, but to short-circuit those aspects of our single reality that appear disconnected, thereby taking a stand against nonexistence:

> There is no equality, no rivalry, only the complicity of that which is extant in a conspiracy against emptiness and nonbeing. Love the existence of the thing more than the thing itself, and your being more than yourselves—this is the highest precept of Acmeism. [. . .] A = A: what a beautiful poetic theme. Symbolism was weary and bored with the law of identity, Acmeism makes it its watchword. [. . .] In this way, having acknowledged the sovereignty of the law of identity, poetry receives as its lifelong feudal possession all that exists, without conditions or limitations. Logic is the empire of the unexpected.[27]

Existence is always self-identical for Mandel'shtam, as it would soon be for Levinas. Here, again, we may think of Schulz's "extreme monism of substance." We may also think of Heidegger's 1935 definition of art's function as disconcealing "in its own way the Being of beings."[28] Mandel'shtam, too, subscribes to a monism wherein the poetic word unveils the secret connections among everything that exists, a "word as such" that is unbounded, "without conditions or limitations," the lord in "the empire of the unexpected." As Victor Terras has remarked, for Mandel'shtam it is the poetic word that allows the poet to collapse temporal distinctions by cutting a diachronic axis across time:

> Time is Mandel'shtam's friend because it creates values, because it enriches a man, as it enriches mankind. Kierkegaard speaks of two possible ways to conquer time: that of the knight who has faithfully waited fifteen years for his damsel and is finally rewarded—he has *killed* time; and that of the husband who has been loyally and happily married for fifteen years—he has *saved* time and preserved it in eternity. Kierkegaard observes that it is the husband who lives "poetically," not the knight. Mandel'shtam has precisely this latter attitude toward time: a man who is true to his humanity is enriched, ennobled, elevated by time; it adds plenitude, integrity, and value to his life. Of him it can be said that "[Odysseus] returned, full of time and of space."[29]

While Terras accurately describes time's function in Mandel'shtam, he is overly enthusiastic about the "plenitude" it affords. After all, such broad access across time and space threatens to eliminate historical contingency, and therefore individuality as well, a tragic dimension already expressed in the poem Terras cites, Mandel'shtam's 1917 lyric "A stream of golden mead flowed from the bottle . . ." (Zolotistogo meda struia iz butylki tekla . . .). The poem is melancholic; Odysseus, "full of time and space," suffers greatly for that fullness. Though all he wants is to return to the secure insularity of Ithaca, he is the quintessential epic wanderer, as homeless as he is timeless.

As we have also seen with Schulz and Platonov, however much we may cleave to the ideal of identity or association, it is impossible to hold either position for very long before we are dislodged by the gravitational pull of the other—or, for that matter, the Other. In this framework, Leszek Kołakowski's description of our "metaphysical horror" in the face of either extreme is particularly fitting, because "if nothing really exists except the Absolute, then the Absolute is nothing; and if nothing really exists except myself, then I am nothing."[30] This nothingness, as Kołakowski correctly indicates, is inescapable: "The Cartesian ego is a kind of black hole: it can suck in anything (except an alter-ego) and nothing can escape from it. Ineffable and uncommunicable, conceptually unconstructible, one might properly call it Nothing."[31] Yet it is the hopelessness of the thinking subjects' striving against this Nothing that we find emotionally compelling in the literature of in-betweenness. In this regard, what Jarzębski writes of Schulz could apply just as well to Mandel'shtam: "Schulzian man is characterized by *incompleteness, inadequacy*. He would like to know the entire world and the mystery of Being, yet he is condemned to a brief life in delimited space."[32] In the vain hope of disrupting the Nothing that is a self-identical Absolute, of breaking its insurmountable totality into interconnected parts, Mandel'shtam reconfigures Acmeism's poetics of identity, with its hierarchy of cultural values, into a poetics of short circuits across space, time, myth, and lived praxis, where hierarchies are replaced by gradations of relative proximity and distance.

Mandel'shtam's ideal of identity in "The Morning of Acmeism" therefore undergoes its own transmutation into short circuits that, in connecting disparate elements into broadly expressive networks, point to the particularity of lived experience even as they gesture toward the universal interconnectedness of Being. He articulates this conceptual slippage as early as 1921, in his lyrical essay "The Word and Culture" (Slovo i kul'tura): "Poetry is the plow that digs into time, such that the deep layers of time, its black earth, are turned up. But there are epochs when mankind, not satisfied with the here and now, longing for deeper layers of time, like a plowman, craves the unbroken earth of time. Revolution in art inevitably leads to classicism. Not because David reaped Robespierre's harvest, but because that's what the earth wants."[33] Here we immediately notice a significant shift in metaphor. Poetry is no longer the lord or landowner whose "lifelong feudal possession" is the totality of existence, "all that exists, without conditions or limitations," but is rather both the plowman and his instrument, working the land, cutting through that totality, turning up the "black earth" of time. Mandel'shtam is moving toward a poetics not of identity but of simultaneity and temporal interconnection, which he then counters with what he regards as the neoclassical impulses of artistic revolution. The metaphor is especially telling. The plowman, disaffected with the present, longs for the Absolute, the "unbroken earth of time." The Russian word *tselina*, "unbroken" or "virgin soil," is a perfect expression of that distant wholeness (*tselost'*). By digging into the *tselina* and turning it up from the bottom, Mandel'shtam effectively neutralizes temporal succession, as Gregory Freidin explains:

> Mandel'shtam called for the appearance of a poet who would be powerful enough to stop time and whose word would be capable of freezing the moment in recollection in the same way that the lifting up of the Host during the Mass suspends temporality and produces anamnesis. The Host is atemporal and the priest transfers its attribute to time itself. Likewise the word, transformed into a node of memory by the poet, can operate according to the principle of

sympathetic magic and tame the devouring time (a eucharistic anamnesis).[34]

Poetry's capacity to cut into time results in a kind of glossolalia, since the poet seems to speak "in a language of all times, of all cultures," and Mandel'shtam goes so far as to call this contemporary poetry, "in all its complexity and internal resourcefulness, naive."[35] Once again, this naivety should be understood in its epistemological sense, and not as a generic attack on the poetry of the immediate post-Revolutionary period.[36] That is, Mandel'shtam underscores the poet's necessarily naive stance toward the incongruities of interconnected spaces and times, the naivety that makes these connections possible. If poetry is "the plow that digs into time," then the poet must suspend the critical apparatus that tells him, for instance, that Petersburg and Leningrad do not coexist in the same temporal frame, even though they are literally the same space.

From the Ideal of Identity to the Action of "Hellenism"

Mandel'shtam elaborates on these interconnections in "On the Nature of the Word," which belongs to the same period of intense reflection on poetic utterance preceding his half-decade hiatus from writing poems. His inquiry becomes all the more urgent because of what he perceives as "the quickening of the tempo of the historical process": "Thanks to a change in the amount of content in an event arriving at a known interval of time, the understanding of a unit of time has become unstable, and it is not by chance that contemporary mathematical science has advanced the principle of relativity."[37] At the same time as Platonov was writing "Audible Steps," projecting his views on social revolution through a reading of Einstein's theories, Mandel'shtam was taking a similar approach in reformulating his poetics.[38] Too much happens in a single moment. The instant, overburdened with content, becomes attenuated as it fills with interconnections between the present and the nonpresent, or between time and timelessness. Mandel'shtam seeks a solution that will preserve a sense of totality while also recognizing the interconnections of many parts—a solution that will, in effect, hold the singular (identity) and the interconnected (infection) in tenuous balance. In a manner that we have already come to expect from those whose confrontation with spatial-temporal relativity leads to a loss of home or self, Mandel'shtam turns to Bergson:

> In order to save the principle of unity in the whirlwind of changes and the unceasing flow of phenomena, contemporary philosophy, in the person of Bergson, [. . .] offers us the study of a system of phenomena. Bergson regards phenomena not in the order of their

> subordination to the law of temporal consecution, but rather in the order of their spatial breadth. He is interested solely in the internal connection of phenomena. He frees this connection from time and regards it separately. In this sense, interconnected phenomena constitute a kind of fan, the blades of which one can spread in time, but which at the same time gives way to a wholly comprehensible turning.[39]

In the waving fan, we know that each blade is present individually, but what we see is motion, a blurred disk moving around a central axis. Mandel'shtam is recycling a similar analogy from Bergson's *Creative Evolution,* where the philosopher compares our mental conceptualization of continuity to the illusion of motion in film, the actor's "successive attitudes" blurring into a single, observable "becoming": "We take snapshots, as it were, of the passing reality, and, as these are characteristic of the reality, we have only to string them on a becoming, abstract, uniform and invisible, situated at the back of the apparatus of knowledge, in order to imitate what there is that is characteristic in this becoming itself."[40] Mandel'shtam's waving fan likewise demands that the thinking subject integrate his detached observation and his personal intuition. Motion veils particularity, while an insistence on the particular masks a movement that belongs equally to reality—"like a prismatic top," Proust remarks, "that spins too quickly and seems only grey, when, on the other hand, in our musings we reflect, we seek, so as to return to the past, to suspend the perpetual motion by which we are borne along, gradually we see once more appear, side by side, but entirely distinct from one another, the tints which in the course of our existence have been successively presented to us by a single name."[41] The integration of the particular and the universal marks a crucial moment in the development of Mandel'shtam's aesthetic philosophy, as it forms the basis of what he terms the "Hellenism" of the Russian language (more on this momentarily). Mandel'shtam has, in a certain sense, rendered Bergson an instrument of history, whose overflow of content has necessitated the development of a system that divorces temporal sequence from the meaning attached to phenomena. Through a maneuver that is cleverer than Bergson would have likely approved, Mandel'shtam allows history to dehistoricize itself. History, the poet seems to say, calls for this philosophical solution, but the solution burns away "the law of temporal consecution," leaving only "the internal connection of phenomena."[42]

In his study of the autobiographical roots of Mandel'shtam's poetics, Evgenii Pavlov points out that for Mandel'shtam the poetic utterance is not only the embodiment of these internal connections (an "internal richness") but the product of the poet's recognition of them, which collapses the historical into the subjective: "In *the moment* of recognition both the experience of subjectivity and the experience of history are fused together."[43]

This "recognition" (*uznavanie*) recalls Viacheslav Ivanov's interplay of "cognition" (*poznanie*) and "penetration" (*proniknovenie*), insofar as the lyric subject perceives internal connections among those things that exist outside him and then merges his own subjectivity with those same connections. Such internal connections form the conceptual bridge between Mandel'shtam's earlier notion of the "word as such" and Schulz's temporal "short circuits." Phenomena are connected not only synchronically—that is, to other phenomena in a given moment—but also diachronically, and thus to a vast store of information that comes before and after, what Pavlov calls "the experience of history." Because "the law of temporal consecution" has been subverted, "before" and "after" also prove conceptually inconsequential.

While I find these interconnections most legible in Mandel'shtam's frequent recourse to rhetorical figures of repetition, especially paregmenon and antanaclasis, Omri Ronen has argued that similar internal resonances appear when Mandel'shtam appropriates lines from other poets: "Considering these repetitions with regard to synchrony and diachrony in poetics, one might say that the poetry of the past, entering the new text 'as it should be, and not as it was,' is subject to synchronization and semantic refraction, but the poetic text based on such fragments, insofar as the original meaning of the fragments remains unchanged, seems to coexist with the refracted one, diachronically correlated with its sources."[44] Quotation, just as much as aural and etymological resonances within words, creates a short circuit across time, a sense that separate temporal spheres are folded into one another. Mandel'shtam's metaphor of the waving fan is therefore particularly apt, allowing us to imagine phenomena interconnected via a central axis while also rejecting a sense of linearity, hierarchy, or progress. As an image evoking spatial-temporal confusion, the fan blades will also resurface in the next chapter through Nikolai Zabolotskii's lyric poem "Red Bavaria" and Vítězslav Nezval's long poem *Edison*.

Because temporal sequence no longer appears as a determinant of value, we may detect a hint of derision in Mandel'shtam's later characterization of Acmeism as "longing" or "nostalgia for world culture." After all, his reflections on poetics in the 1920s affirm his conviction that the whole of culture is always already available to us, so long as we are capable of recognizing its hidden connections to immediate experience. When he declares, in "On the Nature of the Word," that "[t]he theory of progress in literature is the crudest, most repulsive aspect of scholastic ignorance," he is saying that literature, like science, requires a principle of connection in the way we read as well as in the way we write.[45] And this rescue occurs within a discourse on freedom and escape, not from infinity—Mandel'shtam's metaphor of interconnected phenomena as a waving fan is also infinite—but from linearity and simple causality. "Hellenism" is what Mandel'shtam calls this capacity of poetic utterance to connect the individual to a reality that transcends spatial-temporal determinism:

> Hellenism is the conscious encirclement of man with implements instead of indifferent objects, the transformation of these objects into implements, the humanization of the surrounding world, the warming of that world with the most subtle teleological warmth. [. . .] Hellenism is a system in the Bergsonian sense of the word, one that man unfolds around him, like a fan of phenomena that have been freed from temporal dependence, that have been subordinated to an internal connection through the human "I."[46]

While clearly reflecting his lifelong interest in the Mediterranean tradition, "Hellenism" for Mandel'shtam is a quality inherent in—but not always recognized or exploited by—the Russian language itself. He has reconfigured "the word as such," formerly an expression of the self-identity of the Absolute, by placing the individual *between* singularity and totality. Instead of A = A ("what a beautiful poetic theme"), Mandel'shtam proposes "Hellenism" as a cascade of processes with the individual at their center, "consciously" surrounded by things for his use, instead of objects that are "indifferent" or, more accurately, "undifferentiated" (*bezrazlichnye*).

Despite his objection to notions of progress, Mandel'shtam does not mind teleology of the "most subtle" order, as Clare Cavanagh has observed.[47] The tools placed at the subject's disposal should serve a purpose, but that purpose cannot be predetermined by historical necessity. In this way, "Hellenism" fosters an attack on both proletarian literature, in which the entire representation of the world is predetermined by a sense of historical utility, and such literary programs as Symbolism and Futurism, in which the objects represented seem to have an arbitrary relationship to their use.[48] Surrounded by objects for his use, Mandel'shtam's subject is connected to the world, which is also "humanized" in the process. Hilary Fink states this succinctly: "[W]hen Mandel'shtam writes of the Hellenistic nature of the Russian word, he is referring to the way in which language connects us to the world in which we live, connects our 'here and now' to what has already been, in the same way that duration is the means by which the past is preserved in the present. Through both the Hellenistic word and the intuition of duration, one is able to attain a more unified vision of the self in the world, and therefore in time."[49] The individual stands at the intersection of phenomena, "freed from temporal dependence," whose thick interconnections can only be unveiled by the word, which itself contains the "internal connection" to which the phenomena have been subordinated. What happened where and in what sequence is no longer assigned a stable position within a hierarchy of values. Instead, the poetic word restores the primordial link between the singular subject (the bearer of the word) and totality.

But this is a difficult situation, as we see, for example, in the short lyric "With the majestic world I was but childishly connected . . ." (S mirom derzhavnym ia byl lish' rebiacheski sviazan . . . , 1931). The poem's speaker rejects memory, though he still cannot help but admit the connections he seems to deny:

> С миром державным я был лишь ребячески связан,
> Устриц боялся и на гвардейцев глядел исподлобья—
> И ни крупицей души я ему не обязан,
> Как я не мучал себя по чужому подобью.[50]
>
> [With the majestic world I was but childishly connected, / I was afraid of oysters and looked frowningly on the guards, / And I am not obliged to it with a single grain of my soul, / Just as I have not been tormenting myself in another's image.]

This tension is not a consequence of Mandel'shtam's travels and long poetic silence after 1925. It develops from his earlier poetic philosophy, only now it requires the lyric subject either to give up on his dream of integrating all time or to be pulled apart by the disparate times and phenomena in which his very being consists. Thus Akhmatova recalls that for Mandel'shtam memory was not an intellectual faculty so much as a creative act: "He did not know how to remember, or rather, for him it was a kind of different process I won't endeavor to name now, but one undoubtedly close to the creative act. (An example: Petersburg in *The Noise of Time,* as seen by the radiant eyes of a five-year-old child.)"[51]

In rejecting narratives of progress, artistic or otherwise, Mandel'shtam also rejects a narrow reading of Darwinian evolution, maintaining instead that science consists of "connections," not of endless causality: "Science, constructed on the principle of connection, and not of causality, rescues us from the pointless infinity of evolutionary theory, to say nothing of its vulgar henchman, the theory of progress."[52] This helps account for the poet's preference for the evolutionary theories of Jean-Baptiste Lamarck, whose belief that acquired traits could be passed on to one's offspring clearly resonated with Mandel'shtam's sense of deep interconnections across time. "If all that is living leaves but a mark," he writes in his poem "Lamarck" (1932), "When the short, escheated day is done, / On the shifting ladder of Lamarck / I'll occupy the final rung."[53] The poem's central "anxiety," as Galin Tihanov elegantly puts it, is "whether we can insist on being distinctly human [. . .] while still hoping to remain inseparably united with nature in the whole variety of its living forms."[54]

One can easily see how statements such as Mandel'shtam's on the theory of progress, the "vulgar henchman" of evolutionary theory, could run afoul of Marxist ideologues, whose politics accepted historical and social evolution as a foregone conclusion, and who assumed that the telos of that evolution would inevitably be achieved in the Marxist state. Mandel'shtam rejects this notion of historical consequence as a Hegelian "pointless infinity" (*durnaia beskonechnost'*), which we might also translate as "bad" or "evil" infinity, that from which science must "rescue" (*izbavit'*) or, in a more spiritual vein, "redeem" us.[55]

But why this intractable rejection of progress? Because the poetic utterance, the "word as such," should have no gravitational pull, either toward abstract symbolism or toward strict literalism. As Irina Paperno persuasively argues, "for Mandel'shtam the word has, as it were, a dual nature. Its meaning cannot be limited either to the symbolic or to the direct, denotative meaning. In metaphorical terms the word's nature is neither 'absolute' nor 'substantial,' 'material,' or 'corporeal.'"[56] Of course, the word in Mandel'shtam performs both abstracting and denotative functions, but it does not tend (or progress) toward one or the other. Rather, Mandel'shtam tries to maintain his utterances, however tenuously, in the intermediate space between the literal and the purely symbolic.

Mandel'shtam's celebrated poem "I returned to my city . . ." (Ia vernul'sia v moi gorod . . . , also called "Leningrad," 1930) is exemplary in this respect, since it demonstrates how the reestablishment of lost connections simply propels the lyric "I" into the painful economy of recovery and loss. It turns out that one *can* step into the same river twice. The much harder part is stepping back out.

Living in the Past: Mandel'shtam's "I Returned to My City . . ."

The struggle to return is a principal theme in the literature of intermediacy, whether it is a return to the past, to one's childhood, to a place, or eventually to the possibility of return itself. In "I returned to my city . . . ," Mandel'shtam knows that return can never be definitive, that the return to the city of his youth announced in the poem's opening line is impossible, since the Petersburg he had known no longer exists. At the same time, I disagree strongly with the interpretation that for Mandel'shtam "all connections between contemporary Leningrad and the St. Petersburg of his memory have vanished," as Jane Gary Harris suggests.[57] For Mandel'shtam's poem enacts the recognition that *he himself* is the connection between the city he remembers and the one he is now experiencing. He is the nexus between one spatial-temporal frame and another.

Я вернулся в мой город, знакомый до слёз,
До прожилок, до детских припухлых желёз.

Ты вернулся сюда, так глотай же скорей
Рыбий жир ленинградских речных фонарей.

Узнавай же скорее декабрьский денёк,
Где к зловещему дёгтю подмешан желток.

Петербург! я ещё не хочу умирать:
У тебя телефонов моих номера.

Петербург! у меня ещё есть адреса,
По которым найду мертвецов голоса.

Я на лестнице чёрной живу, и в висок
Ударяет мне вырванный с мясом звонок.

И всю ночь напролёт жду гостей дорогих,
Шевеля кандалами цепочек дверных.[58]

[I returned to my city, familiar down to the tears, / To the veins, to the swollen glands of childhood. // You returned to this place, so quickly gulp down / Fish oil from Leningrad's riverside lampposts. // Recognize all the more quickly the little December day, / Where yolk was mixed into ominous tar. // Petersburg! I do not wish to die yet. / You have my telephone numbers. // Petersburg! I still have the addresses / By which I will find the voices of the dead. // I live on a back staircase, and in [my] temple / The bell ripped out with [its] flesh strikes me. // And the whole night through I am waiting for dear guests, / Shaking the shackles of the door chains.]

By December 1930, when Mandel'shtam penned the poem, the intellectual and cultural vibrancy of the pre-Revolutionary capital had been largely drained from the city. Moscow had become the capital in 1918, and the Sovietization of culture that followed the Civil War was not kind to what had been the locus not only of Russia's imperial administration but also of its pretensions toward Europeanization, its bourgeois industrialism, and its aristocratic *patrimoine*.[59] The poem's opening stanza frames the theme of return explicitly as a return to childhood. Leningrad is *his* city. But instead of expressing his ownership through demonstrations of geographic familiarity, which we will come to see as an important feature of Nikolai Zabolotskii's *spatial* manipulations of the same city in the same period, Mandel'shtam takes command of memory. The poet lays claim to his hometown by enumerating its echoes in his own body, leaving the reader to puzzle over whether the "tears," "veins," and "swollen glands of childhood" belong to the poet, other(s), or the city itself. Mandel'shtam emphasizes that he has returned to a mnemonic space just as much as to a physical one. In this way, the poem delineates an expedition to recover what can be found only by short-circuiting the temporal frame of the adult to that of the child.

The poem's political overtones, no doubt magnified by the fact of the author's arrest and death in 1938, have received considerable attention from other readers, generally at the expense of the equally powerful epistemological content.[60] Absent that foreknowledge, however, the poem's autobiographical details relate with surprising directness to congruities between the poet's past and his present. Mandel'shtam frequently addresses the Petersburg theme in poems written before 1925, and in this way "I returned to my city . . ." represents a threefold return.[61] It marks, first of all, the *biographical* return to a city, now called Leningrad, after a peripatetic five years spent in Moscow, Kiev, the Crimea, and Armenia. It is simultaneously a *formal* return to the lyric poem, which he had all but abandoned during the same period. Finally, and in a way that seems hardly separable from the other two, it is a *thematic* return to a subject that, while not quite dormant (Mandel'shtam set his 1927 novella *The Egyptian Stamp* in Petersburg), had been supplanted by Armenia in the poet's geographic imagination. The space that emerges here is more than a city: it is the poet's long-neglected lyric collaborator.

The poem's temporal construct uses its associative chains to link the past with the present. The first such link in the poem is "swollen glands," a common affliction in Petersburg's cool, damp climate. (While researching this book in Petersburg, I, too, came down with an acute case of tonsillitis, complete with high fever and Dostoevskian delirium.) Mandel'shtam notes at the end of *The Noise of Time* that Vladimir Gippius, his teacher, was "prone to tonsillitis," which was also the illness he most feared, since it "interferes with speech."[62] In adulthood, Mandel'shtam, too, suffered from an acute fear of losing his ability to speak.

As a biographical and textual fact, this fear of silence generally receives an existential reading: the poet fears silence because he is a poet to his core, and deprived of the faculty of speech he would, like the Underground Man or the narrator of Beckett's *The Unnamable,* cease to exist. My own tendency is to shy away from this Romantic vision, at least insofar as we can distinguish between the poet's existence and the sense he makes of it. For Mandel'shtam appears to understand, as much in *The Noise of Time* as in "I returned to my city . . . ," that the speaker goes on in his existence even when deprived of speech. Indeed, his dread stems not from a fear of his own nonbeing but from a visceral sense of the limbo such being would entail, that is, banishment to the same "tongue-tied" state that he remembers from childhood, the "flight" from which Gasparov identifies as the first, Acmeist stage of Mandel'shtam's poetic development. The notion that "speech is the metaphysical organ of man" applies as much to Mandel'shtam as it does to Schulz, since it is only through language that we are able to draw together discrete points in space and time that remain disconnected and beyond sense in the absence of the poetic word.

But since the city has changed in the interim between childhood and the adult poet's return, in the poem's second and third stanzas Leningrad tauntingly resists the possibility of collaboration: "You returned to this place, so quickly gulp down / Fish oil from Leningrad's riverside lampposts." Having returned to Leningrad-Petersburg, the city proclaims to the poet, it is now time for you to take your bitter medicine, the cod-liver oil whose unpleasant taste would have been all too familiar to Mandel'shtam from his youth. (The popularity of cod-liver oil as a dietary supplement for children rose at the end of the nineteenth century. It was used as a prophylactic against arthritis and rickets, among other ailments.) Here, however, Mandel'shtam conflates the cod-liver oil forced on the child with the oil once used to light the streetlamps lining Leningrad's canals. Although the poet will address his city as "Petersburg," it has not carried this name since 1914.

The poem's reference to fish oil is just one of several motifs that, as Irina Surat has noted, Mandel'shtam has recycled from *The Egyptian Stamp*.[63] It also dates Mandel'shtam's mnemonic transposition with surprising accuracy, though the dates extend to a period well before the poet's birth. The network of street lamps had evolved and expanded continuously since the city's founding in the early eighteenth century, and the stench of burning oil, which at times included cod-liver oil, was once a common displeasure of life in the Northern Capital, though not so much in Mandel'shtam's day. That may be beside the point, since for Mandel'shtam a fleeting association—frequently, as here, between an architectural detail in the present and the historical past it conjures—will suffice to connect the poet to an expansive temporal arc. All the poet has to do is recognize the connection to manifest it.

The city demands that he do just that, and that he do so quickly. In addition to the "fish oil," in the poem's most challenging couplet the city orders the poet to recognize a December day in which "ominous tar" was mixed together with egg yolk. Once again, the line is less mysterious once we parse out its components, and even though Mandel'shtam's associative method rarely lends itself to an unequivocal or unambiguous reading, the couplet resonates most powerfully when we treat it the same way as the preceding couplet, that is, as a conflation of the biographical present and the remembered past. The oppressively short December days during which Mandel'shtam composed the poem—the poet uses the diminutive for "day," *denek*—allow scant traces of light as the sun circles pitifully above the horizon. Mandel'shtam, then living in a cramped space under the back stairs of his brother Evgeny's apartment on Vasilevsky Island, might have had in mind the familiar appearance of this faint daylight as it scatters over the waters of the Neva emptying into the Gulf of Finland. Kiril Taranovsky has also suggested that yolk and tar register visually as yellow and black, the colors of the Russian imperial standard—a black, double-headed eagle on a yellow background—which Nadezhda Mandel'shtam also notes as having its own "ominous" suggestion in her late husband's imagination.[64]

But another, equally important association that connects this couplet to the "fish oil" has been widely overlooked: coal tar is a common treatment for psoriasis, another frequent ailment in the damp, cold climate and drafty quarters of the Northern Capital. Mixing coal tar with yolk creates a fast-drying topical ointment that, like fish oil, has a strong, unpleasant odor. The poet may in fact be suggesting a memory that is as much olfactory as visual. Returning to his hometown, he is immediately confronted with the modest displeasures and humiliations of childhood, with his own mnemonic space now short-circuited to Leningrad in the era of Stalin, when the city itself attempts to prod the poet into aborting his mission of return and merely to accept, "gulp down," and "recognize" the fact that the home he had left—both physically and lyrically—no longer exists.

The poem's rapid shift from the first-person indicative in the opening couplet to the second-person imperative in the second and third couplets creates the inherently dialogic structure of call-and-response. An early redaction, in fact, sets each of the first, second, and third stanzas off in quotation marks, emphasizing that they emanate from a different speaker from that of the rest of the poem.[65] In the standard version, without quotation marks, the fact that the poet has integrated the voice of the city into his own monologue suggests that this Leningrad is, perhaps, merely a double for the speaker, a reading that is reinforced by the lack of markings designating the imperative stanzas as separate speech.

Omri Ronen has noted not only that such internal dialogue recalls Bakhtin's model for unfinalized speech but that Mandel'shtam was fully conscious of the effect, both in his invention of interlocutors and in his frequent appropriation of others' lines and motifs.[66] Were it not for these grammatical and metaphorical complexities, Ronen argues, we would not have to contend with the kinds of "enigmas" that we encounter in poems like "I returned to my city . . ."[67] Indeed, the capacity for metaphor to shift through accumulated associations was a centerpiece of Mandel'shtam's poetics; for Lidiia Ginzburg, it is the most distinctive feature of what she identifies as the poet's "middle" period (and his second collection, *Tristia,* published in 1922).[68] This is verbal bricolage of a highly refined order. The opposite approach to metaphor, an approach that Mandel'shtam explicitly rejects in his major essay "Conversation about Dante" (Razgovor o Dante, 1933), is what he calls "Heraclitean metaphor." This is the metaphor deployed and immediately withdrawn once it has served its purpose, "emphasizing so powerfully the fluidity of what happens and, with such flourishes, crossing it out" when its work is done.[69] In the Heraclitean view, it would seem, one cannot step into the same metaphor twice.

We can easily isolate the specific rhetorical devices by which Mandel'shtam achieves his decidedly non-Heraclitean metaphor. Throughout his career, and especially following the October Revolution, Mandel'shtam demonstrates an uncanny talent for antanaclasis and especially for paregmenon, the same transformative repetition of word roots that I have already noted at the center of Platonov's verbal art. In fact, Mandel'shtam cleverly uses paregmenon in his description of Dante's metaphors "emphasizing so powerfully the fluidity of what happens and, with such flourishes, crossing it out": the Russian words he uses for "emphasize" (*podcherkivat'*), "flourish" (*roscherk*), and "cross out" (*perecherkivat'*) are all derived from the same root, *-cherk-*, meaning "strike" or "quick movement." In a formulation about the nonaccumulation of meaning, Mandel'shtam takes us from emphasis to its opposite, with considerable flourish of his own.

His grammar exhibits comparable hybridity. In the fourth stanza of "I returned to my city . . ."—the poem's midpoint—Mandel'shtam hybridizes the grammatical form of what has come before, switching back from the second person to the first and returning to the indicative mood from the imperative, all the while preserving the direct address in which the city had challenged the poet. By calling Leningrad "Petersburg" anaphorically in this and the following stanza, Mandel'shtam connects his mnemonic city with his current experience: "Petersburg, I do not wish to die yet. / You have my telephone numbers. // Petersburg, I still have the addresses / By which I will find the voices of the dead." The city is immediately accessible to the poet, since he can always call upon the voices of the dead by retracing the residences they once occupied. The reverse is true as well, since the city can always reach the poet.

Here we witness the dissolution of both spatial and temporal particularity. In the discomfort and isolation of his current lodgings, the entire city appears to be at the poet's fingertips. He does not need to provide the city with a new phone number, for the totality of the old ones will serve the city just as well as old addresses will serve the poet. The repetition of "Petersburg" finds a parallel repetition in *eshche*—"still" or "yet"—which underscores the duration or persistence of the old in the new. Just as the poet is ever accessible to the city—"vulnerable" might be more appropriate—the dead, whose ranks he is not yet ready to join, are ever accessible to him as well.

The telephone, a technology emblematic of modern interconnectivity, here returns to myth as divine, if sinister, communication. Mandel'shtam has explored this theme before, notably in his 1918 poem "Telephone" (Telefon), in which the modern technology of communication appears as both the messenger of the gods and the destroyer of dreams, reverie and wake-up call in one. It also appears in *The Egyptian Stamp*, where Mandel'shtam compares the pointless effort to call the authorities—"vanished, dormant, like perch"—to calling "Proserpina or Persephone, not yet reachable by telephone."[70] Mandel'shtam's double reference to the queen of the underworld, calling her by both her Latin and her Greek names, arises from a transformative association of the words *telefon* and *Persefona,* catching the aural similarity of their respective roots, Greek *phōnē,* "sound," and *phonē,* "killing." In fact, Mandel'shtam had long conceived of Petersburg-Leningrad as the city of the dead, writing in 1916—and referring to the city by its Hellenized name, even as he uses the Roman name for Persephone—"We will die in transparent Petropol, / Where Proserpina rules over us."[71] For Mandel'shtam, the easy, even casual connectivity of the telephone would always portend a threat to individuality, especially in the 1930s, when, as Nadezhda Mandel'shtam would recall, "people were always being 'hauled in' and asked for information about our thoughts and feelings," in "interviews" that could not be refused, "even though they were unofficial and generally arranged on the telephone, as in a Kafka novel."[72]

Despite the poet's declaration in "I returned to my city . . ." that he does "not wish to die yet," the poem is not principally about the fear of mortality. As Ryszard Przybylski has argued, the speaker of "Leningrad," who continues to have access to the material of the past, rather dreads that this access will be cut off. In this sense, death implies more a discontinuation of the past than a cancellation of the present, or else a realization of the poet's fear of silence, a silence that Mandel'shtam describes in "Silentium" (1910) as "both music and word, / And therefore the undisturbed connection / Of all that is living."[73] Przybylski sees this drama playing out in the dialogue between poet and city:

> This division of consciousness into "I" and "you" arose out of an acutely painful sense of the divided life which now occurs in two spheres: in personal, intimate time, in poetic reality, which owes its unity to memory (the individual on the synchronic plane), and in external time, which is composed of scattered historical moments that tear consciousness into pieces, into a series of capricious and discreet "yous" (the individual on the diachronic plane) if the poet does not integrate them into his "I," his own system. An essential condition of continued existence is the transposition of the city into the Eternal Now. This signifies a "first death," but Mandel'shtam does not fear such a death. After such a death Petersburg and his friends can still exist. The poet fears the "second death," complete destruction, which does not allow existence in mythic reality, in memory.[74]

In Przybylski's reading, the "first death" is the instant of short-circuiting, of creating a tenuous unity between "external time" and the poet's "mythic reality." Bakhtin proposed a similar temporal framework with his notion of "great time" (*bol'shoe vremia*), a detemporalization of the literary canon that allows important writers from different eras to appear in conversation with one another. Mandel'shtam's poem does not address cultural greatness, certainly, but it very clearly posits that we are in conversation with whoever—and whatever, and even *wherever*—has entered our consciousness. Present consciousness is constituted by the confluence of data points across time, and this is why the poet is so afraid of being deprived of this access, which would be tantamount to a loss of the present. It would seem that the poet is afraid not only of a loss of access to his personal myth but—and here I am moving well beyond Przybylski's reading—he also realizes how his access to multiple temporalities necessarily destabilizes the Self within "external time."

The poet conveys this anxiety through the assonant masculine rhymes in the central stanzas, which may strike the reader's ear like a moan of pain: *umirát', u tebiá, nomerá, u meniá, adresá, golosá*. At the heart of a poem of unwavering formal discipline, we hear an inarticulate cry. This leads us to the closing two stanzas, which are the most suggestive of a fear of arrest. Mandel'shtam describes the sound of the doorbell as a blow or pistol shot to the head, and the bell chain literally as *kandaly*, "shackles," shaken by the "dear guests." Tempting as it may be to read these details as references to political oppression, and without our excluding that possibility, the most direct biographical reference here is to the discomfort of the poet's living situation and the fact that his quarters meant that he was constantly disturbed by the sound of the doorbell and people moving up and down the stairs.[75] What is especially impressive about "I returned to my city . . ." is how, in a poem of fourteen lines that locate the main speaker unambiguously in a closed room, we find a dramatic continuum between the pre-Revolutionary past and the Stalinist present, and an equally dramatic dialogue between the poetic subject, who calls out for Petersburg, and his Other, who responds as Leningrad.[76]

This dynamic again calls to mind Schulz's story "Solitude," in which the speaker expropriates himself in order to establish contact with the Self-as-Other. Schulz's narrator may imagine a door to compensate for the lack of egress from his imagined space, but no such egress exists. Likewise, the speaker of "I returned to my city . . ." is going nowhere: his doorbell is a weapon, his door lets death in, his city confuses the real and the remembered. Unlike what we find in Schulz, however, in "I returned to my city . . ." the speaker's double is not presented as an image of himself, but as a voice responding to the speaker's own. Oddly, the city's response points to the very short circuit it seeks to foreclose. The poet returns in time as much as he returns to a familiar space, and it is that space's reassertion of the present, as contemporary Leningrad, that short-circuits the present to the past, or time to timelessness. Once Mandel'shtam has instantiated this hybrid temporality, for which the urban space of Petersburg-Leningrad serves as spatial metaphor, the speaker's principal concern becomes the *inescapability* of the system he has created.

The Short Circuit as a Movement against Time

That freedom from temporality menaces us with its own inescapability is already evident in work Mandel'shtam composed at the time the Soviet state was established. A prime example is his 1922 poem "The Age" (Vek), which, to borrow a term from "On the Nature of the Word," "humanizes" the poet's own epoch by infusing it, on the one hand, with an almost human emotional sensitivity, and by assigning it, on the other, the ambiguous physical menace of an untamed beast. As we have seen in "I returned to my city . . . ," the lyric subject seems to project himself into an interlocutor in the poem's opening gesture, though in this instance the Self-as-Other is embodied in time rather than in the urban space of Leningrad: "*My* age, *my* beast, who could manage / To gaze into your pupils / And with his blood fuse / The vertebrae of two centuries?" Like "I returned to my city . . . ," the poem then focuses on the difficulty of reintegrating the selves, now reimagined as discrete temporalities split off from one another, a situation portrayed in the poem as a mortal wound.

Век мой, зверь мой, кто сумеет
Заглянуть в твои зрачки
И своею кровью склеит
Двух столетий позвонки?
Кровь-строительница хлещет
Горлом из земных вещей,
Захребетник лишь трепещет
На пороге новых дней.

Тварь, покуда жизнь хватает,
Донести хребет должна,
И невидимым играет
Позвоночником волна.
Словно нежный хрящ ребёнка,
Век младенческий земли.
Снова в жертву, как ягнёнка,
Темя жизни принесли.

Чтобы вырвать век из плена,
Чтобы новый мир начать,
Узловатых дней колена
Нужно флейтою связать.

Это век волну колышет
Человеческой тоской,
И в траве гадюка дышит
Мерой века золотой.

И ещё набухнут почки,
Брызнет зелени побег,
Но разбит твой позвоночник
Мой прекрасный жалкий век!
И с бессмысленной улыбкой
Вспять глядишь, жесток и слаб,
Словно зверь, когда-то гибкий,
На следы своих же лап.

Кровь-строительница хлещет
Горлом из земных вещей
И горящей рыбой мещет
В берег тёплый хрящ морей.
И с высокой сетки птичьей,
От лазурных влажных глыб
Льётся, льётся безразличье
На смертельный твой ушиб.[77]

[My age, my beast, who will manage / To peer into your pupils / And with his own blood fuse / The vertebrae of two centuries? / Blood-the-builder gushes / From the throat of earthly things, / The parasite merely cowers / On the threshold of new days. // A creature, so long as there is enough life, / Should carry [its] spine to the end, / And the wave plays / With an invisible vertebra. / Like the tender cartilage of a child / The infantile age of the earth. / Again as a sacrifice, like a lamb, / They have brought the crown of life. // To wrest the age from captivity, / To begin the new world, / It is necessary to bind with a flute / The knees of knotty days. / It is the age that rocks the wave / With human longing, / And in the grass a viper's breathing / With the golden measure of the age. // And still the buds are swelling, / The shoot of green spurts out, / But your spine is smashed, / My beautiful, pitiable age! / And with a senseless smile / You look backward, savage and weak, / Like a beast that once was lithe, / At the prints of your own paws. // Blood-the-builder gushes / From the throat of earthly things / And the warm cartilage of seas / Crashes upon the shore as a blazing fish. / And from a high net of birds, / From moist, sky-blue lumps, / It pours, it pours indifferently / Upon your fatal injury.]

The opening lines of "The Age" call to mind two poems that likewise depict the lyric subject's desire for and horror in the face of absolute vision.

The first is Blake's "The Tyger" (1794): "Tyger! Tyger! Burning bright, / In the forests of the night, / What immortal hand or eye / Could frame thy fearful symmetry?" Mandel'shtam does not seem to have had any serious relationship with Blake's work, but beyond Mandel'shtam's occasional pitching into the lexicon of eighteenth-century poetry and the fact that the two poems are composed in the same meter, Blake, too, regards his subject as a beast within indeterminate time ("in the forests of the night").[78] The second, a prose poem, belongs to Miłosz, who in *Road-Side Dog* (Piesek przydrożny, 1997), one of his last books, connects animality with atemporality: "Tiger cubs grow up, learn to hunt, have their own families, while old tigers die or are killed—deaths, the manner of which we can scarcely imagine—and this is repeated innumerable times, and the deer they have caught for lunch also fall innumerable times, and all this is happening in a *now* that knows neither past, nor future."[79] Krzysztof Michalski's reading of this passage presents human consciousness as the intrusion of an illusory temporality into an otherwise timeless repetition: "Nature, this argument suggests, does not know irreversible time, does not know a past that has been lost forever. It is always the same, infinitely repeated gestures, forms, and figures, a ritual dance in which nothing new can happen."[80] The same could be said of the natural world in Mandel'shtam. The only problem is that the human being always brings human time with him, which puts the task of short-circuiting into special relief. For the individual who uses the poetic word to reconstitute Nature's timelessness is attempting to strike out definitions that he himself has introduced. In other words, having brought time into the world, the poet uses poetry to undo what he has done. The struggle against time is once again a struggle against oneself.

We get a strong sense of this struggle in "The Age" simply by virtue of the poet's refusal to tell us which "two centuries" the awaited hero might fuse. In Blake, only an "immortal hand or eye / Could frame [the] fearful symmetry" of the beast. What makes this problem of perception especially resonant with Mandel'shtam's time—with his own "age," as well as with his manner of representing time as such—is that, as Paul Valéry notes in his *Cahiers,* "Einstein created a *point of view,* but not one where any human eye could be located."[81] In "The Age," Mandel'shtam struggles with the problem of how to situate oneself in time when the very experience of time distorts temporality.

As C. J. G. Turner points out, some interpretations of "The Age" have been intent on seeing it as a historical allegory on the October Revolution, which requires us to regard the "two centuries" as the nineteenth and the twentieth. Turner, on the other hand, rejects such a reading and presents "The Age" as a reinterpretation of the myth of Orpheus and Eurydice.[82] We can expand the poem's potential cultural referents further to include a distinctly Christian theme: in the antepenultimate line of the second stanza, Mandel'shtam describes the "age of the earth" as "infantile," a word that picks up the cue of the "child" that closes the previous line, which in turn rhymes with the "lamb" metaphorically sacrificed in the penultimate line. Given that this image is constructed within the larger context of how "[t]o begin the new world," the Christian overtones are unmistakable. When we add to these possibilities a consideration of the poem's feudal and eighteenth-century lexicon, and when we further consider the poem in light of Mandel'shtam's own statements about the function of time in poetic utterance, it becomes clear that we should read the poem's many temporal echoes as a refusal to belong to any of them.

While Mandel'shtam refuses to allow any one temporal-thematic sphere to dominate over the others, throughout the poem he maintains a carefully balanced tension between individual agency and universal indifference. This is the poem's focus, as Alain Badiou proposes in a promising recent interpretation: "There is an incompatibility of sorts between the ontology of life [. . .] and the theory of voluntaristic discontinuity. But the incompatibility constitutes the acting subjectivity of the beast-century."[83] The poem animates this incommensurability by assigning it a biological conceit, a "beast" divided between the timelessness of "the ontology of life" and the "voluntaristic discontinuity" brought about by individual agency.

In characteristic fashion, the poem draws together historical, mythic, religious, and literary source material through paregmenon and by following semantic resonances from one image to the next. The "vertebrae" of the poem's fourth line suggest the "spine" or "spinal column" (*khrebet*) in the second line of the second stanza, as well as in *zakhrebetnik,* "parasite" or "hanger-on," near the end of the first. This spinal column serves in turn as the poem's central metaphor: time is a skeletal core that must be held together by the "blood" of the thinking subject. "Blood-the-builder" (*Krov'-stroitel'nitsa*) appears in both the first and last stanzas, framing the poem's content as it "gushes / From the throat of earthly things," and these lines actually do short-circuit separate times within the poem's compositional history, since Mandel'shtam appended the last stanza (and thus the second iteration of the key lines) to the 1922 poem only in 1936, when he was living in internal exile in Platonov's hometown of Voronezh.[84] Between the first iteration and the last, the lines' meaning undergoes a crucial, if subtle, shift. In the first stanza, self-sacrifice or even political violence seems to stand behind the *zakhrebetnik*'s fear "[o]n the threshold of new days," a sense that is intensified in the second stanza, when "[a]gain as a sacrifice, like a lamb, / They have brought the crown of life." How we then read the reappearance of "Blood-the-builder" at the end of the poem depends on how we interpret the central octet.

At first glance, there is nothing remarkable about the poem's interior stanzas, at least insofar as they express a time philosophy that we have already encountered in Mandel'shtam's theoretical prose. The poet suggests that music, often a figure for poetry in Mandel'shtam and here represented by a flute, is necessary if we are to break out of repetition and to begin a new world: "To wrest the age from captivity, / To begin the new world, / It is necessary to bind with a flute / The knees of knotty days." This appears to be in keeping with Mandel'shtam's concept of "Hellenism," in which poetic binding or connection—*sviaz'*—plays an essential role. Crucially, the word that Mandel'shtam uses for "knees," *kolena,* also means "generations" or "degrees of descent." The poet tells us that the "new world" will begin only once music—or poetic utterance—binds the "generations" or "degrees of descent" of "knotty" or "awkward" days. This short-circuiting recalls the fused vertebrae of centuries in the first stanza, but it also suggests, in its binding, a forestalling of a narrative of historical progress, which the poet distrusts. As Badiou suggests, this tension is irresolvable, since the very same binding of temporal-thematic spheres that characterizes true poetic utterance also threatens the lyric subject with death. Mandel'shtam captures this double bind effectively in the stanza's last image: "And in the grass a viper's breathing / With the golden measure of the age." An animal whose entire body is a spinal column, the snake provides an excellent image for the fusing of different temporal-thematic spheres in a single organism. But the fact that Mandel'shtam uses a word for a *poisonous* snake—*gadiuka,* "viper"—demands that we not ignore the dangers inherent in temporal fusing, especially the danger that the thinking subject will be lost or obliterated in the process.

Mandel'shtam's method of allowing word roots and aural cues to suggest the semantic movements of his verse only intensifies this sense of confusion and dread. In the poem's third stanza, for example, Mandel'shtam flirts with a clever form of catachresis: not "knotty knees," but the "knees / Of knotty days"; not "golden age," but the "golden measure of the age," itself a suggestion of menacing repetition and infinite self-similarity, a golden ratio. Then, in the fourth stanza (the closing stanza in the poem's 1922 version), the escape (*pobeg*) implied by the earlier "wrest the age from captivity" becomes the "shoot of green" (*zeleni pobeg*), while the "gushing" (*khlestat'*) of "Blood-the-builder" becomes the "spurting" (*bryznut'*) of the green shoot. Both verbs refer primarily to the action of blood or rain, laying the semantic foundation for the pouring rain that closes the poems's final redaction. As Mandel'shtam addresses his "beautiful, pitiable age," the renewal suggested by the "shoot of green" is mitigated by its connection to the gushing of blood and, in the last stanza, to the rain pouring "indifferently" (*bezrazlich'e*) over the age-as-injured-animal.

The crucial difference between "Blood-the-builder" in the first stanza and in the last consists in the injury done to the age, which has again been transformed into a figure of pointless repetition. We note the "senseless smile" of a "beast that once was lithe," now reduced to looking "[a]t the prints of your own paws." Because the age's spinal column is "smashed" (*razbit*, literally, "broken into pieces"), it no longer holds disparate temporal-thematic spheres together, and "Blood-the-builder" no longer serves as a builder at all. In this way, the failure of the age to maintain short circuits across time becomes the poet's own failure. And because the poetic "word as such" consists in precisely these short circuits, the age's "fatal injury" becomes the poet's as well. "The Age" demonstrates both the intermediate subject's need to create short circuits across time and the impossibility of maintaining them. This is why Badiou presents this poem as describing a "threshold," which, in order to maintain itself as threshold, can only be approached without ever being crossed: "Poetically, the century has viewed itself as both the impossibility of a crossing and as the tracks leading to it, as the in-between of trace and destination."[85] The thinking subject can remain childishly naive about what distinguishes one time from another only to a point. While the "word as such" connects him to many times and places, he also must contend with his own historical contingency, his existence in a real here and now that smashes eternity to pieces.

The lyric subject in Mandel'shtam's poems often senses that he is split between his own lived praxis and his parallel existence in a distant, mythic "age of genius" (Schulz's term), as the poet expresses succinctly in the penultimate stanza of "Slate Ode" (Grifel'naia oda, 1923):

> Кто я? Не каменщик прямой,
> Не кровельщик, не корабельщик—
> Двурушник я, с двойной душой,
> Я ночи друг, я дня застрельщик.[86]
>
> [Who am I? Not a straightforward bricklayer, / Nor a tile layer, nor a sea captain— / I'm a double-dealer, with a double soul, / I'm a friend of night, I'm the instigator of day.]

This "double-dealer" attempts to split himself between timelessness and time, night and day, and to exist in them, as it were, simultaneously. Such a split requires that he remain intentionally naive about the paradox of his own existence.

Mandel'shtam repeatedly animates this paradox in and through poetic utterance; one must say "in and through," for the poem that demonstrates the paradox is also the device through which it is enacted. In "No, never was I anyone's contemporary . . ." (Net, nikogda, nichei ia ne byl sovremmenik . . . , 1924), which belongs to the same period as "The Age" and "Slate Ode," Mandel'shtam situates his double in a different century.

> Нет, никогда, ничей я не был современник,
> Мне не с руки почёт такой.

О, как противен мне какой-то соименник—
    То был не я, то был другой.

Два сонных яблока у века-властелина
    И глиняный прекрасный рот,
Но к млеющей руке стареющего сына
    Он, умирая, припадёт.

Я с веком поднимал болезненные веки—
    Два сонных яблока больших,
И мне гремучие рассказывали реки
    Ход воспалённых тяжб людских.

Сто лет тому назад подушками белела
    Складная лёгкая постель,
И странно вытянулось глиняное тело—
    Кончался века первый хмель.

Среди скрипучего похода мирового
    Какая лёгкая кровать!
Ну что же, если нам не выковать другого—
    Давайте с веком вековать.

И в жаркой комнате, в кибитке и в палатке
    Век умирает, а потом—
Два сонных яблока на роговой облатке
    Сияют перистым огнём.[87]

[No, never was I anyone's contemporary, / Such an honor makes me uneasy. / Oh, how repulsive I find someone with the same name— / That was not I, it was another. // The age-and-sovereign has two sleepy eyeballs / And a beautiful clay mouth, / But into the fainting arm of [his] aging son / He, dying, falls. // I raised [my] ailing eyelids with the age— / Two large, sleepy eyeballs, / And the roaring rivers told me / The course of fevered human affairs. // A hundred years ago, a light, collapsible bed / Shone white with linens, / And a clay body stretched out strangely— / The age's first intoxication was coming to an end. // Amidst the squeaky march of the world, / Such a light bed! / Well then, if it's not up to us to forge another, / Then let us grow older with the age. // And in the sweltering room, in covered wagon and tent, / The age is dying, but then— / Two sleepy eyeballs on the cornea / Are shining with a feathery fire!]

The creation of a doppelganger requires a special psychosemantic maneuver in which Self and Other are asserted simultaneously in the same entity. Mandel'shtam performs this efficiently in the first stanza by both asserting and rejecting an implied equivalence. The person "with the same name" (one word in Russian, *soimmenik*) is "repulsive" (*protiven*) because he is the "obverse" or "opposite" (alternative translations of the same *protiven*), as a mirror image whose similarity compels the lyric subject to declare, "That was not I, it was another."

Yet the Other is also the Self: both appear as the "two sleepy eyeballs" of the "age-and-sovereign" (the alliterative *vek-vlastelin*), a semantic hybrid that recalls "Blood-the-builder" from "The Age." Here, Mandel'shtam's use of the word *iabloka* is unrelentingly ambiguous. On the one hand, it seems to refer specifically to the "eyeball," *glaznoe iabloko,* of the "age-and-sovereign." On the other, it appears to refer literally to "apples," the biblical symbol of the sin of knowledge—it is the same word in Russian—especially in the last stanza, where the apples shine "on the cornea." Mandel'shtam establishes a clear parallel between these eyes/apples and the relationship between the "I" and its Other, with the poem's semantic-temporal spheres layered around them. The poem invites us to follow these threads without unknotting them, since their interconnection forms the basis for both their philosophical content and their lyric craft.

Similarly, the "age-and-sovereign" demands that we remain flexible in our reading of *vek,* "age" or "century." Rather than referring to a clearly delineated historical period or century, this "age" is closer in concept to Bergsonian *durée,* an eternal moment that may encompass other imperfective temporal frames, as when the poet puns on the homophonic equivalence of "eyelids" (*veki*) and "ages" (*veki*): "I raised [my] ailing eyelids [*veki*] with the age [*S vekom*]."[88] Here we may recall how in "The Age" Mandel'shtam deliberately distinguishes between "age" (*vek*), which he uses to refer ambiguously to the injured totality of time, and "century" (*stoletie*), which is historically defined.[89] We should also note that in "I returned to my city . . . ," "The Age," and "No, never was I anyone's contemporary . . ." alike, the poet shows a clear preference for imperfective verbs of process. Like Bruno Schulz, he steers away from intimations of completed action, even (or especially) when he is referring to death. For Mandel'shtam, the subject dies but is never definitively dead.

This is the ontological condition faced by the "age-and-sovereign," said to be "dying," as well as by the dying double in the previous century: "The age's first intoxication was coming to an end." N. I. Khardzhiev, who edited the first major selection of Mandel'shtam's verse in the post-Stalinist period, identifies this double with Byron, who died in Greece one hundred years before Mandel'shtam composed the poem.[90] But such attempts at defining a clear historical correspondence, however suggestively they may recall Lukács's characterization of the Romantic life-philosophy as "an art of dying," belie the poet's efforts to blur referents from moment to moment.[91] In the second stanza, for instance, the two eyeballs/apples of the "age-and-sovereign" may suggest the speaker and his double in another century. In the third stanza, the same two eyeballs/apples, revealed by the lifting of "ailing" eyelids that could just as easily be "sickly centuries," suggest spheres in which the Self and Other exist simultaneously but separately, even as they belong to the single "age-and-sovereign." The same "age-and-sovereign" is said to be dying and to have a "beautiful clay mouth," while the double is dying as his "clay body stretched out strangely."

From its very first line, "No, never was I anyone's contemporary . . ." extracts the thinking subject from time and then reconnects him to multiple semantic-temporal spheres at once.[92] These short circuits reach their climax in the last stanza, which situates us again in the room of the dying double, but now again "the age is dying." The "two sleepy eyeballs" make their third appearance, but the fact that the "[t]wo sleepy eyeballs on the cornea / Are shining with a feathery fire!" indicates that the word *iabloka* may refer to apples (whose red skin suggests fire), or else that they are eyes shining in the eyes of another viewer.[93]

As we have come to expect from Mandel'shtam, the poet uses paregmenon to warp conventional language. The poem's key words, variations on *iabloko* ("apple," "eyeball") and *vek* ("age, century," but in the plural "eyelid"), shift meaning with each iteration, strengthening the internal associations orchestrated in the poem. This is perhaps most significant in the second half of the penultimate stanza: "Well then, if it's not up to us to forge another, / Then let us grow older with the age." There is some ambiguity regarding the antecedent of "another": the Russian form *drugogo* may be an animate accusative form, in which case it refers to the Other, or else it may be a genitive of negation, which would mean it refers to the age. Such ambiguity would not be out of step with the rest of the text. More importantly, the poet's exhortation changes the polyptoton of a set expression, *vek vekovat',* meaning simply "to live out one's days," into something extraordinary. Since the poem frames "the age" as *durée,* and since it stubbornly refuses to portray death as a completed process, it modifies the received *vek vekovat'* to *s vekom vekovat',* "to age *with* the age." In this gesture, Mandel'shtam again binds the thinking subject to an indeterminate time, underscoring the matrix in which short circuits between incongruent histories and traditions become possible. Or as Gregory Freidin puts it, "Mandel'shtam presented the poet as a martyr who must look straight into the Vii-like eyes of the age, reading in them the mortifying record of its terrors—all in order to establish the continuity of culture between the dead old Russia and the new Russia of his own day."[94]

Whether we see the poet as a martyr here is debatable. After all, it is the poet himself who cultivates his naivety regarding what differentiates real time and myth, the mature adult consciousness and the unfinalized world of childhood. Is his communion with "the age" a deliberate intervention, or does it merely express an ontological condition? Considered within the broader context of Mandel'shtam's thinking about poetry and the world, it must be both.

Mandel'shtam's philosophy of poetic utterance tends naturally toward the catastrophism that we see so readily in his later work, and which has been recognized less readily in Western criticism than in Russian or Polish. This may be because the paradigm of catastrophe as a structural feature of a cultural or metaphysical system, rather than the annulment of that system, is counterintuitive to Western narratives of progress, whereas it was sufficiently ingrained in interwar Eastern Europe for Kafka to declare that the fall from paradise is not before or after us, but *both at once*. "The Expulsion from Paradise," Kafka noted to himself, "is eternal in its principal aspect: this makes it irrevocable, and our living in this world inevitable, but the eternal nature of the process has the effect that not only could we remain forever in Paradise, but that we are currently there, whether we know it or not."[95] A more orthodox eschatology would hold that the world is coming to an end, and we must either prepare for it or accept the futility of preparation. The catastrophism of Mandel'shtam, from *Tristia* on, consists in the recognition that existence is already a catastrophe. The end of the world is a continuous feature of the world's temporal structure. Or, as Czesław Miłosz would conclude in what has since become his most celebrated lyric, "A Song on the End of the World" (Piosenka o końcu świata, 1943), "There will be no other end of the world, / There will be no other end of the world."[96]

If it seems idiosyncratic to use Miłosz to illuminate intermediacy in Mandel'shtam, and vice versa, it is only because Miłosz's catastrophism, usually treated historically in Polish scholarship, has been all but ignored in Anglo-American criticism. This neglect was engineered in no small way by Miłosz himself, who was careful not to expose Western readers to anything he deemed so excessively of a time and place that his Anglophone audience would find it too exotic or alien. Thus only one of the thirteen poems that make up Miłosz's first book, a cycle knowingly entitled *A Poem on Frozen Time* (Poemat o czasie zastygłym, 1933), is included in his English-language oeuvre.[97] But it is this composition that most clearly grounds Miłosz's early work in spatial-temporal intermediacy and exposes the line of continuity between the Polish poet and his older Russian contemporary.

Between Selves: Czesław Miłosz's Lyric Word

Born on his mother's ancestral estate in Lithuania, Miłosz enjoyed an idyllic childhood in the countryside before the family moved to Vilnius in 1920. Miłosz's poetic ambitions blossomed in the two distinct settings in which he spent his youth: on the one hand, the multicultural, cosmopolitan city, and on the other, the family home in the provinces, where he read voraciously from his father's library. In his imagination, he would revisit both settings frequently throughout a writing career spanning two continents and nearly eight decades. When he first entered literary history, however, Miłosz was still a student at Stefan Batory University (now the University of Vilnius), where, despite having switched his major from Polish literature to law, he was drawn most insistently to the lectures in literature and philosophy of Marian Zdziechowski, a noted authority on messianism, and assumed a central position in Żagary, a memorably dynamic student literary group.[98] It was under their auspices that Miłosz published *A Poem on Frozen Time*.

In contrast to the poems in *Rescue* (Ocalenie, 1945) and later—that is, the poems upon which Miłosz built his international reputation in the postwar period—*A Poem on Frozen Time* generally eschews specific historical allusions and locations.[99] Miłosz would eventually dismiss this small collection as juvenilia, the product of one early phase in his development as a writer and thinker.[100] But in this work we can discern a preoccupation with how the poet might use the word to locate himself within an ever-shifting confluence of space, time, and matter, a question that would remain for Miłosz a lifelong metaphysical puzzle. And despite their very different prosody—Miłosz prefers vers libre to Mandel'shtam's formalism—the four declarative sentences that make up the closing quatrain of "Morning" (Rano) could easily have been spoken by Mandel'shtam:

> Kocham materię, która jest tylko lustrem wirującym.
> Kocham ruch mojej krwi jedyną świata przyczynę.
> Wierzę w zniszczalność wszystkiego co istnieje.
> Aby nie zgubić drogi, mam na ręku siną mapę żył.[101]
>
> [I love matter, which is only a spinning mirror. / I love the motion of my blood, the only cause of the world. / I believe in the destructibility of everything that exists. / So as not to lose my way, I have a blue map of veins on my arm.]

For the young Miłosz, as for Mandel'shtam, the work of the poet is a struggle for existence; recall that Mandel'shtam's artist "wants no other paradise than Being." What, then, is this existence, and how do we experience it? The individual knows Being only insofar as he is the intersection of the world's many vectors, such that matter is nothing more than a "spinning mirror" whose turning, like that of Mandel'shtam's "fan whose blades one can spread in time," reflects ourselves back to us. And like Mandel'shtam in "I returned to my city . . . ," it is only by looking to his own body that Miłosz, using his veins as a guide, can navigate the imagined space of "Morning."

Although Miłosz was an avid reader of Russian literature from an early age, he developed a strong interest in those writers and thinkers who figure prominently in Mandel'shtam's intellectual development, especially Vladimir Soloviev and Viacheslav Ivanov, only after his emigration to the

United States, where he introduced Dostoevsky to a generation of students at the University of California, Berkeley.[102] There, his course on contemporary European poetry featured more poems by Mandel'shtam than by any other poet.[103] Already in his earliest published work, however, Miłosz projects questions about the scale of individual subjectivity through shifting representations of lyric time and space. And like Mandel'shtam, Miłosz will exploit epic naivety as the short circuit between adult experience and childhood memory. The Polish title of *A Poem on Frozen Time* prepares us for this maneuver, replacing the conventional term for a lyric poem, *wiersz,* with the higher-style *poemat,* which refers to long poems of a heroic or epic nature, though the cycle consists of only thirteen lyric poems. Of these, the prose poem "Hushabye" (Luli) offers the most explicit instance of this short-circuiting:

> Łącząc zdanie lub linie na płótnie trzeba wiedzieć, że nie zamkną w sobie firmamentu. Nawet wznosząc się Fokkerem na wysokość 5000 metrów—płyniesz na dnie świata jak na dnie okrętu. Malutkie twoje prace i niegodne twego życia dzieła, jeżeli je porównasz z szybkością krwi gnającej po tętnicach. Dlatego wiem, że od pracy nad zaczętym obrazem wolisz samotną włóczęgę po nadrzecznych ponurych dzielnicach. Tam patrzysz na galary z piaskiem, słuchasz śpiewów i z wysokości bulwaru oglądasz posiłek robotników pod przęsłami mostów. Wtedy ty niepodległy krążysz nad swą opuszczoną głową, jak prymitywny duch wyobrażony przez wyznawców prosto. Znowu rozważasz wizje znikomości. Ciało rozkładasz. Na geometryczne figury, płaty i łączysz je nowym sposobem. Rozdzierasz za nogi proroków a szyje pęknięte krwawo, dymią ci w myślach jak ziemia przecięta stalowym dziobem. Życie własne niczego już ci nie przesłania—chcesz ornamenty z poległych ułożyć na chropawych płaszczyznach ziemskiej kuli. A w domach pod którymi przechodzisz z pięściami zaciśniętymi w kieszeniach, dzieciom matki jak tobie twoja 20 lat temu śpiewają luli do snu, luli.[104]

> [Connecting a sentence or lines on canvas, one must know they won't close the firmament within them. Even ascending in a Fokker to a height of 5,000 meters—you sail on the bottom of the world as at the bottom of a warship. Your efforts are tiny, your works unworthy of your life, if you compare them with the speed of the blood driving through your arteries. This is why I know that, rather than working on the painting you've started, you prefer a solitary stroll through bleak neighborhoods by the riverside. There you look on the sand barges, you listen to singers and, from the height of the boulevard, you watch the workers eating beneath the spans of bridges. Then,

> independent, you circle over your own lowered head, like a primitive spirit imagined simply by believers. Again you ponder visions of insignificance. You dismantle your body. Into geometric figures, pieces, and you connect them in a new way. You tear at the legs of the prophets, and necks, bloodily broken, fill your thoughts with smoke, like earth split with a steel beak. Your own life no longer obscures anything: out of the fallen you want to make ornaments on the globe's gravelly plains. And in the houses, which you pass with your fists clenched in your pockets, mothers sing to their children, as yours did twenty years ago, *hush little baby* . . .]

Just as Mandel'shtam tells us that poetry turns up "the black earth" of time, Miłosz compares the result of artistic activity to "earth split with a steel beak," so that what begins with writing or drawing—"a sentence or lines on canvas"—ends in the disruption of the experiential status quo, shown here in the disintegration of the body and the obliteration of the Self. At the same time, this disintegration, which is just as much the individual's integration into surroundings that his artistic efforts cannot contain, is only partial. Miłosz controls the possibilities suggested by the poem's discrete gestures by framing each associative movement within clear oppositions: speaker and addressee, work and leisure, integration and disintegration, war and peace. These oppositions are built upon the poem's underlying dichotomy between the poet's present and his infancy twenty years earlier; each of the poem's specific details begs to be situated in both times at once. By the time Miłosz composed this poem, the Fokker mentioned in the second sentence was already a civilian aircraft, though the Dutch firm was notorious for having constructed warplanes for the German army during World War I. Similarly, "the bottom of the world" is equated to "the bottom of a warship." Even the image of the "workers eating beneath the spans of bridges" is cautiously expansive, since Polish *posiłek* can refer either to a meal or to military reinforcements.

Tempting as it may be to read the poem's war images as presaging what would befall Europe at decade's end, their proper temporal orientation is toward the past. We should be cautious not to overdetermine the distinction, since the whole point is that temporal distinctions collapse within the lyric subject. In "Hushabye," a poem self-consciously presented as a meditation on the limits of artistic representation, Miłosz conflates the memory of World War I with the present life of an unnamed artist walking through the city. Accordingly, in the poem's closing gesture toward childhood memory, the speaker compares the self-consolation of an adult to the reassurances an adult might offer a child.

"I love the movement of my blood, the sole cause of the world," Miłosz declares in "Morning." In "Hushabye," too, we find that man is the measure of all things, since it is only through the vantage of his own person that the individual can encounter the world. And yet the poet is painfully aware of what Lukács calls "the incommensurability of soul and work": "Your efforts are tiny, your works unworthy of your life, if you compare them with the speed of the blood driving through your arteries." This is why the artist ends the poem with "fists clenched in [his] pockets," unable to act as he goes by, resolvedly (or petulantly) forcing himself to observe real life rather than manufacture a false one.

Historical circumstances add special urgency to the poet's epistemological crisis, but the crisis nevertheless remains fundamentally more epistemological than historical. Jan Błoński has suggested that Miłosz's epistemology of the word necessarily encompasses history, since it is only within historical experience that our failure to contain the world within ourselves becomes evident: "This means that the main thing [for Miłosz] is the ability to sum up human experience, the experience of language first of all. This is why he demands to be rooted in tradition [. . .]. For the richness of speech and experience is available to us only through historical memory."[105] It is in this sense somewhat ironic that certain of his Anglophone admirers are fixated on reading Miłosz for moral pronouncements on history.[106] In the immediate postwar period, by contrast, Miłosz was regarded by Marxist critics as the antithesis of a "poet of history." Jan Kott, for example, reacting to Miłosz's *Rescue*, the first book of poems published in liberated Poland, lamented the immateriality and ahistoricity of catastrophism in general, and of Miłosz's poems in particular. He accuses writers like Miłosz of turning their backs on material history: "They took simple images apart, they freely scrambled what you see and hear and used them to construct their hideous visions. Poetic hallucinations overthrew the world of values, they destroyed the material world."[107] Kott's zeal notwithstanding—he openly mocks "the poet [who] makes faces at himself in the mirror, dances and croons, 'There will be no other end of the world'"—his description of catastrophist predilections comports extremely well with a poem like "Hushabye."[108]

Aleksander Fiut, consistently among Miłosz's most astute readers, proposes a third way between myopically historical or epistemological treatments of this poet. Miłosz does not ignore history, as Kott asserts, nor does he hew closely to direct historical representation. Instead, Fiut argues, he recognizes time as belonging to a monistic continuum, such that the "the end of the world occurs without interruption, for it is always possible, always potentially present in the sacral dimension of human existence."[109] Fiut questions whether filing Miłosz's early work under the headword "catastrophism" may therefore be misleading. If, as Fiut suggests, "the life of an individual or species becomes the matrix of events locked in the rhythm of all existence, moving from peak to decay to annihilation," then it should make no difference to Miłosz's epistemological crisis whether fascism or Stalinism destroys Europe.[110] Fiut situates Miłosz appropriately within a tradition of Christian, primarily Catholic, eschatology, but instead of expecting a return to paradise lost in the imagined past, Miłosz defers the arrival of paradise into an infinitely receding future. Fiut neatly sums up Miłosz's position: "A metaphysical, rather than historical, perspective in evaluating change in human history; a monistic, rather than dualistic, system of values; a linear, rather than cyclical, conception of time; and finally a future, rather than past, projection of a positive utopia."[111] If I were to modify Fiut's reading, it would only be to underscore its resonance with Kafka's aphorism about Paradise and the nature of the eternal, that it sweeps aside every either-or and replaces it with a both-and. This is the source of the anxiety that has been called "catastrophist" in Miłosz's early poems. The poet realizes that the cataclysm is not on its way, just around the corner. Existence is already the cataclysm, because there is no other world into which one might escape.

Time and the Self: Miłosz's Passing Away

Einstein's early influence on the young Miłosz was generally positive and came filtered through the mentorship of Oscar Vladislas de Lubicz Miłosz (1877–1939), his distant cousin. Miłosz would recall that Oscar, a minor Symbolist poet who wrote in French and later became Lithuania's representative to the League of Nations, "believed that [Einstein's] theory of relativity had opened a new era of mankind—an era of harmony, reconciliation between science, religion and art. The positive consequence of Einstein's discoveries was the elimination of Newtonian time and space as infinite and the introduction of time and space that underlies our cosmology and its concept of the big bang. I approached Einstein with enormous reverence."[112]

Even in his early career, however, Miłosz understood that Einstein's new description of spatial-temporal reality could only complicate the task of subjective self-definition, since it relativizes our relations with the world around us. The exuberance with which Oscar Miłosz greeted Einstein's new description of reality could not, for the younger Miłosz, mitigate the difficulty and danger of situating ourselves in space and time. On the contrary, the task was now that much more challenging. "For the island of the philosophizing horses," Miłosz would later quip, "was *outopos,* utopia, the banner of our bifurcation into here and there, into inside and outside, or, if you prefer, into a body imprisoned within its passing and a mind soaring above it."[113]

Miłosz illustrates this bifurcation explicitly in "Hushabye." His early poems dramatize the struggle to locate oneself within the cosmic flow of Being, which appears as an effort, probably futile, to escape. *Probably* futile, for Miłosz hopes, sometimes weakly, but consistently. Just as we have seen in Mandel'shtam's "I returned to my city . . . ," in "Hushabye" temporal intermediacy results in a kind of out-of-body experience, with the poem's addressee breaking out of himself and observing his own body from above: "Then, independent, you circle over your own lowered head, like a primitive spirit imagined simply by believers." Doubling, we have already come to expect, is one of the most consistent tropes of intermediacy, and in "Hushabye" Miłosz splits the poem's hero from himself to create an observational loop: no longer in an airplane soaring above this landscape, the wanderer must now see himself as part of the landscape. This is an early instance of what Kazimierz Wyka identified as early as 1946 as the cinematographic movement in Miłosz, opening on a small, specifically delineated object and panning out cinematographically to reveal context and interrelations that become increasingly unwieldy as the scene is populated, a strategy that the poet maintained so consistently in his later career that Helen Vendler later rebranded it "Miłosz's manner."[114] Absorbed into space, broken apart "into geometric figures," the wanderer moves toward self-obliteration before returning to himself. In "Hushabye," the poet, failing to be identical with himself, also tries and fails to be fully absorbed into his surroundings.

Writing from his Argentine exile in the early 1950s, Witold Gombrowicz captured Miłosz's oscillation between identity and infection in a polemical essay in the pages of *Kultura,* émigré Poland's most important cultural periodical. He opens with a delightful epigram:

> I am Miłosz, a Miłosz I must be
> Being Miłosz, a Miłosz I'd rather not be
> The Miłosz in me I kill so as to be
> All the more a Miłosz . . .
>
> Which tells us: that man's essence is development, but development occurs in the course of constant suicide. We must destroy in ourselves that which is in order to reach that which will be. And this freedom, with which Miłosz breaks out of the world without a moment's hesitation—this is precisely the bitter maturity of our time—a maturity won under the tremendous pressure of a history that affected him deeply.[115]

Gombrowicz taps into Marshall Berman's "tragedy of development" on the social plane, only here the tragedy plays out between Miłosz and himself, within a dialectic of self-realization and self-obliteration. If Gombrowicz's critique strikes us as reductive, it is because he locates Miłosz's struggle for and against self-definition strictly in a historical framework. That is, Gombrowicz seems to have in mind Miłosz's striving toward a poetry of definable historical responsibility and moral authority, which in itself may constitute a rejection of narrowly autobiographical or philosophical concerns. But what

Gombrowicz writes about Miłosz applies especially to Miłosz's early poems, where these tensions are less neatly resolved. In particular, we can look at a poem like "Hushabye" as the product of a young poet's struggle with the limitations of art, which offers no ultimate resolution to crisis. Art will not allow the poet to remain coterminous with himself, nor will it dissolve him into his surroundings, nor will it bind him definitively with another time. Perhaps most importantly, art will not free the artist from the equally powerful, equally painful attractions of identity and infection, nor from his sense of participating simultaneously in a historical present and a mythic past.

Like Mandel'shtam, Miłosz ultimately sees poetry as a struggle between identity and infection, and this remains true even much later in his career, long after most other hints of catastrophism have faded. He says as much in the penultimate stanza of his 1968 poem "Ars Poetica?," the question mark portending an uncertainty that might easily be taken as antithetical to the poem's programmatic title:

> Ten pożytek z poezji, że nam przypomina,
> jak trudno jest pozostać tą samą osobą,
> bo dom nasz jest otwarty, we drzwiach nie ma klucza,
> a niewidzialni goście wchodzą i wychodzą.[116]
>
> [This is the benefit of poetry, that it reminds us / how difficult it is to remain oneself, / because our house is open, there's no key in the door, / and invisible guests come and go.]

The thinking subject strives for self-identity but must nevertheless contend with the encroachment of other thinking subjects. The lyric word, by unveiling connections between images and voices otherwise perceived in isolation, reminds us that the thinking subject is never entirely self-identical, however much he may strive to be. Miłosz states this even more explicitly in his 1954 essay "Sunday in Brunnen" (Niedziela w Brunnen): "I am, or at least, I try to be, identical with myself, though I am well aware that the collective, our adapting to it, shapes us imperceptibly. But in this refusal to divide myself into compartments, each of which contains other residents—or passengers—lies the novelty of what I would like to become."[117]

Even as he strives for self-identity, Miłosz recognizes that the Self is inconceivable without the Other. In this he does not differ from Mandel'shtam, a poet whom he came to admire greatly.[118] Yet as much as they share in their approaches to temporal intermediacy, Miłosz and Mandel'shtam are separated by a key epistemological difference. Mandel'shtam's interwar poetics emphasizes the *word* as identity and totality. For him, the lyric word short-circuits a vast store of temporal-semantic information, opening a space or "zone of contact" where present and nonpresent, myth and lived praxis, coincide. Miłosz moves in the opposite direction. He sees the individual as already compromised by the invasion of Others, and he attempts to use poetic utterance to delimit these interconnections, neutralizing the semantic cross-fertilization so typical of Mandel'shtam's poems, though he knows that this is impossible. Accordingly, the paregmenon and related rhetorical devices that we frequently see in Mandel'shtam appear in Miłosz primarily to emphasize the unity of opposites.

The tension between the singularity of lived praxis and the totality of the world, the "incommensurability of soul and work," would vex Miłosz for the rest of his life. "What is there to do if the gaze does not have absolute power," he asks in a prose poem, "*Esse*" (1954), "such that it could absorb objects with the intoxication of speed, leaving behind it only the emptiness of an ideal form, a sign like a hieroglyph, with its simple drawing of an animal or bird?"[119] The poet insists that he can achieve only a semblance of the purity of vision he longs for, referring to himself ironically in "A Confession" (Wyznanie, 1986) as "not entirely clairvoyant."[120] Thus Fiut describes Miłosz as caught between competing visions of self and world, which means that every act of creation confronts the poet with a choice he steadfastly refuses to make: "either the identification of the world with its creator, an illusion of fullness at the cost of violating natural law and giving up sensory evidence, or precision and detailed exactness of presentation of individual objects with the tacit agreement that it is futile to search for a unifying principle either in the subject or in the reality surrounding him."[121] The first path is tantamount to self-obliteration: the poet gains privileged access to the totality of Being, but by being absorbed into the Absolute he loses himself in the process. The second path spells self-isolation, since a pretense toward objectivity presumes that we, too, are disconnected from everything around us. Even if Miłosz would like to subscribe to Mandel'shtam's philosophy of the word, this would only affirm his intermediacy as an ontological fact, since, as Stanisław Barańczak has suggested, "[t]he mediation of language means that naming reality causes a constant and intractable tension between the general and the concrete: the 'problem of universals' cannot be resolved."[122]

Which returns us once again to temporality, for it is through his Heraclitean concept of time that Miłosz copes with—again, without resolving or exiting—what Kazimierz Wyka calls the "antitheticalness of the Miłosz lyric."[123] We might regard this "antitheticalness"—*antytetyczność*—as the poetic analogue of what Iablokov identifies as "reversibility" in Platonov. Along these lines, Miłosz would later recall a critique he received from Pope John Paul II, an ardent reader of Miłosz: "Well, he said you make one step forward, one step back. I answered, Holy Father, how in the twentieth century can one write religious poetry differently?"[124]

Even in his advanced years, Miłosz would recall that for his high school graduation examination he had chosen the topic of "the river of time," and that he had received top marks.[125] In 1953, in a beautiful expression of Rilke's notion of the Open, the poet would write, "And he who, in what is, / Finds calm, order, and the eternal moment, / Passes without a trace."[126] The "eternal moment" is a superb example of Miłosz using catachresis to unify opposites. Drawing together contradictory temporal concepts, he is unifying timelessness and time and, as Michel Masłowski has observed, the immaterial with the material: "The 'eternal moment' is extracted from the continuous movement of terrestrial life, biological and historical; existential fragments are thereby extended through [. . .] symbolization. The poet carries them out of space-time, into a *pleroma* that could be called the world's memory, the memory of God, or the restitution awaited in its plenitude at the end of time."[127]

The theological terms of Masłowski's description, which presents Miłosz as attempting to restore the experiential "moment" to the *pleroma* of cosmic or divine powers, aptly reflects the nonseparation between the religious and the metaphysical in Miłosz's understanding of how things pass. Miłosz, who described this passing variously in terms of Heraclitus and, in *Native Realm* (Rodzinna Europa, 1958), as having possibly made him an "inadvertent pupil of Bergson," first engaged Bergson's ideas seriously in the late 1930s, when he took an interest in William James and Jacques Maritain, Bergson's Catholic disciple.[128] Maritain would help Miłosz clarify the conflict between intuition and experience, as well as the corresponding conflicts between identity and infection (in ontology) and between pure art and practical ethics.[129] In his 1943 essay on Witkiewicz, written while he was translating Maritain, Miłosz formulates his position on art explicitly as being between aesthetics and ethics: "It should be obvious from this sketch that art exists between two extremes. On one side it is threatened by a freedom purchased at the cost of renouncing its influence on human relations, as can be seen in the proponents of 'pure poetry,' 'pure form,' and 'art for art's sake.' On the other side, it is threatened by enslavement to social ideas."[130]

The fact that Miłosz is always striving to balance himself between the demands of art and ethics in his writing has sometimes been lost on his audience, particularly in the West, where attention to his historical or moral authority has made his poetry and philosophy seem less conflicted than they are. But Heraclitus would always lurk in the background of these efforts, reminding Miłosz that the Self will eventually dissolve into the flow of Being. In the introductory note to *For Heraclitus* (Dla Heraklita, 1984–85), a late series of poems and fragments, Miłosz openly ponders which reality is the more reliable, the experiential or the intuitive: "Which reality is true? Is it the first one, austere, which injures us, overpowers us, deceives us with its promises, or the second one, purified, more beautiful, perhaps like that which incorporeal ghosts see?"[131] The poet knows that absolute vision, the kind of clairvoyance that might allow him to bridge the gulf between these two versions of reality, is beyond his power. This is why he resorts to naivety.

Miłosz's longing for spiritual contact, for what Witkiewicz calls "metaphysical feeling," is palpable throughout his work. He was also acutely aware that he was bound to lived praxis. For Miłosz, a carefully cultivated naive vision helps bridge the gap not only between the historical present and the nonpresent but also (and by extension) between lived praxis and the spirit level, as he elaborates in *For Heraclitus*:

> But there is yet a third reality, and it's hard to say how true it may be: that which we find preserved in the language of human speech or pictures, always incomplete, crushed into crumbs, fragments, and composed anew according to the law of selection, that is, form. My century, the twentieth, imposed on me a multiplicity of such evidence of constant change, of the "acceleration of history," providing memoirs, novels, leaving schools of painting in its wake, but most of all the "period photograph" and a strip of film from the beginnings of cinema. In comparison with reality that has been experienced and never preserved this was a drop in the ocean, but without a doubt in my imagination scenes I myself have watched overlap with others from reading, from visits to museums of modern art, from film.[132]

Miłosz, who goes on to say that much of his poetic art is based on an effort to "halt" or "freeze" moments of experience in literature, also acknowledges what Błoński has appropriately termed the "dialogism" of his poetic oeuvre.[133] Błoński suggests that Miłosz's work, rather than being strictly concerned with lived praxis, on the one hand, or Christian metaphysics, on the other, is intimately intertwined with a vast archive of intertextual references, which include Christian mysticism, classical and contemporary literature, and modern art.[134] The same is true of Mandel'shtam.

We can quite easily broaden Błoński's definition of dialogism in Miłosz to encompass a more Bakhtinian sense of the unfinalized thinking subject, of multiple voices in conversation with one another. These voices grow out of Miłosz's intertexts, and, much as we have already seen in Mandel'shtam, they occasionally occur as multiple voices within poems or poem cycles.[135] Miłosz's "third reality" is the site of short circuits, a middle ground, the nexus between the particularity of experience, which he repeatedly emphasizes as being too vast for art to capture, and the immaterial Absolute.

In this regard, literature performs two basic functions. First, it stops time or, more accurately, "preserves" experience. Miłosz describes this third reality as "preserved," *utrwalona,* which shares its root with *trwać,* "to last"; other derived forms of *trwać* appear frequently in Miłosz, which reflects his common interests with Bergson, whose durée is *trwanie* in Polish. Another key word for Miłosz, *minąć*, "to pass," appears often as the reversal or antithesis of lasting. A typical instance of this dialectic appears in the late poem "To a Hazel Tree" (Do leszczyny, 1997), in which Miłosz reflects on his 1997 visit to the landscape of his childhood and addresses that landscape directly:

> Jest coś z heraklitejskiej zadumy, kiedy tutaj stoję,
> Pamiętający siebie minionego
> I życie, jakie było, a też jakie być mogło.
> Nic nie trwa, ale trwa wszystko: ogromna stałość.[136]

> [There's a bit of Heraclitean reverie as I stand here, / Recalling my past self / And life as it was, but also as it might have been. / Nothing lasts, but everything lasts: an enormous constancy.]

The second function of literature for Miłosz, clearly bound to the first, is that it short-circuits experiential reality and intertexts, which are themselves short circuits within literature. This allows for potentially endless recursion between the poem and lived praxis. As the poem attempts to stop time and hold the moment, that moment immediately becomes infected with images, myths, and ideas that destabilize it, expanding the breadth of the original experience.

As comfortable as Miłosz had become with this in-betweenness by the late 1980s, when *For Heraclitus* was written, in the early 1930s he found it much more unsettling. At the age of nineteen, he undertook a correspondence with the noted poet and novelist Jarosław Iwaszkiewicz, who in 1918 had cofounded *Skamander*, a major literary monthly with an artistic program comparable in many respects to that of the Acmeists in Russia. In one of his earliest letters to Iwaszkiewicz, Miłosz describes his "intellectual content" as including biology, Stanisław Ignacy Witkiewicz, Henri Brémond, *poésie pure,* and Paul Valéry. Quoting Witkiewicz, Miłosz describes himself seeking a "metaphysical feeling of the strangeness of existence."[137] At the same time, he asserts in a postscript, "I would like to be an orthodox Catholic. How impressed I am by that bridge suspended in empty space. A construction that is self-contained, self-standing, not concerned with grasping the truth of the external world—a kind of Gothic. To be able to create but one poem so closed and objective!!!"[138] Even allowing for his youthful exuberance in writing what is essentially a fan letter, the interests and ambitions that Miłosz offers by way of self-presentation are those that he will pursue for much of his career. Like Mandel'shtam, he takes as his ideal the image of Gothic architecture, wishing for this perfectly self-contained structure to represent both himself and the poetic word, but he is undecided as to whether the path toward this perfection is through faith or natural science. He is drawn equally to both, as well as to intuition and empiricism, to "pure poetry" and to clearly comprehensible descriptions of lived experience. Appropriately, during this period Miłosz was also fascinated with Russian Constructivism, which likewise sought to create art objects with social utility and practical purpose, but which often relied on abstract, geometric forms to do so, much as the artist-wanderer in "Hushabye" must distintegrate into a jumble of "geometric shapes" in order to return to himself.[139]

In his early writings, Miłosz repeatedly projects these tensions onto a twofold return, to both the place of his youth and to a childlike sense of that youth being fixed in an eternal, mythic durée. The richness of such an operation should not be underestimated: Miłosz, a child of the Lithuanian countryside, would forever assign that landscape special significance as a space outside history, as a point of origin that, like the Absolute, could reabsorb him, freeing him from himself. We see this, for example, in the following lines from "Hymn" (Hymn, 1935), a mystical meditation from Miłosz's second collection, *Three Winters* (Trzy zimy, 1936):

> Toczcie się, rzeki; podnoście swoje ręce,
> stolice! Ja, wierny syn czarnoziemu, powrócę do czarnoziemu
> jakby życia nie było,
> jakby pieśni i słowa tworzyło
> nie moje serce, nie moja krew,
> nie moje trwanie,
> ale głos niewiadomy, bezosobowy,
> sam łopot fal, sam wiatrów chór, samo wysokich drzew
> jesienne kołysanie.[140]
>
> [Flow on, rivers; raise your arms, / capitals! I, a faithful son of the black earth, will return to the black earth / as though life had never been, / as though the songs and words were made / not by my heart, not by my blood, / not by my duration, / but by an unknown voice, impersonal, / the very crashing of waves, the very chorus of winds, the very rocking / of tall trees in autumn.]

This speaker longs for immediacy, which also implies universality, in the sense of universal access to everything that is, as well as in the sense that the poet's "songs and words" would emanate from beyond his corporeal (heart, blood) and incorporeal being (duration). Unlike the poems in the cycle *A Poem on Frozen Time,* here Miłosz begins to play with rhetorical devices of repetition and transformation, especially anaphora and the lyric refrain, which in "Hymn" is addressed perhaps to God or to some vision of the Absolute: "There is no one between you and me."[141] Miłosz's oft-expressed longing for immediacy appears here as a desire for return to the "black earth" of his fatherland. The mythic status assigned to black earth in Eastern European literature may call for its own study, but for Miłosz and Mandel'shtam it is clearly associated with deep time, whether as time itself, as Mandel'shtam projects, or as the point of origin and return, as we find in Miłosz. This is, literally as well as figuratively, the ground of Miłosz's "fatherland"—*ojczyzna,* from *ojciec,* "father"—the term that Miłosz consistently applies to Lithuania. In both concept and consequence, this strategy links Miłosz to the Polish Romantic tradition of the national bard, especially in that we readily hear an echo of Adam Mickiewicz's *Pan Tadeusz,* the 1834 verse novel that opens, "O Lithuania! my fatherland!" More important than the actual land of Miłosz's birth is the mythic idea of that land as Father, and just as Platonov and Schulz repeatedly express a desire to be reunited with the figure of the Father, Miłosz wishes to be reabsorbed into his fatherland.[142]

This is a problematic operation, however. For Miłosz, a return to the fatherland means a return to a youth that is beyond time, which can be accomplished only by short-circuiting the experiential present to the mythic past. In fact, Miłosz self-consciously conceives of youth or childhood as temporal intermediacy, a suspension of time:

> Ale pomiędzy państwami powstającymi z dna mórz,
> pomiędzy zgasłymi ulicami, na miejscu których
> wzniosą się góry ze spadłej zbudowane planety,
> wszystkiemu, co minęło, wszystkiemu, co minie,
> broni się młodość, czysta jak słoneczny kurz,
> ani w dobrym, ani w złym nie rozmiłowana,
> pod twoje olbrzymie nogi podesłana,
> abyś ją gniótł, abyś po niej szedł,
> abyś poruszał swoim oddechem koło,
> a od jego ruchu drżała znikoma budowla,
> abyś jej głód, a innym dawał sól, wino i chleb.[143]

> [But between states, which arise from the bottom of the sea, / between burnt-out streets, in whose place / mountains have risen, built from a fallen planet, / against everything that has passed, everything that passes, / youth defends itself, as pure as solar dust, / enamored of neither good nor evil, / spread out before your huge feet, / for you to crush it, for you to walk on it, / for you to turn the wheel with your breath, / and from its turning the slight structure trembled, / for you to give youth hunger, and others salt, wine, and bread.]

"Youth" is innocence, but innocence is a potentially disastrous position, "enamored of neither good nor evil," both mythically everlasting and dangerously naive, which is to say that it submits to a collapse of mythic and historical times. Miłosz's attenuated syntax locates youth in a valley amid the massive remnants of an unnamed catastrophe, and from this privileged position youth ignores the passage of things, rendering historical time mythic. But much as Miłosz longs for purity, for youth "as pure as solar dust" (in contrast to the "fallen planet"), he understands that the addressee must introduce the order and definition that are synonymous with adulthood, crushing youth, turning "the wheel with your breath," jump-starting the steady and reliable progression of history. The crushing of eternal, mythic youth at the feet of time recalls the smashing of reality that Miłosz describes in the introduction to *For Heraclitus*. Whenever form is introduced into shapeless, unbounded atemporality, that eternity must be crushed and compacted. This is a loss, but a necessary one. Without it, no utterance would be possible, as Miłosz makes clear in "*Esse*" and elsewhere.

Unfortunately, temporal short-circuiting must falter in the face of articulable experience. That is, in using short circuits to connect discrete times and places or a temporal history with the timelessness of myth, the poet's only intervention is to unveil the fundamental interconnectedness of Being. As urgent as such a project undoubtedly was in the interwar period, one wartime example—Miłosz's cycle *The World: A Naive Poem,* written from Nazi-occupied Warsaw—illustrates how important it can be as an affirmation of reality. For as uncomfortable as it is to recognize the Self as stretched between real time and myth, in the face of wholesale destruction, particularly a kind underpinned by false narratives of time and matter, an affirmation of reality may be the only salvation. Or as Miłosz puts it near the beginning of *The Captive Mind* (Zniewolony umysł, 1953), "It was only toward the middle of the twentieth century that the inhabitants of many European countries came, in general unpleasantly, to the realization that their fate could be influenced directly by intricate and abstruse books of philosophy."[144]

The Return to the Fatherland: Miłosz's *The World: A Naive Poem*

In "House of Youths" (Dom młodzieńców, 1930), the penultimate poem in *A Poem on Frozen Time,* Miłosz asks what it is that really passes away, our nostalgia for youth, or external time: "Will our magnificent youth really pass sometime / Or is it rather the earth and the huge horizon that will pass?"[145] The poem is set in a house in Lithuania, where the residents literally shine with the glory of their youth, and where the stories they tell one another conflate memory and imagination: "All the intricate adventures / From the revolution on the Volga and even dreams / We tell each other honestly."[146] The first and last stanzas of this poem form a dialogue between themselves, the question of the beginning being answered with the absolute certainty of the end: "Will the earth pass? Is it the huge horizon that will pass? / No. We're the ones who have to pass."[147] Miłosz's key words are the same here as they would be in "Hymn," building a basic opposition between that which "passes" and that which is so "huge" that it dwarfs the individual in both space and time. Or, to be more precise, the "earth" and "horizon" are everlasting: they exist beyond space and time.[148] What distinguishes "House of Youths" from the later "Hymn" is that the youths of the poem, who willfully collapse historical realities (the "revolution on the Volga") with fantasy ("dreams"), decide that they must pass out of the timelessness of their youth and into historical time, whereas in the more mystical "Hymn" youth must be stamped out, and form must be forcibly introduced into formlessness.

Miłosz, ever drawn to purity, formlessness, and myth, revisits this tension repeatedly. While he does not believe in the possibility of immediate access to the essence of things, he also remains wary of the strictures of definition. He constantly reminds us that he is a product of his time and place, so that his very concept of time and place is relative. He says as much in "Metaphysical Pause" (Metafizyczna pauza, 1980), an essay that the poet fittingly composed as a dialogue with himself:

> Q. What distinguishes space in the twentieth century from space in the last [nineteenth] century?
>
> A. It is no longer a kind of aquarium in which the galaxies are floating. Space is relative, that is, where there is no relation between Point A and Point B, there is no space. In other words, beyond the limits of the universe there is no infinitely expansive space.
>
> Q. Nor time?
>
> A. Nor time. Eternity is not a line extending into infinity.[149]

This is a remarkably conflicted vision of space-time. The thinking subject, according to Miłosz, is once again the measure of all things, since it is up to him to posit a "Point A and Point B," without which space and time simply do not exist. The paradox, captured perfectly by Miłosz's suggestion that eternity is not infinite, derives from the Einsteinian model of the universe as simultaneously finite and unbounded. Miłosz posits that there is nothing—no space, no time—beyond the limits of the finite universe, but the very relativity of the space-time he describes suggests potentially infinite combinations of points and lines standing in relation to one another. Thus, in rejecting a limit in his view of space-time, Miłosz nevertheless asserts the existence of "eternity," using the Polish word *wieczność*, whose root, *wiek*, refers to an age, epoch, or century, a convenient way of defining one's own relation to time.[150]

Miłosz and Mandel'shtam share a nostalgia for the lost world of childhood, certainly, but they are not taking us on a stroll down memory lane. The primary goal of short-circuiting the present to the past is to unveil the connection of historical lived praxis to the eternal and primal. Toward the end of *The Noise of Time*, Mandel'shtam lays these purposes—and their naive device—bare:

> I want not to talk about myself, but to trace the age, the noise and germination of time. My memory is hostile to everything personal. If it were up to me, I would only wince when remembering the past. [. . .] I repeat—my memory is not loving, but hostile, and it works not on reproducing, but on purging the past. [. . .] Where the epic of happy generations speaks in hexameters and the chronicle I have a lacuna, and between me and the age a lapse, a ditch filled with noisy time, a place set aside for my family and domestic archive.[151]

Instead of personal memory, there is a gap, a zone of metaphysical static that must be granted form—in a poem, in a memoir, in a domestic archive—in order to connect the poet, however tenuously, with the mythic age lost on the other side of the noise.[152] As we have already seen, Mandel'shtam's interwar poetics is founded on just these kinds of tenuous short circuits, the interconnection of lived praxis with the mythic "age" of childhood—Schulz's "age of genius"—though the same short circuits foreclose all possibility of escape.

Miłosz's poetics of the fatherland operates by a very similar principle, though Miłosz, like Mandel'shtam, takes momentary refuge in his access to a mythic past. In the "Space" section of his essay "Notes on Exile" (1975, written in English), Miłosz describes the utility of these short circuits across space-time:

> Imagination, always spatial, points north, south, east, and west of some central, privileged place, which is probably a village from one's childhood or native region. [. . .] Exile displaces that center or rather creates two centers. Imagination relates everything in one's surroundings to "over there"—in my case, somewhere on the European continent. It even continues to designate the four cardinal points, as if I still stood there. At the same time the north, south, east, and west are determined by the place in which I write these words.
>
> Imagination tending toward the distant region of one's childhood is typical of literature of nostalgia (a distance in space often serves as a disguise for a Proustian distance in time). Although quite common, literature of nostalgia is only one among many modes of coping with estrangement from one's native land. The new point which orients space in respect to itself cannot be eliminated, i.e., one

> cannot abstract from one's physical presence in a definite spot on the Earth. That is why a curious phenomenon appears: the two centers and the two spaces arranged around them interfere with each other or—and this is a happy solution—coalesce.[153]

Here, again, we are treated to a center-out architectonics of imagination, a spatial-temporal model that demands that the cardinal directions from one's point of origin—in this case, the mythic origin of one's childhood, a loosely defined space "somewhere on the European continent"—retain their significance as coordinates for orientation, though they are in fact altered by the subject's placement in a new space, "determined by the place in which I write these words." Miłosz acknowledges the temporal, Proustian quality of an "[i]magination tending toward the distant region of one's childhood" (distant in time, as well as in space), but he also insists that the poet cannot submit completely to the timelessness of memory or myth, that "one cannot abstract from one's physical presence in a definite spot on the Earth." This is typical of Miłosz's powerful historical consciousness, which does not allow the poet to indulge his fanciful descent into the myth of childhood for long before the timelessness of that myth is corrupted by the passage of time, much as we see in "Hymn," as well as in the poems of Mandel'shtam. Unlike Mandel'shtam, however, Miłosz does not often linger on the ominous inescapability that results from spatial-temporal destabilization. It is in part for this reason that Marek Zaleski calls Miłosz a poet of repetition: "For Miłosz, time, reality, and poetry are inseparable, and their common denominator is repetition [. . .]. Miłosz declares himself programmatically as a poet of the word 'is.' But not only. He is also a poet of the word 'was.' And the border between this 'is' and 'was' becomes effaced."[154] After a long career of reiterating this intermediacy—which is itself the failure to reimmerse oneself in the timeless myth, as well as the failure to break from it entirely—Miłosz is pleased to remain locked within this oscillation between myth and history, to circulate within its endless repetitions.

Such optimism, however, does not characterize the earlier periods of Miłosz's writing life. In closing a 1942 letter to Miłosz, the novelist Jerzy Andrzejewski implored the poet to save himself and his countrymen from the horrors of history: "Dear Czesław, I can already see the swastikas, banners, and portable shrines on the horizon. If you are sleeping, wake up; if you are eating, abandon your food, your work, and your house. Come to the rescue."[155] To the extent that it is given to poets to come to the rescue, he did. *Rescue*, which appeared in December 1945, reprints Miłosz's 1936 collection *Three Winters* with a generous selection of poems written from 1935 to 1945, in France as well as in occupied Poland. Two proems set the tone for the collection as a whole: "Preface" (Przedmowa), which asks pointedly, "What is poetry which saves / Neither nations, nor people?"; and "Escape" (Ucieczka), a poem in which no escape occurs.[156] After these, the first new poem in the collection is "In My Fatherland" (W mojej ojczyźnie, 1937), a poem written before the German invasion, well before Miłosz's work in the diplomatic corps of the postwar Communist government, before his defection and subsequent exile from Poland.

"In My Fatherland" imagines a psychic return to the lakes and woods "[i]n my fatherland, to which I will not return."[157] That is, the poem constructs a space of mnemonic fantasy, an idyll, as closely intertwined with the poet's own sense of Being as with any concrete, historically contingent space. In this respect, the poem anticipates *The World: A Naive Poem* (Świat: Poema naiwne, 1943), one of the two lyric cycles central to *Rescue*. The other, which follows it immediately, is *Voices of Poor People* (Głosy biednych ludzi), which features "A Song on the End of the World."

An arrangement of twenty tightly interwoven lyrics, most of them no longer than three quatrains and written in the style of a nursery rhyme, *The World* attempts to recapture the fantastic and unbounded world of Miłosz's native Lithuania, his personal "somewhere on the European continent." Miłosz uses that world to mitigate real historical catastrophe. He would later say, "*The World* was for me a kind of intuitional initiation of an operation that, only with the perspective of the years, is more or less obvious to me. Indeed, there is an identification with a naive worldview."[158] In the same interview, the poet presents this operation not only as tendentious but also as fundamental to his authorial project, noting that "writing of this kind of work under the conditions of that time was a kind of movement against. It has turned out that my entire oeuvre was a movement against."[159] The world of childhood, a world that seamlessly fuses present experience with timeless imagination, appears here as a naive antidote to the oppressive social and political atmosphere—to say nothing of the physical peril—that the poet endured in occupied Warsaw. Miłosz would repeat analogous maneuvers often throughout his career, notably in his 1955 novel *The Issa Valley* (Dolina Issy).

What is perhaps most interesting about *The World* is that even as the fatherland represented therein is an unbounded space, free from the constraints of historical lived praxis, the Father, who figures significantly in these poems, once again is the lawgiver, the creator of boundaries and order, and therefore the force that must rescue the naive lyric subject from the terror of the boundlessness his short circuits have created. Thus we find in *The World* a dialogic movement between the lyric subject, who uses naivety to escape from history, and the mythic Father, who reintroduces history to rescue the naïf from the terrors of boundlessness. Nowhere is this more evident than in the antepenultimate and penultimate poems, which are composed as a dialogue with each other and, in the first edition of *Rescue*, face each other on opposite pages.

Trwoga

"Ojcze, gdzie jesteś! Las ciemny, las dziki,
Od biegu zwierząt kołyszą się chaszcze,

Trującym ogniem buchają storczyki,
Pod nogą czają się wilcze przepaście.

Gdzie jesteś, ojcze! Noc nie ma granicy,
Odtąd już zawsze ciemność będzie trwała.
Bezdomni, z głodu umrą podróżnicy.
Chleb nasz jest gorzki, wyschnięty jak skała.

Gorący oddech straszliwego zwierza
Zbliża się, prosto w twarze smrodem zieje.
Dokąd odszedłeś, ojcze, jak ci nie żal
Dzieci, w te głuche zabłąkanych knieje."

Odnalezienie

"Tu jestem. Skądże ten lęk nierozumny?
Noc zaraz minie, dzień wzejdzie niedługo.
Słyszycie: grają już pastusze surmy
I gwiazdy błędną nad różową smugą.

Ścieżka jest prosta. Jesteśmy na skraju.
Tam w dole dzwonek w wiosce się odzywa.
Koguty światło na płotach witają
I dymi ziemia, bujna i szczęśliwa.

Tu jeszcze ciemno. Jak rzeka w powodzi
Mgła czarne kępy borówek otula.
Ale już w wodę świt na szczudłach wchodzi
I dzwoniąc toczy się słoneczna kula."[160]

["Terror": "Father, where are you! Forest dark, forest wild, / Thickets rock from the run of the beasts, / Orchids are bursting with poisonous fire, / Wolf traps gape under our legs. // Where are you, Father? The night has no border, / From here the darkness will now last forever. / Homeless, travelers will die from hunger. / Our bread is bitter, as dry as a stone. // The hot breath of a terrible beast / Approaches, pants with its stench in our faces. / Where have you gone, Father, how can you not pity / The children who've strayed into the depths of this forest."

"Discovery": "Here I am. Where does this irrational dread come from? / The night will pass presently, day will dawn in a moment. / Hear it: shepherd's trumpets are already playing, / And the stars wander over their pink trail. // The path is straight. We're on the edge. / Down there a bell is ringing in the village. / Roosters on fences are greeting the light / And the earth is steaming, lush and happy. // Here it is still dark. Like a river in flood / The mist enshrouds the black clumps of bilberries. / But dawn is already entering the water on stilts / And, ringing, the sunny sphere is turning."]

"Terror" explicitly posits an unbounded, mythic space. The children cry out for fear of dangers natural (wild beasts), man-made (wolf traps), and magical (orchids bursting "with poisonous fire"), but they seem most terrified by the limitlessness of their surroundings: "The night has no border, / From here the darkness will now last forever." Homeless wandering, as reliable a marker of intermediacy in Miłosz as it is in Schulz, Platonov, and Mandel'shtam, is here also tied specifically to a lack of spatial-temporal definition. With no concrete center to return to, the children are condemned to wander until they "die from hunger." The repeated calls to the Father take on the tone of a desperate prayer, especially as the children call for his pity in the last stanza. There is a Christian inflection to Miłosz's calling out to the Father, only here the Christian paradigm is turned on its head: instead of calling to the Heavenly Father to rescue them from the perils of their earthly existence, the children call to their earthly father to rescue them from their fairy tale.

"Discovery," its structure identical to that of "Terror," is an antidote to the earlier poem. "Terror" asks the Father, "Where are you?"; "Discovery" answers, "Here I am." Likewise, while "Terror" shows the downside of entering what Miłosz has derisively called an "intuitional" worldview, the Father of "Discovery" criticizes the ensuing dread as "irrational." Most importantly, what the children bemoan as the boundlessness of the night and the endless durée of darkness, the Father counteracts with the notion of passing: not "[t]he night has no border," but "[t]he night will pass presently." Once again, Miłosz constructs this opposition through the contradictory verbs *trwać,* "to last," and *minąć*, "to pass." This call-and-response—between the children and the Father, as well as between semantic oppositions—emerges clearly in the poems' nursery-rhyme structure, with its short sentences and almost singsong rhythm. The Father, in responding to the children, sounds remarkably like them. He reassures the children by pointing out boundaries they do not recognize: a straight path, fences, the forest edge. And yet the poem's last stanza acknowledges this assertion of definitions as an article of faith, for the principal subjects still find themselves enshrouded in mist, "[l]ike a river in flood." The Father, as the voice of authority, assures the children that the historical time of civilization—the stable center, the "central, privileged space, which is probably a village from one's childhood"—exists, but they have all strayed from it and remain lost in the woods. Even the sounds the Father points out—the horns of shepherds, the roosters announcing the dawn—belong more to a pastoral idyll than to any historically contingent space.

In light of Miłosz's oppositional poetics, we can say that Gombrowicz was half wrong when he characterized Miłosz as a poet who "breaks out of the world" using a freedom that is "the bitter maturity of our time." Miłosz,

Gombrowicz says, thinks that history calls on him to be mature, but this is an oversimplification belied by Gombrowicz's own assertion that Miłosz must destroy himself in order to become himself. The maturity represented by history in Miłosz, the steady progress of time introduced by the Father, is always only half of the picture. The other half is immaturity, the myth of the child. Naivety regarding the incommensurability of the historic and mythic allows them to coexist, especially in the 1930s and early 1940s, what Miłosz would call, at the end of his life, "a period of delayed maturity."[161] *Delayed maturity:* the "old surviving in the new," a moment that seems to last forever.

Chapter 4

✦

A Certain Space of Time: Intermediacy in the Modern Polis (Nikolai Zabolotskii, Vítězslav Nezval)

> You are walking through it howsomever. I am, a stride at a time. A very short space of time through very short times of space.
>
> —James Joyce

In *The World,* Czesław Miłosz projects his adult sense of the world through the voice of a child. Or, if not exactly a child, then a monster, a hybrid of the adult and his child self, imperfectly remembered, fully imagined. Miłosz was then about the same age as Schulz had been when he started cultivating a similar method, first in his graphic work, then in his letters to his fiancée, and finally in fiction. Constantly tracking their own coordinates in space and time, these writers felt themselves caught between definition and dissolution, and they sensed that every movement, every gesture, alters their constitution relative to everyone and everything around them. Such is the sense of perpetual displacement in Schulz and Platonov, where characters' very sense of space becomes less certain the further they move from a point of origin. Similarly, in the poems of Mandel'shtam and Miłosz from the same period, the intermediate temporality of the lyric subject consists in movement, though of a slightly different kind: their present is not a fixed point in time, but a moving target pressing into the future even as it drags along the residue of the past. Recognizing himself as multiple selves distributed across space and time, this version of the individual subject declares, after Walt Whitman, "I am large, I contain multitudes." Or, as Mandel'shtam puts it in an early lyric,

> Дано мне тело—что мне делать с ним,
> Таким единым и таким моим?

[. . .]
Я и садовник, я же и цветок,
В темнице мира я не одинок.[1]

[I've been given a body—what am I to do with it, / so singular and so much my own? // [. . .] // I am the gardener, I am also the bloom, / In the prison of the world I am not alone.]

Or else, as Nikolai Zabolotskii puts it in the opening lines of his 1937 poem "Metamorphoses" (Metamorfozy),

Как мир меняется! И как я сам меняюсь!
Лишь именем одним я называюсь,—
На самом деле то, что именуют мной,—
Не я один. Нас много. Я—живой.[2]

[How the world changes! How I myself am changing! / Though I am called by my one name,— / In fact what they call me— / Is not me alone. We are many. I am alive.]

Cosmic universalism, as I have already noted, came in many flavors in interwar Eastern Europe, especially in the Soviet Union, where the dictatorship of the proletariat promised (or threatened) to transform the metaphysical ideal into habitus. Artists and scientists alike redoubled their interest in the "philosophy of the common task," the eclectic system of Nikolai Fedorov that brought together Orthodox theology, science fiction, and biological universalism, ultimately maintaining that technological advances would allow us to resurrect the dead by recovering their dispersed matter. Unlike those who might speculate, with Proust, that "perhaps the resurrection of the soul after death is to be conceived as a phenomenon of memory," several prominent thinkers in Russia believed that it was rather a potential within matter.[3] Aleksandr Bogdanov, whose writings about immortality and the unity of life and matter had a decisive influence on Platonov, subscribed to a similar hope that biological renewal would soon make death obsolete. At the Russian University of Prague, Nikolai Lossky (1870–1965), forced to leave the Soviet Union in 1922, was further systematizing his model of "the world as an organic whole," maintaining that the knowing subject, the individual human self, is a "supertemporal and superspatial being, intimately connected with the whole world": Lossky, too, offers consubstantiality as the basis for possible resurrection and immortality.[4] And Konstantin Tsiolkovskii (1857–1935), an early theorist of rocketry and space travel, argues in his most important philosophical treatise for the possibility of universal consciousness.

The intensity of this interest in cosmism returns us once again to the Dante master plot described by Lukács and Bakhtin. In reading the architecture of

Dante's journey in the *Commedia*, they see the outward movement into the cosmic *polis* as an inward movement into the poet's own soul, where he encounters a range of characters who, in good Freudian fashion, are both himself and not-himself, born of historical contingency or timeless myth, yet in the special setting of Dante's poem condemned to enact the poet's own reflections on time-bound human activity and the eternal order.[5] As an earthly being passing through the divine, the poet is the point where time and eternity collapse together. Change here is marked not by the passage of earthly time, but by the passage of the poet through a space that is, in fact, himself. Thus George Santayana describes Dante's world as caught between the cosmic and the individual, a "golden cage in which his soul sings."[6]

In the literature of intermediacy, this "golden cage" is modeled most frequently on modern urban spaces. Writers wishing to emphasize the destabilization of space as one moves out from the center may focus on the provincial town, as we have seen in Schulz and Platonov. Others, including the Russian poet Nikolai Zabolotskii and the Czech poet Vítězslav Nezval, take us on lyrical walking tours of real urban spaces in the midst of dramatic social and industrial transformations—for these poets, Leningrad and Prague, respectively. Or else it is the poets who are caught in a process of endless metamorphosis. The Dantean split between the cosmic and the individual renders the distinction moot.

The Polis as Carnival: Zabolotskii's "Red Bavaria"

"How the world changes! How I myself am changing!" When the Soviet Union declared its existence by treaty on December 30, 1922, Zabolotskii had been living for just a year in Petrograd, a student of literature at the Pedagogical Institute. Lossky had just departed Russia in September, exiled alongside 160 prominent intellectuals.[7] The public disagreement between Einstein and Bergson over the nature of space-time had just taken place in Paris that April.

Zabolotskii had arrived from Moscow, where he'd been studying literature at the First Moscow University and medicine at the Second, though he had been raised some five hundred miles to the east, in a rural area north of Kazan. In Petrograd, too, Zabolotskii entertained the possibility of becoming a professional scientist, but his interest in the sciences was inextricable from his interests in philosophy and literature, which soon won over.[8] The young poet was torn, as Robin Milner-Gulland points out, between competing visions of man and nature, stability and mutability, "that of flux and relativity throughout the natural world (the popularity of Einstein in Soviet Russia at the time is worth noting), and that of the perfectibility of Nature by (or rather, helped by) man."[9] Nature, a realm of endless potential and fecundity, competes with mankind, an agent of rational order, and Zabolotskii seems to have been especially excited when mankind limits nature or, better yet, nature destabilizes the human.

An omnivorous reader of poetry, literary theory, and philosophy—the hasty sale of his personal library and the loss of many of his papers following Zabolotskii's 1938 arrest sadly preclude a more detailed intellectual pedigree—the young poet was particularly drawn to Khlebnikov and Mandel'shtam, two poets for whom the metaphysics of time proved especially fruitful as a poetic theme.[10] He eventually developed friendships with several luminaries of critical theory, including Lidiia Ginzburg, Iurii Tynianov, and Boris Eikhenbaum. Zabolotskii also actively sought writers whose thinking mirrored his own interest in the consubstantiality of Being, leading to an active correspondence with Tsiolkovskii in the last years of the reclusive philosopher's life.[11]

Zabolotskii spent his two-year military service in what had now been renamed Leningrad, where he found several young writers, including Daniil Kharms and Aleksandr Vvedenskii, who were similarly keen on reflecting "the massive, revolutionary shift of culture and everyday life so characteristic of our time."[12] This language, which Zabolotskii drafted for the 1927 manifesto of the Association for Real Art, or Oberiu (Ob"edinenie real'nogo iskusstva; ObeRIu), reflects a profound desire to move beyond mere dissatisfaction with the aesthetics or execution of contemporary art. The Oberiuty, as these writers came to be known, suggest that our understanding of reality itself has changed, and that it is now incumbent upon art to reflect those changes by adopting a "new attitude," or *mirooshchushchenie*—a philosophical term that literally translates to a "feeling" *(oshchushchenie)* of or for the "world" *(mir)*. In this respect, the Oberiuty would agree with Mandel'shtam's declaration in "The Morning of Acmeism" a decade earlier that "for the artist, attitude [*mirooshchushchenie*] is the weapon and the means, like the hammer in the hands of the mason, and the sole reality is the artwork itself."[13]

Zabolotskii's interest in the mutability of space-time and the consequent blurring of the boundaries of individual existence found immediate purchase in Leningrad at the end of the New Economic Policy (NEP), a sometimes chaotic hybrid of Communist state ownership and private enterprise meant to energize a young and unevenly developed economy. "After I left the army I found myself surrounded by the last years of NEP," Zabolotskii recalled in 1948, two years after his release from internal exile in Kazakhstan. "I found the rapacious life of all manner of businessmen and entrepreneurs deeply alien and hostile. The satirical portrayal of that life became the theme of my poems from 1927 and 1928, which subsequently composed the book *Columns*."[14] Ginzburg offers a comparable assessment of these poems, emphasizing their "grotesque" straddling of "ideals" and "antivalues": "At its very core the lyric—in a sense the exposition of a person's ideals and life values, though also of his antivalues—is in the grotesque, in unmasking and satire. In *Columns,* the world of antivalues is the world of the bourgeois understanding of life, reflected in words deliberately compromised, be they broadly quotidian or decidedly bookish, 'beautiful' words."[15] Ginzburg recognizes that Zabolotskii's grotesqueries are not merely the expressions of a poet at play, but rather reflect a worldview, the poet's "ideals and life values," certainly, "though also his antivalues." For Zabolotskii, these values and antivalues are reflected together throughout the urban landscape. The lyric subject's relation to them necessarily shifts as he moves through the city, as Irene Masing-Delić puts it, "able to unmask an Old World where the absurd (or what should not be) is considered normal and the normal (or what should be) is considered absurd."[16]

This light, almost matter-of-fact treatment of the uncanny is symptomatic of intermediacy, and it has served as a basis for earlier comparisons between Zabolotskii, Platonov, Kafka, and others.[17] Zabolotskii, a self-avowed monist, saw no contradiction between the "normal" and the "absurd." Of his friend, the prolific author Nikolai Chukovskii notes that Zabolotskii "labeled as 'dualism' any contradistinction between the spiritual life and the material, any incomprehension of their identity, their complete unity."[18] Nikita Zabolotskii, the poet's son and literary executor, recalls that "even at the very beginning of his independent creative life, [Zabolotskii] contemplated the interplay of all that exists in the world, the nature of the connections between people, animals, and plants."[19] Many of his poems, especially those that appear later in his career, use lyric intersections to blur contrasts between urban Soviet society and the traditionally agricultural or "natural" countryside, two worlds with which Zabolotskii was intimately familiar.[20] But the intermediacy of the Zabolotskii lyric is most clearly featured in his poems written from the period of NEP and the First Five-Year Plan (1928–32). The exceptionally subtle urban phantasmagoria of these poems show this poet caught quite literally in between a past that will not die and a future that will never come.

Zabolotskii achieves this vision by situating his lyric perspective between the material traces of the old world and objects that bespeak a future not yet fully achieved. The point of view projected by these poems is typically disembodied—another parallel with Platonov, though we might just as easily refer to the out-of-body experience orchestrated by Miłosz in "Hushabye." And like Schulz's representations of Drohobycz—or, closer to home, Mandel'shtam's "I returned to my city . . ."—the poems in *Columns* are remarkable in that they can be read both as imaginative fancy and, with some modest flexibility on the part of the reader, as literal representations of confusion in the modern polis. In "Red Bavaria," for example, the poem that opens *Columns,* the interior of a NEP-era bar in downtown Leningrad seems a world unto itself, since we initially see it as it would appear through a bottle, "In the wilderness of a bottley paradise":

В глуши бутылочного рая,
где пальмы высохли давно,—
под электричеством играя,
в бокале плавало окно;
оно на лопастях блестело,
потом садилось, тяжелело;
над ним пивной дымок вился . . .
Но это описать нельзя.

И в том бутылочном раю
сирены дрогли на краю
кривой эстрады. На поруки
им были отданы глаза.
Они простерли к небесам
эмалированные руки
и ели бутерброд от скуки.

Вертятся двери на цепочках,
спадает с лестницы народ,
трещит картонною сорочкой,
с бутылкой водит хоровод;
сирена бледная за стойкой
гостей попотчует настойкой,
скосит глаза, уйдёт, придёт,
потом, с гитарой наотлёт,
она поёт, поёт о милом:
как милого она кормила,
как ласков к телу и жесток—
впивался шёлковый шнурок,
как по стаканам висла виски,
как, из разбитого виска
измученную грудь обрызгав,
он вдруг упал. Была тоска,
и всё, о чём она ни пела,—
в бокале отливалось мелом.

Мужчины тоже все кричали,
они качались по столам,
по потолкам они качали
бедлам с цветами пополам;
один—язык себе откусит,
другой кричит: я—иисусик,
молитесь мне—я на кресте,
под мышкой гвозди и везде . . .
К нему сирена подходила,

и вот, колено оседлав,
бокалов бешеный конклав
зажёгся как паникадило.

Глаза упали точно гири,
бокал разбили—вышла ночь,
и жирные автомобили,
схватив под мышки Пикадилли,
легко откатывали прочь.
Росли томаты из прохлады,
и вот, опущенные вниз—
краснобаварские закаты
в пивные днища улеглись,
а за окном—в глуши времён,
блистал на мачте лампион.

Там Невский в блеске и тоске,
в ночи переменивший кожу,
гудками сонными воспёт,
над баром вывеску тревожил;
и под свистками Германдады,
через туман, толпу, бензин,
над башней рвался шар крылатый
и имя «Зингер» возносил.[21]

[In the wilderness of a bottley paradise, / where the palms dried out long ago,—/ playing beneath electric lighting, / the window was swimming in the goblet; / it flashed on the fan blades, / then it settled down, grew heavy; / a beery smoke twisted above it . . . / But there's no way to describe that. // And in that bottley paradise / sirens trembled on the edge / of a crooked stage. As collateral / eyes had been surrendered to them. / Toward the heavens they stretched / enameled arms / and ate a sandwich out of boredom. // The doors are twisting on chains, / the folk fall down the stairs, / they crackle [their] cardboard shirtfronts, / they lead the round dance with a bottle; / a siren, pale behind the counter, / treats guests to liquor, / she narrows her eyes, goes out, comes back, / then, with a guitar held out, / she sings, she sings about [her] beloved: / how she nursed [her] beloved, / how gentle on her body, and cruel, / the silken lace dug in, / how whiskey clung to the glasses, / how, having splattered his exhausted chest / from [his] shattered temple, / he suddenly fell. There was longing, / and no matter what she sang,— / in the goblet it was poured out in whitewash. // The men, too, all were shouting, / they were rolling along the tables, / they were swinging along the ceilings, / half bedlam, half flowers; / one bites off his own tongue,

/ another shouts: I'm a little Jesus, / pray to me—I'm on the cross, / nails under [my] armpits and everywhere . . . / The siren went up to him, / and so, she having sat upon his knee, / the frantic conclave of goblets / lit up like a chandelier. // The eyes fell down like weights, / they smashed the goblet—out came night, / and greasy automobiles, / having taken the Piccadilly under the arm, / rolled lightly forward. / Tomatoes grew out of the cool, / and so, lowered down, / the sunsets of the Red Bavaria settled down into the bottoms of beer barrels, / and outside the window—in the wilderness of times, / a lampion shone on a pole. // There Nevsky Prospect, in brightness and longing, / having changed its skin in the night, / its praises sung in sleepy horns, / was disturbing the sign above the bar; / and under the whistles of Hermandades, / through fog, crowd, gas, / a winged globe broke out above the tower / and raised the name "Singer."]

Zabolotskii's poem takes a classic drinking poem of the pre-Revolutionary era, Blok's "The Stranger" (Neznakomka, 1906), and transforms Blok's representation of barroom bacchanalia into a portrait of universal confusion. Yet Zabolotskii is surprisingly literal in his depiction of the actual Red Bavaria, which was located below street level on the corner of Nevsky Prospect and the Griboedov Canal, across the street from the stately Singer Sewing Machine Building. This area boasts a rich heritage of nightmare fiction, featuring prominently in such texts as Nikolai Gogol's "The Nose" and Dostoevsky's *The Double,* and the bar likewise harkened back to the nineteenth century.[22] But while the setting is real, Zabolotskii immediately plays with reflection and refraction of the observed world, the "wilderness" or "disorder" of the "paradise" inside a bottle, already suggestive of a timeless, curved space. The bar is packed and raucous, yet the observational point of view is both quiet and unpeopled: we see everything from the perspective of being *inside* a bottle. Instead of a window, which would admit light downward into the subterranean venue, we see its reflection on the surface of liquid in a goblet. This light then shines upward into the ceiling fan, where it ultimately blurs with a smoke that is neither image nor object but indeterminacy itself, so that Zabolotskii closes the first stanza by resigning from his own descriptive task: *No eto opisat' nel'zia*—"But there's no way to describe that."

So let's try it one more time, he seems to say with the second stanza, starting again from the beginning and populating the stage with actors rather than objects. Or, more precisely, he elides the distinction between objects and people, since it is unclear whether the "sirens" he now places in the "bottley paradise" are barmaids, elements of interior decor, or even a glimpse of the mermaid caryatids adorning the façade of the Singer Building across the street. (Recall that the bar is situated below the street, so that the view the windows afford its patrons is angled to the upper floors of nearby buildings.) By reading the poem's "sirens" strictly as barmaids, some of Zabolotskii's readers overdetermine what the poet clearly intends as intricately connected metaphors—the very enactment in language of Zabolotskii's metaphysics.[23] That Zabolotskii launches this transition from "sirens," creatures who represent the hybridity of person and thing, only underscores the power of associative blending. The depiction of image and action, meanwhile, maintains a tenuous ambiguity. Are the sirens' "enameled hands" the painted fingernails of young women, or are they more literally the enameled "arms"—Russian *ruka* means both—of statuary? Does the song of lost love floating through the bar issue from a performer, or is it imagined as echoing from those mermaids on the Singer Building across the street? Like the smoke above the spinning fan blades, everything blends together, or rather, everything is thickly interconnected, so that one refraction leads immediately to the next.

The spatial-temporal consequence of this intermingling, which we see materially as consubstantiality and linguistically in the concatenated metaphor, is the gradual breakdown in the speaker's sense of rootedness in space and time. His perspective transitions from the point of origin—the view from the bottle—to "the edge / of a crooked stage," or from the center of the bar to the periphery on the street. Zabolotskii uses space much the same way as Platonov and Schulz do, allowing one's movement from the center out toward a noncenter to generate associative transformations of one thing into another. In fact, it is worth noting generally that while the poem is set unambiguously in Leningrad, this Leningrad is to be a meeting place of many worlds, whether we look at the "Bavaria" in the poem's title; the later nod toward London with the mention of "Picadilly," a NEP-era cinema two blocks east along Nevsky; or, in the poem's closing stanza, the suggestion of medieval Spanish "hermandades" and the unmistakably American and capitalist associations with the Singer Sewing Machine Company. So long as Zabolotskii can keep everything in motion, it will be possible for us to be everywhere at once. It is the variable motion of all these elements that allows us to see different space-times moving relative to each other.

The temporal dimension of "Red Bavaria," meanwhile, appears in the collision of the old and new that was characteristic of Soviet urban life under the New Economic Policy. This accounts for the prominence of Christian images, which for Zabolotskii recall the cyclicality of time inscribed within the traditional Orthodox worldview, a time rooted in recurring feasts and faith in Christ's rebirth. Against this cyclicality, Zabolotskii presents the linearity of the Industrial Age, with its insistence on social and technological progress. Despite having been an atheist at the time he wrote *Columns,* Zabolotskii recognizes that the Soviet progress narrative has not yet triumphed over the cyclicality of the religious calendar.[24] On the contrary, he explores the chaotic results of the old and new temporal schemes colliding with each other.

This admixture is evident not only in Zabolotskii's commingling of the religious and the profane, or of the capitalist with the Communist, but even in the light sources described in "Red Bavaria." At the beginning of the poem, we see by *elektrichestvo,* "electric lighting," a loaded word in the early Soviet period, as electrification was one of the most potent and immediate symbols of progress toward the Soviet future. Among Lenin's most famous formulas is his announcement to the Conference of the Russian Communist Party, Moscow Guberniia, in 1920: "Communism is Soviet power plus the electrification of the entire country, since without electrification it will be impossible for us to advance industry."[25] And yet the light source toward the end of the poem is a traditional *panikadilo,* or Orthodox chandelier. Again, we find "the old surviving in the new at every step."

In the antepenultimate stanza of "Red Bavaria," one of Zabolotskii's drunken revelers declares himself a "little Jesus"—*iisusik*—a religious reference that resonates with the image of the church chandelier and the goblet. As Sarah Pratt has suggested, Zabolotskii's frequent play with religious imagery paints him as a kind of holy fool whose "poetic vision itself rests upon the concept of transfiguration."[26] The world of Zabolotskii's early poems, Pratt argues, is an Old Russian "anti-world," one whose general disorder contrasts with the hierarchical reversals of Bakhtin's carnival spaces.[27] But in reading Zabolotskii, such contrasts cannot be categorical, since the interplay of order and disorder, of cohesion and chaos, demonstrates a persistent overlap of world and antiworld. As the poem progresses, it becomes increasingly difficult to distinguish relics of the old world from inventions of the new, the mythic from the real.

Once again, we need to look to the associative structure of the author's metaphors to appreciate their significance for his metaphysics.

Zabolotskii's Metaphor: The View from Between

On September 26, 1926, Zabolotskii wrote a letter to fellow Oberiut Aleksandr Vvedenskii and gave it to Kharms to deliver. Kharms kept the letter instead, as it could not have improved the cohesion of an already fractious group. In his letter, Zabolotskii takes Vvedenskii to task for failing to appreciate the proper function of metaphor, which, Zabolotskii insists, should have an expansive "associative range" that stretches out beyond logical thought: "An unusual interlacing of objects, ascribing them extraordinary qualities and properties, not to mention extraordinary actions. Formally speaking, this is a line of metaphor. All metaphor, so long as it is alive and new, is illogical. [. . .] But an old metaphor, whether Acmeist or Futurist, has easily faded away. The renewal of metaphor could come only by extending its associative range."[28] Zabolotskii situates his description of metaphor relative to the two most vocal antagonists of the literary avant-garde, noting that metaphors get tired regardless of their orientation toward the past (Acmeists) or the future (Futurists). His suggestion that metaphorical language renews itself by extending its associative range, meanwhile, should remind us of similar pronouncements from both Schulz and Mandel'shtam: the former, in his notion that metaphorical "short circuits" restore "conductivity" to language; the latter, in the circular image—what I have translated as "associative range" is more properly "associative circle," *assotsiativnyi krug*—that harkens back to Mandel'shtam's image of the word as a waving fan. In fact, Mandel'shtam's projection of the lyric word through architectural metaphors appears in early Zabolotskii as well, at least insofar as the Russian title of his first collection, *Stolbtsy,* could be translated as "scrolls" as well as "columns."

Metaphor is "illogical" in much the same way as Northrop Frye would later define it, as "not so much an assertion that A is B"—such an assertion would ignore the "obvious unreality" of the claim—"as an annihilation of the space separating A and B."[29] In Frye's formulation, metaphor is inherently a spatial-temporal operation, canceling the space of distinction, though only for a limited time: sooner or later, one has to acknowledge that A *is not* B. It is on this last point, however, that Frye's position diverges instructively from that of Zabolotskii. For according to Zabolotskii's model, a metaphor dies not when we acknowledge its unreality, but when we allow it to ossify to the point of not realizing it as metaphor at all. The word "stiffens," Schulz says, just as Mandel'shtam's reading of Dante leads him to conclude, as Struve puts it, that "poetic speech is diametrically opposed to the ossification of nature, to lexical inertia."[30] Instead of simply reasserting the metaphor, which reduces it to cliché or formula, we renew it by keeping it in motion, waving the fan faster, creating new short circuits.

This is Zabolotskii's method throughout *Columns*. Instead of the "annihilation of the space separating A and B," we find the poet situating himself, or at least his lyrical self-construct, *in between* the two points of comparison. Thus he serves as the nexus between them, the very embodiment of the interconnection that the poet assumes exists a priori among all things. As the poet moves around the city, the points of comparison change, and so too does the thinking subject who represents their intersection. Objects that catch the poet's attention function as coordinates, but because these coordinates are always shifting, the poems convey a sense of constant flux, confusion, and transformation, thereby frustrating the poet's effort at articulation. At times he is simply stumped, as we see already in the first stanza of "Red Bavaria," when he tells us that the scene he has been describing defies description. With its frenetic action and repeated references to light and vision, Zabolotskii suggests that consubstantiality has to be seen—it must be unmasked—if it is to be understood.

Zabolotskii's insistence on the gaze stems from his early interest in visual art, and especially in the representation of internal dynamism in the Analytic Art of Pavel Filonov (1883–1941). Filonov had occupied a prominent position in the avant-garde art world of Petrograd in the 1910s, having developed a visual style that evokes internal dynamics, as distinct from Cubism's attention to surfaces. Filonov's compositional method, which he called "universal flowering" (*mirovoi rastsvet*), sought to conquer time by translating it into a two-dimensional picture plane. The result, a jumble of variegated facets that the viewer is challenged to recombine in multiple ways, forming several represented objects from a limited set of geometric figures, observes an internal dynamism not unlike that of "Red Bavaria," particularly insofar as the appearance of chaos dissipates the more the viewer becomes aware of how the painting's elements are interconnected.

Filonov, a minor poet in his own right, worked closely with other poets, especially Khlebnikov. (In November 1913, when Mandel'shtam felt compelled to call Khlebnikov out to duel for an apparently anti-Semitic poem that Khlebnikov had recited at the Stray Dog Cabaret, Filonov was asked to serve as a second alongside Viktor Shklovsky. The actual duel never occurred, and the incident had no lasting effect on the poets' friendship and mutual admiration.)[31] Filonov's efforts to use "universal flowering" to render the internal dynamism of time in two-dimensional space are essential to any reading of Zabolotskii's attempt to do the same in the lyric poem.

Typical of Filonov's method is a painting from the time of Zabolotskii's arrival in Petrograd. Depending on how the viewer recombines the painting's geometric units, the aptly named canvas *Triumph over Eternity* (Pobeda nad vechnost'iu, 1920–21; figure 4.1) reveals faces and architectural elements that emerge from and recede back into the picture plane. Filonov plays with refraction and recombination by aligning the edges of his compositional units, creating leading edges that extend toward the center from the painting's left-side corners. These lines enclose the painting's clearest zone of (relative) stability, the head whose profile dominates the composition's left side. This center-out principle, the sense that the refraction of elements becomes increasingly chaotic the further we move out from a point of stability, is equally operative in Zabolotskii's "Red Bavaria," in which space and perspective become more unstable as we move out from "the wilderness of a bottley paradise." Additionally, Filonov's painting conveys a strong sense of relative movement within the static image. Much of the painting appears to be in motion, as clusters of geometric shapes lean to the left or right, breaking down into smaller pieces or coalescing into larger structures. That motion, however, is anything but uniform. Larger elements in the upper left are noticeably less dynamic than those in the lower middle. This is why it is much easier for the viewer to hold the head in profile as a fixed shape.

Figure 4.1. Pavel Filonov, *Triumph over Eternity* (Pobeda nad vechnost'iu, 1920–21; oil on canvas). *Paintings of 1930s-1920s [sic]/ Zhivopis' 20–30kh godov,* ed. A. M. Muratov (St. Petersburg: Khudozhnik RSFSR, 1991). Original in the collection of the Russian State Museum, St. Petersburg.

With its mixed metaphors and sound repetitions, Zabolotskii's lyric is the verbal analogue to Filonov's canvas. In this light, I find myself unable to agree with Darra Goldstein's assertion that, in the poems in *Columns,* "Zabolotskii used fragmentation of time and space as a poetic device, without fully plumbing the extent of its meanings."[32] For it is quite clear to me that this fragmentation is not solely the mechanism by which the poet portrays the carnival atmosphere of the NEP-era city—though it does serve this purpose very effectively. Rather, Zabolotskii's fragmentation of space and time in these poems *is* their meaning, an expression of what Andrei Bitov calls the "internal pitch" that draws together "the *practice* of Tsiolkovskii and [. . .]

the art of Filonov, Platonov, and Zabolotskii."[33] Goldstein's reading of time in Zabolotskii's early poems is conditioned by her elegant treatment of his work following his return from eight years' imprisonment and exile in 1946, a "fissure in time" that, Goldstein tells us, "Zabolotskii learned how to drop through [. . .] and thus escape the immediate circle of his present-tense life": "He was able to achieve a sense of time that is neither present, nor past, nor future, but free of standard perceptions."[34] From this perspective, which frames the nullification of time as a lyric guarantor of freedom, it is easy to understand how the temporal manipulations of Zabolotskii's earlier poems might seem purely stylistic; these manipulations of time are, at any rate, inadequate to the project of spiritual liberation that Goldstein ascribes to the poet. But I regard this as a misreading of those early poems. Instead of canceling past, present, and future, Zabolotskii collapses them. If the poems in *Columns* fail to provide transcendence or escape, it is only because there is no transcendence or escape to be had.

There is, however, the reprieve from definition that is afforded by relative motion in space. In the poem "Soccer" (Futbol, April 1926), the relative motion of players on a soccer field allows what would otherwise be a strictly delimited space to expand toward universality, frustrating the forward's progress toward the goal. This effect is most pronounced in the poem's second stanza:

> Свалились в кучу беки,
> опухшие от сквозняка,
> и вот—через моря и реки,
> просторы, площади, снега—
> расправив пышные доспехи
> и накренясь в меридиан,
> слетает шар.[35]

> [The fullbacks have collapsed in a pile, / puffed out from the draft, / and so—across seas and rivers, / expanses, squares, snows— / having straightened out its magnificent armor / and leaning in toward the meridian, / the ball drops down.]

Like "Red Bavaria," "Soccer" is composed in iambic tetrameter with an eccentric rhyme scheme that tends toward alternating rhyme but introduces enclosed or coupled rhymes to heighten the poem's drama. Visually, that drama grows from the poem's contrast of static and dynamic elements: a forward rushing through space versus fullbacks who have "collapsed in a pile." As the ball flies through the air, space dilates, so that the geography that the ball traverses now encompasses "seas and rivers, / expanses, squares, snows." The striker's shot arcs toward its mark, but instead of crossing the goal line, as we might expect, it leans "into the meridian," a longitudinal line marking vast geographic space. The word "armor," which soon pops up again in the poem "Motion" (Dvizhenie, 1927), refers in both poems to any exterior surface, with no differentiation between the surface of a person and that of an object. Even as the soccer field expands to become the world, the ball is also an *imago mundi:* instead of the conventional term for a soccer ball, *miach,* Zabolotskii uses *shar,* "sphere" or "globe." Indeed, both the soccer ball and the field are representatives of planetary space seen simultaneously at different scales, with one arcing over and finally collapsing into the other. As in "Red Bavaria," space is refracted by concatenated metaphors: the field becomes the entire world, but the ball is also that world.[36]

Once again, the subject's passage through this relativistic spatial-temporal construct, where everyone and everything are consubstantial, is the engine that drives the continuous transformation we see in the poem. Perhaps the simplest instantiation of this metamorphosis in movement in *Columns* is the eight-line poem "Motion":

> Сидит извозчик, как на троне,
> Из ваты сделана броня,
> И борода, как на иконе,
> Лежит, монетами звеня.
> А бедный конь руками машет,
> То вытянется, как налим,
> То снова восемь ног сверкают
> В его блестящем животе.[37]
>
> [The cabbie sits, as on a throne, / His armor made of cotton, / His beard, as in an icon, / Just lies there, jingling with coins. / But the poor horse waves his arms, / Now stretches out, like a burbot, / Now once again eight legs are gleaming / Within his brilliant belly.]

Zabolotskii's frequent opposition between the sacred and the profane appears here in the one person of the cabbie, who simultaneously represents a figure from a religious icon and a capitalist profiteer, his beard "jingling with coins." The horse pulling the carriage also belongs to two worlds at once. In one, he is motionless, elongated, even fishlike, "like a burbot," an ugly bottom-feeder.[38] In the other, he is moving so fast that he appears to have a blur of eight legs. Blurring, it happens, is the poem's principal visual activity, as Zabolotskii repeatedly draws our attention to the various flashes of light implied by "armor," "coins," and the sleek "burbot," as well as by the verb *sverkat',* "to gleam," and the participial adjective *blestiashchii,* "brilliant." And yet the cabbie, who collects his fare while exploiting the labor of his "poor horse," sits motionless, even as his coach moves at full

Figure 4.2. Dziga Vertov, stills from *Man with a Movie Camera* (1929)

speed. In this way, Zabolotskii suggests not only relative motion, as he has already done in "Red Bavaria" and "Soccer," but also the marked contrasts inherent in older technologies, contrasts that newer means of transportation (such as the automobiles in "Red Bavaria") serve to highlight.

In treating these gradual technological shifts, Zabolotskii was tapping into one of the main currents of the era's visual culture. Dziga Vertov's most influential film, *Man with the Movie Camera* (Chelovek s kinoapparatom, 1929), produced in the same year that saw the publication of Zabolotskii's *Columns,* provides an especially compelling example. A nonnarrative film consisting entirely of interspliced documentary footage, Vertov's masterwork pays particularly close attention to perspectival shifts relative to different means of transportation. In one noteworthy sequence, Vertov jump-cuts back and forth between shots of a moving locomotive (from a stationary position), passengers in a horse-drawn carriage (shot in motion), passengers in an automobile (shot in motion), and the cameraman in a moving car seen filming passengers riding in an adjacent carriage (figure 4.2). This last shot, filmed from another moving car, shows the camera operator and the nearby passengers moving relative to one another and to the pedestrians along the adjacent sidewalk. Note that one woman in the horse-drawn carriage in the middle shot has her arm raised: she is mocking the cameraman in the car, obsessively cranking the camera, an amusing instance of the old way of life mocking the new.

In addition to their evocation of relative motion, G. B. Filippov has observed that several of Zabolotskii's early poems, including "Movement," lend themselves to a cinematic reading by suggesting the time-lapse effect of multiple stills placed one on top of the other.[39] This montage effect aligns Zabolotskii with Bergson's use of the cinematograph in explaining temporal continuity, as well as with Mandel'shtam's description of the poetic word as a column that cuts across time. What Zabolotskii's play with the transformative potential of movement intimates, and what Vertov's film demonstrates visually, is that the chaos of a NEP-era bar or Leningrad traffic coalesces into the continuity of change—the blur of the horse's legs in "Motion," the lights at the end of "Red Bavaria"—when the individual's perspective merges with the scene he is observing.

Zabolotskii's eagerness to immerse himself in consubstantiality mitigates the anxieties inevitably generated by the chaos around him, but it comes at a high price. When he melts into his shifting surroundings, the observer's individuality is revealed as an illusion. Indeed, the lyric "I" in *Columns* often seems little more than a vantage point. Yet here, too, we find an inner dynamism, a shuttling between individuality and collectivity that both threatens the individual and situates him, a condition that Hans Gumbrecht regards as generally symptomatic of the era:

> Knowledge is always contingent upon—and true or false in relation to—the position of the observer. This means that economic and social instability will seem a nightmare only to those who have a great deal to lose. But it also means that a situation which different observers agree to see as unstable when they look at it from a certain perspective can turn into the stability of change when it is seen from the next higher level. Intellectuals and writers, however, are still obsessed with finding the one and only appropriate distance between themselves and the objects of their gaze.[40]

The double motion toward "the stability of change" and "the only appropriate distance" between observer and object is an essential feature of the in-betweenness expressed in Zabolotskii's early poems. It is also wholly consistent with debates among the Oberiuty about the appropriate distance between the viewer and the object. As Nikita Zabolotskii points out, the Oberiuty attempted early on to navigate two different ways of contemplating the object. The more conventional view regarded the object in relation to the thinking subject's perception. The other view, which lends itself to the phantasmagoria we associate with Zabolotskii, attempted to imagine the life of the object beyond the subjectivity of the observer.[41] In this way, writers like Zabolotskii and Platonov simply tap into what Lev Anninskii defines as "the common language of their epoch," that is, their particular way of "projecting the global mystery play of the spirit—with equally tragic results and consequences."[42] Like the cameraman in *Man with the Movie Camera*, constantly shifting his perspective to encompass a whole that includes himself, Zabolotskii's lyric "I" also attempts to move with the object of his gaze and, at the same time, to preserve his individuality as a thinking subject. Unfortunately, the endless transformations that result from this movement may destabilize the very definitions upon which individuality is grounded.

The Soviet city under the New Economic Policy fostered a menacingly carnivalesque atmosphere, fertile ground for a language of transformation and dynamic universalism that was nevertheless not unique to Soviet realia. Elsewhere in Central and Eastern Europe, the dramatic sociopolitical changes that followed World War I extended "the common language" of spatial-temporal transformation, as well as its consequent entrapment of the individual, to like-minded writers across the region. Vítězslav Nezval's longer poem *Edison*, published as its own volume in 1928 and reprinted in *Night Poems* (Básně nocí) the following year, presents an exceptional analogue in Czech poetry to what Zabolotskii does with the city in Russian, with movement both freeing the lyric subject from fixedness in space and time and, by the very same operation, depriving him of the security of his own individuality.

Lyric Confusion: Nezval's Poetism between Reality and Representation

Vítězslav Nezval was born and spent his early years far removed from the center of national culture; in this he was no different from Zabolotskii or, for that matter, most other authors who took to exploring ontological in-betweenness in this period. Nezval's father was a schoolmaster in a diminutive village in Moravia, where the future poet enjoyed a provincial upbringing until the end of World War I. After he was drafted into the Austrian army, his military career lasted only a few weeks, after which he studied law for a semester in Brno before moving to Prague.

Prague in the 1920s was an unusually vibrant site of cross-cultural dialogue, energized in no small part by the presence of émigré intellectuals, including Nikolai Lossky, who had settled there in the early days of the Soviet state. The city boasted a highly industrialized urban zone and diverse communities of Czechs, Germans, and Jews, as well as the cultural energy that came from the city's having been elevated to the status of national capital in 1918. The connection between figures like Lossky and Nezval was circumstantial, though hardly trivial. We might even regard it as emblematic of how discourses moved among the sometimes insular ethnic and intellectual communities of interwar Prague: by the mid-1920s, Lossky had become active in the Philosophical Society, which discussed epistemology and Husserl's phenomenology and was attended by key members of the Prague Linguistic Circle, who in turn shared the poetics of Khlebnikov, Mayakovsky, and others with Nezval and his cohort.[43] Sixteen years after his arrival in the capital, in his poem "The Walker of Prague" (Pražský chodec, 1936), Nezval would recall the sense of simultaneous fascination and alienation he experienced as a *nouveau arrivé* in what would become his adopted city:

> Jednoho dne v dubnu 1920 jsem přijel po prvé do Prahy
> Na nádraží smutném jak popel se choulil zástup nešťastníků
> Byli to vystěhovalci

Také jsem tu spatřil svět kterému nebudu nikdy rozumět
Poledne houkalo byl soumrak nádražní budova se táhla až do předměstí.[44]

[One day in April 1920 I arrived for the first time in Prague / At the station sad as ash cowered a crowd of wretches / They were emigrants / Here I also caught sight of a world that I will never understand / The midday whistled it was twilight the station stretched all the way to the suburbs.]

Despite the young poet's initial bewilderment among crowds of people fleeing for the New World—in an environment where time speeds up and space dilates, noon flows immediately into dusk, and the train station expands into the distance—Prague quickly became Nezval's home and lifelong artistic collaborator. This is also the phase of Nezval's mercurial career, before his devotion to Surrealism and subsequent Stalinist period, that most insistently explores themes of intermediacy. Like the Oberiuty, the young poet actively sought to combine the principles of competing avant-garde movements in such a way as to elide the distinction between poetic utterance and everyday life.[45] Together with the artist and theorist Karel Teige (1900–1951), Nezval introduced their program, which they called "Poetism" (Poetismus), in the pages of the literary journal *Host* in 1923.

Like the lyric concepts and methods of Mandel'shtam, Miłosz, and Zabolotskii, and like Bergson's model of temporal continuity, Poetism looks to cinematic technology to formulate a new way of representing the individual experience of time and space. In his 1924 essay "The Aesthetics of Film and Cinematography," Teige, the more disciplined theoretician of the two, frames his discussion of Poetism in terms of the cinema, Einsteinian relativity, and the hybridization of cultures in the modern polis:

Perhaps one should say that today a person experiences many more impressions than a person did in the Middle Ages. We are people of an express mentality, of a stirred and ravished sensibility, whose elasticity allows all kinds of developmental possibilities. [. . .] The speed of modes of transportation, just like the theories of Einstein, have furnished us with a new and correct knowledge of space and time. The world is neither a paradise nor the garden of childhood, nor is it the hell of labor. It is simply a spatial-temporal continuum, and its art is—*a chronospatial poem*. [. . .] Americanized Europe is becoming a single, chaotic, and cinematic supercity, and the social transformation playing out therein will sooner or later make of it a harmonic, international city.[46]

Teige does not tell us whether the "chronospatial poem" he proposes should take the shape of a film, a photograph, or a text, and this is very much to the point.[47] As Teige goes on to say, "Poetism maintains that today, now that artistic tradition has been laid to rest, there is but a *single* art with *many forms,* and it is a living *poetry.*"[48] Given the upheavals of this Einsteinian age, of life in "a single, chaotic, and cinematic supercity," Teige argues for art that interacts dynamically and is eventually contiguous with everyday life.

This fusion of art and life was hardly unprecedented, and to some extent it recapitulates what Russian Symbolist aestheticians of the pre-Revolutionary era termed *zhiznetvorchestvo,* or "life creation," which, as Michael Wachtel puts it, "suggests both a synthesis of the two constituent elements (creation *and* life) as well as the creation *of* life (that is, divine creation)," though without defining what this "life" is.[49] Poetism, as Teige understood it, draws specifically on modern urban life for its subject matter, often foregrounding images of the city while shifting subjective emotional or psychological responses to the background. At the same time, Teige perceives everyday life in the new age as tending toward boundlessness, so that Poetism should also be formally unbounded, a notion that Teige expresses in contrast to the rigors of Constructivist design: "Constructivism has rigorous laws. Poetism, free and limitless, knows neither statutes nor restrictions. It is the art of life, and thus expresses itself rather by a kind of gentle, harmonic, living *bon ton.*"[50]

Even more liberationist zeal greets the Poetist project in the memoirs of Václav Černý (1905–1987), a major theorist who regarded Nezval's *Edison* as a landmark event in Czech literature: "The poetic word of Poetism was typically antirealistic; its aesthetics was an outgrowth of the old French tradition of Romanticism—Baudelaire—Symbolism—poetic Modernism beginning with Futurism; its expressive praxis was the Czech offshoot of Apollinaire's poetic Cubism. Its central concept was the concept of *liberation;* it liberated meanings for pleasure and toward pleasures; it trusted in *free imagination* and its inspirational *play.*"[51] But it is one thing to posit the limitlessness of imaginative art, and it is quite another thing to instantiate that limitlessness in the artwork. In his own highly lyrical manifesto of Poetism, "Parrot on a Motorcycle; or, On the Craft of Poetry" (Papoušek na motocyklu čili o řemesle básnickém, 1924), Nezval criticizes poetic tradition for imposing "ideology, subject, and logic" on the poem, foreclosing any sense of continuity in the change of experience and the experience of change: "I am in constant contact with my digestion. All the senses operating. 36 antennae and instinct eternally flowing. All things coalesce toward one point on the chessboard. The resolution of trembling and its directional—this is the sensibility."[52] The poem, according to Nezval, should communicate this "constant contact with [. . .] digestion," such that no image or subject dominates the composition or, by extension, its interpretation. Hybridization, the coalescing of all elements toward a focal point, is essential to lyrical expression, and it is already enacted in Nezval's description. He draws together the Bergsonian concept of duration and a metaphor from physics, that of resolving speed and direction into a vector. According to Nezval, the poet achieves this hybridization through associative leaps of sound and sense, as well as through Whitmanesque metaphors strung together by anaphora. His lyric method is in this respect quite similar to Zabolotskii's. By allowing the poem to generate itself, with each utterance suggesting its next iteration through assonance and unconscious associations of image and idea, the poet remains within the lyric occasion, never contemplating it from outside: "Ceaseless penetration. Always a different mix. The law of association, no other power than that which commands my thirst and my passions."[53]

Later, in his *Modern Poetic Movements* (Moderní básnické směry, 1937), Nezval would describe the Poetism of *Edison*, an aesthetic he had by then abandoned for Surrealism, as a hybrid of the major artistic currents of his time: "Poetism shared with Futurism a fondness for big-city realities and speed; with Cubism a demand for the peculiarity of poetic means of expression; with Surrealism, with which it was born almost simultaneously and which it to some extent anticipated, an inclination toward spontaneous expression (not driven by a preliminary plan and logico-rational demands), an emphasis on associative thought and free, autonomous imagination."[54] And yet what is remarkable about Nezval's Poetism is how difficult he finds it to remain beyond the grasp of "ideology, subject, and logic"—that is, how hard it is to stay within the very flux that Poetism takes for both subject and substance. Nezval's shift to Surrealism is a retreat from that discomfort, and his subsequent move toward Socialist Realism may be regarded as an even more dramatic withdrawal from confusion and nondefinition.[55] In Nezval's Poetist projects, on the other hand, the thinking subject is always split between his own individuality and the collective, the old and the new, and ultimately between the real and the imagined. Nezval's associative poetics in the 1920s leads to a grotesque collision of images and to a sense that the poetic utterance is generating itself through aural and word-root associations, an effect reminiscent of Mandel'shtam, Zabolotskii, and the young Miłosz. "While the unity of art and life was very much a part of the modernist credo, in his strictness Zabolotskii risked confusing the two," Darra Goldstein observes, a point that applies just as well to Nezval in his Poetist phase: "The seriousness with which he approached all aspects of his life suggests that he did not hold his being entirely distinct from his art."[56]

Motion Sickness: Nezval's *Edison*

In the long anaphoric chains that Nezval draws in *Edison*, we see the mind of the poet attempting to formalize free association, to free himself through "associative thought" enacted formally on the page. Instead of expanding the semantic reach of his metaphors, however, the formal constraints of anaphora and end rhyme often mire them in essentially logical oppositions. In *Edison*, a meditation on individual action in times of social and technological transformation, Nezval does not attempt to resolve these tensions. If anything, the poem celebrates them.

Naše životy jsou truchlivé jak pláč
Jednou k večeru šel z herny mladý hráč
venku sněžilo nad monstrancemi barů
vzduch byl vlhký neboť chýlilo se k jaru
avšak noc se chvěla jako prérie
pod údery hvězdné artilerie
které naslouchali u politých stolů
pijáci nad sklenicemi alkoholů
polonahé ženy v šatě z pávích pér
melancholikové jako v podvečer

bylo tu však něco těžkého co drtí
smutek stesk a úzkost z života i smrti
[. . .]

Skláněje se z mostu uviděl jsem stín
sebevrahův stín jenž padal do hlubin
bylo tu však něco těžkého co pláče
byl to stín a smutek hazardního hráče
řekl jsem mu probůh pane co jste zač
odvětil mi smutným hlasem nikdo hráč
bylo tu však něco smutného co mlčí
byl to stín jenž jako šibenice trčí
stín jenž padal z mostu; vykřikl jsem ach!
ne vy nejste hráč! ne vy jste sebevrah!

Šli jsme ruku v ruce oba zachráněni
šli jsme ruku v ruce v otevřeném snění
za město kde počínaly Košíře
z dálky mávaly nám noční vějíře
nad kiosky smutku tance alkoholů
šli jsme ruku v ruce nemluvíce spolu
[. . .]

Kolik vynálezců udělalo krach

hvězdy nevyšinuly se z věčných drah
pohleďte jak tisíc lidí klidně žije
ne to není práce to ani energie
to je dobrodružství jako na moři
uzamykati se v laboratoři
pohleďte jak tisíc lidí klidně žije
ne to není práce to je alchymie
[. . .]

Vždycky znovu žít a míti mánii
jedenkrát jste uzřel v Pensylvánii
noc a obloukovou lampu u Bakera
pocítil jste smutek tak jako já včera
nad poslední stránkou svého románu
jako akrobat jenž přešel po lanu
jako matka která porodila dítě
jako rybář který vytáh plné sítě
jako milenec po sladké rozkoši
jako z bitev kráčející zbrojnoši
jako země v poslední den vinobraní
jako hvězda která hasne za svítání
jako člověk náhle ztrativší svůj stín
jako Bůh jenž stvořil růži noc a blín
jako Bůh jenž touží stvořit nová slova
jako Bůh jenž musí tvořit vždycky znova
[. . .]

Naše životy se nikdy nevrací
umíráme v troskách iluminací
jako jepice a jako blesky hromů

už se vznáší světla mezi listím stromů
už se chvěje v sněhu elektrický drát
už se blíží doba světlých promenád
už se budou hledat duše pod röntgenem
jako ichthyosauři pod neogenem
už se blíží k ránu zlatá rafie
už jsme svědky kinematografie
už nám budou zaháněti vypínače
strašidelné stíny hazardního hráče
už se nesou výkřiky a tleskání
už se Edison svým hostům uklání[57]

[Our lives are woeful like lamentation / Once a young gambler came out of the casino toward evening / outside it was snowing over the monstrances of bars / the air was moist for it was tending toward spring

/ and yet the night was trembling like a prairie / under the impact of starry artillery / which they were listening to at bespattered tables / the drunks over glasses of alcohols / half-naked women dressed in dresses made of peacock feathers / melancholic as early evening // yet here was something heavy that crushes /sorrow longing and anxiety from living and dying [. . .] // Leaning over the bridge I saw a shadow / the shadow of a suicide falling to the depths / yet here was something heavy that weeps / it was the shadow and the sorrow of the gambling man / I said to him for God's sake who or what are you / he answered me in a sorrowful voice no one a gambler / yet here was something sad that keeps silent / it was a shadow that protrudes like a gallows / a shadow that was falling from the bridge; I screamed out oh! / no you are no gambler! no you are a suicide! // We walked hand-in-hand both of us rescued / we walked hand-in-hand in an open dream / beyond the town where Košíře began / from a distance the fans of night were waving at us / over the kiosks dances of alcohols of sorrow / we walked hand-in-hand together saying nothing [. . .] // How many inventors have come up with nothing / the stars have not popped out from their eternal paths / watch how a thousand people peacefully live on / no that isn't work nor is it energy / it's an adventure like on the sea / to shut themselves inside a laboratory / watch how a thousand people peacefully live on / no that isn't work it's alchemy [. . .] // Ever again to live and have a mania / once in Pennsylvania you beheld / the night and an arc lamp at Baker's / you felt sorrow just like mine yesterday / on the last page of my novel / like an acrobat who has crossed the wire / like a mother who has born a child / like a fisherman who has pulled up a full net / like a lover after sweet rapture / like squires marching back from battles / like the earth on the last day of the grape harvest / like a star that disappears at dawn / like a person who has suddenly lost his shadow / like God who created the rose night and henbane / like God who longs to create new words / like God who must always create anew [. . .] // Our lives never return / we are dying in the ruins of illuminations / like the mayfly and like thunder and lightning // already lights are rising among the leaves of trees / already electrical wire is trembling in the snow / already the age of illuminated promenades is approaching / already souls will be sought out under the X-ray / like the ichthyosaur under the Neogene / already the golden raffia is approaching morning / already we are witnesses to the cinematograph / already our switches will be thrown / by the terrifying shadows of the gambler / already shouts and applause will rise / already Edison is bowing to his guests]

Edison reads as a self-generating riff. Roman Jakobson, a powerful influence on Nezval and other members of the Czech avant-garde, argues that Nezval's "childlike rhymes" create "a united front to keep the word from being treated like a fetish."[58] One could indeed argue that the obsessive repetition of certain sounds within words, to say nothing of the anaphoric repetitions that are so essential to Nezval's poetics, *is* fetishistic, though the fetish occurs on the word-root or phonemic level. Regardless, Jakobson's meaning is clear: he points out that Nezval's rhymes expand the associative range of his poetic utterance, frustrating our natural gravitation toward semantic clarity. As one sound builds off the sound it repeats, the repetitions begin to suggest Giorgio Agamben's definition of glossolalia, the intermediate space between sense and pure speech, "not the pure utterance of inarticulate sounds but rather a 'speech in glosses,' that is, a speech whose meaning is unknown."[59]

Rather than standing against the real, Nezval regards such haphazard collisions as the very substance of modern life, in which one always finds "a trembling"—*chvění*—the word Nezval uses in "Parrot on a Motorcycle" when he describes Poetism as a vector, "[t]he resolution of trembling and its directional." In the opening stanza of *Edison*, this trembling shows up in time and space: "the night *was trembling* like a prairie." As we find in the middle stanzas of "Red Bavaria," the lyric perspective is situated both outside and inside, with a view to the snow "over the monstrances of bars"—a blending of the sacred and profane worthy of Zabolotskii—and a simultaneous view of the tables, drinkers, and women inside the bar. One ultimately wonders whether in the word *monstrance* Nezval might not have heard an echo of *monstrum*, "monster." Even the women assume an animal appearance in their "dresses made of peacock feathers."

Edison presents this confusion as a universal condition, a merciless monism that conflates an urban bar with a prairie. This confusion is the root of the poem's existential melancholy: "yet here was something heavy that crushes / sorrow longing and anxiety from living and dying." The word Nezval uses to express this "anxiety," *úzkost*, derives from the adjective *úzký*, a spatial descriptor meaning "narrow" or "cramped." There is truly a sense in which the lyric subject, situated uncomfortably between life and death, is crushed by the world's chaos. Nezval adds a temporal component with *stesk*, "longing" or "nostalgia," suggesting the individual's inability to break with the past. That these lines are repeated as a mutable refrain throughout the poem intensifies their impact, not only because they remind the reader of the poem's existential theme, but also because the ontological condition they describe is an endlessly repetitive cycle, a constant reminder of the subject's entrapment.

Nezval thus poses a simple opposition between two ways of navigating the chaos of the modern city. The figure of Thomas Alva Edison, to whom the poem is dedicated, represents genius, the power to create a unique, inimitable course through the world's confusion. The creative persona, Edison the artist, is already evident in the dedication, before the poem proper begins:

Edisonovi
jenž stvořil víc světel
nežli Bůh sopek
vynálezci nové epochy
Američanu
hrdinovi XX. století
a všech věků
tuto malou odyseu
básník Evropan Čech
Vítězslav Nezval[60]

[To Edison / who created more lights / than God volcanoes / to the inventor of a new epoch / to an American / to a hero of the twentieth century / and all eras / this little odyssey / poet European Czech / Vítězslav Nezval]

In a world of infinite possibilities, the "inventor of a new epoch" finds his own course through infinite potential. The phrasing has a simple but elegant double meaning: Edison is representative of a new epoch, but it is also because of his efforts that a new epoch has been invented. Edison is, as Mandel'shtam says of himself, gardener and flower in one. He can navigate "this little odyssey" in a straight line, without wandering or leaving anything to chance. His foil is the unnamed gambler, the poem's antihero, whose currency is chance and pure association—the opposite of Edison's singular genius.

Though he would not mourn the passing of the old world, Nezval is nevertheless painfully aware that the new world heralded by the inventiveness of Thomas Alva Edison has not yet arrived. In the broader context of interwar letters, Edison stands as a figure not simply of the new life but of the point where the new life and the old intersect. Iurii Olesha captures Edison's symbolic representation of both modern ingenuity and a bygone time with his ironic description of Volodia Makarov, in his novella *Envy* (Zavist', 1927), as "the Edison of the new century."[61] By the time of his death in 1931, the same year as the completion of the Soviet Union's plan for national electrification, the real-life Edison's most significant inventions were already decades old, and while electric light had become a normal part of urban life in Central Europe, electrification remained a potent symbol of modern progress. Edison was, as Karel Čapek described him in an obituary, more an "alchemist" than a scientist, a characterization that resonates strongly with Nezval's poem. For Edison, according to Čapek, had struck a Faustian bargain for the birth of the Modern Age.[62] A *Faustian* bargain, because he had introduced a new world into an old one that had not yet died away.

Whether we see poems like "Red Bavaria" or *Edison* as marking a clean philosophical or aesthetic break from the past, in fact, is decisive for how we read the indeterminate wanderings of their respective lyric subjects. For if the point of these poems is to extoll the excitement of life in the modern polis for its own sake, then their intermediacy would seem to be an illusion that merely heightens the poems' drama. And there were certainly readers for whom a book like *Columns* marked a historical discontinuity, as when Boris Filippov describes Zabolotskii's first book as ushering in a new era, or when Anna Akhmatova rejected Filippov's assertion in her notebooks, remarking that "what really ended in 1929 was the shadow of freedom, and what began was not a 'Red Bavaria,' but Stalinism."[63] So does this work represent the beginning of an era, or the end of one? It serves both purposes effectively because the temporality of the urban wanderer blends past and future. Before we return—for we must always return—to Nezval's treatment of the Edison theme, the notion of the continuity of the old *within* the new deserves further elaboration, especially since it plays a key role in the early poetics of both Nezval and Zabolotskii.

Immaturity; or, Time Incommensurate with Itself

Immaturity—in a metaphysical sense, certainly, though just as often manifest simply as the persistence of childhood into one's adult years—is a consistent feature of intermediacy. The persistence of the old in the new appears in the prose works of Schulz and Platonov as the protagonists' incompleteness or psychological immaturity. In the poems of Miłosz and Mandel'shtam, past and future are bound together by what I have been calling (after Adorno) the "epic naivety" of the lyric subject. Similarly, Zabolotskii and Nezval were particularly adroit at conveying the *feeling* of the urban wanderer as that of being trapped *between* times.

In his poem "The New Life" (Novyi byt, 1927), for example, Zabolotskii portrays the Soviet leap into the future comically as an infant rushing into adulthood. Though set in Moscow, this Moscow is a strange conflation of the city and the country, of urban factories and idyllic fields, and eventually of outside and inside. Old women are running around grieving, we might assume, for the lost past, but there is no time to grieve, because "[t]he new life's already knocking at the door." Nor, it seems, is there any time to waste on such conventions of the old life as baptism or, more to the point, growing up: "an infant ostensibly grows into a man, / but the new life is at full gallop."

Выходит солнце над Москвой,
старухи бегают с тоской:
куда, куда идти теперь?
Уж новый быт стучится в дверь!
Младенец нагладко обструган,
сидит в купели как султан,
прекрасный поп поёт как бубен,

паникадилом осиян;
прабабка свечку выжимает,
младенец будто бы мужает,
но новый быт несётся вскачь—
младенец лезет окарач.
Ему не больно, не досадно,
ему назад не близок путь,
и звёзд коричневые пятна
ему наклеены на грудь.
Уж он и смотрит свысока
(в его глазах—два оселка),
потом пирует до отказу
в размахе жизни трудовой,
гляди! гляди! он выпил квасу,
он девок трогает рукой
и вдруг, шагая через стол,
садится прямо в комсомол.

А время сохнет и желтеет,
стареет папенька-отец
и за окошками в аллее
играет сваха в бубенец.
Ступни младенца стали шире,
от стали ширится рука,
уж он сидит в большой квартире,
невесту держит за рукав.
Приходит поп, тряся ногами,
в ладошке мощи бережёт,
благославить желает стенки,
невесте—крестик подарить . . .
—Увы!—сказал ему младенец,—
уйди, уйди, кудрявый поп,
я—новой жизни ополченец,
тебе-ж—один остался гроб!
Уж поп тихонько плакать хочет,
стоит на лестнице, бормочет,
уходит в рощу, плачет лихо;
младенец в хохот ударял—
с невестой шепчется: Шутиха,
скорей бы час любви настал!

Но вот знакомые скатились,
завод пропел: ура! ура!
и новый быт, даруя милость,
в тарелке держит осетра.

Варенье, ложечкой носимо,
успело сделаться свежо,
жених проворен нестерпимо,
к невесте лепится ужом,
и председатель на-отвале,
чете играя похвалу,
приносит в выборгском бокале
вино солдатское, халву,
и, принимая красный спич,
сидит на столике кулич.

Ура! Ура!—заводы воют,
картошкой дым под небеса,
и вот супруги на покое
сидят и чешут волоса.
И стало всё благоприятно:
приходит ночь, ушла обратно,
и за окошком через миг
погасла свечка-пятерик.[64]

[The sun is rising over Moscow, / old ladies are running with longing: / where, where to go now? / The new life's already knocking at the door! / An infant, clean-shaven, / is sitting in the [baptismal] font like a sultan, / the lovely priest is singing like a tambourine, / illuminated by the [church] chandelier; / the great-grandmother draws out a candle, / an infant ostensibly grows into a man, / but the new life is at full gallop—/ the infant is crawling on all fours. / He feels no pain, no irritation, / the way back is not nearby, / and the brown spots of stars / are affixed upon his chest. / He is already watching from on high / (in his eyes—two whetstones), / then he feasts until he's full / in the swing of the life of labor, / look! look! he's drunken kvass, / he touches girls by the hand / and suddenly, striding across the table, / he sits straight down in the Komsomol. // Yet time is drying out and yellowing, / [his] pappy-daddy grows old, / and past little windows on the lane / the marriage broker is ringing her bell. / The infant's step has grown broader, / his arm grows broader from steel, / he's already sitting in a large apartment, / he holds [his] bride by the sleeve. / The priest arrives, his legs shaking, / in [his] little palm he's guarding relics, / he wishes to bless the walls, / to gift the bride a little cross . . . /—Alas!—the infant said to the priest,— / get out, get out, you curly-headed priest, / I am the militiaman of the new life, / all that's left for you is the grave! / Now the priest wants to cry softly, / he stands on the staircase, he mumbles, / he goes out to the grove, he's crying bitterly; / the infant was breaking into a roar— / he whispers to his bride: "My joker, / soon the hour of love would be

> upon us!" // So then the acquaintances rolled up, / the factory sang out: hooray! hooray! / and the new life, showing its favor, / brings a sturgeon on a plate. / Preserves, carried on a little spoon, / managed to be made fresh, / the groom, unbearably nimble, / clings to [his] bride like a grass snake, / and the master of ceremonies, now full, / playing his praise to the couple, / in a Vyborg [wedding] goblet brings / soldier's wine, halva, / and, taking up [its] red speech, / on the little table stands a kulich. // Hooray! Hooray!—the factories call out, / a potato-like smoke up to the heavens, / and so the spouses at leisure / sit and brush [their] hair. / And everything has turned out well: night arrives, it's left again, / and an instant later, behind the little window, / the little five-point candle has gone out.]

The image of the new life moving swiftly forward, without regard for the ability of mere humans to keep up, suggests a broad understanding of the Russian word *byt*. While I have translated this term as "life," it actually refers to habitus more generally, the whole way of life of a community in a specific space and time. Since *byt* signifies the everyday as such, Zabolotskii picks up on the oddity of declaring a "new" one, tantamount to *a new everyday*. The concept is in tension with itself: novelty implies an identifiable break with what came before, whereas the everyday implies constancy and repetition. This internal tension is represented in Zabolotskii's poem by the "infant," who, as Masing-Delić points out, demonstrates the failure of the NEP-era city to achieve a clean break with the past: "These bloated babes are the generation that had received History's legacy, the opportunity to radically renew life on ground cleared by the Revolution, but had refused to shoulder historical responsibility, remaining infantile and immature. Instead of building the future, this generation reverted to the past in the form of NEP values; parasitically profiting from the resurrected past, they create nothing new themselves."[65] Though the infant is full of youthful energy, his maturation is supposed to progress slowly, in due time. But there is no time, Zabolotskii tells us, since "the new life is at full gallop." Just as the old women are thrown into a panic by the new life's sudden (and apparently unwelcome) arrival, sweeping them away into the past, the infant has no time to waste on growing up, for in the same movement the new life sweeps him into the future.

Masing-Delić is therefore correct when she goes on to argue that the infants in Zabolotskii's early poems are "hylics," materialists who remain unfinalized by material, such that the same incompleteness that appears as a source of freedom in Bakhtin takes a much darker turn in Zabolotskii: "But if in Bakhtin's carnival world, this is a positive and concrete act of communicating with reality, in Zabolotskii's city, the openness of the human body is a sign of terrifying incompleteness and the hallmark of mortality."[66] We should tread carefully over this last point. The "terrifying incompleteness" of Zabolotskii's figures is tragic, certainly, but it also enables them to perform and undergo the transformations that are the source of their power, as Masing-Delić also notes.[67] In "The New Life," Zabolotskii courts this tension and exploits it both to assert a vision and to travesty it in the same breath. Instead of the new life representing temporal continuity, here it is a temporal break quite literally on the other side of the door. Instead of the infant living through the durée of his own life, he must hurry to catch up with the new one.

At first, the intrusion of the new life demands that the infant very quickly assume the behaviors of adulthood: "look! look! he's drunken kvass, / he touches girls by the hand / and suddenly, striding across the table, / he sits straight down in the Komsomol." Though still an infant, the child acts like a man, drinking kvass, taking an erotic interest in women, and instantly becoming a *komsomolets,* a member of the All-Union Leninist Young Communist League. This does not mean, however, that the infant is growing up. On the contrary, Zabolotskii tells us explicitly in the poem's first stanza that an infant "ostensibly"—*budto by*—grows up, but there's no time for that here. Even as the child increasingly acts like an adult, the poet insists on referring to him as an infant. And yet this infant is "the militiaman of the new life," so it falls to him to drive out the priest who opens the poem, transforming the imperative "look! look!" into "get out, get out!"

In the poem's penultimate stanza, the infant is already enjoying his wedding feast, where the spiritual authority represented by the priest in the old life has been supplanted by a *kulich,* or traditional Easter round cake, somehow "taking up [its] red speech." At this, the poem's climactic moment, Zabolotskii offers a symbolic blending of old and new, a familiar holiday food that evokes—whether in language written in icing or yet another instance of hallucinatory conflation—Communist rhetoric. The poet seems to delight in the wide valence of the color red: in Orthodoxy it is associated with the blood and kingdom of Christ; in politics, it is emblematic of Socialism. And in "The New Life" it is both, since the religion of Soviet ideology blends syncretically with the Orthodox practices it would ostensibly supplant. This is all the more obvious in Zabolotskii's original version of the poem, which the publisher had found too risqué. There, it is not the round *kulich* that stands on the table, but *Il'ich*—that is, an image of Lenin.[68]

The new life is a guest at the infant's wedding feast, and its presence fosters a bacchanalian atmosphere that Zabolotskii conveys not only through the driving rhythm of run-on sentences and his signature juxtaposition of peculiar images but more importantly through equally peculiar locutions that frustrate our sense of linear temporality. The jam on the banquet table, for instance, "managed to be made fresh"—*uspelo sdelat'sia svezho*—suggesting either that it reversed time or, at the very least, came out fresh-made of its own accord. Like much of what we hear in these NEP-era lyrics, Zabolotskii's phrasing hints at a set expression from the world of commerce, namely, *sdelat'sia srochnym,* or "to mature," as one might say of a bond—the kind of private investment that was common under the New Economic Policy and yet clearly antithetical to the new life that Soviet Communism promised.

The infant, meanwhile, appears several times in Zabolotskii's poems from this period. Notably, his poem "Immaturity" (Nezrelost', 1928) offers much the same content as "The New Life," only with an inverted temporal structure: instead of the infant racing into manhood in order to experience adult pleasures, in "Immaturity" a seductress suddenly materializes—quite literally out of thin air—to tempt the infant with sex, but the child refuses to mature. Such reversal, orchestrating an elaborate scheme in one poem only to flip it over later, is yet another instantiation of the "undoing" or *obratimost'* that is symptomatic of the literature of intermediacy. In Zabolotskii, these reversals work much the same as they do for Platonov, Schulz, Mandel'shtam, and Miłosz. By pairing every claim or structure with its equally potent counterclaim or counterstructure, the author neutralizes the possibility of progress or escape. In *Columns,* there can be no movement toward definition, the future, or individuality without a corresponding movement in the opposite direction, toward immaturity, the past, or the collective. In a less heterodox Soviet text, a strictly Einsteinian approach might paint an unambiguously materialist, well-defined textual universe, as Lev Nikulin does in his 1932 novel *Time, Space, Motion* (Vremia, prostranstvo, dvizhenie), a text that revels in its *lack* of ambiguity and concludes with the exclamation, "Greetings, maturity! Beautiful, rational, and hopeful maturity!"[69]

Zabolotskii's approach, by contrast, eschews maturity as insistently as it resists rationality. The poet shows the old worldview colliding inconclusively with the new, a collision that creates only fractured glimpses of the world, a textual orchestration of what Filonov's Analytic Art produces visually. In fact, Zabolotskii's "The New Life" calls to mind Sofi'ia Zaklikovskaia's 1927 painting *The Old and New Life* (Staryi i novyi byt), in which past and future are mashed beautifully together (figure 4.3). We might reasonably suppose that Zabolotskii knew this painting, which Zaklikovskaia produced at the same time as Zabolotskii was working on his similarly titled poem, since the poet and the painter were friends and both disciples of Filonov in the 1920s.

In a brief essay on Zabolotskii's legacy, the poet Ol'ga Sedakova speculates that he may not have achieved the fame of many of his contemporaries because "the poetic world of Zabolotskii did not take on any kind of final, precise completeness"—*zavershennost',* which we could just as easily translate as "maturity."[70] Indeed, the young Zabolotskii's poetic universe is predicated on incompleteness, on the frustration of the reader's attempts to define his world. These poems reflect an existence continuously in flux, locked in eternal transformation, where the very notions of "completeness" and "maturity" are revealed as laughably naive and held up for ridicule. As we have seen

Figure 4.3. Sof'ia Zaklikovskaia, *The Old and New Life* (Staryi i novyi byt, 1927; oil on canvas). *Paintings of 1930s-1920s [sic]/ Zhivopis' 20–30kh godov,* ed. A. M. Muratov (St. Petersburg: Khudozhnik RSFSR, 1991). Original in the collection of the Russian State Museum, St. Petersburg.

most dramatically in Schulz, and as we will see in Vítězslav Nezval's follow-up to *Edison*, continuous transformation is not necessarily a laughing matter.

Nezval's Sign of the Times

Instead of the bright world of tomorrow, Zabolotskii and Nezval's early poems cast the individual into endless metamorphoses, chaos in the half-hearted guise of order, and dying without death. These themes are strongly intimated in *Edison*—in the recurring suggestion of suicide, for example, as well as in the interplay of the gambler and the inventor—but Nezval delineates them even more starkly in *Time Signal* (Signál času, 1931), a companion piece to the earlier poem. Here, Nezval lays bare just how frightening spatial-temporal collapse can be.

Naše životy jsou tvrdé krajíce
Každodenně trochu umírajíce
modelujem svoje embryální hlavy
jednou tomu řekli nemoc jindy zdraví
je to tentýž měsíc vždycky jiná čtvrt

Naše životy jsou sto let dlouhá smrt
[. . .]

zmocnil se mne divný nostalgický zmatek
který způsobily dráty od sluchátek

spletené jak modré cévy bez krve
všiml jsem si toho dneska po prve
rychle zapojil jsem kontakt přijimače

Pojala mne úzkost hazardního hráče
[. . .]

noc je zířivá jak Etna která soptí
v tom však uslyšel jsem stakatový hlas

Z pražské hvězdárny se hlásil k slovu čas
[. . .]

Deset hodin orloj na radnici bije
z přítomnosti je už vráska historie
není absolutna v této panice
všecko splývá nevíš kde jsou hranice
vyvolávám ztěží matné snímky dění
pranic netrvá a všecko je i není
byli stavitelé sfing a pyramid
byli kupčíci jež vyhnal z chrámu Žid
byly amfiteatry a katakomby
kněží nevolníci dusičnaté bomby
lidé poslouchali slepě vladaře
byly doby kdy je vezli na káře
bylo bezvládí a byla éra států
byla diktatura proletariátu
přijde čas kdy zmizel pojem rodiny

není věčnosti jsou jenom hodiny

Signál zanikl jak slzy příliš vřelé
vystřídal jej hlučný pozdrav hlasatele
je to hydra jež má statisíce hlav

očekáváš s hrůzou pořad denních zpráv

Vidím Rusko Balkán Anglii a Čínu
[. . .]

Kolik událostí tolik různých not
je mně líto kdož nenalezli bod
na kterém už není ostrých protikladů
který dává nový hlubší smysl hladu
na němž rovnoběžky sbíhají se zas

je to klam však lze tím umlčeti čas
[. . .]

A pak nemám míti strach že někdo chroptí
svět je Etna v níž to stále uvnitř soptí
brzy přijde čas a láva vyrazí
tisíc požárů se vznítí od sazí
[. . .]

srdce slábne slábne avšak ještě buší
chtěl bys beze zbytku proměnit svou duši
v nové tvary v nové věcné bytosti
Všichni tvůrci umírají s lítostí!
[. . .]

V knihovně je tisíc nedočtených stránek
aniž zavřels knihu překvapil tě spánek
zájem o sto věcí vlídně utuchá
rozplývá se starost tíseň předtucha
mozek spí a srdce mechanicky bije
sen tě vede panoptikem poesie
kterou uvědomili si nemnozí
včleněn v tisíceré metamorfosy
ztrácíš zbytek staré štvané osobnosti
slavní vědátoři jak jste v spánku prostí
strážník tancuje a sloup tě zatýká
mizí všecka stará problematika
prožil osud květin vlků lvů a sobů
umíráš a ihned zase vstáváš z hrobu
malé gesto z kraje v kraj tě přenese
a tak strašně nerad probouzeje se
[. . .]

Pocit oříšek ty rozbíjíš mu hlavu
snové kosatce z nichž lisujeme šťávu
která zachvátí tě jako alkohol
miliony cest a jednu z nich si zvol
všecky vedou lidským labyrintem k smrti
měním se jak mění měsíc svoje čtvrti
je to stále tatáž bílá substance
chorál za rakví a píseň do tance
slina polibku a trpká slina hoře
křehkost fontány a kanonáda moře
chanson plískanic a vůně soboty
balet propadlišť i démant nahoty

Odpusťte mi dobrá příští pokolení
žil jsem v době kdy se rytmus stále mění[71]

[The lives we are living are solid slices / Dying each day by little bits and pieces / we give our embryonic heads a form / whether taken for health or taken for harm / no matter the quarter the moon's still the same // Our lives are a death that's a hundred years long [. . .] // then I was gripped by strange nostalgic disorientation / it was telephone cords that caused this conflation / all tangled up like bloodless blue veins / I caught sight of this today for the very first time / quickly I ran to hook up the receiver // I was seized by the dread of the gambler [. . .] // night is brilliant like an Etna which erupts / but in this I heard a staccato voice // From the Prague observatory time declared itself to the word [. . .] // The clock [orloj] on the Town Hall strikes ten / the present has now become a wrinkle of history / there is no absolute in this panic / everything is tangled you don't know where the borders are / I develop barely faded photos of events / nothing at all lasts and everything is and is not / there were the builders of sphinxes and pyramids / there were the profiteers the Jew drove from the temple / there were amphitheaters and catacombs / priests serfs nitrogen bombs / people listened blindly to the ruler / there were times when they were carried on a cart / there was lawlessness and there was an era of states / there was a dictatorship of the proletariat / there will come a time when the concept of family will vanish // there is no eternity there are only hours [clocks] / The signal has faded like tears too sincere / It's been switched out for the newsreader's noisy greeting / it's a hydra with hundreds of thousands of heads // you await the slate of daily news with horror // I see Russia the Balkans England and China [. . .] / There are as many notes as events / I'm sorry for those who haven't found the point / within which there are no longer sharp distinctions / which gives a new deeper meaning to hunger / in which parallels converge again // it's a lie but one can use it to silence time [. . .] // And then I do not have to fear that someone is expiring / the world is an Etna inside of which it is always erupting / soon the time will come and the lava will break through / a thousand fires will be ignited from the soot [. . .] // the heart weakens it weakens and yet still beats / you'd like to transform your soul without remnant / into new shapes into new material beings / All creators die with regret! [. . .] // In the library there are a thousand unread pages / without your having closed the book sleep surprised you / occupation with a hundred things amiably subsides / worry distress apprehension melt away / the brain sleeps and the heart mechanically beats / sleep carries you in a wax museum of poetry / which few have remarked / incorporated in thousandfold metamorphoses / you lose what's left of your old goaded personhood / famous eggheads like you are simple in sleep / the constable dances and the column seizes you / the entire old problematic fades away / he's survived the fate of flowers wolves lions and reindeer / you die and right away rise from the grave / a small gesture will carry you from region

> to region / and you waking up so terribly unhappy [. . .] // A feeling a nut you smash its head / dreamed-up irises from which we press the juice / that engulfs you like alcohol / millions of roads and pick one / all lead by a human labyrinth to death / I change just as the moon changes its quarters / it is always the same white substance / a funereal hymn and a song for dancing / saliva of a kiss and the acrid saliva of grief / fragility of a fountain and the cannonade of the sea / chanson of sleet and aromas of Saturday / a ballet of trapdoors and the diamond of nudity // Forgive me good future generations / I lived in an era when the rhythm was constantly changing.]

Nezval started writing *Time Signal* after reading a newspaper report that Thomas Alva Edison had fallen ill. The poem, then, is an elegy written in anticipation of the subject's demise. In letters to František Borový, his publisher, Nezval suggests that he had composed the poem before actual news of Edison's death reached him, then continued to make adjustments to the poem as he reflected on Edison's death after the fact.[72] In this way, the composition straddles the actual event to which it refers, a fact that Nezval augments by subtitling it "A Panachyda for Edison" (Panichida za Edisona). (A *panachyda* is an Orthodox funeral rite consisting of a long prayer for the departed to be spoken after decease but before burial.) The poem's subtitle also refers us to an earlier text, namely, "Panychida" [*sic*], by Vilém Závada (1905–1982). Published in 1927 and dedicated to Nezval, the poem is a lament for those who died in World War I, and it helps signal Poetism's turn toward recognizing the tragedy of interconnection.

Though *Time Signal* extends the meditation on change that Nezval had started with *Edison*, here the tone is markedly darker. Unlike the lyric "I" of *Edison*, who manages to praise genius despite the sense that he is caught in a chain of endless transformation, the speaker of *Time Signal* finds no pleasure in his failure to break free from existence. At best, he can turn the melancholic lament that serves for the opening line and refrain of *Edison*—"Our lives are woeful like lamentation"—and transform it into an expression of time's infinite divisibility: "The lives we are living are solid slices / Dying each day by little bits and pieces." Slices of what? Of time, certainly, but also of the greater totality of existence. What is most intriguing here is the adjective *tvrdé*, "hard" or "solid," since hardness suggests greater definition than the theme of mutability will allow. This, however, is the root of the poet's despair. The life of the individual is solid enough to be recognized as a life, but the "slice" is not a whole unto itself; there is no "my life" here, only the collective "our lives." "No matter the quarter the moon's still the same," Nezval declares, and an unexpected stanza break allows us a moment to ponder this emblem of internal dynamism, of difference within the same, before he completes the couplet: "Our lives are a death that's a hundred years long."

In *Time Signal*, Nezval challenges us to consider the metaphysical implications of technological synchronization, one of the most momentous innovations, so to speak, of the Industrial Age. Many of the poem's images, thrown together according to an associative principle already hinting at Nezval's burgeoning interest in Surrealism, suggest timepieces. Even the moon that closes the opening stanza should remind us of a clock, since Czech *čtvrt*, "quarter," can refer to a lunar phase or a fifteen-minute interval, just as it does in English. (Czech *měsíc* also means both "moon" and "month.") While the hands are always moving around the face of the clock, Nezval seems to say, the clock itself remains unchanged, a symbol of dynamic flux within an immutable Absolute.

In a poem whose central dilemma is the fact that time *has* been defined—and that it is now possible to listen to the chimes of synchronized clocks or, better yet, to pick up one's telephone and learn the exact time—this may seem a surprising revelation. And yet the precision of modern chronography causes Nezval's speaker real consternation. He knows from his own experience of time that such clean definitions are untrustworthy, that the intertwined telephone cords mirror the infinite tangle of vessels within our own bodies: "then I was gripped by strange nostalgic disorientation / it was telephone cords that caused this conflation." The situation that Nezval portrays here refers us back to the existential problem posed by the shift from Bergsonian time to Einsteinian relativity: Does our time belong to us, or is it something that connects us inextricably to one another? If we are deeply interconnected within time, then how individual can we be? Modern technology allows connections across space that, in turn, trigger unsettling connections across time. In this regard, we may recall Mandel'shtam's tragic play with telephones and nostalgia in "I returned to my city . . . ," written only a few months earlier.

As soon as the poem's speaker hooks up his telephone, he finds himself "seized by the dread of the gambler," Edison's foil from Nezval's earlier poem. But instead of the speaker watching the gambler cast himself from the bridge, as he does in *Edison*, the telephone wire connects him to this doomed, melancholic double. For Nezval, as for Mandel'shtam, interconnection implicates time not only in individual and collective experience but in the very essence of the poetic word: "From the Prague observatory time declared itself to the word." Set off portentously as its own stanza, this line's Czech phrasing, *se hlásil k slovu čas*, may be understood quite conventionally as the announcement of standard time—it completes the rhyme of *stakatový hlas*, the "staccato voice" that announces the hour from the Štefánik Observatory, which opened on Petřin Hill in 1928—or it may be taken to mean that time has *claimed* the word, in the sense of time having seized or spoken for language, or even of astronomical observation having served to reduce time to a communicative unit. In a single line, we find an emblem for the power of science to define something as fluid and slippery as time, but we may also come away with the opposite reading, the sense that the word—poetic utterance as such—is overfull with potential and has lost its specificity. What is true of the Absolute must also apply to a poetic utterance that reflects it. If the word can mean everything, it also means nothing.

As the speaker becomes increasingly aware of his "nostalgic disorientation," the poem's creative consciousness comes into greater conflict with itself. The fifteenth-century *orloj,* or astronomical clock, on Prague's medieval Town Hall strikes ten. Instead of bringing us back to earth, however, this specification of time creates a small ripple, "a wrinkle of history" that shocks us out of "the present," since "there is no absolute in this panic," "everything is tangled you don't know where the borders are," "nothing at all lasts and everything is and is not." This version of the Absolute is a chaos of interconnected parts, Schulz's "extreme monism of substance."

Time Signal, like *Edison* before it, is a lyric unveiling of the deep interconnection of space, time, matter, and energy. Prague's astronomical clock itself embodies this unity of the cosmic and the local. It features a conventional clock dial above, while its lower section describes the movements of the heavenly bodies. At the top of the hour, mechanical figures warn onlookers against vanity: a sculpture of a man turns toward his mirror as a skeleton raises his hourglass. In thinking about how this structure connects the human experience of time with the cosmic indifference to same, Nezval was undoubtedly influenced by contemporaneous representations, such as the one produced by Josef Čapek, Karel Čapek's older brother and sometime collaborator, for Bohuslav Reynek's second poetry collection, *Fish Scales* (Rybí šupiny, 1922).[73] Nezval, who in 1937 published a brief study of the elder Čapek's poems, was likely familiar with his image of the clock tower, its face so prominent as to appear to be moving off the tower and into the foreground (figure 4.4).[74] The clock dial is counterbalanced on the viewer's left by a large star, suggesting the cosmic or astronomical dimension of time.[75] But with the minute and hour hands of equal size and the interval between them noticeably blank on the clock face, it is impossible for us to tell what time it is. Most importantly, the urban space appears to fold inward around the clock tower. Like the speaker of *Time Signal*, the viewer does not know "where the borders are."

Developing "barely faded photos of events" scattered widely across time and space, the poet's consciousness expands rapidly as well. Film arises yet again as a figure for memory and temporal interconnection; we are not to assume that the poem's speaker is actually developing film, if for no other reason than that the images he mentions include "the builders of sphinxes and pyramids" and "the profiteers the Jew drove from the temple," "barely faded" despite their antiquity, a frenetic mishmash of times and places, "priests serfs nitrogen bombs"—in a word, the old life colliding with the new. Thus Nezval, ever attentive to words that can expand the range of his metaphors, deploys the Czech *vyvolávat,* "to develop" film, though the word's primary definition would be "to summon," as one would a memory or a spirit, which is precisely what the poet sets out to do in his lyrical unveiling. "I see Russia the Balkans England and China," he soon declares,

Figure 4.4. Josef Čapek, illustration for Bohuslav Reynek's *Fish Scales* (Rybí šupiny, 1922; block print). Bohuslav Reynek, *Fish Scales* (Ann Arbor: Michigan Slavic Publications, 2001).

and we might easily think of Zabolotskii's soccer ball hurtling "across seas and rivers, / expanses, squares, snows." What is interesting about his perusal of past events is that most of these images also contain the core of their own undoing. There were moneychangers in the Temple, surely, but there was also a Savior who drove them out. There were amphitheaters where people congregated for their entertainment, and there were catacombs where they congregated in death. "Lawlessness" and "an era of states" go hand in hand, though they are opposites; the same could be said of "dictatorship" and "proletariat."[76] Each of these is a piece of a constantly changing whole, and it is therefore only natural that one thing should feed into another in a chain of continuous transformation.

As the poem goes on, Nezval shades this transformation with temporal, geological, and biological implications, beginning with the theme of night turning to day that runs through both *Time Signal* and *Edison*. Contradictory notions shape and feed into one another, as parallels converge again / it's a lie but one can use it to silence time." Once relativized, these notions are infinitely mutable, if only we succeed in finding a perspective where the contradiction dissolves.

One such point would be the hyperbolic geometry developed in the mid-nineteenth century by the Russian mathematician Nikolai Lobachevskii and subsequently employed by Einstein in describing special relativity, to which Nezval slyly alludes with his "parallels" that "silence time": parallel lines can converge in Lobachevskii's framework, and while this fact contradicts everyday experience, it paves the way for Einstein's revolutionary revision of the geometry of space-time. The reader may wonder why one would wish to silence time in the first place, and the answer lies in Nezval's untiring invocation of cyclicality and repetition. Night and day feed into each other; parallel lines must run together in order for them to split apart again; there must be both silence and timelessness in order for us to hear the chime of the clock tower.

Because Nezval's cosmogony subsists in the repetitive coalescence of time and matter and the sudden emergence of fleeting, singular events and entities, there is in effect no reason for him to mourn Edison's passing. The elegiac project self-destructs, since the poet is merely mourning the transformations to which both he and the deceased belong in equal share: "And then I do not have to fear that someone is expiring / the world is an Etna inside of which it is always erupting." The consubstantiality of people and things appears here in an elemental light. As "an Etna," the world is dynamic, even violent flux disguised as constancy. Similarly, we can read the poet's declaration that "soon the time will come" not as the arrival of "the time," of the promised future, but simply as the precipitation of a singular event—"soon . . . *time* will come"—which will then be reabsorbed into chaos. "You'd like to transform your soul without remnant," he remarks, "into new shapes into new material beings"; we would like to maintain a consciousness that observes what becomes of our matter once it is no longer "ours" in the strict sense. While the "extreme monism of substance" guarantees these transformations, it simultaneously limits the intellect's access to them, which is why "[a]ll creators die with regret."

In a manner reminiscent of Bakhtin's "eventness," in *Time Signal* Nezval insists that the world outside human time is pure potentiality. And just as Bakhtin's "eventness" seems to disinherit the author as a creative agent, this view of time threatens to undermine the entire model of genius Nezval has put forward in *Edison*, since it takes agency out of the hands of the individual and attributes singularity to the event per se. Though Nezval and his Edison would like to use transformation to stave off death, death is a transformation that acts on the inventor, who is the instrument, rather than the agent, of transformation. As Antonín Jelínek notes, death does not "change or influence the meaning and value of the life of the one who digs in and creates. The end of the inventor's life in [*Time Signal*] is not an image of metaphysical horror before death, but an image of sadness over a finished life-work and over unfulfilled plans, unrealized possibilities."[77]

Nezval's vision of Edison's death is thus also a vision of rebirth. And if that rebirth is melancholic, it is not only because death marks "unfulfilled . . . possibilities," as Jelínek suggests, but also because it reifies Being as an inescapable chain of metamorphoses: "incorporated in thousandfold metamorphoses / you lose what's left of your old goaded personhood / [. . .] / you die and right away rise from the grave." Maintaining the opposition between dream and waking life already established in *Edison*, Nezval imagines Edison's death as complete absorption into dream life, where distinctions and definitions break down and we are in closest contact with the primordial chaos. Death does not free us from the "thousandfold metamorphoses" of Being. On the contrary, death is the mechanism driving these transformations. Through death, the material of one's body serves new purposes, and the consequences of one's efforts, and even the remnants of one's energies, find their way into the living world. As Nezval puts it elsewhere in *Time Signal,* "the soul's thread transformed into a cord / gives life to millions of phones."[78]

Toward the end of the poem, the pacing of the poet's associations becomes increasingly frenzied as he turns away from Edison and concentrates on the inescapability of these changes. Shifting among the first, second, and third person, Nezval blurs the boundary between the poem's speaker and his ostensible subject. Death is posited as an inevitable, if trivial, change: inevitable, because all roads "lead by a human labyrinth to death"; trivial, because—and here Nezval returns to the moon as an emblem of dynamism—"I change just as the moon changes its quarters / it is always the same white substance." There follows a litany of free associations not unlike those we see throughout Nezval's oeuvre.[79] But this barrage of images does not cancel the constancy of change or the fact that change cannot negate the consubstantiality of all things, "always the same white substance." In begging the forbearance of "good future generations" as the poem reaches its conclusion, Nezval does not wish to be released from time—this would be impossible—but notes that "I lived in an era when the rhythm was constantly changing." A poem that opened as an attempt to account for the age ends up apologizing for the age's ultimate unaccountability.

Like Dante in the *Commedia,* Nezval and Zabolotskii take us on walking tours of urban spaces that also reflect the soul of the lyric subject. And because these spaces are constructed as intermediate zones, they reflect intermediate souls, individuals lost in a boundlessness that had initially promised them freedom. In this way, the implications of spatial-temporal intermediacy in interwar literature reach to the very core of what constitutes subjective experience and its representation in literature. Intermediacy implies a deep, often tortured interconnection between Self and Other, finitude and the Absolute, reality and myth. But when we are talking about the experience of Being, we should also bear in mind the artificiality—and perhaps also the necessity—of such divisions. "The possible is seen as abstract and vague, while the real is seen as thick and weighty, as 'being' or 'existing,'" Henri Lefebvre notes. "But the possible enters the real. It appears there: it announces and invokes its presence within it, and then sets about destroying it and negating it."[80] The possible within the real is beauty in destruction, Schelling's formulation that *Schönheit ist das Unendliche endlich dargestellt*—"Beauty is the infinite made finite."

By this standard, however, intermediacy resists beauty. For unfinalizability corrupts definition from within, such that what initially appears fully formed is thwarted by its dynamic, ill-formed core—its *immaturity*. "Herein lies the ultimate metaphysical problematic of life," the Bergsonian philosopher Tomáš Trnka announced in 1923: "that it is a continuum, without boundaries, and at the same time a delimited 'I.'"[81] This problematic will be the focus of the last chapter.

Chapter 5

When You're Not Really Feeling Yourself: Immaturity and the Double (Karel Čapek, Witold Gombrowicz, Richard Weiner)

I have hardly anything in common with myself . . .

—Franz Kafka

When Czesław Miłosz describes the 1930s as a period of "delayed maturity," he is reiterating some of the central questions for the authors of intermediacy. Do we experience Being as a succession of finite boundaries, or do we enjoy direct communion with the Absolute? Is it possible for a lack of definition—whether historical, as in myth, or developmental, as in immaturity—to exist *within* definition (history, maturity)? Is the thinking subject a singular, delimited entity, or does he contain infinite potential?

Karel Čapek responds to these questions in a remarkable image that appears halfway through his novel *The Meteor* (Povětroň, 1933–34)—and thus also at the exact midpoint of the three-novel sequence that has come to be known as his "noetic trilogy." The Clairvoyant, as one of the novel's central characters is called, is asked to provide a précis of his craft, of his particular way of experiencing Being, to which he responds:

> "It's as if you'd filmed a person's life from his birth to this moment, and then you placed all those images one on top of the other and projected all of them simultaneously. You say: what a jumble! Yes, because the present blends with the past, everything overlaps, and all that remains is the shape of the life, something indescribable and exceedingly personal: something like a personal aura, in which everything is deposited—" His nose became tragically petrified. "Everything, *even the future,*" he gasped.[1]

Like Mandel'shtam, Čapek lifts his cinematic description of durée from Bergson, whose work he knew well. For the Clairvoyant, time is a continuum; the individual frames suggested by the simile simply expose the limitations of the technology in capturing that continuity. This continuum also has a particular shape—a "personal aura"—that can be intuited by the attentive observer. Actual history, experiential reality as it might be known in the discrete moments of a person's life, is of secondary importance. Instead, the Clairvoyant recombines individual moments in order to concentrate on "all of them simultaneously," to see the "shape of the life." Čapek refers to that shape with the word *tvar,* conventionally a physical or geometric "shape," but etymologically linked to *tvář,* a "visage" or "face," and the resonance is effective: the Clairvoyant's art is to intuit the essence of the other person, to reconstruct another's identity by inserting himself into it.

When we regard identity as perfect self-equivalence, the Clairvoyant's method seems paradoxical. But the dialogic interaction implied by intersubjectivity is inherently paradoxical, since it is constructed in the middle ground between two opposite worldviews. The first recognizes each thinking subject as a self-contained universe unto himself, a finite, self-identical being. The second, monistic worldview negates individuality altogether, since all people and things belong to the same substance, which means that individual existence is an illusion. The Clairvoyant, however, stakes out a middle position: the individual remains an individual, but his existence is meaningful only insofar as he is open to contact with the Other. The discomfort of intermediacy lies in how the thinking subject navigates the straits between finitude and the Absolute, which is also necessarily a question of how the Self is constituted in space-time.

This chapter examines the dialectical movement by which the individual's sense of incompleteness, or immaturity, leads to overdefinition, which is most frequently manifest as doubling. Čapek leads our way into these dark woods. His colleague Richard Weiner and the Polish novelist Witold Gombrowicz will meticulously fail to lead us out.

Karel Čapek versus the "Ultimate Metaphysical Problematic"

Most of the writers discussed in this book achieved lasting fame late in their careers or posthumously. Quite often, they have been described as being "ahead of their time," yet this could not be further from the truth: they were decisively of their time and place, though perhaps in ways that have demanded some historical distance for us to appreciate. Unlike the writers to whom I compare him, Karel Čapek was hardly obscure. By the mid-1920s, he had already achieved international fame with his play *Rossum's Universal Robots* (also known as *R. U. R.,* 1920), which introduced the neologism *robot* (his brother Josef's invention), premiered in New York and London in 1923, and in 1924 became the first theatrical production from an independent Czechoslovakia to be staged in Paris.[2] This success led to the quick translation and international distribution of many of Čapek's subsequent works.

Čapek's beginnings were far more modest. His father, a doctor, was the son of farmers, and Čapek was born in Malé Svatoňovice, a small village near what is today the Czech border with Poland, in 1890. Raised in nearby Úpice, he attended high school in Hradec Králové, Brno, and finally Prague, where he began studying philosophy at Charles University. The trajectory of his university education then bears an odd similarity to that of Osip Mandel'shtam. In the winter of 1910, when Mandel'shtam had just returned to St. Petersburg from Heidelberg, Čapek was continuing his study of philosophy at Berlin's Frederick William University (now Humboldt University). He spent the following spring at the Sorbonne, which Mandel'shtam had left in 1909. Unlike Mandel'shtam, who never completed his university education, Čapek received his doctorate in philosophy in 1915 with a dissertation on "The Objective Method in Aesthetics with Regard to Fine Arts" (Objektivní metoda v estetice se zřením k výtvarnému umění).

The tension between subjective experience and objective reality, and by extension between particularity and the Absolute, would be a lifelong preoccupation for Čapek, especially as it relates to the problem of representation, whether to ourselves or for others.[3] In 1922, he published his first full-length novel, *The Absolute Factory* (Továrna na absolutno), a tragicomedy in which a technological breakthrough creates unlimited free energy, but the global euphoria is cut short when the by-product, little pockets of the Absolute, swallows up large parts of the world. In February of the same year, just a few months before the disagreements between Einstein and Bergson assumed an air of public theater at the Société de Philosophie in Paris, Čapek published one of the longer installments of his essayistic sequence *A Critique of Words* (Kritika slov), in which he takes aim at some of the most vexing Czech clichés of his time, such as "Ism" (Ismus), "Mereness" (Pouhost), "Relative" (Relativní), "Experience" (Zkušenost), and "Conflict, Struggle" (Boj, zápas). Čapek takes issue with how an age of mass communication reduces language—and, by extension, the things to which words refer—to slogans and misrepresentations. Although he insists consistently on keeping language accessible to the general reader, oversimplification is antithetical to his theory of the word, which, in its artistic function, subsists in its broadly interconnected multiplicity, in the accumulation of meanings from associations, etymologies, and historical usage. Čapek's philosophy of language, as Jindřich Toman points out, eschews the abstraction of scientific linguistics and privileges the word as "a common possession of the speaker's community."[4] Perhaps this is why, in his brief discourse on "Mereness," Čapek assumes the voice of God, who chastises Adam for the act of naming described in Genesis 2:20: "Adam, in no thing have I ever created any kind of mereness; everything is multifaceted and auspicious, full of possibilities and folds. Adam, the fault rests in your eyes: from my tiger you have made a mere beast, from my matter mere materialism, from my reality mere realism—poor Adam!"[5]

Čapek laments the impoverishment of language or, more accurately, the misuse of language to impoverish the reality to which it refers. "Mereness" in language corrupts the "multifaceted" nature of existence. As in Mandel'shtam's poem "The Age," the invocation of the tiger resonates with William Blake's lyric expression of an existence that defies simple definition. For Čapek, such definitions also have a distinctly ideological overtone: as God chastises Adam—and, by extension, the New Man—for his reductionism, Čapek deforms the standard Czech suffix *-ismus* into the international form *-ism*. The New Man does not turn matter into *materialismus*, a variegated philosophical worldview, but rather into *materialism,* a craven effort to define the world. Čapek draws this effect out by conspicuously using words of Czech origin (*hmota*, "matter"; *skutečnost*, "reality") to represent the richness of the world, while Latinate terms (*materiál*, *realita*) align more easily with the–*isms* he derides ("materialism," "realism").

Of equal interest for understanding Čapek's approach to language is what he then does with the word "Relative," one of the philosophical key words of his era:

> "Relative" is a wise [i.e., wise-sounding] and modern word; values and truths are relative, as are space and time, concepts and certainties, science and human experience: in short, everything is relative, even absolute alcohol: son, if you want to be wise, believe absolutely that everything is relative. [. . .] Forgive me—I don't wish to play with words, but if I said that everything is relative, then I've let slip something quite un-relativistic. For the sinful word "everything" reeks of stubborn and hidden absolutism.[6]

Čapek's satirical potshot against the same "multifaceted" quality he had praised in the world moments before might very well have pleased the man who had made relativity such a staple of interwar discourse. After all, Einstein's insistence that relativity theory describes an objective world, and that it therefore has nothing to do with the moral or conceptual relativism with which it was often conflated, had been frequently ignored by those who were unwilling or unable to give his ideas serious consideration. Not that Einstein would agree with Čapek's conclusions. Čapek rejects the totality of the Absolute, the "stubborn and hidden" everything whose fundamental nature Einstein endeavored to describe. Over and against Einstein's monistic allegiances, Čapek proposes a compromise between the defined and the undefined, between the stable and the relative, and he does so in strikingly Einsteinian language, concluding that "[there are] truths that do not lie [and] beings that are perfect and infinite."[7] Against Einstein's finite yet unbounded universe, Čapek perhaps unwittingly posits individual "beings" that are infinite and perfect. Whether one is speaking of general concepts or specifically of the individual's passage through space and time, Čapek insists on a middle ground between strict definition and formlessness. His relativity is real, but it is *not* absolute, since there always remains a point of stability, not "merely" as an inertial frame of reference (as Einstein would insist) but as a universal standard.[8]

Such vacillation between finitude and boundlessness, between the individual and the collective, and ultimately between the universal and the relative has deep roots in Čapek's early philosophical career, in which he sought applications of Pragmatism to the imaginative arts, even to those areas of avant-garde activity abstracted far from the concerns of the everyday.[9] In his conversations with Tomáš Garrigue Masaryk (1850–1937), the professor of philosophy who had brought Nikolai Lossky to Prague and the first president of an independent Czechoslovakia, Čapek gives due consideration to the interplay between scientific or empirical knowledge and myth, noting that "we literary folk can't let go of mythic-ness [mytičnost]," to which the philosopher-statesman responds:

> Nor, sir, can we philosophers. The poet differs from the scientist and the philosopher insofar as philosophy has quite appropriately been called a novel of ideas; the poet and artist think in images, the scientist and philosopher in concepts. And yet the scientist can in no way dispense with imagination, or, to borrow Goethe's terminology: exact imagination [fantazie exaktní]. The spiritual evolution of the individual and society consists in the gradual abandonment of simpleminded myth and the adoption of a critical understanding. The mythic [mytickost] yields to science, but traces of myth remain in science and new myths are made—what can I say, man is a mythophile.[10]

In an accidental echo of Bruno Schulz's remarks about the "mythicization of reality," Masaryk suggests—and Čapek seems to agree—that within the practical definitions provided by modern science there remains a nonempirical tendency toward the timelessness of legend. The philosopher and the literary artist share the task of negotiating this collision of boundaries with boundlessness.[11]

For Čapek, the task of negotiating between definition and boundlessness in no way abandons the progress narrative that is so essential to Western modernity, and that assumes particular gravity in a geopolitical entity struggling to define itself, as was the case in interwar Czechoslovakia. Whether one is speaking of the individual or society, Masaryk suggests, progress means "the gradual abandonment of simpleminded myths." And yet fantasies and myths will remain an essential feature of any human discourse, a core of antimodernity within modernity, of "the old surviving in the new," of timelessness within time. It is therefore wholly appropriate that Čapek entitles this portion of his conversations with Masaryk "Noetics: A Theory of Knowledge" (Noetika—teorie poznání).

In Western philosophy, "noetics" refers generally to an act of mind through which the thinking subject comes to an understanding of the world. Notably for Husserl, who read Čapek's conversations with Masaryk shortly before his own death, "noetics" refers to an intentional thought act, the imposition of the thinking subject's mind on the vastness of the world.[12] The term became attached to Čapek's trilogy almost immediately, as did the darker implications of what these novels say about human individuality. Reviewing the trilogy's last installment in 1935, Jan Blahoslav Čapek—no relation to the novelist—noted that "with Čapek's trilogy we are dealing not only with his curious and calculating intellect, not only with his insistent psychologism and noetic passion," but also with the horror that comes with our realization that the individual is always bombarded by a plurality of other subjects: "This plurality affords us a broader understanding, certainly; but is it always a plus? [. . .] The integrity of our individuality is too pressing a problem, especially today."[13]

The Individual as Group Project: Karel Čapek's *The Meteor*

With the author's reputation already secured in the 1920s, Čapek's "noetic trilogy" began to make its way almost immediately into the international literary marketplace, with the trilogy's first installment, *Hordubal,* already available in English, German, Polish, and Russian translations before the outbreak of the Second World War.[14] In the Soviet Union, this and other works by Čapek were enthusiastically promoted by Andrei Platonov, who reviewed them under a pseudonym. Platonov especially admired Čapek's masterful use of dialogue, as well as his fusion of the fantastic and the real.[15]

The "noetic trilogy," in fact, consists almost entirely of dialogues among characters whose incompatible perceptions of each other's lives reveal deep fissures between subjective experience and objective reality. In the first American monograph devoted to Čapek's literary legacy, William Harkins suggests that this is why the novels seem fantastical, despite the fact that their action is rooted mostly in domestic conversation. "The conventional, 'realistic' novel assumes that reality is single and objective," Harkens notes, whereas "the novel of introspective experience, on the other hand, suggests that it is relative and subjective. Čapek avoids both extremes, for he is seeking to reconcile subjectivity and objectivity, relativism and absolutism, pluralism and monism."[16] While this is a fitting description of the trilogy, we can appreciate more of the subtlety of Čapek's project if we soften Harkins's language. For Čapek does not *avoid* both extremes, but rather embraces them simultaneously; he does not seek to *reconcile* the individual and the Absolute, but to demonstrate the ways in which Being consists in the movement from one pole to the other. In a trilogy that is principally concerned with individual identity, no identity will find stable resolution.[17]

This is the case in each of the three texts, of which *The Meteor* is the most overtly allegorical. That is, whereas the first and third novels are quite plausible—*Hordubal* is in fact a thinly veiled retelling of an actual and widely publicized murder—in *The Meteor* Čapek sets up an outlandish, highly schematic situation to demonstrate how the thinking subject is constructed between Self and Other.

The novel is set around a hospital bed. A pilot who has literally fallen out of the sky in a fiery plane lies horribly burned and unconscious, a bundle of white bandages. Case X, as he is known, has no documents, and there is no hope that he will survive to tell his own story, so it falls to the people around him to fill in the details of his missing identity, to provide a face for a man who has been defaced, both physically and metaphysically. The Sister of Mercy, the Poet, and the Clairvoyant each take turns telling the man's story, with the Surgeon and the Internist voicing their approbation and doubts. The Poet begins by describing the situation in terms of the same orphanhood, homelessness, and defacement that we have seen in the works of Bruno Schulz, Andrei Platonov, and others, positing that this man "had no mother" because of the very fact of his anonymity: "After all, Case X has neither face nor name, he has no identity, he's Unknown."[18] The central dilemma, that the man before them is both "unknown" and faceless, is a refrain repeated throughout the text. Even the Surgeon, otherwise quite reserved, shouts it in despair toward the beginning of the novel.[19] This nonidentity puts an unusual spin on the fact that all the other characters, even as they struggle to provide Case X with a life narrative, are themselves neither named nor physically described in any detail.

The reason for this lack of detail is quite simple, if more than a little troubling. For Čapek, as for the other authors of intermediacy, individuality is always only a provisional state, a momentary and ultimately theoretical definition. Actual existence, on the other hand, occurs between individuals, in instances of the "free and familiar contact" posited by Bakhtin. Accordingly, the very being of the thinking subject is incompleteness, the unfinalized status of the Bakhtinian hero. Storytelling becomes both the occasion and the enactment of contact, and its reach extends well beyond the textual bounds of the tale being told, as Lubomír Doležel indicates: "The spoken word of the story-teller is one fundamental component of the prime story-telling situation; the other, no less important, is the direct contact between the story-teller and his audience. Not only is there a 'feedback' from the audience to the story-teller, but the two roles are easily interchangeable: telling of stories can be passed on as a relay, because all listeners are potential story-tellers."[20] Along the same lines, Wolfgang Schwartz has observed that the trilogy's "multiperspectival structure" creates "a particular tension between monologism and dialogism," such that the movement between singularity and multiplicity becomes "the structural dominant" of the three novels.[21] Even as the speakers attempt to define the stranger's individuality in *The Meteor,* their own participation in that process of definition undermines the very individuality they seek to recover, to say nothing of their own individuality. For at the same time as the speakers infect Case X with their being, projecting the content of their own subjectivity onto the blank screen of his bandages, Case X infects them in turn, becoming an integral part of their consciousnesses. And because Case X is himself nameless, the characters who help constitute his being must remain nameless as well.

The methods by which the Sister of Mercy, the Clairvoyant, the Poet, and the Internist construct Case X's existence each demonstrate essentially the same compromise between empirical analysis and intuitive synthesis. The differences between their tales are purely formal: Case X appears to the Sister of Mercy in a dream; the Clairvoyant "sees" the general contour of his existence; the Poet writes a story about the stranger; the Internist offers a complicated diagnosis. And yet each speaker describes his method as part-logical, part-intuitive. "What I see does not suffice," the Poet explains. "I want to know more—and that's why I invent stories. [. . .] And, man, I know what fiction is, I know how it's done: let us say, one part experience, three parts imagination, two parts logical deduction, and the rest is clever calculus: so that it'll be new, so it'll be timely, so that above all something will be resolved or proven and, above all, so it'll have an impact."[22] In what Čapek has calculated as a move against the reader's intuition, the Poet insists that his work is not entirely imaginative, and Čapek has carefully chosen words that resonate with scientific and mathematical discourse: *zkušenost,* which in Czech is synonymous with *empirie* ("empiricism"); *kombinace,* which signifies "deduction" in logic and "combination" in mathematics; *kalkul,* meaning "calculus," which speaks for itself; and *časové,* which contains *čas,* "time," though *příhodný* might have been a more suitable word to signify "timely." The Poet is not interested solely in artistic timeliness but also in the capacity of his story to delimit time, for the infinite must be made finite if it is to be conveyed to another, to "have an impact." The Poet's aim, as he later describes in a letter that accompanies his written testimony—he tells his story in absentia, through text—is to formulate reality, if not the one that is, then at least the one that might be: "I'll tell you the theorem of metaphysical madness: the possibility that would be, among all possibilities, the only one possible, *would be reality.* Behold, the *idée fixe* of the visionary: to hunt down reality with the deceptions of fantasies. If you think that we're satisfied to manufacture illusions, you are mistaken; our mania is more monstrous: we strive for reality itself."[23] "Existence is the artist's greatest ambition," Mandel'shtam has told us, and Čapek's Poet would seem to agree. This "mania is more monstrous" than pure imagination, yet the monster here is not the hybrid of man and bird that one finds in Schulz's stories. Instead, Čapek posits a philosophical monster, the intermingling of observation and intuition, of fact and fiction, and eventually of the determinate and the infinite. With his rejection of pure illusion, this is a poet whom Plato might not have ejected from the Republic.

The Clairvoyant is the Poet's collaborator in this art. He does not represent a sharp departure from the Poet, as one might initially suppose. Both the Clairvoyant and the Poet posit a particular form of attention to reality, and the Clairvoyant is equally adamant in his denials of pure fantasy: "I am not a visionary; I am an analyst; true reality does not reveal itself to us; it must be extracted through methodical labor, through analysis and concentration."[24] This form of analysis, of course, also includes the kind of synthesis we see in the Clairvoyant's analogy of stacking film stills and looking through all of them at once. That is, the process both characters employ to see Case X's life involves as much assembly as disassembly.

In the various retellings of the life of Case X, there persists a sense that the analysis and synthesis of the poor man's life amount to much more than the construction of a coherent narrative. The fleeting order that arises from this process is the very basis of Being, as the Sister of Mercy points out in reference to her dream of Case X: "All things would collapse before us into mere dreams if there were no order within them; order is something that occurs only in actual things. This dream frightened me so, because I found more coherence in it than dreams tend to have; and I can only tell it in the way that I understand it now."[25] The Sister of Mercy suggests that what differentiates dreams from reality is that the latter possesses a much higher degree of *souvislost,* which here appears to mean "coherence," though a broader translation would be "consistency," "association," or "connection." The deep interconnection between thinking subjects, their inherent intersubjectivity, is the underlying theme of Čapek's novel. Each of the speakers is both an observer of and a participant in the individual called Case X, whose appearance to the Sister of Mercy in a dream forces her to contradict her own dismissal of fantasy: order, she claims, "occurs only in actual things." Her dream, therefore, is more than the "mere dreams" she rejects.

Even the Internist, who might otherwise represent a purely empirical alternative to all these intuitivist maneuvers, proclaims his methodological in-betweenness: "our *ars medica,* it's fifty percent intuition."[26] Whether one is speaking of the analysis of what has been observed or the synthesis of one's impressions into a coherent whole—here the two processes are in fact dynamically intertwined—this interplay between empiricism and intuition, and therefore between what stands objectively outside the individual thinking subject and what originates from within him, composes both the observer and the person observed. As Thomas Ort has recently noted, for Čapek intuition is the complement of reason, not its antithesis, insofar as it forms the very basis of what Nancy calls "being-with," a subjectivity predicated on the interpenetration of other subjectivities: "[Intuition] meant breaching the high walls of the identities erected around our selves and recognizing that each individual is an ever-shifting compound of experiences, qualities, and fates—a 'crowd' of major and minor constituents."[27] In *The Meteor,* the subjectivity of Case X will ultimately be composed of many voices that originate outside him, yet all of which are presumed by the speakers to harmonize with the variegated selfhood within him. The Clairvoyant explains:

> Assume that life is a kind of sounding, that a person makes a sound, that his thoughts, memory, and subconscious make a sound; and his past resonates within that and any other moment; it is an enormously complex and infinitely polyphonic sound, in which both the present and the past are an eternal fading and harmonizing of the tonics and neighboring tones; the entire past colors the sound of the present. Assume that within us, too, these same waves vibrate with a transmission from outside, at least insofar as we stand in relation to a person who broadcasts his frequency into space—as we all do, as we all do; that harmony is weaker or stronger; it depends on our tuning, on our sensitivity and alertness, and on the intensity of the given relation.[28]

Once again, the Clairvoyant offers a colorfully Bergsonian description of intersubjectivity. In fact, quasi-Bergsonian, since the depiction of the past and present harmonizing with one another is less suggestive of absolute continuity than of concurrence: the past runs alongside and finds points of contact with the present, "coloring" it. Urs Heftrich offers an especially intriguing reading of Čapek's *The Meteor* as grappling with Bergson's concept of intuition, though I would relax his stark designations of the Clairvoyant as an intuitionist and the Poet as an analyst.[29] In my reading, each of the characters in *The Meteor* fuses the synthetic with the analytic, as well as the intuitive with the empirical, a fusion that seems very much the point of Čapek's novel. Furthermore, the basic integrity of the individual is destabilized by the sheer multiplicity of the voices that sound within him, "an enormously complex and infinitely polyphonic sound," a notion that again recalls what Bakhtin describes as the unfinalizability of the hero in a polyphonic text. Along these lines, Gary Saul Morson and Caryl Emerson correctly warn against conflation of Bakhtin's notion of polyphony, which affects the truth-value of authorial utterance and therefore "has to do with the position of the author in a text," and heteroglossia, which "describes the diversity of speech styles in a language."[30] Each novel in Čapek's "noetic trilogy" does, in fact, display a high degree of heteroglossia, since each of the novels' speakers employs an idiosyncratic style of speech, the aggregate of which helps constitute the author's rebellion against the unity of novelistic form. That integrity is destabilized because there is no reference to a stable, objective center, a "real time" that stands outside all thinking subjects. Instead, the subject is infected by "a transmission from outside." For the Clairvoyant, as for all of Čapek's characters, every thinking subject is both a transmitter "who broadcasts his frequency into space"—though we each have not one frequency, but many, which come together in an "infinitely polyphonic sound"—and a receiver who tunes in to the transmissions of others, a process that is both voluntary and involuntary, both empirical, a matter of calculated and systematic observation, and intuitive, a matter of filling in gaps in the perceived data with the data of one's own consciousness.

The Clairvoyant's analogy describes an interpretive process. Each of Čapek's characters is an interpreter, receiving and reprocessing the broadcasts of other characters. And this description of interpretation applies just as well to the experience of Being. In interpreting the text, the interpreter (the theorist, the critic, the translator) places himself between the text and the audience, tuning in to both and, one hopes, broadcasting toward both in a way that changes text, audience, and interpreter alike. This discussion gives us a sense of the in-betweenness of the interpreter, but it does not explain why these characters commit themselves to their descriptions of a man whose death is assured from the very beginning. What compels them toward interpretation?

Part of the answer, as Peter Bugge points out in his reading of Čapek's symbolic use of death and illness, lies in the fact that Čapek rarely depicts death other than as a motivator for metaphysical inquiry: "But the proximity of death here bears no relation to pathology in life. Death is supposed to help answer the question of whether it is possible to understand human life, be it the life of another person *(Hordubal, The Meteor)* or our own life *(An Ordinary Life)*." [31] In light of my reading, we could expand Bugge's comment to note that *Hordubal* and *The Meteor* are also about individual subjectivity, just as *An Ordinary Life* addresses notions of collective Being.

The Meteor is finally about the necessity and the impossibility of an escape from Being, from one's attachment to time and the encroachment of the Other, as well as from the threat of self-containment. Again, it is the Clairvoyant who articulates this anxiety most clearly in spatial-temporal terms:

> I have the feeling of the immense expanse of his life: in this man there is much space, a lot of sea, but he was not a traveler. You see, the living space of the traveler is measurable; but here— There is no goal of any kind; there's no fixed point from which one could determine distances and directions. [. . .] We should start out from a person's last breath in order to grasp what form his life had and what meaning belongs to whatever he lived through. Only with death are the youth and birth of a person finished. [. . .] But I can't, I can't. What misery this is, our understanding in time! [32]

What I have translated as "understanding" is Čapek's meaningful deployment of a common word, *chápání*, from the verb *chopit*, "to grasp or comprehend," but etymologically rooted in the Latin *capere,* "to catch." This is what we mean in English when we say "I get it," an expression of understanding that also conveys grasping and absorption, and this is very much what Čapek seems to have in mind: we are only comprehensible to ourselves and each other in time. But this also means that we are "caught," *stuck* in time. And because "there's no fixed point from which one could determine distances and directions," there is no exit from this man's life, and therefore no way of regarding it from outside as a self-contained whole. Case X remains immersed in Being, *condemned to Being,* and the Clairvoyant is stuck there with him.

Elsewhere, in one of his many rebellions against the observational method he otherwise espouses, the Poet agrees: "I'll tell you, man, it's strange: it's not entirely certain that this life was merely thought up; and when I look at it like that, I'd say that it was *my own life.* It's me. I am both this sea and this man."[33] The sea, which Case X is believed to have crossed in his plane before the fateful crash, is also the novel's convenient central metaphor for undelimited space and, in particular, the undefined space of the stranger's own being. As the Clairvoyant says, "in this man there is much space, a lot of sea." The Poet offers a provisional clarification:

> Dear fellow, the world is great, greater than our experience; it's made from a handful of facts and a whole universe of possibilities. Everything that we don't know is here as a possibility, and every fact is one little bead on the rosary of previous and future eventualities. It's no use: if we are to investigate a person, we have to enter into that world of conjectures, we have to snoop around his potential past and future steps; we have to pursue him with our own imagination if he is to reveal himself to us in his own invisible lifelikeness. It is simply an indifferent matter [je prosto lhostejno] whether it's all made up or all real; [. . .] both are woven from the pure and infinite fabric of possibility, in which everything is based, including that which actually is.[34]

As also happens in the Clairvoyant's explanations of his craft, the Poet folds his description of an interpretive method into a description of Being, expressed in terms of what Bakhtin calls "eventness." Past and future collapse into the pure, open-ended potential of the moment. The observer becomes "indifferent"—*lhostejný*—to the distinction between the actuality before him and the infinite possibilities that stand just off to the side. While Čapek's characters acknowledge that there is such a thing as actuality, the possibility that has been realized, they persist in their belief that this actuality is inextricable from an expansive "universe of possibilities" that are yet to be realized. Again we are reminded of Bakhtin's description of the author as a presence who simply observes the actions of his characters, guessing at the possible interconnections between them.

In Bakhtin, the fact that these possibilities remain undefined is the very source of freedom. In the literature of intermediacy, it is because these possibilities are undefined that Being is itself inescapable. Manifold possibilities constitute, in the words of the Poet, a "Mare Tenebrarum"—a "Sea of Darknesses"—that describes our Being.[35] As the Clairvoyant points out, for Case X there is always "this emphatic stress on the 'I,' which no person can escape."[36] Indeed, escape is the overarching theme of each retelling of Case X's life. In the Poet's narrative, the stranger flees initially toward the Caribbean because he—the Poet—sees the Antilles as the point from which he might be able to escape Being: "It's simply that somewhere there is the place of my *escape*; I may never get there, but it's a region that, for me, exists more powerfully than the countries I've been in."[37] By now we should expect Čapek's phrasing to suggest philosophical connotations beyond the literal. Of the many words he could have chosen to signify "domain" or "region," he chooses *končina,* derived from *konec,* "end." Unless one can see an end or boundary, there is no possibility of escape, and the Poet freely admits that he may never reach his own escape point.

Nor will Case X, whom the Poet repeatedly calls "the man who didn't arrive"—*člověk, který nedoletěl.* This sobriquet bears a pleasant, if likely inadvertent, echo of the one Franz Kafka applies to the protagonist of his first novel, *Amerika,* whose original title was *Der Verschollene*—literally, *The Man Who Disappeared.* Both monikers demonstrate that the thinking subject has left but has not arrived, that he is continuously in transit. More than any of the names that might be assigned to him, "the man who . . ." is the most accurate, since we can never really know who this man is. His journey remains open-ended.

Similarly, the Clairvoyant describes an early stage in the life of Case X as an attempted escape from Self: "He had to break himself apart. It was his internal fate, actually something quite like a flight from a task that was beyond his strength."[38] In the Sister of Mercy's dream narrative, Case X appears to say as much on his own behalf: "If true reality is something that is, and therefore endures, then I fled from reality; it was a cursed flight, for I have not found [reality] again."[39] If reality is the closest we can get to a determinate point amid the vastness of pure potential, a flight from reality is tantamount to a flight into indeterminacy. Case X also makes this point as he speaks through the Poet: "If I call it flight, then it's an escape into the very middle of things, where everything clashes together, where the ages are mated within a perverse mixing of cultures."[40] In the "perverse mixing of cultures," we hear the voice of a rank colonialist, as the Poet believes Case X to have been, but no matter, since this man will never succeed in escaping from himself. On the contrary, his tightly bandaged, faceless torso is a perfect figure for self-enclosure, and yet this is not why his "I" is inescapable. For even while unconscious and insensate, he continues to infect Being for those around him and to be infected by them in turn.

That Was Now, This Is Then: Immaturity and Čapek's *An Ordinary Life*

The insistence on intersubjectivity appears across Čapek's "noetic trilogy." In these three novels, the fact that the thinking subject is not finalized may allow him access to others, but it also prevents him from achieving an integral and self-contained identity. Čapek's characters sense their own immaturity, an incompleteness that opens them to others and, consequently, forecloses any possibility that they can be entirely one with themselves.

It was only after Čapek had finished the trilogy's last installment in 1934 that he appended an afterword outlining the rationale behind his treatment of intersubjectivity, essentially echoing the pronouncements already available to us from the mouths of his characters:

> How cruelly great and complex, how spacious reality is, when it has enough room for so many different interpretations! But it is no longer this chaos, it is a distinct multiplicity; it is no longer uncertainty, but polyphony [. . .]. We perceive the world through what we ourselves are, and perceiving the world we discover ourselves. Thank God, now we are home again; we are from the same fabric as this multiplicity of the world; we are at home in this expansiveness and innumerability, and we can respond to these great many voices. No longer is there just an "I," but we the people; we can make ourselves understood through the many languages that are within us. [. . .] And this most common life is yet infinite; the value of every soul is boundless. [. . .] [T]he life of man is too great for him to have just one face and to be seen all at once.[41]

If this exuberant declaration had appeared at the beginning of Čapek's trilogy instead of at the end, its optimistic tone might have suggested to the reader that these books end happily for any of their principal characters. The individual becomes a democracy unto himself, unfinalized, open to infinite connections with those around him. Unfortunately, the unfinalizability of Čapek's characters, their immaturity, leaves them frustrated and confused, longing for elusive definition.

In chapter 3, I considered how lyric speakers in the poems of Osip Mandel'shtam and Czesław Miłosz sometimes affect naivety in order to reestablish their access to an unfinalized past. Immaturity describes the same interconnection of past, present, and future, though we might say that the polarity is here reversed. The adult does not short-circuit backward toward childhood. Rather, immaturity is the childhood that persists and never fades within the adult. It is a lack of definition that opens the thinking subject to infection by other thinking subjects. Immaturity corrupts identity from within. If the ideal of Mandel'shtam and Miłosz is, to reiterate Bruno Schulz's formulation from his letter to Andrzej Pleśniewicz, "to mature into childhood," Čapek instead emphasizes the child within the mature adult.[42] In *The Meteor,* the Sister of Mercy's tale suggests repeatedly that immaturity is the initial cause of Case X's problems, as when she speaks on his behalf about the romantic crisis that she believes precipitated his flight: "Today I know that she was further along than I, that everything was resolved in her and nothing in me, that she was mature, and I remained a confused, immature, irresponsible guy. [. . .] In me there was none of the fullness of a person whom I would surrender to her. [. . .] Know that my escape was the escape of an insolvent debtor. I remained in debt to her for my very self."[43] This is an effective description of immaturity as in-betweenness, a sense that one is never fully formed and always owes the debt of oneself to the Other.[44]

We find a similar operation in the trilogy's first novel, *Hordubal.* Returning to the small village and family he had left for eight years of labor in America proves impossible for the eponymous hero, who narrates the first half of the novel. In his absence, Juraj Hordubal's wife has aged and taken a lover, and his village has made modest steps toward modernization. But Hordubal does not see these changes: he continues to live as though no time has passed. When he is murdered halfway through the novel, Čapek treats the reader to two more perspectives on his life and his world, first from the lead detectives, then from the court. But as Craig Cravens has demonstrated, even those who attempt to describe Hordubal's life in his absence appropriate his verbal idiosyncrasies in their telling, effectively hybridizing the language of the protagonist, other characters, and the narrator in a way that is deeply resonant with, and may have been partially inspired by, Dostoevsky's technique in *The Double.*[45] Even in death, Hordubal speaks and thinks like a child, incapable of regarding critically anything that does not conform to his simplistic and outmoded sense of the way his life had been eight years earlier. This is why, as Hordubal's wife and her lover are being prosecuted for his murder, his neighbor describes the decedent as a man who was blank on the inside, who "walked like a body without a spirit."[46] *Hordubal* resembles *The Meteor* insofar as both tell the story of a man who traverses the sea but cannot reach his destination.

But it is the trilogy's last installment, *An Ordinary Life,* that presses the theme of metaphysical immaturity most insistently. Like the burned man in *The Meteor,* the hero of *An Ordinary Life* remains anonymous. Instead of having his life told by those around him, however, the narrator tells his own life story, though he cannot do so without the interference of the many voices within him. This is the greater sense of Čapek's understated title: *obyčejný* means "ordinary," but it also contains and is derived from the noun *obyčej,* "custom," and thus radiates a sense of repetition and universality. These voices, each a double for a narrator who claims to have lived an undistinguished, "ordinary" life, are with him from earliest childhood. Childhood, in turn, is a consistent reference point in the novel, and the principal narrator describes it as a separate world that exists outside of time:

> At play, a solitary child forgets himself and everything around him, and his forgetting is outside of time. The broader surroundings are pulled into the social play of children, and their communal world is dominated by the laws of the seasons. Easter, holidays and Christmas, the fair, carnival and festival—these are important dates and deep rifts in time. The year of children has its own order; it is ceremonially compartmentalized according to seasons of the year; the solitary child plays with eternity, but the pack of children plays with time.[47]

The narrator repeatedly calls our attention to how he had been mostly solitary as a child, though he had enough social interaction to notice seasons and holidays, the "deep rifts in time." And yet the solitary child, who must make his own world "outside of time," remains unfinished, and his world remains unfinalized within the adult speaker. The narrator contains many voices that have populated his being for as long as he can remember, and they are constantly contradicting, reversing, and undoing each other. We learn that the hero was *both* solitary *and* sociable, and that these competing tendencies led him to construct separate worlds within himself. One, that of the affable child with many friends and aspirations, grows up to become a railroad employee and an adoring husband. The other never grows up but rather harbors a core of incompleteness, an unfinished world within.

As the novel progresses, Čapek complicates this neat dichotomy between the child who grows into an adult and the adult who remains a child. More and more voices invade the protagonist's life narrative, and each of these voices is matched or in some way attributed to the influence of an ancestor or dead relative. Most important of these is the occasionally mentioned presence of a brother, who died before the protagonist could have had any firsthand knowledge of him, and who serves as a phantom double, a parallel life that *might* have been. Of course, in a narrative built on reversals and self-contradictions the speaker's assertion of immaturity, "that even today I am a child who has his own secret world," will find resistance in equally numerous declarations of maturity and self-enclosure: "I am a mature and complete person who supports himself with exhausting and joyless work."[48] The tension of opposites drives its own, self-perpetuating dialogue between Self and Other, between individuality and plurality, between synthesis and analysis. The hero asserts his singularity, and that singularity is split asunder: "Eight lives that compose my life; and I know that if I had time enough and a clearer head, a whole series of them would emerge, perhaps completely unconnected, perhaps the kind that only existed once and lasted but a moment."[49]

Nothing new can come of this, because the very notion of "newness" requires clear delineations of past, present, and future. The coexistence of different times, of "the old surviving in the new," is a zone not of novelty, but of endless transformation, reiteration, repetition with difference. The hero of *An Ordinary Life* is left having to assert his individuality *and* his plurality repeatedly, and often in the same breath:

> But at the same time, no matter which of these fates I lived or which of these figures I was, I was always this "*I*," and this "I" was ever the same and didn't change from the beginning to the end. That's the strange thing. So is this "I" something that is *above* those figures and their destinies, something higher, singular, and unifying, is it perhaps what we call a soul? And yet this "I" didn't have any content *of its own*, it was now the hypochondriac and then the hero, and it was nothing that might float above them![50]

This self-contradictory chain goes on, with the narrator thinking by turns that he has mastered the voices within him—that he is "above" them—and that he is simply an aggregate of those voices. The very process of defining the "I" against the dialogic interplay of voices and the distinct life paths they represent becomes a dialogic process in itself. The hero shuttles back and forth between asserting the primacy of the Self and recognizing its disintegration into many selves.

Finally, just as he is thinking one last time about the brother-Other he never knew, the protagonist alights on the fact that the supremacy of the "I" is merely an illusion, a means of coping with the menace of nondefinition:

"Maybe every one of us is a sum of people which accumulates from generation to generation. And perhaps by now we're anxious because of this infinite diversification; that's why we want to escape it, and we accept some kind of collective 'I' that might simplify us."[51] Čapek employs a set colloquial expression, *je nám úzko,* to express the anxiety of this identity crisis, but the phrasing is especially potent when read through its literal, spatial meaning: *úzko* means "tight," "narrow," "cramped," a stock description of existential angst in the closed room of identity. In this case it is not the singularity but rather the multitude of selves within the "I" that makes it unbearable. Thus the thinking subject imposes his "collective 'I'" on the multitude in order to consolidate the "infinite diversification" of the Self into a manageable, definable whole. In this regard, Čapek's "collective 'I'" is an especially masterful turn: *davový* comes from *dav,* "crowd" or "throng," so that *davové já* expresses the analytic breakdown and the synthetic reconstitution of the Self simultaneously in a single phrase, yet another instance of wordplay fusing contradictory semantic elements.

It is difficult not to read these reflections on the Self also as a commentary on the compositional logic behind the "noetic trilogy." Because the three novels consist primarily of the narration of *potential* lives, and because Čapek consistently draws our attention to the fact that any number of other narratives might apply equally well to these protagonists, the reader is invited to collaborate with the author in imagining those as-yet unrealized possibilities. The "noetic trilogy" thus invites the reader to assume the role of the Bakhtinian author, following Čapek's characters and guessing at the interconnections between their actions. The hero is unfinalized in large part because, to reiterate the musings of *An Ordinary Life,* the "I" has no content of its own. The hero has the potential to undertake any number of potential actions, each representing another potential narrative to be written. The narrator of *An Ordinary Life* follows as many of these threads as he can before his imminent death.

Going Nowhere Fast: Witold Gombrowicz's Synthesis versus Analysis (+ Infinity)

In 1933, the same year that Čapek published *Hordubal,* Witold Gombrowicz published his *Memoir of a Time of Immaturity* (Pamiętnik z okresu dojrzewania), a collection of stories that adopt a grotesquely satirical stance toward the same issues of identity and infection that Čapek addresses in his "noetic trilogy." Like Čapek, Gombrowicz recognizes that the tension between the self-contained "I" and the encroachment of others around him is ultimately irresolvable: the individual thinking subject remains forever locked in a struggle with others over his own selfhood. As in the "noetic trilogy," the structure of Being in Gombrowicz's fiction is dialogic, without any ultimate resolution or finalization.

An excellent instantiation of this dynamic is the story "Philidor Lined with Child" (Filidor dzieckiem podszyty). As though to demonstrate the remarkable philosophical consistency of his work, Gombrowicz's story, which was written in 1935, first appeared as a chapter in his 1937 novel *Ferdydurke*. It was then retroactively appended to his debut collection of stories when it was reissued in 1957 under the new title *Bakakaj*.[52] "Philidor Lined with Child" is the story of Philidor, Professor of Synthetology at the University of Leiden, the Netherlands, whose principal methods Gombrowicz describes as "addition + infinity" and "multiplication + infinity." The name of Philidor's discipline, "Synthetology," is a neologism that parodies the academic institutionalization of theoretical-philosophical discourse, with which Gombrowicz was extremely well acquainted, but the word *seems* like it should carry more meaning. In general, Gombrowicz took great pleasure in making quasi-allusions that *might* be meaningful, part of a lifelong fascination with *our* need, as readers in and of the world, to make meaning. Thus, if we dig around to see whether Gombrowicz took the name "Philidor" from the eighteenth-century French chess master François-André Danican-Philidor, we will find that Gombrowicz did, and that this is not supposed to matter, which we know because, when the text was translated into French, Gombrowicz insisted that the hero be called "Philifor," so that the name would sound as odd in French as it does in Polish.[53] Or we might wonder whether there is an equally sly, if arbitrary, reference here to the "syntetologia" of the Portuguese economist José Ferreira Borges (1786–1838). Not that we are being asked to examine Gombrowicz's text through the lens of arcane Iberian political economy. On the contrary: there are no such connections to be made, but Gombrowicz wants us to sense that such connections are *almost* there, just out of reach, so that we might experience both the temptation to achieve Philidor's "Higher Synthesis" and the impossibility of doing so. Another colorful example of this meaningless gravitation toward meaning is the title *Bakakaj*, which Gombrowicz took from the name of one of the streets where he lived in Buenos Aires. Shortly before his death, he commented in a letter that he named the book "the way we name dogs, simply to tell one from the other."[54]

"Philidor Lined with Child" animates the antagonism between synthetic interconnections and analytic definitions. Much as Philidor's career may seem to serve a "Higher Synthesis," Gombrowicz warns us otherwise: "Yet a spiritual phenomenon of this magnitude could not *not* trigger its own counterphenomenon in nature, in the sense of the Newtonian principle of action and reaction, and so an equally brilliant Analyst was also quickly born in Colombo and, having attained a doctorate as well as a professorship of Higher Analysis at Columbia, quickly worked his way to the highest ranks of a scientific career."[55] Consistent with the endless transformations and doubling of the thinking subject that one finds in the literature of in-betweenness, Gombrowicz posits a double for Philidor, and he calls this double simply "Anti-Philidor." It is only fitting that Anti-Philidor should be born, as it were, in response to the advent of Philidor ("so an equally brilliant Analyst was also quickly born"), and where else but on the opposite side of the globe? (The actual antipode of Leiden is somewhere near New Zealand, but for Gombrowicz's purposes Sri Lanka will do.) In "Philidor Lined with Child," "Higher Analysis" meets "Higher Synthesis." The existence of one character depends upon, is entangled with, and communicates to the existence of the other. The champion of multiplicity confronts the defender of the monistic Absolute. Let the dismemberment begin.

Dismemberment, we soon learn, is Anti-Philidor's area of expertise: "He worked deconstructively, and his specialty was the deconstruction of a person through enumeration, particularly by flicking. And thus, by means of a flick to the nose, he spurred the nose into self-contained being, by which the nose moved spontaneously in all directions, to the horror of its owner."[56] Gombrowicz's hyperlogical grotesquery is amusing, but it is also deeply troubling. For what does it say of our individuality when we can be so easily broken down into parts, each of which has its own "self-contained being"—*samoistny byt,* literally, "a being that exists on its own"? What it appears to mean for Gombrowicz is that the thinking subject is always *subject* to attacks from the Other, certainly. But in addition to highlighting the attempts of the Other to penetrate the Self from without, Gombrowicz follows Čapek in pointing to the Self's vulnerability from *within*. Philidor's sense that he is a complete and internally unified whole, serving the "Higher Synthesis," is pure illusion. Instead, the unity of the Professor of Synthesis is merely a mask to protect him from the Professor of Analysis. At the same time, it may appear that Anti-Philidor's analytic method is a shield to protect him from being unified from outside. Yet Philidor and Anti-Philidor are best understood not by their equal and opposite methods, but by their shared phobia: Philidor, the servant of a "Higher Synthesis," is afraid of the loss of the Self through disintegration *in* the world, whereas Anti-Philidor, the servant of a "Higher Analysis," is afraid of the loss of the Self through absorption *by* the world. For them both, intersubjectivity is unavoidable and intolerable. Philidor attempts to absorb Anti-Philidor and his mistress into the larger synthesis of culture, declaring, "There is a God! Honor! Synthesis!"[57] Philidor cannot win, however, because Gombrowicz endeavors to transform dichotomy into dynamic, to move, as Zbigniew Majchrowski has put it, "from a system of alternatives (either/or) into a system of antinomy, from the sphere of historiosophy into the sphere of sociology."[58] Accordingly, Anti-Philidor must counter Philidor, trying to dismember Philidor and his wife through his reference to, or his "flicking" at, parts rather than wholes, which Philidor describes stiffly as "a terrible anarchy, a terrible breakdown in order."[59]

Anti-Philidor wins the first round, calling attention to Mrs. Philidor's leg in a way that leaves her slowly disintegrating in a hospital bed. Philidor wishes to counter by calling the analyst out to a duel, that great equalizer of Polish Romantic culture, but he fails, because in performing the traditional gesture of slapping Anti-Philidor's cheek, he can only hit a part, and not the whole: "You can catch my cheek, but not me—not me! There is no me at all! There is no me!"[60] The first task for Philidor, then, is to establish an ontological ground upon which Anti-Philidor might be subject to synthesis. As we will see in a moment, this is where Gombrowicz demonstrates the interpenetration of the strictly temporal and the timeless.

Because the Professor of Analysis has "analyzed" Mrs. Philidor into parts, Philidor decides to synthesize his opponent's mistress into a unified whole, just long enough to slap Anti-Philidor into a duel. The duel, Philidor reasons, can only end in victory, since a duel for one's honor is itself done in the service of synthesis, of culture: "If he falls, by that death he will pay tribute to Synthesis; if he kills me, then he kills by a synthetic mechanism. Thus mine will be a triumph from beyond the grave."[61] But he cannot slap Anti-Philidor until he synthesizes Anti-Philidor's mistress, and he achieves this by giving her money. Even this bribe is no simple task. For if Anti-Philidor can "spur . . . [a] nose toward self-contained being" by flicking it, Philidor will not be able to synthesize the analyst's clever mistress without offering her an uncountable sum. That is, if she can divide and subdivide Philidor's offer into manageable parts, analysis will continue to win over synthesis. Thus Philidor liquidates all his assets, offering the mistress all that he has. Unable to analyze the sum placed before her, both Anti-Philidor and his mistress find themselves unexpectedly synthesized into a whole. Then—slap!

The synthesist wants to offer a sum that cannot be returned, and which therefore draws the recipient into a zone of contact that cannot be closed: the gift must be assimilated in toto. As his master stroke, atop the overwhelming sum he has placed before Anti-Philidor and his mistress, he adds a single, shiny *grosz* (one penny), the monetary embodiment of indivisibility itself. Jacques Derrida describes this delay between gift and countergift as a displacement of time, such that the unspoken contract of exchange cannot be completed immediately:

> [T]he *syn-*, the *syn*thesis, the *sys*tem, or the *syn*tax that joins together gift and exchange is temporal—or more precisely temporizing—difference, the delay of the term or the term of delay that dislocates any "at the same time." The identity between gift and exchange would not be immediate and analytical. It would have in effect the form of an *a priori* synthesis: a synthesis because it requires tem-

> porization and *a priori*—in other words necessary—because it is required at the outset by *the thing itself*, namely by the very object of the gift, by the force or the virtue that would be inherent to it.[62]

In like fashion, the synthesist strives to divorce the gift from its completion in an exchange, so that instead of the temporizing difference that Derrida says will separate the gift and countergift, there is a *de*-temporizing effect: the opening of an indeterminate space for contact. Anti-Philidor has no way to analyze this gift, and therefore no way to complete the exchange. And their zone of contact will remain open if, as Philidor expects, one of them dies in the duel that follows. One professor will give death to the other, but that gift cannot be reciprocated.

But there is a serious miscalculation here, and it reveals itself when we more closely examine the zone of synthetic contact Philidor thinks he is opening. For what Philidor does not seem to realize is that he is already a priori locked in a system of reciprocal exchange—intersubjectivity itself—and that he will never be able to achieve his ideal of "Higher Synthesis," since he is himself an individual. Philidor cannot be alone in the world, since a mirror opposite, an Anti-Philidor, has also come into being to reciprocate his existence. Nor is Philidor wholly representative of "Higher Synthesis," because he remains an individual thinking subject, with individual characteristics and contingencies. And Anti-Philidor is not wholly representative of "Higher Analysis," either, since he possesses an individuality that is more than the sum of its (or his) parts. Both antagonists are in between synthetic unity and analytic multiplicity, and each tends toward one in the vain hope of canceling the other (and, more importantly, *his* Other).[63] The opposition each would seek to resolve in his own favor is too symmetrical to be resolved. The story's narrator, one of Philidor's assistants, suddenly realizes this tactical error as he is looking at the parties to the duel: Philidor versus Anti-Philidor, the wife versus the mistress, and two seconds on each side. "And then I understood what it was that I dreaded," he remarks. "It was symmetrical: the situation was symmetrical, and in this one found its strength, but also its weakness."[64]

Philidor, who has the first shot, misses, but according to his synthetic reason, that should not—in the fullest, logical sense of the phrase—make any difference. If he dies, his will be a "synthetic" death. But Anti-Philidor has something else in mind: he shoots off Mrs. Philidor's finger, so that Philidor must shoot off the mistress's finger with his subsequent shot, and so on. The duel goes on for a very long, undefined time. This scene of dismemberment echoes the breakdown of the body into geometric shapes in Miłosz's "Hushabye," itself a figure for the interplay of analysis and synthesis: "You dismantle your body. Into geometric figures, pieces, and you connect them in a new way." When, at the end of Gombrowicz's story, the old professor nostalgically recalls the great event, the narrator exclaims: "'[B]ut Professor, you're speaking like a child!' To which the senile old man replied: 'Everything is lined with child.'"[65]

Is Everything Lined With Child? Immaturity and Familiar Contact

Gombrowicz, whose play with language nearly always points to philosophical consequence, refers to Philidor as *zdziecinniały*—"senile"—in which we find the words *dziecię* and *dziecina,* "child." (*Dziecina* in particular is a word that might be applied to an adult who displays childish or age-inappropriate behavior.) At the same time, he is a *starzec,* an "old man." Therefore, before the Professor even has a chance to declare that "[e]verything is lined with child," we already have a verbal description of the phenomenon. Being "lined with child" means being the aggregate of different times, of the well-defined, closed, finalized, mature adult without, and of the shapeless, open, unfinalized, immature child within. Derrida is quite right when he says that the gift reveals the madness of "at the same time," since it refers to different times, as it were, simultaneously. Gombrowicz constructs a milieu of "free and familiar contact" in which he recognizes a core of unfreedom. After all, if Being consists only of reciprocity and exchange, if there is nothing but intersubjectivity, then both self-identity and absolute collectivity are mere illusions: the subject will never escape into himself, and he will never be absorbed into the totality of the Absolute.

In 1935, when Gombrowicz wrote "Philidor Lined with Child," the Polish author published a remarkably similar reading of Cervantes to the one advanced by Bakhtin just six years earlier. In the popular periodical *Kurier Poranny,* Gombrowicz reflects on this in-betweenness in Cervantes:

> Perhaps future ages will manage to cast a solid bridge over the chasm between the private cosmos of each and the general cosmos for all. At present, we see the chasm growing ever deeper. Because, on the one hand, the isolated human *individuum,* propped up by nearly every cultural trend, by science, art, ethics, and even the civil and criminal law, becomes increasingly greedy and demanding. And, on the other hand, the mighty unities of the higher order, like the State, or the Nation, are all the more violent in their imposition of one common way of feeling, in the name of the necessity of collective life.
>
> Reading *Don Quixote,* [. . .] we see that certain treasures of the soul can fall under the pressure of a cosmos for everyone. We see the insane elasticity and vulnerability of reality, its as yet not completely clarified nature, its—one wishes to say—unfreedom.[66]

It was typical of Gombrowicz to use a brief comment about a recent book or translation as an occasion for his own philosophical musings on literature and society. In his reading of *Don Quixote,* Gombrowicz airs tensions both social and metaphysical, and while he seems to be particularly concerned with the synthetic impositions of the nation, he is also wary of the "isolated human *individuum,*" which is becoming "increasingly greedy and demanding" in a culture still in thrall to the Romantic cult of individualism. Reality, Gombrowicz contends, is both elastic and vulnerable, both solid and "as yet not completely clarified." This is the root cause of "unfreedom," since we cannot hope to bridge "the chasm between the private cosmos of each and the general cosmos for all." And this, finally, is what Gombrowicz means when he has the old professor declare, "Everything is lined with child." There is a reality, yes, but it contains within itself an unfinished core. There is time, but it contains timelessness. There are windmills, but they are also giants.

The Mythicization of Reality Redux

Jerzy Jarzębski complicates this reading of Gombrowicz's Bakhtinian subplot with his suggestion that there can be no real dialogue in Gombrowicz, because Gombrowicz guards his "I" too jealously: "Defending the independence of one's own 'I' thus becomes a trap: indeed, the 'I' flees the deformations flowing from outside, but it is also unable to constitute itself in full, constantly enclosing itself within the limits of its phantasms. [. . .] It is therefore as if the writer sought the road to outside through the body."[67] This might indeed be the case in Gombrowicz's early stories if we were to read them strictly as depictions of a particular reality, even if that reality is admittedly phantasmagoric. Then the duel between Philidor and Anti-Philidor would seem completely nondialogic, a mechanical exchange of symmetrical gestures.

But the structure of Gombrowicz's tales—a structure that repeats itself with exceptional freshness and vigor in each iteration—suggests that they are themselves hybrids of the real and the mythic. Or, more accurately, they are attempts to construct the mythic within the scaffolding of the real, so that among the various hints at the everyday, historically contingent world we find a gathering of timeless, *essential* social acts. Witness, for example, the duel between the Professor of Synthesis and the Professor of Analysis, a purely structural exchange, but an essentially dialogic exchange nonetheless. Likewise, the body, which is so often the currency of dialogic exchange in Gombrowicz, is less a "real," historically contingent body, and more a mythic body, a pure symbol. This is why one feels little shock, let alone grief, at the slow dismemberment of Mrs. Philidor and her counterpart. Whether one considers these characters as synthetic whole or analytic part, they are merely instruments in an economic exchange between the hero and his double.

Still, it would be inaccurate to claim Gombrowicz as an absurdist, since he insists, at times with monomaniacal zeal, that he is fashioning a language that, in a vein we can easily identify with Bakhtin, clearly and accurately reflects reality as it is, and not just the delimited forms we have inherited. "It seems to me personally," he wrote between *Memoirs of a Time of Immaturity* and *Ferdydurke*, "that literature suffers simply from a lack of the most common reality. Because the evolution of concepts in society does not keep up with the evolution of facts, our culture on any given scale occurs in a sort of vacuum, our language is anachronistic, our sense—the same, and we are slaves of many forms that we have long since outdistanced through life."[68] As we have seen throughout our tour of the literature of intermediacy, the problem of accessing reality once again comes down to finding a language capable of manifesting the fundamental interpenetration of subjects and matter, corrupting the delimited forms imposed on us by a received culture.

This is Bruno Schulz's "mythicization of reality" par excellence, the gradual, necessarily incomplete transformation of historically contingent reality into timeless, repeatable, potentially open-ended episodes. As one finds in Proust or Joyce, the dressing of a social reality may remain, but the spatial-temporal underpinnings of that reality are destabilized.[69] Gombrowicz, a friend of Schulz who shared his admiration for Proust and Joyce, underscores this dynamic interaction between myth and reality in his comments on *Don Quixote:*

> In *Don Quixote* we have two levels—the higher level, where the timeless, magnificent drama between subjectivism and objectivism, the individual and the group, dream and waking life plays out; and there is a lower, everyday, practical level, where we watch a nutcase's amusing war with the truth of common sense, where the nutcase takes a lashing. And similarly, today we too are split between two levels. In the depths of [our] soul we know and feel a terrible conflict between our person, ever-so-unbridled, and the laws of the universal world, but that doesn't keep us from sleeping, eating, or riding the tram. [. . .] There is a Don Quixote in each of us, but on the periphery of a Sancho Panza.[70]

What Gombrowicz says about the two levels of engagement in *Don Quixote* applies beautifully to his own work, as well as to Karel Čapek's "noetic trilogy." These texts instantiate "the timeless, magnificent drama between subjectivism and objectivism, the individual and the group," but they are also demonstrations of recognizable people acting poorly in social situations and being duly punished for their immaturity, which is almost as much behavioral as it is metaphysical.

The point here is to recognize the reality of this in-betweenness within and through everyday experience. Such is the case, for example, in the story that opens Gombrowicz's *Memoir from a Time of Immaturity.* In "The

Honorable Kraykowski's Dancer" (Tancerz Mecenasa Kraykowskiego, 1933), an anonymous narrator cuts into line at the theater, and a haughty lawyer grabs him by the collar and—literally and figuratively—puts him in his place. This narrator, who is dying from increasingly severe epileptic seizures, seeks continuous contact with the attorney, who, predictably, wants nothing to do with him. There ensues a game of cat and mouse as the narrator resorts to baroque strategies for maintaining contact with the object of his obsession: the hero follows Kraykowski, writes letters to the lawyer's mistress, and so on, all in the hope of deepening a contact that Kraykowski himself had initiated. The narrator's purpose in stalking Kraykowski is as simple as it is horrifying. A dying man, he wants nothing more or less than to propagate his own being through "free and familiar contact" with another.

The Honorable Kraykowski and the story's protagonist strive toward two fundamentally opposed ideals of Being. The attorney, with his high social and professional standing, his wealth, his traditional marriage, and his equally traditional love affair, occupies a world of rules and manners that secure him from unwanted contact with the ineffable, the unclean, the immature. In this regard, it is unsurprising, albeit a little ironic, that it is the attorney who initiates contact with the narrator in the story's opening passage, and precisely because the narrator has violated the rigid etiquette of the theater. The narrator immediately begins to fetishize this unexpected contact: "—just then someone grabbed me by the collar from behind and coldly—so coldly—pulled me away from the little window and pushed me to the appropriate place, that is, to where the line ended. My heart was pounding, I was out of breath—isn't it murderous when someone is all of a sudden grabbed by the collar in a public establishment?—but I looked around: it was a tall, freshened-up, fragrant lordship with trimmed mustache."[71] Appropriate to his profession as a keeper of the law, the Honorable Kraykowski will not stand for so flagrant an affront to his sense of propriety as some rapscallion cutting into the front of a line. As the attorney instructs his companions, "We must teach them, teach them untiringly, or else we will never cease to be a nation of Zulus."[72] Kraykowski's colonialist sense of cultural immaturity is palpable: he sees Poland as a backward, disorderly nation, one in which the integrity of one's identity is constantly being compromised by immature behavior. To achieve his ideal of Being, the attorney must impose necessary limits on behavior and, by extension, on interhuman contact. Kraykowski is equal to himself, coterminous with himself, identical to himself, and this is how he would prefer it. Avoiding unwanted contact with the Other means remaining secure in one's own form, however artificial that form may be.

What the attorney does not realize is that he has already infected the narrator, not merely in the powerful impression he makes with his grandeur but in the very fact that he is "freshened-up, fragrant": the narrator *smells* the attorney, and insofar as the attorney's perfumed and powdered presence marks his identity, the narrator breathes that identity in. The balance of the story then describes the hero's efforts to return the favor by making Kraykowski realize that they are ontologically intertwined. The protagonist's behavior recalls the hero of Dostoevsky's *Notes from Underground*, who also requires contact with those he shuns in order to be assured of his own existence. But unlike Dostoevsky's hero, who in his misguided way seeks not only contact with but the respect of society, Gombrowicz's narrator puts a very low premium on outward displays of social recognition. Of much greater importance is the task of devising novel methods to unveil the a priori bond between Self and Other.

At first, these machinations require the speaker to follow Kraykowski, to attach personal consequences to the attorney's actions. Soon, however, the narrator decides that the only way not to be defined by Kraykowski is to *un*-define *him*. This leads to an ingenious scene in which the hero enters Kraykowski's favorite pastry shop and pays for a month's supply of the napoleons the attorney enjoys as a daily treat: "[N]othing is so difficult and delicate, so holy even, as human personhood, nothing can equal that voraciousness of mysterious connections that grow faint and pointless among strangers, in order to enchain them in a slightly monstrous bond. Imagine an attorney who leaves a public restroom, reaches for his fifteen grosze, and is informed that the bill—has already been settled. What does he feel then?"[73]

It is because of statements like these that we can say definitively that the story's hero is not merely trying to torment Kraykowski, even when he attempts to sabotage the attorney's love affair, but that he has a much more fundamental ontological project in mind. Kraykowski, as a creature of social convention, takes appropriately conventional refuge in identity: he is a self-contained entity, a molded and delimited social form striving to be equal to himself. Kraykowski tries to exist in spite of his contact with the world, which he strives to hold at bay through a prescriptive propriety. The story's hero, on the other hand, is expansive; he pursues contact with others because he understands that it is through this contact that he exists at all. In contrast to Kraykowski's conventional identity, his equality with himself, the story's narrator demonstrates the notion that not only one's existence but one's essence are dependent on the coexistence of another. As Jean-Luc Nancy explains, all people and things are coessential: "Coessentiality signifies the essential sharing of essentiality, sharing in the guise of assembling, as it were."[74] The narrator *needs* to share his essence—his very being—with Kraykowski, and this need is made all the more urgent by the fact that the narrator's health is growing steadily worse. This is not to say that Kraykowski does not need the narrator as well; on the contrary, their relationship is one of mutual infection, which is the basis, and not merely a possible scenario, of existence. The crucial difference is that Kraykowski idealizes identity without infection and tries to find refuge there, whereas the narrator recognizes the possibility for continued existence through infection, even if only as pure material, leading us to his final assault: "I could suddenly expire on the street, under a fence, and in that case—I'd have to write a note—may they forward my corpse to the Honorable Kraykowski's address."[75]

Contagious Laughter (Judging a Book by Its Cover)

The narrator of "The Honorable Kraykowski's Dancer" seeks what Nancy calls the "essential sharing of essentiality," but the attorney does not wish to share. As I have suggested, this problem is reiterated time and again in Gombrowicz's work, and it was understood especially well by Bruno Schulz, who made it the conceptual basis for the book cover he designed for Gombrowicz's 1937 novel *Ferdydurke* (figure 5.1). Years later, from the discomfort of his long exile in Argentina, Gombrowicz would recall how he sent one of his first printed copies of the novel to Schulz, who had been unexcited by the project's early drafts. Gombrowicz tells us that Schulz read the finished text insatiably over the course of a single day. Taking short breaks from his reading, Schulz walked several times to the post office in Drohobycz and wired Gombrowicz news of his excitement and enthusiasm.[76]

In the image that Schulz had designed for the novel's cover, heads and limbs struggle to emerge from a single tree trunk, a core that they all share. A few small houses appear in the background, perhaps to hold out the possibility of a more concrete, recognizable world just a little further off from where we happen to be. Schulz's drawing is an incisive visual exegesis, one that distills Gombrowicz's consistent exploration of intersubjectivity as the inevitable basis of Being. The image illustrates the consubstantiality, the deep interconnection, of various thinking subjects, all of whom are in some way immature, unfinalized. This incompleteness leaves them open to infectious contact from others, and the expressions on the figures' faces convey both the hilarity and the agony of this sharing of essences.

After the publication of *Ferdydurke,* Gombrowicz continued to develop this problematic in subsequent writings. In "The Rat" (Szczur), which was first published in *Skamander* in 1939 and included in *Bakakaj* in 1957, Gombrowicz presents a clear delineation of infection as freedom and identity as tyranny. In fact, we can read "The Rat" as a kind of rewriting of "The Honorable Kraykowski's Dancer" that intensifies the earlier story's antagonism *ad absurdum.* Instead of a society attorney as the defender of order and identity, we have a retired appellate judge named Skorabkowski. Instead of an idiosyncratic but mostly harmless stranger as the perpetrator of infection, we have the unforgettable Hooligan, whose nature is so excessive that no one can control it: "He was born in the middle of nowhere on

Figure 5.1. Bruno Schulz, cover of Witold Gombrowicz's *Ferdydurke* (1937; ink on paper). Bruno Schulz, *Księga obrazów,* ed. Jerzy Ficowski (Gdańsk: Słowo/obraz terytoria, 2012).

an expansive plain, grew up in forests, mountains, valleys, and expanses, and never slept in closed quarters, which lent him a particularly massive nature—an expansiveness of the soul—and fostered the outpouring of his disposition."[77] The Hooligan's nature is so "expansive," in fact, that when he sings at night, all the dogs and people within earshot sing with him: "And desperate dogs called back along their pickets, howling deafly and darkly. And finally this howling even infected the people. And the entire neighborhood howled longingly, deafly, and blackly, directly at the moon, which shone down palely."[78] After "The Honorable Kraykowski's Dancer," the reader cannot be surprised that Judge Skorabkowski must resist the Hooligan's expansiveness, and resist he does. In fact, he traps the Hooligan, locks him in his basement, and sets about finding a means of shrinking the Hooligan's nature. That is, Skorabkowski attempts to impose form where there had been only expansiveness, identity where there had been only infection.

In "The Rat" Gombrowicz offers two essential innovations to the themes introduced in "The Honorable Kraykowski's Dancer." First, the absolute freedom enjoyed by the Hooligan is anything but benign: as Skorabkowski points out, he murders indiscriminately. Second, even the expansive Hooligan has something with which he would rather *not* associate, or "be-with": a rat. The fear of being infected by the rat, of sharing its ratty essence, drives the Hooligan into the safety of identity; his expansiveness shrinks. Later, after he escapes, the Hooligan himself realizes the threat of infection, of the mutual sharing of essence. As Gombrowicz puts it, "he wasn't certain whether his painful association with one of these rodents over many years hadn't left in him something attractive to rats in general."[79] The rat is what the Hooligan has been for Skorabkowski: infection's threat to identity and selfhood. Skorabkowski's footman, and thus his assistant in torture, clearly articulates the fear of such infection, not just with regard to the Hooligan but in general: "[The footman] cursed the absolute mercilessness of the rat, cursed these horrible and somehow appalling associations within nature, cursed the limitlessness of mercilessness."[80]

When we look once again at Bruno Schulz's etching, we find a visual representation of this very same "limitlessness of mercilessness"—*bezgraniczność niemiłosierności*—which locks the Bakhtinian subplot in a double bind. For both Čapek and Gombrowicz, immaturity fosters a boundlessness that comes at a high price: it means that we are all incomplete and interconnected, consubstantial, bound to each other. Lacking a secure identity, the thinking subject is constantly infecting others and being infected by them. If such ontological intercourse eliminates boundaries, it also asks us to question the value of a world where even mercilessness is unbounded. The literature of intermediacy tells us that we have no choice but to play this game. It also tells us that we can never win.

Shame and Doubling: *Ferdydurke*

The plot of *Ferdydurke* is simple. Józio, a writer and an unmistakable stand-in for Gombrowicz himself, is abducted by Pimko, his old schoolmaster. Pimko drags Józio back to the schoolhouse, where he must then relive all the humiliations of adolescence. In each chapter, Józio has a chance to escape his captivity, but first he must endure some embarrassing crisis. And because he retreats from these crises, his adventures become a chain of repeated failures. Each time Józio approaches an uncomfortable boundary he withdraws back into his degrading imprisonment.

The novel's central question is whether an individual can ever be completely self-contained or, on the other hand, fully dispersed in the social collective. Józio's dilemma is not simply how to reclaim his mature existence but how to reconcile his internal lack of definition—his immaturity—with his well-formed, adult exterior. That is, Józio embodies intermediacy from the beginning, and not simply as a consequence of his abduction. In the opening pages of *Ferdydurke* Gombrowicz furnishes us with everything we need to understand the metaphysical construct of his narrative:

> On Tuesday I awoke at that soulless, dim hour when night has in fact already ended, but dawn has not yet managed to begin in earnest. Suddenly awakened, I wanted to rush by taxi to the station, for it seemed to me that I was going away—at just the next minute I was heartbroken to realize there was no train awaiting me at the station, no hour had struck. I was lying in the murky light, and my body was unbearably afraid, oppressing my spirit with terror, my spirit oppressed my body, and the most minute fiber seized up in anticipation that nothing would happen, nothing would change, nothing would ever occur, and no matter what I undertook, nothing, nothing would come of it.[81]

Gombrowicz places Józio in a strangely open-ended temporal confinement: night has ended, but day has not yet begun. This is the same intermediate temporality in which Schulz's father exists beyond death, a "commercial traveler" who returns after nightfall and leaves again before morning. Like Gregor Samsa in *The Metamorphosis,* our hero awakens in fright of missing a train, but before long he realizes that nothing will happen—that, in fact, nothing will *ever* happen. With no temporal boundary to cross, he is already a captive, and he feels his captivity as his body and spirit mutually oppressing one another. In a chapter appropriately called "Abduction" (Porwanie), he is stuck between times, though he will soon discover that his anxiety does not stem from a sense that time is not moving forward, but that it is, in effect, repeating itself. Józio finds that his very being is essentially bifurcated into mature and immature essences bound together, so that everything that happens in his adult life inscribes within itself the image of a shameful immaturity:

> The dream that vexed me in the night, the one that woke me, was an exponent of dread. In a reversal of time that should be forbidden to nature, I saw myself as I had been when I was fifteen or sixteen—I

> had shifted into youth—and standing in the breeze, on a rock, right next to the mill by the river, I was saying something, I heard my own long-buried voice, chicken-like and squeaky, I saw a not fully grown nose on a not fully formed face and too large hands—I felt the unpleasant consistency of that intermediate, transitory phase of development. I awoke in laughter and horror, because it seemed to me that the way I am today, at thirty, was mimicking and making fun of the unfledged pipsqueak I had been, and then he was mimicking me—and by the same token—that we were both mimicked by ourselves.[82]

In the notion of self-mimicry as self-mockery, we already find the roots of doubling, of the expropriation of the Self. In this sense, it is worth noting that my English translation of the passage loses the original's insistence on first-person action: it could be put, "the I who I am today, at thirty, *am* mimicking" myself. In his nightmare, Józio discovers a chain of mimetic activity within himself, with his youthful self-image comically, horribly mirroring his older self-image in a continuous, unbroken loop, a scene that will repeat itself in the novel's third chapter, where two youths fight a duel by making faces at each other. The circularity of this process provides an excellent figure for the function of one of the novel's richest motifs, the *pupa,* "tushy" or "bottom." The *pupa* represents the hero's immaturity or, more accurately, the unfinalized component of his Self, inextricable from his personhood. It plays two roles in the novel, both as enslaver and temporary liberator. It prevents Józio from defining himself, so that as he is being dragged back to school he declares, "The idiotic, infantile *pupa* was paralyzing, removing any possibility of resistance."[83] At the same time, Józio reaches for this pervasive immaturity whenever his humiliating circumstances precipitate a crisis, since immaturity liberates him from a society that demands maturity and resolve.

Many scholars have noted that for Gombrowicz immaturity is an inherent and inescapable condition of Being.[84] Immaturity helps us understand Józio's individuality as a compromise, the "intermediate, transitory phase" between the elusive freedom of formlessness and the solidity of form. Because it is inextricable from Being, the *pupa*, as a figure for immaturity, can neither be eliminated nor ignored, and this dooms Józio's struggle from the beginning. For Józio's ultimate goal, to keep his past from regurgitating itself into his present, is tantamount to a struggle to escape Being. And this struggle, while doomed to failure, necessitates the expropriation of the Self into a double, the exteriorization of the Self that, through mimicry and mockery, brings the thinking subject to a shameful awareness of Being.

Emmanuel Levinas describes this process extremely well in his essay "On Escape" (De l'évasion, 1935). Contemporary with *Ferdydurke,* it marks Lévinas's early departure from Heidegger:

> Existence is an absolute that is asserted without reference to anything else. It is identity. But in this reference to himself, man perceives a type of duality. His identity with himself loses the character of a logical or tautological form; it takes on a dramatic form[. . . .] In the identity of the I, the identity of being reveals its nature as enchainment, for it appears in the form of suffering and invites us to escape. Thus, escape is the need to get out of oneself, that is, *to break that most radical and unalterably binding of chains, the fact that the I is oneself.*[85]

The "duality" that Levinas posits is precisely what we witness in Józio's repeated encounters with mimicry, instances of mimesis that take on the character of a confrontation with the Self. The most widely discussed such instance, which has become common currency in Polish popular culture, is the scene in chapter 3, "Catching and Further Crushing" (Przyłapanie i dalsze miętoszenie), in which Józio and his classmates engage in a duel of face making, imitating one another to establish a kind of existential supremacy.[86] In his dream, however, Józio faces an image not of an immature Other, but of the immature component of his own being, from which he cannot escape.

As if this manifestation of the Other were not clear enough, just before Pimko abducts Józio—for his re-maturation by means of dematuration—Gombrowicz literalizes the immature double Józio has seen in his dream: "I realized that I was not alone. There was someone other than me in the corner, next to the stove, where the light had not yet reached—another person was in the room. . . . And again the dryness in the mouth, the beating of the heart, the halting of the breath—that was me, myself, standing by the oven. This time it was no dream—there was actually a double standing by the stove."[87] This moment is the linchpin of both the novel's plot and its philosophical structure. Gombrowicz tells us that the double in Józio's room is afraid, that it does not wish to return the protagonist's gaze, and this displacement from the Self, in which the double does *not* wish to meet the subject's gaze, signifies the shame of Being. Józio immediately recognizes the dual nature of this apparition, both himself and not, both present and absent, "something alien, imposed, a kind of compromise between the external world and the internal one."[88] Gombrowicz explicitly posits the intermediacy of the thinking subject. For the protagonist, with a redoubled will toward escape into an existence that is both singular and whole, reaches for his writing instruments, his pen and blank paper, in order to devise a work that will define and distinguish him, that will in effect *be* him, and that will therefore abolish his compromised existence and secure his individuality: "I start to write the first pages of my very own work, just like me, identical with me, arising straight out of me."[89] But Józio never succeeds in composing a work coterminous with himself, because just as he seizes this opportunity for self-definition, Pimko enters. Józio puts up no resistance. He is, after all, inextricable from his immaturity, his *pupa*, which cannot be eliminated.

The drama of *Ferdydurke* consists in the repeated failure to achieve what Levinas calls "excendence," an escape from Being, and this failure is bound to both memory and shame. Memory, because the hero is tormented by the recollection of his immaturity, of the disorderly, unruly, disobedient world of his youth, and this makes him feel that his very existence is collapsing and that he must escape, though flight is impossible, since memory cannot be outrun. Shame, because according to Levinas shame arises from our inability to escape Being, and from the fact that this failure is obvious to all gazes directed toward us:

> Shame does not depend—as we might believe—on the limitation of our being, inasmuch as it is liable to sin, but rather on the very being of our being, on its incapacity to break with itself. Shame is founded upon the solidarity of our being, which obliges us to claim responsibility for ourselves. [. . .] It is therefore our intimacy, that is, our presence to ourselves, that is shameful. It reveals not our nothingness but rather the totality of our existence. Nakedness is the need to excuse one's existence. Shame is, in the last analysis, an existence that seeks excuses. What shame discovers is the being who *uncovers* himself.[90]

Writing twenty years later, Jean-Paul Sartre makes the opposite claim about shame. Because shame arises from the gaze of the Other, whose freedom the "I" wishes to claim for himself, it has the effect of reifying identity: "Shame reveals to me that I *am* this being, not in the mode of 'was' or of 'having to be,' but *in-itself*."[91] But these models of shame are not mutually exclusive for Gombrowicz. On the contrary, his construction of shame requires the endless repetition of movement in both directions: the thinking subject attempts to flee his own identity, but he also flees the Other. These flights are both necessary and impossible. The thinking subject can never be completely coterminous with himself in the way Levinas describes, and he can never assent to "being-with." Instead, Gombrowicz posits an uncomfortable middle ground between these ideals, an intermediacy that is at once comic and horrifying. This is why Józio wakes up "in laughter and horror."

Levinas reveals for us the basic mechanism behind the appearance of the double. In the absence of the Other, Gombrowicz invents another in whose eyes immaturity—that is, his disorder and excess—is shameful. One of the paradoxes of shame in the Western imagination, as Bernard Williams notes, is that it both binds one person to another and prompts an impulse to flee.[92] This effect can be seen even in the absence of the Other. After all, the thinking subject need only imagine the Other's gaze in order to posit a sense of shame.

As Janusz Margański further suggests, the thinking subject must then waver between the ideal of an unknowable Absolute and contact with ethically independent thinking subjects, a movement between Self and Other:

> In fact, Gombrowicz always confronts his heroes with this antinomy [. . .]. Man, wishing to extract himself from the oppression of painful mediations, ravenous for unmediated relations with his neighbor or his God, reaches innocently for forms of discourse fixed in tradition, for a deep-rooted symbolic. And this is also where we get the compulsion toward repetition and constant parody. And this is also where we get the attempt to appropriate set modes of discourse through parody and the attempt to create—following the "death of God"—other interhuman relations. And this is also where we get the wound that constantly appears in the "I" who is thinking about God.[93]

In this formulation, the individual's quest—for definition, on the one hand, or contact, on the other—is always doomed. In striving for contact with the Other, that Other is sometimes an ethically independent thinking subject (the "neighbor"), sometimes the self-identical Absolute ("God"). The individual seeks these "unmediated relations" to escape the Self, which is shameful. But Gombrowicz's characters cannot escape from the Self, and the shame of their failure only makes them all the more dependent on the Other. Gombrowicz, in fact, raises this bonding power of shame to the level of abject addiction, asserting that "man is most deeply dependent on his reflection in the soul of another person, though it may be the soul of a moron."[94] The fact that the individual is dependent—*uzależniony*, "addicted"—on the Other's concept of him guarantees that he can never be alone, though the shame that remains an essential condition of that scrutiny simultaneously drives him to panic and flight. The result is a constantly alternating movement toward and away from the Self—his memory, his immaturity and maturity—as reflected "in the soul of another person." This vacillation is manifest in the appearance of the double.

Giorgio Agamben, in his description of Levinas's "uncovering of oneself" as "expropriation and desubjectivization," renders the link between shame and doubling even more explicit:

> It is as if our consciousness collapsed and, seeking to flee in all directions, were simultaneously summoned by an irrefutable order to be present at its own defacement, at the expropriation of what is

> most its own. In shame, the subject thus has no other content than its own desubjectification; it becomes witness to its own disorder, its own oblivion as a subject. [. . .] [W]hoever experiences shame is overcome by his own being subject to vision; he must respond to what deprives him of speech. [. . .] [Shame] is nothing less than the fundamental sentiment of being *a subject,* in the two apparently opposed senses of this phrase: to be subjected and to be sovereign.[95]

Afraid to look up, Józio's cowering double is "overcome by his own being subject to vision," and Józio, pressured by his "being *a subject,*" attempts throughout the novel to escape into both senses of that word, into the security of a sovereign self-identity and the illusory freedom of nondefinition. Being a subject means having only enough definition to recognize oneself as a Self, one who overlaps with other selves and is subject to them. Józio cannot stand his own identity—his self-singularity, which the appearance of his double paradoxically serves to emphasize—and in this sense is complicit in his own abduction, the process by which he is subjected once again to all the humiliations of adolescence. At the same time, he finds the trials to which he is repeatedly subjected equally unbearable, and this compels him to escape back into his self-singularity, his "sovereignty." Recall that Józio's first reaction to the appearance of his double is a desperate attempt *to write,* to reconstitute his identity through language. He has been mortified by the reception of his book, Gombrowicz's own *Memoir from a Time of Immaturity,* which had been viciously attacked by critics, who saw the author as immature and tried to shame him into silence.[96]

Gombrowicz revisits the link between shame and silence several times throughout *Ferdydurke,* most notably in the chapter entitled "Preface to Philidor Lined with Child" (Przedmowa do Filidora dzieckiem podszytego), where he writes about the poet-prophet so secure in his selfhood that accusations of immaturity can no longer stifle him, for he is beyond shame. He writes that "the poet-prophet of sound philosophy is fixed so firmly in himself that not even stupidity and immaturity are able to frighten or harm him—with head raised high, he can express himself and make himself manifest in his own indolence, whereas you are now barely in a state to express anything, for terror has taken away your voice."[97] Józio, however, is not a "poet-prophet of sound philosophy" who is "fixed [. . .] in himself." Instead, he is open and exposed to the world, which constantly threatens him with its shame-inducing gaze. Gombrowicz incorporates this enforced silence into the novel's closing passages, when we find Józio and Zosia, the young woman whom Józio has kidnapped, sitting together and unsure what to do now that the captive has performed his own kidnapping. Each character is entirely incapable of articulating these shameful circumstances to the other. For each, the presence of the Other makes such an explanation both necessary and impossible: "I didn't know what to do. I couldn't explain and voice to Zosia what had happened on the estate, for I was ashamed, but anyway, I didn't find the words. Whereas she probably figured it out more or less, for she was ashamed, too, and she really couldn't voice it."[98] Gombrowicz assembles an analogically repetitive, chiasmic chain: the captive becomes the captor, but unable to "voice" his experience—*wyjęzyczyć*, literally, "to express in language"—he feels only shame. This shame is itself infectious, and Zosia, the captive's captive, feels it as well. But she is also incapable of expressing it in language.

Zosia herself functions as a double of the protagonist, at least insofar as she clearly mirrors key aspects of his interiority, and the doubling that we have already witnessed in the novel's opening chapter serves as the prototype for this mirroring. The various instances of emotional infection and interpersonal entanglement that we find amply evidenced in *Ferdydurke* ultimately stem from and reflect that initial moment, in which the protagonist is entangled with no Other but with his Self. Typically for Gombrowicz, the doubling of the synthetic whole echoes the symmetry of analytic parts. Józio says of his encounter with the double, "Furtively, from under the blanket, I looked as though not at myself, and I saw that face, which was mine and not-mine. . . . That's my nose . . . that's my mouth . . . those are my ears, my home."[99]

Decades later, Gombrowicz would recycle this scene in the second volume of his *Diary* (Dziennik, 1957–61). In Buenos Aires, where he spent twenty years of exile, Gombrowicz receives an unexpected visit from his friend Simon, who remarks that his daughter has just been horribly scalded by a pot of boiling water. She is still in the hospital; Simon does not know what to do with himself. Gombrowicz and Simon sit facing each other, unable to say anything, and Gombrowicz tells us:

> Yet I went silent, he went silent, and we sat, so to speak, nose-to-nose. One-on-one. Hand-to-hand. Leg-to-leg. Knee-to-knee. One-on-one. Until this stupid identity in this, my room, started to bug me, and I think, how is it that he repeats me, I repeat him, one-on-one—suddenly the scalding of the child scalded me until I hissed—and then, I see, though so similar, we can't go on sitting here, and in general it's better not to sit but get out, get out, get out, a way out, any, an expulsion, a distancing, became pressing, burning![100]

We are drawn again to the signature inventory of body parts, the arms and legs of Gombrowicz finding their necessary counterparts in those of Simon. But we should be especially intrigued by Gombrowicz's annoyance at "this stupid identity in this, my room." Gombrowicz uses the word "identity" in a metaphysical, rather than a conventional, sense: he is referring to their equivalence, not to their status as individuals. This draws the two distinct individuals, Gombrowicz and Simon, into an uncomfortable, "stupid" congruence. "Stupid" because this mirroring is infinitely self-referential, and because the two individuals should not be identical, especially in Gombrowicz's own domestic space. In a similar way, Józio emphasizes that the unbearable expropriation of Self, the appearance of the double, occurs in his own home. This is what makes such an identity "stupid," since it underscores the intrusion of the Other into the ontological zone of the Self.

The Double and Repetition

It should not be possible for one to be equivalent to another in the same way as one is equivalent to oneself. Or so the thinking subject, pained by the encroachment of the Other, would like to think. In fact, this intrusion of the Other is a basic function of Being, and Gombrowicz does not oppose it so much as he points out—repeatedly, in one colorful example after another—that it compels us to attempt an escape. It does not matter whether such a flight is from the Self or from the Other in whom the Self is mirrored, since both escapes are ultimately impossible. The urgent need to flee, to break out of this unwholesome identity—with oneself, with the Other—remains real. But Gombrowicz's phrasing already forecloses the possibility of any such escape, since he describes the need to flee as *palące,* literally "burning," though also a conventional word for "urgent," as it is in English. This picks up the connotative cue of the child's scalding, which Gombrowicz already feels through his symmetry with Simon. Thus the author's need to escape inscribes within itself the very same association from which escape becomes necessary.

Obsessively, Gombrowicz expresses this need with repetitions that fetishize the word. One word leads necessarily to another, "hand-to-hand," "one-on-one." Nothing can be uttered without it meeting its echo or mirror image. For Gombrowicz—and, in fact, we have already seen this in Schulz, Platonov, Mandel'shtam, Miłosz, Zabolotskii, and Nezval—the language of intermediacy is inherently repetitive, and the repetitions of sounds, words, and sentiments create loops that divorce language from its conventional communicative function. As I have suggested earlier, one may think of Samuel Beckett's late-Modernist repetitions as the far extreme of this approach to language. In *Waiting for Godot* or *The Unnamable,* repetition demonstrates the use of language as a placeholder for what is not, or cannot be, said. Or, to consider the same issue diachronically, these obsessive repetitions detach the content of language from its historical function, since that which is infinitely repeatable can no longer be historically contingent. In repeating the same words over and over, Gombrowicz's speaker sacrifices historically contingent narrative to myth, the repeatable, historically noncontingent utterance par excellence. This is what Theodore Adorno meant when he wrote, in reference to theoretical discussions of Culture with a capital "C," "Fetishism gravitates toward mythology."[101] Repetition releases its content from linear temporality, ultimately rendering it self-equivalent, self-identical.

Following the critical commonplace that Gombrowicz often seems to write the same book over and over, Hanjo Berressem suggests that the author suffers from a "literary repetition compulsion" that is tied to the thinking subject's—and, by extension, the author's—difficult and painful relationship with the reality around him: "This compulsion causes the 'fractal' character of Gombrowicz's work, which is not only concerned with the inevitably broken character of human reality, but which is also basically self-similar; specific forms and structures are repeated obsessively on various levels. In these condensations and displacements the trauma is reconstructed, a reconstruction that becomes the subject's enigmatic and ambivalent truth."[102] It is striking how easily we could apply this same formulation to any of the authors of intermediacy. Especially in the fiction of Platonov, Schulz, Čapek, and (we shall see) Weiner, repetition is in part this same continuous "reconstruction." But in the process of reconstruction, the original trauma—the death of the Father, the loss of one's own sense of individual identity—is itself reconstituted, propelling the thinking subject toward new flights. Meanwhile, the reconstruction of the world, a repetition with difference, represents the compromise between lived praxis and myth, an intermediary position that the thinking subject experiences as an "enigmatic and ambivalent truth."

In both the *Diary* and *Ferdydurke,* the consequence of identity is predictably the same: the individual must try to escape, to break free of this shameful self-equivalence, even though such an escape is ultimately impossible, since there can be no escape from Being. There is a basic difference between the two scenarios presented in the *Diary* and *Ferdydurke*, however, insofar as the double in the novel appears as the literal desubjectification of the subject, the *ex*-propriation of his Self from himself, whereas in the *Diary* we find the reverse movement, the *ap*-propriation of the Other into the Self, if only momentarily. But I would suggest that for Gombrowicz, an author who assigns vital importance to all things "interhuman," the difference between splitting off from oneself and absorbing the Other into oneself is a difference of polarity rather than of quality.

Gombrowicz's "interhuman church" (*kościół międzyludzki*), so named initially in his play *The Marriage* (Ślub, 1953), is a zone of interpersonal contact beyond the bounds of culturally prescribed institutions, Gombrowicz's personal formulation of "free and familiar contact." According to Jerzy Jarzębski, the notion of the interhuman church arises out of Gombrowicz's "fundamental ambivalence": "assiduously fleeing all manner of social and ideological systems, at the same time he desperately sought some kind of new principle on which it might be possible to base his communication with Others, with the world; he sought a lasting middle ground, around which he could organize his own personhood."[103] Jarzębski goes on to note that even this concept, once established, provided Gombrowicz scant consolation. The splitting of the Self is merely the obverse of ontological intercourse with the Other, and both movements create an intimacy that is shameful, whether it reveals our vulnerability to the Other or, to reiterate Levinas's point, our "presence to ourselves," an ontological condition from which there is no escape. The double emerges in these texts as the literalization of this intimacy, and the countless interpersonal entanglements in Gombrowicz emerge from this primal, *intra*-personal dynamic of subjectification and desubjectification.

Gombrowicz explains this dynamic in unusually direct language in a 1951 letter to Martin Buber. Shortly before writing to Buber in Jerusalem, Gombrowicz had been given a Spanish translation of the Jewish philosopher's *What Is Man?* (Das Problem des Menschen, 1948) by his close friend Alejandro Rússovich, who later relayed the one passage that made an especially strong impression on Gombrowicz, and which we may also read as encapsulating Gombrowicz's thinking about interhuman relations:[104]

> The fundamental fact of human existence is neither the individual as such nor the aggregate as such. Each, considered by itself, is a mighty abstraction. The individual is a fact of existence in so far as he steps into a living relation with other individuals. The aggregate is a fact of existence in so far as it is built up of living units of relation. [. . .] The view which establishes the concept of "between" is to be acquired by no longer localizing the relation between human beings, as is customary, either within individual souls or in a general world which embraces and determines them, but in actual fact *between* them.[105]

Gombrowicz sensed a kindred ontological tendency in Buber and sent him a manuscript of *The Marriage*. Buber's initial response, insisting that the play is not really dramatic, since Gombrowicz's characters are not "separate and self-contained," helped Gombrowicz clarify his position on the potential dialogism within our own interiority. "Can't there be drama," Gombrowicz asks in his letter to Buber, "not between people, but in a person himself? If someone suffers from an incurable disease—isn't the drama realized between himself and his disease? If someone is confronted with his fate, with his destiny—must that necessarily play out through the mediation of people?"[106] For Gombrowicz, as for Čapek in *An Ordinary Life,* it is not only conceivable but necessary that such internal conflicts play themselves out within the individual thinking subject. And yet Gombrowicz's own tendency is to externalize these conflicts through a double, the "'I' in an alien domain." That is, what occurs within the individual echoes outward into interpersonal action, wherein the subject not only casts himself outward, as we see at the beginning of *Ferdydurke,* but also creates and resists the identification of himself with others, as we see in the *Diary.* In his letter to Buber, Gombrowicz moves quickly from asserting a drama within the subject to rejecting the possibility of "separate and self-contained" people altogether: "[I] cannot provide a conflict between people who exist 'on their own,' as you say, because my vision, my intuition rests precisely on the fact that there are no people 'on their own.' My hero's drama is not a confrontation with other people, but merely with the forces that arise *from people, between* people."[107] For Gombrowicz, the subject oscillates continuously between his own subjectification and desubjectification. He is always singular—or sovereign—because he cannot escape his own being. But at the same time, he is always plural—or subjected to his others—because the Other exposes him to Being. The sudden impulse to escape, as constant a motif in *Ferdydurke* as it is in much of the rest of Gombrowicz's oeuvre, represents both a fundamental need and an inevitable failure. Taken together, flight and failure form a repetitive loop.

Time and Time Again: Repetition as a Revolt against Temporality

There are many well-documented reasons for why Gombrowicz might have felt a literal need to defend his personhood, against his family background, the painful last gasps of Polish aristocratic culture, his own literary and artistic ambitions, and even the critics who had attacked his first book, *Memoirs from a Time of Immaturity. Ferdydurke* provides a wealth of material for those who read its individual episodes with an eye toward Gombrowicz's parody of cultural conditioning. But there is also a powerful metaphysical dimension to Gombrowicz's approach to individuality. At the level of character development, this approach concerns the spatial distribution of the thinking subject's existence, which is not limited to his own body, but rather extends to others and, in the extreme case, is fully expropriated into the body of the double. At the larger structural level, Gombrowicz's approach is equally a rebellion against time, which in *Ferdydurke* is relentlessly repetitive.

The novel's central problematic is a form of repetition, the repetition of childhood in adulthood. Józio, however, remains an adult despite his imprisonment; we could even go so far as to say that his imprisonment consists of the incommensurability of the times to which he is attached. This existential condition describes the temporal schema of the novel as a whole, and thus of the subjectivity the novel systematically describes. "In 'between' the Adult and the Youth, we can discover our real humanity," Eryk Pieszak writes of

Gombrowicz. "A real person is someone who is 'suspended between.'"[108] Enacting this suspension, each time Józio approaches an uncomfortable boundary, rather than transgress it, he withdraws back into his own unfreedom. The same shame that I have discussed in reference to the repetition of the Self in the double also drives Józio to panic and flight. The result is a constantly alternating movement toward and away from the individual's own Self.

Repetition: that which is born from a will toward momentary self-liberation—a retreat from crisis—but which must cancel out the possibility of total escape, for each withdrawal from crisis promises a return to crisis. Søren Kierkegaard draws what is perhaps the most elegant link between recollection and repetition, viewing them as opposite polarities of the same phenomenon: "Repetition and recollection are the same movement, except in opposite directions, for what is recollected has been, is repeated backward, whereas genuine repetition is recollected forward."[109] At first glance, Kierkegaard's concept of repetition as a forward projection of the material of recollection is enticingly appropriate for the hero of *Ferdydurke*. Józio, after all, does not spend the novel sitting around and reminiscing about his youth, but is actually forced to relive it—though differently, of course, as an adult. He must reexperience the feeling of inexperience of which he is so ashamed. Yet Gombrowicz complicates this model considerably, for the repetition of crises reemphasizes the immaturity of the hero's soul, not his maturity or self-realization. Repetition for Gombrowicz signals the hero's inability to transgress, to realize the full potential of the crisis as a separation from his unfree circumstances (*crisis*, from Greek *kritein,* "to separate"). The crisis, or what Kierkegaard calls the "ordeal," is a "*temporary* category" ("it *eo ipso* is defined in relation to time and therefore must be annulled in time") because it is seen from the other side of what Kierkegaard calls the "thunderstorm," the moment of separation.[110] Simply put, the ordeal is a discrete event, since it must be viewed from within an eternity wherein the ordeal is no longer taking place. Instead of definitive crisis or ordeal, however, Gombrowicz exposes us to repetition: we are always inside the event, because the event never stops taking place.

In his notes and papers, Kierkegaard writes that individual freedom begins as a desire that fears repetition, becomes enslaved by it, and is reborn into sagacity, which attempts to contextualize and thus stave off repetition, but fails. Enchained by repetition again, freedom then "breaks forth in its highest form, in which it is qualified in relation to itself."[111] Gombrowicz's protagonist seems perfectly capable of desiring freedom and, consequently, of fearing the repetition that locks him in, but it is not until the last chapter that he appears to emerge into complete consciousness of the *pupa* and of the endless repetition that it embodies. This, of course, is not the "highest form" of freedom that Kierkegaard posits, but merely a sagacity that no longer fears repetition, giving way to a recognition of its inevitability. In artfully repetitive terms, Gombrowicz tells us at the end of the novel that there is no escape from repetition: "For there is no escape from one's mug, except into another mug, and from a person one may take refuge only in the embrace of another person. But from the *pupa* there is absolutely no escape."[112]

Jan Kott, whom I mentioned in chapter 3 for having criticized what he perceived as the immateriality and ahistoricity of Milosz's wartime poems, offers an admirably blunt assessment of Gombrowicz's condition: "Even the best party becomes a hell if you cannot leave it."[113] He goes on to describe an all-night party he attended in a Warsaw apartment in 1943. As day was approaching, Kott says he heard a knocking sound coming from an adjoining room and, upon further investigation, found two men knocking their heads in unison against the floor before rising to face each other, matching grimace for grimace, frown for frown. "Already there were a few of us who had been infected by Gombrowicz," Kott recalls, "or more precisely by *Ferdydurke*."[114] The two duelists in this instance were Czesław Miłosz and Jerzy Andrzejewski.

Note that the adventures we encounter in chapter after chapter of Gombrowicz's novel are not merely a rehashing of earlier action, though the basic pattern of entrapment and flight into further entrapment remains the same. Rather, each ordeal is inflected with an accumulating knowledge of the ordeals that precede it, eventually pushing Józio toward sagacity in the last chapter, each time leaving him a surplus of possibility from his earlier inability to transgress. This becomes clear in the novel's eleventh chapter, "Preface to Philibert Lined with Child" (Przedmowa do Filiberta dzieckiem podszytego), the second chapter to be called a "Preface." Here, the speaker—who appears to fuse Józio with the authorial voice of Gombrowicz himself—reflects on the inevitability of such repetitions: "And again a preface . . . and I'm enslaved to the preface, I can't dispense with the preface, and I must have a preface, for the law of symmetry demands that 'Philibert Lined with Child' answer 'Philidor Lined with Child,' and the preface to 'Philibert Lined with Child' must answer the preface to 'Philidor Lined with Child.' Though I would wish it, I cannot, I can't, I just can't evade the iron laws of symmetry, as well as of analogy."[115] Gombrowicz knows—as does Józio—what has come before in the telling of *Ferdydurke*. Rather than release him/them from having to repeat what has already been said, this knowledge demands repetition. The very same equal and opposite wills toward synthesis and analysis that we have already seen in "Philidor Lined with Child" drive the novel as a whole. Józio himself is constantly moving between the analytic impulse, which separates him from others, and the synthetic, which integrates him with them. That he is aware of his own enslavement to this process does not release him from it. Each instantiation of this dynamic is simultaneously a new experience and a recapitulation of what has come before.

In fact, as Mark C. Taylor points out in reference to Kierkegaard, it is the failure of transgression, and therefore the retention of all the potential that transgression would cancel, that makes each repetition new: "The irreducible outside of transgression prevents repetition from becoming the return of the same. Repetition is the return of absolute Difference. [. . .] As the return of a difference that identity cannot incorporate, and an Other that the same cannot assimilate, repetition subverts the recollection upon which speculative philosophy is based."[116] This formulation helps us understand why Gombrowicz's protagonist is always perplexed and indecisive and cannot commit to a single transgression. While we, from our privileged standpoint as readers, recognize patterns of repetition in Józio's narrative, and while he himself manages to admit to a kind of deterministic formal repetition in "Preface to Philibert Lined with Child," Józio is ultimately overwhelmed by the "irreducible outside of transgression." This "difference that identity cannot incorporate" is not quite coterminous with immaturity, but immaturity remains for Gombrowicz the absence of an ordering principle that could contain or efface this difference, this surplus. Time and again we witness Józio's inability to "assimilate" an Other who contains this immaturity, whether it is the double of himself he sees in his room in the novel's first chapter or the seemingly impenetrable youthfulness of the young girl he abducts toward the end of the novel. Even her family name, Młodziak—from *młody,* "young"—points to the immaturity that torments Józio.

The last clause of Taylor's formulation, that "repetition subverts the recollection upon which speculative philosophy is based," might give us pause vis-à-vis Gombrowicz. For while the novel is not a treatise in speculative philosophy, recollection (such as the recollection of one's immature youth) is an essential component of these repetitive adventures. Furthermore, Taylor asserts, via Maurice Blanchot, that repetition "marks 'the end of philosophy' and 'the beginning of writing.'"[117] In *Ferdydurke,* Gombrowicz seems to offer us an alternative to this conclusion, because if writing is itself the transgression (as Gombrowicz illustrates in the novel's opening chapter, and as Taylor concurs), then it is repetition that *prevents* the transgression from taking place.[118] Shaken by the appearance of his double, "an Other that the same cannot assimilate," Józio sits down to write, to formulate himself within the definitive bounds of language, but Pimko steals him away before he can put pen to paper.

Repetition is also more generally a subversion of time and of the progress that time seems to promise. In another treatment of Kierkegaard, Arne Melberg suggests that, although repetition occurs in a time that we might call "now," this "now" is a different temporal category than that which exists in the absence of repetition: "The temporal dialectics of 'repetition' suspends temporal sequence [. . .]. [T]he *now* that is always an *after* actually comes *before*—it is the *now* of 'the instant,' the sudden intervention in sequential time, the caesura that defines what has been, makes it possible to tell its story and makes way for the 'new.'"[119] To "suspend . . . temporal sequence" is precisely what Gombrowicz demonstrates with repetition, since it is the linear progression of events that, in moments of crisis, promises to lead Józio to unknown consequences he would rather not face. In place of these consequences he substitutes a pattern of repetitions, until every present becomes "the instant," that is, a present that inscribes its own past within itself and, in a sense, falls short of being a present at all. As Melberg tells us, "The instant is never pure presence: it always carries a past."[120]

The novel's repetitions reveal that Józio is as apprehensive about the fixed propriety of maturity as he is about the disorder and uncertainty of immaturity. In other words, he is as disturbed by the definition and restriction of form as he is by the overabundance of formlessness: "we are always ceaselessly looking for form, and we revel in it or suffer by it, and we adapt to it or violate and smash it, or we allow it to shape us, Amen."[121] Gombrowicz's hero calls for form when the formlessness of reality is most overwhelming, and yet he comes to abhor it when it approaches, because "our form pervades us, imprisons us from within as much as from without."[122] In reference to Bakhtin, Dostoevsky, Schulz, and Miłosz, Jean-Pierre Salgas notes that, for Gombrowicz, the "Form of the World" is the God who may or may not be dead: "In Witold—the old pupil of pathology (Schulz) and sociology (Miłosz), and in childhood an avid reader of Gogol and Dostoevsky—there is something of a Rabelaisian return to the Russian's [*sic*] questions concerning man after the death of God . . . Since for the Pole (on the periphery of Europe, neither a Frenchman, nor a German, nor a Russian) God is first of all the Form of the World."[123] Salgas, for whom Gombrowicz is a "Dostoevsky in the style of Rabelais," regards Gombrowicz as neither here nor there, at once trying to find his place (as person, as artist) in a world where he is undeniably marginal, and where received definitions (language, culture, genre) offer little consolation.[124] In this fight against form, Gombrowicz repeatedly points to the *pupa*, the unrelenting infantilism that, like the determinism of form, also has the power to terrify. There is no way out, either through order or through disorder, which is why Gombrowicz's protagonist chooses eternal vacillation. So long as repetition occurs, there is no need for Józio to choose between maturity and immaturity. He can remain tentatively between them and exist only in the repeated "instant," eluding both absolute definition and overwhelming excess.

Doubling the Double: Richard Weiner's *The Game of Quartering*

When we reexamine the thematic substructure of the double in its relation to shame, speechlessness, and the gaze of the Other, we find that Central European literature between the world wars is rife with instantiations of the same basic mechanism. The themes of identity and escape were of equal concern to Richard Weiner, whose work offers many avenues of fruitful comparison to Gombrowicz and Čapek.

Weiner, a Paris correspondent for the Czech daily newspaper *Lidové noviny,* was just resuming his literary activities at the time Gombrowicz, fleeing the paternalistic pressures of family and cultural life in Poland, arrived in France. But as we have already seen, there is no escape, and Janusz Margański points out that even Gombrowicz's flight to Paris was culturally prescribed: young Polish men from prosperous families were regularly sent to Paris to receive Western culture.[125] And according to Margański, Gombrowicz was ambivalent about the forms of cultural production he encountered in Paris: "Gombrowicz did not chase after Modernism; admittedly, he observed and analyzed it, but he also fled from it."[126]

Unlike Gombrowicz, Weiner had already established himself as a poet and prose author by the time he relocated to Paris in 1919, where he became a full-time journalist. Jindřich Chalupecký, Weiner's best postwar critic, describes this move as a "double escape": "An escape from his Czech surroundings, and just as much an escape from his own calling as a writer."[127] While living in Paris in the 1920s, Weiner wrote hundreds of Czech-language feuilletons, addressing issues that ranged from Surrealist aesthetics to the cultural significance of Marcel Proust. At the same time, he participated directly in the international artists' group Le Grand Jeu, which included the French poets René Daumal (1908–1944) and Roger Gilbert-Lecomte (1907–1943) and the Czech painter Josef Šíma (1891–1971).[128]

Distinct from the burgeoning French Surrealist movement, Le Grand Jeu sought, as Martin Tharp explains, "less an aesthetic than an ethic: the project of Rimbaud not only to transgress but in fact [to] dissolve all [borders] separating life from art, and finally even life from death."[129] In late 1925, Šíma began experimenting with the use of prisms in painting, and he explained his method of capturing "the unity of the world" to Weiner, who shared his ideas at the time: "Regardless of how diverse the material, it is 'one.' This monism lends unpredictable dimensions to reality. In this reality memory is reflected in the mirror of the present moment, from the perspective of the future."[130] For Šíma, monism consists not only in the ultimate unity of all things but also in the fusion of past, present, and future. Present experience becomes an extension of past memory. At the same time, the present is tied inextricably to the future, which it anticipates. Weiner's second phase of literary production, which lasted from 1927 to 1933, demonstrates both the influence of Le Grand Jeu and Weiner's increasingly problematic relationship to this perspective on space-time and matter.[131]

The most important product of this last wave of activity is *The Game for Real* (Hra doopravdy, published 1933). Weiner's last work, and one of his most challenging, is a masterful instantiation of the themes of doubling, interpersonal infection, and entrapment. Consisting of two thematically intertwined novellas, *The Game for Real* opens in much the same way as *Ferdydurke,* with the unbearable doubling of the protagonist. Yet a significant difference in this first novella, entitled *The Game of Quartering* (Hra na čtvrcení, 1929–31), is that it opens not with the hero at home, but on his way home.

On the Metro, the unnamed hero of *The Game of Quartering* encounters a strange double, though not of himself. This man is the spitting image of Vicente Escudero, the Spanish flamenco dancer who was a Paris sensation in the 1920s, and he starts to follow the narrator, who then has difficulty returning home. In fact, new doubles appear, and they foreclose a definitive return to the protagonist's domestic space: it is late at night, and the narrator cannot open his own door because there is an equal and opposite force pushing against it from the other side. Daniela Hodrová has noted the symbolic significance of setting as Weiner illustrates this aporia, in what is supposed to be the transitional space between the outer world and the domestic space, an "'estrangement' of dwelling" similar to what we find in Dostoevsky and Kafka, and with the same effects: "Subsequently, his doubles appear in the apartment. Times and places start to permeate each other in prose; the subject's identity is called into question."[132]

In a productive comparison between Weiner and Franz Kafka, Lubomír Doležel focuses on the opening of *The Game of Quartering* as emblematic of Weiner's metaphysics, which requires "emissaries of the invisible world" to penetrate the unity of the visible:

> This first encounter between the visible and the invisible worlds in Weiner's novel indicates the specificity of Weiner's semantics: There is no clear and strict demarcation between the visible and the invisible worlds. Weiner's typical semantic device is that of metamorphosis, a device of converting, transforming individuals of the invisible world into agents of the visible world and vice versa. In contrast to Kafka's semantics, a typical character of Weiner is a "split individual," existing simultaneously or alternatively both in the visible, and in the invisible worlds.[133]

This "split individual" is itself oxymoronic: one cannot be both "split" and "individual" without forming some kind of double of oneself. Along the same lines, Alfred Thomas, writing against a Czech reception that has generally viewed Weiner's notoriously difficult language as self-neutralizing, makes the significant point that Weiner's insistence on paradoxical phrasing "abolishes the artificial separation between [true and false]: two conflicting truth claims coexist in the same word or phrase."[134] Thus the language of Weiner's fiction becomes the very mechanism of reflexivity, the substance that both constitutes and corrupts the Self, as Daniela Hodrová has noted with regard to Weiner, Čapek, and similarly self-reflexive authors of their time: "Hypothecizing and relativizing, the 'openness' of plot that reflects the relative nature of 'open' knowledge also signifies the openness and layeredness of the semantic structure, the tendency toward ambivalence and polysemy, toward a game of indirect, perhaps hidden meanings that is yet another form of distancing literature from reality or, more precisely, the form by which literature transforms nonliterary reality into literary reality."[135] In this way, Weiner's play with language becomes the means by which the "ambivalence and polysemy" of real-life existence is imported into what we might otherwise see as the closed, unchanging, strictly delimited world of the literary text—"the form by which literature transforms nonliterary reality into literary reality."

Gombrowicz's protagonist manages to produce multiple doubles by mapping his interiority onto the Other(s) he encounters; Weiner's protagonist will do the same. In the opening passages of *The Game of Quartering*, the hero discovers reflections of himself repeatedly in his immediate surroundings, eventually finding them in his own home. What the hero does not understand is how the Other(s) can get into his house when only he has the key. But then he realizes that the Other has no difficulty being attached to the hero, since the two are one:

> But who exactly is this stranger behind my door, of whom I should have been terrified but was not terrified, who assumed my terror *within himself*, and around whose corporeal being—for he is corporeal—I step with such stubborn indifference, as if around my own shadow? Who is this unexpected intruder into my bachelor life's daily rhythm who, all things considered, does nothing to spoil it? Under whose gaze, watchful yet remote, am I pretending to be disinterestedly inspecting my ground-floor apartment, my abode, where it is so easy for a stranger to intrude, no differently today than any other (when I am invariably alone)? For God's sake, who is he, paradoxically present, a man so *rare* that it's almost like he's not here, and under whose haunting, haunted supervision I perform an array of passes suited to an inspector, after which I lie down *fully aware* that I can sleep peacefully, that I am alone, that I am still alone despite the fact that he's with me?! I am not bothered, not at all bothered by this someone, whom I see and do not regard.[136]

The scene is at first comic. For the double, as we have seen in Gombrowicz and Čapek, is the Self *and* the Other, the expropriation of the Self *as* Other. The double is, to borrow Julia Kristeva's useful term, the *abject,* the unfinished being of the individual set outside him.[137] This is why the hero feels like he should be afraid, and yet he is not afraid. He states with absolute certainty that this Other is "corporeal," and yet he can follow him around the apartment "as if around my own shadow." The narrator characterizes the Other as "this unexpected intruder into my bachelor life's daily rhythm," and yet the Other "does nothing to spoil it."

These paradoxes, which the protagonist recognizes as such when he calls the Other "paradoxically present," go on and on. The Other's gaze is "watchful yet remote," and this is entirely appropriate, since the Other is both here and not-here: "I am still alone despite the fact that he's with me." Weiner develops the paradox further by switching fluidly between proximal and distal demonstrative adjectives in the original, referring to the Other by turns as "this" and "that." As an expropriation of the Self, the double confronts the thinking subject with the reality of an entanglement with the Other and, at the same time, with the isolation of his own identity. Gombrowicz represents the incommensurability of these two selves through immaturity, the unfinished "I" longing for contact, versus the adult "I" longing for self-enclosure. Weiner calls it a "bachelor life"—likely a veiled reference to his own homosexuality—which is conceptually comparable to Gombrowicz's term: *staromládenecký život,* literally "the life of an old-young man," a life that this narrator implies should be solitary, though he is at pains to emphasize how much the "paradoxical presence" of another does not upset him.

Both Gombrowicz and Weiner assure their readers that the appearance of the double is no dream, though it is strongly associated with the dream life, as we have also seen throughout our tour of intermediacy. When the double appears to Józio at the beginning of *Ferdydurke,* the latter has just awoken from a troubling dream. When the double appears in *The Game of Quartering,* the narrator is about to go to bed, an act that will require him simply to accept the double's presence "*fully aware,*" as a necessary condition of Being. Maryna Miklaszewska, the Polish translator of *The Game for Real,* describes the artistic program of Le Grand Jeu specifically in terms of cultivating such an awareness, "to maintain oneself in a state of constant readiness, in expectation of such a time as would allow them to cross the boundary between self and world and find themselves at that boundary-point [. . .] that is their ultimate goal."[138] For André Breton and his disciples, Miklaszewska goes on to note, such a maneuver would lead to a liberating "happy madness," a "convenient dodge," whereas for Weiner and Le Grand Jeu the same method brought "genuine madness, taken to an extreme, 'with no way out.'"[139]

The opening of *The Game of Quartering* illustrates the hopelessness of the individual's entrapment. For Weiner, as for Gombrowicz and Schulz, the gaze of the thinking subject does not meet that of his double or, more generally, of the Other who would seem to repeat him. In the first chapter of *Ferdydurke,* Józio's double cowers in the corner, refusing to return his gaze. In Schulz's story "Solitude," the speaker's mirror image also refuses to look him in the eye, so that one can view the Other only "sort of in profile." In *The Game of Quartering,* the speaker is likewise unable to see any of several potential doubles except in profile, as when he observes his dubious friends Mutig and Fuld: "And I came to the realization that if I am seeing them both in profile, then they are facing each other. And it crossed my mind (as if for the first time) that whenever I attempted to overcome his supposed virtue, Fuld would always, and without exception, stand so that I could not see him other than in profile."[140] Mutig and Fuld mirror each other, but they also mirror the narrator in an inescapable associative chain. Indeed, the protagonist of Weiner's text sees himself mirrored in several other characters, and he sees them mirrored in each other as well.

The reader may continue to wonder why the individual cannot catch the gaze of his double. One reason—and this speaks to the ontological structure of the double—is that to do so would imply the completion of an exchange, or the closing of the circuit, between the Self and the Self-as-Other. We can imagine how, hypothetically, this would constitute the reintegration of the Self, since the distance between the Self and the Other would collapse in the meeting of their gaze. In the most extensive study of Weiner's prose to date, Steffi Widera suggests that, particularly in Weiner's early work, the motif of the double occurs in a syncretic Judeo-Christian framework, in which shame splits the Self, which is then reintegrated in a moment of redemption (Erlösung), itself consummate with death's reintegration of the Self into the Absolute.[141] What complicates this model for the later work, and especially for *The Game for Real,* is how Weiner generally refuses to reintegrate the thinking subject and his double. When such redemption seems possible, it is then frustrated by repetition.

As Gombrowicz demonstrates in *Memoir from a Time of Immaturity, Ferdydurke,* the *Diary,* and elsewhere, when the individual is mirrored in another—whether that Other is truly an independent thinking subject or simply a double of the Self—shame holds open the circuit of intersubjective exchange. That is, shame expresses both the subject's need for and failure to attain Levinas's "excendence," to escape from Being. The double manifests that failure by being one with the subject and, at the same time, outside the subject. The double, as an intermediate state situated between identity and alterity, cannot be recovered by an immediate gaze or verbal communication. Faced with his own reflection in another, the individual cannot catch the Other's gaze, because this would be tantamount to catching his own gaze. He cannot speak, because his shame prevents him from communicating with himself, a condition that Leonard Neuger describes as "auto-incommunicability," rendering even language nonsyntagmatic and ultimately nonnarrative.[142]

Weiner takes this problematic to new heights. In *The Game of Quartering*, the narrator eventually finds that the presence of the double eliminates all possibility for true solipsism. The hero can see himself outside himself, but he can no longer see himself in a mirror:

> But the fact that I was face-to-face *with myself* was not the eeriest thing; eerier still was the ardor with which my thought was trying to persuade my hesitating senses that this was no delusion; eerier still was the certainty that my senses, at just this moment my sight, had begun to live outside of my thought. [. . .] I was on my feet, a step before the tall mirror over the fireplace—I say before the tall mirror over the fireplace, knowing with sun-like clarity that I'm in front of the mirror—which, however, did not answer me. And again: eerier than this betrayal of me, who despite an unspoken but age-old pact did not issue forth from those depths, was my ardent, gloomily high-spirited thought, trying to persuade my startled senses not to be afraid, not to run away, that there was nothing to worry about, that this empty mirror was a correct mirror, *that this was how it had to be.*[143]

"*This was how it had to be*": Weiner recognizes that the expropriation of the Self in the form of a double expresses a necessary and inescapable condition of Being. Indeed, what would it say about the ontological structure of the double if the hero *could* see himself simultaneously in the room and in the mirror? In this passage, the speaker's difficulty is not in reconciling his psyche with the fact that the mirror "did not answer" him—*neodpovídalo,* which also suggests withholding speech—but in suppressing the visceral reaction of his "startled senses" against what seems an unnatural phenomenon, one that Gombrowicz has told us "should be forbidden to nature." And yet the narrator realizes the paradox of being "face-to-face" with himself. He tells us that eerier than the appearance of the double was the way in which his thought (*myšlenka,* also "idea," "concept") attempted to convince his senses not to rebel against this necessary condition of Being. Weiner underscores the paradox adjectivally, describing his thought as "gloomily high-spirited." And just as the speaker's senses "seemed to live outside of my thought," his thought seems to live outside his being, at least insofar as the thought is strange enough for the thinker to be surprised by it.

Faced with his double, Weiner's hero recognizes in an equally Gombrowiczean manner the extent to which he is both sovereign and subject. Then, in a wonderful demonstration of the dynamics of shame and defacement, the narrator calmly states, "He stole my face; he stole my face." To which one of his interlocutors asks, "Which one?"[144] Here we might recall Agamben's formulation about shame: "It is as if our consciousness collapsed and, seeking to flee in all directions, were simultaneously summoned by an irrefutable order to be present at its own defacement, at the expropriation of what is most its own." The protagonist of *The Game of Quartering* constantly wants to escape from his own existence, but at the same time he must bear witness to his own defacement, a process that is reiterated with every Other he encounters.

The Walk of Shame: Weiner's *The Game for the Honor of Payback*

The second part of *The Game for Real*, entitled *The Game for the Honor of Payback* (Hra na čest za oplatku, 1930–31), repeats the doubling motif of the first, but it also elaborates the role of shame in manifesting the double. Here the protagonist is named, but he is known only as Hanba—literally "shame," "dishonor"—and the story follows his psychological torment in having missed the opportunity to slap a man named Mr. Steel, who has offended him.[145] Like the protagonist of *The Game of Quartering*, however, this hero feeds off his own shame: "he was ashamed [. . .] and relished his shame."[146] He also spends a great deal of time in front of the mirror. But unlike the narrator of *The Game of Quartering*, Hanba *sees* himself in the mirror, which is consistent with his early confession to Zinaida, the servant to whom he tries—and fails—to relate: "I don't know how to exteriorize."[147] Weiner elaborates on what this might mean in a passage late in the novel, when the hero is looking at a man on the street who is himself looking at his mirror image in a shop window:

> He is so immersed in affectionate and deferential self-regard that the dense flow of passers-by has as if spat him out and forsaken him, as punishment for his having betrayed the community of the street; he's been left alone; but then what is solitude to someone whose plethoricity is such that he is a community unto himself? Has the street cast him out? He's swept it away again. He and his image have fallen in love with each other with so unfussy an ardor that it was actually the two of them, irresistible, invincible, who had been in control; he was in control. [. . .] And now it is the snoop [i.e., Shame, the hero] who is walking past the mirror: he has cast a fleeting sidelong glance . . . whom does he see? An elderly child. And this disastrous kitchen boy of moral petitions says: "That one there looks after himself; when we look after ourselves we become self-confident. Look after yourself!"[148]

Weiner is a little tongue-in-cheek in his treatment of his hero's solitude, which is more generally a source of torment. The man and his mirror image are in love with each other, to the exclusion of the outside world. But this does not matter, since the stranger is a Whitmanesque universe unto himself: he, too, contains multitudes. Weiner coins a neologism, *pletoričnost* ("plethoricity"), to illustrate the inherent multiplicity of the Self, the sense that the individual is "a community unto himself." When the hero looks into the same mirror, however, he experiences shame instead of self-confidence, since he sees himself as a grotesque hybrid of child and adult. While Gombrowicz constructs the notion of immaturity as an expansive cosmos within the individual, here Weiner reaches for the remarkably similar notion of the "aged" or "elderly child" (*obstárlé dítě*). It is almost as a wicked afterthought that he makes this child—the unfinalized core of the hero—speak back to the hero, admonishing him for his slovenly appearance and the lack of self-confidence it fosters. Weiner uses the word *sebevědomý,* "self-assured" or "self-confident," though etymologically the word suggests self-awareness, and one senses that this meaning might apply as well. Self-aware, the stranger takes comfort in his own "plethoricity." Lacking self-awareness, the hero feels only shame and rejection, a sense that he is neither a self-contained whole, nor an integral part of a larger community. Zdeněk Vašíček refers to this condition ironically as Weiner's *neosobnost,* his "impersonality," noting that "this is not the life-problem of man as an individual; it is a question of humanity's very existence."[149]

Gombrowicz would most likely agree. In his *Testament,* he describes *Ferdydurke* as an attempt to defend his individuality, his personhood.[150] By examining shame and doubling in Gombrowicz and Weiner, we discover how that defense is doomed to fail. For these authors, the impossibility of escape is a foregone conclusion even before the story of that escape begins. Yet the hero must try to escape nonetheless, simply because this is how the game of Being is played. We cannot win, but we still have to play.

The result, Bohumil Novák noted shortly after the publication of *The Game for Real,* is "a world of hell, of night and nightmares": "Time, space, and causal relations between phenomena, relations that are entirely internal—here everything is transformed into a dream that is so incomprehensible that it becomes excruciating and horrifying, into a mortal game that is ultimately life itself and thus played for real."[151] Novák errs, I think, in his insistence on Weiner's interiority and self-enclosure, a notion he then contradicts by drawing our attention, as more recent readers have done, to Weiner's consistent use of catachresis.[152] Like those of Platonov, Schulz, Mandel'shtam, and others, Weiner's unexpected word combinations may initially strike the reader as malapropism or substandard usage, but the paradoxes they create, like Schulz's desire to "mature into childhood," enact the very same intermediacy they describe.

One passage from *The Game for the Honor of Payback,* also cited by Novák, illustrates this point exceptionally well: "When he [Hanba] went out the next morning and headed for the square, he knew, even before he locked up, that he was no longer there: he had been replaced by his legend. A legend without beginning or end, a narrative as yet illegible, but therefore almost more credible than him, than the banal mediocrity of his impoverished existence."[153] It is in the moment of leaving a domestic space that Hanba suddenly realizes his absence as its own infinitely expansive narrative, full of possibility. Weiner describes this narrative as a *pověst,* "legend" or "tale," a term that applies specifically to narrative forms irreducible to specific facts or real-life circumstances, freed from the tyranny of authorship, "without beginning or end." In other words, the subject's absence invites the Other to fill in missing details, such that the actual reader enters into a dialogue with the fictional character, creating a more "credible" him than could arise from the text, whose fixed forms only deceive.[154] But as Petr Málek reminds us, this dialogue carries none of the freedom that Bakhtin might ascribe to it, since "the oscillation between diegesis (the narrated world) and exegesis (the act of narration)" entraps the thinking subject, resulting in "existential discord and personal stress."[155]

The two narratives that make up Weiner's *The Game for Real* are each structured around formal repetitions analogous to those in Gombrowicz's *Ferdydurke,* and they serve similar ends. Like Józio, Weiner's protagonists discover that the repetition of their person in their doubles is also the repetition of time, a repetition of the familiar with unfamiliar differences. The narrator of *The Game of Quartering* realizes this early on, when he is still learning to cope with the presence of strangers in his apartment. In a strikingly Gombrowiczean manner, he then turns to us, the readers, and helps us formulate the structure of this repetition:

> Imagine that every day you eat from the same plate with a floral print; you know it so well that it would not escape you were it replaced by a plate with slightly different flowers. But one day you take a closer look and discover a tiny, heretofore overlooked flaw. Go on, try—how should I put this?—try to entrance it; fix your eyes on it; a moment later, and you're looking at a kind of intimate unreality; the one reality, irrefutable, since it's quotidian, remains solely this heretofore overlooked flaw; it's like the sole discernible shape in a fog, only you don't know "where to put it." [. . .] It was no different with my uninvited guests. They were strangers to me; they became estranged from me all at once, but not as much so as my own apartment, albeit still familiar and unaltered to my eyes. They were somehow more real than it was. They were strangers, unfamiliar, and yet theirs was an assigned unfamiliarity, promised; only I didn't know "where to put them."[156]

The narrator's own understanding of the strangers in his apartment is formulated in terms of repetition and familiarity. The intruders—who, as I have already indicated, present themselves as expropriations of the protagonist's own interiority—precipitate a crisis of difference within the otherwise self-replicating chain of the everyday. The question for the narrator then becomes a problem of how to assimilate this difference, how to reintegrate it into the repetitive chain, "where to put it." Weiner establishes a clear distinction between the unreal and the real, the "kind of intimate unreality" and the "one reality, irrefutable." This distinction is based in turn on a corresponding opposition between the repeated, everyday, "quotidian" reality and the unique, instantaneous, and "unfamiliar."

There is a conceptual challenge in Weiner's analogy of the flawed dinner plate: How does the "flaw," the crack in everyday experience represented by the presence of strangers in the narrator's apartment, become immediately normalized, so that the mundane, domestic space of the apartment becomes estranged? This clever maneuver underscores why the repetitiveness of Weiner's texts is, in his own careful calculation, so terribly claustrophobic: the strangers in the apartment are themselves reflections of the narrator's interiority, and they are therefore more domestic than the domestic space around them. Weiner immediately drains the uncanny from an otherwise uncanny circumstance, flipping it upside down. The strange is accepted as normal, "assigned," "promised." The everyday becomes strange. And the thinking subject is left to deal with the impenetrable remainder, the flash of the uncanny, the "flaw" that tells him that the reality he has known is now an unreality, though that unreality seems more real than what he had known before. The horror of the thinking subject in Weiner's texts is the incomprehension of someone whose reality has been replaced with an unreality and who, to his own horror, wholly accepts that substitution.

Whereas Doležel refers to this as a divide between the "visible" and "invisible" worlds, forming the basis of his comparison of Weiner and Kafka, Věra Linhartová, in her critical postscript to the 1967 edition of *The Game for Real,* puts the same incommensurability into geometric terms: "The basic conceptual pair of Weiner's internal geometry consists of the notions of a circle and a straight line. The basic motivating force leading to this relationship and, consequently, also to the motion of that pair is the tendency toward rectification of the circle, a rectification that is naturally a component of a geometry that is no longer static, but projective, and according to whose laws his world is arranged."[157] By "rectification of the circle," Linhartová is referring to a conceptual process by which the circular line becomes straight. In part because of their response to Constructivist design and poetics, the authors of intermediacy often respond well to non-Euclidean geometric models; one thinks of Platonov or Schulz in their construction of space, or of Miłosz's early references to pure geometry, or of Mandel'shtam's architectural metaphors for the construction of poetic utterance. Linhartová's geometric vision of Weiner's work is particularly apt because it functions as both a spatial and a temporal metaphor. Spatially, it is very difficult to map out his characters' movements, largely because mundane spaces are made strange, despite their remaining "familiar and unaltered to [the] eyes." In a way that is remarkably similar to what we see in Schulz's stories, the cyclical, repeatable, everyday spaces of one's domestic sphere are subtly transformed and "estranged." Temporally, that which normally repeats itself may continue to do so, but it repeats itself with difference. The circle and the straight line distort one another, so that there is neither pure repetition nor pure difference. Linhartová's reference to projective geometry is especially useful here, because it connects us to perspectival shifts in the visual arts—to which Weiner, in part through his friendship with Josef Šíma, was well attuned—as well as to the unorthodox notion, drawn from projective geometry, that parallel lines can eventually meet. In this connection, we may recall Nezval's reference to hyperbolic geometry and the meeting of parallel lines in *Edison*.

And isn't "repetition with difference" another way of characterizing the continuous transformations we find throughout the literature of intermediacy? Isn't it another way of formulating the uncomfortable collapse of past, present, and future, which prevents the thinking subject from living—as Gombrowicz declares in *Ferdydurke*—"only by today's problematic"? This is certainly the case for Hanba, the protagonist of *The Game for the Honor of Payback,* whose existential imprisonment Weiner describes at the beginning of the text as the moment of being shocked *out* of the present: "His hands, till now folded beneath his head, have shifted; they slide, they grope, they stretch. They jerked, righted themselves, they were pondering. They've sensed as it were a new, unknown state. It was strange; it was an awakening. It was the recognition that he who until now had not known anything about himself beyond that he is, had also already been, and would yet be. It was him discovering duration and sequence, it was the discovery of past and future."[158] Weiner—who, like Schulz, delights in the uncanny within the mundane—essentially reconstructs the dynamic we have just seen in *The Game of Quartering.* A man who is otherwise perfectly content to live a meaninglessly repetitive existence is shocked into a sense of the "strange" within his most immediate and familiar space, in this case encompassing his own hands. He becomes differently aware of his own familiarity, which now contains within itself "a new, unknown state." The Czech word *skupenství* refers to a physical "state," and it suggests a particular arrangement or order of components. Here, Hanba recognizes the familiarity of his world, but he feels that this world has been rearranged. Like Józio's dream of the double or the appearance of strangers in the apartment in *The Game of Quartering,* this sense of the uncanny comes from *within* the protagonist, and his "awakening" is in fact an awakening-into-dream, since it is the "invisible" world, the world of spatial-temporal displacement, doubling, and transformation, that will now become his real life.

Weiner's protagonist suddenly discovers "duration and sequence," and once again the author's choice of words is highly significant. For a philosophically minded author working in Paris in the 1920s, "duration" is an unmistakably Bergsonian term. Indeed, we can easily regard Weiner's description as the collapse of Einsteinian relativity into Bergsonian durée, since the hero, a man who until now has seen time relative only to his own present experience, suddenly becomes uncomfortably aware of the duration of past, present, and future. "The breaking apart of the eternal is agony (which is why we long for the eternal)," Radim Vondráček notes in reference to Weiner and Čapek, "but at the same time it is an essential foundation of human existence, as much so in Weiner's prose as in that of the Čapek brothers. Without this foundation, without living through moments, there can be no real-life orientation in time and space; there is only a kind of dwelling in nothingness."[159]

This is the basic antinomy faced by Weiner: the *horror vaccui* of nothingness or the "agony" of definition in time and space, of one moment following another without connection or meaning. The word Weiner uses for "succession" or "sequence," *řetěz,* literally means "chain": the hero, until now a creature of the present, finds himself enchained to past and future. This enchainment anticipates the novella's central dilemma, the protagonist's need to return an insult from the past that overwhelms his present and directs him toward future action. Whereas Dostoevsky treats the same plotline in *Notes from Underground* as a struggle to recover one's social identity, in *The Game for the Honor of Payback* the protagonist has a purely existential goal, the recovery of his self-singularity, his presentness. He must find Mr. Steel and slap him, closing the circuit of exchange that was opened with Steel's insult.

At the end of the novella, the protagonist, who has been wavering throughout the text between action and inaction, ultimately comes to the realization that his pursuit of self-singularity is futile. Zinaida, the servant to whom he fails to relate at the beginning of the text, has nearly drowned in his presence, and the protagonist is being held for questioning by the police:

> He was looking into the underside of his greasy cap, reading there that life begins just when we have *sensed* (but sensed the way we perceive smells, tastes, or lights) that it is a spiral, which in the instantaneous point of the "I" is just beginning, and then—ever more vertiginously and centrifugally—it spins out into being without end and without beginning, and that we are wed to freedom just in that moment when we have no choice but *not to place* a pause between today and tomorrow, I and thou, here and anywhere.[160]

In a few moments, in this same office, Hanba will meet Mr. Steel again, and at the police detective's insistence Steel will deliver the slap that (it turns out) Hanba had felt but never received, and that has therefore been forestalled for the entire text. For now, though, the protagonist contemplates his own nonsensical existence, as he does repeatedly from the novella's opening passages. Gazing at an appropriately circular geometry, the underside of his cap, he learns to "read" life as pure intuition and fellow feeling, a "spiral" starting out from the singular, "instantaneous point of the 'I'" and eventually spinning outward to encompass all times, places, and others. This reintegration into the Absolute allows no privileged position for the Self, no "pause between today and tomorrow, I and thou, here and anywhere." The moment "we are wed to freedom" comes only when we reach a limit or boundary, when we "have no choice."

It is remarkable that Weiner's protagonist, who is self-obsessed in all senses of the term, would come to characterize such self-obliteration as "freedom." What value can there be in freedom without the independence of the Self? When Mr. Steel finally does slap Hanba, it would seem to open a new interval or exchange, one that we might imagine Hanba attempting to close after the novella's end. Weiner leaves us to wonder whether this protagonist will ever be one with himself, as he wishes to be for most of the text, or fully absorbed in the Absolute, as he wishes to be just before Mr. Steel slaps him at the police station. *The Game for Real* is constructed around the repetitiveness of these vacillations, as Václav Černý observed in a brief 1937 reflection on Weiner's work: "In *The Game for Real* [. . .] the world changes into an apparition, a muddle, a grotesque grimace of nothingness, where the plains of dream and waking life, of hallucination and reality, intermingle, without one being truer than the other. [. . .] A hundred times the poet conquers and overwhelms reality with his poetic work, and a hundred times he is obliged to battle it again."[161] We, too, are enjoined to fight against reality in Weiner's work, though it is perhaps unclear which reality we are fighting, so entangled do "the plains of dream and waking life" become.

In an act of visual exegesis on a par with Bruno Schulz's frontispiece to Gombrowicz's *Ferdydurke,* Josef Šíma, who had also been a central actor in the development of Weiner's poetics, provides an excellent précis of *The Game for Real* in his frontispiece to the 1967 edition (figure 5.2). A disembodied face, a mask with no eyes, floats behind vertical bars. Identity, the mask suggests, is both illusory and necessary. How could it be any other way? The individual thinking subject is always striving to be wholly himself, but this is not possible. Weiner's text dramatizes the struggle for selfhood or for self-obliteration, for an escape from the prison of identity or the discomfort of fellow feeling. Both flights are doomed to failure, but this does not prevent the struggle from recycling itself time and again, repeating itself

Figure 5.2. Josef Šíma, frontispiece for Richard Weiner's *The Game for Real* (1967; ink on paper). Richard Weiner, *Hra doopravdy* (Prague: Mladá fronta, 1967).

with just enough difference for the panicked subject to believe that somehow, somewhere, there might be a way out.

Instead of a way out, however, there is only repetition. It is the repetitive quality of Bruno Schulz's stories, in which the Father dies and fades away, only to die again in the subsequent text. It is the repetitiveness of Andrei Platonov's narratives, in which time is never progressive, and progress is never achieved. It is Karel Čapek or Witold Gombrowicz repeating the same story over and over, discovering that no matter how many different ways it is told, the story remains the same. And it is ultimately repetition that drives the poetics of Osip Mandel'shtam, Nikolai Zabolotskii, and Vítězslav Nezval, with each word, sound, or image suggesting the echo of a similar word, sound, or image, and with each anaphoric chain instantiating difference within repetition. For these authors, there can be no boundary beyond repetition itself, a point that Czesław Miłosz puts into the mouth of the "prophet" in "A Song on the End of the World." Nothing happens, nothing changes, and the doubters are certain that the world is not ending. To which the prophet, who is working in his garden, answers: "There will be no other end of the world, / There will be no other end of the world."[162] Though I've mentioned this before, it bears repeating.

Conclusion

> The ancient prophets are like children. For what is the Book of Revelation when you have Albert Einstein's *On Relativity*?
>
> —Kazimierz Wyka

Strange, weird, unsettling, disturbing, uncanny, Kafkaesque: these words have been applied so frequently to the works I discuss in this book that the terms themselves might easily be dismissed as critical cliché or journalistic reduction. There is indeed plenty in these characterizations to make us wary, especially when they are taken to describe Eastern European literature more generally. In the Western popular imagination, they resonate perfectly with stereotypes of Eastern Europe as darkly mysterious, the "blank spots" on the cultural map that, as Miłosz quips, "could have easily borne the inscription *Ubi leones* (Where the lions are)," a "domain of wild beasts" dotted with such unfamiliar place names as "Prague (mentioned sometimes because of Kafka), Warsaw, Budapest, and Belgrade."[1] Those of us who take a special interest in this literature know that there is plenty there that hardly fits the preconception, including work that represents everyday life in terms that differ little from Western norms, whatever they may be. If writing is motivated by rebellion and Mandel'shtam's "literary spite"—if it is always produced *na przekór,* "in opposition to," as Miłosz described his own writing—then my own book is offered against the assumption that Eastern European literature in general, and interwar Modernism specifically, is unfathomably Kafkaesque. Mind you, I do not reject the term "Kafkaesque" or the sense of entrapment and inescapability it implies. Rather, I argue that when we call attention to the spatial-temporal destabilization we encounter in certain specimens of Eastern European Modernism, as well as to their attendant feeling of discomfort and doom, we are responding to the specific ontological paradigm represented therein. As a critical framework, intermediacy is a demystification of a thematic structure that is frequently acknowledged but rarely treated systematically. As a poetics of metaphysical "unfreedom" in interwar

Eastern Europe, intermediacy moves us from a recognition of an oddity to a description of its quiddity.

This is in part why I have approached in-betweenness comparatively, as a phenomenon present across literary genres and in several national traditions. Treated in isolation, the strangeness of each of the writers I have discussed in this book appears as idiosyncrasy, which can only elevate their value within any system of artistic values that privileges outsiders, rebels, and being "ahead of one's time." The fact that these writers are strange *in the same way,* that they all adopt in-betweenness as a central theme in their writing, and that the thematic substructure of this intermediacy is consistent across so large and varied a body of work suggests a broader cross-cultural phenomenon than individual artistic genius could adequately explain.

We have seen this substructure unfold from the initial destabilization of the individual's spatial-temporal definition to embrace a stock of tropes that lend intermediacy its unsettling atmosphere: orphanhood, homelessness, indifference, naivety, metamorphosis, immaturity, repetition, and doubling. When we consider how these tropes are arrayed in the given text, we find first that they map cleanly onto spatial-temporal categories. The doubling of the thinking subject, for example, is a spatial analogue to repetition in time. Likewise, homelessness is a spatial representation of the isolation and loss experienced in its temporal mode as orphanhood. Indifference and naivety are two sides of the same coin: one is a failure to distinguish between objects in space, the other a deliberate cancellation or "short-circuiting" of distinctions in time. Metamorphosis, in which we see a dramatic change in how people and things occupy space, reflects the dynamism of immaturity, "the old surviving in the new," the mutability of the individual expressed as a problematic within time.

It should come as no surprise that these tropes fall just as cleanly within the spheres of individuality or collectivity, singularity or totality. After all, our definition in space and time—"location" may be a more fitting term—is the most fundamental constituent of our sense of Self, as well as of the relation of that Self to its milieu, "the outside world assigned to it as the arena and substratum of its actions." A revolution in the way we conceive of space and time naturally leads to a revolution in how we conceive of ourselves *through* space and time. These shifts are ongoing, inescapable, and troubling, as Elizabeth Grosz has argued:

> The Kantian conception of subjectivity is a metaphysical correlate of Newtonian physics, and the decentered Freudian subject conforms to the relativity of an Einsteinian universe. Perhaps the postmodern subject finds its correlative in the virtuality of cyberspace and its attendant modes of respatialization. Such conceptions are both ways of negotiating our positions as subjects within a social and cosmic

> order, and representations that affirm or rupture preexisting forms of subjectivity.[2]

Whether these renegotiations "affirm or rupture preexisting forms of subjectivity," they can produce the persistent anxiety that is a distinctive feature of the literature of intermediacy; we wouldn't dream of applying the word "Kafkaesque" to a text that leaves us feeling contented and reassured. The affirmation of our subjectivity confronts us with ourselves, with our limitation and isolation as thinking subjects, compelling us to flee toward the Other, or else toward the Absolute. The rupture of our subjectivity challenges our very sense of who or what we are in the world, so that we flee in the opposite direction, into the security of the Self, however illusory that security proves to be. Vacillation between these extremes appears formally in these works as structural and verbal repetition.

I have argued throughout this book that what distinguishes intermediacy in interwar Eastern Europe from the breakdown of spatial-temporal boundaries that we recognize in contemporaneous artifacts of Western European late Modernism is its special orientation toward the freedom such breakdown engenders. Authors like Proust, Joyce, and Mann collapse time and expand space in order to empower the inhabitants of their respective story worlds, allowing them to manipulate those worlds and to reshape them as a reflection of their own souls. The authors of intermediacy, all of them writing from within a broader public discourse on how to reshape state, society, and even nature, announce the hellishness of freedom, its "limitlessness of mercilessness." Like the hero of Sigizmund Krzhizhanovskii's "Quadraturin," they are prisoners of the infinite. For what good is it to have a home when you cannot find your way out?

Intermediacy means that there is no way out, even in death, a point that Schulz illustrates beautifully in the last story in his last book, enticingly called "My Father's Last Escape" (Ostatnia ucieczka ojca, 1936). Such a title might suggest the limit, the border, the escape route that we have been looking for; even the initial adjective, *ostatnia,* suggests the "final," the "ultimate." The tragic irony is that all of Schulz's representations of the death of the Father are "escapes," flights from the family, but not from Being. "My Father's Last Escape" describes yet another death, yet another transformation, yet another failure of the thinking subject to distinguish between reality and myth. Repetition makes death a formality, or at least a symptom of the mutability of forms:

> At that time my father had already definitively died. He died many times, never quite completely, always with certain reservations that demanded the revision of that fact. Some good came of it. By thus breaking his death down into installments, my father accustomed us to the fact of his departure. We grew indifferent to his increasingly

> diminished returns, each more pitiful than the last. The physiognomy of his already absent person dispersed, as it were, in the room where he lived; it branched out, at certain points creating bizarre knots of likeness with unlikely clarity.[3]

In my treatment of in-betweenness, I have discussed several rhetorical devices that foster a sense of unfinalizability, among them the use of imperfective verbs to convey open-ended, repetitive processes. This is a favorite device in Schulz, Mandel'shtam, and Nezval, and Schulz uses it to especially strong effect in "My Father's Last Escape." Here, two verb forms appear almost side by side to describe Jakub's death. The first form, "had . . . died," is unmistakably perfective, expressing a limit, since Jakub had died "definitively." But immediately thereafter, Schulz repeats the verb in an imperfective form, *umierał,* and then tells us why: Jakub died "many times." The "already" of the first sentence is replaced by the repeated "always" of the second, an instance of the very same "revision" that the second sentence describes. Once again, the family "grew indifferent" to Jakub's changes, and he continues to change. Although he is already dead, the remainder of the text describes Jakub's ongoing metamorphosis. In "My Father's Last Escape," Jakub transforms into a creature reminiscent of a crab or scorpion, though it is difficult to tell exactly, since the metamorphosis is never complete.

Schulz's language in this passage describes a frustrated economic exchange, a death that is paid out in "installments" or "on credit," a situation of "increasingly diminished returns." Death in Schulz always leaves a remainder, "certain reservations" that prevent the contract from being closed completely and therefore require further "revision," recapitulation, repetition. Such a death is aporetic, though not entirely for the reasons Derrida describes in his *Aporias,* where death cannot be fully experienced because of the difficulty (or impossibility) of defining the boundaries of that experience.

In his discussion of Heidegger, Derrida points out three possibilities for death: ending, the absolute moment that cannot be known or communicated; perishing, which belongs to speechless animals, and therefore also cannot be communicated; and "demise," or *Ableben,* "an intermediate phenomenon [*Zwischenphenomenon*]," which belongs to human beings and is communicable only as process.[4] This last category, demise, most closely describes death in the literature of intermediacy. But whereas the demise of the thinking subject can be expressed in language, it ends in a death that cannot. Schulz gets around this problem by skipping over that final moment of boundary and disappearance, repeatedly looping back to the process of Jakub's demise. The "ending" as such never occurs.

This may have been what Kafka had in mind in a remarkable aphorism about death as continuation: "The cruelty of death lies in the fact that it brings the real sorrow of the end, but not the end."[5] For Kafka, just as for

Schulz, death merely punctuates the repetitive structure of metamorphosis. When the authors of intermediacy mourn, as Platonov's characters continually mourn, or as Schulz's narrator mourns the demise of his father, they in effect feel the "real sorrow" of the passing of a form, not of the passing of essence. That essence can never achieve a definitive break from Being; at most, it may pass out of temporality, into the mythic age of an ancestor. Mircea Eliade describes this movement in *The Myth of the Eternal Return, or, Cosmos and History* (Le mythe de l'éternel retour: archétypes et répétition, 1949): "The transformation of the dead person into an 'ancestor' corresponds to the fusion of the individual into an archetypal category. [. . .] The transformation of the dead into ghosts, and so on, in a certain sense signifies their reidentification with the impersonal archetype of the ancestor."[6] By short-circuiting real time and the mythic past—the "mythicization of reality"—Schulz transforms the archetypal Father back into the historically contingent Jakub, who then repeatedly fades away, only to return again in the next story.

This textual universe's lack of definitive boundaries is the root of its unfreedom. Freedom requires limits on the world, on time, and on the thinking subject. Along these lines, Hannah Arendt describes a freedom that arises out of limitation, out of the inherent differences between individuals in their capacities to act. Following Epictetus, she writes that "[t]he 'science of living' consists in knowing how to distinguish between the alien world over which man has no power and the self of which he may dispose as he sees fit."[7] For Arendt, freedom without limits is no freedom at all, since the thinking subject can express selfhood only in a contingent act: "Only where the I-will and the I-can coincide does freedom come to pass."[8]

Arendt is generally interested in political freedom, but her formulation applies just as well to metaphysical freedom. In a 1976 lecture on "Freedom and Responsibility," Emmanuel Levinas describes "finite freedom" precisely as a relation to the Other, whose presence underscores that which belongs uniquely to the Self: "Finite freedom consists in doing what is our vocation, that is, in doing what no one other than myself can do. Limited in this way by the other, it remains freedom."[9] When the boundaries between Self and Other break down, as they necessarily do in the literature of intermediacy, it is no longer possible for us to say where the Self ends and the Other begins. Thus the thinking subject no longer has access to free acts, since there is no longer any quality or idea that remains uniquely his own.

Interwar intermediacy faded from view in the immediate aftermath of World War II, though it was already dissipating as social and political circumstances in Central and Eastern Europe began to deteriorate in the late 1930s. By the time of the Great Terror in the Soviet Union, Stalinism's grip on Soviet culture had successfully neutralized the indeterminacy and ambiguity that dominates the literature of in-betweenness: there is no "in-between" in Stalinism. Even Einstein's physics came repeatedly under fire for its perceived philosophical incompatibility with Marxism.[10] Nikolai Zabolotskii was arrested in 1938 and charged with anti-Soviet activity; he spent the next six years in labor camps, ruining his health. Osip Mandel'shtam died the same year in a transit camp, the official report said, "of heart failure." ("This is as much to say," his widow would later remark, "that he died because he died: what is death but heart failure?")[11] Andrei Platonov's son was arrested during the same period. When he returned to his family from a labor camp in 1940, he brought a severe case of tuberculosis, from which the author would also die a decade later.

With the exception of Czesław Miłosz, whose long career displays an exceptional talent for adaptation and reinvention, the fates of most of the remaining authors of intermediacy likewise read as existential nightmares that they might have authored themselves. In Czechoslovakia, Vítězslav Nezval passed quickly from Poetism to Surrealism, only then to become a dedicated Stalinist during the war, which neither Richard Weiner nor Karel Čapek lived to see. Weiner died in 1937 after living for several excruciating years with stomach cancer, which had been repeatedly misdiagnosed until shortly before it killed him. Čapek died of pneumonia in December 1938, but this allegedly did not prevent the Gestapo from trying to hunt him down, just to make sure that his death had not been a sham. In Poland, Bruno Schulz did not survive the war; he was shot in the street by a German officer in November 1942 while fetching a loaf of bread. Witold Gombrowicz, meanwhile, suffered an uncannily Gombrowiczean fate. Having boarded a transatlantic cruise in 1939, he arrived in Buenos Aires one week before the Nazi invasion and found himself stuck in Argentina with no money and no Spanish. Relying on a conservative Polish émigré community for his survival, he spent the war in extreme poverty and isolation.

But this does not mean that the paradigm of intermediacy disappears altogether. There is, first of all, a large body of writing belonging to the interwar period that can be read productively within this framework. In addition to works I have not discussed by the same writers I have, several of the figures who dwell on the periphery of this study would warrant their own sustained treatments as authors of intermediacy. These include Sigizmund Krzhizhanovskii, Marina Tsvetaeva, Boris Pil'niak, and Stanisław Ignacy Witkiewicz, to name just four. Others, such as the Czech novelist Vladislav Vančura (1891–1942), the Hungarian novelist Miklós Szentkuthy (1908–1988), and the Croatian novelist Miroslav Krleža (1893–1981)—especially his 1932 novel *The Return of Filip Latinovicz* (Povratak Filipa Latinovicza)—present opportunities for further exploration. In interwar Poland, the short fiction of Kazimierz Truchanowski (1904–1994) bore so close a resemblance to Bruno Schulz's that the former was publicly accused of plagiarism.[12]

In the postwar period, we find an obvious echo of intermediacy in the works of writers around the world who were directly inspired by this literature and continued to explore the consequences of spatial-temporal destabilization. These include Camus, Sartre, Beckett, and Borges, as well as the Serbian author Danilo Kiš (1935–1989) and the Czech theorist Daniela Hodrová (1946-), herself among our most perceptive readers of intermediacy. Magda Romanska has recently argued that the theater of Tadeusz Kantor (1915–1990) extended the legacy of Bruno Schulz in postwar Poland.[13] Paul Auster's *The New York Trilogy* (1985–86) and Don Delillo's *Cosmopolis* (2003), which is dedicated to Auster, also come to mind. Armed with these more recent texts, we can even reevaluate the spatial-temporal constructs of Proust, Mann, and Joyce, especially considering the tension between scientific and mythic motifs in their works.[14] The French novelist Yves-Michel Ergal, for example, has taken this approach to Proust and Joyce in particular, suggesting that the conflation of the adult artist and his young self is not "a prodigy upon whom the older writer likes to linger, and who constitutes a figure at once autobiographical and mythological; he remains just as much in an intermediary reality."[15] As an interpretive paradigm, intermediacy offers an abundance of comparative work still for us to perform.

But should we? How much lighter our lives might be were we to leave off such questions altogether and live in blissful—and now, necessarily, willful—ignorance of our entrapment between singularity and totality, so that we might then remain like Tristram Shandy's Uncle Toby, "who, of all things in the world, troubled his brain the least with abstruse thinking;—the ideas of time and space [. . .], with a thousand other inquiries and disputes about INFINITY, PRESCIENCE, LIBERTY, NECESSITY, and so forth, upon whose desperate and unconquerable theories, so many fine heads had been turned and crack'd."[16] Alas, freedom and necessity, identity and difference, infinity and definition in space and time—to acknowledge one is already to situate oneself in both. We cannot experience our connection to the world, whether we are talking about our participation in a system of economic exchange or the "metaphysical feelings" aroused by art, without relinquishing a concomitant measure of our own autonomy, that is, our freedom. But we cannot reclaim that autonomy without its attendant sense of profound isolation, the *horror vacui* of our solitude in the universe—and in ourselves.

APPENDIX

Osip Mandel'shtam, "I returned to my city . . . " (1930), as it appears in *Literaturnaia gazeta* (Nov. 1932), as "Leningrad." Seven couplets, dactyllic tetrameter, all masculine rhyme.

Я вернулся в мой город, знакомый до слёз,
До прожилок, до детских припухлых желёз.

> The second and third stanzas switch from the first person to the second as the city speaks back to the lyric "I." M. augments the call-and-response effect by making each sentence coterminus with its stanza in the original.

Ты вернулся сюда, так глотай же **скорей**
Рыбий жир ленинградских речных фонарей.

Узнавай же **скорее** декабрьский денёк,
Где к зловещему дёгтю подмешан желток.

> As M. shifts to addressing the city directly in the fourth and fifth stanzas, he relies on the assonance of the stressed *a* to create a sound profile evocative of a cry of despair.

Петербург, я ещё не хочу умир**а**ть:
У теб**я** телефонов моих номер**а**.

Петербург, у мен**я** ещё есть адрес**а**,
По которым найду мертвецов голос**а**.

Я на лестнице чёрной живу, и в висок
Ударяет мне вырванный с мясом звонок.

И всю ночь напролёт жду гостей дорогих,
Шевеля кандалами цепочек дверных.

I returned to my city, familiar to tears,
To the veins and red tonsils of my childhood years.

—You returned to this place, **hurry up** and choke down
Fishy oils from the lamps cast all over this town.

—**Hurry up** and remark the December that woke
To an ominous tar all mixed up with the yolk.

Piterbúrg, I'm not ready to submit to death's law.
You still have all my numbers; I'll wait for your call.

Piterbúrg, I'm in awe of the dead that I saw
When their voices came raw from unwelcoming walls.

My back entryway silent, with pain in my head
From the bell ringing through, tearing flesh as it sped,

All night long **I** await dearest guests on my floor
And the moment they'll tug at the chain by my door.

With *skorée,* "faster," the city impresses upon the lyric "I" the urgency of his mnemonic exercise.

The poem begins and ends in the first person, but the *return* to the first person is also the dialogic process of returning to the space of childhood: the city speaks to the poet as "Leningrad," but the poet addresses the city as "Petersburg," a name it has not had since 1905.

Osip Mandel'shtam, "No, never have been anyone's contemporary . . . " (1924), as published in 1925. Six quatrains, alternating iambic hexameter-tetrameter, alternating feminine-masculine rhyme.

At the end of the first stanza, the reversal of the verb and negative adverb, not strictly necessary to preserve the iambic rhythm, allows M. to make a positive statement of self-negation: "That *was* not-I," i.e., the Other.

Нет, никогда, ничей я не был современник,
Мне не с руки почёт такой.
О, как противен мне какой-то соименник,
То был не я, то был другой.

The duonym "age-and-sovereign" refers ironically to the age as a self-sufficient *detemporalization* of time, the aging son upon whose arm the age falls as he dies. In calling the age's mouth both "lovely" and "clay," M. suggests how such detemporalization is both seductive and false: thus the grammatical dysjunction that divides the stanza.

Два сонных **яблока** у **века-властелина**
И глиняный прекрасный рот,
Но к млеющей руке стареющего сына
Он, умирая, припадёт.

Я **с веком** поднимал болезненные **веки**—
Два сонных яблока больших,
И мне гремучие рассказывал реки
Ход воспалённых тяжб людских.

The fourth and fifth stanzas suggest that at the height of Romanticism, which M. historicizes in reference to a specific number of years (contrasting the atemporal designation "the age," though *vek* can also refer to a century), the "age-and-sovereign" might still hold to a mythic lack of temporal boundaries, whereas the poet in the present must suffer the passing of time.

Сто лет тому назад подушками белела
Складная лёгкая постель,
И странно вытянулось глиняное тело,—
Кончался века первый хмель.

Среди скрипучего похода мирового
Какая лёгкая кровать!
Ну что же, если нам не **выковать** другого,—
Давайте с веком **вековать**.

И в жаркой комнате, в кибитке и в палатке
Век умирает, а потом
Два сонных яблока **на роговой облатке**
Сияют перистым огнём.

The poem's lexical field is generated from four instances of paranomasia, labeled 1 through 4.

No, never was I anyone's contemporary,
For such an honor offends itself.
Cognomens merely make me feel contrary,
That was not I, but someone else.

Two sleepy **apples in the eyes** of **age-and-sovereign,**
He has a lovely mouth of clay,
But as he dies he falls upon the fading arm
Of a son who continues to age.

Together **with the age** I raised my ailing **eyelids**—
Two sleepy apples in the eyes,
And I was told in what the roaring streams did
Of the course of fevered human affairs.

A hundred years ago, shining white with linens,
An airy, well-proportioned bed,
The body made of clay stretched strangely and unrisen,—
The age's first drunk coming to an end.

Amidst the squeaky din of the world's marching forward,
How lightly that bed was arranged!
Well then, if it won't fall to us **to forge** another,
Let us **grow older** with the age.

And in sweltering bedchamber, in tent and covered wagon
The age is dying, but then
With feathery fire **on the plate of the cornea**
Two sleepy eyeballs shine.

The quadruple negation that opens the poem, though gramatically unremarkable in Russian, adds emotional force to the poet's rejection of being a "contemporary," which for M. refers to a person bound to historical time.

1 *Iabloka,* "apples," is also "eyeballs," typically in the anatomical compound *gláznye iábloka.* The equivalence between Self/Other rejected in the first stanza becomes the two "sleepy eyeballs" of the dying age in the second.

2 M. plays on the similarity between *vek,* "age" or "century," and *véka,* eyelid. The speaker places himself in the position of the age, lifting his "eyelids" "with the age" in the third stanza, "aging" "with the age" in the fifth.

3 *Výkovat',* "to forge," becomes *vekovát',* "to age," emphasizing that an age or era, as a detemporalization of time's passing, is an artificial, made thing. Since we cannot "forge another," we must grow older with the one we have.

4 In the poem's penultimate line, instead of *rogováia obolóchka* for "cornea," where *obolóchka* literally means "covering" or "encasement," M. gives us *rogováia oblátka,* where the latter word, though linked by etymology, refers to the "wafer" consumed with the Eucharist, or else to a "tablet" of medicine. In this way, the poem's closing gesture melds the motif of the eyes with the Last Rites we might suppose would be performed on the dying individual. In dying with human time, the age is again recycled into timelessness.

Nikolai Zabolotskii, "Red Bavaria" (1926), as it appears in *Columns* (1929), pp. 7–9. Six stanzas, iambic tetrameter, with idiosyncratic rhymes preferring the couplet to alternation, feminine to masculine.

Z. shifts the metrical profile from the first stanza to the second to create a sense of acceleration. The first stanza consists of eight lines with no enjambment. The second, by contrast, is one line shorter; five of the seven lines are enjambed.

В глуши бутылочного рая,
где пальмы высохли **давно**,—
под электричеством играя,
в бокале плавало окно;
оно на лопастях блестело,
потом садилось, тяжелело;
над ним пивной дымок вился…
Но это описать нельзя.

Z. begins his portrait anew by paraphrasing the opening line of the first stanza in the opening line of the second.

Literally setting a "stage," Z. delights in images of mixture, of the collision of the old and the new. The fronds of the dried-out palms suggest the "blades" of the fans now spinning overhead. The electrical lighting frees the window, a less miraculous source of interior illumination, to "play," its reflection "swimming" in the goblet.

И в том бутылочном раю
сирены дрогли на краю
кривой эстрады. На поруки
им были отданы глаза.
Они простерли к небесам
эмалированные руки
и ели бутерброд от скуки.

Vódit' khorovód, "dance the round," is a set expression, though one whose word-root repetition fits smoothly into Z.'s compositional method, particularly in this stanza, which sees *stóikoi* transformed into *nastóikoi*, as well as a rapid succession of words ending *-iot*.

Like Nezval, and in a manner reminiscent of Whitman, Z. relies heavily on anaphora to create chains of verbal transformation in lines that are themselves about transformation. The keyword for this mechanism is *kak* (*jak* in Nezval, usually a relative pronoun in Whitman), which introduces similes that become increasingly mixed.

Вертятся двери на цепочках,
спадает с лестницы народ,
трещит картонною сорочкой,
с бутылкой **водит хоровод**;
сирена бледная за **стойкой**
гостей попотчует **настойкой**,
скосит глаза, уйдёт, придёт,
потом, с гитарой наотлёт,
она поёт, поёт о милом:
как милого она кормила,
как ласков к телу и жесток—
впивался шёлковый шнурок,
как по стаканам висла виски,
как, из разбитого виска
измученную грудь обрызгав,
он вдруг упал. Была тоска,
и всё, о чём она ни пела,—
в бокале отливалось мелом.

In the blankness of bottley heaven,
where the palm trees' best days were **long past,—**
at play beneath electrical lighting
the window swam around in the glass;
it flashed on the blades as they spun,
grew heavy as it settled down,
a beery smoke curling above it...
Though there are no words to describe it.

And at that bottley heaven's edge
the sirens trembled on the stage,
uneven. They'd been paid,
on bond, many sets of eyes.
They reached for the skies
with arms beautifully glazed
and at sandwiches, unfazed.

The doors are swinging on their fetters,
the people cascade down the stairs,
they flap their shirtfronts made of paper
and bottle-**dance away their cares;**
a siren, pale behind the **counter,**
is treating guests to nips of **liquor,**
she looks away, steps out, comes back,
and then, a guitar across her lap,
she starts to sing, sings of her love:
how she had nursed her love to health,
how tender toward its cruel embrace—
her flesh was bit by silken lace,
how whiskey clung around their glasses,
how he, exhausted chest in masses
bespattered from his shattered head,
collapsed in but an instant, dead.
This misery, and all she sang,
poured out as whitewash in the stein.

Lit., "in the backwoods," "in the middle of nowhere," from the root *glukh-*, "remote," also the root of *glukhoi*, "deaf." Coupling this with *rai*, "paradise" or "heaven," Z. immediately situates us in an ambiguous, unpopulated space.

Lit., "long ago." After situating us "nowhere" in the first line, Z. emphasizes our belatedness in time.

Lit., "But this is impossible to describe." The poem stops short, only to start again in the new stanza.

A stylized reference to the cheap cardboard dickeys worn by the male clientele. That the people, *naród*, "tremble" synecdochally with their shirtfronts suggests that they, too, are made of cardboard. Z.'s phrasing plays on the idiom *treshchát' kak soróka*, "to titter like a magpie."

Lit., "How tender toward the body, and cruel," the phrase echoes the Russian expression *Láskovyi teliónok dvukh mátok sosiót*, lit., "A tender calf sucks from two mothers," comparable to the English "You catch more flies with honey than with vinegar." Z. transforms *láskovyi teliónok*, "tender" or "affectionate calf," into *láskov k télu*, "tender" or "gentle toward the body," while pairing the idiom's image of suckling with the siren's ambiguous suggestion of having "nursed" her lover.

One of the simplest forms of antanaclasis available in Russian is the transformation of a reflexive verb into its transitive form, or vice-versa. Here, the conversion of *kachát'sia*, "to stagger, wobble, pitch (intransitive)," to *kachát'*, "to swing, pitch (transitive)" drives a broader hypermetabole: between the two verbs *po stolám*, "along the tables," becomes *po potolkám*, "along the ceiling," so that flowers and "bedlam" are literally "half-and-half," *popolám*, split between high and low. This lays the foundation for the blending of the sacred and the profane in the second half of the stanza.

Мужчины тоже все кричали,
они **качались** по столам,
по потолкам они **качали**
бедлам с цветами пополам;
один—язык себе откусит,
другой кричит: я—**иисусик**,
молитесь мне—я на **кресте**,
под мышкой гвозди и везде...
К нему сирена подходила,
и вот, колено оседлав,
бокалов бешеный **конклав**
зажёгся как **паникадило**.

The peculiar perspective that opens the poem—we initially see the bar from inside a bottle—is reprised in the antepenultimate stanza, in which the smashing of a wine glass exiles us from the preceding brightness and gaiety, and even from the bar itself. The play of light on the street extends the poem's play with space and time, as the British name of the "Piccadilly" movie house harkens back to the "bedlam" of the preceding stanza, which also prepares us for this moment aurally: "Piccadilly" sounds like "panikadilo," and the cry of the "Little Jesus" with nails "under my arm" becomes the "Piccadilly" also grabbed *pod mýshki,* "under" or "by the arms."

Глаза упали точно гири,
бокал разбили—вышла ночь,
и жирные автомобили,
схватив **под мышки Пикадилли**,
легко откатывали прочь.
Росли томаты из прохлады,
и вот, опущенные вниз—
краснобаварские закаты
в пивные днища улеглись,
а за окном—**в глуши времён**,
блистал на мачте лампион.

The movement from "bedlam" to "Picadilly" in the penultimate stanza sets the stage, as it were, for more extensive spatial blending in the final stanza: the Spanish "Hermandades," as well as the Singer Manufacturing Company building and its strong association with American-made sewing machines. This is embodied, quite literally, in the "winged globe" that graces the building to this day.

Там Невский в блеске и тоске,
в ночи переменивший кожу,
годками сонными воспёт,
над баром вывеску тревожил;
и под свистками **Германдады**,
через туман, толпу, бензин,
над башней рвался шар крылатый
и имя "**Зингер**" возносил.

Авг. 1926

The men were also all a-shout,
they **pitched** among and over tables,
their bedlam washing in and out
with flowers **pitched** up toward the gables;
one of them's biting off his tongue,
another shouts that he's **God's son,**
upon the **cross**—give me your prayers,
nails under my arm and everywhere.
The siren then approached this guy,
they all lit up like a **chandelier,**
the wild **conclave** of glasses cheered
when she had perched upon his knee.

Lit., "upon the cross" we find "a Little Jesus." The poem turns our attention upward, only then to debase the identification with the deity by using the diminutive *iisúsik*. The religious conceit then allows Z. to present the revelers as a "wild conclave." Even the "chandelier" to which they are compared is a *panikadílo,* i.e., the large array of candles hanging down from the ceiling of an Orthodox church.

Like weights, the eyes dropped suddenly,
they smashed the glass—and out came night,
the automobiles ran greasily,
having grabbed **the arm of Piccadilly**,
and smoothly forward, out of sight.
From the cool air tomatoes grew,
and then, drawn quickly down,
they came to rest at the bottom of brew—
the Red Bavaria's setting suns,
while out the window—**in the wilderness of times,**
a pole with a lantern continued to shine.

In offering the Red Bavaria as a symbol, or even the epicenter, of spatial-temporal collapse, the poem is most explicit in how it bookends its contents between "the wilderness of bottley paradise," *glush' butýlochnogo ráia*, at the beginning of the poem, and "the wilderness of times," *glush' vremén,* at the end.

There Nevsky, light and grief, alas,
taking the night to change its skin,
will raise a song of sleepy whistles,
over the bars it's disturbed the sign;
and beneath the **Hermandades**' calls,
through fog, and crowd, and also gas,
a winged globe towered above it all
and lifted **Singer's** name.

August 1926

NOTES

Introduction

The epigraph is from Robert Musil, *The Man without Qualities,* vol. 1, *A Sort of Introduction and Pseudoreality Prevails,* trans. Sophie Wilkins and Burton Pike (New York: Vintage, 1996), 274. Appropriately, Franco Moretti offers the same passage as the first epigraph to his intriguing visual reduction of literary history, which constitutes a spatialization of temporal data, and vice-versa. See Franco Moretti, *Graphs, Maps, Trees: Abstract Models for a Literary History* (London: Verso, 2005).

1. See, for example, Stanisław Barańczak, "Antynomie 'bycia w świecie,' albo Kobieca sztuka pośredniczenia," in his *Ironia i harmonia* (Warsaw: Czytelnik, 1973), 129–49.

2. See, for example, Neil Cornwell, *The Absurd in Literature* (Manchester: Manchester University Press, 2006). Cornwell's slippery definition of the absurd casts an extremely large net, in which several of the authors I will discuss are caught, though Cornwell's treatment of their similarities is largely superficial.

3. For a discussion of the "Kafkaesque" in its epistemological and spiritual dimension, see A. Kiarina Kordela, "Kafkaesque: (Secular) Kabbalah and Allegory," in *Freedom and Confinement in Modernity: Kafka's Cages,* ed. A. Kiarina Kordela and Dimitris Vardoulakis (New York: Palgrave Macmillan, 2011), 127–58. For the legal and administrative use of "Kafkaesque," see especially Jack Greenberg, "From Kafka to Kafkaesque," in Franz Kafka, *The Office Writings,* ed. Stanley Corngold, Jack Greenberg, and Benno Wagner, trans. Eric Patton and Ruth Hein (Princeton, N.J.: Princeton University Press, 2009), 355–71.

4. Tzvetan Todorov, *The Fantastic: A Structural Approach to a Literary Genre,* trans. Richard Howard (Ithaca, N.Y.: Cornell University Press, 1975), 174.

5. Ibid., 173.

6. Bruno Schulz, *Opowiadania, wybór esejów i listów,* ed. Jerzy Jarzębski (Wrocław: Ossolineum, 1989), 368. Kafka qtd. in Walter Benjamin, "Franz Kafka," in his *Illuminations: Essays and Reflections,* ed. Hannah Arendt, trans. Harry Zohn (New York: Schocken, 1968), 116.

7. Hans Ulrich Gumbrecht, *In 1926: Living at the Edge of Time* (Cambridge, Mass.: Harvard University Press, 1998), 339.

8. Michael Beddow, *The Fiction of Humanity: Studies in the Bildungsroman from Wieland to Mann* (Cambridge: Cambridge University Press, 1982), 233–34. Lorraine Daston and Peter Galison demonstrate the extent to which this insistence on objective fact was peculiar to nineteenth-century epistemology.

See Lorraine Daston and Peter Galison, *Objectivity* (New York: Zone Books, 2007).

9. Thomas Vargish and Delo E. Mook, *Inside Modernism: Relativity Theory, Cubism, Narrative* (New Haven, Conn.: Yale University Press, 1999), 22. Vargish coins the term in his entry for "Modernism" in *The Routledge Encyclopedia of Philosophy,* ed. Edward Craig, vol. 6 (London: Routledge, 1998), 447–49.

10. Milan Kundera, *The Art of the Novel,* trans. Linda Asher (New York: Harper and Row, 1988), 81.

11. Robert Walser, *Jakob von Gunten,* trans. Christopher Middleton (New York: New York Review of Books, 1999), 109.

12. Kundera, *The Art of the Novel,* 3–22. Kundera does not sufficiently distinguish between the artistic or philosophical methods of these writers. His project, admittedly, is to lump them together as having collectively rebelled against verisimilitude in the construction of narrative space-time and, in the process, against History, with a capital "H."

13. Michel Foucault, *Security, Territory, Population: Lectures at the College de France, 1977–1978,* ed. Michel Senellart, trans. Graham Burchell (New York: Picador), 20. Foucault's note 37 provides useful references to the conceptual heritage of "milieu" in Newton and Lamarck.

14. Hugh Kenner, *Flaubert, Joyce and Beckett: The Stoic Comedians* (Urbana, Ill.: Dalkey Archive Press, 2005), 97.

15. Among recent book-length studies, see Sarah Tribout-Joseph, *Proust and Joyce in Dialogue* (London: Legenda, 2008). For a strong general reading of the relationship between relativity theory and literary representation, see Michael H. Whitworth, *Einstein's Wake: Relativity, Metaphor, and Modernist Literature* (Oxford: Oxford University Press, 2001), particularly the fourth chapter.

16. Angus Fletcher, *Time, Space, and Motion in the Age of Shakespeare* (Cambridge, Mass.: Harvard University Press, 2007).

17. Michael W. Clune, *Writing Against Time* (Stanford, Calif.: Stanford University Press, 2013).

18. Martin Hägglund, *Dying for Time: Proust, Woolf, Nabokov* (Cambridge, Mass.: Harvard University Press, 2012).

19. Stephen Kern, *The Modernist Novel: A Critical Introduction* (Cambridge: Cambridge University Press, 2011), 125.

20. Sara Danius, *The Senses of Modernism: Technology, Perception, Aesthetics* (Ithaca, N.Y.: Cornell University Press, 2002), 192.

21. Kundera, *The Art of the Novel,* 11–12.

22. Galin Tihanov, "Why Did Modern Literary Theory Originate in Central and Eastern Europe? (And Why Is It Now Dead?)" *Common Knowledge* 10.1 (Winter 2004): 61–81.

23. In the year before writing the story, Krzhizhanovskii participated in a seminar on relativity theory led by the Soviet geologist Vladimir Vernadskii. Sigizmund Krzhizhanovskii, *Sobranie sochinenii v piati tomakh,* vol. 1, ed. Vadim Perel'muter (St. Petersburg: Symposium, 2001), 18, 684n.

24. Marcel Proust, *The Guermantes Way,* trans. C. K. Scott Moncrieff (New York: Modern Library, 1925), part 2, 234.

25. See especially the "Preface: On Scientific Cognition" in G. W. F. Hegel, *Phenomenology of Spirit,* trans. A. V. Miller (Oxford: Oxford University Press, 1977), 1–45.

26. I have written elsewhere about the fluidity with which "Eastern Europe" has been defined in the postwar reception of Eastern European literature. See Benjamin Paloff, "East Is Always Further East," *East European Politics and Societies* 28.4 (November 2014): 687–92.

27. Mikhail Epstein, "Russo-Soviet Topoi," trans. Jeffrey Karlsen, in *The Landscape of Stalinism: The Art and Ideology of Soviet Space,* ed. Evgeny Dobrenko and Eric Naiman (Seattle: University of Washington Press, 2003), 285; Natalia Poltavtseva, "The Husserlian, the Cosmicist and the Pushkinian in Platonov," *Essays in Poetics: The Journal of the British Neo-Formalist Circle* 27 (Autumn 2002), 105; Alain Badiou, *The Century,* trans. Alberto Toscano (Cambridge: Polity, 2007), 24; William E. Harkins, *Karel Čapek* (New York: Columbia University Press, 1962), 143.

28. Erich Fromm, *Escape from Freedom* (New York: Henry Holt, 1994). First published in 1941, Fromm's book is primarily concerned not with metaphysics, but with political freedom. He nevertheless advances a theory of anxiety in freedom similar to that which energizes metaphysical debate in the twentieth century: the individual is horrified both by his individuality and by his belonging to a collective.

29. Marshall Berman, *All That Is Solid Melts into Air: The Experience of Modernity* (New York: Penguin, 1982), 43.

30. Ibid., 37–86.

31. Iurii Davydov traces Modernism's renewed interest in speculative metaphysics to German Romanticism: "This same two-sidedness of artistic and metaphysical impulses that Thomas Mann established in reference to 'the intellectual novel' of our century was already characteristic of the German Romantics, the majority of whom were no strangers to philosophy; indeed, they were inwardly drawn toward it. Even then, art strove to become 'a species of metaphysics,' and metaphysics 'a species of art.'" Iurii Davydov, *Begstvo ot svobody: Filosofskoe mifotvorchestvo i literaturnyi avangard* (Moscow: Khudozhestvennaia literatura, 1978), 12–13. But while we see this interpenetration of philosophy and literature following a long trajectory, from the high Romanticism of Goethe to the late-Romantic philosophy of Nietzsche, there remains an indispensable distinction between Romanticism's revolt against verisimilitude and the Modernist revival of indeterminacy in literature. In Romantic texts, the efforts of protagonists and lyric subjects to grasp otherness are consistently formulated as an individual striving to bridge the gaps between lived praxis and the sublime, between the material world and the spirit level, between human helplessness and divine omnipotence. Thus Faust conjures Mephistopheles from within the strict confines of his study and under the oppressive weight of his worldly ambitions. Though he catches a glimpse of the other world's power, he does not succeed in entering that other world. Davydov's work is noteworthy in the broader context of Modernist studies because, in what appears to be a case of convergent evolution, he articulates a reading of Modernism that is very close to Berman's and based on many of the same primary texts, yet the two books—Davydov's

is provocatively titled after Fromm's *Escape from Freedom*—were published almost simultaneously on opposite sides of the Iron Curtain.

32. Berman, *All That Is Solid Melts into Air,* 70.

33. Georg Lukács, *Soul and Form,* trans. Anna Bostock (Cambridge, Mass.: MIT Press, 1974), 54.

34. Michel Foucault, *The Order of Things: An Archaeology of the Human Sciences* (New York: Vintage, 1970), 48–49.

35. In "Discourse in the Novel" (Slovo v romane, 1934–1935), Bakhtin writes: "The language of the poetic genre is the one and only *Ptolemaic world,* outside of which there is nothing, and nothing is needed. The idea of a multiplicity of linguistic worlds, much like those of sense or expression, is organically inaccessible to poetic style. The world of poetry, regardless of how much contradiction or intractable conflict the poet has revealed therein, is always devoted to the one, indisputable word." Orig: "Язык поэтического жанра—единый и единственный *птолемеевский мир,* вне которого ничего нет и ничего не нужно. Идея множественности языковых миров, равно осмысленных и выразительных, органически недоступна поэтическому стилю. Мир поэзии, сколько бы противоречий и безысходных конфликтов ни раскрывалось в нём поэтом, всегда освещен единым и бесспорным словом." M. M. Bakhtin, *Sobranie sochinenii v semi tomakh,* ed. S. G. Bocharov and V. V. Kozhinov, vol. 3 (Moscow: Iazyki Slavianskikh Kul'tur, 2012), 39. Despite Bakhtin's insistent denial of the coexistence of "a multiplicity of linguistic worlds" in the lyric poem, several scholars have successfully rebutted his claim and applied his discourse models to poetry. See especially David H. Richter, "Dialogism and Poetry," *Studies in the Literary Imagination* 23.1 (Spring 1990): 9–27; Michael Eskin, "Bakhtin and Poetry," *Poetics Today* 21.2 (Summer 2000): 379–91; and the concurrent treatment in Eskin's *Ethics and Dialogue in the Works of Levinas, Bakhtin, Mandel'shtam, and Celan* (Oxford: Oxford University Press, 2000), 114–25.

36. See Albert Einstein, *Relativity: The Special and the General Theory,* trans. Robert W. Lawson (London: Routledge, 2001), 27–39.

37. Gary Saul Morson, *Narrative and Freedom: The Shadows of Time* (New Haven, Conn.: Yale University Press, 1994), 119.

38. Sigizmund Krzhizhanovskii provides a colorful illustration, this time in his description of the hero in the European *Reiseroman,* or travel novel, written just before his short story "Quadraturin." In a formulation that could just as easily belong to Lukács or Bakhtin, Krzhizhanovskii tells us that the novel of wandering consists in the conflation of inner and outer events, and therefore of the psychological novel and the adventure novel. Krzhizhanovskii, *Sobranie sochinenii v piati tomakh,* vol. 4, 686–89.

39. This whimsical detail has sometimes been chalked up to Kafka's ignorance of American geography. In preparing the incomplete manuscript for publication, Max Brod (who originated the title *Amerika*) corrected the detail about the bridge, and in his preface to the first American edition Klaus Mann remarks that Kafka's "only sources of information were the few books he had read—and his own poetic imagination." Klaus Mann, preface, in Franz Kafka, *Amerika,* trans. Willa Muir and Edwin Muir (New York: Schocken, 1974), xii. This per-

spective, however, does not adequately reflect the fact that the geography of Kafka's story worlds, especially in his novelistic projects, is always based on his native Prague, which is similarly bisected by the Vltava.

40. Jorge Luis Borges, "On Exactitude in Science," in his *Collected Fictions*, trans. Andrew Hurley (New York: Penguin, 1998), 325.

41. Benjamin, "Franz Kafka," 120.

42. Orig.: "Отменяется всякая *дистанция* между людьми и вступает в силу особая карнавальная категория—*вольный фамильярный контакт между людьми.*" M. M. Bakhtin, *Problemy poetiki Dostoevskogo,* in his *Sobranie sochinenii v semi tomakh,* vol. 6 (Russkie slovari, 2002), 138.

43. Georg Lukács, *The Theory of the Novel*, trans. Anna Bostock (Cambridge: MIT Press, 1971), 122.

44. Erich Fromm, whose "escape from freedom" I have already mentioned as an effective entry into the theme of intermediacy, in fact identifies the hero of Kafka's *The Castle* as the epitome of the "powerlessness of man" in the modern age. Fromm, *Escape from Freedom,* 132.

45. C. S. Lewis, *The Lion, the Witch and the Wardrobe* (New York: HarperCollins, 2000), 59.

46. Georges Poulet, *La Pensée indéterminée, III. De Bergson à nos jours* (Paris: Presses Universitaires de France, 1990), 207.

47. Orig.: "Разобраться в мире значило для [Достоевского]—помыслить все его содержания, как одновременные, *и угадать их взаимоотношения в разрезе одного момента.*" M. M. Bakhtin, *Problemy tvorchestva Dostoevskogo,* in his *Sobranie sochinenii v semi tomakh,* vol. 2 (Russkie slovari, 2000), 37.

48. Franz Kafka, *The Complete Stories,* ed. Nahum N. Glatzer (New York: Schocken, 1971), 430. The translation is by Willa Muir and Edwin Muir. Orig.: "Sancho Pansa, der sich übrigens dessen nie gerühmt hat, gelang es im Laufe der Jahre, in den Abend- und Nachtstunden, durch Beistellung einer Menge Ritter- und Räuberromane seinen Teufel, dem er später den Namen Don Quichote gab, derart von sich abzulenken, daß dieser dann haltlos die verrücktesten Taten ausführte, die aber mangels eines vorbestimmten Gegenstandes, der eben Sancho Pansa hätte sein sollen, niemandem schadeten. Sancho Pansa, ein freier Mann, folgte gleichmütig, vielleicht aus einem gewissen Verantwortlichkeitsgefühl dem Don Quichote auf seinen Zügen und hatte davon eine große und nützliche Unterhaltung bis an sein Ende." Franz Kafka, *Kritische Kafka-Ausgabe: Nachgelassene Schriften und Fragmente,* ed. Jost Schillemeit, vol. 2.1 (Frankfurt: S. Fischer, 1992), 38.

49. Orig.: "чтобы жить, надо быть незавершённым, открытым для себя[.]" M. M. Bakhtin, "Avtor i geroi v esteticheskoi deiatel'nosti," in his *Sobranie sochinenii v semi tomakh,* vol. 1 (Russkie Slovari i Iazyki Slavianskoi Kul'tury, 2003), 95.

50. Maurice Blanchot, *The Space of Literature,* trans. Ann Smock (Lincoln: University of Nebraska Press, 1982), 27.

51. Orig.: "Historia mego stawania się to dzieje ciągłego przystosowywania się mego do mych dzieł literackich." Witold Gombrowicz, *Dziennik, 1957–1961,* vol. 8 of *Dzieła* (Kraków: Wydawnictwo Literackie, 1986), 18.

52. Early in her study of Tsvetaeva, Olga Peters Hasty remarks that the poet's "confrontations with death [. . .] urge her to new connections that course

through time and space to make the past endure in the future and to nullify the effects of physical separation." Olga Peters Hasty, *Tsvetaeva's Orphic Journeys in the Worlds of the Word* (Evanston, Ill.: Northwestern University Press, 1996), xiii. This observation alone may invite a comparison between Tsvetaeva's approach to death and immortality and what we will observe in Platonov and Schulz. As we will see, however, for Platonov and Schulz separation and association go hand-in-hand, as do liberation and entrapment.

53. Indeed, this is how Eleanor Honig Skoller accounts for the paucity of women, relative to men, producing "experimental" fiction in the postwar era, work that "is among other things highly self-reflexive and frequently marked by attempts to break the old forms, blur the genres, make indistinct the line between fiction and non-fiction (criticism, history, and philosophy), and release the tension between the warring opposites characteristic of Western thought, such as inside/outside, presence/absence, truth/lie, fiction/reality, and even masculine/feminine." Eleanor Honig Skoller, *The In-Between of Writing: Experience and Experiment in Drabble, Duras, and Arendt* (Ann Arbor: University of Michigan Press, 1993), 3. Marianne DeKoven offers a similar accounting in her "Male Signature, Female Aesthetic: The Gender Politics of Experimental Writing," in *Breaking the Sequence: Women's Experimental Fiction,* ed. Ellen G. Friedman and Miriam Fuchs (Princeton, N.J.: Princeton University Press, 1989), 72–81. While we should remain cautious not to conflate late-Modernist texts from Central and Eastern Europe with subsequent postmodernist currents, the general effort to neutralize "warring opposites" is common to both.

54. Marcel Proust, *On Art and Literature: 1896–1919,* trans. Sylvia Townsend Warner (New York: Carroll and Graf, 1997), 303–4.

Chapter 1

The chapter epigraph is from E. M. Cioran, *History and Utopia,* trans. Richard Howard (Chicago: University of Chicago Press, 1987), 37.

1. Published in 1927, in the thick of the public discourse on space and time, Martin Heidegger's construction of subjectivity in *Being and Time* is, among other things, an attempt to answer these questions. Heidegger writes: "Again, the perception of what is known does not take place as a return with one's booty to the 'cabinet' of consciousness after one has gone out and grasped it. Rather, in perceiving, preserving and retaining, the Da-sein that knows *remains outside as Da-sein.* In 'mere' knowledge about a context of the being of beings, in 'only' representing it, in 'solely' 'thinking' about it, I am no less outside in the world together with beings than I am when I *originally* grasp them." Martin Heidegger, *Being and Time: A Translation of* Sein und Zeit, trans. Joan Stambaugh (Albany: State University of New York Press, 1996), 58.

2. Peter Galison argues persuasively for the need to view the technological and conceptual changes during the late nineteenth century as mutually conditioning cultural pressures: "What emerged in the late nineteenth century was not merely the issue of a particular invention—coordinated clocks certainly existed before then. Instead, Europe and North America experienced a dramatic, global alteration in the place and density of electrodistributed time. Linked clocks of

the late nineteenth century covered the world. Circles of such wide-spanning technologies pulled each other along. Trains dragged telegraph lines, telegraphs made maps, maps guided rail-laying. All three (trains, telegraphs, maps) contributed to a growing sense that long-distance simultaneity made the question, What time is it now somewhere else? at once practical and evocative. When we read Einstein's and Poincaré's many discussions of the new ideas of time and space cast in the lexicon of automobiles, telegraphs, trains, and cannons, we are seeing the conditions under which these questions became commonplace." Peter Galison, *Einstein's Clocks, Poincaré's Maps: Empires of Time* (New York: W. W. Norton, 2003), 312–13.

3. Stephen Kern, *The Culture of Time and Space, 1880–1918* (Cambridge, Mass.: Harvard University Press, 1983), 71–72.

4. When Bergson and Einstein were both appointed to the Intellectual Committee of the League of Nations (with Bergson as president), it was widely reported in the world press, as was Einstein's conspicuous absence from the committee's inaugural meeting in Geneva. "His absence caused considerable comment," the *New York Times* noted portentously. "Bergson Heads League Scholars' Committee," *New York Times,* Aug. 2, 1922, 7.

5. Edmund Husserl, *The Crisis of European Sciences and Transcendental Phenomenology: An Introduction to Phenomenological Psychology,* trans. David Carr (Evanston, Ill.: Northwestern University Press, 1970), 5.

6. Ibid. For Husserl's definition of "physicalistic rationalism," see especially 65–67.

7. Aleksandr Blok, "Krushenie gumanizma," in his *O literature,* 2nd ed., ed. T. N. Bedniakova (Moscow: Khudozhestvennaia literatura, 1989), 323.

8. E. M. Cioran, *The Temptation to Exist,* trans. Richard Howard (Chicago: Quadrangle Books, 1968), 42–43.

9. Lukács, *Soul and Form*, 28–41.

10. Ibid., 36.

11. Lukács, *The Theory of the Novel*, 97. It is worth noting that the movement in Lukács's early, pre-Marxist thinking is paradoxically directed *away* from deterministic interpretive models. In *Soul and Form*, Lukács remarks that in Romantic literature the soul manifests itself through gesture, which allows it to achieve the "eternal certainty" of form (29). Five years later, in his discussion of Cervantes, Lukács destabilizes form and gesture alike, since the incommensurability of soul and form leaves only performance.

12. Lukács, *The Theory of the Novel,* 97. Lukács does not limit his treatment to Romantic literature, but rather presents the evolution of novelistic discourse as a continuum from Cervantes to Dostoevsky, who he suggests may initiate a new phase in the novel's development.

13. Orig.: "Прошлое тесно. Академия и Пушкин непонятнее гиероглифов. Бросить Пушкина, Достоевского, Толстого и проч. и проч. с парохода Современности." From the Futurist manifesto "A Slap in the Face of Public Taste" (Пощёчина общественному вкусу, 1912), signed by Mayakovsky, Khlebnikov, David Burliuk, and Aleksandr Kruchenykh (see Vladimir Maiakovskii et al., "Poshchechina obshchestvennomu vkusu," in *Literaturnye manifesty ot simvolizma do nashikh dnei,* ed. S. B. Dzhimbinov [Moscow: XXI Vek/

Soglasie, 2000], 142–43). Mandel'shtam and Zabolotskii, the best representatives of intermediacy in the Russian lyric poem in the 1920s and 30s, did not practice *zaum,* but Khlebnikov's practice was instrumental for them (through both admiration and rejection) as they formulated their own aesthetic and philosophical positions. See Gerald Janecek, *ZAUM: The Transrational Poetry of Russian Futurism* (San Diego: San Diego State University Press, 1996), 330–36.

14. It is for this reason that the Russian Futurists took such an active interest in the writings of young children and the mentally deranged, in whom the ego cannot hold the id behind its floodgates.

15. That Kundera's French-language texts never acknowledge Lukács's influence is curious, especially since the author directs us toward Lukács in one of his earliest reflections on the relationship between epic and novel, also called *The Art of the Novel* (Umění románu, 1961), which focuses on the interwar Czech novelist Vladislav Vančura. There, Kundera cites Lukács as the first to recognize how literary representation after 1848 shifted its attention from reflecting universals (a tree in a narrative simply stands for whatever the reader might imagine a tree to be) to particular surfaces (the tree is now the one specific tree that the author had in mind). Kundera refers to Lukács's later writings on Realism, his least heterodox and therefore the least likely to arouse the censor's suspicions, but this is the closest he comes to acknowledging the conceptual genealogy of "the depreciated legacy of Cervantes." Milan Kundera, *Umění románu: Cesta Vladislava Vančury za velkou epikou* (Prague: Československý spisovatel, 1961), 147.

16. Lukács, *The Theory of the Novel,* 152.

17. Michael Holquist and Katerina Clark, *Mikhail Bakhtin* (Cambridge, Mass.: Harvard University Press, 1984), 99.

18. Mikhail Gasparov, "M. M. Bakhtin in Russian Culture of the Twentieth Century," in *Critical Essays on Mikhail Bakhtin,* ed. Caryl Emerson (New York: G. K. Hall, 1999), 85.

19. Adam Phillips explains the significance of the escape act for the modern consciousness as a public demonstration of boundaries and their flexibility: "[W]e transgress *in order to find out if we can escape; to find out just what the servants of justice, the instigators of the law, are made of.* [. . .] It was perhaps the decadence of Houdini—and the culture that nurtured him—that unlike Daedalus and Icarus he had to invent things to escape from, that as an absurdist jack-of-both-trades he had to look for things to escape from and invent ways of escaping." Adam Phillips, *Houdini's Box: The Art of Escape* (New York: Vintage, 2002), 78.

20. Consistent with the metaphysical interests of the interwar period, Bakhtin was not the only one working on the construction of time and space in canonical works, and some contemporaneous critics of Bakhtin's book were quick to point out the tenuousness of his (mis)application of these principles to Dostoevsky. See, for example, G. Voloshin, "Prostranstvo i vremia u Dostoevskogo," *Slavia* (Prague) 12.1–2 (1933): 162–72, excerpted in *M. M. Bakhtin: Pro et contra,* vol. 1 (St. Petersburg: RKhGU, 2001), 200–201.

21. Bakhtin revised his study of Dostoevsky and reissued it in 1963 as *Problems of Dostoevsky's Poetics* (Проблемы поэтики Достоевского). Because I treat

Bakhtin's work on Dostoevsky as a vital snapshot of how interwar approaches to space and time relate to subjectivity and individual freedom, I rely primarily on the earlier version of the book. Instances where I draw on the 1963 revision are clearly noted as such.

22. Bakhtin takes these earlier critics to task in the opening pages of *Problems of Dostoevsky's Creative Work*. Among the major critics singled out by Bakhtin as having given us a "monologic" reading are Vasilii Rozanov and Lev Shestov.

23. A. F. Koni, "Fedor Mikhailovich Dostoevskii (Dostoevskii kak kriminalist, 1881)" and "F. M. Dostoevskii," in his *Sobranie sochinenii v vos'mi tomakh,* vol. 6 (Moscow: Izdatel'stvo "Iuridicheskaia literatura," 1968), 406–45.

24. Vladimir Chizh, *Dostoevskii kak psikhopatolog* (Moscow: M. Katkov, 1885).

25. Arkhiepiskop Antonii [Khrapovitskii] and Vladimir S. Soloviev, *F. M. Dostoevskii kak propovednik khristianskogo vozrozhdeniia i vselenskogo pravoslaviia* (Moscow: Pechatnia A. I. Snegirevoi, 1908). Following the October Revolution, Antonii became the first head of the Russian Orthodox Church in exile.

26. James P. Scanlan, *Dostoevsky the Thinker* (Ithaca, N.Y.: Cornell University Press, 2002).

27. Orig.: "свобода и самостоятельность их в самой структуре романа по отношению к автору." M. M. Bakhtin, *Problemy tvorchestva Dostoevskogo,* in his *Sobranie sochinenii v semi tomakh,* vol. 2 (Russkie slovari, 2000), 19.

28. This rejection of moral imperatives demonstrates one of the major limits of Kant's influence on the young Bakhtin.

29. Despite his interest in dramatic dialogue, Bulgakov's interpretation of Dostoevsky's "symbolic tragedies" remains predictably close to the religious core of Dostoevsky criticism up to that time: "For Dostoevsky, just as for ourselves listening intently to his testaments, the Russian tragedy is chiefly religious—a tragedy of faith and disbelief. [. . .] For him there is only one certainty in life, a single truth—Christ." S. N. Bulgakov, "Russkaia tragediia," in his *Sochineniia v dvukh tomakh,* ed. I. B. Rodnianskaia (Moscow: Nauka, 1993), 501. In his deployment of two words for truth, we can appreciate the poetics of Bulgakov's own adoration of Christ-in-Dostoevsky: he moves from the *pravda* ("truth") of everyday life to the *istina* (higher, gospel "Truth") of Christ. Even as Bulgakov's suggestion of the dramatic in Dostoevsky's works points to a formal element within his prose method, the main event for the critic—and, he asserts, for Dostoevsky as well—is precisely this movement from the truth of the world to the Truth of God.

30. Viacheslav Ivanov, "Dostoevskii i roman-tragediia," in *Rodnoe i vselenskoe,* ed. V. M. Tolmachev (Moscow: Respublika, 1994), 294. The last section of Ivanov's essay, which was published separately as "Excursus: The Foundation Myth in *Demons,*" is a direct response to Bulgakov's text; both appeared in the April 1914 issue of *Russian Thought* (Russkaia mysl').

31. Bakhtin, *Problemy tvorchestva Dostoevskogo,* 17.

32. Viacheslav Ivanov, "Dostoevskii i roman-tragediia," 295.

33. Jean-Luc Nancy, *Being Singular Plural,* trans. Robert D. Richardson and Anne E. O'Byrne (Stanford, Calif.: Stanford University Press, 2000), 30.

34. Viacheslav Ivanov, "Dostoevskii i roman-tragediia," 295.
35. Ibid., 296.
36. Orig.: "Главные герои Достоевского, действительно, в самом творческом замысле художника *не только объекты авторского слова, но и субъекты собственного непосредственно значащего слова.*" M. M. Bakhtin, *Problemy tvorchestva Dostoevskogo,* 12.
37. Ibid., 16–17. As it happens, Bakhtin applied the same critique to Viacheslav Ivanov as a poet, noting in his lectures on Russian literature that Ivanov created no new forms, but that he executed ingenious instantiations of the forms he had inherited. See R. M. Mirkina's notes to Bakhtin's lectures in the 1920s, "Zapisi lektsii po istorii russkoi literatury," in Bakhtin, *Sobranie sochinenii v semi tomakh,* vol. 2, 320–21.
38. It is believed Bakhtin was working on a "prototext" to his Dostoevsky book as early as 1922. See the editor's note to Bakhtin, *Sobranie sochinenii v semi tomakh,* vol. 2, 431–32.
39. Orig.: "Поэтому и миры героев, планы романа, несмотря на их различную иерархическую акцентуацию, в самом построении романа лежат рядом в плоскости сосуществования (как и миры Данте) и взаимодействия (чего нет в формальной полифонии Данте), а не друг за другом как этапы становления." Bakhtin, *Problemy tvorchestva Dostoevskogo,* 40.
40. Albert Camus, *The Rebel,* trans. Anthony Bower (New York: Vintage, 1956), 264. Bakhtin names Camus, among others, in "O polifonichnosti romanov Dostoevskogo," an interview with the Polish journalist and translator Zbigniew Podgórzec, in Bakhtin, *Sobranie sochinenii v semi tomakh,* vol. 6, 461.
41. Thaddaeus Zielinski [Tadeusz Zieliński], *Die Behandlung von gleichzeitiger Ereignisse im antiken Epos, Erster Theil* (Leipzig: Dieterich'sche Verlagsbuchhandlung, 1901).
42. Gary Saul Morson and Caryl Emerson, *Mikhail Bakhtin: Creation of a Prosaics* (Stanford, Calif.: Stanford University Press, 1990), 64–68.
43. Morson, *Narrative and Freedom,* 22.
44. Orig.: "Если бога нет, то какой же я после того капитан?" F. M. Dostoevskii, *Polnoe sobranie sochinenii v tridtsati tomakh,* vol. 10 (Leningrad: Nauka, 1974), 180.
45. Orig.: "Событие может быть ясно и отчётливо для участника в его поступке во всех своих моментах. Значит ли это, что он его логически понимает? Т. е. что ему ясны только общие, транскрибированные в понятия моменты и отношения? Нет, он ясно видит и этих индивидуальных единственных людей, которых он любит, и небо, и землю, и эти деревья, [. . .] и время, вместе с тем ему дана и ценность, конкретно, действительно утверждённая ценность этих людей, этих предметов, он интуирует и их внутренние жизни и желания, ему ясен и действительный и должный смысл взаимоотношений между ним и этими людьми и предметами." Bakhtin, *Sobranie sochinenii v semi tomakh,* vol. 1, 30–31.
46. Given the difficulty of dating his early notebooks precisely, we cannot be certain when Bakhtin first encountered the ideas of Max Scheler. It is clear, however, that Bakhtin became familiar with *The Nature of Sympathy* shortly after its publication. He also knew the more religious phenomenology of Edith

Stein, whose 1917 dissertation *On the Problem of Sympathy* (Neues zum Problem der Einfühlung) is referenced in both Scheler's book and Bakhtin's notes. (Stein was, with Martin Heidegger, a student and secretary of Husserl.) This demonstrates not only that Bakhtin was inspired by Viennese phenomenology at the turn of the century but that he kept up with its ongoing development in the interwar period.

47. Max Scheler, *Wesen und Formen der Sympathie: Der "Phänomenologie der Sympathiegefühle,"* 2nd ed. (Bonn: F. Cohen, 1923). For a representative sampling from this and other works by Scheler, see Max Scheler, *On Feeling, Knowing, and Valuing,* ed. Harold J. Bershady (Chicago: University of Chicago Press, 1992).

48. Orig.: "И это событие не может быть в целом транскрибировано в теоретических терминах, чтобы не потерять самого смысла своей событийности, того именно, что ответственно знает и на чём ориентируется поступок. Неправильно будет полагать, что эта конкретная правда события, которую и видит и слышит и переживает и понимает поступающий в едином акте ответственного поступка—несказáнна, что её можно только как-то переживать в момент поступления, но нельзя отчётливо и ясно высказать. Я полагаю, что язык гораздо более приспособлен высказывать именно её, а не отвлёченный логический момент в его чистоте." Bakhtin, *Sobranie sochinenii v semi tomakh,* vol. 1, 30–31.

49. Ibid., 131.

50. Thomas Seifrid, *The Word Made Self: Russian Writings on Language, 1860–1930* (Ithaca, N.Y.: Cornell University Press, 2005), 211.

51. Friedrich Nietzsche, *The Will to Power,* ed. Walter Kaufmann, trans. Walter Kaufmann and R. J. Hollingdale (New York: Vintage, 1967), 283.

52. Orig.: "Автор не только видит и знает всё то, что видит и знает каждый герой в отдельности и все герои вместе, но и *больше* их, причём он видит и знает нечто такое, что им принципиально не доступно, и в этом всегда определённом и устойчивом *избытке* видения и знания автора по отношению к каждому герою и находятся все моменты завершёния целого[.] [. . .] Своею завершённостью и завершенностью события жить нельзя, нельзя поступать; чтобы жить, надо быть незавершённым, открытым для себя—во всяком случае во всех существенных моментах жизни, надо ценностно еще предстоять себе, не совпадать со своею наличностью." Bakhtin, *Sobranie sochinenii v semi tomakh,* vol. 1, 95.

53. Ibid., vol. 6, 461–62.

54. Galin Tihanov, *The Master and the Slave: Lukács, Bakhtin, and the Ideas of Their Time* (Oxford: Oxford University Press, 2000), 65–66.

55. Bakhtin describes "great time" in several notebook entries in the years before his death, but he never succeeded in elaborating the concept in a complete work. In his notebooks, he writes of important and lasting literature: "The works smash the limits of their own time, they live in the ages, i.e., *in great time,* moreover frequently (and magnificent works—always) a more intense and full life than in their own contemporaneity." Orig: "Произведения разбивают грани своего времени, живут в веках, т. е. *в большом времени,* притом часто (а великие произведения—всегда) более интенсивной и полной жизнью, чем

в своей современности." Bakhtin, *Sobranie sochinenii v semi tomakh,* vol. 6, 454.

56. Orig.: "Термин этот употребляется в математическом естествознании и был введён и обоснован на почве теории относительности (Эйнштейна). Для нас не важен тот специальный смысл, который он имеет в теории относительности, мы перенесём его сюда—в литературоведение—почти как метафору (почте, но не совсем) [. . .]." M. M. Bakhtin, "Forma vremeni i khronotopa v romane," in his *Sobranie sochinenii v semi tomakh,* vol. 3, 288.

57. Morson and Emerson, *Mikhail Bakhtin: Creation of a Prosaics,* 367.

58. Bernhard F. Scholz, "Bakhtin's Concept of 'Chronotope': The Kantian Connection," in *The Contexts of Bakhtin: Philosophy, Authorship, Aesthetics,* ed. David Shepherd (Amsterdam: Harwood, 1998), 154.

59. Orig.: "Основной категорией художественного видения Достоевского было не становление, а *сосуществование и взаимодействие.* Он видел и мыслил свой мир по преимуществу в пространстве, а не во времени." Bakhtin, *Sobranie sochinenii v semi tomakh,* vol. 6, 36.

Chapter 2

The chapter epigraph is from Thomas Mann, *The Magic Mountain,* trans. John E. Woods (New York: Vintage, 1995), 4.

1. Jakub Schulz (1846–1915) was forty-six when Bruno, his last child, was born. For most of Bruno's childhood Jakub was in poor health, suffering from chronic tuberculosis and, later, cancer. Because he was no longer capable of maintaining the family business, Jakub's ill health forced the family to liquidate the shop several years before his death and move, in 1910, to a modest house on Floriańska Street, where both of Schulz's parents died, and where he produced his major literary and graphic works. See Jerzy Ficowski, *Regiony wielkiej herezji i okolice: Bruno Schulz i jego mitologia* (Sejny: Pogranicze, 2002), 24; and Wiesław Budzyński, *Schulz pod kluczem* (Warsaw: Bartelsmann, 2001), 32–41. The importance of Drohobycz to Schulz's life and literary creation has been examined thoroughly, particularly by Budzyński, in his *Schulz pod kluczem*, 48–67, and in his book-length history of the town and its most famous resident, *Miasto Schulza* (Warsaw: Prószyński i S-ka, 2005). A more compact treatment of the connections between Schulz's childhood home and his literary imagination appears in Jerzy Ficowski, *Regions of the Great Heresy: Bruno Schulz, a Biographical Portrait,* trans. Theodosia S. Robertson (New York: W. W. Norton, 2003), 92–102.

2. Orig.: "W taką noc niepodobną iść Podwalem ani żadną inną z ciemnych ulic, które są odwrotną stroną, niejako podszewką czterech linij rynku." Schulz, *Opowiadania*, 60.

3. Orig.: "Nazywam je sklepami cynamonowymi dla ciemnych boazeryj tej barwy, którymi są wyłożone." Ibid.

4. In addition to those titles treated specifically in this chapter, stories especially illustrative of the center-out principle include "August" (Sierpień), the opening story of *Cinnamon Shops;* "Pan" (Pan); "The Street of Crocodiles" (Ulica Krokodyli); and "The Gale" (Wichura).

5. Jerzy Jarzębski, *Prowincja centrum: Przypisy do Schulza* (Kraków: Wydawnictwo Literackie, 2005), 92.

6. Orig.: "[Z]wielokrotniają się, plączą i wymieniają jedne z drugimi ulice. Otwierają się w głębi miasta, żeby tak rzec, ulice podwójne, ulice sobowtóry, ulice kłamliwe i zwodne. Oczarowana i zmylona wyobraźnia wytwarza złudne plany miasta, rzekomo dawno znane i wiadome, w których te ulice mają swe miejsce i swą nazwę, a noc w niewyczerpanej swej płodności nie ma nic lepszego do roboty, jak dostarczać wciąż nowych i urojonych konfiguracyj." Schulz, *Opowiadania*, 59–60.

7. Orig.: "[T]ę wieloraką polifonię architektoniczną." Ibid., 71.

8. Orig.: "Coraz bardziej umacniało się w nas przekonanie, że cała ta burza była tylko donkiszoterią nocną, imitującą na wąskiej przestrzeni kulis tragiczne bezmiary, kosmiczną bezdomność i sieroctwo wichury." Ibid., 89. Jarzębski points out that "imitation" is one of Schulz's "keywords" and applies "to all those spheres of reality that encompass the new, the recent, while taking after the form and function of things rooted in history and tradition." Jarzębski, *Prowincja centrum*, 92. While this is certainly the case in many instances, it is not so here, where the metaphor is considerably more complex: the weather (storm) is a function of time (night), which behaves like a literary character (Don Quixote) in an expressly performative space (the "stage"). We will see a comparably rich chain of imitations in the Father's "imitations" of cockroaches in the stories "Cockroaches" (in the present chapter) and "Father's Last Escape" (treated in the conclusion).

9. The dates provided for Platonov's novels refer to the years of composition. Neither work was published in Platonov's lifetime; the novels first appeared in the West in the 1960s and '70s, nearly half a century after their composition. The dates provided for Schulz's two collections of connected stories refer to the year of publication. (N.B.: *Cinnamon Shops*, when it appeared, was postdated to 1934, according to the publishing conventions of the time.) Persuasive evidence suggests that Schulz wrote *Cinnamon Shops* between 1930 and 1932, the same period as his correspondence with Debora Vogel, from which the stories arose. Many of the stories in *Sanatorium under the Sign of the Hourglass* were in fact composed in the late 1920s, before those collected in *Cinnamon Shops*, making Schulz's activities in artistic prose roughly contemporary with the writing of *Chevengur* and *The Foundation Pit*. See Ficowski, *Regions of the Great Heresy*, 57–62.

10. Jarzębski comments on this problem in an amusing footnote: "As we know, one must be careful when it comes to 'reality' in literature, but it happens that in the case of 'Cinnamon Shops' Schulz is exceptionally clear in suggesting the correspondence of the story's initial realia to the realia of Drohobycz. I followed the beginning of little Józef's course [. . .] one late November evening in 1992, amazed at the degree to which everything corresponded with Schulz's story: starting at the Municipal Theater, along Podwale, which begins from that point, to the recesses of the rear walls of the houses along the square, along with their maze of annexes. But in this maze of recesses 'reality' ends, and there begins the dream about the world, along with the vision of those fantastic shops." Jarzębski, *Prowincja centrum*, 10 n2. I am particularly grateful to Professor

Jarzębski for guiding me along this same course during my visit to Drohobycz in 2008.

11. Besides Cubism, which among artistic movements has received the most critical attention with regard to the reconceptualization of space and time in the early twentieth century, German Expressionism is especially noteworthy for its spatial distortions in both film and painting, and its aesthetic influence on Schulz is immediately obvious in his prose and graphic work.

12. Bruno Schulz, *Księga listów,* ed. Jerzy Ficowski, 2nd ed. (Gdańsk: Słowo/obraz terytoria, 2002), 198.

13. Michał Paweł Markowski, *Polska literatura nowoczesna: Leśmian, Schulz, Witkacy* (Kraków: Universitas, 2007), 242–44.

14. See, for example, Michał Chmielowiec, "Zdarzenie bezdomne," *Kultura: Tygodnik literacki, artystyczny i społeczny* 3.13 (1938): 5; Włodzimierz Pietrzak, "Bluszcz na ruinach," *Prosto z mostu* 27 (1938): 7; and Marjan Promiński, "Nowości literackie," *Sygnały* 40 (March 1, 1938), 5.

15. Among postwar critics, one camp, generally of a Structuralist critical persuasion, focused on the writers' thematic correspondences, which are considerable by any measure, and noted the fact that Schulz not only was an early and enthusiastic reader of Kafka in the original but also lent his name to the first Polish translation of *The Trial.* Consequently, Schulz is often mentioned by nonspecialists as having translated Kafka into Polish, but this is inaccurate. His fiancée, Józefina Szelińska, translated *The Trial* in 1936, and Schulz, who was both fluent in German from early childhood and well acquainted with the culture of the Austro-Hungarian bureaucracy, corrected the translation, added a preface, and arranged for its publication. It was decided that, because Schulz had already attained some notoriety with *Cinnamon Shops,* he would be credited as the translator on the title page, as he continues to be in more recent reprintings. See Ficowski, *Regions of the Great Heresy,* 112. Notable appearances of this error of fact include W. G. Sebald, "The Undiscover'd Country: The Death Motif in Kafka's *The Castle,*" *Journal of European Studies* 2 (1972), 30. In the postwar reevaluation of Schulz's legacy, critics were quick to dispute whether the authors' similarities suggest direct influence, the kind of convergence that indicates different writers feeding off a shared zeitgeist, or even, as Isaac Bashevis Singer suggested, a Romantic convergence of spirit, declaring that "between Schulz and Kafka there is something that Goethe calls *Wahlverwandschaft*"—the term we now translate conventionally into English as "elective affinity"—"an affinity of souls that you have chosen for yourself." Philip Roth, *Shop Talk: A Writer and His Colleagues and Their Work* (Boston: Houghton Mifflin, 2001), 79. We may wonder, however, whether this comparison would have occurred to Singer absent Roth's question, which he also poses to Aharon Appelfeld in a separate conversation (21–22). Roth, an ardent admirer of Kafka and Schulz, was especially keen to promote the latter, lesser-known author among English-language readers, having published the first American edition of Schulz in 1977 in the series *Writers from the Other Europe,* which Roth edited for Penguin from 1974 to 1989. Yet this was not the first time that Singer had drawn the comparison, having already done so in his 1965 review of the first English-language edition of *Cinnamon Shops,* published as *The Street*

of Crocodiles, which he then quotes at length in his review of *Sanatorium under the Sign of the Hourglass* fifteen years later. Isaac Bashevis Singer, "A Polish Franz Kafka," The *New York Times,* July 9, 1978, BR1. The same question remains relevant for my reading of intermediacy, particularly in light of the fact that an eclectic mix of commentators consider thematic correspondences between Schulz and Kafka "superficial," as J. M. Coetzee has characterized them. J. M. Coetzee, *Inner Workings: Literary Essays, 2000–2005* (New York: Penguin, 2008), 74. The most imposing voice in the latter camp belongs to Jerzy Ficowski, Schulz's biographer, who consistently rejects the notion that Schulz was aping the literary project of his older, more famous contemporary, and who dismisses the similarity between Schulz's transformations and that of Gregor Samsa by calling the latter "inexplicable" and a "*deus ex machina.*" Ficowski, *Regions of the Great Heresy,* 117. Elisabeth Goślicki-Baur, in her own discussion of transformation in Schulz, supports Ficowski's position, if less stridently: "Although many aspects of their work demonstrate a similarity, they do not lend themselves well to direct juxtaposition." Elisabeth Goślicki-Baur, *Die Prosa von Bruno Schulz* (Frankfurt: Peter Lang, 1975), 78 n2. Schulz began reading Kafka in the original German at least as early as 1927, which makes Schulz's interest in him approximately contemporary with the earliest stirrings of his own literary ambition. The prose styles of the two authors are undoubtedly dissimilar, yet the argument against the comparison is unconvincing, at least to this reader. In particular, Ficowski's claim that "[t]heir worlds are diametrically opposed, their artistic motifs quite different, and their philosophies distant from one another" is hyperbolic to the point of error. Ficowski, *Regions of the Great Heresy,* 101.

16. Mieczysław Jastrun, "Poza rzeczywistością historyczną," *Kuźnica* 1.1 (June 1, 1945), 14.

17. Artur Sandauer, "Rzeczywistość zdegradowana: Rzecz o Brunonie Schulzu," in his *Zebrane pisma krytyczne,* vol. 1 (Warsaw: Państwowy Instytut Wydawniczy, 1981), 573.

18. Orig.: "Kafka znalazł dla tych spraw nieuchwytnych i niewyrażalnych w języku ludzkim—jak gdyby adekwatną cielesność, jakiś materiał zastępczy, w którym buduje i wyprowadza aż do najdrobniejszych szczegółów strukturę sprawy." Bruno Schulz, "Posłowie do polskiego przekładu *Procesu* Kafki," in his *Opowiadania,* 413.

19. See Jacques Lacan, "The Subversion of the Subject and the Dialectic of Desire in the Freudian Unconscious," in his *Ecrits: A Selection,* trans. Alan Sheridan (New York: W. W. Norton, 1977), 311, 316.

20. Orig.: "[S]ą one samoistną rzeczywistością poetycką, okrągłą, ze wszech stron zamkniętą, w sobie uzasadnioną i spoczywającą." Schulz, "Posłowie do polskiego przekładu *Procesu* Kafki," 414.

21. Orig.: "Kafka widzi niezwykle ostro realistyczną powierzchnią rzeczywistości, [. . .] ale jest to dla niego luźny naskórek bez korzeni, który zdejmuje jak delikatną powłokę i nakłada na swój transcendentny świat, transplantuje na swą rzeczywistość." Ibid.

22. See Viktor Shklovsky, *Theory of Prose,* trans. Benjamin Sher (Urbana, Ill.: Dalkey Archive Press, 1991), 1–14. We could also extend this line of thinking to the early, formative practices of Bakhtin, Voloshinov, and Medvedev.

23. For the story's dating, see Ficowski, *Regiony wielkiej herezji i okolice*, 58.

24. Orig.: "Czasem widzę się w lustrze. Rzecz dziwna, śmieszna i bolesna! Wstyd wyznać. Nie widzę się nigdy *en face*, twarzą w twarz. Ale trochę głębiej, trochę dalej stoję tam w głębi lustra nieco z boku, nieco profilem, stoję zamyślony i patrzę w bok. Stoję tam nieruchomo patrząc w bok, nieco w tył za siebie. Nasze spojrzenia przestały się spotykać." Schulz, *Opowiadania*, 311.

25. While the text pertains more to the speaker's manner of perceiving than to his appearance, it also comports well with the latter, at least with regard to the impression Schulz's manner left on those around him. Maria Budratzka-Tempele, a young artist who knew Schulz immediately after World War I, says that "when he looked at someone, that person would have the impression of being looked at askance." In 1921, when she was twelve, Irena Kejlin-Mitelman met Schulz in the spa town of Kudowa, on the Czech border, and describes his appearance as "hunched over, as if closed within himself." Jerzy Ficowski, ed., *Bruno Schulz: Listy, fragmenty, wspomnienia o pisarzu* (Kraków: Wydawnictwo Literackie, 1984), 42, 45.

26. Orig.: "Czy mam zdradzić, że pokój mój jest zamurowany? Jakżeż to? Zamurowany? W jakiż sposób mógłbym zeń wyjść?" Schulz, *Opowiadania*, 312. Another instance of the mirror that refuses to return the narrator's image appears in the title story of *Sanitorium under the Sign of the Hourglass*. *Opowiadania*, 257.

27. In Schulz, this kind of spatial distortion goes hand in hand with temporal indeterminacy, and these have received considerable attention in the critical literature. An exemplary semiotic treatment of Schulz's spatial and temporal distortions can be found in Jerzy Jarzębski and Teresa Jarzębska, "Uwagi o semantyce przestrzeni i czasu w prozie Brunona Schulza," in *Studia o Prozie Brunona Schulza*, ed. Kazimiera Czaplowa (Katowice: Uniwersytet śląski, 1976), 49–72. The authors effectively tie Schulz's treatment of matter and space to the seasonal cycles specified in his prose, an interpretive thread that is taken up again in Grzegorz Korecki, "Kategorie czasu w Prozie Brunona Schulza," *Przegląd Humanistyczny* 25.1–2 (1981): 139–59.

28. Orig.: "Muszę sobie tylko wyobrazić drzwi, dobre stare drzwi, jak w kuchni mego dzieciństwa, z żelazną klamką i ryglem. Nie ma pokoju tak zamurowanego, żeby się na takie drzwi zaufane nie otwierał, jeśli tylko starczy sił, by mu je zainsynuować." Schulz, *Opowiadania*, 312.

29. I often think of this as "the *X-Files* model" of narrative memory, in reference to the popular American television show broadcast from 1993 to 2002. This program was unusual for its time insofar as it both gestured toward a single, overarching plot and broke the conventions of serial narrative by refusing to advance that plot significantly. From one episode to the next, its protagonists appear to have little or no memory of important discoveries made in preceding episodes.

30. There were just over eighty thousand inhabitants in Platonov's hometown at the time of his birth, whereas Drohobycz counted fewer than twenty thousand.

31. Joseph Brodsky, "Catastrophes in the Air," in his *Less than One: Selected Essays* (New York: Farrar, Straus & Giroux, 1986), 292.

32. For a review of this program, its results, and its antecedents in pre-Soviet environmental engineering, see Stephen Brain, "The Great Stalin Plan for the Transformation of Nature," *Environmental History* 15 (October 2012): 670–700.

33. Viktor Shklovsky, *Third Factory,* trans. Richard Sheldon (Urbana, Ill.: Dalkey Archive Press, 2002), 77. Of course, all of the rivers Shklovsky mentions continue to exist, though in some cases their courses were substantially altered from their historical norm by the major land reclamation projects of the First Five-Year Plan.

34. Despite Platonov's demonstrations of faith in socialism in his journalistic prose from the early 1920s, his philosophical roots, as we will see later, were far from strictly Marxist. The poet Semen Izrailovich Lipkin, who knew Platonov from the early 1940s, recounts that Platonov's materialist philosophy was generally pantheistic, after the philosophical tradition of Nikolai Fedorov. S. Lipkin, "Golos druga," in *Andrei Platonov: Vospominaniia sovremennikov, Materialy k biografii,* ed. N. V. Kornienko and E. D. Shubina (Moscow: Sovremennyi pisatel', 1994), 123. For a general discussion of the influence of Fedorov, Aleksandr Bogdanov, and others on Platonov's early philosophical development, see Elena Tolstaia, *Mirposlekontsa: Raboty o russkoi literature XX veka* (Moscow: RGGU, 2002), 289–323; and Thomas Seifrid, *Andrei Platonov: Uncertainties of Spirit* (Cambridge: Cambridge University Press, 1992), 20–31.

35. Stephen Kotkin, *Magnetic Mountain: Stalinism as a Civilization* (Berkeley: University of California Press, 1995), 30.

36. Platonov's *Chevengur* was slated for publication and reached the point of author-corrected page proofs before it was withdrawn by the publisher. The text of *The Foundation Pit* exists in handwritten manuscript and author-corrected typescript only.

37. Orig.: "[Общий дом . . .] куда войдёт на поселение весь местный класс пролетариата[.]" Andrei Platonov, *Kotlovan: Tekst, materialy tvorcheskoi istorii,* ed. N. A. Groznova et al. (St. Petersburg: Nauka, 2000), 190. This sentence belongs to a passage that bears a question mark in the earliest handwritten manuscript. While most print editions include the entire passage as written, it is omitted from the most recent: Andrei Platonov, *Kotlovan,* in his *Sobranie sochinenii v vos'mi tomakh,* ed. N. V. Kornienko, vol. 2 (Moscow: Vremia, 2009), hereafter cited as *Kotlovan.* The lacuna occurs on 422.

38. Eliot Borenstein suggests that the incorporeal in Platonov is a specifically feminine principle, an argument that is well suited to the texts he explicitly discusses, including "A Story about Many Interesting Things" (Rasskaz o mnogikh interesnykh veshchakh, 1923) and the early essay "The Soul of the World" (Dusha mira, 1920). Eric Naiman, meanwhile, describes the body metaphor in Platonov's early journalistic writings in terms of its deindividuation, that is, its striving toward a "collective corporeality." We should note, however, that by the more ambitious works of the late 1920s—when the author himself was ideologically less strident and undoubtedly chastened by the course of the Soviet project in the first years under Stalin—Platonov was just as apt to show both men and women as fragile bodies that project the state of the souls they contain, i.e., starvation, satiety, transition, etc. See Eliot Borenstein, *Men without*

Women: Masculinity and Revolution in Russian Fiction, 1917–1929 (Durham, N.C.: Duke University Press, 2000), 195–96; and Eric Naiman, *Sex in Public: The Incarnation of Early Soviet Ideology* (Princeton, N.J.: Princeton University Press, 1997), 72.

39. Brodsky, *Less than One,* 290.

40. Orig.: "По вечерам Вощев лежал с открытыми глазами и тосковал о будущем, когда всё станет общеизвестным и помещённым в скупое чувство счастья." Platonov, *Kotlovan,* 449. Unless otherwise noted, all quotations from *The Foundation Pit* are drawn from the redaction in Platonov, *Sobranie sochinenii v vos'mi tomakh,* vol. 3 (2009).

41. In the most extensive treatment of Platonov's poetic language, Mikhail Mikheev points to another lexical element in the same sentence about Voshchev that supports this interpretation, albeit by a different path. Platonov's use of the word *skupoi,* which I have translated as "meager" (it could also be rendered as "miserly"), often refers to something in short supply and to be guarded jealously so that it might be available to future generations: "The point is that at this moment, for Voshchev as well as for the other diggers in the foundation pit, there is not yet any cause for joy; they merely console themselves with hope and live by thinking that their actions will at least bring it closer, that they will preserve and maintain it for later, for the future." Mikhail Mikheev, *V mir Platonova cherez ego iazyk: Predlozheniia, fakty, istolkovaniia, dogadki* (Moscow: MGU, 2003), 154.

42. We might also describe Voshchev's attitude toward the future as a melancholic affliction, in the Freudian sense, insofar as the object of his longing cannot be fully grasped, since the future has not yet arrived. See Sigmund Freud, "Mourning and Melancholia," in his *The Penguin Freud Reader,* ed. Adam Phillips (New York: Penguin, 2006), 310–25.

43. A more common, though still nonstandard, use of the verb is *toskovat' za* with the instrumental case, which further emphasizes the notion that the pining subject comes after the object of his longing. Platonov deploys his unusual use of the preposition *o* again in an aside about the cynical Kozlov that was ultimately cut from the typescript: "Kozlov extracted a mote from his bony nose and looked to the side, as though he were longing for freedom, though in fact he was not longing for anything." Orig.: "Козлов вынул соринку из своего костяного носа и посмотрел в сторону, точно тоскуя о свободе, но на самом деле ни о чём не тосковал." Andrei Platonov, *Kotlovan,* in Pushkinskii Dom, St. Petersburg, fond 780, item 8 (hereafter referenced as Pushkinskii Dom 780.8); Platonov, *Kotlovan: Tekst, materialy tvorcheskoi istorii,* 193–94. (The omitted text would otherwise appear in Platonov, *Kotlovan,* 424.) Again, the verb is future oriented, since we can reasonably infer from Platonov's Marxist ideology and from Kozlov's contrary character that the freedom for which Kozlov would be longing—if, in fact, he had been longing for anything—is that of an unrealized future, not of the pre-Revolutionary past. Platonov himself may have been uneasy about the direct suggestion that the freedom of the Soviet future has not yet been made manifest.

44. Epstein, "Russo-Soviet Topoi," 285.

45. Svetlana Boym, *The Future of Nostalgia* (New York: Basic Books, 2001), 49.

46. Orig.: "Погибнет-ли Эсесерша подобно Насте или выростет [sic] в целого человека, в новое историческое общество?—это тревожное чувство и составляло тему сочинения, когда его писал автор. Автор мог ошибиться, изобразив в виде смерти девочки гибель социалистического поколения, но эта ошибка произошла лишь от излишней тревоги за нечто любимое, потеря чего равносильна разрушению не только всего прошлого, но и будущего." Pushkinskii Dom 780.8, 125. This text concludes the novel only in its most recent print redaction: Platonov, *Kotlovan,* 534. The feminine *esesersha* seems to be peculiar to Platonov's lexicon. We can assume that at a certain stage of Platonov's authorial process he had intended for this passage to close the text of *The Foundation Pit,* since "The End" (Конец) is crossed out at the bottom of the previous page and moved to the end of Platonov's handwritten addendum.

47. Orig.: "Эх ты, эсесерша наша мать!" Platonov, *Kotlovan,* 508.

48. Shortly after Nastia's arrival, Safronov, whose officious verbiage muddles his allegiance to ideology, greets her "as an element of the future" (как элемент будущего). Platonov, *Kotlovan,* 456. That he immediately falls back to sleep indicates an ironic stance toward this designation, but Platonov is at least half-serious, as his expurgated conclusion indicates: Nastia is indeed "an element of the future," but she has been transplanted into the present, where she will inevitably fail to thrive.

49. E. A. Iablokov, *Na beregu neba: Roman Andreia Platonova* Chevengur (St. Petersburg: D. Bulanin, 2001), 10–17.

50. See Sigmund Freud, *The Standard Edition of the Complete Psychological Works of Sigmund Freud,* ed. James Strachey et al., vol. 10 (London: Hogarth Press, 1955), 235–36; and vol. 20 (1959), 119–20.

51. Orig.: "[. . .] будущий человек найдёт себе покой в этом прочном доме, чтобы глядеть из высоких окон в простертый, ждущий его мир." Platonov, *Kotlovan,* 423. Note the double duty performed by the word *pokoi,* which Platonov most likely meant in its formal reference to a room or chamber, though its primary definition is "peace" or "rest" (also in the sense of "eternal rest"), suggesting that the proletarian house only exists in some version of the afterlife, that is, in the ahistorical future, where the future man "will find his peace."

52. Yeats's poem "The Second Coming," from *Michael Robartes and the Dancer* (1921), addresses the imminence of apocalypse, but it is also about repetition, about a world that keeps on spinning, even though it is spinning out of control, "Turning and turning in the widening gyre." W. B. Yeats, *The Collected Poems of W. B. Yeats,* 2nd ed., ed. Richard J. Finneran (New York: Scribner, 1996), 187.

53. On the Soviet theory of the future's arrival, see Andrzej Walicki, *Marxism and the Leap to the Kingdom of Freedom: The Rise and Fall of the Communist Utopia* (Stanford, Calif.: Stanford University Press, 1997), 269–79.

54. Ibid., 44–45.

55. Regarding Platonov's interest in Einstein, see N. V. Kornienko's commentary on the manuscript of Platonov's play *Noev kovcheg, Novyi mir* 9 (1993), 137–38.

56. Orig.: "Социальная революция—ворота в царство сознания [. . .] Это [наука] не будет теперешней наукой, тлеющей в университетах, лабораториях

и библиотеках. Это будет бушующее пламя познания, охватившее все города, все улицы, все существа нашей планеты." Andrei Platonov [as A.P.], "Slyshnye shagi: Revoliutsiia i matematika," *Voronezhskaia kommuna* (January 18, 1921), in Andrei Platonov, *Sochineniia,* ed. N. V. Kornienko, vol. 1.2 (Moscow: IMLI RAN, 2004), 147.

57. Orig.: "Они тождественны, они—одно. [. . .] Несовершенство нашего сознания в том, что я, например, не мог понять сразу эту формулу, а сначала почувствовал её[.]" Ibid., 147–48.

58. Poltavtseva, "The Husserlian, the Cosmicist and the Pushkinian in Platonov," 105, 106–7. While I would soften Poltavtseva's characterization of Platonov's shift from traditionalism to modernity, which is never fully executed, she correctly identifies his application of modern, future-oriented, "enlightened" concepts to the atemporal, "mythological paradigm" of his upbringing: "Platonov belonged culturally and genetically to a strong Russian tradition of archaic and traditionalist culture with all the attendant cultural mechanisms (the mythological paradigm) but subsequently moved over to the logical, rationalistic modern European 'enlightened' paradigm, and [. . .] he tried for a certain period to use the logic of this paradigm to reinterpret the old cultural and symbolic world to which he was accustomed" (101). Valerii V'iugin follows the demiurgic quality of Platonov's hero a step further, encompassing the German post-Romantic tradition that had such a marked influence on Schulz as well: "It is difficult in reading Platonov to dispense with the line of the 'god-man,' including Feuerbach and Nietzsche. In Platonov's world, man does not rely from beginning to end on the Someone's participation. He refashions the world himself (successfully or not, this is another question), and it is in this that his actions are close to Fedorov's." V. Iu. V'iugin, *Andrei Platonov: Poetika zagadki: Ocherk stanovleniia i evoliutsii stilia* (St. Petersburg: Izdatel'stvo Russkogo Khristianskogo Gumanitarnogo Instituta, 2004), 293.

59. Orig.: "До самого вечера молча ходил Вощев по городу, словно в ожидании, когда мир станет общеизвестен. Однако ему по-прежнему было неясно на свете, и он ощущал в темноте своего тела тихое место, где ничего не было, но ничто ничему не препятствовало начаться. Как заочно живущий, Вощев делал своё гулянье мимо людей, чувствуя нарастающую силу горюющего ума и всё более уединяясь в тесноте своей печали." Platonov, *Kotlovan,* 419.

60. Orig.: "[. . .] устало длилось терпение на свете, точно всё живущее находилось где-то посредине времени и своего движения: начало его всеми забыто и конец неизвестен, осталось лишь направление во все стороны." Platonov, *Kotlovan,* 467.

61. M. A. Dmitrovskaia, "Zagadka vremeni: A. Platonov i O. Shpengler," in *Logicheskii analiz iazyka: Iazyk i vremia,* ed. N. D. Arutiunova and T. E. Ianko (Moscow: Indrik, 1997), 302–13. Dmitrovskaia offers many excellent examples on 306–8.

62. The "tightness" (*tesnota*) of Voshchev's spiritual space also recalls the word frequently used by Dostoevsky to describe the living quarters of his protagonists, notably of the Underground Man and Raskolnikov. But the difference between Dostoevsky and Platonov is extremely telling. For Dostoevsky, the dank, cramped quarters of the exterior world indicate the mounting psy-

chological confinement of his protagonists, who fail repeatedly to comprehend their own inner worlds. For Platonov, on the other hand, it is the inner space that fosters psychic delineations, and the outer space that remains mysterious and daunting. The author describes Voshchev not only as empty on the inside but also as being wholly aware of his emptiness—through immediate "feeling," Platonov's principal mode of contact with the world. See, for example, part 2, chapter 6, of *Notes from Underground,* in which the Underground Man's room is described as "tight, cramped, and low" (Orig.: "В комнате узкой, тесной и низкой"), and part 2, chapter 5, of *Crime and Punishment,* in which Raskolnikov's living space is also described as "cramped and low" (тесная и низкая). Dostoevskii, *Polnoe sobranie sochinenii v tridtsati tomakh,* vol. 5, 152, and vol. 6, 111, respectively.

63. V. Iu. V'iugin, "Povest' 'Kotlovan' v kontekste tvorchestva Andreia Platonova," in Platonov, *Kotlovan: Tekst, materialy tvorcheskoi istorii,* 13.

64. Orig.: "Он ожидал, когда же там будет вынесена резолюция о прекращении вечности времени, об искуплении томительности жизни." Platonov, *Kotlovan,* 471.

65. Seifrid, *Andrei Platonov: Uncertainties of Spirit,* 146.

66. Orig.: "Эту песню он слышал ещё в детстве, её пели солдаты русско-японской войны. И теперь её поют,—и одинаково, как в то давнее время, небо было покрыто туманной жарой, а солнце пустынно светило над всею безлюдной ветхостью [var.: над всём сиротством] земли. Значит, Вощев зря пропадёт жизнь—она не меняется, она как замершее детство и в ней нет истины на конце. [. . .] Горе всеобщего состояния начинало мучить Вощева, он чувствовал всю наружную жизнь, как свою внутренность, и хрипел горлом, открыв рот для сообщения.

—Чиклин, а где-ж марксизм? Кругом слабые места [var.: люди] и одно пустое, вечное время, у меня опять здоровье пропадет . . .

—Да вот именно-то!—сказал Чиклин.—Тут дом нужен, а тут порожняк лежит, поневоле у тебя нужда свербит. Но мы управимся, мы всю пустоту загромоздим." Pushkinskii Dom 780.8, 56. The variants are from Platonov, *Kotlovan: Tekst, materialy tvorcheskoi istorii,* 204.

67. Orig.: "[О]ни видели мир уже доделанным до конца[.]" Pushkinskii Dom 780.8, 56.

68. Seifrid, *Andrei Platonov: Uncertainties of Spirit,* 29.

69. Orig.: "Снежный ветер утих; неясная луна выявилась на дальнем небе, опорожнённом от вихрей и туч,—на небе, которое было так пустынно, что допускало вечную свободу, и так жутко, что для свободы нужна была дружба." Platonov, *Kotlovan,* 508.

70. Miroslav Drozda, "Umělecký prostor v próze Andreje Platonova," in *Východoevropská moderna a její evropský kontext,* vol. 1, ed. Ladislav Zadražil (Prague: Nakladatelství Karolinum, 1999), 127.

71. Lukács writes: "German Romanticism, although it did not always completely clarify its concept of the novel, drew a close connection between it and the concept of the Romantic; and rightly so, for the novel form is, like no other, an expression of this transcendental homelessness." Lukács, *The Theory of the Novel,* 41.

72. Georg Lukács, *History and Class Consciousness: Studies in Marxist Dialectics,* trans. Rodney Livingstone (Cambridge, Mass.: MIT Press, 1971), 146.

73. Ibid., 250.

74. Ibid., 156.

75. See V. I. Lenin, *The State and Revolution,* trans. Robert Service (New York: Penguin, 1992), especially chapter 5 ("The Economic Base of the Withering Away of the State"), 75–92.

76. "Копёнкин любил мать и Розу одинаково, потому что мать и Роза было одно и то же первое существо для него, как прошлое и будущее живут в одной его жизни." Platonov, *Chevengur,* 165. Unless otherwise noted, citations of *Chevengur* refer to the redaction in Platonov, *Sobranie sochinenii v vos'mi tomakh,* vol. 3.

77. Aleksandr Bogdanov, *Empiriomonizm,* vol. 1 (Moscow: S. Dorovatovskii i A. Charushnikov, 1905), 23.

78. "Дванов считал, что надо к матери, равно к умершему брату, итти не прямым путём верной преданности и вечных воспоминаний, а обходным—через коммунизм и победу над природой: тогда будут самые лучшие встречи [. . .]" Andrei Platonov, *Chevengur,* in Pushkinskii Dom 780.34, 2.147–48 (278), hereafter cited as Pushkinskii Dom 780.34.

79. "[Копёнкин] сам вполне присоединился к убеждению Дванова и решил дождаться раскопки могил." Ibid., 2.68 (154).

80. "[О]н видел смерть как другую губернию, которая расположена под небом, будто на дне прохладной воды,—и она его влекла." Platonov, *Chevengur,* 16. This line was a later addition to the manuscript: it is inserted in pen on 5.

81. Orig.: "Александр Дванов не слишком глубоко любил себя, чтобы добиваться для своей личной жизни коммунизма, но он шёл вперёд со всеми, потому что все шли и страшно было остаться одному, он хотел быть с людьми, потому что у него не было отца и своего семейства. Чепурного же, наоборот, коммунизм мучил, как мучила отца Дванова тайна посмертной жизни, и Чепурный не вытерпел тайны времени и прекратил долготу истории срочным устройством коммунизма в Чевенгуре,—так же, как рыбак Дванов не вытерпел своей жизни и превратил её в смерть, чтобы заранее испытать красоту того света." Platonov, *Chevengur,* 318. There is a peculiar inconsistency in the text insofar as Platonov refers to the "fisherman Dvanov," whereas at the beginning of the novel (17) we are told that young Sasha is taken in by Mavra Fetisovna Dvanova, and Sasha appears to take that family name.

82. Orig.: "[. . .] я теперь скоро умру к тебе [. . .]." Ibid., 31. Emphasis added.

83. Borenstein, *Men without Women,* 261.

84. Orig.: "[О]н ещё внутри весь живой, только снаружи помер." Platonov, *Chevengur,* 304.

85. "Инженер Прушевский уже с двадцати пяти лет почувствовал стеснение своего сознания и конец дальнейшему понятию жизни, будто тёмная стена предстала в упор перед его ощущающим умом. И с тех пор он мучился, шевелясь у своей стены, и успокаивался, что, в сущности, самое срединное, истинное устройство вещества, из которого скомбинирован мир и люди, им

постигнуто, вся насущная наука расположена ещё до стены его сознания, а за стеною находится лишь скучное место, куда можно и не стремиться. Но всё же интересно было—не вылез ли кто-нибудь за стену вперёд." Platonov, *Kotlovan,* 429.

86. Bruno Schulz, "Bruno Schulz do St. I. Witkiewicza," in Schulz, *Opowiadania,* 444–45.

87. Orig.: "Но в человеке ещё живёт маленький зритель—он не участвует ни в поступках, ни в страдании—он всегда хладнокровен и одинаков. Его служба—это видеть и быть свидетелем, но он без права голоса в жизни человека и неизвестно, зачем он одиноко существует. Этот угол сознания человека день и ночь освещён, как комната швейцара в большом доме." Platonov, *Chevengur,* 104.

88. F. W. J. von Schelling, *Ages of the World,* trans. Judith Norman, published with Slavoj Žižek, *The Abyss of Freedom* (Ann Arbor: University of Michigan Press, 1997), 123. The translation is based on Schelling's 1813 revision of "Ages of the World" (Die Weltalter).

89. Later in the same work, Schelling absorbs this duality into a world model rooted in opposing wills, one that strives toward positive contact with the world (love), and another, negative will that rejects the world (wrath). "Unconditioned freedom," he writes, "is not a characteristic of particular actions; it is rather the capacity to be entirely one or entirely the other of two contradictory things." Ibid., 171. Indeed, the thinking subject strives toward "absolute freedom" but does not attain it, since one cannot be absolutely oneself, nor absolutely absorbed into the collective. Schelling makes a halfhearted attempt to reassert a provisional monism within this duality by suggesting the existence of a tertiary will, one that encompasses both contradictory wills within itself. This effort toward reintegration of the parts into an ideal of the whole resonates with our authors' own failed efforts toward recovery of the lost world.

90. In *On the Nature of Sympathy,* Scheler defines several grades of sympathetic experience, from "feeling-in-common" to "emotional infection" and, eventually, "emotional identification," in which the "I" completely absorbs another subject (idiopathic identification) or is absorbed by him (heteropathic identification). See Scheler, *On Feeling, Knowing, and Valuing,* 54–68. Such absolute values, of course, are impossible, but it is the striving toward consequential contact between thinking subjects that so fascinates Bakhtin and resonates so powerfully with the literature with which his narrative theories are most kindred.

91. Miłosz Bukwalt, *Literackie portrety żydowskich ojców w prozie Brunona Schulza i Danila Kiša* (Wrocław: Wydawnictwo Uniwersytetu Wrocławskiego, 2003), 35.

92. Orig.: "Прушевский шёл на котлован впереди неизвестных людей. Письмо сестре он отправил и хотел теперь упорно действовать, беспокоиться о текущих предметах и строить любое здание в чужой прок, лишь бы не тревожить своего сознания, в котором он установил особое нежное равнодушие, согласованное со смертью и с чувством сиротства к остающимся людям." Platonov, *Kotlovan,* 433.

93. Orig.: "Юзик не откликнулся, на минуту был слышен сиротливый ветер [. . .]." Boris Pil'niak, *Golyi god,* in his *Sobranie sochinenii v shesti tomakh,* vol. 1, ed. K. Andronikashvili-Pil'niak (Moscow: Terra-Knizhnyi Klub, 2003), 133.

94. V. I. Lenin, *Polnoe sobranie sochinenii v 55-x tomakh,* 5th ed., vol. 39 (Moscow: Gosudarstvennoe izdatel'stvo politicheskoi literatury, 1963), 380.

95. Kafka, *The Complete Stories,* 89, translation by Willa Muir and Edwin Muir. Orig.: "Als Gregor Samsa eines Morgens aus unruhigen Träumen erwachte, fand er sich in seinem Bett zu einem ungeheueren Ungeziefer verwandelt." Franz Kafka, *Kritische Kafka-Ausgabe: Drucke zu Lebzeiten,* ed. Hans-Gerd Koch (Frankfurt: S. Fischer, 1994), 115.

96. Without rejecting this hypothesis, Michael Ryan suggests alternatively that "Samsa" refers us back to Schopenhauer's understanding of *Samsara,* the concept of reincarnation and rebirth in several Eastern religions, and that the two etymologies might coexist: "The malaise of being alone could fit with the idea of *Samsara.*" Michael P. Ryan, "Samsa and *Samsara:* Suffering, Death, and Rebirth in 'The Metamorphosis,'" *German Quarterly* 72.2 (Spring 1999), 136.

97. By very different means, Harold Skulsky arrives at a similar conclusion, noting that "Gregor is a tragic hero whose home is closed to him even though he is in it, and for whose recognition there is no 'rational' basis. [. . .] Even in what is *recognizably* a person, the essence of its personhood and the object of our compassion amount to behavior and nothing more. For a person, so conceived, to be *disfigured* is in a measure to disintegrate; to be transformed as Gregor is transformed is no longer to exist." Harold Skulsky, *Metamorphosis: The Mind in Exile* (Cambridge, Mass.: Harvard University Press, 1981), 192–93.

98. In German, this difference between species of indifference is more pronounced. In the metaphysics to which I refer here, from the Idealism of Schelling through the phenomenology of Heidegger, *Indifferenz* refers to the lack of difference or failure to differentiate on a basic ontological level. *Gleichgültigkeit,* on the other hand, refers to indifference in its quotidian sense of not having a preference.

99. Orig.: "[Н]овый мир будет строиться из вечного материала, который никогда не придёт в бросовое состояние." Platonov, *Chevengur,* 174.

100. Iablokov, *Na beregu neba,* 12.

101. Orig.: "[Д]ействительно любил и чувствовал лишь готовое изделие,—то, во что превратилось посредством труда человека и что дальше продолжает жить самостоятельной жизнью." Platonov, *Chevengur,* 41.

102. Orig.: "сочувствие паровозу." Ibid., 22. Zakhar Pavlovich's conversation with the train occurs on 59–60. Most of Platonov's characters express a basic ontological connection with mechanical objects at some point in the novel.

103. Orig.: "Захар Павлович спешил работать в день, чтобы как можно больше мёртвых природных вещей превратить в изделия [. . .] и через это сделать куски вещества живыми телами—похожими на человека, и даже лучше его." Pushkinskii Dom 780.34, 46.

104. Orig.:"Он хотел бы, чтобы мир действительно был бесконечен, дабы колёса всегда были необходимы и изготовлялись беспрерывно на общую радость, но никак не мог почувствовать бесконечности." Platonov, *Chevengur,* 42.

105. Orig.: "Дванов лежал в траве Чевенгура, и, куда бы ни стремилась его жизнь, её цели должны быть среди дворов и людей, потому что дальше ничего нет, кроме травы, поникшей в безлюдном пространстве, и кроме неба, которое своим равнодушием обозначает уединённое сиротство людей на земле." Ibid., 339.

106. Orig: "Люди в куче живут и лично видятся—зачем им почта, скажи пожалуйста! Здесь, брат, пролетарии уже вплотную соединены!" Ibid., 209.

107. Orig.: "Наше гибельное время и неизбежную смерть чувствовал тогда живо и грустно. Мне жаль было мечущихся бесприютных людей, объединённых и покинутых [. . .]; по молодости я мечтал о другой и мирной судьбе—о каком-то глубоком человеческом сознании, видящем события в мире прежде их появления,—о богатстве вселенной, которое удовлетворит всякую жадность жизни и о каком абсолютном сердечном чувстве веры в значение человека, как завоевателя и спасителя бушующей природы, уничтожающей самое себя. Всё это я обдумывал много раз—теперь меня интересовало превращение мыслей в событие." Pushkinskii Dom 780.34, unpaginated leaf 43.

108. This macabre, darkly comic scene actually recapitulates a moment in *Chevengur* when such a transformation does *not* happen: Chepurnyi walks into the "common house"—again, *obshchii dom,* the same term applied to the proletarian construct in *The Foundation Pit*—and is annoyed that the sparrows fly away in fear: "I was relying on you! [. . .] You're our kindred bird, now you need fear nothing—there are no more bourgeois: please, live here!" Orig.: "На вас я надеялся! [. . .] Вы наша кровная птица, только бояться теперь ничего не следует—буржуев нету: живите, пожалуйста!" Platonov, *Chevengur,* 256.

109. Orig: "Медведь перестал колотить и, отошедши, выпил от жажды полведра воды. Утерев затем своё утомлённо-пролетарское лицо, медведь плюнул в лапу и снова приступил к труду молотобойца." Platonov, *Kotlovan,* 501. Platonov underscores Misha's belonging to the collective by noting that he is forging a horseshoe for "a certain individual peasant," expressed by the etymologically redundant *dlia odnogo edinolichnika.*

110. Orig.: "Девочка всё время следила за медведем—ей было хорошо, что животное тоже есть рабочий класс,—а молотобоец глядел на неё как на забытую сестру, с которой он жировал у материнского живота в летнем лесу своего детства." Ibid., 503.

111. Orig.: "[О]бнажённые ноги были покрыты густым пухом, почти шерстью, выросшей от болезней и бесприютности, какая-то древняя, ожившая сила превращала мёртвую ещё при её жизни в обрастающее шкурой животное." Ibid., 458.

112. Orig.: "Czas mego ojca i mój własny czas już do siebie nie przystawały." Schulz, *Opowiadania,* 265.

113. Orig.: "Mieszkaliśmy w rynku, w jednym z tych ciemnych domów o pustych i ślepych fasadach, które tak trudno od siebie odróżnić. Daje to powód do ciągłych omyłek. Gdyż, wszedłszy raz w niewłaściwą sień i na niewłaściwe schody, dostawało się zazwyczaj w prawdziwy labirynt obcych mieszkań, ganków, niespodzianych wyjść na obce podwórza i zapominało się o początkowym celu wyprawy, ażeby po wielu dniach, wracając z manowców dziwnych i splątanych

przygód, o jakimś szarym świcie przypomnieć sobie wśród wyrzutów sumienia dom rodzinny." Ibid., 13.

114. Jarzębski, *Prowincja centrum,* 110. Jarzębski's remarks, which come decades after his groundbreaking interpretive work on Schulz in *The Novel as Self-Creation* (Powieść jako autokreacja, 1984), respond in part to a dominant thread in Schulz criticism that frames the discussion of center and periphery in terms of Schulz's biography, according to which it was long believed that he had spent very little time outside his hometown of Drohobycz, having made only very brief trips to Vienna—almost seven hundred kilometers west—in the early twentieth century and one trip to Paris in his lifetime. Recent scholarship has shown, however, that Schulz spent long stretches of several months at a time in Vienna during the First World War, prompting a closer consideration of how centers and peripheries fit into Schulz's prose as a matter of narrative design. See Paolo Caneppele, "Bruno Schulz w Wiedniu," trans. K. Sobczyński, in *W ułamkach zwierciadła: Bruno Schulz w 110 rocznicę urodzin i 60 rocznicę śmierci,* ed. Małgorzata Kitowska-Łysiak and Władysław Panas (Lublin: Towarzystwo Naukowe Katolickiego Uniwersytetu Lubelskiego, 2003), 533–45.

115. "Dominantą jego nastroju była jakaś nieokreślona i zasadnicza żałość, sieroctwo i bezradność—niezdolność do zapełnienia czymś pustki życia pomiędzy sensacjami posiłków. [. . .] Nawet jeszcze w głębi snu, w którym potrzebę oparcia się i przytulenia zaspokajać musiał, używając do tego własnej swej osoby, zwiniętej w kłębek drżący—towarzyszyło mu poczucie osamotnienia i bezdomność." Schulz, *Opowiadania,* 47–48.

116. Schulz introduces the language of portraiture with the passage's first word, *dominanta* ("the dominant"), which in Polish belongs primarily to the visual arts—that is, to Schulz's professional sphere—and refers to the most striking or dominant element in a visual composition. Meanwhile, in his invocation of "loneliness," Schulz skips the abstract noun *samotność,* which signifies "solitude" in Schulz's story of the same name, in favor of the gerund *osamotnienie,* derived from the verb *osamotnić,* "to leave alone," or eventually from *osamotnieć,* "to feel lonely." Schulz's use of *osamotnienie* reinforces loneliness as a process or character trait rather than a momentary emotion or impression.

117. F. W. J. Schelling, *Bruno; or, On the Natural and the Divine Principle of Things,* ed. and trans. Michael G. Vater (Albany: State University of New York Press, 1984), 177.

118. Orig.: "*Sklepy cynamonowe* dają pewną receptę na rzeczywistość, statuują pewien specjalny rodzaj substancji. Substancja tamtejszej rzeczywistości jest w stanie nieustannej fermentacji, kiełkowania, utajonego życia. Nie ma przedmiotów martwych, twardych, ograniczonych. Wszystko dyfunduje poza swoje granice, trwa tylko na chwilę w pewnym kształcie, ażeby go przy pierwszej sposobności opuścić. [. . .] Ktoś jest człowiekiem, a ktoś karakonem, ale ten kształt nie sięga istoty, jest tylko rolą na chwilę przyjętą, tylko naskórkiem, który za chwilę zostanie zrzucony. Statuowany tu jest pewien skrajny monizm substancji, dla której poszczególne przedmioty są jedynie maskami." Bruno Schulz, "Bruno Schulz do St. I. Witkiewicza," in Schulz, *Opowiadania,* 444–45.

119. Schelling, *Bruno; or, On the Natural and the Divine Principle of Things,* 158–59.

120. Orig.: "Jest godne uwagi, jak w zetknięciu z niezwykłym tym człowiekiem rzeczy wszystkie cofały się niejako do korzenia swego bytu, odbudowywały swe zjawisko aż do metafizycznego jądra, wracały niejako do pierwotniej idei, ażeby w tym punkcie sprzeniewierzyć się jej i przechylić w te wątpliwe, ryzykowne i dwuznaczne regiony, które nazwiemy tu krótko regionami wielkiej herezji." Schulz, *Opowiadania,* 32.

121. Orig.: "W chłodnym półmroku zamkniętych firanek stał on tam, jak za życia, na jednej nodze, w pozie buddyjskiego mędrca, a gorzka jego, wyschła twarz ascety skamieniała w wyraz ostatecznej obojętności i abnegacji." Schulz, *Opowiadania,* 81. The word I have translated as "curtains" is *firanki,* an almost ubiquitous Polish window treatment consisting of a long drape of sheer or translucent material that strains natural light and produces the "semidarkness" Schulz describes.

122. This graphic, though unfinished, is not a casual sketch; we have at least one extant projection for the same image.

123. "[Jakub] nie mógł też wróść w żadną realność i unosił się wiecznie na peryferii życia, w półrealnych regionach, na krawędziach rzeczywistości." Schulz, *Opowiadania,* 81.

124. "Mój ojciec poruszał się wieloczłonkowym skomplikowanym ruchem dziwnego rytuału, w którym ze zgrozą poznałem imitację ceremoniału karakoniego. [. . .] Podobieństwo do karakona występowało z dniem każdym wyraźniej—mój ojciec zamieniał się w karakona." Ibid., 84.

125. "Represented events are, in most cases, repeatable familiar activities, occurring many times in [the] boring atmosphere of the small town. [. . .] The events 'loosen' from the thread of time, they do not participate in the story, do not push the plot onwards." Krzysztof Stala, *On the Margins of Reality: The Paradoxes of Representation in Bruno Schulz's Fiction* (Stockholm: Stockholm University Press, 1993), 56–57. Stala focuses on "repeatable familiar activities," such as the household chores that occupy so much of Schulz's attention. But in their imperfective repetition, detached "from the thread of time," Jakub's transformations, too, are familiar household events, infinitely repeatable, always in process.

126. "[P]rzestaliśmy go odróżniać, zlał się w zupełności z tym czarnym niesamowitym plemieniem." Schulz, *Opowiadania,* 84.

127. Friedrich Nietzsche, *Thus Spoke Zarathustra,* in his *The Portable Nietzsche,* ed. and trans. Walter Kaufman (New York: Penguin, 1968), 125.

128. Caroline Walker Bynum, *Metamorphosis and Identity* (New York: Zone Books, 2001), 31.

129. I agree with Bynum wholeheartedly when she calls hybridity dialogic in a Bakhtinian sense, remarking that "[i]ts contraries are simultaneous and in conversation with each other," and that "hybrids both destabilize and reveal the world." Ibid., 160.

130. A substantial portion of Schulz's graphic work is collected in the Muzeum Literatury im. Adama Mickiewicza in Warsaw. A comprehensive catalogue of the collection has been published: Wojciech Chmurzyński, *Bruno Schulz, 1892–1942: Rysunki i archiwalia ze zbiorów Muzeum Literatury im. Adama Mickiewicza w Warszawie* (Warsaw: Muzeum Literatury im. Adama Mickiewicza, 1992).

131. Małgorzata Kitowska-Łysiak, "Wizje kobiecości w *Xiędze bałwochwalczej:* Salome i Androgyne," in *Czytanie Schulza: Materiały międzynarodowej sesji naukowej Bruno Schulz—w stulecie urodzin i w pięćdziesięciolecie śmierci,* ed. Jerzy Jarzębski (Kraków: Instytut Filologii Polskiej UJ, 1994), 251–63.

132. Orig.: "Tu ojciec mój zaczął budować przed naszymi oczyma obraz tej wymarzonej przez niego *'generatio aequivoca,'* jakiegoś pokolenia istot na wpół tylko organicznych, jakiejś pseudowegetacji i pseudofauny, rezultatów fantastycznej fermentacji materii. Były to twory podobne z pozoru do istot żywych, do kręgowców, skorupiaków, członkonogów, lecz pozór ten mylił. Były to w istocie istoty amorfne bez wewnętrznej struktury, płody imitatywnej tendencji materii, która, obdarzona pamięcią, powtarza z przyzwyczajenia raz przyjęte kształty. Skala morfologii, której podlega materia, jest w ogóle ograniczona i pewien zasób form powtarza się wciąż na różnych kondygnacjach bytu." Schulz, *Opowiadania,* 40–41.

133. Arthur Schopenhauer, *The World as Will and Representation,* vol. 1, trans. E. F. J. Payne (New York: Dover, 1969), 145.

134. Orig.: "W kątach siedziały nieruchomo wielkie karakony, wyogromnione własnym cieniem." Schulz, *Opowiadania,* 14.

135. Orig.: "[C]zuł, nie patrząc, że przestrzeń obrasta go pulsującą gęstwiną tapet, pełną szeptów, syków i seplenień." Ibid., 15.

136. "Chciałem cię już od dawna zapytać: prawda, że to jest on?—I chociaż nie wskazałem nawet spojrzeniem na kondora—matka odgadła od razu, zmieszała się bardzo i spuściła oczy." Ibid., 82.

137. Julia Kristeva, *Time and Sense: Proust and the Experience of Literature* (New York: Columbia University Press, 1996), 301.

138. Ibid., 303.

139. Orig.: "Nie dręcz mnie, drogi—mówiłam ci już przecież, że ojciec podróżuje, jako komiwojażer, po kraju—przecież wiesz, że czasem w nocy przyjeżdża do domu, ażeby przed świtem jeszcze dalej odjechać." Schulz, *Opowiadania,* 85.

140. Orig.: "To, co Pan mówi o naszym sztucznie przedłużonym dzieciństwie—o niedojrzałości—dezorientuje mnie trochę. Gdyż zdaje mi się, że ten rodzaj sztuki, jaki mi leży na sercu, jest właśnie regresją, jest powrotnym dzieciństwem. Gdyby można było uwstecznić rozwój, osiągnąć jakąś okrężną drogą powtórnie dzieciństwo, jeszcze raz mieć jego pełnię i bezmiar—to byłoby to ziszczeniem 'genialnej epoki,' 'czasów mesjaszowych,' które nam przez wszystkie mitologie są przyrzeczone i zaprzysiężone. Moim ideałem jest 'dojrzeć' do dzieciństwa. To by dopiero była prawdziwa dojrzałość." Schulz, *Księga listów,* 113–14. In his letter to Pleśniewicz, Schulz was responding to the latter's recently published remarks on the work of both Schulz and Gombrowicz. This is why Schulz refers to "our art": he is referring at least initially to his own work and Gombrowicz's.

141. Michał Okłot, "Maturing into Childhood: An Interpretive Framework of a Modern Cosmogony and Poetics," *Alif: Journal of Comparative Poetics* 27 (2007), 135.

142. Marta Bartosik, *Bruno Schulz jako krytyk* (Kraków: Universitas, 2000), 115.

143. Ibid., 39–45.

144. Orig.: "Ale i wiedza nie jest niczym innym, jak budowaniem mitu o świecie, gdyż mit leży już w samych elementach i poza mit nie możemy w ogóle wyjść." Schulz, *Opowiadania,* 367.

145. Jan Błoński, *Biedni Polacy patrzą na getto* (Kraków: Wydawnictwo Literackie, 1994), 126.

146. Karl Jaspers, *Truth and Symbol,* trans. Jean T. Wilde, William Kluback, and William Kimmel (New Haven, Conn.: College and University Press, 1959), 58. Platonov continued to address the themes of childhood and a child's experience of the world until the end of his career. See N. G. Poltavtseva, "Tekst i intertekst v detskikh rasskazakh A. Platonova 50-kh godov," in *Tvorchestvo Andreia Platonova: Issledovaniia i materialy,* vol. 2 (St. Petersburg: Nauka, 2000), 58–69.

147. Platonov uses Kopenkin's simplicity to extraordinary emotional effect, but this also opens the risk of misreading Kopenkin as having a mental defect. For example, in Lev Dodin's stage adaptation of Platonov's novel, which premiered in 1999 and is now part of the regular repertoire of the Malyi Dramaticheskii Teatr in St. Petersburg, Kopenkin is presented comically as a lumbering man-child.

148. Orig.: "Ликвидируй кулака как класс. Да здравствует Сталин, Козлов и Сафронов. Дядя Чиклин, Сталин только на одну каплю хуже Ленина, а Будённый на две. Привет бедному колхозу, а кулакам нет." Platonov, *Kotlovan*, 483.

149. Orig.: "Вместо людей активист записывал признаки существования: лапоть прошедшего века, оловянную серьгу от пастушьего уха, штанину из рядна и разное другое снаряжение трудящегося, но неимущего тела." Ibid., 514.

150. Meerson defines *neostranenie* as follows: "If defamiliarization displays the quotidian anew, as the unknown, then non-defamiliarization is a refusal to acknowledge that the unknown or new is unusual, such that this refusal to acknowledge unusualness often assumes outrageous forms and, in any event, no longer occurs as aesthetically neutral." Ol'ga Meerson, *Svobodnaia veshch': Poetika neostraneniia u Andreia Platonova* (Oakland: Berkeley Slavic Specialties, 1997), 10.

151. Jean Piaget, *The Child's Conception of the World,* trans. Joan Tomlinson and Andrew Tomlinson (Totowa, N.J.: Littlefield, Adams, 1969), 153.

152. Platonov, *Sobranie sochinenii v vos'mi tomakh,* vol. 1, 464.

153. Orig.: "Сон ребёнка—песнь пророка." "In Sleep" (Vo sne), ibid.

154. See, for example, Thomas Seifrid's reading of the story "The Priest" (Pop, 1920), in *Andrei Platonov: Uncertainties of Spirit,* 47–48.

155. Several studies treat the connection between Modernist Primitivism and representations of the child world in language and visual media. See, for example, Yuri Molok, "Children's Drawing in Russian Futurism," trans. Sophy Thompson, in *Discovering Child Art: Essays on Childhood, Primitivism, and Modernism*, ed. Jonathan Fineberg (Princeton, N.J.: Princeton University Press, 1998), 55–67. Molok provides an efficient summary of the influence of child language and psychology on Symbolists, Acmeists, and Futurists.

156. Theodore W. Adorno, *Notes to Literature,* vol. 1, ed. Rolf Tiedemann, trans. Sherry Weber Nicholsen (New York: Columbia University Press, 1991), 24. As Tiedemann notes, Adorno wrote "On Epic Naivety" for *Dialectic of Enlightenment,* his joint project with Max Horkheimer (xiii). Although we do not have a precise indication of where the fragment would be situated in the larger work, it is easy to see how it fits conceptually in the book's broader outline of a dialectical relationship between myth and Enlightenment rationality: "The principle of immanence, the explanation of every event as repetition, which enlightenment upholds against mythical imagination, is that of myth itself. The arid wisdom which acknowledges nothing new under the sun, because all the pieces in the meaningless game have been played out, all the great thoughts have been thought, all possible discoveries can be construed in advance, and human beings are defined by self-preservation through adaptation—this barren wisdom merely reproduces the fantastic doctrine it rejects: the sanction of fate which, through retribution, incessantly reinstates what always was. Whatever might be different is made the same. [. . .] The identity of everything with everything is bought at the cost that nothing can at the same time be identical to itself." Max Horkheimer and Theodore W. Adorno, *Dialectic of Enlightenment: Philosophical Fragments,* ed. Gunzelin Schmid Noerr, trans. Edmund Jephcott (Stanford, Calif.: Stanford University Press, 2002), 8. Horkheimer and Adorno correctly discern the repetitive, self-nourishing dynamic of *Identitätsphilosophie:* the self-identity of the Absolute can only come at the expense of individual identity, which, as difference, negates the totality of the Absolute. Horkheimer and Adorno remark this oscillation between totality and particularity, between formlessness and definition, and it is in this context that "On Epic Naivety" should be read.

157. Adorno, *Notes to Literature,* vol. 1, 24–25. The tension that Adorno posits between the universal, timeless myth and the particular, contingent narrative also resonates powerfully with Husserl's universal idealism. (Husserl had been the subject of Adorno's doctoral dissertation in 1924.) Husserl suggests in his *Logical Investigations* (Logische Untersuchungen, 1900–1901) that "all fundamental logical distinctions [are] categorical" rather than essential, and that they pertain "to the pure form of possible objects of consciousness as such." Edmund Husserl, *Logical Investigations,* vol. 1, trans. J. N. Findlay (London: Routledge, 2001), 240. Along these lines, Husserl goes on to discuss how identity can never be defined as "alikeness," but rather suggests a total self-equivalence that, in its resistance to difference, defies definition per se (242). It is a short leap from Husserl's description of identity to that put forward by Heidegger in *Identity and Difference,* which suggests that identity is the self-equivalence of essence(s). Adorno breaks away from Husserl in his suggestion that the particularity of narrative is not merely a category for mental contemplation. Instead, this particularity is an *essential* difference that distinguishes narrative from myth, which remains immured in its own universality.

158. Orig.: "[. . .] зону максимального контакта с настоящим (современностью) в его незавершённости [. . .]"; "эпический мир отделён от современности, то есть от времени певца (автора и его слушателей), абсолютной эпической дистанцией." M. M. Bakhtin, "Epos i roman: O met-

odologii issledovaniia romana," in his *Literaturno-kriticheskie stat'i* (Moscow: Khudozhestvennaia literatura, 1986), 399, 401.

159. Orig.: "Эпический мир завершён сплошь и до конца не только как реальное событие отдалённого прошлого, но и в своём смысле и своей ценности: его нельзя ни изменить, ни переосмыслить, ни переоценить." Ibid., 405.

160. Orig.: "Но в этом и нет беды, ибо структура целого повторяется в каждой части, и каждая часть завершена и кругла, как целое." Ibid., 419.

161. Roman Ingarden, *The Literary Work of Art: An Investigation on the Borderlines of Ontology, Logic, and Theory of Literature,* trans. George G. Grabowicz (Evanston, Ill.: Northwestern University Press, 1973), 246.

162. Schulz's essay has been translated as "The Mythologizing of Reality," which is generally how it is known in English-language criticism, as in Bruno Schulz, *Letters and Drawings of Bruno Schulz,* ed. Jerzy Ficowski, trans. Walter Arndt (New York: Fromm, 1988), 115–17. For our purposes, however, this translation is misleading. As we will see, Schulz does not intend for us to understand *mityzacja* as the formulation of a "mythological" vision of reality, one that would filter actual experience through analogues in archetypal characters and plot lines. Rather, he views poetic language as the technology that restores mythic timelessness to personal experience, which is otherwise governed by temporal distinction and separation. Schulz's "mythicization" makes everyday reality "mythic," not "mythological."

163. Orig.: "Poezja odpoznaje te sensy stracone, przywraca słowom ich miejsce, łączy je według dawnych znaczeń." Schulz, *Opowiadania,* 366.

164. Schulz could not have known the work of Bakhtin or Adorno. But he did have at least a passing familiarity with Ingarden, who was an active correspondent of Witkiewicz's, and made a point of requesting that Ingarden's books be sent to him from Warsaw in a letter dated August 30, 1937, to Romana Halpern, whom he had met through Witkiewicz. It is unclear whether she ever fulfilled his request, though she was a particularly helpful friend to Schulz in the 1930s, rendering him a number of practical and administrative services over the three years of their active correspondence. Schulz, *Księga listów,* 147.

165. Schulz, *Opowiadania,* 446.

166. Schulz documents his special admiration for these authors in several letters and occasional prose. His preference for Rilke is explicit, as he states in a 1934 letter to Arnold Spaet, a Germanist, translator, and friend of Stanisław Przybyszewski and Julian Tuwim. See Schulz, *Księga listów,* 41. In the same year, he wrote to Rudolf Ottenbreit that for some time he had been most delighted by Rilke, Kafka, and Mann, all of whom he read in the original. Schulz, *Księga listów,* 59. In the aforementioned letter to Witkiewicz, he cites Mann's *Jacob and His Brothers,* which Schulz read in the original German, beginning with the publication of the tetralogy's first volume in 1933, the same year that Schulz's own *Cinnamon Shops* was published, though Schulz had been reading Mann voraciously for many years.

167. In one of his more powerful essays on language from the interwar period, Martin Heidegger recognizes in Rilke's concept of "the Open" an analogy to his own notion of Being as the ground of existence. Martin Heidegger, "What Are

Poets For," in his *Poetry, Language, Thought,* trans. Albert Hofstadter (New York: Harper and Row, 1971), 106–8.

168. Agamben not only demonstrates how Heidegger inverts Rilke's privileging of animal nonconsciousness over human consciousness but also shows how this inversion was itself unresolved by Heidegger in 1929–30: "The animal is at once open and not open—or, better, it is neither one nor the other: it is *open in a nondisconcealment* that, on the one hand, captivates and dislocates it in its disinhibitor with unmatched vehemence, and, on the other, does not in any way disconceal as a being that thing that holds it so taken and absorbed. Here, Heidegger seems to oscillate between two opposite poles, which in some ways recall the paradoxes of mystical knowledge—or, rather, nonknowledge." Giorgio Agamben, *The Open: Man and Animal,* trans. Kevin Attell (Stanford, Calif.: Stanford University Press, 2003), 59.

169. Along these lines, Schulz regarded Rilke's *New Poems* (1907) as "his work at its peak," finding the later *Duino Elegies* (1922)—where we find Rilke's description of "the Open"—and *Sonnets to Orpheus* (1922) "oversophisticated and esoteric." Schulz, *Księga listów,* 129.

170. Orig.: "Proces usensowiania świata jest ściśle związany ze słowem. Mowa jest metafizycznym organem człowieka. Jednakowoż słowo z biegiem czasu sztywnieje, ustala się, przestaje być przewodnikiem nowych sensów. Poeta przywraca słowom przewodnictwo przez nowe spięcia, które z kumulacji powstają." Schulz, *Opowiadania*, 367–68.

171. There is an intriguing ambiguity in Schulz's formulation. The Polish word *przewodnik,* "conductor," refers more commonly to a "guide," and *przewodnictwo,* "conductivity," to "leadership" or "guidance." This is deliberate: Schulz believes that the word requires constant renewal through the accumulation of new meanings, since the word is always slipping toward ossification. Poetic language, then, is never stable. It is rather a navigational point, a polestar, toward which the author strives.

Chapter 3

The chapter epigraph is from Lenin, *The State and Revolution,* 89.

1. Bakhtin, *Literaturno-kriticheskii stat'i,* 420.
2. Bakhtin, *Sobranie sochinenii v semi tomakh,* vol. 3, 155.
3. A number of scholars have used Bakhtin's own discourse models to challenge his intemperate remarks on poetry and monoglossia. Michael Eskin does so by emphasizing the self-subversive quality of Bakhtin's notion of responsibility: "Poetic speech reveals itself—ironically, given Bakhtin's putative repudiation of poetry on metalinguistic grounds—as metalinguistically more significant than novelistic discourse precisely because it turns a person's indelible existential answerability for his or her acts (including speech acts) into one of its artistically constitutive moments." Eskin, "Bakhtin on Poetry," 388. Graham Pechey, meanwhile, suggests that certain poets—he turns to Blake—present an allegorized self turned apostrophically toward a range of addressees, opening an unfinalized, dialogic space: "Like Bakhtin, Blake poses discourses of integral personification against those rationalizing discourses that reify everything

they touch." Graham Pechey, "Not the Novel: Bakhtin, Poetry, Truth, God," in *Bakhtin and Cultural Theory,* ed. Ken Hirschop and David Shepherd, 2nd ed. (Manchester: Manchester University Press, 2001), 76.

4. Osip Mandel'shtam, *Sobranie sochinenii v chetyrekh tomakh,* vol. 2, ed. P. Nerler and A. Nikitaev (Moscow: Art-Biznes-Tsentr, 1993), 388.

5. Ralph Dutli, *Mandelstam: Meine Zeit, mein Tier: Ein Biografie* (Zurich: Ammann, 2003), 56–63.

6. Though his time in Germany ranks among the least-detailed portions of the poet's biography, university records and other documentary evidence suggest that Mandel'shtam's time in Heidelberg was devoted primarily to the study of medieval French literature and Venetian Renaissance art. See Thomas A. Beyer, Jr., "Osip Mandel'shtam and the University of Heidelberg: Three Documents," *Slavonic and East European Review* 65.2 (April 1987): 236–37.

7. The term "Acmeism" first appeared in print in 1913 in the journal *Appolon,* whose editorial interests bridge the aesthetic leap from Symbolism to Acmeism, and whose 1910 publication of Mikhail Kuzmin's "On Beautiful Clarity" (О прекрасной ярости) has been widely credited with initiating Acmeism as a self-conscious, if generally ill-defined, literary movement. Recently, however, John Malmstad and Nikolay Bogomolov have called this reading into question, arguing instead that Kuzmin's article, when read in the context of an ongoing feud between *Apollon*'s editors and Viacheslav Ivanov, appears as a rejection of artistic programs as such. From the other side, Akhmatova categorically rejected the notion that Kuzmin was an Acmeist. See John E. Malmstad and Nikolay Bogomolov, *Mikhail Kuzmin: A Life in Art* (Cambridge, Mass.: Harvard University Press, 1999), 165–73.

8. Nadezhda Mandel'shtam, *Vospominaniia,* ed. Iurii Freidin (Moscow: Soglasie, 1999), 296.

9. Mikhail Gasparov, "Poet i kul'tura: Tri poetiki Osipa Mandel'shtama," in Osip Mandel'shtam, *Pol'noe sobranie stikhotvorenii,* ed. Mikhail Gasparov and A. G. Mets (St. Petersburg: Akademicheskii Proekt, 1997), 59. This version of Gasparov's essay, which introduces Biblioteka Poeta's second attempt to present Mandel'shtams poetic works (after an earlier volume, incomplete and often inaccurate, published in the so-called blue series in 1973 and edited by N. I. Khardzhiev, with an introduction by A. L. Dymshitz), differs slightly from its original composition. As an introductory essay, it defines "The Three Poetics of Osip Mandel'shtam," whereas the earlier version, "Osip Mandel'shtam: Tri ego poetiki," suggests merely that Gasparov intends to outline "three of his poetics," leaving the possibility of others.

10. O. Mandel'shtam, *Sobranie sochinenii v chetyrekh tomakh,* vol. 1, 178–79.

11. Orig.: "Подобно тому, как существуют две геометрии—Эвклида и Лобачевского, возможны две истории литературы, написанные в двух ключах: одна—говорящая только о приобретениях, другая—только об утратах, и обе будут говорить об одном и том же." Ibid., 219.

12. Ibid., vol. 2, 290–91.

13. Orig.: "Но, к величайшему сожалению, память и дело быстро разошлись, не пошли рука об руку. Будущники и пассеисты очень быстро очутились в

двух враждующих станах. Будущники огульно отрицали прошлое; однако это отрицание было не чем иным, как диетой. Из соображений гигиены они запрещали себе чтение старых поэтов или читали их под сурдинку, не признаваясь в этом публично. Точно такую же диету прописали себе и пассеисты. Я решаюсь утверждать, что многие почтённые литераторы до последного времени, когда они были к этому вынуждены, не читали своих современников." Ibid., 294.

14. In this respect, Mandel'shtam would likely have agreed with Manfred Hinz's assessment that Futurism and Passéism were essentially the same in their respective treatments of historical time: "Futurism has to presume that no historical change has ever occurred and will never occur, because the future is also without history. In this tautological antithesis of a timeless space of past and an equally tuneless space of future, the distinction between Futurism and Passéism is in danger of perishing." Manfred Hinz, "The Future and Catastrophe: The Concept of History in Italian Futurism," in *The Promise of History: Essays in Political Philosophy,* ed. Athanasios Moulakis (Berlin: Walter de Gruyter, 1985), 188.

15. Orig.: "Блоку футуризм противопоставил Хлебникова. Что им сказать друг другу? Их битва продолжается и в наши дни, когда нет в живых ни того, ни другого. Подобно Блоку, Хлебников мыслил язык как государство, но отнюдь не в пространстве, не географически, а во времени. Блок—современник до мозга костей, время его рухнет и забудется, а всё-таки он останется в сознании поколений современником своего времени. Хлебников не знает, что такое современник. Он гражданин всей истории, всей системы языка и поэзии. Какой-то идиотический Эйнштейн, не умеющий различить, что ближе—железнодорожный мост или «Слово о полку Игореве». Поэзия Хлебникова идиотична—в подлинной, греческом, неоскорбительном значении этого слова." O. Mandel'shtam, *Sobranie sochinenii w chetyrekh tomakh,* vol. 2, 296.

16. Nikita Struve, *Osip Mandel'shtam* (London: Overseas Publications Interchange, 1990), 123.

17. Stuart Goldberg, *Mandel'shtam, Blok, and the Boundaries of Mythopoetic Symbolism* (Columbus: Ohio State University Press, 2011), 106.

18. Orig: "У отца совсем не было языка, это было косноязычие и безъязычие." O. Mandel'shtam, *Sobranie sochinenii v chetyrekh tomakh,* vol. 2, 361, 363.

19. Orig.: "По существу, отец переносил меня в совершенно чужой век и отдалённую обстановку." Ibid., 362.

20. Orig.: "Существовать—высшее самолюбие художника. Он не хочет другого рая, кроме бытия." Ibid., vol. 1, 177. Note that in this context "самолюбие" can be translated not only as "ambition" but also as "vanity."

21. Emmanuel Levinas, *On Escape,* trans. Bettina Bergo (Stanford, Calif.: Stanford University Press, 2003), 55. Levinas's construction of shame in this text, which marks his early departure from Heidegger, will figure strongly in chapter 5.

22. Orig.: "Эта реальность в поэзии—слово как таковое." O. Mandel'shtam, *Sobranie sochinenii v chetyrekh tomakh,* vol. 1, 177.

23. Orig.: "[В] акмеизме [слово] впервые принимает более достойное вертикальное положение и вступает в каменный век своего существования." Ibid., 178.

24. T. S. Eliot, "Tradition and the Individual Talent [1919]," in his *Selected Prose of T.S. Eliot,* ed. Frank Kermode (New York: Harcourt, 1975), 36–44.

25. While his interest in the Mediterranean tradition does not distinguish Mandel'shtam from the Symbolists, Ryszard Przybylski suggests that it does help us differentiate him from other Acmeists, who focused instead on the Russian canon (Akhmatova) or the New Testament (Gumilev): "It was Mandel' shtam, then, to whom fell the task of fusing the classical tradition with the modern Russian poetry of our century." Ryszard Przybylski, *An Essay on the Poetry of Osip Mandelstam: God's Grateful Guest,* trans. Madeline G. Levine (Ann Arbor, Mich.: Ardis, 1987), 174.

26. Orig.: "Строить можно только во имя «трёх измерений», так как они есть условие всякого зодчества. [. . .] Строить—значить бороться с пустотой, гипнотизировать пространство." O. Mandel'shtam, *Sobranie sochinenii v chetyrekh tomakh,* vol. 1, 179.

27. Orig.: "Нет равенства, нет соперничества, есть сообщничество сущих в заговоре против пустоты и небытия. [. . .] Любите существование вещи более самой вещи и своё бытие больше самих себя—вот высшая заповедь акмеизма. [. . .] А = А: какая прекрасная поэтическая тема. Символизм томился, скучал тождества, акмеизм делает его своим лозунгом [. . .]. Таким образом, признав суверенитет закона тождества, поэзия получает в пожизненное ленное обладание всё сущее без условий и ограничений. Логика есть царство неожиданности." Ibid., 180.

28. Martin Heidegger, "The Origin of the Work of Art," in his *Poetry, Language, Thought,* trans. Albert Hofstadter (New York: Harper and Row, 1971), 39.

29. Victor Terras, "The Time Philosophy of Osip Mandel'shtam," *Slavonic Review* 109 (July 1969), 346–47.

30. Leszek Kołakowski, *Metaphysical Horror,* trans. Agnieszka Kołakowska (Chicago: University of Chicago Press, 2001), 23.

31. Ibid., 73.

32. Jerzy Jarzębski, "Wstęp" (introduction), in Schulz, *Opowiadania,* lxvii.

33. Orig: "Поэзия—плуг, взрывающий время так, что глубинные слои времени, его чернозем, оказываются сверху. Но бывают такие эпохи, когда человечество, не довольствуясь сегодняшним днём, тоскуя по глубинным слоям времени, как пахарь, жаждет целины времён. Революция в искусстве неизбежно приводит к классицизму. Не потому, что Давид снял жатву Робеспьера, а потому, что так хочет земля." Osip Mandel'shtam, "Slovo i kul'tura," in his *Sobranie sochinenii v chetyrekh tomakh,* vol. 1, 213.

34. Gregory Freidin, *A Coat of Many Colors: Osip Mandel'shtam and His Mythologies of Self-Presentation* (Berkeley: University of California Press, 1987), 194.

35. Orig.: "В священном исступлении поэты говорят на языке всех времён, всех культур. [. . .] Современная поэзия, при всей своей сложности и

внутренней исхищренности, наивна." O. Mandel'shtam, *Sobranie sochinenii v chetyrekh tomakh,* vol. 1, 216.

36. While the tone of Mandel'shtam's essay sometimes shifts ambiguously, such that it is not always completely clear which attitudes with respect to the poetic word he approves or disdains, it is punctuated throughout with lines of verse by Mandel'shtam and by poets he admired, projecting an unironic stance at least toward his own formulations.

37. Orig.: "Поставленный мною вопрос приобретает особенную остроту благодаря ускорению темпа исторического процесса. [. . .] Благодаря изменению количества содержания событий, приходящихся на известный промежуток времени, заколебалось понятие единицы времени, и не случайно современная математическая наука выдвинула принцип относительности." Osip Mandel'shtam, "O prirode slova," in his *Sobranie sochinenii v chetyrekh tomakh,* vol. 1, 217.

38. Viacheslav Vs. Ivanov thus demonstrates that Mandel'shtam's late poems, and particularly his "Verses on an Unknown Soldier" (Stikhi o neizvestnom soldate, 1937), refer back to an understanding of relativity that dates to his formulations in poetics from the early 1920s. See Viach. Vs. Ivanov, "'Stikhi o neizvestnom soldate' v kontekste mirovoi poezii," in *Zhizn' i tvorchestvo O. E. Mandel'shtama: Vospominaniia, materialy k biografii, "novye stikhi," kommentarii, issledovaniia,* ed. S. S. Averintsev et al. (Voronezh: Izdatel'stvo Voronezhskogo Universiteta, 1990), 356–66.

39. Orig.: "Чтобы спасти принцип единства в вихре перемен и безостановочном потоке явлений, современная философия, в лице Бергсона, [. . .] предлагает нам учение о системе явлений. Бергсон рассматривает явления не в порядке их подчинения закону временной последовательности, а как бы в порядке их пространственной протяженности. Его интересует исключительно внутренняя связь явлений. Эту связь он освобождает от времени и рассматривает отдельно. Таким образом, связанные между собой явления образуют как бы веер, створки которого можно развернуть во времени, но в то же время он поддаётся умопостигаемому свёртыванию." O. Mandel'shtam, *Sobranie sochinenii v chetyrekh tomakh,* vol. 1, 217–18.

40. Henri Bergson, *Creative Evolution,* trans. Arthur Mitchell (New York: Modern Library, 1944), 332.

41. Proust, *The Guermantes Way,* 5–6.

42. On the debt Mandel'shtam's thinking owes to Bergson, see Francis Nethercott, "Elements of Bergson's *Creative Evolution* in the Critical Prose of Osip Mandel'štam," *Russian Literature* 30 (1991): 455–66; Anne Faivre-Dupaigre, "Toska po edinstvu: O vliianii Bergsona na rannego Mandel'shtama," *Russian Literature* 42 (1997): 137–51; and Hilary L. Fink, *Bergson and Russian Modernism, 1900–1930* (Evanston, Ill.: Northwestern University Press, 1999), 64–77. Fink's consideration is especially useful insofar as she points out Mandel' shtam's misprision vis-à-vis Bergson: "The 'connection among phenomena' that Bergson considers, while 'liberated' from *linear* time, gains its very essence and unity within what Bergson terms *real* time, or the indivisible time of duration. While Mandel'shtam redresses this inaccuracy [. . .] it is important to keep in mind his former tendency to appropriate Bergsonian philosophy as a means of

escaping time altogether, a central concern of Russian modernists in general" (*Bergson and Russian Modernism,* 69). While the desire to escape from historical time is indeed a central issue for Mandel'shtam, we should temper Fink's last claim—shared by Faivre-Dupaigre ("Toska po edinstvu," 142)—by reemphasizing that Mandel'shtam is also a poet of history, and that he wavers between the escape Bergson might afford and a tendency toward the concrete and historically contingent in his verse. As Nadezhda Mandel'shtam notes, Mandel'shtam "did not, like Berdiayev and the Symbolists, seek to escape into some realm of pure spirit from the earthly confines of our everyday here and now. [. . .] To M., as a self-styled Acmeist, three-dimensional space and life on earth were essential because he wanted to do his duty by his 'host'—he felt that he was here to build, which can only be done in three dimensions." Nadezhda Mandel'shtam, *Hope against Hope,* trans. Max Hayward (New York: Atheneum, 1970), 263–64.

43. Evgenii Pavlov, *Shok pamiati: Avtobiograficheskaia poetika Val'tera Ben'iamina i Osipa Mandel'shtama,* trans. Aleksandr Skidan (Moscow: Novoe Literaturnoe Obozrenie, 2005), 134.

44. Omri Ronen, *Poetika Osipa Mandel'shtama* (St. Petersburg: Giperion, 2002), 25.

45. Orig.: "Теория прогресса в литературе—самый грубый, самый отвратительный вид школьного невежества." O. Mandel'shtam, *Sobranie sochinenii v chetyrekh tomakh,* vol. 1, 219.

46. Orig.: "Эллинизм—это сознательное окружение человека утварью вместо безразличных предметов, превращение этих предметов в утварь, очеловечивание окружающего мира, согревание его тончайшим телеологическим теплом. [. . .] Эллинизм—это система в бергсоновском смысле слова, которую человек развертывает вокруг себя, как веер явлений, освобождённых от временной зависимости, соподчинённых внутренней связи через человеческое я." Ibid., 227.

47. Cavanagh notes that "Mandel'shtam is not [averse] to turning the systems and theories of the new regime to his own ends in the essays, though the state he warily commends would not have recognized itself in his idiosyncratic portraits. At his most optimistic, he sees [his] Hellenism and Soviet Marxism as a nearly perfect fit: each system is profoundly teleological, and each is guided by a goal of a global, truly human-centered economy at once universal and domestic." Clare Cavanagh, *Osip Mandelstam and the Modernist Creation of Tradition* (Princeton, N.J.: Princeton University Press, 1995), 150. Where we may soften Cavanagh's language is in her reference to the "profoundly teleological" character of Mandel'shtam's Hellenistic word. Mandel'shtam's Hellenism is indeed teleological, but as I have already indicated, Mandel'shtam's understanding of telos is itself idiosyncratic. For Mandel'shtam, the purpose of the poetic utterance is tied to its immediate use, not to an ultimate goal or endpoint. On the contrary, he disavows the notion of determinate evolution that is so much a part of the Marxist theory of history.

48. Mandel'shtam goes on to criticize Andrei Belyi and other Symbolists on precisely these grounds, because they do not recognize the Hellenism of the Russian word. O. Mandel'shtam, *Sobranie sochinenii v chetyrekh tomakh,* vol. 1, 221.

49. Fink, *Bergson and Russian Modernism,* 65.

50. Osip Mandel'shtam, *Polnoe sobranie stikhotvorenii,* ed. M. L. Gasparov and A. G. Mets (St. Petersburg: Akademicheskii Proekt, 1997), 195–96.

51. Anna Akhmatova, "Mandel'shtam," in her *Sobranie sochinenii v shesti tomakh,* ed. S. A. Kovalenko, vol. 5 (Moscow: Ellis Lak, 2001), 21.

52. Orig.: "Наука, построенная на принципе связи, а не причинности, избавляет нас от дурной бесконечности эволюционной теории, не говоря уже о её вульгарном прихвостне—теории прогресса." O. Mandel'shtam, *Sobranie sochinenii v chetyrekh tomakh,* vol. 1, 218.

53. Orig.: "Если всё живое лишь помарка / За короткий выморчоный день, / На подвижной лестнице Ламарка / Я займу последнюю ступень." O. Mandel'shtam, *Polnoe sobranie stikhotvorenii,* 213.

54. Galin Tihanov, "Contextualizing Bakhtin: Two Poems by Mandel'štam," *Russian Literature* 50.2 (2001), 175. In an especially forceful challenge to Bakhtin's dismissive attitude toward the lyric poem, Tihanov argues that Bakhtin's writings from the 1930s pick up conceptually where "Lamarck" leaves off.

55. I am grateful to Jonathan Bolton for pointing out the Hegelian precedent in Mandel'shtam's characterization of infinity.

56. Irina Paperno, "On the Nature of the Word: Theological Sources of Mandel'shtam's Dialogue with the Symbolists," in *Christianity and the Eastern Slavs,* vol. 2, *Russian Culture in Modern Times,* ed. Robert P. Hughes and Irina Paperno, California Slavic Studies 17 (Berkeley: University of California Press, 1994), 299.

57. Jane Gary Harris, *Osip Mandelstam* (Boston: Twayne, 1988), 105.

58. O. Mandel'shtam, *Polnoe sobranie stikhotvorenii,* 194.

59. On the Sovietization of culture in Petrograd, particularly after Lenin's death in 1924, see Katerina Clark, *Petersburg: Crucible of Cultural Revolution* (Cambridge, Mass.: Harvard University Press, 1995), 183–200.

60. A number of otherwise productive readings of the poem are thus weighed down by the political reading. See, for example, Peter Zeeman, *The Later Poetry of Osip Mandelstam: Text and Context* (Amsterdam: Rodopi, 1988), 100–102; Victor Terras, "Death of a Poet: Osip Mandelshtam," in *Enemies of the People : The Destruction of Literary, Theater, and Film Arts in the 1930s,* ed. Katherine Bliss Eaton (Evanston, Ill.: Northwestern University Press, 2002), 80; and Struve, *Osip Mandel'shtam,* 38.

61. Mandel'shtam's many Petersburg-themed poems include "I'm cold. Transparent spring . . ." (Мне холодно. Прозрачная весна . . . , 1916), "In transparent Petropol we will die . . ." (В Петрополе прозрачном мы умрём . . . , 1916), "A wandering flame on a terrible height . . ." (На страшной высоте блуждающий огонь . . . , 1918), "In Petersburg we'll meet again . . ." (В Петербурге мы сойдёмся снова . . . , 1920), and "Concert in the Train Station" (Концерт на вокзале, 1921).

62. O. Mandel'shtam, *Sobranie sochinenii v chetyrekh tomakh,* vol. 2, 390–91.

63. Irina Surat, "Poet i gorod: Peterburgskii siuzhet Osipa Mandel'shtama," *Zvezda* 5 (2008), 197.

64. Kiril Taranovsky, *Essays on Mandel'štam* (Cambridge, Mass.: Harvard University Press, 1976), 57–61.

65. An early version of the poem, without a title, with markings indicating reported speech, and with other variations in the verses, is reprinted in O. Mandel'shtam, *Sobranie sochinenii v chetyrekh tomakh,* vol. 3, 307.

66. Ronen, *Poetika Osipa Mandel'shtama*, 38–42. Among other poets who use intertextual references dialogically, Ronen singles out Khlebnikov, Mayakovsky, Zabolotskii, and Joseph Brodsky.

67. Ibid., 28–29.

68. Lidiia Ginzburg, *O lirike* (Moscow: Intrada, 1997), 347. The critical division of Mandel'shtam's poems into three phases, roughly broken by the October Revolution and the poet's five-year break from writing poems in the late 1920s, seems to begin with Ginzburg's discussion of "the poetics of association," which was first published in 1964. We have already seen Mikhail Gasparov working from the same model.

69. Orig: "с такой силой подчеркивающей текучесть явления и такими росчерками перечеркивающей его." O. Mandel'shtam, *Sobranie sochinenii v chetyrekh tomakh,* vol. 3, 236.

70. Orig.: "звонил в милицию, звонил правительству—исчезнувшему, уснувшему, как окунь, государству. С тем же успехом он мог бы звонить к Прозерпине или к Персефоне, куда телефон ещё не проведён." Osip Mandel'shtam, *Sobranie sochinenii v chetyrekh tomakh,* vol 2., 478. I am grateful to Mikhail Krutikov for calling this lovely passage to my attention.

71. Orig.: "В Петрополе прозрачном мы умрём, / Где властвует над нами Прозерпина." O. Mandel'shtam, *Polnoe sobranie stikhotvorenii,* 134.

72. N. Mandel'shtam, *Hope against Hope,* 86, 87.

73. Orig.: "Она и музыка и слово, / И потому всего живого / Ненарушаемая связь." O. Mandel'shtam, *Polnoe sobranie stikhotvorenii*, 94.

74. Przybylski, *An Essay on the Poetry of Osip Mandelstam: God's Grateful Guest*, 146.

75. It is interesting that both the political and nonpolitical readings of the poem competed with one another immediately after Mandel'shtam wrote it. Showing the poem to a Russian editor, Mandel'shtam was told in no uncertain terms that it was the sort of composition that could get the author arrested. The poem was nevertheless published in *Literaturnaia gazeta* in 1932.

76. Anna Lisa Crone and Jennifer Day expand this model of doubling significantly in their reading of the poem. Instead of a simple expropriation of Self in the form of a double, they suggest that the poem contains multiple selves, most of them dead, which is why the speaker claims to have many telephone numbers. Such a reading can be easily assimilated into my discussion. Anna Lisa Crone and Jennifer Day, *My Petersburg/Myself: Mental Architecture and Imaginative Space in Modern Russian Letters* (Bloomington, Ind.: Slavica, 2004), 174–75. Where I would disagree with Crone and Day is in their framing their discussion of the poem as a reversal of time. In my reading, the poet does not attempt to *reverse* time, but rather short-circuits the present to the past, so that both temporalities coexist.

77. Osip Mandel'shtam, *Polnoe sobranie stikhotvorenii,* 169–70.

78. For example, in the last stanza, Mandel'shtam's use of the present active verb *meshchet* to describe the "crashing" of a "fiery fish" against the shore

(the verb is generally attached to crashing light, that of the sun or lightning, or to a gaze) belongs more to the era of Catherine the Great than to Mandel'shtam's own. See, for example, Aleksandr Sumarokov's "Oda gosudaryne imperatritse Ekaterine Vtoroi na vziatie Khotina i pokorenie Moldavii" (1769): "Минерва росска громы мещет [. . .]"; the Fourth Song of Mikhail Kheraskov's *Chesmesskii boi* (1771): "Кровавые лучи в Средземны волны мещет [. . .]"; or Gavriil Derzhavin's "Dokazatel'stvo Tvorcheskogo bytiia" (1796): "[Солнце] мещет огнь очей своих."

79. Orig.: "Młode tygryski dorastają, uczą się polować, zakładają swoje rodziny, stare tygrysy umierają czy giną—jak, nie umiemy sobie przedstawić—i powtarza się to niepojęta ilość razy, niepojęta też ilość razy padają schwytane na obiad jelenie, a wszystko to odbywa się w znającym ani przeszłości, ani przyszłości *teraz*." Czesław Miłosz, *Piesek przydrożny* (Kraków: Znak, 2011), 265. This passage is omitted from the English-language edition, *Road-Side Dog*, trans. Czesław Miłosz and Robert Hass (New York: Farrar, Straus and Giroux, 1998).

80. Krzysztof Michalski, *The Flame of Eternity: An Interpretation of Nietzsche's Thought*, trans. Benjamin Paloff (Princeton, N.J.: Princeton University Press, 2012), 152. Miłosz's poem also begs to be read in the context of his long friendship with Tadeusz Kroński, an important Marxist philosopher, whom he called *Tygrys* ("Tiger"). Their discussions, especially in the decade before Kroński's death in 1958, often centered on the problem of how to engage the world philosophically when nature is utterly indifferent to the definitions that such engagement requires. See Czesław Miłosz, *Rodzinna Europa* (Kraków: Wydawnictwo Literackie, 2001), 290–334.

81. Paul Valéry, *Cahiers/Notebooks*, vol. 5, ed. Brian Stimpson, trans. Paul Gifford et al. (Frankfurt: Peter Lang, 2010), 73.

82. C. J. G. Turner, "On Osip Mandel'shtam's Poem 'Vek,'" *Slavic and East European Journal* 20.2 (Summer 1976): 148–54.

83. Badiou, *The Century*, 16. Note that Badiou subscribes to the simplest historical reading of the "two centuries" as the pre- and post-Revolutionary eras.

84. For a short, carefully documented account of the Mandel'shtams' stay in Voronezh, see Oleg Lekmanov, *Zhizn' Osipa Mandel'shtama: Dokumental'noe povestvovanie* (St. Petersburg: Zvezda, 2003), 181–97.

85. Badiou, *The Century*, 24.

86. O. Mandel'shtam, *Polnoe sobranie stikhotvorenii*, 176–78.

87. Ibid., 181–82.

88. *Veki* is an archaic plural form of *vek*, still used in such set expressions as *v koi-to veki*, "for all time."

89. In conventional Russian speech, *vek* refers generally to a "century."

90. N. I. Khardzhiev, editorial note in Osip Mandel'shtam, *Stikhotvoreniia*, ed. N. I. Khardzhiev, 2nd ed. (Leningrad: Sovetskii pisatel', 1974), 285.

91. Lukács, *Soul and Form*, 54.

92. In an extremely thorough analysis of the lexical-semantic components of Mandel'shtam's oeuvre, L. G. Panova concludes that there is a line of development that, at the beginning of Mandel'shtam's career, recognizes only the moment and eternity, but that later becomes cyclical, and eventually linear: "The

straightening of Time passes through several stages: time in the form of spirals (everything is repeated, but not as it was before), and historical time (time composed of centuries or historical epochs)." L. G. Panova, *"Mir," "prostranstvo," "vremia" v poezii Osipa Mandel'shtama* (Moscow: Iazyki Slavianskoi Kul'tury, 2003), 371. While I disagree with Panova's ultimate conclusion that Mandel'shtam's temporal schema became quite linear in the last two decades of his life, her categories are quite useful. My reading argues that Panova's two major temporal schemes, the "spiral" and the "historical," fuse together in many of Mandel'shtam's poems of the 1920s and 1930s.

93. In archaic English the pupil of the eye was also described as an "apple." This appellation, so to speak, is preserved in the figure of speech "apple of my eye." It is also worth noting that conventional Russian uses the diminutive form *obolochka* to refer to the "cornea," whereas *oblatka* refers more commonly to a "wafer" or "host," with the attendant religious connotations.

94. Freidin, *A Coat of Many Colors*, 165.

95. Franz Kafka, *The Zürau Aphorisms,* ed. Roberto Calasso, trans. Michael Hofmann and Geoffrey Brock (New York: Schocken, 2006), 65.

96. Orig.: "Innego końca świata nie będzie, / Innego końca świata nie będzie." Czesław Miłosz, *Wiersze,* vol. 1, ed. Aleksander Fiut (Kraków: Znak, 2001), 208. All quotations from Miłosz's poems refer to his five-volume *Wiersze* (2001–9) unless otherwise noted.

97. Translations executed or approved by the author are included in Czesław Miłosz, *New and Collected Poems (1931–2001)* (New York: Ecco, 2001).

98. Although the Żagary poets did not model themselves after the Russian Acmeists, who evidently had little or no direct influence on the group's intellectual activities, it is worth noting that, like Mandel'shtam, Żagary sought to collide the concrete details of a sometimes incomprehensible present with the symbolic and psychic potentials of classical literature. Jerzy Kwiatkowski points out that Żagary had no aesthetic program—an announcement on the first page of Żagary's journal's first issue declares, "We are making no group, school, or movement"—but that its members' aesthetic writings emphasize "suggestiveness, constructivism, making-mundane, the cult of fact," and "instead of emotionality a dictatorship of the intellect." Jerzy Kwiatkowski, *Dwudziestolecie międzywojenne* (Warsaw: Wydawnictwo PWN, 2001), 41–42. In his own *The History of Polish Literature,* Miłosz notes that Józef Czechowicz, one of the major poets of interwar catastrophism, was "the first to translate some of the little-known foreign poets of the avant-garde," including Mandel'shtam. Czechowicz's first collection of poems, *Stone* (Kamień, 1927), shares its title with Mandel'shtam's debut collection of 1913. Miłosz describes his own catastrophist second book, *Three Winters* (Trzy zimy, 1936), as follows: "Its rush to symbols, set unexpectedly into lines with a classicist ring, alludes to calamities of cosmic amplitude." Miłosz, *The History of Polish Literature,* 2nd ed. (Berkeley: University of California Press, 1983), 411–413.

99. A notable exception is the poem "Against Them" (Przeciwko nim), composed, as the epigraph states, "On the occasion of Blachowski's trial for the murder of Gaston Koehler-Badin." The text refers to the murder of a Swiss foreman at the textile factory in Żyrardów, in central Poland. It is one of Miłosz's most explicitly leftist poems.

100. Czesław Miłosz, *Podróżny świata—Rozmowy z Renatą Gorczyńską* (Kraków: Wydawnictwo Literackie, 2002), 10.

101. Miłosz, *Wiersze* vol. 1, 12.

102. Miłosz notes that Zdziechowski, his teacher at Stefan Batory University, was steeped almost exclusively in Russian and French philosophy and Modernism, especially in Soloviev, but he also treats Zdziechowski as an old-fashioned thinker. Miłosz, *Podróżny świata—Rozmowy z Renatą Gorczyńską,* 9. See also Czesław Miłosz, "O historii polskiej literatury, wolnomyślicielach i masonach," in his *Prywatne obowiązki* (Kraków: Wydawnictwo Literackie, 2001), 150–82. There, Miłosz remarks that Russian Symbolism, with a tradition that begins in the philosophy of Soloviev and leads to the "classical perfection" of Mandel'shtam, differs from French Symbolism in that it is "remarkably 'substantive'" (172). The notion that poetry should be substantive (Miłosz uses the word *treściowy,* which we might also translate as "material" or "having content") is very important to Miłosz, and that he might locate such content in some Symbolist poetry is not as surprising as it might seem, since Miłosz struggled with the idea that poetry should have content that was intellectually, emotionally, and historically intelligible, and he was attracted to Stanisław Ignacy Witkiewicz's theory of an art that consisted of Pure Form. In his 1943 essay on Witkiewicz, Miłosz writes: "If I oppose that element which Bremond called the *ineffable,* it only seems so. In actual fact I criticize Pure Form because of my love for it, because, longing for paradise, one may deny oneself the return if that return would be merely a pollution." Orig.: "Jeżeli przeciwstawiam się temu pierwiastkowi, który Bremond nazwał *ineffable,* to tylko pozornie. W istocie krytykuję Czystą Formę przez miłość do niej, bo wolno, tęskniąc do raju, zabronić sobie powrotu, gdy ten powrót byłby tylko skażeniem." Czesław Miłosz, "Granice sztuki (St. I. Witkiewicz z perspektywy wojennych przemian)," in his *Zaczynając od moich ulic* (Kraków: Znak, 2006), 93.

103. Irena Grudzińska-Gross, *Czesław Miłosz and Joseph Brodsky: Fellowship of Poets* (New Haven, Conn.: Yale University Press, 2009), 90.

104. Czesław Miłosz, *Poemat o czasie zastygłym* (Vilnius: Koło Polonistów Słuchaczy Uniwersytetu Stefana Batorego, 1933), 10. Some later editions of this poem print it with line breaks, as we see for example in the 1993 edition of Miłosz's collected poems. See Czesław Miłosz, *Wiersze,* vol. 1 (Kraków: Znak, 1993), 83. In its first edition, however, this is clearly a prose poem, justified against both margins, and I have preferred that original format here. The original prose formatting has been reproduced in the most recent, authoritative edition of Miłosz's collected works. See Miłosz, *Wiersze* [2001], vol. 1, 17.

105. Jan Błoński, "Bieguny poezji," in his *Wszystko, co literackie: Pisma wybrane,* vol. 1, ed. Jerzy Jarzębski (Kraków: Wydawnictwo Literackie, 2001), 179.

106. Typical of reading Miłosz as a "poet of history" are Edward Hirsch's pronouncement that Miłosz's "work was initiated by the apocalyptic fires of history," in his *Poet's Choice* (New York: Harcourt, 2006), 99; Jerry Harp's characterization of Miłosz as a "poet of history," in his introduction to *A Poetry Criticism Reader,* ed. Jerry Harp and Jan Weissmiller (Iowa City: University of Iowa Press, 2006), 13; and, most dramatically, Al Alvarez's description of Miłosz as "a poet

of memory, a witness; his real heroes are the dead to whom his poems make reparation"—a position that received a pointed rebuke from Miłosz himself. See Al Alvarez, "Witness," *New York Review of Books* 35.9 (June 2, 1988), 21; and Czeslaw Miłosz, "A Poet's Reply," *New York Review of Books* 35.12 (July 21, 1988), n.p. Clare Cavanagh subjects Miłosz's English-language reception to an evenhanded critique in her *Lyric Poetry and Modern Politics: Russia, Poland, and the West* (New Haven, Conn.: Yale University Press, 2009), 237–55.

107. Jan Kott, *Po prostu* (Warsaw: Książka, 1946), 108.

108. Ibid., 109.

109. Aleksander Fiut, *The Eternal Moment: The Poetry of Czesław Miłosz*, trans. Theodosia S. Robertson (Berkeley: University of California Press, 1990), 78. In the revised Polish edition of Fiut's classic study, he situates himself explicitly "between" Kott and Błoński, though the latter does not appear in this connection in the English translation. See Aleksander Fiut, *Moment wieczny: Poezja Czesława Miłosza* (Kraków: Wydawnictwo Literackie, 1998), 119.

110. Fiut, *The Eternal Moment*, 73.

111. Ibid., 83.

112. Robert Faggen, "Czesław Miłosz: The Art of Poetry LXX," *Paris Review* 36.133 (Winter 1994), 250.

113. Orig.: "Bo wyspa filozofujących koni to było *outopos*, utopia, znamię naszego rozdwojenia na tu i tam, na wewnątrz i zewnątrz, czy, jeżeli kto woli, na uwięzione na przemijaniu ciało i na szybujący nad nim umysł." Miłosz, *Piesek przydrożny*, 292.

114. Kazimierz Wyka, "Ogrody lunatyczne i ogrody pasterskie" [1946], in his *Rzecz wyobraźni*, 2nd ed. (Warsaw: Państwowy Instytut Wydawniczy, 1977), 281; Helen Vendler, "A Lament in Three Voices," *New York Review of Books* 48.9 (May 31, 2001), http://www.nybooks.com/articles/archives/2001/may/31/a-lament-in-three-voices/ (accessed March 7, 2013).

115. Orig.: "Jestem Miłoszem, Miłoszem być muszę
Będąc Miłoszem, Miłoszem być nie chcę
Miłosza w sobie zabijam ażeby
Bardziej Miłoszem być . . .
Co się wykłada: że istota człowieka jest rozwój, a rozwój dokonuje się na drodze nieustannego samobójstwa. Musimy uśmiercić w sobie to, co jest, ażeby dojść do tego, co będzie. I ta swoboda, z jaką Miłosz, bez chwili wahania, odrywa się od swojego świata, to właśnie gorzka dojrzałość naszego czasu—dojrzałość zdobyta pod potężnym, głęboko przez niego przeżytym, ciśnieniem historii." Witold Gombrowicz, "Przeklęte zdrobnienie znowu dało mi się we znaki (Obrońcom poetów w odpowiedzi)," in Miłosz, *Zaczynając od moich ulic*, 144.

116. Miłosz, *Wiersze*, vol. 3 (2003), 79.

117. Orig.: "Jestem, a przynajmniej staram się być tożsamy ze sobą, choć przecie wiem, że zbiorowość, dostosowanie się do niej, nas niepostrzeżenie kształtuje. Ale w tej odmowie dzielenia swojej osoby na przedziały, z których każdy zawiera innych mieszkańców—czy pasażerów, leży nowość tego, czym chciałbym zostać." Czesław Miłosz, "Niedziela w Brunnen," in his *Metafizyczna pauza*, ed. Joanna Gromek (Kraków: Znak, 1989), 21.

118. Miłosz, *Prywatne obowiązki,* 130.

119. "Co można zrobić, jeżeli wzrok nie ma siły absolutnej, tak, żeby wciągał przedmioty z zachłyśnięciem się szybkości, zostawiając za sobą już tylko pustkę formy idealnej, znak, niby hieroglif, który uproszczono z rysunku zwierzęcia czy ptaka?" Miłosz, *Wiersze,* vol. 2 (2002), 255.

120. Miłosz, *Wiersze,* vol. 4 (2004), 154. It is worth noting that the religious connotation of the poem's title differs from what the English translation "A Confession" might suggest. While the Polish word "wyznanie" can be used to signify a confession of deeds or sins, its more standard reference is to a confession of faith, as in a creed. Thus Miłosz's poem, which is written in the tone of a confession of sins—"Dear Lord, I loved strawberry jam / And the dark sweetness of a woman's body"; orig.: "Panie Boże, lubiłem dżem truskawkowy / I ciemną słodycz kobiecego ciała"—can ultimately be read not as apologia, but rather as a semiautobiographical *ars poetica.*

121. Fiut, *The Eternal Moment,* 10–11.

122. Stanisław Barańczak, "Język poetycki Czesława Miłosza: Wstępne rozpoznanie," in *Poznawanie Miłosza: Studia i szkice o twórczości poety,* ed. Jerzy Kwiatkowski (Kraków: Wydawnictwo Literackie, 1985), 431.

123. Kazimierz Wyka, "Płomień i marmur" (1937), in his *Rzecz wyobraźni,* 263.

124. Faggen, "Czesław Miłosz: The Art of Poetry LXX," 249.

125. Miłosz, *Podróżny świata,* 10.

126. Orig.: "A kto w tym, co jest, / Znajduje spokój, ład i moment wieczny, / Mija bez śladu." Czesław Miłosz, "Notatnik: Brzegi Lemanu," in his *Wiersze,* vol. 2, 163.

127. Michel Masłowski, "Miłosz et le religieux," in *Czesław Miłosz et le vingtième siècle,* ed. Maria Delaperrière (Paris: Institut d'études slaves, 2006), 219.

128. Czesław Miłosz, *Rodzinna Europa* (Krakow: Wydawnictwo Literackie, 2001), 124.

129. Coincidentally, after studying with Bergson at the Sorbonne, Maritain attended the University of Heidelberg, anticipating the educational career of Mandel'shtam.

130. Czesław Miłosz, *Legends of Modernity: Essays and Letters from Occupied Poland, 1942–1943,* trans. Madeline G. Levine (New York: Farrar, Straus & Giroux, 2005), 142.

131. Orig.: "Która rzeczywistość jest prawdziwa? Czy ta pierwsza, surowa, która nas rani, obezwładnia, zwodzi obietnicami, czy ta druga, oczyszczona piękniejsza, może taka, jaką widzą duchy bezcielesne?" Miłosz, *Wiersze* vol. 4, 168. The sequence *For Heraclitus* belongs to the book *Chronicles* (Kroniki, 1987).

132. Orig.: "A jest jeszcze rzeczywistość trzecia, trudno orzec, na ile prawdziwa: ta, którą znajdujemy utrwaloną w języku ludzkiej mowy czy obrazów, zawsze niepełna, rozbita na okruchy, fragmenty, i składana na nowo wedle prawa selekcji, czyli formy. Mój wiek dwudziesty napierał na mnie wielością takich świadectw o bezustannej zmianie, o 'historycznym przyspieszeniu', podsuwając pamiętniki, powieści, następując po sobie szkoły malarstwa, nade wszystko

jednak 'fotografię z epoki' i taśmę filmową od początków kina. W porównaniu z rzeczywistością doznaną a nigdy nie utrwaloną była to kropla w morzu, ale niewątpliwie w mojej wyobraźni nakładały się na siebie sceny, które sam oglądałem, i te, które przyszły z lektur, z wizyt w muzeach nowoczesnej sztuki, z filmu." Ibid., 169.

133. Ibid., 169–70. For "halting," Miłosz uses the Polish word *zatrzymywanie,* which can refer both to stopping movement or suspending time. Both senses apply here.

134. Jan Błoński, "Wzruszenie, dialog i mądrość," in *Poznawanie Miłosza: Studia i szkice o twórczości poety,* ed. Jerzy Kwiatkowski (Kraków: Wydawnictwo Literackie, 1985), 363–80.

135. See, for example, the poems "Dialogue" (Dialog, 1934) and "Song" (Pieśń, 1934), both from *Three Winters.* A dialogic section of *The World: A Naive Poem* will be discussed below.

136. Miłosz, *Wiersze,* vol. 5, 85. Other noteworthy examples of the tension between lasting and passing in Miłosz's work include: "A Moral Treatise" (Traktat moralny, 1947), "A Treatise on Poetry" (Traktat poetycki, 1957), "Oeconomia divina" (1973), and "Rivers" (Rzeki, 1980).

137. Czesław Miłosz, letter to Jarosław Iwaszkiewicz (December 11, 1930), in Czesław Miłosz and Jarosław Iwaszkiewicz, *Portret podwójny,* ed. Barbara Toruńczyk and Robert Papieski (Warsaw: Zeszyty Literackie, 2011), 10–11. In later life Miłosz would often repeat that he had originally intended to pursue biology or forestry as a profession. See, for example, Miłosz, *Podróżny świata,* 8.

138. Orig: "Chciałbym być prawowiernym katolikiem. Tak mnie imponuje ten most zawieszony w próżni. Konstrukcja w sobie zamknięta, samowystarczalna, niekusząca się o uchwycenie prawdy świata zewnętrznego—jakby gotyk. Móc stworzyć choć jeden wiersz tak zamknięty i obiektywny!!!" Miłosz, letter to Iwaszkiewicz, 12.

139. Miłosz published a brief notice listing what he saw as the precepts of Russian Constructivism in *Żagary* in 1931. See Czesław Miłosz, *Przygody młodego umysłu* (Kraków: Znak, 2003), 39.

140. Miłosz, *Wiersze,* vol. 1, 73.

141. Orig.: "Nikogo nie ma pomiędzy tobą i mną." Ibid.

142. See, for example, the poem "Fatherland" (Ojczyzna, 1932) in *A Poem on Frozen Time,* as well as *In Search of the Fatherland* (Szukanie ojczyzny, 1992), one of Miłosz's last essay collections.

143. Miłosz, *Wiersze,* vol. 1, 74–75.

144. Czeslaw Miłosz, *The Captive Mind,* trans. Jane Zielonko (New York: Vintage, 1981), 3.

145. Orig.: "Czy naprawdę kiedyś młodość nasza wspaniała przeminie / Czy raczej przeminie ziemia i pusty, olbrzymi nieboskłon?" Miłosz, *Wiersze,* vol. 1, 25.

146. Orig.: "Wszystkie zawiłe przygody / Z dni rewolucji nad Wolgą i nawet sny / Mówimy sobie szczerze." Ibid.

147. Orig.: "Czy przeminie ziemia? Czy przeminie olbrzymi nieboskłon? / Nie. Przeminąć trzeba nam." Ibid.

148. Miłosz revisits this dynamic in "Dawns" (Świty, 1932), which appears in *Three Winters*, a poem similarly set in a house in Lithuania, and in which human activity is framed from an increasingly cosmic perspective. As Stanisław Barańczak demonstrates, "[t]ime also flows on the macro-scale: from the past through the present and toward the future, from youth through maturity and toward old age." Stanisław Barańczak, *Pomyślane przepaście: Osiem interpretacji* (Katowice: Wydawnictwo Uniwersytetu Śląskiego, 1995), 19.

149. Orig.: "P. Czym różni się przestrzeń w dwudziestym wieku od przestrzeni w wieku ubiegłym? O. Nie jest to rodzaj akwarium, w którym pływają galaktyki. Przestrzeń jest względna, tj. tam, gdzie nie ma stosunku pomiędzy punktem A i punktem B, nie ma przestrzeni. Innymi słowy, poza obrębem wszechświata nie ma przestrzeni nieskończenie rozciągłej. P. Ani czasu? O. Ani czasu. Wieczność nie jest linią przedłużającą się w nieskończoność." Czesław Miłosz, "Metafizyczna pauza, czyli pytania i odpowiedzi," in his *Metafizyczna pauza*, 77.

150. Thus when Miłosz gathered the transcripts of his conversations with the late Futurist poet Aleksander Wat into a monumental oral autobiography, he entitled it *My Century* (Mój wiek, 1977).

151. Orig.: "Мне хочется говорить не о себе, а следить за веком, за шумом и прорастанием времени. Память моя враждебна всему личному. Если бы от меня зависело, я бы только морщился, припоминая прошлое. [. . .] Повторяю—память моя не любовна, а враждебна, и работает она не над воспроизведением, а над отстранением прошлого. [. . .] Там, где у счастливых поколений говорит эпос гекзаметрами и хроникой, там у меня стоит знак зияния, и между мной и веком провал, ров, наполненный шумящим временем, место, отведённое для семьи и домашнего архива." O. Mandel'shtam, *Sobranie sochinenii v chetyrekh tomakh*, vol. 2, 384.

152. The mythic time Mandel'shtam wishes to recover is not necessarily that of his lost Jewish heritage. As Efraim Sicher has argued, the mythic past for Mandel'shtam refers first of all to an unbounded St. Petersburg remembered from childhood. Whether Jewishness is alternatively a marker for restrictive definitions, as Sicher argues, is another matter entirely. See Efraim Sicher, "The 'Color' of Judaism: Timespace Oppositions in the Synaesthesia of Osip Mandel'shtam's *Shum Vremeni*," in *Aspects of Modern Russian and Czech Literatures*, ed. Arnold McMillin (Columbus, Ohio: Slavica, 1989), 31–54.

153. Czesław Miłosz, "Notes on Exile," in his *To Begin Where I Am: Selected Essays* (New York: Farrar, Straus and Giroux, 2001), 16–17. In a note appended to the Polish-language version of the same text, Miłosz elaborates on this last point in reference to the poems he wrote in California: "This is why my poetry written in California is a poetry simultaneously about my native district, conjoined, as it were, into one, and additionally, my poetry delves, as it were, into the depths, historically into the past of the region I come from. Those who know such poems of mine as, for example, 'When I Went to Siedmiogród' [actually "Bells in Winter" (Dzwony w zimie), from the 1974 cycle *Where the Sun Rises and Sets* (Gdzie wschodzi słońce i kędy zapada)], know that I go all the way back to the sixteenth century and identify myself with an Arian returning from my native district to his brethren in Siedmiogród." Orig.: "Dlatego moja poezja pis-

ana w Kalifornii jest poezją równocześnie mojego rodzinnego powiatu i poezją Kalifornii, zrośniętych niejako w jedno, przy czym poezja moja drąży niejako w głąb, historycznie w przeszłość tego obszaru, z którego się wywodzę. Ci, którzy znają takie moje wiersze jak np. 'Kiedy jechałem do Siedmiogrodu' wiedzą, że sięgam nawet do XVI wieku i identyfikuję się z arianinem, który z mojego rodzinnego powiatu wraca do Siedmiogrodu do swoich współbraci." Czesław Miłosz, *Noty o wygnaniu/Notes on Exile* (Łomża: Norbertinum, 2006), 11–12.

154. Marek Zaleski, *Zamiast: O twórczości Czesława Miłosza* (Kraków: Wydawnictwo Literackie, 2005), 172–73.

155. Jerzy Andrzejewski, undated letter to Czesław Miłosz (1942), in Miłosz, *Legends of Modernity: Essays and Letters from Occupied Poland, 1942–1943*, 172.

156. Orig.: "Czym jest poezja, która nie ocala / Narodów ani ludzi?" Miłosz, *Wiersze*, vol. 1, 139.

157. Orig.: "W mojej ojczyźnie, do której nie wrócę." Miłosz, *Wiersze*, vol. 1, 142.

158. Orig.: "Można więc powiedzieć, że *Świat* był dla mnie jakimś intuicyjnym przystąpieniem do operacji, która dopiero z perspektywy lat jest dla mnie mniej więcej oczywista. Rzeczywiście, tam jest identyfikacja z naiwnym poglądem na świat." Miłosz, *Podróżny świata*, 65.

159. Orig.: "Tak, ale pisanie tego rodzaju utworów w ówczesnych warunkach było jakimś chodzeniem na przekór. Tak wypadło, że cała moja twórczość była chodzeniem na przekór." Ibid., 66.

160. Miłosz, *Wiersze*, vol. 1, 204–5.

161. Czesław Miłosz, "Notes to the 1996 Polish Edition," in his *Legends of Modernity*, 260. Miłosz characterizes his book as "a memoir from a period of delayed maturity," a play on the title of Gombrowicz's first book, *Memoir from a Time of Immaturity* (Pamiętnik z okresu dojrzewania, 1933).

Chapter 4

The chapter epigraph is from James Joyce, *Ulysses* (New York: Vintage, 1990), 37.

1. O. Mandel'shtam, *Polnoe sobranie stikhotvorenii*, 91–92. Bolesław Leśmian expresses a similar cosmism in a posthumous poem, "I'm here in earthly darkness—and am, as yet, afar" (Tu jestem—w mrokach ziemi i jestem—tam jeszcze).

2. Nikolai Zabolotskii, *Polnoe sobranie stikhotvorenii i poem*, ed. Nikita Zabolotskii (St. Petersburg: Akademicheskii Proekt, 2002), 205.

3. Proust, *The Guermantes Way*, 113.

4. N. O. Lossky, *History of Russian Philosophy* (New York: International Universities Press, 1951), 252. While he was teaching in St. Petersburg, Lossky made a strong impression on a number of young intellectuals, perhaps most intriguingly on Mikhail Bakhtin, who found in Lossky's intuitivist approach a way out of the neo-Kantian orthodoxies that had otherwise absorbed him. M. M. Bakhtin, *Besedy s V. D. Duvakinym* (Moscow: Soglasie, 2002), 63–64.

5. Erich Auerbach observes that "the men who appear in the *Comedy* are already removed from earthly time and temporal destiny," allowing Dante "to represent the entire earthly, historical world of his knowledge and experience as

already subjected to God's final judgment, so that each soul occupies the place assigned to it by the divine order." Erich Auerbach, *Dante: Poet of the Secular World,* trans. Ralph Manheim (New York: New York Review Books, 2007), 86.

6. George Santayana, *Three Philosophical Poets: Lucretius, Dante, and Goethe* (Cambridge, Mass.: Harvard University Press, 1910), 208.

7. For more on the circumstances surrounding the mass exodus of Russian scientists and philosophers, see M. Osharov, "To Alien Shores: The 1922 Expulsion of Intellectuals from the Soviet Union," *Russian Review* 32.3 (July 1973): 294–98.

8. A. Makedonov, *Nikolai Zabolotskii: Zhizn', tvorchestvo, metamorfozy* (Leningrad: Sovetskii pisatel', 1968), 12–13.

9. R. R. [Robin] Milner-Gulland, "Zabolotsky: Philosopher-Poet," *Soviet Studies* 22.4 (April 1971), 601.

10. Robin Milner-Gulland points out that Zabolotskii's affection for the works of Khlebnikov and Mandel'shtam was unusual, given his general rejection of "all residual influence from such figures as Akhmatova, Maiakovskii, Esenin, Blok, and Symbolism generally." Robin Milner-Gulland, "Nikolai Zabolotskii (1903–1958)," *Slavonica* 9.2 (November 2003), 123.

11. Tsiolkovskii's cosmic philosophy has widely been regarded as a major influence on Zabolotskii, though it may be more accurate to describe their conceptual similarities as an elective affinity or meeting of minds. Zabolotskii had already published *Columns* and written his most important longer philosophical poems, "The Triumph of Agriculture" (Торжество земледелия, 1929–30) and "Mad Wolf" (Безумный волк, 1931), by the time he wrote his first letter to Tsiolkovskii, dated January 7, 1932. There Zabolotskii remarks that he had only just recently begun to read Tsiolkovskii's work on the future of mankind, and he asks the philosopher to send him more books. Tsiolkovskii obliged him. See Nikolai Zabolotskii, *Sobranie sochinenii v trekh tomakh,* vol. 3, ed. E. Zabolotskaia and Nikita Zabolotskii (Moscow: Khudozhestvennaia literatura, 1984), 308–9.

12. Orig: "Громадный революционный сдвиг культуры и быта, столь характерный для нашего времени." Nikolai Zabolotskii, "Obshchestvennoe litso Oberiu. Poeziia Oberiutov," in his *Sobranie sochinenii v trekh tomakh,* vol. 1, 521.

13. Orig.: "[М]ироощущение для художника орудие и средство, как молоток в руках каменщика, и единственное реальное—это самое произведение." Osip Mandel'shtam, "Utro akmeizma," in his *Sobranie sochineniia v chetyrekh tomakh,* vol. 1, 177.

14. Orig.: "По выходе из армии я попал в обстановку последних лет нэпа. Хищнический быт всякого рода дельцов и предпринимателей был глубоко чужд и враждебен мне. Сатирическое изображение этого быта стало темой моих стихов 1927–1928 годов, которые впоследствии составили книжку «Столбцы»." Nikolai Zabolotskii, "Avtobiografiia," in his *Sobranie sochinenii v trekh tomakh,* vol. 1, 492. While we can readily accept what Zabolotskii says here about his own subject matter in that period of great social transformation, it is also useful for us to bear in mind that this written statement comes from a writer who had spent eight of the previous ten years insisting that he was a good

Soviet citizen, wrongfully imprisoned and exiled. That is, while there is certainly a satirical edge to Zabolotskii's early poems, they are much more than the sharp jabs at businessmen and entrepreneurs Zabolotskii describes here. Nor was the Soviet city under the New Economic Policy anything new to Zabolotskii when he left the army, since he had served just across the Neva from downtown Leningrad, on the Vyborg Side, mostly as an editor of a military newspaper.

15. Lidiia Ginzburg, "Zabolotskii dvadtsatykh godov," in her *Zapisnye knizhki, Vospominaniia, Esse* (St. Petersburg: Iskusstvo-SPB, 2002), 478.

16. Irene Masing-Delić, *Abolishing Death: A Salvation Myth of Russian Twentieth-Century Literature* (Stanford, Calif.: Stanford University Press, 1992), 245.

17. The inclusion of Zabolotskii in this comparison is merely implicit in Angela Livingstone, "Meditations on Strangeness in Other Writers," in *"Strannaia" poeziia i "strannaia" proza,* ed. E. A. Iablokov and I. E. Loshchilov (Moscow: Piataia strana, 2003), 289–303. Livingstone's essay is devoted primarily to defining "strangeness" vis-à-vis the uncanny in Platonov, Kafka, and Freud, but it appears in an anthology of essays primarily dedicated to Zabolotskii (and printed to honor his centenary), and many of her observations apply to him as well. The link between Zabolotskii and Platonov is more explicit in the preceding essay from the same collection, E. A. Iablokov, "'Bezumnyi volk' N. Zabolotskogo i 'vol'chi' motivy v literature 1920-kh godov," 275–88. Sarah Pratt, meanwhile, notes that both Platonov and Zabolotskii were irritated by the tendency of critics to read their phantasmagoria as foolishness, whereas both authors believed they were accurately depicting their environment: "Like Zabolotskii, Platonov was plagued by readers' perceptions of satire where it very likely did not exist and by readers' negative responses to the apparently limited mental and moral abilities of the characters he created." Sarah Pratt, *Nikolai Zabolotskii: Enigma and Cultural Paradigm* (Evanston, Ill.: Northwestern University Press, 2000), 113.

18. Nikolai Chukovskii, "Vstrechi s Zabolotskim," in *Vospominaniia o Zabolotskom,* ed. E. V. Zabolotskaia and A. V. Makedonov (Moscow: Sovetskii pisatel', 1977), 230.

19. Nikita Zabolotskii, *Zhizn' N. A. Zabolotskogo* (St. Petersburg: Logos, 2003), 95.

20. See, for example, Iosip Uzharevich (Josip Užarević), "Mir nad mirom: Problema 'dvoemiriia' v lirike Nikolaia Zabolotskogo," *Russian Literature* 56.1–3 (July 2004): 297–311.

21. Nikolai Zabolotskii, *Polnoe sobranie stikhotvorenii i poem,* 311–12.

22. Founded in 1863, the Bavaria brewery, which ran the downtown bar, added "Red" to its name after the Bolsheviks came to power; it continued to operate into the twenty-first century in a complex north of the city center.

23. See, for example, Darra Goldstein, *Nikolai Zabolotskii: Play for Mortal Stakes* (Cambridge: Cambridge University Press, 1993), 56; and Pratt, *Nikolai Zabolotskii: Enigma and Cultural Paradigm,* 124–26, who compares these ambiguous images to those of Aleksandr Blok's 1906 poem "The Unknown Woman" (Незнакомка), to which Zabolotskii's poem seems to respond.

24. According to his friend Nikolai Sboev, in the 1920s Nikolai Zabolotskii was an almost imposing atheist who saw the world in terms of complex material

systems. N. Sboev, "Mansarda na Petrogradskoi," in *Vospominaniia o Zabolotskom,* 2nd ed., ed. E. V. Zabolotskaia, A. V. Makedonov, and N. N. Zabolotskii (Moscow: Sovetskii pisatel', 1984), 44, quoted in Nikita Zabolotskii, *Zhizn' N. A. Zabolotskogo,* 86–87.

25. Lenin, *Polnoe sobranie sochinenii,* vol. 42, 30.

26. Pratt, *Nikolai Zabolotskii: Enigma and Cultural Paradigm,* 5.

27. Ibid., 129–33.

28. Orig.: "Необычное чередование предметов, приписывание им необычайных качеств и свойств, кроме того—необычайных действий. Говоря формально—это есть линия метафоры. Всякая метафора, пока она ещё жива и нова,—алогична. [. . .] Но старая метафора легко стерлась—и акмеистическая, и футуристическая. Обновление метафоры могло идти лишь за счёт расширения ассоциативного круга." Quoted in Nikita Zabolotskii, *Zhizn' N. A. Zabolotskogo,* 107.

29. Northrop Frye, "The Koine of Myth," in his *Myth and Metaphor: Selected Essays, 1974–1988,* ed. Robert D. Denham (Charlottesville: University Press of Virginia, 1990), 7.

30. Struve, *Osip Mandel'shtam,* 238.

31. Shklovsky provides an amusing account of this incident in Serena Vitale, *Shklovsky: Witness to an Era,* trans. Jamie Richards (Urbana, Ill.: Dalkey Archive Press, 2012), 102–3.

32. Goldstein, *Nikolai Zabolotsky: Play for Mortal Stakes,* 103.

33. Andrei Bitov, "Piat'desiat let bez Platonova," in his *Piatoe izmerenie: Na granitse vremeni i prostranstva* (Moscow: Izdatel'stvo Nezavisimaia Gazeta, 2002), 68.

34. Goldstein, *Nikolai Zabolotsky: Play for Mortal Stakes,* 103–4.

35. Nikolai Zabolotskii, *Stolbtsy* (Leningrad: Izdatel'stvo Pisatelei v Leningrade, 1929), 13. This is the third stanza in more recent redactions: Nikolai Zabolotskii, *Polnoe sobranie stikhotvorenii i poem,* 74–75.

36. This collision of the real with the imagined does not bar us from reading the poem allegorically, as Irene Masing-Delić does, suggesting that the beleaguered striker is a Soviet hero struggling for immortality, and that the opposing defense represents "self-satisfied NEP men." See Masing-Delić, *Abolishing Death,* 264–65. Such an allegorical reading, in fact, redoubles the poem's failure to define its reality. In the poem, the soccer field, defined by the conventions of the game, becomes indistinguishable from an expansive mythic space. But in the allegorical reading, this movement from reality to myth is reversed: the players, who appear as mythic archetypes in the poem, draw comparison to the historically contingent businessmen of the NEP-era city.

37. Nikolai Zabolotskii, *Polnoe sobranie stikhotvorenii i poem,* 80.

38. It is an amusing coincidence that the Polish word for "burbot," *miętus,* is also the name of one of the most decisively immature characters in Witold Gombrowicz's novel *Ferdydurke* (1937), discussed in the next chapter. For both Zabolotskii and Gombrowicz, the burbot represents slowness and lack of development.

39. G. B. Filippov, *Russkaia sovetskaia filosofskaia poeziia: Chelovek i priroda* (Leningrad: Izdatel'stvo Leningradskogo universiteta, 1984), 136–37.

40. Gumbrecht, *In 1926: Living at the Edge of Time,* 340–41.

41. See Nikita Zabolotskii, *Zhizn' N. A. Zabolotskogo,* 118–21.

42. L. Anninskii, "Nikolai Zabolotskii: 'Ia sam iznemogal ot schast'ia bytiia . . . ,'" in *Nikolai Zabolotskii: Pro et contra,* ed. T. V. Igoshchevaia and I. E. Loshchilov (St. Petersburg: RKhGA, 2010), 649.

43. Jindřich Toman, *The Magic of a Common Language: Jakobson, Mathesius, Trubetzkoy, and the Prague Linguistic Circle* (Cambridge, Mass.: MIT Press, 1995), 105. Peter Demetz reports that the members of Devětsil and the Prague Linguistic Circle met regularly in separate rooms of the same café, the Národní Kavárna, and also frequented the Slavia, "a Prague showplace often visited by Albert Einstein and Thomas Mann." Peter Demetz, *Prague in Black and Gold: Scenes in the Life of a European City* (New York: Hill and Wang, 1997), 354; for his part, Nezval would later come to be highly regarded in Russia (224–25). After World War II, Nezval's poems were also widely translated into Russian. The two poems discussed in this chapter, *Edison* and *Time Signal,* were translated by the poets David Samoilov and Boris Pasternak, respectively. A generous selection of Nezval's poems in Russian translation was published in 1960, with an afterword by Nazim Hikmet: Vítězslav Nezval, *Izbrannoe,* ed. S. Shchipacheva (Moscow: Izdatel'stvo inostrannoi literatury, 1960). For a summary of Nezval's presence in Russian poetry after 1945, see I. V. Toksina, ed., *Vitezslav Nezval: Bibliograficheskii ukazatel'* (Moscow: Izdatel'stvo "Kniga," 1967).

44. Vítězslav Nezval, *Praha s prsty deště [1936]* (Prague: Akropolis, 2000), 10.

45. This fusion of art and everyday life was taken to a comic extreme by Kharms and Vvedenskii, Zabolotskii's most celebrated collaborators among the Oberiuty. For them, the banality of everyday experience and language becomes the very substance of art.

46. Karel Teige, "Estetika filmu a kinografie," *Host* 3.6–7 (April 1924), 144.

47. The contributions of Teige and Nezval to *Host* were first volleys, rather than the ultimate formulation of Poetism. Teige followed his *Host* essay with publications in the avant-garde journal *ReD,* notably his "Manifesto of Poetism" (Manifest poetismu) in 1927. For a treatment of Poetism's evolution through its manifestos, see Lenka Bydžovská, "The Avant-Garde Ideal of Poeisis: Poetism and Artificialism during the Late 1920s," trans. Karolina Vočadlo, in *Karel Teige: L'Enfant Terrible of the Czech Modernist Avant-Garde, 1900–1951,* ed. Eric Dluhosch and Rotislav Švacha (Cambridge, Mass.: MIT Press, 1999), 47–63.

48. Teige, "Estetika filmu a kinografie," 145.

49. Michael Wachtel, *Russian Symbolism and Literary Tradition: Goethe, Novalis, and the Poetics of Vyacheslav Ivanov* (Madison: University of Wisconsin Press, 1994), 144.

50. Teige, "Estetika filmu a kinografie," 149.

51. Václav Černý, *Paměti I (1921–1938)* (Brno: Atlantis, 1994), 158. Although a more detailed analysis falls outside the bounds of this study, I would like to note the hand of Karel Čapek in the conceptual genealogy of Poetism. Čapek's early translations of French poetry, and most importantly his 1919 translation

of Apollinaire's "Zone" (as "Pásmo"), had a serious impact on the Devětsil poets, and especially on Nezval, who wrote an appreciative introduction, "The Guide of Young Poets," to the 1936 book publication of Čapek's translations. See Vítězslav Nezval, "Průvodce mladých básníků," in Karel Čapek, *Básnické počátky/Překlady,* vol. 24 of *Spisy* (Prague: Český spisovatel, 1993), 55–61.

52. Orig.: "Jsem v neustálém kontaktu se svým trávením. Všecky smysly v chodu. 36 antén a instinkt věčně protékající. Všecky se slévají k jedinému bodu šachovnice. Souhrn chvění a jeho šipky—hle senzibilita." Vítězslav Nezval, "Papoušek na motocyklu čili o řemesle básnickém," *Host* 3.9–10 (July 1924), 220.

53. Orig.: "Neustálé pronikání. Vždy jiná směs. Zákon asociace, nejiná síla než ta, jež ovládá mou žízeň a mé vášně." Ibid., 221. Nezval's notion of "penetration" (pronikání) bears an inadvertent echo of Viacheslav Ivanov's notion of "penetration" (проникновение), the basis of the latter's theory of authorial sympathy. The difference is that Ivanov's notion pertains expressly to forms of interhuman contact, whereas Nezval seems to envision a broader interpenetration of all people and things.

54. Orig.: "Poetismus měl s futurismem společnou zálibu ve velkoměstských skutečnostech a v rychlosti, s kubismem požadavek svébytnosti básnických výrazových prostředků, se surrealismem, s nímž se zrodil takřka současně a jejž do jisté míry anticipoval, sklon k spontánnímu, předběžným plánem a logicko-rozumovými požadavky neřízenému vyjadřování se, zdůrazňování asociativního myšlení a volné samočinné obrazotvornosti." Vítězslav Nezval, *Moderní básnické směry* (Prague: Československý spisovatel, 1966), 220.

55. In this regard, the contrast between the poems Nezval produced in the mid-1930s and those composed during the war is dramatic, both thematically and formally. The free-verse, highly associative, and ahistorical poems of his Surrealist phase are replaced, in *Historical Portrait* (Historický obraz, 1945), by propagandistic declarations in unvarying, seven-stanza clusters of tercets. Vítězslav Nezval, *Historický obraz: Básně z let 1939–1945* (Prague: Melantrich, 1945).

56. Goldstein, *Nikolai Zabolotskii: Play for Mortal Stakes*, 62–63.

57. Vítězslav Nezval, *Edison* (Prague: Plejada, 1928), 11–13, 27, 28, 35.

58. Roman Jakobson, "What Is Poetry," in his *Language in Literature,* ed. Krystyna Pomorska and Stephen Rudy (Cambridge, Mass.: Harvard University Press, 1987), 376. Jakobson briefly describes his friendship with a number of interwar Russian, Czech, and Polish poets—including Julian Tuwim and Kazimierz Wierzyński—in his *My Futurist Years,* ed. Bengt Jangfeldt, trans. Stephen Rudy (New York: Marsilio, 1992), 63.

59. Giorgio Agamben, *The End of the Poem: Studies in Poetics,* trans. Daniel Heller-Roazen (Stanford, Calif.: Stanford University Press, 1999), 66.

60. Nezval, *Edison,* iii.

61. Iurii Olesha, *Zavist', Ni dnia bez strochki, Rasskazy* (Moscow: Izvestiia, 1989), 64.

62. Karel Čapek, "Kouzelník z Menlo Parku," in his *Od člověka k člověku II,* vol. 15 of *Spisy* (Československý spisovatel, 1991), 542–43. Čapek titled his obituary "The Wizard of Menlo Park," and Edison's international reputation for modern-day wizardry resonated with Nezval's conception of the modern,

which encompassed a broad sense of inventiveness. Another of Nezval's most important Poetist compositions from the period is "The Astonishing Wizard" (Podivuhodný kouzelník, 1930), which was collected, together with *Edison* and later *Time Signal,* in subsequent redactions of Nezval's poetry collection *Night Poems* (Básně noci, 1930, 1948).

63. Anna Akhmatova, *Pobeda nad sud'boi,* ed. N. I. Kraineva, vol. 1 (Moscow: Russkii put', 2005), 64.

64. Nikolai Zabolotskii, *Stolbtsy,* 29–31.

65. Masing-Delić, *Abolishing Death,* 249.

66. Ibid., 261.

67. Ibid., 259.

68. This version of the poem is printed in Nikolai Zabolotskii, *Polnoe sobranie stikhotvorenii i poem,* 316–17.

69. Orig.: "Да здравствует зрелость! Прекрасная, разумная и надёжная зрелость!" Lev Nikulin, *Vremia, prostranstvo, dvizhenie,* in his *Sochineniia v trekh tomakh,* vol. 1 (Moscow: Goslitizdat, 1956), 263. This text is not to be confused with Nikulin's 1931 text, published under the same name in 1934 in very different form.

70. Ol'ga Sedakova, *Proza* (Moscow: En Ef Kiiu/Tu Print, 2001), 666.

71. Vítězslav Nezval, *Signál času: Panichida za Edisona* (Prague: František Borový, 1931), 9–13, 15, 17, 19, 23.

72. Vítězslav Nezval, *Depeše z konce tisíciletí: Korespondence Vítězslava Nezvala,* ed. Marie Krulichová, Milena Vinařová, and Lubomír Tomek (Prague: Československý spisovatel, 1981), 44–47.

73. Bohuslav Reynek, *Rybí šupiny* (Petrkov: U Německého Brodu, 1922).

74. Vítězslav Nezval, *Josef Čapek: Studie* (Prague: František Borový, 1937).

75. It is unclear whether Čapek deliberately shaped this star as a Star of David, though such a reading of the image is plausible, especially as the star appears just behind and to the left of the clock tower. If we are oriented to face Prague's *orloj,* the star would then sit low in the northern sky. It could just as easily be the North Star. But a few hundred meters north of the Old Town Square is Josefov, Prague's Jewish Quarter, with its own peculiar artifact of timekeeping: the clock on the tower of the Jewish Town Hall has Hebrew letters instead of arabic numerals, and its hands move counterclockwise.

76. Notably, Nezval expunged these sentiments from the poem after his conversion to Socialist Realism.

77. Antonín Jelínek, *Vítězslav Nezval* (Prague: Československý spisovatel, 1961), 52.

78. Orig.: "nitka duše proměněná ve drátek / dává život milionům sluchátek." Nezval, *Signál času: Panichida za Edisona,* 20.

79. In their treatment of the function of litany in *Edison,* Magda van Duijkeren and Miloš Stejskal make an interesting argument differentiating the litanies in the poem as a whole. In litanies structured by anaphora pertaining to the lyric "I," they suggest, the anaphoric lines are autosemantic, their meaning independent of their context. In litanies structured by anaphora pertaining to the figure of Edison, the words are synsemantic, dependent on their context for complete meaning. While such opposition is perhaps too schematic for my

own consideration of *Edison*, this reading ultimately provides a different path by which the lyric "I" and his subject become fused as the poem progresses. See Magda van Duijkeren and Miloš Stejskal, "Funkce litanických řad v Nezvalově 'Edisonu,'" in *Czech Studies: Literature, Language, Culture/České studie: Literatura Jazyk Kultura*, ed. Mojmír Grygar (Amsterdam: Rodopi, 1990), 203–27.

80. Henri Lefebvre, *Critique of Everyday Life, Vol. 2, Foundations for a Sociology of the Everyday*, trans. John Moore (London: Verso, 2002), 195.

81. Tomáš Trnka, "Problém individua," *Naše doba* 30.10 (Sept. 1923), 603.

Chapter 5

The chapter epigraph is from Franz Kafka, *The Diaries, 1910–1923*, ed. Max Brod (New York: Schocken, 1949), 252.

1. Orig.: "'Je to, jako byste filmovali život člověka od narození až do tohoto okamžiku, a pak všechny ty obrázky položili na sebe a promítli je všechny současně. Řeknete: jaká změť! Ano, neboť splývá přítomnost i minulost, všechno se překrývá, a zbývá jen tvar života, něco nepopsatelného a nesmírně osobního: něco jako osobní aura, ve které je uloženo vše'—Nos mu tragicky ustrnul. 'Všecko, *i budoucnost*,' vydechl." Karel Čapek, *Hordubal, Povětroň, Obyčejný život*, vol. 8 of *Spisy* (Československý spisovatel, 1984), 172. All subsequent citations of *Hordubal, Povětroň, Obyčejný život* refer to this edition.

2. The play's strong reception sparked predictable excitement back in Prague. See H. Jelínek, "*R. U. R.* v Paříže," *Lumír* 51.4 (1924): 218–19.

3. In his doctoral dissertation, Čapek refers but once to Bergson, and in such a way as to suggest that this apostle of subjective experience might be regarded alongside Schopenhauer and Jean-Marie Guyau as an objectivist "metaphysician of beauty," for whom nature *might be* treated as an aesthetic object, at least insofar as Bergson's essay *On Laughter* (1899) refers to the "true reality of the thing, stripped of its conceptual outer layer." See Karel Čapek, *Univerzitní studie*, ed. Miloš Pohorský (Prague: Československý spisovatel, 1987), 209–10.

4. Jindřich Toman, "Karel Čapek, Karl Kraus, and the Theory of the Phrase," in *On Karel Čapek*, ed. Michael Makin and Jindřich Toman (Ann Arbor: Michigan Slavic Publications, 1992), 104.

5. Orig.: "Adame, nikde a v ničem nestvořil jsem nějaké pouhosti; všechno je mnohostranné a slibné, plné možnosti a kliček. Adame, vina je ve tvých očích; z mého tygra jsi udělal pouhé zvíře, z mé hmoty pouhý materialism, z mé skutečnosti pouhý realism—ubohý Adame!" Karel Čapek, "Kritika slov," in his *O umění a kultuře II*, vol. 18 of *Spisy* (Československý spisovatel, 1985), 132.

6. Orig.: "'Relativní' je slovo moudré a moderní; relativní jsou hodnoty i pravdy, relativní je prostor i čas, pojmy a poznatky, věda a zkušenost lidská, relativní je zkrátka všechno, i absolutní alkohol; synu, chceš-li moudrým býti, věř absolutně, že všechno je relativní. [. . .] Promiňte, nechci si hráti se slovy; ale řekl-li jsem, že všechno je relativní, uklouzlo mi tím něco docela nerelativistického; neboť hříšné slovo 'všechno' páchne zarytým a tajným absolutismem." Ibid., 132–33.

7. Orig.: "[Jsou] pravdy, které se neklamou [a] bytosti, jež jsou dokonalé a nekonečné." Ibid., 134.

8. Although he appears to have had at least a moderate technical understanding of special relativity, Čapek openly mocked its esoteric mathematics and apparent distance from everyday life, for example, in his 1926 feuilleton "On Relativism" (O relativismu): "As far as concerns Einstein's relativism, I'll say openly that I don't understand it, just as I don't understand certain religious mysteries, the logic of history, infinite space, the wisdom of statesmen, and other things." (Pokud se týče relativismu Einsteinova, pravím upřímně, že mu nerozumím, tak jako nerozumím některým náboženským tajemstvím, logice dějin, nekonečnému prostoru, státnické moudrosti, a jiným věcem.) Karel Čapek, *O umění a kultuře III*, vol. 19 of *Spisy* (Československý spisovatel, 1986), 25. It is interesting that the esoterica to which Čapek compares Einstein—religion, history, statecraft—are all major subjects of inquiry in his fiction and journalism.

9. Čapek treats American Pragmatism in greater philosophical detail in a study subsequent to his dissertation: *Pragmatism; or, The Philosophy of Practical Life* (Pragmatismus čili filozofie praktického života, 1918). Both works are republished in his *Univerzitní studie.*

10. Karel Čapek, *Hovory s T. G. Masarykem,* vol. 20 of *Spisy* (Československý spisovatel, 1990), 219–20.

11. In his popular biography of Franz Kafka, Frederick Karl suggests that it was this emphasis on transformation that distinguished Czech Modernism from the Modernist forms it borrowed wholesale from Paris and Vienna. This is an oversimplification. Whether Čapek and Kafka knew each other personally or followed each other's work remains an open question. At the very least, they had several mutual friends, though they moved in largely separate circles. Johannes Urzidil, a German-language author who knew both Čapek and Kafka in Prague, says in a personal letter to George Gibian that there was "sort of a glass-wall [. . .] even between the most liberal Czechs and Germans," and that while the Germans often discussed their Czech counterparts, the separation was maintained mostly from the Czech side. See Frederick Karl, *Franz Kafka: Representative Man* (New York: Fromm, 1993), 25; and George Gibian, "Karel Čapek's Apocrypha and Franz Kafka's Parables," *American Slavic and East European Review* 18.2 (April 1959), 238 n1.

12. Ivan Blecha, *Edmund Husserl a česká filosofie* (Olomouc: Nakladatelství Olomouc, 2003), 32.

13. Jan Biahoslav Čapek, "Karel Čapek: *Obyčejný život,*" *Naše doba* 42.1 (1935): 308.

14. The entire trilogy was published between 1934 and 1936 by George Allen Unwin in the English translation of Marie Weatherall and Robert Weatherall. The first German translation of *Hordubal* appeared in 1933, the same year it was published in Czech. The same novel was published in a Russian version by Goslitizdat in 1937. The first Polish translation of both *Hordubal* and *An Ordinary Life* appeared in 1935, published by J. Przeworski, in the translation of Paweł Hulki-Laskowski. An excerpt of the Polish translation of *Hordubal* appeared in the June 23, 1935, issue of *Tygodnik Ilustrowany,* whose contributors included Bruno Schulz, Czesław Miłosz, and Witold Gombrowicz: "Wyjątek z powieści *Karola Czapka—Hordubal,* która w tłumaczeniu Pawła Hulki-Laskowskiego ukaże się nakładem J. Przeworskiego," *Tygodnik Ilustrowany* 76.25 (June 23,

1935), 488. For a summary of Čapek's publication and theatrical history in Poland, see Halina Janaszek-Ivaničková, *Karel Čapek* (Warsaw: Czytelnik, 1985), 142–45.

15. Andrei Platonov, *Razmyshleniia chitatel'ia* (Moscow: Sovetskii pisatel', 1970), 197; Viach. Vs. Ivanov, "Andrei Platonov i Chapek: Fantasticheskii realizm," in his *Izbrannye trudy po semiotike i istorii kul'tury, Tom 2: Stat'i o russkoi literature* (Moscow: Iazyki russkoi kul'tury, 2000), 646.

16. Harkins, *Karel Čapek*, 143.

17. For this reason I disagree with Harkins's suggestion that the three novels, taken in order, form a Hegelian dialectic of thesis, antithesis, and synthesis, with *Hordubal* positing a conflict between the subjective and the objective, *The Meteor* between multiple instances of objectivity, and *An Ordinary Life* between multiple instances of subjectivity. While this is an accurate description of the novels' narrative devices, Harkins's formulation suggests the emergence of a stable solution to the problem of identity that is, in fact, nowhere present in the text. Ibid., 142.

18. Orig.: "Byl chlapec, který neměl matky. [. . .] Případ X přece nemá tváře ani jména, nemá totožnost, je Neznámý." Čapek, *Hordubal, Povětroň, Obyčejný život,* 205.

19. Ibid., 139.

20. Lubomír Doležel, *Narrative Modes in Czech Literature* (Toronto: University of Toronto Press, 1973), 98.

21. Wolfgang F. Schwartz, "(De)Konstruction von Erinnerung und Biographie als Element der Zyklisierung bei Karel Čapek: Die 'noetische Trilogie,'" in *Zyklusdichtung in den slavischen Literaturen,* ed. Reinhard Ibler (Frankfurt: Peter Lang, 2000), 490–91.

22. Orig.: "Mně nestačí, co vidím; chci vědět víc—a proto vymýšlím povídačky. [. . .] A já vím, člověče, co to fikce je, já vím, jak se to dělá: řekneme, jeden díl zkušenosti, tři díly fantazie, dva díly logické kombinace, a ostatek je chytrácký kalkul: aby to bylo nové, aby to bylo časové, aby se v tom něco řešilo nebo dokazovalo a hlavně, hlavně aby to působilo." Čapek, *Hordubal, Povětroň, Obyčejný život*, 133.

23. Orig.: "Řeknu vám větu metafyzického šílenství: možnost, která by mezi všemi byla jediná možná, *byla by skutečností.* Hle, fixní idea fantastů: honit skutečnost oklikami přeludů. Myslíte-li, že nám stačí vyrábět iluze, jste na omylu; naše mánie je obludnější: pokoušíme se o samu skutečnost." Ibid., 194.

24. Orig.: "Nejsem visionář, jsem analytik; pravá skutečnost se nám nezjevuje; musí být vytěžena přísnou prací, analýzou a soustředěním." Ibid., 171.

25. Orig.: "Všechny věci by se nám rozpadly v pouhé sny, kdyby v nich nebyl nějaký pořádek; pořádek je něco, co je jen v skutečných věcech. Proto mne ten sen tak poděsil, že jsem v něm našla víc souvislosti, než mívají sny; a nemohu jej vypravovat než tak, jak mu rozumím teď." Ibid., 144. Note that the Sister of Mercy characterizes dreams as *pouhý,* the same word Čapek criticizes for its reductionism in the most substantial installment of A Critique of Words.

26. Orig.: "[N]áše ars medica, to je na padesát procent intuice." Ibid., 161.

27. Thomas Ort, *Art and Life in Modernist Prague: Karel Čapek and His Generation, 1911–1938* (New York: Palgrave Macmillan, 2013), 156. Ort goes

on to note that, for Čapek, "the true value of intuition lay in its creation of the possibility of empathy" (197). This is certainly the case as it pertains to Čapek's social values and democratic ideals, though I must emphasize that even these values and ideals grow out of the author's core epistemology, such that a failure to empathize reflects a fundamental misapprehension of Being as such.

28. Orig.: "Myslete si, že život je jakési znění, že člověk zní, že zní jeho mysl, paměť i podvědomí; i jeho minulost souzní v tomto a kterémkoliv okamžiku; je to nesmírně složitý a nekonečně mnohohlasý zvuk, ve kterém je přítomno i minulé věčným dozníváním a spoluzněním vrchních a vedlejších tónů; celá minulost zabarvuje zvuk přítomnosti. Myslete si, že i v nás se přenosem zvenčí rozkmitají tytéž vlny, aspoň pokud jsme v nějakém vztahu k člověku, jenž vysílá do prostoru svůj kmitočet—jako každý z nás, každý z nás; to souznění je slabší nebo silnější; to záleží na našem ladění, na naší citlivosti a pozornosti a na intenzitě daného vztahu." Čapek, *Hordubal, Povětroň, Obyčejný život*, 174.

29. Urs Heftrich, "Karel Čapeks Auseinandersetzung mit Henri Bergson," *Zeitschrift für Slavische Philologie* 50.2 (1990), 369.

30. Morson and Emerson, *Mikhail Bakhtin: Creation of a Prosaics*, 232–33.

31. Peter Bugge, "Nákaza světa: Nemoc a epidemie v dílech Karla Čapka z konce třicátých let," *Česká literatura* 47.3 (1999), 242–43.

32. Orig.: "Mám pocit ohromného životního rozsahu; v tom člověku je mnoho prostoru, mnoho moře, ale nebyl cestovatelem. Rozumíte, životní prostor cestovatelův je měřitelný; ale tady—Chybí tu jakýkoliv cil; není tu pevného bodu, od kterého by bylo možno určit vzdálenosti a směry. [. . .] Měli bychom vyjít od posledního dechu člověka, abychom pochopili, jakou podobu měl jeho život a jaký význam náleží čemukoliv, co prožil. Teprve smrtí je hotovo mládí i narození člověka. [. . .] Ale nemohu, nemohu. Jaká bída je naše chápání v čase!" Karel Čapek, *Hordubal, Povětroň, Obyčejný život*, 177.

33. Orig.: "Ach, člověče, to je to divné: ono není tak docela jisto, že ten život byl jenom vymyšlen; a když se tak na to dívám, řekl bych, že to byl *můj vlastní* život. To jsem já. Já jsem to moře i ten muž." Ibid., 204.

34. Orig.: "Milý člověče, svět je veliký, větší než naše zkušenost; je udělán z hrsti faktů a celého vesmíru možnosti. Všecko, co nevíme, je tu jako možnost, a každý fakt je jedna kulička v růženci předchozích i budoucích eventualit. Nic platno, jdeme-li za člověkem, musíme se pustit do toho světa dohadů, musíme čenichat jeho možné kroky minulé i příští; musíme ho stíhat svou fantazií, má-li se nám zjevit ve své neviditelné živosti. Je naprosto lhostejno, je-li celý vymyšlen nebo celý skutečný; [. . .] oba jsou upředeni z čisté a nekonečné látky možnosti, ve které je uloženo vše, i to, co skutečně jest." Ibid., 199.

35. Ibid.

36. Orig.: "[T]en prudký přízvuk na já, jemuž neuniká nikdo z nás lidí." Ibid., 189.

37. Orig.: "Prostě tam někde je místo mého *útěku;* nikdy tam asi nepřijdu, ale je to končina, jež existuje pro mne silněji než země, ve kterých jsem byl." Ibid., 206.

38. Orig.: "Musel se rozbít. To byl jeho vnitřní osud, vlastně cosi jako únik před úkolem, který byl nad jeho síly." Ibid., 183–84.

39. Orig.: "Je-li pravá skutečnost něco, co jest, a co tudíž trvá, tedy jsem utekl před skutečností; byl to zatracený útěk, neboť jsem ji už nenašel." Ibid., 156.

40. Orig.: "Říkám-li tomu únik, tedy je to útěk do samého středu věcí, kde se všechno utkává, kde se páří věky ve zvrhlém míšení kultur." Ibid., 225.

41. Orig.: "Jak ukrutně veliká a složitá, jak prostorná je skutečnost, když v ní je dost místa pro tolik různých interpretací! Ale není to už takový chaos, je to zřetelná mnohost, už to není nejistota, nýbrž mnohohlasost [. . .] [P]oznáváme svět skrze to, co jsme sami, a poznávajíce svět objevujeme sebe samotné. Chválabohu, teď už jsme zase doma; jsme ze stejné látky jako ta mnohost světa; jsme doma v té rozloze a nesčíslnosti a můžeme odpovídat těm přemnohým hlasům. Už není jen já, ale my lidé; můžeme se domluvit mnohými jazyky, které jsou v nás. [. . .] I ten nejobyčejnější život je ještě nekonečný, nesmírná je hodnota každé duše. [. . .] [Ž]ivot člověka je příliš veliký, aby měl jen jedinou tvář a mohl být přehlednut najednou." Ibid., 399–400.

42. It is a peculiar coincidence that during the same period that Karel Čapek composed the "noetic trilogy," Josef Čapek devoted himself primarily to child portraiture and to illustrations for children's books. Oleg Malevič reports that Josef Čapek's interest in art *for* children lasted from 1928 until about 1934, though he would later remain interested in art *by* children. When a Prague gallery invited visitors to vote for their favorite items in an exhibition of child art, Čapek signed his comment card, "Josef Čapek, an old child." Oleg Malevič, *Bratři Čapkové,* trans. Hana Štěpánková (Prague: Ivo Železný, 1999), 207–9.

43. "Dnes vím, že ona byla dál než já, že v ní bylo rozhodnuto vše a ve mně nic, že ona byla zralá a já zůstal zmateným, nedorostlým, neodpovědným chlapcem. [. . .] Nebylo ve mně plnosti člověka, kterého bych jí odevzdal. [. . .] Vězte, že můj útěk byl útěkem insolventního dlužníka. Zůstal jsem jí dlužen sama sebe." Karel Čapek, *Hordubal, Povětroň, Obyčejný život,* 154.

44. In this regard, it is worth noting that education, the period of one's social and intellectual maturation, is etymologically linked to "completion" in Czech and Polish. The Czech word *vzdělaní* refers conventionally to "education," though etymologically it is rooted in the process of "making something to completion," from the verb *dělat,* "to make." This echo is even stronger in Polish, in which "education" is *wykształcenie,* or the process whereby something is "fully formed," from *kształt,* "form, shape." As a final attestation of one's maturity, the diploma received upon completion of secondary education is *maturita* in Czech, *matura* in Polish.

45. Craig S. Cravens, "Čapek's *Hordubal* and Dostoevsky's *The Double:* Madness and Free-Indirect Discourse," *Comparative Literature* 52.1 (2000): 53–71.

46. Orig.: "Ano, vídala Hordubala, chodil jako tělo bez ducha." Čapek, *Hordubal, Povětroň, Obyčejný život,* 113.

47. Orig.: "Osamělé dítě ve své hře zapomíná na sebe a na všecko, co je kolem, a jeho zapomenutí je mimo čas. Do společné hry dětí je vtaženo i širší okolí a jejich pospolitý svět je ovládán zákony ročních dob. [. . .] Velikonoce, prázdniny a vánoce, jarmark, pouť a posvícení, to jsou důležitá data a hluboké předěly v čase. Rok dětí má svůj řád, je obřadně rozčleněn podle ročních období; osamělé dítě si hraje s věčností, kdežto dětská smečka s časem." Ibid., 280–81.

48. Orig.: "i dnes jsem dítě, které má svůj tajný svět "; "[J]sem dospělý a hotový člověk, který se živí úmornou a neradostnou prací." Ibid., 292, 304.

49. Orig.: "Osm životů, které skládají můj život; a já vím, kdybych měl víc pokdy a jasnější hlavu, že by se jich našla ještě řada, třeba docela nesouvislých, třeba takových, které byly jen jednou a trvaly jenom okamžik." Ibid., 378.

50. Orig.: "Ale přitom, ať jsem žil kterýkoli z těch údělů nebo byl kýmkoli z těch figur, byl jsem to vždycky *já,* a to já bylo pořád totéž a neměnilo se od začátku až do konce. To je to divné. Je tedy to já cosi, co je *nad* těmi figurami a jejich osudy, něco vyššího, jediného a jednotícího, je to snad to, čemu říkáme duše? Ale vždyť to já nemělo žádný *svůj* obsah, jednou bylo tím hypochondrem a jednou tím hrdinou, a nebylo ničím, co by se vznášelo nad nimi!" Ibid., 379.

51. Orig.: "Třeba každý z nás je součet lidí, jenž narůstá z pokolení do pokolení. A třeba už je nám úzko z toho nekonečného rozrůznění; proto mu chceme uniknout a přijímáme nějaké davové já, které by nás zjednodušilo." Ibid., 383.

52. Witold Gombrowicz, *Bakakaj i inne opowiadania,* vol. 1 of *Pisma zebrane*, ed. Zdzisław Łapiński (Kraków: Wydawnictwo Literackie, 2002), 151. All quotations from Gombrowicz's stories will refer to this edition, which is the most complete and authoritative scholarly edition yet produced and is the first in an ongoing scholarly redaction of his collected works. For the dating of the story, see 289.

53. Ibid., 258. Delightful as this observation is, one may disagree with Zdzisław Łapiński when he characterizes "Philifor" as "just as weird to the French as Philidor is for us." Gombrowicz does not seek out names that sound completely absurd. Instead, he is intent on using names that sound like they *should* carry some reference or association but do not in their given cultural context.

54. Ibid., 233.

55. Orig.: "Lecz zjawisko duchowe tej miary nie mogło nie wywołać w naturze swego kontr-zjawiska, w myśl Newtonowskiej zasady akcji i reakcji, dlatego też równie znakomity Analityk rychło urodził się w Colombo i na uniwersytecie Columbia uzyskawszy doktorat tudzież profesurę Wyższej Analizy, szybko wspiął się na najwyższe szczeble kariery naukowej." Ibid., 151.

56. Orig.: "Działał on rozkładowo, a specjalnością jego był rozkład osoby na części za pomocą rachowania, w szczególności za pomocą prztyczków. I tak za pomocą prztyczka w nos pobudzał nos do samoistnego bytu, przy czym nos ruszał się spontanicznie na wszystkie strony ku przerażeniu właściciela." Ibid., 151–52.

57. Orig.: "Jest Bóg! Honor! Synteza!" Ibid., 156.

58. Zbigniew Majchrowski, "'Białe małżeństwo' czyli 'ślub w kościele ludzkim,'" *Teksty* 34.1 (1977), 115.

59. Orig.: "[S]traszna anarchia, straszne rozwydrzenie." Gombrowicz, *Bakakaj i inne opowiadania,* 158.

60. Orig.: "Policzek możesz zahaczyć, ale nie mnie—nie mnie! Mnie nie ma w ogóle! Nie ma mnie!" Ibid., 155.

61. Orig.: "Jeżeli on padnie, to śmiercią swą odda hołd Syntezie—jeżeli zabije mnie, to zabije trybem syntetycznym. Tak więc moje będzie za grobem zwycięstwo." Ibid., 160.

62. Jacques Derrida, *Given Time: I. Counterfeit Money,* trans. Peggy Kamuf (Chicago: University of Chicago Press, 1992), 39–40.

63. This intermediate status of the individual is consistent with what Georg Simmel (1858–1918) described as an ongoing, potentially irresolvable conflict between the Enlightenment-rational model of the individual, which is based on a notion of universality, and the Romantic model, which is rooted in difference: "One force is the yearning for the autonomous personality that bears the cosmos within itself, whose isolation has the great compensation of being identical to all others at its deepest, natural core. The other is the yearning for the incomparability of being unique and different, which is compensated for its isolation by the fact that each person can exchange with another some good that he alone possesses and whose exchange weaves both of them into the interaction of organic parts of the whole." Georg Simmel, "Freedom and the Individual," trans. Richard Albares, in Simmel's *On Individuality and Social Forms,* ed. Donald L. Levine (Chicago: University of Chicago Press, 1971), 225.

64. Orig.: "I wtedy pojąłem, czego się obawiam. To było symetria—sytuacja była symetryczna i w tym się zawierała jej moc, lecz także jej słabość." Gombrowicz, *Bakakaj i inne opowiadania*, 161.

65. Orig.: "[A]leż, Profesorze, pan mówi jak dziecko!' A na to zdziecinniały starzec odparł: 'Wszystko podszyte jest dzieckiem.'" Ibid., 163.

66. Orig.: "Może przyszłe wieki dadzą sobie radę z przerzuceniem solidnego mostu nad przepaścią pomiędzy prywatnym kosmosem każdego, a ogólnym kosmosem dla wszystkich. Obecnie widzimy, że przepaść coraz się pogłębia. Bo z jednej strony—pojedyńcze indywiduum ludzkie, wspomagane przez wszystkie prawie kierunki kultury, przez naukę, sztukę, etykę i nawet prawo cywilne i karne, staje się coraz bardziej zachłanne i wymagające; a z drugiej strony potężne jedności wyższego rzędu, jak Państwo, czy Naród, tym gwałtowniej w imię konieczności życia zbiorowego narzucają jeden wspólny sposób odczuwania. Czytając *Don Kichota,* [. . .] widzimy jakie skarby duszy mogłyby przepaść pod ciśnieniem kosmosu dla wszystkich. Widzimy szaloną elastyczność i podatność rzeczywistości, jej jeszcze nie wyjaśnioną do gruntu naturę, jej, chciałoby się powiedzieć, niewolniczość." Witold Gombrowicz, "*Don Kichot* obecnie," in his *Proza (Fragmenty), Reportaże, Krytyka literacka, 1933–1939,* vol. 12 of *Dzieła*, ed. Jerzy Jarzębski (Kraków: Wydawnictwo Literackie, 1995), 154–55.

67. Jerzy Jarzębski, *Podglądanie Gombrowicza* (Kraków: Wydawnictwo Literackie, 2000), 91.

68. Orig.: "Otóż mnie osobiście wydaje się, że literatura choruje po prostu na brak najzwyklejszej rzeczywistości. Ponieważ ewolucja pojęć w społeczeństwie nie nadąża ewolucji faktów, kultura nasza w danej mierze odbywa się niejako w próżni, język nasz jest anachroniczny, odczuwanie—takoż i jesteśmy niewolnikami wielu form, któreśmy dawno—życiem wyprzedzili." Witold Gombrowicz, "Rzeczywistość i żywotność," in his *Czytelnicy i krytycy: Proza, reportaże, krytyka literacka, eseje, przedmowy,* ed. Maria Rola (Kraków: Wydawnictwo Literackie, 2004), 178

69. Completing this circle, Russell E. Brown has asserted that in his later years Joyce studied Polish in order to read Bruno Schulz. It is an attractive thought, but I have not been able to confirm it, and I find the claim doubtful. Russell E. Brown, *Myths and Relatives: Seven Essays on Bruno Schulz* (Munich: Otto Sagner, 1991), 67. Gombrowicz, meanwhile, cited Joyce's *Ulysses* as the book he

most admired in 1935. Witold Gombrowicz, "[Jaką najciekawszą książkę przeczytałem w r. 1935?]," in his *Proza (Fragmenty), Reportaże, Krytyka literacka, 1933–1939,* 203–4.

70. Orig.: "W *Don Kichocie* mamy dwa poziomy—poziom wyższy, na którym rozgrywa się wieczysty i wspaniały dramat pomiędzy subiektywizmem, a obiektywizmem, jednostką, a grupą, snem i jawą, oraz poziom niższy, codzienny, praktyczny, gdzie oglądamy zabawną wojnę wariata z prawdą zdrowego rozsądku, w której wariat otrzymuje cięgi. Podobnie i my dzisiaj dzielimy się na dwa poziomy. W głębiach duszy znamy i czujemy straszliwy konflikt pomiędzy naszą, jakże wybujałą osobą, a prawami świata powszechnego, ale to nie przeszkadza nam spać, jeść, ani jeździć tramwajem. [. . .] W każdym z nas jest Don Kichot, ale na marginesie Szanszo Pansy." Gombrowicz, "*Don Kichot* obecnie," 155.

71. Orig.: "—wtem ktoś wziął mnie z tylu za kołnierz i zimno—tak zimno—odciągnął od okienka i popchnął na właściwe miejsce, tj. tam, gdzie kończył się ogonek. Serce zabiło mi mocno, zabrakło tchu—czyż to nie jest mordercze, gdy ktoś zostanie naraz wzięty za kołnierz w publicznym lokalu?—lecz obejrzałem się: był to wysoki, wyświeżony, pachnący jegomość z przystrzyżonym wąsikiem." Gombrowicz, *Bakakaj i inne opowiadania,* 13.

72. Orig.: "Trzeba uczyć, niestrudzenie uczyć, inaczej nie przestaniemy być narodem Zulusów." Ibid., 14.

73. Orig.: "[N]ic nie jest tak trudne i delikatne, tyle święte nawet, co osobowość ludzka, nic nie może się równać tej zachłanności tajemnych związków, które rodzą się między obcymi nikłe i bezprzedmiotowe, by skuć nieznacznie potworną więzią. Wyobraźcie sobie mecenasa, który wychodzi z publicznego pisuaru, sięga po piętnaście groszy i dowiaduje się, że rachunek—już uregulowany. Cóż odczuwa wtedy?" Ibid., 18.

74. Nancy, *Being Singular Plural,* 30.

75. Orig.: "Mogę skonać nagle na ulicy, pod płotem, a w takim razie—trzeba napisać karteczkę—niech trupa mego odeślą pod adresem mecenasa Kraykowskiego." Gombrowicz, *Bakakaj i inne opowiadania,* 22.

76. Witold Gombrowicz, *Wspomnienia polskie* (Kraków: Wydawnictwo Literackie, 2002), 126–27.

77. Orig.: "Urodził się on w szczerym polu i na rozległej równinie—wychowywał się po lasach, górach, dolinach i rozłogach—nigdy nie sypiał w zamkniętym pomieszczeniu—i to mu dało specyficzną masywność i szerokość natury—rozległość duszy—kolebiącą rozlewność usposobienia." Gombrowicz, *Bakakaj i inne opowiadania,* 184. My translation of "The Rat" was first published in *Words without Borders,* online at http://www.wordswithoutborders.org/article.php?lab=Rat.

78. Orig.: "A psy zrozpaczone odzywały się po opłotkach, wyjąc głucho i ciemno. A to wycie zarażało w końcu i ludzi. I cała okolica wyła tęsknie, głucho i czarno, prosto w księżyc, który świetniał blado." Gombrowicz, *Bakakaj i inne opowiadania,* 185.

79. Orig.: "Co więcej, nie był też pewny, czy długoletnie i jakże bolesne obcowanie z jednym z tych gryzoni nie pozostawiło w nim czegoś pociągającego dla szczurów w ogóle." Ibid., 193.

80. Orig.: "[Lokaj] przeklinał absolutną niemiłosierność szczura, przeklinał te straszne i jakby bezapelacyjne związki w naturze, przeklinał bezgraniczność niemiłosierności." Ibid., 190.

81. Orig.: "We wtorek zbudziłem się o tej porze bezdusznej i nikłej, kiedy właściwie noc się już skończyła, a świt nie zdążył jeszcze zacząć się na dobre. Zbudzony nagle, chciałem pędzić taksówką na dworzec, zdawało mi się bowiem, że wyjeżdżam—dopiero w następnej minucie z biedą rozeznałem, że pociąg dla mnie na dworcu nie stoi, nie wybiła żadna godzina. Leżałem w mętnym świetle, a ciało moje bało się nieznośnie, uciskając strachem mego ducha, duch uciskał ciało i każda najdrobniejsza fibra kurczyła się w oczekiwaniu, że nic się nie stanie, nic się nie odmieni, nic nigdy nie nastąpi i cokolwiek by się przedsięwzięło, nie pocznie się nic i nic." Witold Gombrowicz, *Ferdydurke,* vol. 2 of *Pisma zebrane,* ed. Włodzimierz Bolecki (Kraków: Wydawnictwo Literackie, 2007), 5.

82. Orig.: "Sen, który mię trapił w nocy i obudził, był wykładnikiem lęku. Nawrotem czasu, który powinien być zabroniony naturze, ujrzałem siebie takim, jakim byłem, gdym miał lat piętnaście i szesnaście—przeniosłem się w młodość—i stojąc na wietrze, na kamieniu, tuż koło młyna nad rzeką, mówiłem coś, słyszałem dawno pogrzebany swój głosik koguci, piskliwy, widziałem nos niewyrośnięty na twarzy niedokształtowanej i ręce za wielkie—czułem niemiłą konsystencję tej fazy rozwoju pośredniej, przejściowej. Zbudziłem się w śmiechu i w strachu, bo mi się zdawało, że taki, jak jestem dzisiaj, po trzydziestce, przedrzeźniam i wyśmiewam sobą niewypierzonego chłystka, jakim byłem, a on znowu przedrzeźnia mnie—i równym prawem—że obaj jesteśmy sobą przedrzeźniani." Ibid., 6.

83. "Idiotyczna, infantylna pupa paraliżowała odbierając wszelką możliwość oporu." Ibid., 21.

84. Among the most recent contributions to this discussion are Francesco Cataluccio, *Niedojrzałość: Choroba naszych czasów,* trans. Stanisław Kasprzysiak (Kraków: Znak, 2006); and Dagmara Jaszewska, *Nasza niedojrzała kultura: Postmodernizm inspirowany Gombrowiczem* (Warsaw: Oficyna naukowa, 2002).

85. Levinas, *On Escape,* 55.

86. Gombrowicz, *Ferdydurke,* 46–62.

87. Orig.: "[S]postrzegłem, że nie jestem sam. Był ktoś oprócz mnie w kącie, koło pieca, gdzie światło jeszcze nie dotarło—drugi człowiek był w pokoju. [. . .] I znowu w ustach susza, bicie serca, zatamowanie oddechu—to ja sam stałem pod piecem. Tym razem nie był to sen—naprawdę pod piecem stał sobowtór." Ibid., 14.

88. Orig.: "[C]oś obcego, narzuconego, jakiś kompromis pomiędzy światem zewnętrznym a wewnętrznym." Ibid., 16.

89. Orig.: "[Z]aczynam pisać pierwsze stronice dzieła mojego własnego, takiego jak ja, identycznego ze mną, wynikającego wprost ze mnie." Ibid.

90. Levinas, *On Escape,* 63–65.

91. Jean-Paul Sartre, *Being and Nothingness: An Essay on Phenomenological Ontology,* trans. Hazel E. Barnes (New York: Philosophical Library, 1956), 262.

92. Bernard Williams, *Shame and Necessity* (Berkeley: University of California Press, 1993), 81–84.

93. Janusz Margański, *Gombrowicz wieczny debiutant* (Kraków: Wydawnictwo Literackie, 2001), 193.

94. Orig.: "Gdyż człowiek jest najgłębiej uzależniony od swego odbicia w duszy drugiego człowieka, chociażby ta dusza była kretyniczna." Gombrowicz, *Ferdydurke,* 9.

95. Giorgio Agamben, *Remnants of Auschwitz: The Witness and the Archive,* trans. Daniel Heller-Roazen (New York: Zone Books, 2002), 106–7.

96. In the most thorough Lacanian treatment of Gombrowicz's prose, Hanjo Berressem provides a savvy reading of this inferiority complex. For Berressem, the thinking subject's shame stems from his inferiority in relation to the symbolic order that has been imposed on him. No matter how well he succeeds in defining himself, there is always a more fully realized set of definitions just out of his grasp. At the same time, the thinking subject recognizes that the definitions culture has provided are inadequate in relation to his own sense of Self: "Gombrowicz is caught in the double bind that, on the one hand, the subject is ashamed of its libidinal inferiority in the light of the ideal symbolic order (the reality principle and the superego) and that, additionally, this shame is heightened by the inferiority of this specific symbolic order in relation to other, better symbolic orders. Gombrowicz's shame, therefore, is the result of both a personal and a cultural inferiority. On the other hand, however, the ego is ashamed of its submission under any, and especially under an inferior, cultural law. Gombrowicz is once more caught in this split between ego and subject. While the imaginary ego is ashamed of the symbolic, Oedipal subject, the subject is ashamed of its libidinous, immature ego. Ultimately, the pleasure principle is ashamed of the reality principle and vice versa." Hanjo Berressem, *Lines of Desire: Reading Gombrowicz's Fiction with Lacan* (Evanston, Ill.: Northwestern University Press, 1998), 113. Berressem's reading adds a structuralist psychological nuance to my consideration of Gombrowicz's ontology.

97. Orig.: "[W]ieszcz o zdrowej filozofii tak mocno jest utwierdzony w sobie, iż nawet głupota i niedojrzałość go nie przestraszają ani mogą mu zaszkodzić—z podniesionym czołem może on się wyrażać i objawiać w swojej indolencji, podczas gdy wy nic prawie nie jesteście już w stanie wyrazić, ponieważ strach wam głos odbiera." Gombrowicz, *Ferdydurke,* 75.

98. Orig.: "Nie wiadomo było, co robić. Nie mogłem wytłumaczyć i wyjęzyczyć Zosi, co się stało we dworze, gdyż wstydziłem się, a zresztą nie znajdowałem słów. Ona zaś prawdopodobnie domyślała się mniej więcej, gdyż również wstydziła się i zgoła nie mogła wyjęzyczyć." Ibid., 235.

99. Orig.: "Ukradkiem spod kołdry patrzyłem jakby nie na siebie i widziałem tę twarz, która była moją i nie moją. [. . .] Oto nos mój . . . oto moje usta . . . oto uszy moje, dom mój." Ibid., 15.

100. Orig.: "Jednakże zamilkłem, on zamilkł i siedzieliśmy, że tak się wyrażę, nos w nos. Sam na sam. Ręka w rękę. Noga w nogę. Kolano w kolano. Sam na sam. Aż mnie drażnić zaczęła ta tożsamość głupia w tym pokoju moim i myślę, jak to jest, że on mnie powtarza, ja jego powtarzam, sam na sam—wtem sparzenie dziecka sparzyło mnie ażem syknął—i wtedy, widzę, choć tacy podobni, nic

tu nie wysiedzimy i w ogóle lepiej nie siedzieć a wyjść, wyjść, wyjść, wyjście, jakiekolwiek, wydalenie się, oddalenie, stało się naglące, palące!" Gombrowicz, *Dziennik, 1957–1961,* 284.

101. Theodore Adorno, "Cultural Criticism and Society," in his *Prisms,* trans. Shierry Weber Nicholsen and Samuel Weber (Cambridge, Mass.: MIT Press, 1983), 24.

102. Berressem, *Lines of Desire,* 282.

103. Jerzy Jarzębski, "Między awangardą a modernizmem: Witkacy, Schulz, Gombrowicz," in his *W Polsce czyli wszędzie* (Warsaw: Wydawnictwo PEN, 1992), 10.

104. Alejandro Rússovich, "Gombrowicz od wewnątrz," in *Tango Gombrowicza,* ed. and trans. Rajmund Kalicki (Kraków: Wydawnictwo Literackie, 1984), 128.

105. Martin Buber, *What Is Man?,* in his *Between Man and Man* (London: Routledge, 2002), 240–241.

106. Orig.: "Czy nie może istnieć dramat nie—między ludźmi, lecz w samym człowieku? Jeżeli ktoś jest chory na nieuleczalną chorobę—czyż dramat nie urzeczywistnia się między nim a jego chorobą? Jeżeli ktoś konfrontuje się ze swoim losem, z przeznaczeniem—czy to musi koniecznie odbywać się za pośrednictwem ludzi?" Witold Gombrowicz, letter to Martin Buber, Buenos Aires (July 25, 1951), Gombrowicz Archive, Beinecke Library, Yale University, gen. MSS. 515, series 1, box 2, item 51.

107. Orig.: "[J]a nie mogę dać konfliktu między ludźmi istniejącymi 'samodzielnie,' jak Pan mówi, gdyż moja wizja, moje wyczucie na tym właśnie polega, że tych 'samodzielnych' ludzi nie ma. Dramat mojego bohatera to nie—konfrontacja z innymi ludźmi, a tylko z mocami, które wytwarzają się *z ludzi, pomiędzy* ludźmi." Ibid.

108. Eryk Pieszak, *Trzy dyskursy o spotkaniu z Innym: Gombrowicza, Schelera i Lévinasa ścieżki spotkania w pobliżu wielkich dróg* (Poznań: Wydawnictwo Poznańskiego Towarzystwa Przyjaciół Nauk, 2003), 77.

109. Søren Kierkegaard, *Fear and Trembling/Repetition,* ed. and trans. Howard V. Hong and Edna H. Hong (Princeton, N.J.: Princeton University Press, 1983), 131.

110. Ibid., 210–13.

111. Ibid., 301–2.

112. Orig.: "Gdyż nie ma ucieczki przed gębą, jak tylko w inną gębę, a przed człowiekiem schronić się można jedynie w objęcie innego człowieka. Przed pupą zaś w ogóle nie ma ucieczki." Gombrowicz, *Ferdydurke,* 241.

113. Jan Kott, *The Theater of Essence and Other Essays* (Evanston, Ill.: Northwestern University Press, 1984), 83.

114. Ibid., 84.

115. Orig.: "I znowu przedmowa . . . i zniewolony jestem do przedmowy, nie mogę bez przedmowy i muszę przedmowę, gdyż prawo symetrii wymaga, aby *Filidorowi dzieckiem podszytemu* odpowiadał *dzieckiem podszyty Filibert,* przedmowie zaś do *Filidora* przedmowa do *Filiberta dzieckiem podszytego.* Choćbym chciał, nie mogę, nie mogę i nie mogę uchylić się żelaznym prawom symetrii oraz analogii." Gombrowicz, *Ferdydurke,* 169.

116. Mark C. Taylor, *Altarity* (Chicago: University of Chicago Press, 1987), 351.

117. Ibid., 352.

118. Ibid., 352–53.

119. Arne Melberg, *Theories of Mimesis* (Cambridge: Cambridge University Press, 1995), 137.

120. Ibid., 141.

121. Orig.: "[Z]awsze, bez przerwy szukamy formy i rozkoszujemy się nią lub cierpimy przez nią i przystosowujemy się do niej lub gwałcimy i rozbijamy ją, lub pozwalamy, aby ona nas stwarzała, amen." Gombrowicz, *Ferdydurke,* 74.

122. Orig.: "Forma nasza przenika nas, więzi od wewnątrz równie, jak od zewnątrz." Ibid., 45.

123. Jean-Pierre Salgas, *Witold Gombrowicz lub ateizm integralny,* trans. Jan Maria Kłoczowski (Warsaw: Czytelnik, 2004), 100–101.

124. Ibid., 100–102.

125. Janusz Margański, *Geografia pragnień: Opowieść o Gombrowiczu* (Kraków: Wydawnictwo Literackie, 2005), 52–54.

126. Ibid., 62.

127. Jindřich Chalupecký, *Expresionisté: Richard Weiner, Jakub Deml, Ladislav Klíma, Podivný Hašek* (Prague: Torst, 1992), 27.

128. Šíma was also a friend of Vítězslav Nezval, who wrote an appreciation of his artwork: Vítězslav Nezval, "Josef Šíma," *Aventinum* 7.33 (1931–32): 267. Šíma composed what has become the most enduring portrait of Nezval, a simple ink-line drawing.

129. Martin Tharp, "Czech Paris: Le Grand Jeu and Richard Weiner," *Estetika* 36.1–3 (1999), 119.

130. Josef Šíma, quoted in Michel Random, *Le grand jeu,* vol. 1 (Paris: Editions Denoël, 1970), 34.

131. For a compact summary of Weiner's influence on Le Grand Jeu, and vice versa, see also Věra Linhartová, *Joseph Sima: Ses amis, ses contemporains* (Brussels: La Connaissance, 1974), 34–36.

132. Daniela Hodrová, "Smysl pokoje," in *Poetika míst: Kapitoly z literární tematologie,* ed. Daniela Hodrová et al. (Prague: H&H, 1997), 231. For "estrangement," Hodrová uses *zcizení,* one of the standard Czech renderings of Shklovsky's *ostranenie,* but also a legal term for the expropriation of property. This makes a pleasant double entendre: Weiner's protagonist, experiencing "estrangement" in his domicile, is also deprived of his right to his own home.

133. Lubomír Doležel, "Radical Semantics: Franz Kafka and Richard Weiner," in *Forms and Functions,* ed. Jürgen Esser and Axel Hübler (Tübingen: Gunter Narr, 1981), 228. In his study of Le Grand Jeu, Michel Random asserts that Weiner was also a personal friend of Franz Kafka and Max Brod, but this is difficult to substantiate, at least on the basis of the memoirs provided by members of Kafka's circle. Random, *Le grand jeu,* 34. Brod does not mention Weiner in his memoir *Der Prager Kreis* (Stuttgart: W. Kohlhammer, 1966), nor does Johannes Urzidil mention him in his *There Goes Kafka,* trans. Harold A. Basilius (Detroit: Wayne State University Press, 1968), though both devote some attention to contemporary developments in Czech letters.

134. Alfred Thomas, *The Labyrinth of the Word: Truth and Representation in Czech Literature* (Munich: R. Oldenbourg, 1995), 107.

135. Daniela Hodrová, "Sebereflexívní román," in *Poetika české meziválečné literatury: Proměny žánrů*, ed. Daniela Hodrová et al. (Prague: Československý spisovaltel, 1987), 173.

136. Orig.: "Ale kým vlastně je ten cizinec za mými dveřmi, jehož jsem se zděsit měl, a nezděsil; jenž vzal moje zděšení *na sebe* a po němž tělesném—neboť byl tělesný—kráčím s netečností tak zatvrzelou jakoby po svém stínu? Kdo je tento nenadálý rušitel rytmu staromládeneckého mého života, a který ho přese vše nehatí? Pod jehož pozorným, ale odlehlým pohledem se dnes nejinak než denně (kdy jsem sám nepochybně) vydávám na apatickou prohlídku přízemního bytu, své noclehárny, kam je cizímu tak snadno vetřít se? Proboha, kdo je to, tento paradoxně přítomný, jenž jsa tak *vzácně*, je právě proto tak, jako by ho nebylo, a pod jehož strašidelně ustrašeným dozorem konám řadu stereotypních ověřovacích hmatů, po nichž ulehnu *s klidným vědomím*, že mohu klidně usnout, že jsem sám, že jsem zase sám, přestože se mnou onen!? Nevadí mi, nevadí tento kdosi, jehož vidím a neznamenám." Richard Weiner, *Lazebník/Hra doopravdy*, vol. 3 of *Spisy* (Prague: Torst, 1998), 220–21. Translations of *Hra doopravdy* are drawn from Richard Weiner, *The Game for Real*, trans. Benjamin Paloff (San Francisco: Two Lines Press, 2015).

137. Kristeva's notion of the abject has been used effectively to treat several topics in Gombrowicz's work, especially his construction of identity. See, for example, Tomislav Z. Longinović, "I, Witold Gombrowicz: Formal Abjection and the Power of Writing in *A Kind of Testament*," in *Gombrowicz's Grimaces: Modernism, Gender, Nationality*, ed. Ewa Płonowska Ziarek (Albany: State University of New York Press, 1998), 33–50; and Katarzyna Jerzak, "Defamation in Exile: Witold Gombrowicz and E. M. Cioran," also in *Gombrowicz's Grimaces*, 177–209.

138. Maryna Miklaszewska, "Wokół paryskiego okresu twórczości Richarda Weinera," *Pamiętnik słowiański* 26 (1976), 171–72.

139. Ibid., 172.

140. "I uvědomil jsem si, že vidím-li je oba z profilu, to že sobě tedy navzájem čelí. I vytanulo mi (jakoby poprvé), že pokaždé, když jsem usiloval o to, jak zmoci domnělou jeho ctnost, Fuld se vždy a bez výjimky stavěl tak, že jsem ho nemohl vidět jinak než z profilu." Weiner, *Lazebník/Hra doopravdy*, 240.

141. Steffi Widera, *Richard Weiner: Identität und Polarität im Prosafrühwerk* (Munich: Otto Sagner, 2001), 246–62.

142. Leonard Neuger, *Ćwiczenia z wrażliwości: Duże i małe szkice literackie* (Katowice: Wydawnictwo Uniwersytetu Śląskiego, 2006), 108.

143. Orig.: "To však, že jsem byl tváří v tvář *sobě*, nebylo nejstrašidelnější; strašidelnější ještě byla horlivost, s níž moje myšlenka domlouvala zdráhajícím se smyslům, že nejde o jejich klam; strašidelnější ještě bylo zjištění, že moje smysly, hned například zrak, se jaly žít mimo mou myšlenku. [. . .] Byl jsem na nohou, skokem před vysokým zrcadlem nad krbem—dím před vysokým zrcadlem nad krbem, a slunojasně věda, že před zrcadlem—, které však neodpovídalo. A zase: strašidelnější než zrada toho, mě, který se navzdory němé, ale odvěčné úmluvě z oněch hlubin nepřihlásil, byla moje horlivá, pochmurně rozjařená myšlenka,

domlouvající poplašeným smyslům, aby se nebály, aby neprchaly, že není proč se starat, že ono zrcadlo prázdné je zrcadlem správným, *že to tak musí být.*" Weiner, *Lazebník/Hra doopravdy,* 282–83.

144. Orig.: "Ukradl mi tvář; ukradl mi tvář." "Kterou?" Weiner, *Lazebník/ Hra doopravdy,* 283.

145. One is reminded of Philidor's inability to slap Anti-Philidor in Gombrowicz's story "Philidor Lined with Child," which is also the fifth chapter of *Ferdydurke.*

146. Orig.: "[S]tyděl se [. . .] a kochal se svým studem." Weiner, *Lazebník/ Hra doopravdy,* 302.

147. Orig.: "Neumím exteriorizovat." Ibid.

148. Orig.: "V láskyplné a uctivé zhlížení sebe je zabrán tak, že ho hutný tok chodců jako by vyplil a zanechal, za trest, že zradil pospolitost ulice; osamël; ale copak je samota jemu, jehož pletoričnost je taková, že je pospolitostí sám sobě? Ulice ho vyvrhla? On zase ji vyhladil. On a jeho obraz zamilovali se navzájem neodolatelní, nepřemožitelní, vládli; vládl. [. . .] A teď jde mimo zrcadlo on, slidič: podíval se letmým bočným pohledem . . . koho to vidí? Obstárlé dítě. A kazisvětský ten kuchtík principiálních petic si povídá: 'Tamten si na sobě dává záležet; když si na sobě dáváme záležet, stáváme se sebevědomými. Dávat si na sobě záležet!'" Ibid., 388–89.

149. Zdeněk Vašíček, *Přijetí podmínek* (Prague: Torst, 1996), 115. Notably, Vašíček couches his reading of Weiner's "impersonality" in a brief discussion of the interpenetration of the mythic and the real, a standard feature of intermediate literature.

150. Witold Gombrowicz, *Testament: Rozmowy z Dominique de Roux* (Kraków: Wydawnictwo Literackie, 1996), 44–45.

151. Bohumil Novák, "Richard Weiner," *Listy pro umění a kritiku* 2 (1934): 136.

152. Ibid., 136–37.

153. Orig.: "Když nazítří ráno vyšel a zamířil k náměstí, věděl dřív ještě, než zamkl, že ho už není: byl nahrazen svou pověstí. Pověstí, bez začátku ni konce, pověstí, zatím nečitelnou, ale proto právě věrohodnější než on sám a než banální průměrnost jeho chudinské existence." Weiner, *Lazebník/Hra doopravdy,* 356.

154. Tomáš Jirsa provides a detailed accounting of a different kind of dialogic interaction in Weiner's fiction, that which arises from the narrator's frequent intrusion into or sudden appearance within the narrative. See Tomáš Jirsa, "Dialog jako způsob existence v díle Richarda Weinera," *Česká literatura* 1 (2008): 73–100.

155. Petr Málek, "Allegories of Absence: Richard Weiner and Karel Čapek," *Central Europe* 9.2 (November 2011), 102.

156. Orig.: "Představte si, že byste jedli denně z téhož kvítkového talíře; znáte jej tak dobře, že by vám neušlo, kdyby jej zaměnili za talíř s kvítky trochu jinými. Ale jednoho dne jste se zadívali pozorněji, i odkryli jste drobný, posud přehlížený kaz. Zkuste to a hleďte jej—jak bych řekl?—hleďte jej fascinovat; upřete naň oči; chvíle, a patříte v jakési zdůvěrněné neskutečno; jedinou realitou nepopěrnou, skoro všední, zbyl právě onen dotud přehlížený kaz; je jakoby jedinou v mlhách jak tak zřetelnou formou, jenomže nevíte, 'kam ji dát'. [. . .] Tak

nějak bylo tomu s nevítanými mými hosty. Byli mi cizí; odcizili se mi zčistajasna, ne však tolik jako vlastní byt, ať si zůstával očím povědomý a nezměněný. Byli jaksi skutečnější než on. Byli to cizinci neznámí, ale byli to neznámí přikázaní, přislíbení; jenomže jsem nevěděl, 'kam je dát.'" Weiner, *Lazebník/Hra doopravdy,* 225.

157. Věra Linhartová, afterword to Richard Weiner, *Hra doopravdy* (Prague: Mladá fronta, 1967), 275.

158. Orig.: "Ruce, složené potud pod hlavou, sebou pohnuly; sunou se, hmatají, natahují se. Škubly sebou, stanuly, zamyslily se. Nahmátly jakoby nové, neznámé skupenství. Bylo to zvláštní: bylo to probuzení. Bylo to poznání, že on, jenž nevěděl o sobě dotud nic víc, než že jest, už také byl a ještě bude. Byl to objev trvání a řetězu, byl to objev minula a budoucna." Weiner, *Lazebník/Hra doopravdy,* 298.

159. Radim Vondráček, "Zářivé hlubiny: Vlastislav Hofman a kouskování věčna," in *Expresionismus a české umění* (Prague: Národní Galerie v Praze, 1994), 198.

160. Orig.: "Patřil do dýnka promaštěné čepice, čta tam, že život počíná tehdy právě, kdy jsme *počuli* (ale počuli, jako čijeme vůně, chuti nebo světla), že je závitnicí, která v mžikovém bodu Já jen začíná, a pak—stále závratněji a odstředivěji—se roztáčí do bytí bez konce a bez začátku, a se svobodou že se ženíme v oné chvíli právě, kdy nemůžeme jinak než *neklást* pomlku mezi dnes a zítra, já a ty, tuto a kdekoliv." Weiner, *Lazebník/Hra doopravdy,* 429.

161. Václav Černý, "Za Richardem Weinerem," in his *Tvorba a osobnost,* vol. 1 (Prague: Odeon, 1992), 592.

162. Orig.: "Innego końca świata nie będzie, / Innego końca świata nie będzie." Miłosz, *Wiersze,* vol. 1, 207–8.

Conclusion

The epigraph is from Wyka, *Rzecz wyobraźni,* 10.

1. Czesław Miłosz, *The Witness of Poetry* (Cambridge, Mass.: Harvard University Press, 1983), 7.

2. Elizabeth Grosz, *Space, Time, and Perversion: Essays on the Politics of Bodies* (New York: Routledge, 1995), 100.

3. Orig.: "W tym czasie ojciec mój umarł był już definitywnie. Umierał wielokrotnie, zawsze jeszcze nie doszczętnie, zawsze z pewnymi zastrzeżeniami, które zmuszały do rewizji tego faktu. Miało to swoją dobrą stronę. Rozdrabniając tak śmierć swą na raty, oswajał nas ojciec z faktem swego odejścia. Zobojętnieliśmy na jego powroty coraz bardziej zredukowane, za każdym razem żałośniejsze. Fizjonomia już nieobcnego rozeszła się niejako w pokoju, w którym żył, rozgałęziła się, tworząc w pewnych punktach przedziwne węzły podobieństwa o nieprawdopodobnej wyrazistości." Schulz, *Opowiadania,* 313.

4. Jacques Derrida, *Aporias,* trans. Thomas Dutoit (Stanford, Calif.: Stanford University Press, 1993), 36–42.

5. Franz Kafka, *The Blue Octavo Notebooks,* ed. Max Brod, trans. Ernst Kaiser and Eithne Wilkins (Cambridge, Mass.: Exact Change, 1991), 53.

6. Mircea Eliade, *The Myth of the Eternal Return, or, Cosmos and History,* trans. Willard R. Trask (Princeton, N.J.: Princeton University Press, 1954), 46–47.

7. Hannah Arendt, *Between Past and Future: Eight Exercises in Political Thought* (New York: Penguin, 1968), 147.

8. Ibid., 160.

9. Emmanuel Levinas, *God, Death, and Time,* trans. Bettina Bergo (Stanford, Calif.: Stanford University Press, 2000), 178.

10. See Alexander Vucinich, *Einstein and Soviet Ideology* (Stanford, Calif.: Stanford University Press, 2001), 56–88.

11. Nadezhda Mandel'shtam, *Hope Against Hope,* 377.

12. See Ficowski, *Regiony wielkiej herezji i okolice,* 390–407.

13. Magda Romanska, *The Post-Traumatic Theater of Grotowski and Kantor: History and Holocaust in* Akropolis *and* The Dead Class (London: Anthem Press, 2014), 229–37.

14. See, for example, Gerald Gillespie, *Proust, Mann, Joyce in the Modernist Context* (Washington, D.C.: Catholic University of America Press, 2003), 85–87.

15. Yves-Michel Ergal, *"Je" devient écrivain: Essai sur Proust et Joyce* (Paris: Editions Interuniversitaires, 1996), 240.

16. Laurence Stern, *The Life and Opinions of Tristram Shandy, Gentleman,* ed. Ian Campbell Ross (Oxford: Oxford University Press, 2009), 150.

WORKS CITED

Adorno, Theodore W. *Notes to Literature*. 2 vols. Ed. Rolf Tiedemann. Trans. Sherry Weber Nicholsen. New York: Columbia University Press, 1991.

———. *Prisms*. Trans. Shierry Weber Nicholsen and Samuel Weber. Cambridge, Mass.: MIT Press, 1983.

Agamben, Giorgio. *The End of the Poem: Studies in Poetics*. Trans. Daniel Heller-Roazen. Stanford, Calif.: Stanford University Press, 1999.

———. *The Open: Man and Animal*. Trans. Kevin Attell. Stanford, Calif.: Stanford University Press, 2003.

———. *Remnants of Auschwitz: The Witness and the Archive*. Trans. Daniel Heller-Roazen. New York: Zone Books, 2002.

Akhmatova, Anna. *Pobeda nad sud'boi* [Triumph over Fate]. 2 vols. Ed. N. I. Kraineva. Moscow: Russkii Put', 2005.

———. *Sobranie sochinenii v shesti tomakh* [Collected Works in Six Volumes]. Ed. S. A. Kovalenko. Moscow: Ellis Lak, 1998–2005.

Alvarez, Al. "Witness." *New York Review of Books* 35:9 (June 2, 1988): 21.

Anninskii, L. "Nikolai Zabolotskii: 'Ia sam iznemogal ot schast'ia bytiia . . .'" [Nikolai Zabolotskii: "I've Been Exhausted by the Joy of Being . . ."]. In *Nikolai Zabolotskii: Pro et contra*, ed. T. V. Igoshchevaia and I. E. Loshchilov, 645–60. St. Petersburg: RKhGA, 2010.

Antonii [Khrapovitskii], Arkhiepiskop, and Vladimir S. Soloviev. *F. M. Dostoevskii kak propovednik khristianskogo vozrozhdeniia i vselenskogo pravoslaviia* [Dostoevsky as a Preacher of Christian Rebirth and Universal Orthodoxy]. Moscow: Pechatnia A. I. Snegirevoi, 1908.

Arendt, Hannah. *Between Past and Future: Eight Exercises in Political Thought*. New York: Penguin, 1968.

Auerbach, Erich. *Dante: Poet of the Secular World*. Trans. Ralph Manheim. New York: New York Review Books, 2007.

Badiou, Alain. *The Century*. Trans. Alberto Toscano. Cambridge: Polity, 2007.

Bakhtin, M. M. *Besedy s V. D. Duvakinym* [Conversations with V. D. Duvakin]. Moscow: Soglasie, 2002.

———. *Literaturno-kriticheskie stat'i* [Articles in Literary Criticism]. Moscow: Khudozhestvennaia literatura, 1986.

———. *Sobranie sochinenii v semi tomakh* [Collected Works in Seven Volumes]. Ed. S. G. Bocharov and V. V. Kozhinov. Moscow: Russkie Slovari and Iazyki Slavianskikh Kul'tur, 1996–.

Barańczak, Stanisław. "Antynomie 'bycia w świecie,' albo Kobieca sztuka pośredniczenia" [The Antinomies of 'Being in the World,' or, The Women's Art of Mediation]. In *Ironia i harmonia*, 129–49. Warsaw: Czytelnik, 1973.

———. "Język poetycki Czesława Miłosza: Wstępne rozpoznanie" [The Poetic Language of Czesław Miłosz]. In *Poznawanie Miłosza: Studia i szkice o twórczości poety,* ed. Jerzy Kwiatkowski, 419–45. Kraków: Wydawnictwo Literackie, 1985.

———. *Pomyślane przepaście: Osiem interpretacji* [Well-Conceived Abysses: Eight Interpretations]. Katowice: Wydawnictwo Uniwersytetu Śląskiego, 1995.

Bartosik, Marta. *Bruno Schulz jako krytyk* [Bruno Schulz as Critic]. Kraków: Universitas, 2000.

Beddow, Michael. *The Fiction of Humanity: Studies in the Bildungsroman from Wieland to Mann.* Cambridge: Cambridge University Press, 1982.

Benjamin, Walter. "Franz Kafka." In Walter Benjamin, *Illuminations: Essays and Reflections,* ed. Hannah Arendt, trans. Harry Zohn, 111–40. New York: Schocken, 1968.

Bergson, Henri. *Creative Evolution,* Trans. Arthur Mitchell. New York: Modern Library, 1944.

"Bergson Heads League Scholars' Committee." *New York Times,* Aug. 2, 1922, 7.

Berman, Marshall. *All That Is Solid Melts into Air: The Experience of Modernity.* New York: Penguin, 1982.

Berressem, Hanjo. *Lines of Desire: Reading Gombrowicz's Fiction with Lacan.* Evanston, Ill.: Northwestern University Press, 1998.

Beyer, Thomas A., Jr. "Osip Mandel'shtam and the University of Heidelberg: Three Documents." *Slavonic and East European Review* 65.2 (April 1987): 236–37.

Bitov, Andrei. *Piatoe izmerenie: Na granitse vremeni i prostranstva.* Moscow: Izdatel'stvo Nezavisimaia Gazeta, 2002.

Blanchot, Maurice. *The Space of Literature.* Trans. Ann Smock. Lincoln: University of Nebraska Press, 1982.

Blecha, Ivan. *Edmund Husserl a česká filosofie* [Edmund Husserl and Czech Philosophy]. Olomouc: Nakladatelství Olomouc, 2003.

Blok, Aleksandr. *O literature* [On Literature]. 2nd ed. Ed. T. N. Bedniakova. Moscow: Khudozhestvennaia literatura, 1989.

Błoński, Jan. *Biedni Polacy patrzą na getto* [The Poor Poles Look at the Ghetto]. Kraków: Wydawnictwo Literackie, 1994.

———. *Wszystko, co literackie: Pisma wybrane* [Everything That Is Literary: Selected Writings]. 2 vols. Ed. Jerzy Jarzębski. Kraków: Wydawnictwo Literackie, 2001.

———. "Wzruszenie, dialog i mądrość" [Emotion, Dialogue, and Wisdom]. In *Poznawanie Miłosza: Studia i szkice o twórczości poety,* ed. Jerzy Kwiatkowski, 363–80. Kraków: Wydawnictwo Literackie, 1985.

Bogdanov, Aleksandr. *Empiriomonizm.* Vol. 1. Moscow: S. Dorovatovskii i A. Charushnikov, 1905.

Borenstein, Eliot. *Men without Women: Masculinity and Revolution in Russian Fiction, 1917–1929.* Durham, N.C.: Duke University Press, 2000.

Borges, Jorge Luis. *Collected Fictions.* Trans. Andrew Hurley. New York: Penguin, 1998.

Boym, Svetlana. *The Future of Nostalgia*. New York: Basic Books, 2001.
Brain, Stephen. "The Great Stalin Plan for the Transformation of Nature." *Environmental History* 15 (October 2012): 670–700.
Brod, Max. *Der Prager Kreis* [The Prague Circle]. Stuttgart: W. Kohlhammer, 1966.
Brodsky, Joseph. *Less than One: Selected Essays*. New York: Farrar Straus, & Giroux, 1986.
Brown, Russell E. *Myths and Relatives: Seven Essays on Bruno Schulz*. Munich: Otto Sagner, 1991.
Buber, Martin. *Between Man and Man*. London: Routledge, 2002.
Budzyński, Wiesław. *Miasto Schulza* [Schulz's City]. Warsaw: Prószyński i S-ka, 2005.
———. *Schulz pod kluczem* [Schulz under Lock and Key]. Warsaw: Bartelsmann, 2001.
Bugge, Peter. "Nákaza světa: Nemoc a epidemie v dílech Karla Čapka z konce třicátých let" [Infection of the World: Illness and Epidemic in Karel Čapek's Works from the Late 1930s]. *Česká literatura* 47.3 (1999): 241–58.
Bukwalt, Miłosz. *Literackie portrety żydowskich ojców w prozie Brunona Schulza i Danila Kiša* [Literary Portraits of Jewish Fathers in the Prose of Bruno Schulz and Danilo Kiš]. Wrocław: Wydawnictwo Uniwersytetu Wrocławskiego, 2003.
Bulgakov, S. N. *Sochineniia v dvukh tomakh* [Works in Two Volumes]. Ed. I. B. Rodnianskaia. Moscow: Nauka, 1993.
Bydžovská, Lenka. "The Avant-Garde Ideal of Poeisis: Poetism and Artificialism during the Late 1920s." Trans. Karolina Vočadlo. In *Karel Teige: L'Enfant Terrible of the Czech Modernist Avant-Garde, 1900–1951,* ed. Eric Dluhosch and Rotislav Švacha, 47–63. Cambridge, Mass.: MIT Press, 1999.
Bynum, Caroline Walker. *Metamorphosis and Identity*. New York: Zone Books, 2001.
Camus, Albert. *The Rebel*. Trans. Anthony Bower. New York: Vintage, 1956.
Caneppele, Paolo. "Bruno Schulz w Wiedniu" [Bruno Schulz in Vienna]. Trans. K. Sobczyński. In *W ułamkach zwierciadła: Bruno Schulz w 110 rocznicę urodzin i 60 rocznicę śmierci,* ed. Małgorzata Kitowska-Łysiak and Władysław Panas, 533–45. Lublin: Towarzystwo Naukowe Katolickiego Uniwersytetu Lubelskiego, 2003.
Čapek, Jan Blahoslav. "Karel Čapek: *Obyčejný život*" [Karel Čapek: An Ordinary Life]. *Naše doba* 42.1 (1935): 308.
Čapek, Karel. *Spisy* [Writings]. 24 vols. Prague: Československý spisovatel/ Český spisovatel, 1981–95.
———. *Univerzitní studie* [University Studies]. Ed. Miloš Pohorský. Prague: Československý spisovatel, 1987.
———. "Wyjątek z powieści *Karola Czapka—Hordubal,* która w tłumaczeniu Pawła Hulki-Laskowskiego ukaże się nakładem J. Przeworskiego" [Excerpt from Karel Čapek's Novel *Hordubal,* Soon to Appear from J. Przeworski, Publisher, Translated by Paweł Hulka-Laskowski]. *Tygodnik Ilustrowany* 76:25 (June 23, 1935): 488.

Cataluccio, Francesco. *Niedojrzałość: Choroba naszych czasów* [Immaturity: The Illness of Our Times]. Trans. Stanisław Kasprzysiak. Kraków: Znak, 2006.

Cavanagh, Clare. *Lyric Poetry and Modern Politics: Russia, Poland, and the West.* New Haven, Conn.: Yale University Press, 2009.

———. *Osip Mandelstam and the Modernist Creation of Tradition.* Princeton, N.J.: Princeton University Press, 1995.

Černý, Václav. *Paměti I (1921–1938)* [Memoirs I]. Brno: Atlantis, 1994.

———. *Tvorba a osobnost* [Creative Work and Personhood]. 2 vols. Prague: Odeon, 1992.

Chalupecký, Jindřich. *Expresionisté: Richard Weiner, Jakub Deml, Ladislav Klíma, Podivný Hašek* [Expressionists]. Prague: Torst, 1992.

Chizh, Vladimir. *Dostoevskii kak psikhopatolog* [Dostoevsky as Psychopathologist]. Moscow: M. Katkov, 1885.

Chmielowiec, Michał. "Zdarzenie bezdomne" [The Homeless Event]. *Kultura: Tygodnik literacki, artystycyny i społeczny* 3:13 (1938): 5.

Chmurzyński, Wojciech, ed. *Bruno Schulz, 1892–1942: Rysunki i archiwalia ze zbiorów Muzeum Literatury im. Adama Mickiewicza w Warszawie* [Bruno Schulz, 1892–1942: Drawings and Archival Materials from the Collections of the Adam Mickiewicz Museum of Literature in Warsaw]. Warsaw: Muzeum Literatury im. Adama Mickiewicza, 1992.

Chukovskii, Nikolai. "Vstrechi s Zabolotskim" [Encounters with Zabolotskii]. In *Vospominaniia o Zabolotskom,* ed. E. V. Zabolotskaia and A. V. Makedonov, 218–33. Moscow: Sovetskii pisatel', 1977.

Cioran, E. M. *History and Utopia.* Trans. Richard Howard. Chicago: University of Chicago Press, 1987.

———. *The Temptation to Exist.* Trans. Richard Howard. Chicago: Quadrangle Books, 1968.

Clark, Katerina. *Petersburg: Crucible of Cultural Revolution.* Cambridge, Mass.: Harvard University Press, 1995.

Clune, Michael W. *Writing against Time.* Stanford, Calif.: Stanford University Press, 2013.

Coetzee, J. M. *Inner Workings: Literary Essays, 2000–2005.* New York: Penguin, 2008.

Cornwell, Neil. *The Absurd in Literature.* Manchester: Manchester University Press, 2006.

Cravens, Craig S. "Čapek's *Hordubal* and Dostoevsky's *The Double:* Madness and Free-Indirect Discourse." *Comparative Literature* 52.1 (2000): 53–71.

Crone, Anna Lisa, and Jennifer Day. *My Petersburg/Myself: Mental Architecture and Imaginative Space in Modern Russian Letters.* Bloomington, Ind.: Slavica, 2004.

Danius, Sara. *The Senses of Modernism: Technology, Perception, Aesthetics.* Ithaca, N.Y.: Cornell University Press, 2002.

Daston, Lorraine, and Peter Galison. *Objectivity.* New York: Zone Books, 2007.

Davydov, Iurii. *Begstvo ot svobody: Filosofskoe mifotvorchestvo i literaturnyi avangard* [Escape from Freedom: Philosophical Mythmaking and the Literary Avant-Garde]. Moscow: Khudozhestvennaia literatura, 1978.

DeKoven, Marianne. "Male Signature, Female Aesthetic: The Gender Politics of Experimental Writing." In *Breaking the Sequence: Women's Experimental Fiction,* ed. Ellen G. Friedman and Miriam Fuchs, 72–81. Princeton, N.J.: Princeton University Press, 1989).

Demetz, Peter. *Prague in Black and Gold: Scenes in the Life of a European City.* New York: Hill and Wang, 1997.

Derrida, Jacques. *Aporias.* Trans. Thomas Dutoit. Stanford, Calif.: Stanford University Press, 1993.

———. *Given Time: I. Counterfeit Money.* Trans. Peggy Kamuf. Chicago: University of Chicago Press, 1992.

Dmitrovskaia, M. A. "Zagadka vremeni: A. Platonov i O. Shpengler" [The Riddle of Time: A. Platonov and O. Spengler]. In *Logicheskii analiz iazyka: Iazyk i vremia,* ed. N. D. Arutiunova and T. E. Ianko, 302–13. Moscow: Indrik, 1997.

Doležel, Lubomír. *Narrative Modes in Czech Literature.* Toronto: University of Toronto Press, 1973.

———. "Radical Semantics: Franz Kafka and Richard Weiner." In *Forms and Functions,* ed. Jürgen Esser and Axel Hübler, 225–29. Tübingen: Gunter Narr, 1981.

[Dostoevsky] Dostoevskii, F. M. *Polnoe sobranie sochinenii v tridtsati tomakh* [Complete Collected Works in 30 Volumes]. 30 vols. Leningrad: Nauka, 1972–90.

Drozda, Miroslav. "Umělecký prostor v próze Andreje Platonova" [Artistic Space in Andrei Platonov's Prose]. In *Východoevropská moderna a její evropský kontext,* vol. 1, ed. Ladislav Zadražil, 125–41. Prague: Nakladatelství Karolinum, 1999.

Dutli, Ralph. *Mandelstam: Meine Zeit, mein Tier: Ein Biografie* [Mandel'shtam: My Age, My Beast: A Biography]. Zurich: Ammann, 2003.

Einstein, Albert. *Relativity: The Special and the General Theory.* Trans. Robert W. Lawson. London: Routledge, 2001.

Eliade, Mircea. *The Myth of the Eternal Return, or, Cosmos and History.* Trans. Willard R. Trask. Princeton, N.J.: Princeton University Press, 1954.

Eliot, T. S. "Tradition and the Individual Talent [1919]." In *Selected Prose of T.S. Eliot,* ed. Frank Kermode, 36–44. New York: Harcourt, 1975.

Epstein, Mikhail. "Russo-Soviet Topoi." Trans. Jeffrey Karlsen. In *The Landscape of Stalinism: The Art and Ideology of Soviet Space,* ed. Evgeny Dobrenko and Eric Naiman, 277–310. Seattle: University of Washington Press, 2003.

Ergal, Yves-Michel. *"Je" devient écrivain : Essai sur Proust et Joyce* ["I" Becomes the Writer: An Essay on Proust and Joyce]. Paris: Editions Interuniversitaires, 1996.

Eskin, Michael. "Bakhtin on Poetry." *Poetics Today* 21.2 (Summer 2000): 379–91.

———. *Ethics and Dialogue in the Works of Levinas, Bakhtin, Mandel'shtam, and Celan.* Oxford: Oxford University Press, 2000.

Faggen, Robert. "Czesław Miłosz: The Art of Poetry LXX." *Paris Review* 36.133 (Winter 1994): 243–73.

Faivre-Dupaigre, Anne. "Toska po edinstvu: O vliianii Bergsona na rannego Mandel'shtama" [The Longing for Unity: On Bergson's Influence on Early Mandel'shtam]. *Russian Literature* 42 (1997): 137–151.

Ficowski, Jerzy, ed. *Bruno Schulz: Listy, fragmenty, wspomnienia o pisarzu* [Bruno Schulz: Letters, Fragments, Recollections about the Author]. Kraków: Wydawnictwo Literackie, 1984.

———. *Regions of the Great Heresy: Bruno Schulz, a Biographical Portrait.* Trans. Theodosia S. Robertson. New York: W. W. Norton, 2003.

———. *Regiony wielkiej herezji i okolice: Bruno Schulz i jego mitologia* [Regions of the Great Heresy and Their Surroundings: Bruno Schulz and His Mythology]. Sejny: Pogranicze, 2002.

Filippov, G. B. *Russkaia sovetskaia filosofskaia poeziia: Chelovek i priroda* [Soviet Russian Philosophical Poetry: Man and Nature]. Leningrad: Izdatel'stvo Leningradskogo universiteta, 1984.

Fink, Hilary L. *Bergson and Russian Modernism, 1900–1930.* Evanston, Ill.: Northwestern University Press, 1999.

Fiut, Aleksander. *The Eternal Moment: The Poetry of Czesław Miłosz.* Trans. Theodosia S. Robertson. Berkeley: University of California Press, 1990.

———. *Moment wieczny: Poezja Czesława Miłosza.* Kraków: Wydawnictwo Literackie, 1998.

Fletcher, Angus. *Time, Space, and Motion in the Age of Shakespeare.* Cambridge, Mass.: Harvard University Press, 2007.

Foucault, Michel. *The Order of Things: An Archaeology of the Human Sciences.* New York: Vintage, 1970.

———. *Security, Territory, Population: Lectures at the College de France, 1977–1978.* Ed. Michel Senellart. Trans. Graham Burchell. New York: Picador, 2009.

Freidin, Gregory. *A Coat of Many Colors: Osip Mandel'shtam and His Mythologies of Self-Presentation.* Berkeley: University of California Press, 1987.

Freud, Sigmund. "Mourning and Melancholia." In *The Penguin Freud Reader,* ed. Adam Phillips, 310–25. New York: Penguin, 2006.

———. *The Standard Edition of the Complete Psychological Works of Sigmund Freud.* 24 vols. Ed. James Strachey et al. London: Hogarth Press, 1953–74.

Fromm, Erich. *Escape from Freedom.* New York: Henry Holt, 1994.

Frye, Northrop. *Myth and Metaphor: Selected Essays, 1974–1988.* Ed. Robert D. Denham. Charlottesville: University Press of Virginia, 1990.

Galison, Peter. *Einstein's Clocks, Poincaré's Maps: Empires of Time.* New York: W. W. Norton, 2003.

Gasparov, Mikhail. "M. M. Bakhtin in Russian Culture of the Twentieth Century." In *Critical Essays on Mikhail Bakhtin,* ed. Caryl Emerson, 83–85. New York: G. K. Hall, 1999.

———. "Poet i kul'tura: Tri poetiki Osipa Mandel'shtam" [The Poet and Culture: The Three Poetics of Osip Mandel'shtam]. In Osip Mandel'shtam, *Pol'noe sobranie stikhotvorenii,* ed. Mikhail Gasparov and A. G. Mets, 5–64. St. Petersburg: Akademicheskii Proekt, 1997.

Gibian, George. "Karel Čapek's Apocrypha and Franz Kafka's Parables." *American Slavic and East European Review* 18.2 (April 1959): 238–47.

Gillespie, Gerald. *Proust, Mann, Joyce in the Modernist Context.* Washington, D.C.: Catholic University of America Press, 2003.

Ginzburg, Lidiia. *O lirike* [On Lyric]. Moscow: Intrada, 1997.

———. *Zapisnye knizhki, Vospominaniia, Esse* [Notebooks, Memoirs, Essays]. St. Petersburg: Iskusstvo-SPB, 2002.

Goldberg, Stuart. *Mandel'shtam, Blok, and the Boundaries of Mythopoetic Symbolism*. Columbus: Ohio State University Press, 2011.

Goldstein, Darra. *Nikolai Zabolotskii: Play for Mortal Stakes*. Cambridge: Cambridge University Press, 1993.

Gombrowicz, Witold. *Bakakaj i inne opowiadania*. Vol. 1 of *Pisma zebrane*. Ed. Zdzisław Łapiński. Kraków: Wydawnictwo Literackie, 2002.

———. *Czytelnicy i krytycy: Proza, reportaże, krytyka literacka, eseje, przedmowy* [Readers and Critics: Prose, Journalism, Literary Criticism, Essays, Prefaces]. Ed. Maria Rola. Kraków: Wydawnictwo Literackie, 2004.

———. *Dziennik, 1957–1961* [Diary]. Vol. 8 of *Dzieła*, ed. Jan Błoński. Kraków: Wydawnictwo Literackie, 1986.

———. *Ferdydurke*. Vol. 2 of *Pisma zebrane*. Ed. Włodimierz Bolecki. Kraków: Wydawnictwo Literackie, 2007.

———. Letter to Martin Buber, Buenos Aires (July 25, 1951). Gombrowicz Archive, Beinecke Library, Yale University, gen. MSS. 515, series 1, box 2, item 51.

———. "Przeklęte zdrobnienie znowu dało mi się we znaki (Obrońcom poetów w odpowiedzi) [Accursed Dimunition Has Made Me Miserable Again (In Response to the Defenders of Poets)]." In Czesław Miłosz, *Zaczynając od moich ulic*, 142–52. Kraków: Znak, 2006.

———. *Proza (Fragmenty), Reportaże, Krytyka literacka, 1933–1939* [Prose (Fragments), Journalism, Literary Criticism 1933–1939]. Vol. 12 of *Dzieła*, ed. Jerzy Jarzębski. Kraków: Wydawnictwo Literackie, 1995.

———. *Testament: Rozmowy z Dominique de Roux* [Testament: Conversations with Dominique de Roux]. Kraków: Wydawnictwo Literackie, 1996.

———. *Wspomnienia polskie* [Polish Memories]. Kraków: Wydawnictwo Literackie, 2002.

Goślicki-Baur, Elisabeth. *Die Prosa von Bruno Schulz* [Bruno Schulz's Prose]. Frankfurt: Peter Lang, 1975.

Greenberg, Jack. "From Kafka to Kafkaesque." In Franz Kafka, *The Office Writings*, ed. Stanley Corngold, Jack Greenberg, and Benno Wagner, trans. Eric Patton and Ruth Hein, 355–71. Princeton, N.J.: Princeton University Press, 2009.

Grosz, Elizabeth. *Space, Time, and Perversion: Essays on the Politics of Bodies*. New York: Routledge, 1995.

Grudzińska-Gross, Irena. *Czesław Miłosz and Joseph Brodsky: Fellowship of Poets*. New Haven, Conn.: Yale University Press, 2009.

Gumbrecht, Hans Ulrich. *In 1926: Living at the Edge of Time*. Cambridge, Mass.: Harvard University Press, 1998.

Hägglund, Martin. *Dying for Time: Proust, Woolf, Nabokov*. Cambridge, Mass.: Harvard University Press, 2012.

Harkins, William E. *Karel Čapek*. New York: Columbia University Press, 1962.

Harp, Jerry. Introduction. In *A Poetry Criticism Reader*, ed. Jerry Harp and Jan Weissmiller, 1–16. Iowa City: University of Iowa Press, 2006.

Harris, Jane Gary. *Osip Mandelstam*. Boston: Twayne, 1988.

Hasty, Olga Peters. *Tsvetaeva's Orphic Journeys in the Worlds of the Word.* Evanston, Ill.: Northwestern University Press, 1996.

Heftrich, Urs. "Karel Čapeks Auseinandersetzung mit Henri Bergson" [Karel Čapek's Dispute with Henri Bergson]. *Zeitschrift für Slavische Philologie* 50.2 (1990): 354–87.

Hegel, G. W. F. *Phenomenology of Spirit.* Trans. A. V. Miller. Oxford: Oxford University Press, 1977.

Heidegger, Martin. *Being and Time: A Translation of* Sein und Zeit. Trans. Joan Stambaugh. Albany: State University of New York Press, 1996.

———. *Poetry, Language, Thought.* Trans. Albert Hofstadter. New York: Harper and Row, 1971.

Hinz, Manfred. "The Future and Catastrophe: The Concept of History in Italian Futurism." In *The Promise of History: Essays in Political Philosophy,* ed. Athanasios Moulakis, 172–203. Berlin: Walter de Gruyter, 1985.

Hirsch, Edward. *Poet's Choice.* New York: Harcourt, 2006.

Hodrová, Daniela. "Sebereflexívní román" [The Self-Reflexive Novel]. In *Poetika české meziválečné literatury: Proměny žánrů* [The Poetics of Interwar Czech Literature: Metamorphoses of Genre], ed. Daniela Hodrová et al., 156–77. Prague: Československý spisovatel, 1987.

———. "Smysl pokoje" [The Meaning of a Room]. In *Poetika míst: Kapitoly z literární tematologie* [The Poetics of Places: Chapters from Literary Thematology], ed. Daniela Hodrová et al., 217–38. Prague: H&H, 1997.

Holquist, Michael, and Katerina Clark. *Mikhail Bakhtin.* Cambridge, Mass.: Harvard University Press, 1984.

Horkheimer, Max, and Theodore W. Adorno. *Dialectic of Enlightenment: Philosophical Fragments.* Ed. Gunzelin Schmid Noerr. Trans. Edmund Jephcott. Stanford, Calif.: Stanford University Press, 2002.

Husserl, Edmund. *The Crisis of European Sciences and Transcendental Phenomenology: An Introduction to Phenomenological Psychology.* Trans. David Carr. Evanston, Ill.: Northwestern University Press, 1970.

———. *Logical Investigations.* 2 vols. Trans. J. N. Findlay. London: Routledge, 2001.

Iablokov, E. A. "'Bezumnyi volk' N. Zabolotskogo i 'vol'chi' motivy v literature 1920-kh godov" [N. Zabolotskii's "Insane Wolf" and "Wolf" Motifs in the Literature of the 1920s]. In *"Strannaia" poeziia i "strannaia"proza* ["Strange" Poetry and "Strange" Prose], ed. E. A. Iablokov and I. E. Loshchilov, 275–88. Moscow: Piataia strana, 2003.

———. *Na beregu neba: Roman Andreia Platonova* Chevengur [At Heaven's Edge: Andrei Platonov's Novel *Chevengur*]. St. Petersburg: D. Bulanin, 2001.

Ingarden, Roman. *The Literary Work of Art: An Investigation on the Borderlines of Ontology, Logic, and Theory of Literature.* Trans. George G. Grabowicz. Evanston, Ill.: Northwestern University Press, 1973.

Ivanov, Viacheslav. *Rodnoe i vselenskoe* [The Native and the Universal]. Ed. V. M. Tolmachev. Moscow: Respublika, 1994.

Ivanov, Viach. Vs. *Izbrannye trudy po semiotike i istorii kul'tury, Tom 2: Stat'i o russkoi literature* [Selected Works in Semiotics and Cultural History, Vol. 2: Articles on Russian Literature]. Moscow: Iazyki russkoi kul'tury, 2000.

———. "'Stikhi o neizvestnom soldate' v kontekste mirovoi poezii" ["Poem of the Unknown Soldier" in the Context of World Poetry]. In *Zhizn' i tvorchestvo O. E. Mandel'shtama: Vospominaniia, materialy k biografii, "novye stikhi," kommentarii, issledovaniia*, ed. S. S. Averintsev et al., 356–66. Voronezh: Izdatel'stvo Voronezhskogo Universiteta, 1990.

Jakobson, Roman. *Language in Literature*. Ed. Krystyna Pomorska and Stephen Rudy. Cambridge, Mass.: Harvard University Press, 1987.

———. *My Futurist Years*. Ed. Bengt Jangfeldt. Trans. Stephen Rudy. New York: Marsilio, 1992.

Janaszek-Ivaničková, Halina. *Karel Čapek*. Warsaw: Czytelnik, 1985.

Janecek, Gerald. *ZAUM: The Transrational Poetry of Russian Futurism*. San Diego: San Diego State University Press, 1996.

Jarzębski, Jerzy. *Podglądanie Gombrowicza* [Gombrowicz's Peeping]. Kraków: Wydawnictwo Literackie, 2000.

———. *Prowincja centrum: Przypisy do Schulza* [Province Central: Notes on Schulz]. Kraków: Wydawnictwo Literackie, 2005.

———. *W Polsce czyli wszędzie* [In Poland, That Is, Everywhere]. Warsaw: Wydawnictwo PEN, 1992.

———. "Wstęp" [Introduction]. In Bruno Schulz, *Opowiadania, wybór esejów i listów* [Stories, Selected Essays and Letters], ed. Jerzy Jarzębski, iii–cxxv. Wrocław: Ossolineum, 1989.

Jarzębski, Jerzy, and Teresa Jarzębska. "Uwagi o semantyce przestrzeni i czasu w prozie Brunona Schulza" [Remarks on the Semantics of Space and Time in the Prose of Bruno Schulz]. In *Studia o Prozie Brunona Schulza*, ed. Kazimiera Czaplowa, 49–72. Katowice: Uniwersytet śląski, 1976.

Jaspers, Karl. *Truth and Symbol*. Trans. Jean T. Wilde, William Kluback, and William Kimmel. New Haven, Conn.: College and University Press, 1959.

Jastrun, Mieczysław. "Poza rzeczywistością historyczną" [Beyond Historical Reality]. *Kuźnica* 1:1 (June 1, 1945): 13–17.

Jaszewska, Dagmara. *Nasza niedojrzała kultura: Postmodernizm inspirowany Gombrowiczem* [Our Immature Culture: The Postmodernism That Gombrowicz Inspired]. Warsaw: Oficyna naukowa, 2002.

Jelínek, Antonín. *Vítězslav Nezval*. Prague: Československý spisovatel, 1961.

Jelínek, H. "*R. U. R.* v Paříže" [*R. U. R.* in Paris]. *Lumír* 51.4 (1924): 218–19.

Jerzak, Katarzyna. "Defamation in Exile: Witold Gombrowicz and E. M. Cioran." In *Gombrowicz's Grimaces: Modernism, Gender, Nationality*, ed. Ewa Płonowska Ziarek, 177–209. Albany: State University of New York Press, 1998.

Jirsa, Tomáš. "Dialog jako způsob existence v díle Richarda Weinera" [Dialogue as a Means of Existence in Richard Weiner's Work]. *Česká literatura* 1 (2008): 73–100.

Joyce, James. *Ulysses*. New York: Vintage, 1990.

Kafka, Franz. *The Blue Octavo Notebooks*. Ed. Max Brod. Trans. Ernst Kaiser and Eithne Wilkins. Cambridge, Mass.: Exact Change, 1991.

———. *The Complete Stories*. Ed. Nahum N. Glatzer. New York: Schocken, 1971.

———. *The Diaries, 1910–1923*. Ed. Max Brod. New York: Schocken, 1949.

———. *Kritische Kafka-Ausgabe: Drucke zu Lebzeiten*. Ed. Hans-Gerd Koch. Frankfurt: S. Fischer, 1994.

———. *Kritische Kafka-Ausgabe: Nachgelassene Schriften und Fragmente*. Ed. Jost Schillemeit. Vol. 2.1. Frankfurt: S. Fischer, 1992.

———. *The Zürau Aphorisms*. Ed. Roberto Calasso. Trans. Michael Hofmann and Geoffrey Brock. New York: Schocken, 2006.

Karl, Frederick. *Franz Kafka: Representative Man*. New York: Fromm, 1993.

Kenner, Hugh. *Flaubert, Joyce and Beckett: The Stoic Comedians*. Urbana, Ill.: Dalkey Archive Press, 2005.

Kern, Stephen. *The Culture of Time and Space, 1880–1918*. Cambridge, Mass.: Harvard University Press, 1983.

———. *The Modernist Novel: A Critical Introduction*. Cambridge: Cambridge University Press, 2011.

Kierkegaard, Søren. *Fear and Trembling/Repetition*. Ed. and trans. Howard V. Hong and Edna H. Hong. Princeton, N.J.: Princeton University Press, 1983.

Kitowska-Łysiak, Małgorzata. "Wizje kobiecości w *Xięgze bałwochwalczej*: Salome i Androgyne" [Visions of Womanhood in *The Book of Idolatry*: Salome and Androgyne]. In *Czytanie Schulza: Materiały międzynarodowej sesji naukowej Bruno Schulz—w stulecie urodzin i w pięćdziesięciolecie śmierci*, ed. Jerzy Jarzębski, 251–63. Kraków: Instytut Filologii Polskiej UJ, 1994.

Kołakowski, Leszek. *Metaphysical Horror*. Trans. Agnieszka Kołakowska. Chicago: University of Chicago Press, 2001.

Koni, A. F. *Sobranie sochinenii v vos'mi tomakh* [Collected Works in Eight Volumes]. Moscow: Izdatel'stvo "Iuridicheskaia literatura," 1966–69.

Kordela, A. Kiarina. "Kafkaesque: (Secular) Kabbalah and Allegory." In *Freedom and Confinement in Modernity: Kafka's Cages*, ed. A. Kiarina Kordela and Dimitris Vardoulakis, 127–58. New York: Palgrave Macmillan, 2011.

Korecki, Grzegorz. "Kategorie czasu w Prozie Brunona Schulza" [Categories of Time in the Prose of Bruno Schulz]. *Przegląd Humanistyczny* 25.1–2 (1981): 139–59.

Kornienko, N. V. Commentary to Andrei Platonov, *Noev kovcheg* [Noah's Ark]. *Novyi mir* 9 (1993): 137–38.

Kotkin, Stephen. *Magnetic Mountain: Stalinism as a Civilization*. Berkeley: University of California Press, 1995.

Kott, Jan. *Po prostu* [Simply]. Warsaw: Książka, 1946.

———. *The Theater of Essence and Other Essays*. Evanston, Ill.: Northwestern University Press, 1984.

Kristeva, Julia. *Time and Sense: Proust and the Experience of Literature*. New York: Columbia University Press, 1996.

Krzhizhanovskii, Sigizmund. *Sobranie sochinenii v piati tomakh* [Collected Works in Five Volumes]. Ed. Vadim Perel'muter. St. Petersburg: Symposium, 2001–10.

Kundera, Milan. *The Art of the Novel*. Trans. Linda Asher. New York: Harper and Row, 1988.

———. *Umění románu: Cesta Vladislava Vančury za velkou epikou* [The Art of the Novel: Vladislav Vančura's Road to the Great Epic]. Prague: Československý spisovatel, 1961.

Kwiatkowski, Jerzy. *Dwudziestolecie międzywojenne* [The Interwar Period]. Warsaw: Wydawnictwo PWN, 2001.
Lacan, Jacques. *Ecrits: A Selection.* Trans. Alan Sheridan. New York: W. W. Norton, 1977.
Lefebvre, Henri. *Critique of Everyday Life, Vol. 2, Foundations for a Sociology of the Everyday.* Trans. John Moore. London: Verso, 2002.
Lekmanov, Oleg. *Zhizn' Osipa Mandel'shtama: Dokumental'noe povestvovanie* [The Life of Osip Mandel'shtam: A Documentary Narrative]. St. Petersburg: Zvezda, 2003.
Lenin, V. I. *Polnoe sobranie sochinenii v 55-x tomakh* [Complete Collected Works in Fifty-Five Volumes]. 5th ed. Moscow: Gosudarstvennoe izdatel'stvo politicheskoi literatury, 1959–65.
———. *The State and Revolution.* Trans. Robert Service. New York: Penguin, 1992.
Levinas, Emmanuel. *God, Death, and Time.* Trans. Bettina Bergo. Stanford, Calif.: Stanford University Press, 2000.
———. *On Escape.* Trans. Bettina Bergo. Stanford, Calif.: Stanford University Press, 2003.
Lewis, C. S. *The Lion, the Witch and the Wardrobe.* New York: HarperCollins, 2009.
Linhartová, Věra. Afterword to Richard Weiner, *Hra doopravdy.* Prague: Mladá fronta, 1967.
——. *Joseph Sima: Ses amis, ses contemporains* [Josef Šima: His Friends, His Contemporaries]. Brussels: La Connaissance, 1974.
Lipkin, S. "Golos druga" [A Friend's Voice]. In *Andrei Platonov: Vospominaniia sovremennikov, Materialy k biografii,* ed. N. V. Kornienko and E. D. Shubina, 120–24. Moscow: Sovremennyi pisatel', 1994.
Livingstone, Angela. "Meditations on Strangeness in Other Writers." In *"Strannaia" poeziia i "strannaia"proza* ["Strange" Poetry and "Strange" Prose], ed. E. A. Iablokov and I. E. Loshchilov, 289–303. Moscow: Piataia strana, 2003.
Longinović, Tomislav Z. "I, Witold Gombrowicz: Formal Abjection and the Power of Writing in *A Kind of Testament.*" In *Gombrowicz's Grimaces: Modernism, Gender, Nationality,* ed. Ewa Płonowska Ziarek, 33–50. Albany: State University of New York Press, 1998.
Lossky, N. O. *History of Russian Philosophy.* New York: International Universities Press, 1951.
Lukács, Georg. *History and Class Consciousness: Studies in Marxist Dialectics.* Trans. Rodney Livingstone. Cambridge, Mass.: MIT Press, 1971.
———. *Soul and Form.* Trans. Anna Bostock. Cambridge, Mass.: MIT Press, 1974.
———. *The Theory of the Novel.* Trans. Anna Bostock. Cambridge, Mass.: MIT Press, 1971.
Maiakovskii, Vladimir, et al. "Poshchechina obshchestvennomu vkusu" [A Slap in the Face of Public Taste]. In *Literaturnye manifesty ot simvolizma do nashikh dnei,* ed. S. B. Dzhimbinov, 142–43. Moscow: XXI Vek/Soglasie, 2000.
Majchrowski, Zbigniew. "'Białe małżeństwo' czyli 'ślub w kościele ludzkim'" ["Unconsummated Marriage," or, "A Wedding in the Human Church"]. *Teksty* 34.1 (1977): 106–21.

Makedonov, A. *Nikolai Zabolotskii: Zhizn', tvorchestvo, metamorfozy* [Nikolai Zabolotskii: Life, Work, Metamorphoses]. Leningrad: Sovetskii pisatel', 1968.

Málek, Petr. "Allegories of Absence: Richard Weiner and Karel Čapek." *Central Europe* 9.2 (November 2011): 83–107.

Malevič, Oleg. *Bratři Čapkové* [The Čapek Brothers]. Trans. Hana Štěpánková. Prague: Ivo Železný, 1999.

Malmstad, John E., and Nikolay Bogomolov. *Mikhail Kuzmin: A Life in Art.* Cambridge, Mass.: Harvard University Press, 1999.

Mandel'shtam, Nadezhda. *Hope against Hope.* Trans. Max Hayward New York: Atheneum, 1970.

———. *Vospominaniia* [Memoirs]. Ed. Iurii Freidin. Moscow: Soglasie, 1999.

Mandel'shtam, Osip. *Polnoe sobranie stikhotvorenii* [Complete Collected Poems]. Ed. M. L. Gasparov and A. G. Mets. St. Petersburg: Akademicheskii Proekt, 1997.

———. *Sobranie sochinenii v chetyrekh tomakh* [Collected Works in Four Volumes]. Ed. P. Nerler and A. Nikitaev. Moscow: Art-Biznes-Tsentr, 1993–97.

———. *Stikhotvoreniia.* Ed. N. I. Khardzhiev. 2nd ed. Leningrad: Sovetskii pisatel', 1974.

Mann, Klaus. Preface. In Franz Kafka, *Amerika,* trans. Willa Muir and Edwin Muir, vii–xviii. New York: Schocken, 1974.

Mann, Thomas. *The Magic Mountain.* Trans. John E. Woods. New York: Vintage, 1995.

Margański, Janusz. *Geografia pragnień: Opowieść o Gombrowiczu* [The Geography of Desires: A Narrative about Gombrowicz]. Kraków: Wydawnictwo Literackie, 2005.

———. *Gombrowicz wieczny debiutant* [Gombrowicz, Eternal Novice]. Kraków: Wydawnictwo Literackie, 2001.

Markowski, Michał Paweł. *Polska literatura nowoczesna: Leśmian, Schulz, Witkacy* [Modern Polish Literature: Leśmian, Schulz, Witkacy]. Kraków: Universitas, 2007.

Masing-Delić, Irene. *Abolishing Death: A Salvation Myth of Russian Twentieth-Century Literature.* Stanford, Calif.: Stanford University Press, 1992.

Masłowski, Michel. "Miłosz et le religieux" [Miłosz and the Religious]. In *Czesław Miłosz et le vingtième siècle,* ed. Maria Delaperrière, 211–230. Paris: Institut d'études slaves, 2006.

Meerson, Ol'ga. *Svobodnaia veshch': Poetika neostraneniia u Andreia Platonova* [A Free Thing: The Poetics of Non-Defamiliarization in Andrei Platonov]. Oakland: Berkeley Slavic Specialties, 1997.

Melberg, Arne. *Theories of Mimesis.* Cambridge: Cambridge University Press, 1995.

Michalski, Krzysztof. *The Flame of Eternity: An Interpretation of Nietzsche's Thought.* Trans. Benjamin Paloff. Princeton, N.J.: Princeton University Press, 2012.

Mikheev, Mikhail. *V mir Platonova cherez ego iazyk: Predlozheniia, fakty, istolkovaniia, dogadki* [Into Platonov's World through His Language: Suggestions, Facts, Interpretations, Guesses]. Moscow: MGU, 2003.

Miklaszewska, Maryna. "Wokół paryskiego okresu twórczości Richarda Weinera" [Concerning the Parisian Period of Richard Weiner's Work]. *Pamiętnik słowiański* 26 (1976): 161–81.

Milner-Gulland, Robin. "Nikolai Zabolotskii (1903–1958)." *Slavonica* 9.2 (November 2003): 123–25.

———. "Zabolotsky: Philosopher-Poet." *Soviet Studies* 22.4 (April 1971): 595–608.

Miłosz, Czesław. *The Captive Mind*. Trans. Jane Zielonko. New York: Vintage, 1981.

———. *The History of Polish Literature*. 2nd ed. Berkeley: University of California Press, 1983.

———. *Legends of Modernity: Essays and Letters from Occupied Poland, 1942–1943*. Trans. Madeline G. Levine. New York: Farrar, Straus & Giroux, 2005.

———. *Metafizyczna pauza* [Metaphysical Pause]. Ed. Joanna Gromek. Kraków: Znak, 1989.

———. *New and Collected Poems (1931–2001)*. New York: Ecco, 2001.

———. *Noty o wygnaniu/Notes on Exile*. Łomża: Norbertinum, 2006.

———. *Piesek przydrożny* [Road-Side Dog]. Kraków: Znak, 2011.

———. *Podróżny świata—Rozmowy z Renatą Gorczyńską* [Passenger of the World: Conversations with Renata Gorczyńska]. Kraków: Wydawnictwo Literackie, 2002.

———. *Poemat o czasie zastygłym* [Poem on Frozen Time]. Vilnius: Koło Polonistów Słuchaczy Uniwersytetu Stefana Batorego, 1933.

———. "A Poet's Reply." *New York Review of Books* 35:12 (July 21, 1988): n.p.

———. *Prywatne obowiązki* [Private Obligations]. Kraków: Wydawnictwo Literackie, 2001.

———. *Przygody młodego umysłu* [Adventures of a Young Mind]. Kraków: Znak, 2003.

———. *Road-Side Dog*. Trans. Czesław Miłosz and Robert Hass. New York: Farrar, Straus and Giroux, 1998.

———. *Rodzinna Europa* [Native Realm]. Kraków: Wydawnictwo Literackie, 2001.

———. *To Begin Where I Am: Selected Essays*. New York: Farrar, Straus and Giroux, 2001.

———. *Wiersze* [Poems]. 3 vols. Kraków: Znak, 1993.

———. *Wiersze* [Poems]. 5 vols. Ed. Aleksander Fiut. Kraków: Znak, 2001–9.

———. *The Witness of Poetry*. Cambridge, Mass.: Harvard University Press, 1983.

———. *Zaczynając od moich ulic* [Beginning with My Streets]. Kraków: Znak, 2006.

Miłosz, Czesław, and Jarosław Iwaszkiewicz. *Portret podwójny* [Double Portrait]. Ed. Barbara Toruńczyk and Robert Papieski. Warsaw: Zeszyty Literackie, 2011.

Molok, Yuri. "Children's Drawing in Russian Futurism." Trans. Sophy Thompson. In *Discovering Child Art: Essays on Childhood, Primitivism, and Mod-*

ernism, ed. Jonathan Fineberg, 55–67. Princeton, N.J.: Princeton University Press, 1998.

Moretti, Franco. *Graphs, Maps, Trees: Abstract Models for a Literary History.* London: Verso, 2005.

Morson, Gary Saul. *Narrative and Freedom: The Shadows of Time.* New Haven, Conn.: Yale University Press, 1994.

Morson, Gary Saul, and Caryl Emerson. *Mikhail Bakhtin: Creation of a Prosaics.* Stanford, Calif.: Stanford University Press, 1990.

Musil, Robert. *The Man Without Qualities,* vol. 1, *A Sort of Introduction and Pseudoreality Prevails.* Trans. Sophie Wilkins and Burton Pike. New York: Vintage, 1996.

Naiman, Eric. *Sex in Public: The Incarnation of Early Soviet Ideology.* Princeton, N.J.: Princeton University Press, 1997.

Nancy, Jean-Luc. *Being Singular Plural.* Trans. Robert D. Richardson and Anne E. O'Byrne. Stanford, Calif.: Stanford University Press, 2000.

Nethercott, Francis. "Elements of Bergson's *Creative Evolution* in the Critical Prose of Osip Mandel'štam." *Russian Literature* 30 (1991): 455–66.

Neuger, Leonard. *Ćwiczenia z wrażliwości: Duże i małe szkice literackie* [Exercises in Sensitivity: Literary Sketches Large and Small]. Katowice: Wydawnictwo Uniwersytetu Śląskiego, 2006.

Nezval, Vítězslav. *Depeše z konce tisíciletí: Korespondence Vítězslava Nezvala* [Dispatches from the End of the Millennium: The Correspondence of Vítězslav Nezval]. Ed. Marie Krulichová, Milena Vinařová, and Lubomír Tomek. Prague: Československý spisovatel, 1981.

———. *Edison.* Prague: Plejada, 1928.

———. *Historický obraz: Básně z let 1939–1945* [Historical Portrait: Poems, 1939–1945]. Prague: Melantrich, 1945.

———. *Izbrannoe* [Selected Poems]. Ed. S. Shchipacheva. Moscow: Izdatel'stvo inostrannoi literatury, 1960.

———. *Josef Čapek: Studie* [Josef Čapek: A Study]. Prague: František Borový, 1937.

———. "Josef Šíma." *Aventinum* 33 (1931–32).

———. *Moderní básnické směry* [Modern Poetic Movements]. Prague: Československý spisovatel, 1966.

———. "Papoušek na motocyklu čili o řemesle básnickém" [Parrot on a Motorcycle; or, On Poetic Craft]. *Host* 3.9–10 (July 1924): 220–23.

———. *Praha s prsty deště [1936]* [Prague with Fingers of Rain]. Prague: Akropolis, 2000.

———. "Průvodce mladých básníků." In Karel Čapek, *Básnické počátky/ Překlady,* vol. 24 of *Spisy,* 55–61. Prague: Český spisovatel, 1993.

———. *Signál času: Panichida za Edisona* [Time Signal: A Panachyda for Edison]. Prague: František Borový, 1931.

Nietzsche, Friedrich. *The Portable Nietzsche.* Ed. and trans. Walter Kaufman. New York: Penguin, 1968.

———. *The Will to Power.* Ed. Walter Kaufmann. Trans. Walter Kaufmann and R. J. Hollingdale. New York: Vintage, 1967.

Nikulin, Lev. *Sochineniia v trekh tomakh* [Works in Three Volumes]. Moscow: Goslitizdat, 1956.

Novák, Bohumil. "Richard Weiner." *Listy pro umění a kritiku* 2 (1934): 136.

Okłot, Michał. "Maturing into Childhood: An Interpretive Framework of a Modern Cosmogony and Poetics." *Alif: Journal of Comparative Poetics* 27 (2007): 131–53.

Olesha, Iurii. *Zavist', Ni dnia bez strochki, Rasskazy* [Envy, Not a Day without a Line, Stories]. Moscow: Izvestiia, 1989.

Ort, Thomas. *Art and Life in Modernist Prague: Karel Čapek and His Generation, 1911–1938*. New York: Palgrave Macmillan, 2013.

Osharov, M. "To Alien Shores: The 1922 Expulsion of Intellectuals from the Soviet Union." *Russian Review* 32.3 (July 1973): 294–98.

Paloff, Benjamin. "East Is Always Further East." *East European Politics and Societies* 28.4 (November 2014): 687–92.

Panova, L. G. *"Mir," "prostranstvo," "vremia" v poezii Osipa Mandel'shtama* ["World," "Space," "Time" in the Poetry of Osip Mandel'shtam]. Moscow: Iazyki Slavianskoi Kul'tury, 2003.

Paperno, Irina. "On the Nature of the Word: Theological Sources of Mandel'shtam's Dialogue with the Symbolists." In *Christianity and the Eastern Slavs*, Vol. 2, *Russian Culture in Modern Times*, ed. Robert P. Hughes and Irina Paperno, California Slavic Studies 17, 287–310. Berkeley: University of California Press, 1994.

Pavlov, Evgenii. *Shok pamiati: Avtobiograficheskaia poetika Val'tera Ben'iamina i Osipa Mandel'shtama* [The Shock of Memory: The Autobiographical Poetics of Walter Benjamin and Osip Mandel'shtam]. Trans. Aleksandr Skidan. Moscow: Novoe Literaturnoe Obozrenie, 2005.

Pechey, Graham. "Not the Novel: Bakhtin, Poetry, Truth, God." In *Bakhtin and Cultural Theory*, 2nd ed., ed. Ken Hirschop and David Shepherd, 62–84. Manchester: Manchester University Press, 2001.

Phillips, Adam. *Houdini's Box: The Art of Escape*. New York: Vintage, 2002.

Piaget, Jean. *The Child's Conception of the World*. Trans. Joan Tomlinson and Andrew Tomlinson. Totowa, N.J.: Littlefield, Adams, 1969.

Pieszak, Eryk. *Trzy dyskursy o spotkaniu z Innym: Gombrowicza, Schelera i Lévinasa ścieżki spotkania w pobliżu wielkich dróg* [Three Discourses on Encountering the Other: Gombrowicz, Scheler, and Levinas's Paths of Encounter Near to Great Roads]. Poznań: Wydawnictwo Poznańskiego Towarzystwa Przyjaciół Nauk, 2003.

Pietrzak, Włodzimierz. "Bluszcz na ruinach" [Ivy on the Ruins]. *Prosto z mostu* 27 (1938): 7.

Pil'niak, Boris. *Sobranie sochinenii v shesti tomakh* [Collected Works in Six Volumes]. Ed. K. Andronikashvili-Pil'niak. Moscow: Terra-Knizhnyi Klub, 2003.

Platonov, Andrei. *Chevengur* [handwritten manuscript]. Pushkinskii Dom, St. Petersburg, fond 780, item 34.

———. *Kotlovan* [The Foundation Pit; typescript]. Pushkinskii Dom, St. Petersburg, fond 780, item 8.

———. *Kotlovan: Tekst, materialy tvorcheskoi istorii* [The Foundation Pit: Text, Materials from Its Creative History]. Ed. N. A. Groznova et al. St. Petersburg: Nauka, 2000.

———. *Razmyshleniia chitatel'ia* [A Reader's Meditations]. Moscow: Sovetskii pisatel', 1970.

———. *Sobranie sochinenii v vos'mi tomakh* [Collected Works in Eight Volumes]. Ed. N. V. Kornienko. Moscow: Vremia, 2009.

———. *Sochineniia* [Works]. Ed. N. V. Kornienko. Moscow: IMLI RAN, 2004.

Poltavtseva, N. G. "The Husserlian, the Cosmicist and the Pushkinian in Platonov." *Essays in Poetics: The Journal of the British Neo-Formalist Circle* 27 (Autumn 2002): 97–113.

———. "Tekst i intertekst v detskikh rasskazakh A. Platonova 50-kh godov" [Text and Intertext in Andrei Platonov's Stories for Children from the 1950s]. In *Tvorchestvo Andreia Platonova: Issledovaniia i materialy,* vol. 2, 58–69. St. Petersburg: Nauka, 2000.

Poulet, Georges. *La Pensée indéterminée, III. De Bergson à nos jours.* Paris: Presses Universitaires de France, 1990.

Pratt, Sarah. *Nikolai Zabolotskii: Enigma and Cultural Paradigm.* Evanston, Ill.: Northwestern University Press, 2000.

Promiński, Marjan. "Nowości literackie" [Literary Novelties]. *Sygnały* 40 (March 1, 1938): 5.

Proust, Marcel. *The Guermantes Way.* Trans. C. K. Scott Moncrieff. New York: Modern Library, 1925.

———. *On Art and Literature: 1896–1919.* Trans. Sylvia Townsend Warner. New York: Carroll and Graf, 1997.

Przybylski, Ryszard. *An Essay on the Poetry of Osip Mandelstam: God's Grateful Guest.* Trans. Madeline G. Levine. Ann Arbor, Mich.: Ardis, 1987.

Random, Michel. *Le grand jeu.* 2 vols. Paris: Editions Denoël, 1970.

Reynek, Bohuslav. *Rybí šupiny* [Fish Scales]. Petrkov: U Německého Brodu, 1922.

Richter, David H. "Dialogism and Poetry." *Studies in the Literary Imagination* 23.1 (Spring 1990): 9–27.

Romanska, Magda. *The Post-Traumatic Theater of Grotowski and Kantor: History and Holocaust in* Akropolis *and* The Dead Class. London: Anthem Press, 2014.

Ronen, Omri. *Poetika Osipa Mandel'shtama* [The Poetics of Osip Mandel'shtam]. St. Petersburg: Giperion, 2002.

Roth, Philip. *Shop Talk: A Writer and His Colleagues and Their Work.* Boston: Houghton Mifflin, 2001.

Rússovich, Alejandro. "Gombrowicz od wewnątrz" [Gombrowicz from the Inside]. In *Tango Gombrowicza,* ed. and trans. Rajmund Kalicki, 121–29. Kraków: Wydawnictwo Literackie, 1984.

Ryan, Michael P. "Samsa and *Samsara:* Suffering, Death, and Rebirth in 'The Metamorphosis.'" *German Quarterly* 72.2 (Spring 1999): 133–52.

Salgas, Jean-Pierre. *Witold Gombrowicz lub ateizm integralny* [Witold Gombrowicz; or, Integral Atheism]. Trans. Jan Maria Kłoczowski. Warsaw: Czytelnik, 2004.

Sandauer, Artur. *Zebrane pisma krytyczne* [Collected Criticism]. 3 vols. Warsaw: Państwowy Instytut Wydawniczy, 1981.
Santayana. George. *Three Philosophical Poets: Lucretius, Dante, and Goethe.* Cambridge, Mass.: Harvard University Press, 1910.
Sartre, Jean-Paul. *Being and Nothingness: An Essay on Phenomenological Ontology.* Trans. Hazel E. Barnes. New York: Philosophical Library, 1956.
Sboev, N. "Mansarda na Petrogradskoi" [Petrograd Mansard]. In *Vospominaniia o Zabolotskom,* 2nd ed., ed. E. V. Zabolotskaia, A. V. Makedonov, and N. N. Zabolotskii, 43–46. Moscow: Sovetskii pisatel', 1984.
Scanlan, James P. *Dostoevsky the Thinker.* Ithaca, N.Y.: Cornell University Press, 2002.
Scheler, Max. *On Feeling, Knowing, and Valuing.* Ed. Harold J. Bershady. Chicago: University of Chicago Press, 1992.
———. *Wesen und Formen der Sympathie: Der "Phänomenologie der Sympathiegefühle"* [Nature and Forms of Sympathy: The "Phenomenology of Sympathetic Feeling"]. 2nd ed. Bonn: F. Cohen, 1923.
Schelling, F. W. J. *Ages of the World.* Trans. Judith Norman, published with Slavoj Žižek, *The Abyss of Freedom.* Ann Arbor: University of Michigan Press, 1997.
———. *Bruno; or, On the Natural and the Divine Principle of Things.* Ed. and trans. Michael G. Vater. Albany: State University of New York Press, 1984.
Scholz, Bernhard F. "Bakhtin's Concept of 'Chronotope': The Kantian Connection." In *The Contexts of Bakhtin: Philosophy, Authorship, Aesthetics,* ed. David Shepherd, 141–72. Amsterdam: Harwood, 1998.
Schopenhauer, Artur. *The World as Will and Representation.* Vol. 1. Trans. E. F. J. Payne. New York: Dover, 1969.
Schulz, Bruno. *Księga listów* [The Book of Letters]. 2nd ed. Ed. Jerzy Ficowski. Gdansk: Słowo/obraz terytoria, 2002.
———. *Letters and Drawings of Bruno Schulz.* Ed. Jerzy Ficowski. Trans. Walter Arndt. New York: Fromm, 1988.
———. *Opowiadania, wybór esejów i listów* [Stories, Selected Essays and Letters]. Ed. Jerzy Jarzębski. Wrocław: Ossolineum, 1989.
Schwartz, Wolfgang F. "(De)Konstruction von Erinnerung und Biographie als Element der Zyklisierung bei Karel Čapek: Die 'noetische Trilogie'" [(De)construction of Memory and Biography as an Element of Cyclicalization in Karel Čapek's "Noetic Trilogy"]. In *Zyklusdichtung in den slavischen Literaturen,* ed. Reinhard Ibler, 487–506. Frankfurt: Peter Lang, 2000.
Sebald, W. G. "The Undiscover'd Country: The Death Motif in Kafka's *The Castle.*" *Journal of European Studies* 2 (1972): 22–34.
Sedakova, Ol'ga. *Proza* [Prose]. Moscow: En Ef Kiiu/Tu Print, 2001.
Seifrid, Thomas. *Andrei Platonov: Uncertainties of Spirit.* Cambridge: Cambridge University Press, 1992.
———. *The Word Made Self: Russian Writings on Language, 1860–1930.* Ithaca, N.Y.: Cornell University Press, 2005.
Shklovsky, Viktor. *Theory of Prose.* Trans. Benjamin Sher. Urbana, Ill.: Dalkey Archive Press, 1991.

———. *Third Factory*. Trans. Richard Sheldon. Urbana, Ill.: Dalkey Archive Press, 2002.

Sicher, Efraim. "The 'Color' of Judaism: Timespace Oppositions in the Synaesthesia of Osip Mandel'shtam's *Shum Vremeni*." In *Aspects of Modern Russian and Czech Literatures*, ed. Arnold McMillin, 31–54. Columbus, Ohio: Slavica, 1989.

Simmel, George. *On Individuality and Social Forms*. Ed. Donald L. Levine. Chicago: University of Chicago Press, 1971.

Singer, Isaac Bashevis. "A Polish Franz Kafka." *New York Times*, July 9, 1978, BR1.

Skoller, Eleanor Honig. *The In-Between of Writing: Experience and Experiment in Drabble, Duras, and Arendt*. Ann Arbor: University of Michigan Press, 1993.

Skulsky, Harold. *Metamorphosis: The Mind in Exile*. Cambridge, Mass.: Harvard University Press, 1981.

Stala, Krzysztof. *On the Margins of Reality: The Paradoxes of Representation in Bruno Schulz's Fiction*. Stockholm: Stockholm University Press, 1993.

Stern, Laurence. *The Life and Opinions of Tristram Shandy, Gentleman*. Ed. Ian Campbell Ross. Oxford: Oxford University Press, 2009.

Struve, Nikita. *Osip Mandel'shtam*. London: Overseas Publications Interchange, 1990.

Surat, Irina. "Poet i gorod: Peterburgskii siuzhet Osipa Mandel'shtama" [The Poet and the City: Osip Mandel'shtam's Petersburg Theme]. *Zvezda* 5 (2008): 178–203.

Taranovsky, Kiril. *Essays on Mandel'štam*. Cambridge, Mass.: Harvard University Press, 1976.

Taylor, Mark C. *Altarity*. Chicago: University of Chicago Press, 1987.

Teige, Karel. "Estetika filmu a kinografie" [The Aesthetics of Film and Cinematography]. *Host* 3.6–7 (April 1924): 143–52.

Terras, Victor. "Death of a Poet: Osip Mandelshtam." In *Enemies of the People: The Destruction of Literary, Theater, and Film Arts in the 1930s*, ed. Katherine Bliss Eaton, 75–87. Evanston, Ill.: Northwestern University Press, 2002.

———. "The Time Philosophy of Osip Mandel'shtam." *Slavonic Review* 109 (July 1969): 346–47.

Tharp, Martin. "Czech Paris: Le Grand Jeu and Richard Weiner." *Estetika* 36.1–3 (1999): 116–23.

Thomas, Alfred. *The Labyrinth of the Word: Truth and Representation in Czech Literature*. Munich: R. Oldenbourg, 1995.

Tihanov, Galin. "Contextualizing Bakhtin: Two Poems by Mandel'štam." *Russian Literature* 50.2 (2001): 165–84.

———. *The Master and the Slave: Lukács, Bakhtin, and the Ideas of Their Time*. Oxford: Oxford University Press, 2000.

———. "Why Did Modern Literary Theory Originate in Central and Eastern Europe? (And Why Is It Now Dead?)." *Common Knowledge* 10.1 (Winter 2004): 61–81.

Todorov, Tzvetan. *The Fantastic: A Structural Approach to a Literary Genre*. Trans. Richard Howard. Ithaca, N.Y.: Cornell University Press, 1975.

Toksina, I. V., ed. *Vitezslav Nezval: Bibliograficheskii ukazatel'* [Vítězslav Nezval: A Bibliography]. Moscow: Izdatel'stvo "Kniga," 1967.

Tolstaia, Elena. *Mirposlekontsa: Raboty o russkoi literature XX veka* [Post-world: Works on Russian Literature in the Twentieth Century]. Moscow: RGGU, 2002.

Toman, Jindřich. "Karel Čapek, Karl Kraus, and the Theory of the Phrase." In *On Karel Čapek*, ed. Michael Makin and Jindřich Toman, 87–108. Ann Arbor: Michigan Slavic Publications, 1992.

———. *The Magic of a Common Language: Jakobson, Mathesius, Trubetzkoy, and the Prague Linguistic Circle*. Cambridge, Mass.: MIT Press, 1995.

Tribout-Joseph, Sarah. *Proust and Joyce in Dialogue*. London: Legenda, 2008.

Trnka, Tomáš. "Problém individua" [The Problem of the Individuum]. *Naše doba* 30.10 (September 1923).

Turner, C. J. G. "On Osip Mandel'shtam's Poem 'Vek.'" *Slavic and East European Journal* 20.2 (Summer 1976): 148–54.

Urzidil, Johannes. *There Goes Kafka*. Trans. Harold A. Basilius. Detroit: Wayne State University Press, 1968.

Uzharevich, Iosip (Josip Užarević). "Mir nad mirom: Problema 'dvoemiriia' v lirike Nikolaia Zabolotskogo" [World over World: The Two-World Problem in Nikolai Zabolotskii's Lyric]. *Russian Literature* 56.1–3 (July 2004): 297–311.

Valéry, Paul. *Cahiers/Notebooks*. Vol. 5. Ed. Brian Stimpson. Trans. Paul Gifford et al. Frankfurt: Peter Lang, 2010.

van Duijkeren, Magda, and Miloš Stejskal. "Funkce litanických řad v Nezvalově 'Edisonu'" [The Function of Litanies in Nezval's "Edison"]. In *Czech Studies: Literature, Language, Culture/České studie: Literatura Jazyk Kultura*, ed. Mojmír Grygar, 203–27. Amsterdam: Rodopi, 1990.

Vargish, Thomas. "Modernism." In *The Routledge Encyclopedia of Philosophy*, ed. Edward Craig, vol. 6, 447–49. London: Routledge, 1998.

Vargish, Thomas, and Delo E. Mook. *Inside Modernism: Relativity Theory, Cubism, Narrative*. New Haven, Conn.: Yale University Press, 1999.

Vašíček, Zdeněk. *Přijetí podmínek* [Accepting Conditions]. Prague: Torst, 1996.

Vendler, Helen. "A Lament in Three Voices." *New York Review of Books* 48:9 (May 31, 2001): 27–31.

Vitale, Serena. *Shklovsky: Witness to an Era*. Trans. Jamie Richards. Urbana, Ill.: Dalkey Archive Press, 2012.

V'iugin, V. Iu. *Andrei Platonov: Poetika zagadki: Ocherk stanovleniia i evoliutsii stilia* [Andrei Platonov: The Poetics of Riddle: A Sketch of the Formation and Evolution of Style]. St. Petersburg: Izdatel'stvo Russkogo Khristianskogo Gumanitarnogo Instituta, 2004.

———. "Povest' 'Kotlovan' v kontekste tvorchestva Andreia Platonova" [*The Foundation Pit* in the Context of Andrei Platonov's Creative Work]. In Andrei Platonov, *Kotlovan: Tekst, materialy tvorcheskoi istorii*, 5–18.

Voloshin, G. "Prostranstvo i vremia u Dostoevskogo" [Space and Time in Dostoevsky]. *Slavia* (Prague) 12.1–2 (1933): 162–72. Excerpted in *M. M. Bakhtin: Pro et contra*, vol. 1, 200–201. St. Petersburg: RKhGU, 2001.

Vondráček, Radim. "Zářivé hlubiny: Vlastislav Hofman a kouskování věčna" [Radiant Depths: Vlastislav Hofman and the Dismemberment of the Eternal].

In *Expresionismus a české umění*, 197–203. Prague: Národní Galerie v Praze, 1994.

Vucinich, Alexander. *Einstein and Soviet Ideology*. Stanford, Calif.: Stanford University Press, 2001.

Wachtel, Michael. *Russian Symbolism and Literary Tradition: Goethe, Novalis, and the Poetics of Vyacheslav Ivanov*. Madison: University of Wisconsin Press, 1994.

Walicki, Andrzej. *Marxism and the Leap to the Kingdom of Freedom: The Rise and Fall of the Communist Utopia*. Stanford, Calif.: Stanford University Press, 1997.

Walser, Robert. *Jakob von Gunten*. Trans. Christopher Middleton. New York: New York Review Books, 1999.

Weiner, Richard. *The Game for Real*. Trans. Benjamin Paloff. San Francisco: Two Lines Press, 2015.

———. *Lazebník/Hra doopravdy*. Vol. 3 of *Spisy*. Prague: Torst, 1998.

Whitworth, Michael H. *Einstein's Wake: Relativity, Metaphor, and Modernist Literature*. Oxford: Oxford University Press, 2001.

Widera, Steffi. *Richard Weiner: Identität und Polarität im Prosafrühwerk* [Richard Weiner: Identity and Polarity in His Early Prose]. Munich: Otto Sagner, 2001.

Williams, Bernard. *Shame and Necessity*. Berkeley: University of California Press, 1993.

Wyka, Kazimierz. *Rzecz wyobraźni* [A Matter of Imagination]. 2nd ed. Warsaw: Państwowy Instytut Wydawniczy, 1977.

Yeats, W. B. *The Collected Poems of W. B. Yeats*. 2nd ed. Ed. Richard J. Finneran. New York: Scribner, 1996.

Zabolotskii, N. [Nikolai]. *Polnoe sobranie stikhotvorenii i poem*. Ed. Nikita Zabolotskii. St. Petersburg: Akademicheskii Proekt, 2002.

———. *Sobranie sochinenii v trekh tomakh* [Collected Works in Three Volumes]. Ed. E. Zabolotskaia and N. Zabolotskii. Moscow: Khudozhestvennaia literatura, 1984.

———. *Stolbtsy* [Columns/Scrolls]. Leningrad: Izdatel'stvo Pisatelei v Leningrade, 1929.

Zabolotskii, Nikita. *Zhizn' N. A. Zabolotskogo* [The Life of N. A. Zabolotskii]. St. Petersburg: Logos, 2003.

Zaleski, Marek. *Zamiast: O twórczości Czesława Miłosza* [Instead: On the Work of Czesław Miłosz]. Kraków: Wydawnictwo Literackie, 2005.

Zeeman, Peter. *The Later Poetry of Osip Mandelstam: Text and Context*. Amsterdam: Rodopi, 1988.

Zielinski, Thaddaeus [Tadeusz Zieliński]. *Die Behandlung von gleichzeitiger Ereignisse im antiken Epos, Erster Theil* [The Treatment of Simultaneous Events in the Greek Epic, Part I]. Leipzig: Dieterich'sche Verlagsbuchhandlung, 1901.

INDEX

Page numbers in italics refer to figures.